AF900172

Applied Demography and Public Health

Applied Demography Series

Volume 3

Series Editor: David A. Swanson

The field of applied demography is largely driven by the quest for the knowledge required by clients, both in public and private sectors, to make good decisions within time and costs constraints. The book series, Applied Demography, provides a forum for illustrating and discussing the use of demographic methods, concepts, and perspectives in a wide range of settings – business, government, education, law, and public policy - as well as the influence of these settings on demographic methods, concepts, and perspectives. The books within the series can be used as resources for practitioners and as materials serving as case studies for pedagogical uses.

For further volumes:
http://www.springer.com/series/8838

Nazrul Hoque • Mary A. McGehee
Benjamin S. Bradshaw
Editors

Applied Demography and Public Health

Springer

Editors
Nazrul Hoque
Department of Demography
Institute for Demographic
and Socioeconomic Research
University of Texas, San Antonio
San Antonio, TX, USA

Mary A. McGehee
Health Statistics Branch
Arkansas Department of Health Center
for Public Health Practice
Little Rock, AR, USA

Benjamin S. Bradshaw
School of Public Health
The University of Texas
San Antonio, TX, USA

ISBN 978-94-007-6139-1 ISBN 978-94-007-6140-7 (eBook)
DOI 10.1007/978-94-007-6140-7
Springer Dordrecht Heidelberg New York London

Library of Congress Control Number: 2013933044

© Springer Science+Business Media Dordrecht 2013
This work is subject to copyright. All rights are reserved by the Publisher, whether the whole or part of the material is concerned, specifically the rights of translation, reprinting, reuse of illustrations, recitation, broadcasting, reproduction on microfilms or in any other physical way, and transmission or information storage and retrieval, electronic adaptation, computer software, or by similar or dissimilar methodology now known or hereafter developed. Exempted from this legal reservation are brief excerpts in connection with reviews or scholarly analysis or material supplied specifically for the purpose of being entered and executed on a computer system, for exclusive use by the purchaser of the work. Duplication of this publication or parts thereof is permitted only under the provisions of the Copyright Law of the Publisher's location, in its current version, and permission for use must always be obtained from Springer. Permissions for use may be obtained through RightsLink at the Copyright Clearance Center. Violations are liable to prosecution under the respective Copyright Law.
The use of general descriptive names, registered names, trademarks, service marks, etc. in this publication does not imply, even in the absence of a specific statement, that such names are exempt from the relevant protective laws and regulations and therefore free for general use.
While the advice and information in this book are believed to be true and accurate at the date of publication, neither the authors nor the editors nor the publisher can accept any legal responsibility for any errors or omissions that may be made. The publisher makes no warranty, express or implied, with respect to the material contained herein.

Printed on acid-free paper

Springer is part of Springer Science+Business Media (www.springer.com)

Foreword

Drs. Hoque, McGehee, and Bradshaw have created a unique work that provides an excellent demonstration of the utility of applied demography in the analysis of key public health issues. It presents the results of analyses that extend our knowledge of how demographic factors impact basic health issues, of social and economic changes impacting and resulting from health events, and demonstrate the utility of demographic methodological applications that contribute to understanding and managing health related events and outcomes. It does so while examining issues important to improving health outcomes, preventing and reducing the incidence of important diseases and disorders, and improving health care. At the same time, the work's analyses provide important insights on how such factors are impacted by key demographic events such as aging, child bearing, and mortality.

The work spans a wide breadth of important health issues related to obesity, depression, diabetes, cancer, hypertension, and other conditions and does so as they impact health in such key treatment areas as health screening, obstetrics, and cardiac and geriatric medicine. It examines interrelated economic, demographic, and social factors on such conditions, including the effects of income mobility, aging, health expenditures, racial/ethnic differentials in infant mortality, and other health-related dimensions. It is also rich in its demonstration of how important demographic techniques have been applied to health-related analyses, including the use of population projections in conjunction with incidence rates to determine the future demand for health services, the use of cause-specific and condition-specific forms of analysis to examine the incidence of diabetes, the use of population density analyses to examine relationships between social and health impacted events such as violent crime, life expectancy analysis in the examination of the effects of aging, and the use of very specific methods such as the Lee-Carter Method and Markov analyses. This work is one that should be of substantial use to both the health care professional and the applied demographic analyst.

This book is also international in its focus. It not only examines dimensions related to domestic United States health related areas in Texas, Florida, and the United States generally, but it also examines multinational issues related to programs from the World Health Organization as well as analyses in India, specifically Kerala,

Liberia, Bangladesh, Great Britain, and Brazil. It should be of interest to those with both domestic and international demographic and health care interests.

The work is noteworthy not only for the breadth of its subject matter and its methodological and geographic content, but also because the chapters are of exceptionally high quality and utility. They provide clear statements of the scope and importance of the work they describe. They delineate and justify the methods used with substantial rigor and provide descriptions of results that will be useful to both the most rigorous demographic methodologist and the health care planner and analysts who want to evaluate their own findings relative to their program development and application efforts. In sum, this is simply an excellent volume that is both methodologically rigorous and pragmatically useful.

I believe the volume will be of substantial utility in general academic courses in the areas of demography and public health and can play a very important role in demographic methods courses in providing explicit examples of the use of the methods and materials of demography and public health analysis. I have decided to use it as a companion text in my demographic methods course next year and believe that the work will be especially useful to my students, many of whom are on their way to medical school and public health careers.

In sum, I highly recommend this text to both academics and practitioners in demography and public health. For both groups, this work will be a useful addition to their professional libraries and an excellent choice as a text for courses in demography and public health.

Rice University Steve Murdock

Foreword

This volume on health demography brings together important topical subjects and useful findings and materials in a single source. Moreover, the book is international. For important topical ideas, we have, for example, two chapters that deal with the determinants and consequences of obesity, respectively. Other topical chapters deal with aging and health care expenditures in the Indian state of Kerala, maternal health in post-war Liberia, density of retail alcohol outlets and crime in the U.S., racial disparities in infant mortality in the U.S., blood pressure control and diabetes in Bangladesh, and retirement and mortality. These discussions and others on important topical subjects are found in this book.

We also find new methodological insights inside this volume. What are the pros and cons of using biological markers, for example? Is the Lee-Carter Method for forecasting mortality applicable to health services planning in Brazil? How can one reliably estimate valid survival and mortality rates from successive cross-sectional surveys? What is the effect of different cancer screening policies and practices in the U.S. and Europe on cancer incidence and mortality? Importantly, general methodological issues involved in the study of again, health, and mortality are also discussed. These are examples of the coverage of methodological issues of high interest to health demographers and others.

Substantive findings of high interest are found throughout this book. In addition to the ones already mentioned, they include obstetric morbidity in India, the relationship of neighborhood resources and adolescent health and risk behaviors in the U.S., health life expectancy in a district of Bangladesh, and the effects of maternal health status and early childbearing on infants and their health.

Last, but not least, this book directly and indirectly provides valuable information on a wide range of data sets, including, among others, the WHO study of global aging and the UK household longitudinal survey. When combined with the international flavor, methodological insights, and substantive findings, knowledge of these data sets should serve to spur new studies and insights. Take your time and be prepared to take notes to keep track of the ideas you get while reading this wonderful book.

Professor of Sociology
University of California Riverside
Riverside, California, USA

David A. Swanson, Ph.D.

Acknowledgements

We wish to thank Evelien Bakker, the senior editor of Springer publications, who made this work possible. Evelien came up with the idea for this book while attending the 2nd Applied Demography Conference, which was held in San Antonio, Texas, on January 10–12, 2010. In that conference, the session on Applied Demography and Public Health Issues gave her the idea of an edited volume, and the editors came up with the title of the book *Applied Demography and Public Health.*

Many persons have contributed to the development of this volume. We thank the authors of the individual chapters for submitting their work for publication in *Applied Demography and Public Health.* Our appreciation is also extended to the reviewers for their timely response to our requests for revisions. All the chapters are peer reviewed, and we would also like to thank those who provided peer reviews and comments for the authors in regard to the chapters in this volume.

We would like to thank Dr. Lloyd Potter, Director of the Institute for Demographic and Socioeconomic Research and former chair of the Department of Demography and Organization Studies at The University of Texas at San Antonio, for sponsoring the Applied Demography Conference and also for providing financial support for this book. We also appreciate the contributions of Patricia Bramwell, Lisa Espinoza, Beverly Pecotte, Jeffrey Jordan, and Eric Quiroz, all with the Institute for Demographic and Socioeconomic Research, who helped with the conference and also with the book. We owe special thanks to Karen White who helped us as a technical editor for the book. We especially appreciate the support of Bernadette Deelen-Mans, the editor of Springer publications, and her staff, as well as the staff at the production office.

Finally, Drs. Bradshaw and McGehee would like to thank Dr. Nazrul Hoque for taking the lead in the development of this volume. Dr. Hoque took the responsibility of assembling a list of possible papers from the conference that he thought would be appropriate for the publication, invited the authors to submit their work for possible publication as book chapter, and submitted the papers for review and revision.

Contents

Part X [illegible]

Chapter 1
Introduction

Nazrul Hoque, Mary A. McGehee, and Benjamin S. Bradshaw

Applied demography is an ever-evolving field that is applicable to a number of disciplines (Siegel 2002; Murdock and Swanson 2008). It is a subfield of basic demography, which is the study of human populations and the size, composition, and spatial distribution of these populations and the related processes of fertility, mortality, and migration. Unlike basic demography which is primarily concerned with increasing knowledge about how these processes lead to demographic change, the focus of applied demography is understanding the consequences of demographic change, including the related social and economic consequences and their application to decisions related to policy development, planning, the distribution of goods and services, etc. in a specific area (Murdock and Ellis 1991).

Public health is about the health of the public – the population – not the health of individual members (Turnock 2008). The emphasis is on the public – on the population itself. Public health and demography have been intimately related for centuries; indeed, it is difficult to separate the two. Because the focus of public health practice is on the population, success or failure of public health efforts are measured with population level data – e.g., rates, ratios, life expectancy, etc. From the time John Graunt (1662) began analyzing vital statistics data in the mid-17th century to the present, demographers have made observations either directly or indirectly on the health of the popu-

N. Hoque (✉)
Department of Demography and Institute for Demographic and Socioeconomic Research, The University of Texas, San Antonio, TX, USA
e-mail: Nazrul.hoque@utsa.edu

M.A. McGehee
Health Statistics Branch, Center for Public Health Practice, Arkansas Department of Health, Little Rock, AR, USA
e-mail: mary.mcgehee@arkansas.gov

B.S. Bradshaw
Management, Policy & Community Health Division, The University of Texas School of Public Health, San Antonio, TX, USA
e-mail: bradshaw@uthscsa.edu

N. Hoque et al. (eds.), *Applied Demography and Public Health*,
Applied Demography Series 3, DOI 10.1007/978-94-007-6140-7_1,
© Springer Science+Business Media Dordrecht 2013

lation with death and birth statistics and measures based on these in conjunction with census and survey information. Demographers have contributed invaluably to public health through development of population estimates and projections and evaluations of the quality of these products. Without good quality estimates and projections, planning for public health services would be nearly impossible. Often, the denominators for public health measures come from work done by applied demographers. Likewise, persons whose primary interest was in public health have made invaluable contributions to demography. This does not mean that public health practice may not include individual level interventions – e.g., assigning nurses to educate new mothers in proper care of infants, immunization programs, etc. – but unlike medical practice, the emphasis is on the population, not on the individual.

In this volume, the usefulness of the methods of applied demography in addressing public health issues is illustrated. This volume is not a complete overview of applied demography and public health and their interrelations. It is a collection of papers that illustrate some of the ways that applied demography can be used to inform or support public health issues. It should also be pointed out that the chapters were not necessarily prepared with "customers" in mind; they originated as papers presented at professional meetings. The work originated in a session at the Applied Demography Conference held in San Antonio, Texas, in January 2010. Some papers from that session are included in the volume. In addition, authors of appropriate papers presented at the annual meeting of the Population Association of America in April 2010 were invited to contribute their work. All contributions were sent for independent review. The editors are grateful to the contributors and the reviewers for their hard work.

This volume is intended for a wide range of users. Applied demographers, health policy makers, social epidemiologists, and social scientists or practitioners in the public and private sectors interested in public health can benefit from the information in this publication. In addition, this volume could be used as an accompanying text for courses in applied undergraduate and graduate demography and public health science courses. The authors' papers provide a number of resources and tools that can be used by these persons in conducting research aimed at promoting public health: (1) information on a variety of health research datasets, (2) different statistical methodologies for analyzing health-related data and developing concepts related to health status, (3) methodologies for forecasting or projecting disease incidences and associated costs, and (4) discussion of demographic concepts used to measure population health status. Also important is the recurring theme of understanding how demographic and socioeconomic characteristics affect public health.

Overview of the Parts and Chapters

The volume is organized into five sections. Part I (Chaps. 2–5) examines the impact of aging on health and health-related expenditures, both in developed and developing countries. Part II (Chaps. 6–9) examines the use of data from cross-sectional surveys, vital statistics, and disease registries to estimate cause-specific mortality rates in the U.S. and Europe. These mortality rates are used by health professionals to examine progress in eliminating disparities in health between different populations. Part III (Chaps. 10–12) provides specific attention to maternal health and morbidity in developed and developing countries – including India, Liberia, and the U.S. Part IV (Chaps. 13–17) provides analyses of special cases, and Part V (Chaps. 18–21) covers methodological issues in public health. All five sections contain examples of how demographic techniques and concepts are related to public health.

Part I

The four chapters in Part I are examples of how demographic techniques can be useful in public health planning. In Chap. 2, Hoque and Howard use population projections and other formal demographic techniques to look at the impact of population growth, an aging population, and changes in the race and ethnic composition of the population on the increase in the prevalence of persons who are overweight and obese and the costs of overweight and obesity. This information will be useful to state health policy makers and administrators. In Chap. 3, Fox and Hutto build on this methodology by looking at the effect of obesity on intergenerational income mobility. Utilizing the National Longitudinal Survey of Youth 1979 data, Fox and Hutto compare the likelihood of upward mobility by obesity status. According to Fox and Hutto, obesity dampens upward mobility and increases downward mobility for overweight women. The chapter by Gorrindo et al. looks at the cross-country comparison of sociodemographic correlates of depression. They use data from the WHO study on global aging and adult health to examine the extent which sociodemographic variables correlate to the depressive conditions across five countries: China, India, Ghana, Mexico, and South Africa. Chapter 5 by Yadawendra Singh illustrates the use of demographic techniques to examine how population aging affects health expenditures and to provide estimates of the cost of managing chronic diseases in the future. Singh examines the burden of aging in terms of health expenditures in Kerala, the Indian state that has the highest proportion of elderly in India. Using methods of empirical analyses, the author found that the proportion of elderly having at least one ailment is much higher in Kerala compared to other Indian states and that per capita out-of-pocket health expenditure for non-elderly in-patient care is higher than that for the elderly. Based on the estimates the author predicted that the burden of managing the cost of diseases will increase significantly in coming future.

Part II

In Chap. 6, Smith, McFall, and Bradshaw use data from the Behavioral Risk Factor Surveillance System survey (BRFSS) and the National Center for Health Statistics to produce estimates of death rates for diabetics. The BRFSS is the world's largest on-going health survey and is conducted in all 50 states, the District of Columbia,

Puerto Rico, the U.S. Virgin Islands, and Guam by the Centers for Disease Control and Prevention (CDC). Bishop-Royse and Eberstein use linked birth and infant death to examine causes of death that contribute to the racial disparities in infant mortality, as well the influence of the social context and maternal sociodemographic characteristics on these disparities (Chap. 7). In Chap. 8, Smith, McFall, and Bradshaw present a method for estimating death rates for subpopulations using successive cross-sectional survey data. In Chap. 9, Garcia and Crimmins compare cancer screening policies in the U.S. and Europe and conclude that countries with the highest screening rates have generally experienced faster decline in mortality. This chapter points out the importance of cancer screening to reduce the death due to cancer, particularly for people 50 years of age and above.

Part III

What are some of the public health issues that can affect fertility levels and fertility decisions in different societies? What are some of the demographic and socioeconomic factors that affect fertility levels and decisions? These questions are addressed in Part III, which focuses on maternal health and morbidity. In Chap. 10, Sontakke and Reshmi use the National Family Health Survey (NFHS) to study obstetric morbidity in India and to examine the relationship between socioeconomic and demographic factors and obstetric morbidity. The findings suggest that level of obstetric morbidity varied among the Indian states. Meadows et al. use data from the Panel Survey of Income Dynamics (PSID) to assess how an adolescent mother's self-rated health status can predict her odds of experiencing childbirth at a young age (Chap. 11). Murty and McCamey use data from a survey of Liberian women (ages 13–49) to examine how selected demographic and socioeconomic factors affect maternal health and morbidity in post-war Liberia. The authors concluded that maternal mortality in Liberia is very high and efforts are underway to develop better health services to the marginalized areas as they struggle to recover from two decades of war (Chap. 12).

Part IV

Part IV addresses various topics that provide excellent examples of the interaction between **demographic characteristics** and processes and their implications for public health policy, health intervention strategies, and health promotion. Also, in this section, a number of **demographic concepts** used to measure the health status of the population are discussed. In particular, the authors provide examples of how spatial distributions or concentrations of the population, population characteristics, and progressions through different lifestages affect health. In Chap. 13, Snedker et al. look at neighborhood characteristics and their influence on adolescent health. This research has clear policy implications for those interested in better understanding the relationship between neighborhood context and individual-level outcomes. Mancha and Zey employ a new methodological approach to explore the relationship between alcohol retail outlet density, population density, and crime (Chap. 14). Mondal et al. use data from 406 hypertensive diabetic patients from the Rajshahi Medical College Hospital and Rajshahi Diabetic Centers in Bangladesh who are receiving treatment for HTN and diabetics to examine the relationship between socio-demographic characteristics and the control of diabetes and hypertension (Chap. 15). Life expectancy, a demographic concept used to measure health status, is the topic of the paper by Tareque et al. This chapter examines the relationship between an active aging index and healthy life expectancy (HLE) in Bangladesh using data collected from the Rajshahi District of Bangaldesh (Chap. 16). Finally, Shim et al. (Chap. 17) present their results of a systematic literature review to address whether type of retirement is a risk factor for mortality.

Part V

The chapters in Part V delve deeper into different methodologies, including demographic methodologies, that can be used to assess and understand factors related to population health. The paper by Kamiya et al. analyzes the relationship between social engagement – or social structure – and health and the biomarkers used to measure this relationship (Chap. 18). Yashin et al. (Chap. 19) discuss an approach to mortality modeling that takes into account the internal and external factors related to health. According to the authors this type of analysis is useful to health practitioners in developing personalized preventive and treatment strategies. McFall and Buck discuss the usefulness of the UK Household Longitudinal Survey as a resource for research in demography and health (Chap. 20). The use of the Lee-Carter method, which combines a demographic model with a times-series method to forecast health services, is illustrated by Rodrigues et al. (Chap. 21). This chapter would be helpful to the health practitioners and policy makers who are concerned about future health care use and costs.

References

Graunt, J. (1662). *Natural and political observations mentioned in a following index, and made upon the bills of mortality*. New York: Evergreen Review, Inc.

Murdock, S. H., & Ellis, D. R. (1991). *Applied demography: An introduction to basic concepts, methods, and data*. Boulder: West View Press.

Murdock, S. H., & Swanson, D. A. (Eds.). (2008). *Applied demography in the 21st century* (pp. 3–10). New York: Springer Science+Business Media B.V.

Siegel, J. (2002). *Applied demography: Applications to business, government, law and public policy*. San Diego: Academic.

Turnock, B. J. (2008). Public health: *What it is and how it works*. Sudbury: Jones and Bartlett Publishers.

Part I
Impact of Aging on Health and Health-Related Expenditure

Chapter 2
The Implications of Aging and Diversification of Population on Overweight and Obesity and the Cost Associated with Overweight and Obesity in Texas, 2000–2040

Nazrul Hoque and Jeffrey Howard

Introduction

Overweight and obesity are major health concerns in contemporary America. The percentage of the population that is considered overweight and obese has increased substantially over the past years for both adults and children. Approximately 133.6 million American adults, or 66.0% of all adults, are either overweight or obese (NIH 2004). Obesity rates have more than doubled since 1990, increasing from 11.6% in 1990 to 26.3% in 2007 (CDC 1991, 2007). This increase is of substantial concern because of the health risks associated with overweight and obesity. Overweight and obesity are related to increased risk for heart disease, type 2 diabetes, and a number of other diseases (Wolk et al. 2001; Calle et al. 2003). Approximately 300,000–400,000 deaths each year in the United States are attributable to overweight and obesity status (Allison et al. 1999; Obesity in America 2004).

In addition to observing differences in the prevalence rate of overweight and obesity for males and females (Baskin et al. 2005; Flegal et al. 2010), higher body mass indices tend to be more prevalent among minority population members due to an association between low socioeconomic status and a variety of other factors such as historical and cultural aspects. African Americans and Hispanics tend to be more likely than non-Hispanic Whites and other groups to have higher Body Mass Index scores. This is due, in large part, to long-term patterns of socioeconomic disparity with African Americans and Hispanics having rates of poverty that are two to three

N. Hoque (✉)
Department of Demography and Institute for Demographic
and Socioeconomic Research, University of Texas at San Antonio, San Antonio, TX, USA
e-mail: Nazrul.hoque@utsa.edu

J. Howard
Department of Demography, University of Texas at San Antonio,
San Antonio, TX, USA

N. Hoque et al. (eds.), *Applied Demography and Public Health*,
Applied Demography Series 3, DOI 10.1007/978-94-007-6140-7_2,
© Springer Science+Business Media Dordrecht 2013

times the levels for non-Hispanic Whites and median income levels that are roughly 60–65% of those for non-Hispanic Whites (US Census Bureau 2008). Because of these differences and the fact that these differences have been evident for decades, African Americans and Hispanics are more likely to purchase and consume high calorie, high carbohydrate foods that are generally less expensive than many lower-calorie fruits, vegetables and lean meat alternatives. For both African Americans and Hispanics decades of impoverishment have led to food consumption patterns based on cultural traditions and cost considerations that are likely to lead to higher likelihoods of being overweight or obese.

Based on data for adults 20 years of age and older from the National health and Nutrition Examination Survey (NHANES) 2007–2008, the age-adjusted overweight and obesity prevalence rates for Hispanics are more than six points higher, while for African Americans the prevalence rates are more than 11 points higher, compared with non-Hispanic Whites. The prevalence rates are 38.7, 44.1, and 32.4% for Hispanic, African American, and non-Hispanic Whites, respectively (Flegal et al. 2010). The prevalence rates for adult population for all race/ethnicity groups are higher compared with young population. Consequently, in areas with more diverse or aging populations, the health and financial implications can present significant concerns for policy makers and health care providers within these communities.

Texas provides an excellent location for an examination of the potential effects and the costs of overweight and obesity because of the prevalence of these conditions in its population and the rapid diversification of its population. Texas had the sixth highest rate of adult obesity among all U.S. states in 2000 at 25.3% and had the fifth highest rate of obese adults in 2001 and 2002 at 24.6 and 25.5, respectively (CDC 2000, 2001, 2002, 2007). Among Texas adults, overweight and obesity prevalence rose from 43.0% in 1990 to 63.0% in 2002. This is an increase of 20 percentage points and a change of 56.5% in only 12 years. The economic burden associated with overweight and obesity in Texas is substantial. In Texas, overweight- and obesity-related direct and indirect costs among adults reached an estimated $11.3 billion during 2000 (Hoque et al. 2010).

Identifying the magnitude of potential future increases in the number of overweight and obese persons in Texas may also be informative for the nation because the current characteristics of Texas' population are similar to those projected for the United States as a whole (U.S. Bureau of the Census 2008). In 2000, Texas had a population that was 53% non-Hispanic White, and by 2004 it had become a majority minority state. In 2000 slightly more than 30% of the Texas population was Hispanic and approximately 12% that was African-American. In 2010, the proportion of non-Hispanic White population decreased to 46.6% while the proportion of Hispanic population increased to 37.5%. The United States population (U.S. Census Bureau 2008) is projected to become a majority minority by 2042 with approximately 30% Hispanics and about 12% African-Americans by midcentury. Texas data, consequently, can offer insights that are relevant to national health and other planning efforts.

In this paper, we demonstrate the importance of data on the projected number of overweight and obese adults to identify the cost of overweight and obesity as well as the relative effects of population growth, change in the age structure, and change in the racial/ethnic composition of the population. Such a decomposition is important because it allows one to identify the detailed causes of such increases and to direct health education efforts toward those segments of the population most likely to experience increases in overweight and obesity. This work provides a clear example of the use of applied and general demographic methods to address a critical area of concern for the nation and its component states.

McCusker et al. (2004) used a cohort-component projection model to project the number of overweight and obese adults and projected annual costs associated with those overweight and obese persons in Texas through the year 2040. This study expands the analysis by McCusker et al. by decomposing the change in the prevalence of overweight and obese adults for successive periods due to (a) the rate of population growth, (b) change in the age structure, and (c) change in the racial/ethnic composition of the population. The importance of understanding these three dimensions in determining overweight and obesity is evident from the demographics of Texas. Texas' population has grown faster than the national population rate during every census since 1850. The Texas population increased by 2.7% annually during the 1970s compared with 1.1% nationally. During the 1990s, Texas populations increased by 2.3% while the U.S. population increased by 1.3%. Although growth has slowed since 2000, the Texas population growth rate is still higher than that for the U.S., 2.1 and 1.0%, respectively, from 2000 to 2010. Texas population of 25.1 million in 2010 may exceed 45 million by 2040.

The median age of Texas population was 28 years in 1980, 30 years in 1990, and 32.3 years in 2000. The median age for the total population of Texas is expected to increase from 32.3 in 2000 to 38.1 in 2040. For the Anglo population it would increase from 38.0 to 46.2 years, for the Hispanic population it would increase from 25.5 to 34.2 years, for the Black population it would increase from 29.6 to 39.8 years, and for the Other population (composed of Asians, American Indians, and other nonwhite, non-Hispanic, non-African American groups) it would increase from 31.1 to 48.7 years. The proportion of the Texas population 65 years of age or older has increased from 9.6% in 1980 to 10.1% in 1990 to and 13.8% in 2000, and it is projected to increase to 20.6% by 2040.

The proportion of the Hispanic population in Texas has increased from 21.0% in 1980 to 25.6% in 1990 and to 32.0% in 2000. The proportion of Other population has increased from 1.4% in 1980 to 2.2% in 1990 and to 3.3% in 2000. By contrast, the proportion of the population that is Anglo population decreased from 65.7% in 1980 to 60.6% in 1990 and to 53.1% in 2000. The proportion of the population that is Black has remained relatively static (11.9% in 1980 and 11.6% in 1990 and 2000).

Both in Texas and nationwide, the prevalence of obesity is higher among Black and Hispanic adults compared to non-Hispanic white adults. In Texas, both the prevalence of overweight and obesity and the number of Hispanic adults are expected to increase during the next four decades. To assess the impact of these changes, we projected (1) the number of normal weight, overweight, and obese adults in Texas through the year 2040, and (2) the costs associated with overweight and obesity. In examining the results presented in this paper, it is important to acknowledge that a variety of factors such as social, economic, resource, and policy factors may have as large or even larger effects on overweight and obesity and the cost associated with overweight and obesity than demographic forces. However, we believe that demographic change will play a major role in determining the future overweight and obese status in Texas as well as in the United States. Thus, we maintain that it is useful to examine the implications of such factors on overweight and obesity for policy purposes.

Methods

The analysis was performed in four stages. The first stage involved the preparation of detailed projections of the population by age, sex, and race/ethnicity in Texas. The second stage involved the derivation of age, sex and race/ethnicity-specific rates for normal weight, overweight, and obesity and multiplication of these rates by the number of persons in the projected population cohorts. The third stage involved the computation of direct and indirect costs associated with overweight and obesity for the base year and multiplication of these costs by the projected number of overweight and obese population to obtain the projected costs associated with overweight and obesity in Texas. The fourth stage involved the computation of decomposition effects due to changes in population growth, age structure, and race/ethnicity composition. The procedures followed in each of these stages are described in the following sections.

Projecting the Population of Texas

Population projections were completed with a cohort-component projection technique. The basic characteristics of this technique are the use of separate cohorts – persons with one or more common characteristics, and the separate projection of each of the major components of population change – fertility, mortality, and migration, for each cohort. These component projections are then combined in the demographic equation as follows:

$$P_t = P_0 + B - D + NM$$

Where P_t=population for the projected year; P_0=population at the base year; B=births between P_0 and P_t; D=deaths between P_0 and P_t; NM=net migration between P_0 and P_t.

The following major steps were performed for the population projections: (1) a baseline set of cohorts was selected for the projection area of interest for the baseline time period; (2) appropriate baseline fertility, mortality, and migration measures were determined for each cohort for the baseline time period; (3) a method was determined for projecting trends in fertility, mortality, and migration rates over the projection period; and (4) a computational procedure was selected for applying the rates to the baseline cohorts to project the population for the projection period.

The four baseline cohorts used in the projections were single-year-of-age cohorts of male and female Anglos (white non-Hispanic persons), Blacks (Black non-Hispanic persons), Hispanics (Spanish-origin persons of all racial and ethnic groups), and Other (persons in all other nonAnglo, nonAfrican American, non-Hispanic racial and ethnic groups). These cohorts were extracted from Summary File 1 of the 2000 Census of Population and Housing. A detailed description of the methods for formulating these race/ethnicity combinations and the projections methodology can be obtained from the authors.

Baseline age and race/ethnicity-specific fertility rates were computed with data from the Texas Department of State Health Services for births by age and race/ethnicity, and the mother's place of residence The numerators for such rates are the average number of births for 1999, 2000 and 2001 for mothers in each age and race/ethnicity group and the denominators are the population counts by age and race/ethnicity in 2000. These data showed total fertility rates for Anglo, Black, Hispanic and the Other racial/ethnic groups in 2000 that were 1.92, 2.05, 2.92 and 1.95 respectively for the State of Texas.

To project fertility rates, we examined the historical patterns and trends in total fertility rates by race/ethnicity. Evaluation of these age and race/ethnicity-specific fertility rates in Texas showed patterns of slightly increased fertility among Anglos from 1990 to 2000. Rates for Blacks showed a decrease of nearly 14% from 1990 to 2000. Hispanic showed a decline of more than 6% from 1990 to 2000. The rates for Other racial/ethnic group decreased from a total fertility rate of 2.04 in 1990 to 1.95 in 2000.

Survival rates by age, sex, and race/ethnicity were computed using the death data from Texas Department of Health for 1999, 2000, and 2001 and 2000 census population. Survival rates were projected assuming that the survival rates of Texas will follow the national trends for the projection period. We computed the ratio of Texas's 2000 age, sex, and race/ethnicity specific survival rates to those of the nation and applied these ratios to the projected survival rates of the U.S. The national rates were obtained from the Population Projections Branch of the U.S. Bureau of the Census (Spencer 1984, 1986, 1989; Hollmann et al. 2000).

Migration is the most difficult component of population projections for which to obtain base rates and projected rates. We used a vital statistics method which is the simplest and most accurate method of estimating net migration (Texas Population Estimates and Projection Program 2006). In this method net migration is equal to population change minus natural increase (births minus deaths). Thus, births and deaths by age, sex, and race/ethnicity were added to and subtracted from the 1990 population to produce an expected 2000 population. This expected population was compared to the actual 2000 census counts to estimate net migration rates for 1990–2000 periods. These rates provided the migration component for population projections.

Four alternative population projection scenarios were developed based on projected trends in fertility and survival rates and alternative assumptions regarding net migration. These scenarios used the same fertility and survival assumptions but three different sets of migration assumptions. One scenario assumed no net migration (that is, the net of in and out migrations are equal to zero or there is no migration) by age, sex, and race/ethnicity, referred to as the 0.0 migration scenario. A second scenario assumed that rates of age, sex, and race/ethnicity specific net migration were equal to one-half of the 1990–2000 rates, referred to as the 0.5 migration scenario. A third scenario assumed a continuation of the 1990–2000 rates of age, sex, and race/ethnicity specific net migration, referred to as the 1.0 migration scenario. A fourth scenario assumed a continuation of the 2000–2004 rates of age, sex, and race/ethnicity specific net migration, referred to as the 2000–2004 migration scenario (For a detailed discussion on population projections, refer to the projection methodology at the TSDC website, which can be accessed at the location noted above).

The 2000–2004 scenario is used for this analysis because we compared the 2010 projected population produced by different scenarios with the census counts of 2010 population and the 2000–2004 scenario is closest to the actual counts. However, as with all other projections, if the assumptions about the future demographic processes are incorrect, the projections will be incorrect. Thus, the 2000–2004 scenario assumes that migration will average 198,290 persons per year throughout the projection period. Total fertility rates for Anglos will decline from 1.92 to 1.72, for Blacks from 2.05 to 1.72, for Hispanics from 2.85 to 2.20 and for Others from 1.95 to 1.86 by 2040. Survival rates for Texas were assumed to follow the national level (i.e., life expectancy will increase by 6 years from 2000 to 2040). If these assumptions are incorrect, the projections will be incorrect. We utilize these projections with full realization of their limitations but with the expectation that although the exact number of persons projected to live in the state in the future is unlikely to be correct, the general trends are likely to be in the direction indicated.

Measures of Prevalence for Normal Weight, Overweight, and Obesity

Individuals are defined as normal weight, overweight, or obese by having a body mass index (BMI) of less than 25.0, between 25.0 and 29.9, and over 30.0 kg/m^2, respectively as defined by the National Institutes of Health (NIH 1998). Estimates of the prevalence of normal weight, overweight, and obesity among Texas adults by age group, sex, and race/ethnicity were derived from data collected during 1999–2002 by the Texas Behavioral Risk Factor Surveillance System (BRFSS), an ongoing telephone survey of state residents' health conditions and behaviors coordinated by the Centers for Disease Control and Prevention. Respondents' self-reported height and weight were used to calculate their BMI (weight in kilograms divided by

Table 2.1 Prevalence rate (per 100) of overweight and obese adults in Texas by age group, sex, and race/ethnicity, 1999–2002

	Male				Female			
Year	Anglo	Black	Hispanic	Other	Anglo	Black	Hispanic	Other
Overweight								
18–24	34.2	38.2	38.6	36.5	16.6	29.9	24.8	12.1
25–34	42.9	37.9	45.7	32.5	22.9	32.4	32.6	16.3
35–44	49.5	49.7	46.7	44.3	26.3	29.1	34.9	27.3
45–54	48.4	41.3	45.7	44.1	29.1	35.6	29.9	30.9
55–64	50.2	50.7	54.4	37.5	31.7	44.7	35.2	35.0
65+	47.3	25.0	46.1	36.1	33.2	33.3	35.4	29.0
All ages	46.5	41.9	45.4	38.1	27.9	33.2	32.0	23.7
Obese								
18–24	13.2	14.7	14.8	1.9	7.1	22.1	15.1	3.4
25–34	19.5	36.8	27.4	14.2	16.3	28.8	29.5	8.7
35–44	23.3	31.6	32.9	12.7	17.9	38.4	32.5	12.5
45–54	26.6	35.7	37.2	22.0	24.8	42.3	37.8	23.5
55–64	26.0	27.4	27.5	15.6	23.2	39.8	41.9	22.5
65+	18.0	39.1	28.1	8.3	17.5	31.5	31.3	22.6
All ages	21.8	32.3	28.3	13.0	18.9	34.2	30.7	13.9

height in meters squared). The age, sex, and race/ethnicity-specific prevalence rates used are presented in Table 2.1.

As shown in totals by race/ethnicity on Table 2.1, Black females have the highest female obesity prevalence at 34.2% followed by Hispanic females at 30.7%, Anglo females at 18.9%, while Other females have the lowest rate of 13.9%. Black males also have the highest male obesity prevalence of 32.3% followed by Hispanic males with 28.3%, Anglo males with 21.8%, and Other males with 13.0%. The prevalence of overweight is highest for Black females at 33.2% followed by Hispanic females at 32.0%, Anglo females at 27.9% and Other females at 23.7%. The prevalence of overweight is highest for Anglo males at 46.5% followed by Hispanic males at 45.4%, Black males at 41.9%, and Other males at 38.1%.

Next we examine the prevalence of overweight and obesity by age and age within each race/ethnicity group. The prevalence of overweight is 20% higher for Anglo males aged 25–34, compared to Anglo females, and 23.2% higher for Anglo males aged 35–44. The overall prevalence of overweight for Anglo males is 18.6% higher than Anglo females (46.5 and 27.9%, respectively). The prevalence of obesity is also higher for Anglo males than females for all age groups. The overall obesity for Anglo males is 2.9% higher than for females. The prevalence of overweight is higher for Black males than females except in the age group 65 and above where the female rate is higher than the male rate. For obesity, female rates are higher than male rates in the 18–24 and 35–64 age ranges, while males are higher for ages 25–34 and 65 and over. For the Hispanic population of all ages the prevalence of overweight is 13.4% higher for males than for females, 45.4 and 32.0%, respectively. For obesity, the Hispanic female prevalence is a little higher than the male rate, 30.7 and 28.3%, respectively. For the Other population of all ages, the overweight prevalence is 14.4% higher for males than for females, 38.1 and 23.7%, respectively. The obesity prevalence for Other females for age 65 and over is 15.3 percentage points higher than the male rate, 23.0 and 8.3, respectively. Obesity prevalence ranged from 3.2% for Other males 18–24 years of age to 39.1% for Black males 65 years of age and over. Overall, the prevalence for obesity is higher for Black and Hispanic populations compared to the Anglo population.

Projected Changes in Prevalence of Overweight and Obesity

In the U.S., the prevalence of overweight and obesity has increased dramatically during the past 20 years. As mentioned in the introduction, obesity rates have increased from 11.6% in 1990 to 26.3% in 2007. The increase in the prevalence of obesity has been so rapid during recent years that the rate of increase is not likely to be sustainable over time. For this reason, the future rates of change in the prevalence of overweight and obese adults were assumed to decrease incrementally over time. Changes in the prevalence of overweight and obesity were based on data from the 1990 to 2002 national BRFSS. The rates of change in prevalence were assumed to slow over time, with prevalence decreasing linearly by one-fourth of the 1990–2002 decade equivalent from 2000 to 2010, and decreasing by an additional one-half of the previous decades' prevalence in each of the next three decades. For comparison purposes another set of projections were completed using constant 1999–2002 prevalence of overweight and obesity. Due to space limitations we do not present the later set of projections.

Projected Costs of Overweight and Obesity

The projected costs of overweight and obesity were derived from previously published direct and indirect cost estimates for the State of Texas. According to 2001 cost estimates for overweight and obesity, total annual direct and indirect costs were $471 for each overweight adult and $2,249 for each obese adult in Texas (McCusker et al. 2004). A more recent study by Dor et al. (2010) estimates the yearly cost at $432 for an overweight man, $524 for an overweight women, $2,646 for an obese man, and $4,879 for an obese woman. Since this is a recent study, we use these 2010 values to project the future cost associated with overweight and obesity in Texas. These are direct medical costs which include both out-of-pocket and insurance-covered expenditures related to physician services, hospital care, and pharmaceuticals. We have not added indirect expenses or the value of lost life to these annual costs. Adding the value of lost life would produce much higher costs. According to Dor et al. (2010), including the values for loss of life would increase the estimated costs to $8,365 for obese women and $6,518 for obese men.

Decomposition Analysis

Finally, we used decomposition techniques to identify how each of the three factors studied affected changes in the number of overweight and obese adults relative to the population base. Decomposition analysis provides a technique for identifying the proportion of a difference between two crude rates that is attributable to each of a set of demographic factors (Kitagawa 1955; Das Gupta 1978). Decomposition analysis is clearly an appropriate technique for discerning how demographic factors will affect the number of overweight and obese adults in Texas at different points in times. By using decomposition techniques, we discern what portion of the change in overweight and obese adults for each of the four time periods (2000–2010, 2010–2020, 2020–2040 and 2000–2040) is attributable to population change, what portion is attributable to change in the age structure, and what portion is attributable to change in race/ethnicity composition occurring between the two periods.

Results

We used all four population projections scenarios to project the number of overweight and obese adults and the costs associated with overweight and obesity in Texas through 2040. The data presented here are for the zero net migration and 2000–2004 migration scenarios. As noted before, we believe that the 2000–2004 scenario is most likely to approximate future levels of population change in Texas, and other scenarios (i.e., 1990–2000) show similar patterns to those shown for the 2000–2004 scenario; the zero net migration scenario provides a projection of population based on natural increase (i.e., the excess of birth over deaths). By comparing results for the zero migration scenario to the 2000–2004 scenario, we can examine the likely impact of migration in overall patterns of population growth. This comparison is important because migrants (particularly immigrants) are likely to have a different prevalence of overweight and obesity than the native born population and thus have potentially dramatic impacts on overweight and obese status.

An Overview of Major Demographic Trends

Table 2.2 provides population data for the adult population (18 years of age and older) in Texas by race/ethnicity for 2000 and projected to 2040 by alternative migration scenarios. According to the 2000–2004 migration scenario, the adult population in Texas is expected to increase from 15 million in 2000 to 34.4 million in 2040. The adult population by race/ethnicity is projected to increase from the year 2000 to 2040 as follows: the non-Hispanic White or Anglo population will increase from 8.5 to 9 million, the Black population will increase from 1.7 to 2.8

Table 2.2 Population 18 years of age and older by race/ethnicity in 2000 and projected to 2040 under alternative projection scenarios for Texas (in thousands)

Year	Anglo	Black	Hispanic	Other	Total
Zero net migration scenario					
2000	8,522.2	1,653.3	4,282.9	506.7	14,965.1
2010	8,921.3	1,895.8	5,272.4	586.3	16,675.8
2020	9,090.6	2,083.1	6,350.9	663.2	18,187.8
2030	9,117.3	2,205.5	7,495.3	726.2	19,544.3
2040	8,862.8	2,239.9	8,451.4	743.2	20,297.3
2000–2004 migration scenario					
2000	8,522.2	1,653.3	4,282.9	506.7	14,965.1
2010	8,951.4	2,011.7	6,680.9	880.6	18,524.6
2020	9,154.7	2,340.4	9,838.1	1,441.3	22,774.5
2030	9,224.0	2,625.2	14,073.3	2,251.4	28,173.9
2040	9,004.1	2,829.5	19,281.9	3,318.3	34,433.8

million, the Hispanic population will increase from 4.3 to 19.3 million, and the Other population will increase from 506,711 persons to 3.3 million (Table 2.2).

The Anglo adult population would account for only 2.6% of net growth from 2000 to 2040, which means the rest of the net growth will come from the minority population, especially the Hispanic population that would account for 77.3% of the net change.

Migration will play an important role in future population change in Texas. The 2000–2004 migration scenario suggest that 72.7% of the net growth in Texas adult population from 2000 to 2040 is likely to be due to net migration.

The total adult population will increase by 130.1% from 2000 to 2040. Although all racial/ethnic groups show population increase during this time; the Anglo population will only increase by 5.7%, the Black population will increase by 71.1%, the Hispanic population will increase by 350.2%, and the Other population will increase by 554.9% (Table 2.3). Under zero net migration scenario, total adult population will increase by only 35.6%, Anglo by 4.0%, Black by 35.5%, Hispanic by 97.3% and Other population by 46.7%.

Increase in Minority Populations

The second major demographic pattern is the trend toward an increasing number and proportion of minority population Table 2.4 presents the percent of the adult population (18 years of age and older) in Texas by race/ethnicity for 2000 and projected to 2040. Based on the 2000–2004 scenario, the proportion of the adult population that is Black is expected to decrease from 11.0% in 2000 to 8.2% in 2040. In this same scenario, the proportion of Hispanic adults is expected to increase from 28.6% in 2000 to 56% in 2040. The proportion of Other adults will increase from 3.4% in 2000 to 9.6% in 2040.

Table 2.3 Percent change for selected time periods for projected adult population by race/ethnicity under alternative projection scenarios for Texas

Year	Anglo	Black	Hispanic	Other	Total
Zero net migration scenario					
2000–2010	4.7	14.7	23.1	15.7	11.4
2010–2020	1.9	9.9	20.5	13.1	9.1
2020–2030	0.3	5.9	18.0	9.5	7.5
2030–2040	−2.8	1.6	12.8	2.3	3.9
2000–2040	4.0	35.5	97.3	46.7	35.6
2000–2004 migration scenario					
2000–2010	5.0	21.7	56.0	73.8	23.8
2010–2020	2.3	16.3	47.3	63.7	22.9
2020–2030	0.8	12.2	43.0	56.2	23.7
2030–2040	−2.4	7.8	37.0	47.4	22.2
2000–2040	5.7	71.1	350.2	554.9	130.1

Table 2.4 Proportion of population 18 years of age and older by race/ethnicity in 2000 and projected to 2040 under alternative projection scenarios for Texas

Age group	Anglo	Black	Hispanic	Other	Total
Zero net migration scenario					
2000	57.0	11.0	28.6	3.4	100.0
2010	53.5	11.4	31.6	3.5	100.0
2020	50.0	11.5	34.9	3.6	100.0
2030	46.6	11.3	38.4	3.7	100.0
2040	43.7	11.0	41.6	3.7	100.0
2000–2004 migration scenario					
2000	57.0	11.0	28.6	3.4	100.0
2010	47.9	11.3	35.9	4.9	100.0
2020	39.7	11.1	42.6	6.6	100.0
2030	32.3	10.5	48.7	8.5	100.0
2040	25.9	9.7	54.0	10.4	100.0

The Aging Population

The trend toward an older age structure in the U.S. and Texas population has been widely discussed elsewhere (Murdock et al. 2003). The projected percent of population by age group and race/ethnicity from 2000 to 2040 for Texas are provided in Table 2.5. The proportion of the total population that is 65 years of age or older is projected to increase from 13.8% in 2000 to 20.6% in 2040. During this period, the proportion of the population 65 years of age or older within each race/ethnicity is projected to increase as follows: the Hispanic population will increase from 8.1 to 13.6%, the Black population will increase from 10.6 to 20.8%, the Anglo population will increase from 17.8 to 31.4%, and the Other population will increase from 6.7 to 32.0% (2000–2004 scenario).

Table 2.5 Percent of adult population by age group and race/ethnicity in 2000 and projected percent of population by age group and race/ethnicity for 2040 under alternative projection scenarios for Texas

Age group	Anglo	Black	Hispanic	Other	Total
Base year 2000					
18–24	11.4	16.4	20.6	15.1	14.7
25–34	17.3	22.8	27.2	27.2	21.1
35–44	21.8	24.2	22.2	23.8	22.2
45–54	19.1	17.0	14.3	18.2	17.5
55–64	12.6	9.0	7.6	9.0	10.7
65+	17.8	10.6	8.1	6.7	13.8
Zero net migration scenario, year-2040					
18–24	9.2	10.9	13.8	7.8	11.2
25–34	14.4	17.2	19.4	13.4	16.8
35–44	14.8	17.4	18.0	15.1	16.4
45–54	15.5	18.1	14.8	12.8	15.5
55–64	14.6	15.0	13.6	13.7	14.1
65+	31.5	21.4	20.4	37.2	26.0
2000–2004 migration scenario, year-2040					
18–24	9.2	11.3	12.4	7.0	11.0
25–34	14.4	17.4	21.5	12.9	18.4
35–44	14.9	17.5	20.5	15.0	18.3
45–54	15.6	18.6	18.1	16.6	17.3
55–64	14.5	14.4	13.9	16.5	14.4
65+	31.4	20.8	13.6	32.0	20.6

Table 2.6 shows the percent change in population from 2000 to 2040 by age group and race/ethnicity. For the total population as well as for each race/ethnicity, the already mentioned population growth can be seen. This can be observed in each age group, yet with great differences in the percent change, the younger age groups are expected to grow considerably less than the older age groups. As noted before, the Anglo population is expected to grow the least (as measured in percent change), while the population that is Hispanic has the highest percent change within all age groups from 2000 to 2040.

Impacts of Demographic Factors on Overweight and Obesity

The projections of the number of overweight and obese adults in Texas are provided in Table 2.7. Under the 2000–2004 migration scenario, the overall number of overweight adults in Texas is projected to increase from 5.5 million in 2000 to 13.6 million in 2040. During this period, the distribution of overweight adults in Texas by race/ethnicity is projected to increase as follows: the Anglo population will increase from 3.1 million to almost 3.5 million, the Black population will increase

Table 2.6 Percent change in population by age group and race/ethnicity from 2000 to 2040 under alternative projection scenarios for Texas

Age group	Anglo	Black	Hispanic	Other	Total
Zero net migration scenario					
18–24	−16.0	−9.4	32.2	−24.1	3.8
25–34	−13.7	1.7	40.6	−27.5	7.6
35–44	−29.2	−2.5	60.2	−7.5	0.4
45–54	−15.5	44.9	105.2	3.7	19.9
55–64	20.1	125.3	249.7	122.2	79.7
65+	84.1	172.4	398.3	716.8	154.5
2000–2004 net migration scenario					
18–24	−14.9	17.9	172.4	201.2	71.7
25–34	−12.4	30.3	253.5	211.8	100.7
35–44	−27.2	24.3	317.0	313.9	89.8
45–54	−13.9	86.8	470.1	498.4	128.1
55–64	21.5	175.3	724.3	1088.8	210.1
65+	86.3	234.0	655.2	3042.9	242.2

Table 2.7 Adult population with overweight and obesity in Texas in 2000 and projected to 2040 by race/ethnicity under alternative projection scenarios (in thousands)

	Overweight				Obese				Total	
Year	Anglo	Black	Hispanic	Other	Anglo	Black	Hispanic	Other	Total over weight	Total obese
Zero net migration scenario										
2000	3,100.3	611.4	1,645.9	157.1	1,698.0	534.9	1,222.3	68.3	5,514.7	3,523.5
2010	3,318.3	721.7	2,087.5	192.9	2,104.4	728.6	1,841.8	101.0	6,320.4	4,775.8
2020	3,440.9	802.2	2,546.3	220.6	2,302.2	878.2	2,424.4	127.1	7,010.0	5,731.9
2030	3,481.1	842.8	3,031.0	240.6	2,362.8	970.7	2,979.7	142.9	7,595.5	6,456.1
2040	3,403.0	856.1	3,439.1	248.4	2,352.5	1,012.5	3,435.9	148.7	7,946.6	6,949.6
2000–2004 migration scenario										
2000	3,100.3	611.4	1,645.9	157.1	1,698.0	534.9	1,222.3	68.3	5,514.7	3,523.5
2010	3,330.3	764.8	2,651.2	288.2	2,109.8	770.3	2,313.3	149.6	7,034.5	5,343.0
2020	3,466.6	899.6	3,977.5	481.1	2,317.6	985.8	3,787.4	279.3	8,824.8	7,370.1
2030	3,524.0	1,002.5	5,727.5	756.3	2,391.5	1,154.8	5,677.0	454.9	11,010.3	9,678.2
2040	3,459.8	1,079.9	7,920.2	1,118.9	2,391.0	1,279.8	7,984.6	685.6	13,578.8	12,341.0

from 611,394 to 1.1 million, the Hispanic population will increase from 1.6 to 7.9 million, and the Other category will increase from 157,143 to 1.1 million.

The number of obese persons in the adult population is projected to increase from 3.5 million in 2000 to 12.3 million to 2040. Within this time, the distribution of obese adults in Texas by race/ethnicity is projected to increase as follows; the Anglo obese population will increase from 1.7 to 2.4 million, the Black population will increase from 534,892 to 1.3 million, the Hispanic population will increase

Table 2.8 Percent change in overweight and obese persons for selected time periods in Texas

	Overweight				Obese				Total	
Year	Anglo	Black	Hispanic	Other	Anglo	Black	Hispanic	Other	Total over weight	Total obese
Zero net migration scenario										
2000–2010	7.0	18.0	26.8	22.8	23.9	36.2	50.7	47.9	14.6	35.5
2010–2020	3.7	11.2	22.0	14.3	9.4	20.5	31.6	25.8	10.9	20.0
2020–2030	1.2	5.1	19.0	9.1	2.6	10.5	22.9	12.4	8.4	12.6
2030–2040	−2.2	1.6	13.5	3.2	−0.4	4.3	15.3	4.0	4.6	7.6
2000–2040	9.8	40.0	109.0	58.1	38.5	89.3	181.1	117.7	44.1	97.2
2000–2004 migration scenario										
2000–2010	7.4	25.1	61.1	83.4	24.3	44.0	89.3	119.0	27.6	51.6
2010–2020	4.1	17.6	50.0	66.9	9.8	28.0	63.7	86.7	25.5	37.9
2020–2030	1.7	11.4	44.0	57.2	3.2	17.1	49.9	62.9	24.8	31.3
2030–2040	−1.8	7.7	38.3	47.9	−0.0	10.8	40.6	50.7	23.3	27.5
2000–2040	11.6	76.6	381.2	612.0	40.8	139.3	553.2	903.9	146.2	250.2

from 1.2 to 8 million, and the Other category of obese persons will increase from 68,297 to 685,643. If we compare 2000–2004 scenario with zero net migration scenario, 69.8 and 61.1% of the growth in overweight and obese population, respectively, is due to migration.

Table 2.8 presents the percent change in overweight and obese persons for selected time periods in Texas. The total overweight adult population will increase by 146.2% from 2000 to 2040. During the projection period, the overweight Anglo adult population will increase by 11.6%, the overweight Black adult population will increase by 76.6%, the overweight Hispanic adult population will increase by 381.2%, and the overweight Other adult population will increase by 612% (2000–2004 migration scenario). The percent change in persons with obesity follows similar patterns with Hispanics having the highest percent change and Anglos having the smallest percent change. The percent change in overweight and obesity decreases steadily over time for all race/ethnicity groups except for Hispanics.

According to the 2000–2004 migration scenario in Table 2.9, the proportion of overweight adults who are Anglo will decrease from 56.3% in 2000 to 25.5 in 2040, the proportion who are Black will decrease from 11.1% in 2000 to 8.0% in 2040, while the proportion who are Hispanic will increase from 29.8% in 2000 to 58.3% in 2040, and the proportion from the Other category will increase from 2.8% in 2000 to 8.2% in 2040 of all overweight persons. The proportion of Anglo obese adults will decrease from 48.2% in 2000 to 19.3 in 2040. The proportion of Black obese adult will decrease from 15.2% in 2000 to 10.4% in 2040. The proportion of Hispanic obese population will increase from 34.7 to 64.7 and Other obese population will increase from 1.9 to 5.6% from 2000 to 2040.

The aging of the population will markedly affect the overweight and obese rates by age groups in the projected years. The effects of aging, as illustrated in Table 2.10, are apparent for all racial and ethnic groups. The prevalence of overweight and

Table 2.9 Percent of adult population that is overweight and obese in Georgia in 2000 and projected to 2040 by race/ethnicity and alternative projection scenarios

	Overweight				Obese					
Year	Anglo	Black	Hispanic	Other	Anglo	Black	Hispanic	Other	Total over weight	Total obese
Zero net migration scenario										
2000	56.3	11.1	29.8	2.8	48.2	15.2	34.7	1.9	100.0	100.0
2010	52.5	11.4	33.0	3.1	44.0	15.3	38.6	2.1	100.0	100.0
2020	49.2	11.4	36.3	3.1	40.2	15.3	42.3	2.2	100.0	100.0
2030	45.8	11.1	39.9	3.2	36.6	15.0	46.2	2.2	100.0	100.0
2040	42.8	10.8	43.3	3.1	33.9	14.6	49.4	2.1	100.0	100.0
2000–2004 migration scenario										
2000	56.3	11.1	29.8	2.8	48.2	15.2	34.7	1.9	100.0	100.0
2010	47.3	10.9	37.7	4.1	39.5	14.4	43.3	2.8	100.0	100.0
2020	39.2	10.2	45.1	5.5	31.4	13.4	51.4	3.8	100.0	100.0
2030	32.0	9.1	52.0	6.9	24.7	11.9	58.7	4.7	100.0	100.0
2040	25.5	8.0	58.3	8.2	19.3	10.4	64.7	5.6	100.0	100.0

Table 2.10 Percent adult population with overweight and obesity in Texas in 2000 and projected to 2040 by race/ethnicity under alternative projection scenarios

	Overweight				Obese					
Age group	Anglo	Black	Hispanic	Other	Anglo	Black	Hispanic	Other	Total over weight	Total obese
Base year 2000										
18–24	8.0	15.1	17.2	12.0	5.8	9.3	10.8	3.0	11.6	8.0
25–34	15.7	21.6	28.0	21.4	15.7	23.1	27.2	23.0	20.3	20.9
35–44	22.7	25.6	23.6	27.4	22.4	26.2	25.4	22.2	23.4	24.1
45–54	20.3	17.5	14.0	21.7	24.7	20.6	18.7	30.8	18.1	22.1
55–64	14.2	11.5	8.8	10.6	15.6	9.5	9.4	12.9	12.2	12.5
65+	19.1	8.7	8.4	6.9	15.8	11.3	8.5	8.1	14.4	12.4
Zero net migration scenario, year-2040										
18–24	6.5	10.4	11.5	6.1	5.5	6.9	7.8	1.6	9.1	6.8
25–34	13.3	16.9	20.0	10.6	15.0	19.2	21.1	11.9	16.5	18.5
35–44	15.1	18.6	18.7	16.6	15.0	17.6	18.8	12.3	17.1	17.2
45–54	15.7	18.1	13.7	14.4	19.9	20.7	18.1	19.4	15.0	19.2
55–64	15.4	18.6	14.9	14.8	17.9	14.8	15.2	17.2	15.5	16.0
65+	34.0	17.4	21.2	37.5	26.7	20.8	19.0	37.6	26.8	22.3
2000–2004 migration scenario, year-2040										
18–24	6.6	10.8	9.6	4.7	5.5	7.1	6.4	1.2	8.5	6.0
25–34	13.3	17.2	21.1	9.0	15.1	19.7	21.7	9.8	17.7	19.5
35–44	15.4	18.9	21.4	15.0	15.2	17.7	21.1	10.7	19.1	18.9
45–54	15.9	18.8	17.4	18.4	20.2	21.5	22.3	24.0	17.2	21.9
55–64	15.6	18.1	16.3	18.4	18.0	14.4	16.0	20.8	16.5	16.5
65+	33.2	16.2	14.2	34.5	26.0	19.6	12.5	33.5	21.0	17.2

Table 2.11 Percent change in adult population that is overweight and obese by age group from 2000 to 2040

Age group	Overweight Anglo	Black	Hispanic	Other	Obese Anglo	Black	Hispanic	Other	Total over weight	Total obese
Zero net migration scenario										
18–24	−10.3	−3.1	39.6	−19.6	30.0	39.5	104.7	17.9	12.4	66.4
25–34	−7.7	8.9	49.2	−22.2	33.6	58.2	117.7	12.6	17.3	75.2
35–44	−26.5	2.1	65.1	−3.6	−7.7	26.3	108.4	20.4	5.3	41.0
45–54	−15.6	44.8	104.9	4.6	11.9	91.0	171.6	36.9	19.2	70.7
55–64	19.9	125.1	255.2	121.5	59.0	194.8	353.9	191.3	84.1	154.5
65+	95.1	181.5	427.5	758.1	133.8	248.0	528.2	905.2	167.8	252.8
2000–2004 migration scenario										
18–24	−6.1	56.2	169.1	217.2	36.2	124.1	292.5	366.0	86.7	173.5
25–34	−3.2	73.8	265.4	236.3	40.1	152.6	425.4	387.1	124.2	240.1
35–44	−22.0	61.1	338.0	342.7	−2.0	100.1	446.8	453.4	108.7	187.5
45–54	−10.2	134.7	501.7	579.6	19.1	210.0	683.1	790.1	143.0	262.1
55–64	26.1	242.4	804.5	1307.0	67.2	348.1	1024.5	1753.4	248.2	383.7
65+	98.8	307.6	716.1	3922.2	138.1	410.5	867.9	4609.7	272.3	405.5

obesity is low for those aged 18–24, is highest for those aged 45–54, and then declines for those 55 and older. However, the largest percent increase in overweight and obesity for all race/ethnicity groups is among those who are 65 years of age and older, except for the Hispanic population. For the Hispanic population the largest increase is among those who are 55–64 years of age.

The percent change that is expected to occur from 2000 to 2040 for the adult population that is either overweight or obese by age group and race/ethnicity is presented in Table 2.11. As could be seen for the total population, the percent change in overweight and obesity is the highest for the older age groups both in zero net migration and 2000–2004 migration scenarios. For age group 65 and above, the overweight population will increase by 272.3% and the obese population will increase by 405.5% from 2000 to 2040 (2000–2004 scenario). The greatest changes can be observed for Hispanics and Other populations both for overweight and obesity.

The annual costs associated with overweight and obesity are expected to increase by 283.8% (Table 2.12); that is from $11.3 billion in 2000 to $36.7 billion in 2040. During this period, the annual costs, in billions, associated with overweight and obesity by race/ethnicity is projected to increase as follows; for the Hispanic population costs will increase from $3.8 to $23.1 billion, for the Anglo population it will increase from $5.7 to $7.7 billion, for the Black population it will increase from $1.6 to $3.5 billion, and for the Other population it will increase from $0.25 to $2.4 billion. In terms of percent change, the projected costs associated with overweight and obesity will increase by 35.1% for Anglos, by 507.9% for Hispanics, by 118.8% for Blacks, and by 860% for the Other population from 2000 to 2040.

Table 2.12 Projected cost associated with overweight and obesity in Texas by race/ethnicity from 2000 to 2040 under alternative projection scenarios (Using 2009 constant dollars and in millions)

	Overweight				Obese				Total		
Year	Anglo	Black	Hspnc	Other	Anglo	Black	Hspnc	Other	Over weight	Obese	Cost
Zero net migration scenario											
2000	1,449.3	290.7	772.4	73.5	4,255.1	1,275.7	3,003.6	173.7	2,585.9	8,708.1	11,294.0
2010	1,550.9	343.2	979.5	90.5	5,277.2	1,734.5	4,517.0	265.4	2,964.1	11,794.1	14,758.2
2020	1,608.8	381.6	1,195.0	103.6	5,817.7	2,082.2	5,970.1	338.7	3,289.0	14,208.7	17,497.7
2030	1,628.2	401.0	1,423.2	113.2	6,009.8	2,288.5	7,371.0	382.5	3,565.6	16,051.8	19,617.4
2040	1,591.7	407.3	1,615.7	116.9	5,990.2	2,380.9	8,511.0	404.2	3,731.6	17,286.3	21,017.9
2000–2004 migration scenario											
2000	1,449.3	290.7	772.4	73.5	4,255.1	1,275.7	3,003.6	173.7	2,585.9	8,708.1	11,294.0
2010	1,556.3	363.5	1,241.3	135.2	5,289.5	1,832.2	5,644.8	390.3	3,296.3	13,156.8	16,453.1
2020	1,620.4	427.6	1,859.8	226.0	5,852.9	2,334.3	9,202.5	739.7	4,133.8	18,129.4	22,263.2
2030	1,647.7	476.3	2,676.0	355.7	6,076.0	2,714.5	13,764.1	1,217.9	5,155.7	23,772.5	28,928.2
2040	1,617.6	513.2	3,698.5	526.6	6,081.3	3,000.7	19,385.4	1,855.9	6,355.9	30,323.3	36,679.2

The Results of the Decomposition Analysis

The results of the decomposition analysis of population change by age and race/ethnicity on overweight and obesity prevalence in Texas are shown in Table 2.13. The first column indicates the total effect of the three factors on the differences in the crude rates of overweight and obesity for the time period indicated. The next three columns decompose the difference in the crude rates due to population change (rate effect), age, and race/ethnicity. The next three columns (columns 5–7) present the change shown in column 2–4 in percentage terms with the sum of the percentages equaling 100% of the change.

The results in Table 2.13 show that change in each of the three factors decomposed will increase the number of overweight and obese persons. This is indicated by the positive values shown for nearly all values in the table for 2000–2040. The population change, or rate effect, is the major determinant of change in overweight and obese status accounting for 60% of the change in overweight and 74% of the change in the number of persons with obese status for the total change period from 2000 to 2040 (2000–2004 Migration Scenario). For this total period, age and race/ethnicity have similar effects, together accounting for 40 and 26% of the change in the number of overweight and obese persons, respectively.

The impact of population growth is pronounced for both overweight and obese adults. The impact of population growth on obesity is higher than that for overweight adults. During 2000–2010, the impact of population growth is 67 and 81.1% for overweight and obesity, respectively. During 2010–2020, the impact is 53.7 and 74.5% for overweight and obesity and the impact of population growth is 53.1 and 62.3% for overweight and obesity during 2020–2040.

The age effect is more pronounced on overweight status during the projection period and has very small effects on obesity. This age effect reflects the aging process expected in the population. For example, although age accounts for 17.6% of the total change in the number of overweight during the period of 2000–2010, almost 31% of the projected change in the number of overweight from 2010 to 2020 is projected to result from the aging of the population, the period when the substantial effects of the aging of the baby boom population will become evident.

Race/ethnicity also has a positive impact on overweight and obesity. Rapid growth in the minority population has a positive impact on the increase in the number of overweight and obese in Texas. The impact of race/ethnicity on the increase in the number of overweight and obese persons is 15.3 and 13.7% during 2000–2010, 15.7 and 22.1% during 2010–2020, and 29.8% on overweight and 38.0% of the increase in the number of obese persons from 2020 to 2040. The rapid increase in the proportion of change accounted for by race/ethnicity over time suggests that (in the absence of change in the prevalence of overweight and obese status among minority populations) as the diversity of the population increases so will the need to address problems related to overweight and obese status.

The results in Table 2.13 also indicate that the combined effects of age and race/ethnicity increase over time. Thus, whereas these two characteristics account for

Table 2.13 Decomposition of the effects of population change, age, and race/ethnicity on overweight and obesity in Texas

		Composition effect due to			Percent of change in total effect due to			Percent of absolute change in total effect due to		
Characteristic	Total effect	Rate effect	Age	Race/ ethnicity	Rate effect	Age	Race/ ethnicity	Rate effect	Age	Race/ ethnicity
Zero net migration scenario										
2000–2010										
Overweight	1.0506	0.6933	0.2728	0.0844	66.00	25.97	8.04	66.00	25.97	8.04
Obese	5.0941	4.2596	0.3896	0.4448	83.62	7.65	8.73	83.62	7.65	8.73
2010–2020										
Overweight	0.6409	0.3652	0.1998	0.0759	56.98	31.18	11.84	56.98	31.18	11.84
Obese	2.8762	2.5428	−0.1569	0.4903	88.41	−5.45	17.05	79.71	4.92	15.37
2020–2040										
Overweight	0.6088	0.2849	0.1452	0.1787	46.79	23.85	29.35	46.79	23.85	29.35
Obese	2.7237	2.0931	−0.2976	0.9282	76.85	−10.93	34.08	63.07	8.97	27.97
2000–2040										
Overweight	2.3003	1.4061	0.5695	0.3248	61.12	24.76	14.12	61.12	24.76	14.12
Obese	10.6939	8.8839	0.0733	1.7367	83.07	0.69	16.24	83.07	0.69	16.24
2000–2004 migration scenario										
2000–2010										
Overweight	1.1232	0.7539	0.1972	0.1720	67.13	17.56	15.31	67.13	17.56	15.31
Obese	5.2975	4.2949	0.2788	0.7238	81.07	5.26	13.66	81.07	5.26	13.66
2010–2020										
Overweight	0.7750	0.4161	0.2374	0.1215	53.70	30.63	15.67	53.70	30.63	15.67
Obese	3.5183	2.6202	0.1224	0.7756	74.47	3.48	22.05	74.47	3.48	22.05
2020–2040										
Overweight	0.6857	0.3640	0.1170	0.2046	53.09	17.07	29.84	53.09	17.07	29.84
Obese	3.4790	2.1659	−0.0080	1.3211	62.26	−0.23	37.97	61.97	0.23	37.80
2000–2040										
Overweight	2.5838	1.5559	0.5666	0.4613	60.22	21.93	17.85	60.22	21.93	17.85
Obese	12.2948	9.1050	0.5152	2.6745	74.06	4.19	21.75	74.06	4.19	21.75

about 33% of the total increase in the number of overweight and 19% of the total increase in the number of obese persons from 2000 to 2010, for 2010 to 2020 these two factors account for 46% of the change in the number of overweight and for 25% of the change in the number of obese. For 2020–2040, the effects of these two factors on the number of overweight remain nearly the same as for those from 2010 to 2020 for the change in the number of overweight but they increase to account for roughly 38% of the total increase in the number of obese.

The results in Table 2.13 clearly show that each of the demographic factors (population growth, aging and diversification) will increase the number of persons who are overweight and obese, in the absence of other changes. Anticipating demographic change is of vital importance for understanding change in these critical health-related statuses.

Conclusions

Overall the results reported here suggest that demographic change will have a substantial impact on the increase in the number of overweight and obese persons in Texas. Results also indicate that each of the major factors of population growth, the aging of the population, and the increasing diversity of the population will lead to increased numbers of overweight and obese persons. Related increases in total demands on health care and other forms of support reflect the projected changes in overweight and obesity in Texas and the costs related to these conditions.

If current trends in the ever-increasing prevalence of overweight and obesity among Texas adults persist, annual costs associated with excess weight could reach $36.7 billion by the year 2040. Even if the prevalence of overweight and obesity among Texas adults remain at the 1999–2002 rates presented in this study, the costs of overweight and obesity will continue to rise as the Texas population increases, ages, and becomes more diverse.

The limitations of this analysis must be recognized, however. Although the number of overweight and obese adults in Texas and the United States is expected to continue to increase, few projections such as those presented here exist that quantify the extent or rate of change. A recent study based on national BRFSS data used a linear time trend to project the prevalence of overweight and obesity among adult men and women in the United States (Sturm et al. 2004). The study estimated that among men, the prevalence of overweight would reach 39% by 2020 and the prevalence of obesity would reach 46%. Among women, the prevalence of overweight was estimated to reach 42% by 2020, and the prevalence of obesity was estimated to reach 38%. These estimates are higher than the projections presented in this report because the estimates in that study are based on a linear time trend. In the current analysis, the rates of prevalence change were assumed to decrease over time since the rapid increase in the prevalence of overweight and obesity in Texas and the United States observed during the 1990s was considered to be unsustainable. If the prevalence of overweight and obesity continued to increase on a linear trend in Texas and reached the levels reported in the published study, the associated annual costs of overweight and obesity in Texas could be much higher than the projected cost of $36.7 billion in 2040.

Although we believe the assumptions underlying our analysis are reasonable given the past and the expected future trends, the projections reported are based on a number of assumptions and limitations that must be acknowledged. First, it must be recognized that projections are subject to considerable error when unforeseen changes alter the historical patterns on which the projections are based. Changes in rates of future population growth, such as declines in the rate of population increase among minority populations, as well as increases or decreases in the prevalence of overweight and obesity due to changes in the population's dietary habits, could affect the accuracy of the projections presented here. In addition, the prevalence estimates for overweight and obesity in Texas are based on self-reported height and weight data, which typically underestimate BMI (Nieto-Garcia et al. 1990). If the actual prevalence of obesity in Texas is higher than this study reports, then both the number of overweight and obese adults and the associated costs might be much higher than those presented herein. However, if the actual prevalence of obesity in Texas is lower than this study reports, then both the number of overweight and obese adults and the associated costs might be much lower than those presented herein. In addition, the definition of overweight and obesity may change over time, and advances in the prevention or the possibility of a cure for overweight and obesity in the next 40 years may reduce the numbers of overweight and obese adults in Texas. The prevalence of overweight and obesity may increase or decrease from the rates we assumed and thus our projections may be an overestimation or an underestimation of the actual numbers of overweight and obese persons in Texas. The reported projections of overweight and obese adults and the costs associated with overweight and obese would be correct if the assumptions hold true in the coming years.

Overweight and obesity statuses are already recognized as the leading health problem facing Texas. Our projections of the number of overweight and obese adults, and the direct and indirect costs associated with overweight and obesity, may be more alarming than previously thought. The economic cost of overweight and obesity is already overwhelming, and the future growth in the overweight and obese population is likely to increase the cost further. Thus, there is a critical need for policies and programs designed to decrease the prevalence of overweight and obesity through both prevention and treatment to address this growing public health problem in Texas and the nation.

The results of the analysis provided here not only suggest the potential magnitude of the increases in the number of overweight and obese persons, the demographic dimensions associated with such increases, and the costs associated with these increases, they also suggest some of the factors that should be considered in the policies developed to address the growth in the number of overweight and obese persons. For example, it is evident that although it may be difficult to alter patterns of population growth, projecting where such growth is likely to occur should assist policy makers in locating and sizing service facilities to address the problems associated with overweight and obese status. Similarly, the critical role played by aging and population diversification over the next 20 years makes evident the need to target educational and prevention programs toward the needs of aging and minority populations. Finally, what is especially critical is to understand that the relationships between such factors as minority status and overweight and obesity stem from social and economic differentials, which are alterable. Programs aimed at reducing socioeconomic disparities may thus also reduce the demand for services resulting from overweight or obese status by reducing the reasons for the disparities in prevalence between minority and other populations.

References

Allison, D. B., Fontaine, K. R., Manson, J. E., Stevens, J., & Vanitalie, T. B. (1999). Annual deaths attributable to obesity in the United States. *Journal of the American Medical Association, 282*, 1530–1538.

Baskin, J.L., Ard, J., Franklin, F., & Allison, D. B. (2005). Prevalence of obesity in the United States. *Obesity Reviews, 6*:5–7.

Calle, E. E., Rodriguez, C., Walker-Thurmond, K., & Thun, M. J. (2003). Overweight, obesity, and mortality from cancer in a prospectively studied cohort of U.S. adults. *The New England Journal of Medicine, 348*, 1625–1638.

Centers for Disease Control and Prevention. (1991, 1999, 2000, 2001, 2002, 2003, 2004, 2007). *Behavioral risk factor surveillance system survey data*. Atlanta: U.S. Department of Health and Human Services, Centers for Disease Control and Prevention. Available online at: http://www.cdc.gov/brfss. Last accessed 2004.

Das Gupta, P. (1978). A general method of decomposing a difference between two rates into several components. *Demography, 15*(February), 99–112.

Dor, A., Ferguson, C., Langwith, C., & Tan, E. (2010). *A Heavy Burden: The individual costs of being overweight and obese in the United States* (Technical Report). Washington, DC: George Washington University.

Flegal, K. M., Carroll, M. D., Ogden, C. L., & Johnson, C. L. (2002). Prevalence and trends in obesity among US adults, 1999–2000. *Journal of the American Medical Association, 288*, 1723–1727.

Flegal, K.M., Carroll, M.D., Ogden, C.L. & Curtin, L.R. (2010). Prevalence and trands in obesity among US adults, 1999-2008. *Journal of the American Medical Association, 303*(3): 235–241.

Hollmann, F. W., Mulder, T. J., & Kallan, J. E. (2000). *Methodology and assumptions for the population projections of the United States: 1999 to 2100* (Population Division Working Paper No. 38). Washington, DC: U.S. Bureau of the Census.

Hoque, N., McCusker, M. E., Murdock, S. H., & Perez, D. (2010). The implications of change in population size, distribution, and composition on the number of overweight and obese adults and direct and indirect cost associated with overweight and obese adults in Texas through 2040. *Population Research and Policy Review, 29*, 173–191.

Kitagawa, E. M. (1955). Components of a difference between two rates. *Journal of the American Statistical Association, 50*, 1168–1194.

McCusker, M. E., Sanchez, E. J., Murdock, S. H., Hoque, N., & Huang, P. P. (2004). *The burden of overweight and obesity in Texas, 2000–2040* (Technical Report). Chapel Hill: Centers for Disease Control and Prevention and University of N. Carolina Available online at: http://www.publichealthgrandrounds.unc.edu/catch/handout_txCost_Obesity_Report.pdf. Last accessed Jan 2008.

Murdock, S. H., White, S., Hoque, M. N., Pecotte, B., You, X., & Balkan, J. (2003). *The new Texas challenge: Population change and the future of Texas*. College Station: Texas A&M University Press.

National Institutes of Health. (1998). *Clinical guidelines on the identification, evaluation, and treatment of overweight and obesity in adults*. Bethesda: Department of Health and Human Services, National Institutes of Health, National Heart, Lung, and Blood Institute.

National Institutes of Health. (2004). National Institute of Diabetes, Digestive and Kidney Diseases. "Statistics related to overweight and obesity: The economic costs." Available online at: http//www.win/niddk.nih.gov/statistics/index.htm. Last accessed Jan 2008.

Nieto-Garcia, F. J., Bush, T. L., & Keyl, P. M. (1990). Body mass definitions of obesity: Sensitivity and specificity using self-reported height and weight. *Epidemiology, 1*, 146–152.

Obesity in America. (2004). *A handbook on obesity in America*. Available online at: http://www.obesityinamerica.org/links/HandbookonObesityinAmerica.pdf. Last accessed Jan 2008.

Spencer, G. (1984). *Projections of the population of the United States, by age, sex, and race: 1983–2080* (Current Population Reports, Series P-25, Number 952). Washington, DC: U.S. Government Printing Office.

Spencer, G. (1986). *Projections of the Hispanic population: 1983–2080* (Current Population Reports, Series P-25, Number 796). Washington, DC: U.S. Government Printing Office.

Spencer, G. (1989). *Projections of the population of the United States, by age, sex, and race: 1988–2080* (Current Population Reports, Series P-25, Number 1018). Washington, DC: U.S. Government Printing Office.

Sturm, R., Ringel, J. S., & Andreyeva, T. (2004). Increasing obesity rates and disability trends. *Health Affairs, 23*, 199–205.

Texas Population Estimates and Projection Program. (2006). *Projections of the population of Texas and counties in Texas by age, sex and race/ethnicity for 2000–2040*. San Antonio: University of Texas at San Antonio, Texas State Data Center. Available on-line at: http://txsdc.utsa.edu/tpepp/projections/Texas_County_Projection_Methodology.pdf.

U.S. Census Bureau. (2008). *Projected population by single year of age, sex, race, and Hispanic origin for the United States: July 1, 2000 to July 1, 2050* [machine-readable file]. Available online at: http://www.census.gov/population/www/projections/files/nation/download/NP2008_D1.csv. Last accessed Feb 2009.

Wolk, A., Gridley, G., Svensson, M., Nyrem, O., McLaughlin, J., Fraumeni, J., & Adami, H. O. (2001). A prospective study of obesity and cancer risk (Sweden). *Cancer Causes & Control, 12*, 13–21.

Chapter 3
The Effect of Obesity on Intergenerational Income Mobility

Liana Fox and Nathan Hutto

Introduction

Obesity has increasingly become a national health concern of epidemic proportions. Recent Centers for Disease Control (CDC) data indicate that the national age-adjusted obesity prevalence reached an all-time high of 34% in 2008, with more than 16% of children and adolescents obese (Flegal et al. 2010). Overall, 68% of U.S. adults are overweight or obese. Overweight and obese individuals are at increased risk of a range of medical conditions, including coronary heart disease, type-2 diabetes, cancer, sleep apnea, and reproductive dysfunction. Medical costs associated with overweight and obesity were $92.6 billion in 1998 and accounted for at least 9% of all national health care spending (Finkelstein et al. 2003). More than 10 years later, the costs have surely increased with obesity's increased prevalence. In addition to health care spending, obesity has many socioeconomic costs, with vast research detailing correlates between socioeconomic status (SES) and weight.

Overweight and obesity are expensive, both nationally and personally. It is estimated that overweight and obesity are responsible for 5–9% of national annual medical costs (Wolf and Colditz 1994; Finkelstein et al. 2003), driven in part by the fact that obese individuals spend $10,000 more in lifetime medical expenses due to related medical conditions (Bhattacharya and Sood 2004). The overweight and obese also experience declines in wages and lifetime earnings compared to those of normal weight (Wada and Tekin 2010). Aside from increased medical costs, a number of mechanisms have been hypothesized to mediate this relationship, including decreased probabilities of marriage (Mukhopadhyay 2008), lower spousal earnings (Averett and Korenman 1996), and labor market discrimination (Baum and Ford 2004).

L. Fox (✉) • N. Hutto
School of Social Work, Columbia University, New York, NY, USA
e-mail: lef2118@columbia.edu

N. Hoque et al. (eds.), *Applied Demography and Public Health*,
Applied Demography Series 3, DOI 10.1007/978-94-007-6140-7_3,

© Springer Science+Business Media Dordrecht 2013

While the relationship between SES and obesity has been widely researched, there have been no studies examining obesity's effect on intergenerational mobility. This paper begins to fill this gap as we look at the impact of obesity on the likelihood of upward and downward mobility. We will also examine differential impacts of obesity on mobility by gender.

Background

While there have been no prior studies examining obesity's direct effect on mobility, there is a substantial body of research on the many pathways through which this relationship could operate. Although causal direction is often difficult to establish in obesity studies because mobility might be endogenous to BMI, obesity is correlated with a number of relevant sociodemographic indicators, such as educational attainment, income, geography, and race and ethnicity (Ogden et al. 2010; Wang and Beydoun 2007; Zhang and Wang 2004). Particularly relevant to this study, Langenberg et al. (2003) found that father's social class in childhood is inversely related to BMI in later adulthood, even after adjusting for one's own social class in middle adulthood. Obesity and its economic outcomes are also differentiated by gender. While only 52% of women are overweight or obese, compared to 69% of men, a number of studies have demonstrated that obesity tends to affect women to a greater degree. Overweight and obese individuals have been shown to have lower wages than peers of normal weight, with much of the wage penalty falling on obese women (Baum and Ford 2004; Han et al. 2008; DeBeaumont 2009). This tendency for lower wages has been attributed to labor market discrimination against obese women. Similarly, Classen (2009a, b) has found that obese and overweight women and women with weights relatively greater than their peers have lower levels of college attainment than women of normal weight; males do not experience these same effects.

Obesity also interacts with marriage and mating. Assortative mating – the tendency for a species to choose a mate with similar phenotypic or cultural characteristics – may contribute to two obese or relatively disadvantaged individuals marrying each other (Hebebrand et al. 2000; Speakman et al. 2007). In their study of obesity and marriage rates, Fu and Goldman (1996) employed Becker's theory on the stylized formulation of assortative mating, which implies that men are more likely to be concerned with their spouse's social and physical characteristics, while females value their future partner's socio-economic characteristics. Their model identified significantly lower marriage probabilities for obese women compared to obese men. In a study of obesity's effect on cohabitation and marriage, Mukhopadhyay (2008) found that after controlling for variables that affect marriage probabilities, obese women were significantly less likely to cohabitate or marry than other women and men of all weight groups.

This paper will examine how overweight and obesity affect intergenerational economic mobility, a relationship that has gone unexplored. The level of intergenerational mobility – that is, movement in the income distribution, relative to parental position – is considered a key indicator of equality of opportunity among a population (Van de Gaer et al. 1998). The presence of opportunity should theoretically erase much of an individual's birth circumstances.

Mobility is usually measured in one of two ways: through occupation and income/earnings. Both measures have a number of methodological limitations – occupations are difficult to rank and income reports are subject to measurement error and recall bias – but are used to answer a variety of research questions. This study will employ family income mobility, as it is measured contemporaneously in the longitudinal dataset (so recall bias is not an issue) and it is a more comprehensive measure of economic well-being than occupational status. Also, as we are interested in breaking out results by gender, we use total family income as opposed to earnings, which would have problematic selection bias as women more frequently leave the paid labor market to raise children and care for other family members, therefore earning $0 in wages.

Data

Our research is based on an analysis of the National Longitudinal Survey of Youth 1979 (NLSY79), a nationally representative longitudinal survey of individuals who were 14–22 years old in 1979 covering a wide range of health and economic questions asked repeatedly throughout the respondent's life. Respondents were interviewed annually from 1979 to 1994 and biannually from 1994 to 2008. The survey's original sample size was 12,686 individuals, with retention rates near 70% over the survey's 27-year duration. Data collection methods have varied over the years. In-person interviews were conducted from 1979 to 1986 and 1988–2000, while telephone interviews were conducted in 1987 and 2002–2008. Computer-assisted interviewing replaced paper-and-pencil interviewing in 1993.

To measure intergenerational mobility, we restrict our survey to individuals who were 14–22 years old and living at home in the years that parental family income was collected so that parental income would have an opportunity to influence child outcomes. We allow parental income to be collected between 1979 and 1982. Additionally, averaging multiple years of income reduces measurement error and gives a better approximation of permanent family income. The sample is restricted to children with parents aged 30–61 at measurement of parents' income so as to avoid measurement error associated with earnings during early career and retirement years, which would differ from the true long-run earnings. We measure child income as a respondent's log family income averaged for all available years between age 35 and 50, approximately the age at which individuals have reached the peak of their earnings potential (Solon 1999). Family income includes all sources of income from individuals in the household older than 14 years old, before taxes or other deductions. All dollar values are converted to 2007 dollars using the Consumer Price Index for Urban Consumers, Research Series (CPI-U-RS).

Body mass index (BMI) is measured between ages 20 and 24, the age at which most respondents would be entering the labor market. We measure obesity using the imperial BMI formula (weight in pounds times 703 divided by height in inches squared) for individuals ages 20–24. Using the National Institute of Health guidelines, individuals with a BMI of 18.5–24.9 are considered normal weight, 25–29.9 overweight, and 30 and above obese. Height and weight questions were asked in 1981, 1982, and 1985. We use linear interpolation to impute the height and weight for 1983 and 1984 so that all individuals have a BMI measurement between ages 20 and 24. Women who were pregnant at the time of BMI measurement are excluded from the sample, unless we were able to obtain another valid BMI measurement during the valid age range.

We restrict our sample to individuals who reported valid parent family income (at age 14–22), BMI (at age 20–24), and family income at age 35–50. After all of these restrictions, the sample size is 6,564 individuals.

Methodology

We follow the standard intergenerational mobility methodology used by many researchers, such as Solon (1992), Hertz (2005) and Bratberg et al. (2007) to measure mobility by examining the correlation between parent family income and child family income. Intergenerational mobility is defined as the income elasticity from one generation to the next. Intergenerational elasticities explain the degree of variation in income that can be explained from the previous generation. Larger elasticities are associated with lower intergenerational mobility in society as one's place in the income distribution is more a function of parental status than individual characteristics or achievements.

When comparing family income across two generations, adjustments must be made to account for life-cycle variation in income. Average log family income from both generations is age-adjusted by regressing income on average parent (or child) age and age-squared and using the residual from the regression (including the constant term) as the income measure (Bratberg et al. 2007).

Once we create age-adjusted log income measures, we regress child family income on parent family income in general and by BMI level (normal, overweight, and obese).[1] Based on analyses of the impact of obesity on wages, we expect that

[1] While both the number of earners and number of children in a household are likely endogenous to total family income and obesity status, we tested an alternative specification as a sensitivity test of our results. Following Deaton (1997) and Hertz (2005), we examined a family size-adjusted model, with total family income adjusted by a family size factor (*F*) equal to: $F = (N_{adult} + 0.5N_{child})^{0.9}$ where N_{adult} is the number of adults in the household over age 18 and N_{child} is the number of children age 17 and below. This factor is raised to the power of 0.9 to capture probable economies of scale that exist in larger households. The family-size adjusted models were somewhat more muted, with the overall elasticity of 0.37 vs. 0.43, and the disparities between groups were very similar.

obesity's effect on mobility will be felt most strongly by women (Register and Williams 1990; Pagan and Davila 1997). As such, we also divide the regression models by gender.

Following the methodology established by Hertz (2005), we augment the results from the regressions with transition matrices. While the regressions estimate the likelihood of movement from one generation to another, transition matrices provide additional information regarding the degree and direction of movement by each parental family income quintile. Transition matrices graphically show the likelihood of movement from one point in the income distribution in the parental generation to all other points in the child's generation.

Results

Table 3.1 provides several sample summary statistics for the overall and BMI-stratified samples. Parents' family income illustrates that the respondents are relatively evenly distributed in childhood. The exception to this is that obese individuals are significantly under-represented in the highest quintile, with a ten point gap from normal weight individuals, and over-represented in the lowest quintile by four points. The gap grows for the obese in adulthood and expands to a seven point gap in the fourth quintile. A small BMI gap also opens up between overweight and normal groups in the second and highest quintile.

The demographic data further underscores the general disadvantage facing the overweight and obese in this sample. Individuals of normal weight are more likely to attain higher levels of education, with, for example, a 6 point gap in college attainment between those who are overweight and those with normal weight and a 12 point gap for the obese group. The overweight and obese are also more likely to be Black or Hispanic. Both of these findings are consistent with previous research. This table also shows that the overweight and obese are less likely to be married and that females are more likely to be obese. We will discuss these trends in further detail later.

Table 3.2 contains age-adjusted bivariate intergenerational income elasticities. These elasticities can be interpreted as intergenerational log income correlations in which an elasticity of 0.43 (as in the full sample) indicates that a 10% difference in parental income would lead to a 4.3% difference in child income. Lower elasticities indicate a higher level of intergenerational mobility, but do not indicate the direction of that mobility. The elasticity for the full sample is consistent with other research that finds intergenerational income elasticities ranging between 0.3 and 0.5 (Solon 1999). The overall elasticities in each BMI category do not deviate much from the full sample elasticity. The exception to this is that obese individuals have an overall elasticity four points lower than the full sample. This indicates that the obese individuals sampled have higher overall mobility and family incomes that deviate substantially from their parents.

Table 3.1 Descriptive statistics

	Overall	BMI status						
		Normal	Overweight	Obese				
	Mean/%	Mean/%	Mean/%	Mean/%	Overweight – normal		Obese – normal	
Parents' family income (ln 2007$)								
Log ave. parent family income	10.65	10.66	10.61	10.51	−6%	*	−15%	***
% in lowest quintile	20%	20%	21%	24%	2%		4%	*
% in second quintile	20%	20%	21%	24%	1%		4%	
% in middle quintile	20%	20%	20%	22%	0%		2%	
% in fourth quintile	20%	20%	19%	19%	−1%		−1%	
% in highest quintile	20%	21%	18%	11%	−2%		−10%	***
Child's Family Income (ln 2007$)								
Log ave. family income (age 35–50)	10.75	10.79	10.67	10.42	−0.13	***	−0.37	***
% in lowest quintile	20%	19%	22%	31%	0.03		0.13	***
% in second quintile	20%	19%	23%	23%	0.04	***	0.03	
% in middle quintile	20%	20%	21%	22%	0.01		0.02	
% in fourth quintile	20%	21%	19%	13%	−0.02		−0.07	***
% in highest quintile	20%	21%	16%	11%	−0.06	***	−0.11	***
BMI								
BMI (age 20–24)	22.93	21.76	26.82	33.45	5.07	***	11.69	***
Race								
% White, non-Hispanic	51%	51%	49%	44%	−0.02		−0.07	**
% Black, non-Hispanic	31%	31%	30%	35%	−0.02		0.04	*
% Hispanic	16%	15%	19%	18%	0.04	***	0.03	

Education								
LTHS	8%	8%	11%	11%	0.03	***	0.03	*
HS	38%	36%	41%	47%	0.05	**	0.11	***
Some college	21%	21%	20%	21%	–0.01		–0.01	
BA+	20%	22%	16%	10%	–0.06	***	–0.12	***
Family status								
% Married	53%	55%	50%	41%	–0.05	**	–0.13	***
% With children	80%	81%	77%	70%	–0.04	**	–0.11	***
Ave. # of kids (if # child>0)	2.39	2.37	2.47	2.45	0.10		0.08	
Basic demographics								
% Female	48%	48%	34%	55%	–0.15	***	0.07	***
Ave. age	44.3	44.3	44.5	44.8	0.27	***	0.58	***
% U.S. born	93%	93%	93%	96%	–0.01		0.03	*
N	6,564	4,732	1,132	310				

***p<0.01; **p<0.05; *p<0.1

Table 3.2 Bivariate intergenerational income mobility estimates

BMI	Overall	Male	Female
Overall	0.4255***	0.4158***	0.4350***
	(0.015)	(0.022)	(0.022)
Normal	0.4245***	0.4123***	0.4387***
	(0.018)	(0.026)	(0.025)
Overweight	0.4608***	0.4372***	0.4102***
	(0.036)	(0.046)	(0.060)
Obese	0.3810***	0.2709**	0.2984***
	(0.080)	(0.122)	(0.108)

Standard errors in parentheses
***p<0.01; **p<0.05; *p<0.1

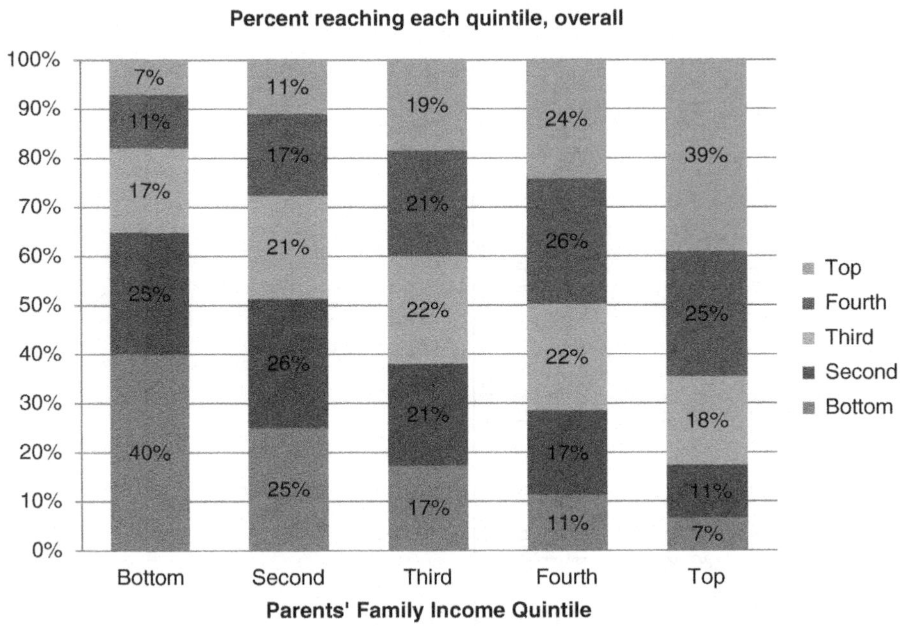

Fig. 3.1 Overall transition matrix

To better understand intergenerational volatility between quintiles and within BMI groups, we examined transition matrices, which show the distribution of adult respondents within each parental income quintile. However, due to small cell sizes in some cases we do not present the full results here. In Fig. 3.1, which illustrates transition in the entire sample, we see results consistent with an overall intergenerational elasticity of 0.43 in that income is relatively stable from generation to

Table 3.3 Mobility direction

	Overall (%)	Normal (%)	Overweight (%)	Obese (%)
Full sample				
Upward	34.6	35.5	32.2**	31.3*
Downward	34.8	34.0	35.6	39.7**
None	30.6	30.5	32.2	29.0
Men				
Upward	34.3	34.7	33.4	36.2
Downward	34.8	34.4	34.9	39.1
None	30.9	30.9	31.7	24.6*
Women				
Upward	35.0	36.3	29.9***	27.3***
Downward	34.8	33.6	37.0*	40.1**
None	30.2	30.0	33.1*	32.6

Asterisks for t-tests between overweight/obese and normal weight categories
***$p<0.01$; **$p<0.05$; *$p<0.1$

generation. For example, 40 and 39% of the sample who began life in the bottom and top parental income quintiles respectively remained in those quintiles in adulthood. Although this "stickiness" is not as strong in other parental quintiles, it is the case that the modal quintile in adulthood aligns with parental quintile.

The results for the normal weight sample are nearly identical to the results overall. These patterns change, however, when we examine transition in the overweight and obese samples. We see much more downward transition and stickiness within the lower income quintiles, while there is much less upward transition. These trends are amplified in the obese sample. Within this group, nearly half of people starting in the bottom quintile remain in the bottom quintile in adulthood, and many obese individuals starting in the second and third quintiles move down to the bottom quintile later in life. Similarly, obese people who begin in the fourth or fifth quintile disproportionately move downward.

Table 3.3 provides another point of mobility comparison by detailing the direction of mobility by BMI level and gender. In the full sample, roughly one-third is each downwardly mobile, upwardly mobile, and not mobile. These results are consistent with normal weight men and women and reflect the findings in the intergenerational elasticities and transition matrices that mobility is relatively stable across populations. However, this is not the case for the overweight and obese sample. Overweight and obese individuals are significantly less likely to be upwardly mobile, and overweight individuals are more likely to be downwardly mobile than normal weight individuals, a trend that appears to be entirely driven by females. Overweight and obese females are significantly less likely to be upwardly mobile and significantly more likely to be downwardly mobile: obese women face a nine percentage point upward mobility penalty and a six percentage point downward mobility penalty compared with normal weight women.

Discussion

These results present a complicated picture of the effect of weight on income mobility. As supported in the literature, obese individuals are more likely than normal weight individuals to come from disadvantaged childhoods and less likely to come from advantaged childhoods. These discrepancies in SES of origin may influence access to opportunity structures – such as education and marriage – that promote mobility. The various measures of elasticity and transition utilized in this paper help identify the mobility trends and magnitude of those trends for individuals across BMI groups. We find that obese individuals have much lower income elasticities than other groups and that obese women experience both significant downward mobility and lack of upward mobility.

The gender differences between men and women, especially obese men and women, are striking. At the outset of this paper, we posited three possible pathways through which obesity could affect intergenerational income mobility: labor market discrimination, differential childhood position, and marriage. The literature clearly supports the hypothesis that overweight and obese women experience labor market discrimination that reduces their wages. Social norms regarding women's appearance exist to a degree not expected for men. Wages of overweight and obese women may suffer because of these norms through employer or customer bias; given that women are more likely to work in customer service-oriented industries, pressure for appearance conformity may be especially hard felt. Men do not tend to suffer the same penalties for appearance, perhaps because expectations for appearance are lower or because men tend to work in non-customer service oriented industries in which appearance matters less. However, because of issues of female selection out of the labor market, this theory is not readily testable in this study.

Obesity also appears to compound disadvantage in our sample, making upward mobility more difficult for those individuals beginning in the lowest income quintiles. Table 3.4 shows that obese women – who have the highest probability of downward mobility – disproportionately begin life in the lower income quintile, while obese men begin in the higher income quintiles. More than twice the proportion of obese women compared to obese men constitutes the bottom quintile of parental income (14% vs. 32%). Conversely, obese men are nearly twice as likely as obese women to be in the fourth and fifth quintiles. These differential starting positions between men and women may limit access to the opportunity structures necessary to be upwardly mobile.

Table 3.4 Parental income distribution of obese individuals by gender

	Obese overall (%)	Obese men (%)	Obese women (%)
Bottom quintile	24	14	32
Second quintile	24	20	26
Third quintile	22	25	20
Fourth quintile	19	26	14
Top quintile	11	14	8

Table 3.5 Percent married by BMI status and gender

	Men (%)	Women (%)
Overall	53	53
Normal	53	57
Overweight	54	42
Obese	55	30

Given that we are examining mobility in terms of family income, it is important to consider the role of marriage and spouse selection. Much like in the workplace, overweight and obese women pay a marriage penalty that men do not, likely because many of the same social norms that exist in the labor market also exist in the marriage market. This penalty may come in the form of simply being unmarried, or by marrying a partner who has lower earnings potential. Because of the same cultural norms that pathologize heaviness among women, heavier men may in fact be seen as prosperous by potential mates because their supposed success has allowed these men to consume more. Table 3.5 illustrates that overweight and obese women are disproportionately unmarried when compared to normal weight women and all men.

This study suffers from two primary limitations. First, after restricting the overall sample to respondents with valid BMI and income data, the sample is reduced by more than half, placing the study at risk for unobserved selection bias. Related to this, the sample sizes for obese respondents are quite small. However, a power analysis of the female sample comparing obese and normal weight women (172 vs. 2,289) found that our sample has 100% power to detect significant effects ($\alpha = .05$) in the t-tests employed to compare differences in proportions. Future studies would benefit from oversampling of overweight and obese individuals. Although outside the scope of this study, it remains unclear what factors mediate the relationship between obesity and income mobility and how these pathways interact with gender. This study is premised on the temporal ordering of parental family income, BMI at labor market entry, and child family income in adulthood. However, it is quite likely that later adult BMI is correlated with young adult BMI and income in adulthood. We cannot adjust for this endogenous and, likely, mediating variable. Future research should attempt to identify the many mediators supported in previous research.

Selected References

Averett, S., & Korenman, S. (1996). The economic reality of the beauty myth. *The Journal of Human Resources, 31*(2), 304–330.

Baum, C., & Ford, W. (2004). The wage effects of obesity: A longitudinal study. *Health Economics, 13*(9), 885–899.

Bhattacharya, J., & Sood, N. (2004). Health insurance, obesity, and its economic costs. In *The economics of obesity: A report on the workshop held at USDA's economic research service* (pp. 21–24), Washington, DC.

Bratberg, E., Nilsen, O. A., & Vaage, K. (2007). Trends in intergenerational mobility across offspring's earnings distribution in Norway. *Industrial Relations, 46*(1), 112–128.

Classen, T. (2009a). The effect of relative weight status on education accumulation (Working paper). http://homepages.luc.edu/~tclass1/

Classen, T. (2009b). Obesity and educational attainment (Working paper). http://homepages.luc.edu/~tclass1/

Deaton, A. (1997). *The analysis of household surveys: A microeconometric approach to development policy*. Baltimore: Johns Hopkins University Press.

DeBeaumont, R. (2009). Occupational differences in the wage penalty for obese women. *The Journal of Socio-Economics, 38*, 344–349.

Finkelstein, E. A., Fiebelkorn, I. C., & Wang, G. (2003). National medical spending attributable to overweight and obesity: How much, and who's paying? *Health Affairs, Supplement, W3*, 219–226.

Flegal, K. M., Carroll, M. D., Ogden, C. L., & Curtin, L. R. (2010). Prevalence and trends in obesity among U.S. adults, 1999–2008. *Journal of the American Medical Association, 303*(3), 235–241.

Fu, H., & Goldman, N. (1996). Incorporating health into models of marriage choice: Demographic and sociological perspectives. *Journal of Marriage and the Family, 58*(3), 740–758.

Han, E., Norton, E. C., & Stearns, S. C. (2008). Weight and wages: Fat versus lean paychecks. *Health Economics, 18*(5), 535–548.

Hebebrand, J., Wulftange, H., Goerg, T., Ziegler, A., Hinney, A., Barth, N., Mayer, H., & Remschmidt, H. (2000). Epidemic obesity: Are genetic factors involved via increased rates of assortative mating? *International Journal of Obesity and Related Metabolic Disorders, 24*, 345–353.

Hertz, T. (2005). Rags, riches, and race: The intergenerational economic mobility of black and white families in the United States. In *Unequal chances: Family background and economic success* (pp. 165–91). New York: Russell Sage Press.

Langenberg, C., Hardy, R., Kuh, D., Brunner, E., & Wadsworth, M. (2003). Central and total obesity in middle aged men and women in relation to lifetime socioeconomic status: Evidence from a national birth cohort. *British Medical Journal, 57*(10), 816–822.

Mukhopadhyay, S. (2008). Do women value marriage more? The effect of obesity on cohabitation and marriage in the USA. *Review of Economics of the Household, 6*(2), 111–126.

Ogden, C. L., Lamb, M. M., Carroll, M. D., & Flegal, K. M. (2010). *Obesity and socioeconomic status in adults: United States 1988–1994 and 2005–2008* (NCHS data brief no. 50). Hyattsville: National Center for Health Statistics.

Pagan, J., & Davila, A. (1997). Obesity, occupational attainment, and earnings. *Social Science Quarterly, 78*, 756–770.

Register, C. A., & Williams, D. R. (1990). Wage effects of obesity among young workers. *Social Science Quarterly, 71*, 130–141.

Solon, G. (1992). Intergenerational income mobility in the United States. *American Economic Review, 82*(3), 393–408.

Solon, G. (1999). Intergenerational mobility in the labor market. In A. Orley & C. David (Eds.), *Handbook of labor economics* (Vol. 3A, pp. 1761–1800). Amsterdam: Elsevier Science BV.

Speakman, J. R., Djafarian, K., Stewart, J., & Jackson, D. M. (2007). Assortative mating for obesity. *American Journal of Clinical Nutrition, 86*(2), 316–323.

Van de Gaer, D., Martinez, M., & Schokkaert, E. (1998). *Measuring intergenerational mobility and equality of opportunity* (Center for Economic Studies, Discussion Paper Series. add:ces9810). Katholieke Universiteit Leuven, Centrum voor Economische Studiën. http://www.econ.kuleuven.ac.be/ew/academic/econover/Papers/DPS9810.pdf

Wada, R., & Tekin, E. (2010). Body composition and wages. *Economics & Human Biology, 8*(2), 242–254.

Wang, Y., & Beydoun, M. A. (2007). The obesity epidemic in the United States – gender, age, socioeconomic, racial/ethnic, and geographic characteristics: A systematic review and meta-regression analysis. *Epidemiologic Reviews, 29*(1), 6–28.

Wolf, A. M., & Colditz, G. A. (1994). The cost of obesity: The U.S. perspective. *Pharmacoeconomics, 5*(Suppl. 1), 34–37.

Zhang, Q., & Wang, Y. (2004). Trends in the association between obesity and socioeconomic status in U.S. adults: 1971 to 2000. *Obesity Research, 12*, 1622–1632.

Chapter 4
A Cross-Country Comparison of Sociodemographic Correlates of Depression in the WHO Study of Global Aging and Adult Health (SAGE)

Tristan Gorrindo, Somnath Chatterji, Paul Kowal, Zachary Epstein, and Maxine Weinstein

Introduction

Depressive disorders are the leading cause of the burden of disease in both middle- and high-income countries (Mathers et al. 2008). With the exception of the African region – where infectious and diarrheal diseases continue to dominate – depressive disorders rank among the top ten causes of disease burden in all WHO regions; globally, they are projected to be the single most important cause in 2030. Alleviating the personal suffering and reducing the economic costs and consequences of this group of disorders is a growing concern and focus for intervention. Relative to physical conditions, psychiatric disorders have been shown to be more disabling and less likely to be treated in some parts of the world (Suliman et al. 2010).

Using data from the WHO Study on global aging and adult health (SAGE), we evaluate the extent and sociodemographic correlates of depressive conditions across five countries: India, China, Ghana, Mexico, and South Africa. Our work focuses on a few correlates – income, sex, age, education, and self-assessed health – that have already been identified as linked to the condition; previous findings regarding these correlates are summarized below. The SAGE data provide an important vehicle for identifying and assessing the characteristics of persons at highest risk of a depressive episode. Unlike most demographic studies, which typically use a form of the CES-D to characterize depressive symptoms, the SAGE data on affective disorders

T. Gorrindo (✉)
Department of Psychiatry, Massachusetts General Hospital, Washington, DC, USA
e-mail: TGORRINDO@PARTNERS.ORG

S. Chatterji • P. Kowal
Measurement and Health Information Systems, World Health Organization (WHO), Genève, Switzerland

Z. Epstein • M. Weinstein
Center for Population and Health, Georgetown University, Washington, DC, USA

N. Hoque et al. (eds.), *Applied Demography and Public Health*,
Applied Demography Series 3, DOI 10.1007/978-94-007-6140-7_4,
© Springer Science+Business Media Dordrecht 2013

allow a diagnosis of depression that is closely consistent with the Diagnostic and Statistical Manual of Mental Disorders (American Psychiatric Association 2000). The DSM diagnosis is important because it allows for comparisons with the extant psychiatric literature. We use the DSM criteria to identify persons who would have been diagnosed as depressed during the previous year and compare that percentage with an estimate of persons who self-report that they were diagnosed, took medication or had other treatment for depression, or had an in- or outpatient visit related to anxiety or depression. We use these measures to estimate (in our five countries) the overall prevalence of a major depressive episode and the extent to which the depressive episode in the past year went undiagnosed or untreated. Finally, we explore the extent to which the correlates explain whether a respondent reported a major depressive episode in the previous year.

Income

Generally, low socioeconomic status is associated with a higher probability of a depressive disorder (Kessler et al. 2003; Lorant et al. 2003). More specifically, in many developing countries, poverty and socioeconomic insecurity have been shown to be associated with higher prevalence of mental health disorders (Patel and Kleinman 2003). But the evidence regarding income is not unmixed. Araya and colleagues, for example, found that that after controlling for other socioeconomic factors, per capita household income was not associated with greater risk of suffering from common mental disorders (Araya et al. 2003), although they did find a significant association between poor living conditions and risk, even in the presence of controls. In India, having a higher standard of living was associated with a lower of risk of suffering from "common mental disorder[s]," – including depression – that are often encountered in community and primary care settings (Goldberg and Huxley 1992; Shidhaye and Patel 2010), while income insecurity and shocks to family income appear to be associated with increased rates of suicide among farmers (Sundar 1999).

In Mexico, among a nationally representative sample, low-income respondents were not only more likely to suffer from depressive symptoms but were also more likely to report severe conditions (Medina-Mora et al. 2005). And – also in Mexico – among the elderly, economic security – primarily food security – was associated with lower prevalence of depression (Guerra et al. 2009).

Turning to Africa, a study of low-income South Africans from three cities – Capetown, Durban, and Port Elizabeth – found that persons with high non-employment income (pensions, disability grants, unemployment insurance, and child support) and persons with less total income over the previous month were more likely to present with depressive symptoms (Hamad et al. 2008). However, this relationship between income and depression was not consistent with findings from a nationally representative sample of South Africans (Stein et al. 2008) or with a small study of a rural South African village that found no relationship between socio-economic status and general psychiatric morbidity (Rumble et al. 1996). We have identified only limited data from Ghana, but a sample of outpatients from a Ghanaian psychiatric hospital was characterized as predominantly "low economic" status (Majodina and Johnson 1983; Tomlinson et al. 2009; Gureje et al. 2010, 2011).

Sex

In most studies, being a woman is one of the more consistent indicators of an individual's lifetime risk of suffering from a mood disorder (Kessler et al. 2003; Medina-Mora et al. 2007; Stein et al. 2008). The correlation between being female and risk of major depression is found across a wide number of countries (Weissman et al. 1996); many studies using self-reported measures or structured interviews find that women are twice as likely as men to suffer from depression (Nolen-Hoeksema 1987).

Lifetime prevalence of major depressive disorder was significantly higher for women than for men in nationally representative samples of South Africans and Mexicans (Medina-Mora et al. 2007; Stein et al. 2008). In a study of suicide risk in South Africa, women were twice as likely to have attempted suicide (Joe et al. 2008). A significant difference in prevalence between men and women was also found in a sample of adults in four Chinese provinces (Phillips et al. 2009) and in a sample of both the in- and outpatients of a Ghanian psychiatric hospital, researchers found that two-thirds of the sample was female (Majodina and Johnson 1983). However, sex is not always a significant indicator of general psychiatric morbidity (see for example, see Rumble et al. regarding rural South African villages) (Rumble et al. 1996).

The effects of poor mental health also vary by sex. For example, Suliman and colleagues found that, among persons suffering from a physical or psychiatric condition in South Africa, women reported significantly less impairment in their ability to function as home managers (Suliman et al. 2010). And women may also cope differently from men: in a comparison of college students from the U.S. and Ghana, women were more likely to engage in ruminative coping when feeling depressed (Eshun 2000).

Education

Some studies show that higher education is associated with a lower risk of suffering from a major depressive disorder (Kessler et al. 2003; Ross and Mirowsky 2006), but the evidence is mixed. Among studies of the elderly community, lower education level was not determined to be a risk factor for depression (Cole and Dendukuri 2003). And Andrade and colleagues (2000) found no significant correlation between education and 12-month comorbidity for mental disorders, i.e., the prevalence of anxiety, mood, and substance-abuse disorders, collectively.

In rural India, greater education among women was a significant predictor of reduced risk of suffering from a common mental disorder (Shidhaye and Patel 2010). Guerra and colleagues (2009), in a study of the elderly Mexican population, found that education attainment and prevalence of a depressive episode are weakly inversely correlated; and in South Africa, the lifetime prevalence of a psychiatric mood disorder and reported depressive symptoms among low-income adults were both found to be significantly higher for individuals with relatively less education (Hamad et al. 2008; Stein et al. 2008). However, among South Africans, persons with more education, just as with income, report that depressive episodes have a wider impact across more domains of their daily lives (Suliman et al. 2010).

Age

The relationship between age and depression is complex. Among a sample of English-speaking U.S. respondents, Mirowsky and Ross found that depression follows a U-shaped pattern with age as levels of depression initially decrease with age before reaching a minimum around age 45 and increasing thereafter (Mirowsky and Ross 1990).

In a sample of the Chinese adult population, Phillips and colleagues found that relative to persons under age 40, mood and anxiety disorders were more prevalent among persons aged 40 years and older (Phillips et al. 2009). And Shidhaye and Patel (2010) found an association between older age and higher rates of depression in their survey of rural Indian women. But not all studies find higher rates among older persons: in Mexico, for example, Medina-Mora and colleagues (2007) found that, relative to persons aged 55 years or older, the risk of depression was higher among younger age groups, with the highest risk among the youngest group (age 18–29). Stein and colleagues' evaluation of the South African population found depression was significantly higher between the ages of 35 and 49 than at ages 65 and over (Stein et al. 2008).

Self-Assessed Health

There is an extensive literature on the relationship between depression and self-assessed health (we return to this question in the discussion); the direction of the causal relationship between the two is unclear and probably reciprocal. Some recent evidence indicates that self-reported overall health is a significant predictor for subsequent depression, but being depressed does not have a significant effect on self-assessed health (Kosloski et al. 2005); other evidence suggests that physical illness increases subsequent depressive symptoms, and depression has a smaller, lagged effect of increasing physical disorder (Aneshensel et al. 1984; Moussavi et al. 2007).

While the causal direction is unclear, the association is strong. Among the adult population of a rural South African village, physical illness was significantly associated with having a mental disorder (Rumble et al. 1996); and in a study of Mexican adults in Tijuana, worse self-assessed health was found to be associated with higher (more depressed) scores on the Center for Epidemiological Studies Depression measure (Vega et al. 1987).

Data and Methods

Our data are drawn from five (China, Ghana, India, Mexico, and South Africa) of the six countries that participated in the WHO SAGE, "as part of a Longitudinal Survey Programme to compile comprehensive longitudinal information on the health and well-being of adult populations and the ageing process." (World Health Organization 2011). Data from the Russian Federation were not available at the time of publication.

The goal of the sampling design was to obtain a nationally representative cohort of persons aged 50 years and older, with a smaller cohort of persons aged 18–49 for comparison purposes. The target sample size was 5,000 households with at least one person aged 50+ years and 1,000 households with an 18–49 year old respondent. In the older households, all persons aged 50+ years (for example, spouses and siblings) were invited to participate. In consultation with the Ministry of Health in China and China CDC, a new sampling design was used for SAGE in China drawn from an existing national surveillance system. In India, a representative sample of six states was included, taking into consideration population size and level of development (World Health Organization 2011).

For each respondent, we created two measures that captured different dimensions of a possible depressive diagnosis. The first, using DSM criteria, captures the essentials of a clinical assessment; the second estimates treatment levels based on the respondent's report of diagnosis, medication or other treatment, or in- and out-patient visits for depression or anxiety.

More specifically, the first measure was based on DSM-IV-TR criteria for a major depressive episode (American Psychiatric Association 2000). Individual questions assessing depression were based on the Composite International Diagnostic Interview (CIDI) version 3.0 (Kessler and Ustun 2004). Using these criteria, we classified respondents as having a major depressive episode if they endorsed a 2 week period within the past year of depressed mood or anhedonia in addition to four or more concurrent symptoms from the following list: loss of appetite, difficulty falling asleep or insomnia, fatigue or low energy, restlessness or slow movement, negative feelings about oneself or loss of confidence, diminished concentration, or thoughts of suicide.

The following questions were used to determine whether survey participants had depressed mood and four or more concurrent symptoms. Respondents met the DSM criterion for sadness/depressed mood if they answered "yes" to the following three items: "During the last 12 months, have you had a period lasting several days when you felt sad, empty or depressed," "Was this period of sadness for more than 2 weeks," and, "Was this period of sadness most of the day, nearly every day?" Respondents met the DSM criterion for anhedonia if they answered "yes" to the following survey items: "During the last 12 months, have you had a period lasting several days when you lost interest in most things you usually enjoy such as personal relationships, work or hobbies/recreation," "Was this period loss of interest for more than 2 weeks," and, "Was this period loss of interest most of the day, nearly every day?"

Respondents met the DSM criterion for appetite disturbance if they answered "yes" to, "During this period, did you lose your appetite?" They met the DSM criterion for sleep disturbance if they answered "yes" to either, "Did you notice any problems falling asleep," or, "Did you notice any problems waking up too early?" They met the DSM criterion for psychomotor agitation or retardation if they answered "yes" to "Did you notice any slowing down in your moving around," or, "During this period, were you so restless or jittery nearly every day that you paced up and down and couldn't sit still?" They met the DSM criterion for decreased energy if they answered "yes" to the following 3 items: "During the last 12 months, have you had a period lasting several days when you have been feeling your energy decreased or that you are tired all the time," "Was this period of low energy for more than 2 weeks," and, "Was this period low energy most of the day, nearly every day?" Respondents met DSM criterion for low self-esteem if they answered "yes" to, "During this period, did you feel negative about yourself or like you had lost confidence?" They met DSM criterion for poor concentration if they answered "yes" to either, "During this period, did you have any difficulties concentrating; for example, listening to others, working, watching TV, listening to the radio," or, "Did you notice any slowing down in your thinking?" Finally, respondents met DSM criterion for suicidal ideation if they answered "yes" to either, "Did you think of death, or wish you were dead," or "During this period, did you ever try to end your life?"

Our estimate of treatment in the past year was based upon a respondent's self-report of taking medications or having other treatment in the past year, or having sought in- or out-patient treatment for anxiety or depression in the past year. Respondents were screened with "Have you ever been diagnosed with depression," and if they said yes, they were asked, "Have you been taking any medications or other treatment for it during the last 12 months?" Respondents were also asked to, "think of," their last three inpatient and three outpatient medical office visits in the last 12 months. They were then asked, "Which reason best describes why you needed this visit?" Subjects were categorized as depressed if they: reported being diagnosed with depression and having taken medications or other treatment in the last 12 months, or if they reported that "Depression or anxiety" was the primary reason for any of their inpatient or outpatient visits in the last 12 months.

In order to control for the cultural influence of stigma towards mental illness, a dichotomous variable was introduced into the regression analysis based on a question that asked participants, "Do you think people who are sad will tell us they are sad?"

We used quintile of permanent income calculated based on household assets and environmental risk factors (having or not having improved water, sanitation, cooking- and heating facilities). A random effects model (xtprobit) (StataCorp 2007) was then used to estimate income as a continuous measure, with that estimate divided into income quintiles. Additional details regarding the calculation can be found in Ferguson and others (Ferguson et al. 2003).

Age was measured in completed years as of the last birthday; the regression models (logit) (StataCorp 2007) include an age squared term to allow for non-linearities at the upper ages in the relationship with depression.

Survey participants were excluded from the analysis if they were missing data for demographic or social characteristics, population weight, measures of depression or treatment, stigma, or if interview data were collected from a proxy respondent.

Results

Descriptive statistics are provided in Table 4.1. There is substantial variation by country in the estimated percentages of depression. Respondents who experienced a DSM-based depressive episode in the past year range from less than 1% in China to almost 8% in India. Reports of treatment for depression range from a low of below 1% in China to over 5% in South Africa (where the report of treatment slightly exceeds the estimate of prevalence). When combined, estimates of prevalence based on DSM criteria or treatment range from just over 1% in China to nearly 9% in Mexico. India and Ghana have the highest levels of respondents who have less than primary education (about 44%); South Africa has the highest percentage with more than secondary education (37%) followed by China with 29%. The highest levels of good or very good self-assessed health are in South Africa and Ghana (60 and 63%, respectively); the highest levels of endorsement of the statement "Do you think that most people who are sad will tell us they are sad," occur in China where nearly three-quarters of the respondents said "yes," and in Ghana (nearly two-thirds said "yes").

We briefly summarize the univariate distributions of survey respondents who were depressed in the past year (according to DSM criteria) and who were treated or sought treatment in the last year by country and by individual covariates (data not shown). For age, across all five countries, lowest levels of depression are found below age 40; Ghana, India, and China show a similar pattern with regard to DSM criteria: higher age is generally associated with higher levels of depression, while Mexico and South Africa show a spike during the middle ages – 40–49 in South Africa and 40–59 in Mexico. In general, treatment patterns mirror estimates of depression, but it appears that a significant proportion of the 50–59 year olds in Mexico are not being treated, and overall, the treatment gap increases with age in China.

Women report higher levels of depression than men in all countries except China; they are more likely to have been treated in the last year in all countries except Ghana. Respondents who are widowed, separated, or divorced have the highest levels of depression; in India and South Africa, levels in this group are especially

Table 4.1 Descriptive statistics by country (percentages except as noted)

	Country				
Characteristic	India	Mexico	South Africa	Ghana	China
Depressed					
DSM	7.69	5.69	4.93	4.33	0.83
Treated last 12 months	1.23	4.48	5.25	0.54	0.34
DSM or treated	8.42	8.74	6.50	4.54	1.04
Education					
<Primary	44.67	25.91	22.45	44.46	19.72
Primary	16.42	25.70	14.43	19.53	18.75
Secondary	15.83	23.64	26.58	10.62	32.44
>Secondary	23.07	24.75	36.55	25.39	29.09
Age					
<20	3.03	(No cases)	(1.10)	1.16	0.91
20–29	20.73	16.03	7.33	11.53	7.78
30–39	25.60	35.52	24.54	27.43	21.36
40–49	26.04	22.19	31.72	35.00	44.32
50–59	12.05	13.05	12.59	9.94	11.52
60–69	7.55	6.67	7.82	6.84	8.22
70–79	3.92	4.65	3.64	2.64	4.77
80+	1.08	(1.79)	1.26	4.42	1.11
Mean (S.D.)	41.04 (14.61)	42.47 (14.37)	42.25 (14.46)	44.36 (14.46)	
Female	49.24	52.88	55.03	50.17	49.01
Marital status					
Marr, cohab	82.18	69.92	50.05	72.57	89.15
Never marr.	9.26	21.00	30.58	8.25	5.62
Div, sep, wid	8.56	9.07	19.37	19.18	5.23
Self assessed health					
Good, V. good	51.35	57.02	60.23	63.44	53.21
Moderate	37.86	35.76	31.71	27.51	35.06
Bad, V. bad	10.79	7.22	8.06	9.05	11.74
People will tell us they are sad	54.42	45.52	49.93	65.13	73.89
N of cases	10,635	2,566	3,111	4,917	13,736

Note: Values in parentheses based on fewer than 50 cases

pronounced (20 and 22%, respectively). Self-assessed health is strongly related to depression (we return to the interpretation of this result in the discussion, see below): levels of depression are lowest among persons who report good or very good health (ranging from virtually 0% in China to nearly 4% in India); mid-range among those who say their health is moderate (from 1.32% in China to a high of 9.51% in India); and highest among respondents who say they are in poor or very poor health (nearly 3% in China and over 35% in Mexico).

Socioeconomic status as measured by permanent income or education shows little consistency across countries in its relationship with depression; indeed, in only a few instances does there appear to be a discernible association. In India, both

Table 4.2 Percentage of population neither depressed nor treated, percentage of depressed (DSM criteria) who have not been treated, and untreated depressed as percentage of sample population by country

Country	Not depressed and not treated	Percentage of depressed who are untreated[a]	Untreated depressed as percentage of sample population[b]
India	91.59	93.46	7.19
Mexico	91.26	74.75	4.26
South Africa	93.52	25.40	1.25
Ghana	95.47	92.21	4.00
China	98.96	85.51	0.71

[a]Persons identified as depressed according to DSM criteria who do not report being treated/Persons identified as depressed according to DSM criteria
[b]Persons identified as depressed according to DSM criteria who do not report being treated/Total sample

income and education are inversely related to depression, but no clear trend in either dimension emerges in any other country.

Finally, we used the question about whether people would say they were sad as a way of getting at whether an admission of depression would be stigmatized. In all countries except India, people who did not endorse the statement were more likely to be depressed (although in Ghana the difference was small as it was in China). In other words, in aggregate, people who felt that there was some stigma attached to the admission of sadness were more likely to be depressed by DSM criteria than people who did not think it would be stigmatizing.

We examine an estimate of "unmet need" for treatment in Table 4.2. First, we looked at a conservative measure of the proportion of the sample in each country who were not depressed in the past year based on the two measures, i.e., who were not depressed according to DSM criteria and who were not being treated or had not sought treatment. By this measure, over 90% of the respondents in all the countries were not depressed in the last 12 months, with values ranging from nearly 99% in China to about 91% in both India and Mexico. We then examine two ways of thinking about the need for treatment. First, we look at the respondents who were diagnosed as depressed by DSM criteria but who did not report treatment as a percentage of the depressed. These figures range from about 25% in South Africa to just above 93% in India. Second, we examine untreated (but depressed) respondents as a percentage of the study population; here the figures range from under 1% in China to above 7% in India.

Our final analyses – logit regressions of a DSM diagnosis of depression on the covariates – are shown in Table 4.3 (which excludes self-assessed health) and Table 4.4 (which includes self-assessed health). Looking at Table 4.3 shows that controlling simultaneously for the covariates does not greatly change the overall picture. Men are less likely than women to be depressed (India, Mexico, and South Africa). Older age is associated with a higher likelihood of being depressed (India, Mexico, Ghana), but the relationship levels off and then declines as evidenced

Table 4.3 Results (coefficients) from regression of DSM diagnosis of depression on sociodemographic characteristics by country

	Country				
Characteristic	India	Mexico	South Africa	Ghana	China
Male	−0.37*	−2.67***	−1.09*	−0.01	0.42
Age (completed years)	0.06***	0.39***	0.28	0.09***	0.15
Age squared	−0.0004	−0.003***	−0.003	−0.0005*	−0.001
Marital status					
Currently married (omitted)					
Single	0.24	−0.62	−0.55	0.04	0.57
Div, sep, widowed	0.72***	−0.96*	2.89***	0.46	1.44
Quintile of permanent income					
Lowest I (omitted)					
II	−0.07	−1.32	1.54*	0.51	−0.32
III	−0.18	0.19	0.31	−0.22	−0.02
IV	−0.49*	0.16	−1.05	−0.44	−1.93***
Highest V	−0.68**	−1.32	−0.89	0.32	0.19
Education					
Less than primary (omitted)					
Primary	−0.07	−0.40	1.28	−1.49**	−1.33**
Secondary	0.09	1.07	1.84*	0.87	0.43
More than secondary	−0.16	0.52	0.58	0.32	−0.20
People will tell us they are sad	0.18	−0.86**	0.10	−0.15	−0.21
Constant	−4.12***	−12.24***	−11.86**	−6.26***	−8.79***
N	10,635	2,566	3,111	4,917	13,736
Pseudo-R^{2a}	.05***	.28***	.48***	.08***	.07***

*p<.05; **p<.01; ***p<.001

[a]p value reflects the significance of Chi squared for the associated Wald statistic

by negative values for the age squared terms (significant in Mexico and Ghana, marginally significant in India (p=.054) and South Africa (p=.063)). Being widowed, divorced, or separated is associated with a higher likelihood of depression everywhere (but statistically discernible in only India and South Africa) except in Mexico where it is associated with a lower likelihood of depression. Once we control for the other factors, income appears to emerge – possibly – as weakly inversely associated; to the extent that we observe statistically discernible results, they seem to show higher levels of depression at lower quintiles of income and lower levels of depression at higher levels of income. Not so for education: no clear pattern emerges even within a country. Nor does a person's assessment of stigmatization of sadness appear to have an effect: it is statistically discernible in Mexico, but when self-assessed health is introduced, on the one hand it loses significance in Mexico, on the other, it attains significance – in the opposite direction – in India. The overall picture does not much change when self-assessed health is introduced (Table 4.4), except that self-assessed health itself is strongly associated with the likelihood that the

Table 4.4 Results (coefficients) from regression of DSM diagnosis of depression on socio-demographic characteristics and self-assessed health by country

	Country				
Characteristic	India	Mexico	South Africa	Ghana	China
Male	–0.28*	–2.31***	–0.98*	0.05	0.60
Age (completed years)	0.05*	0.32***	–0.24	0.08**	0.09
Age squared	–0.0004	–0.003**	–0.003	–0.0005*	–0.001
Marital status					
Currently married (omitted)					
Single	0.25	–0.16	–0.04	–0.05	0.59
Div, sep, widowed	0.73***	–0.66	3.14***	0.40	1.37
Quintile of permanent income					
Lowest I (omitted)					
II	–0.03	–1.09	2.08*	0.53	–0.00
III	–0.15	0.05	0.88	–0.21	0.33
IV	–.41*	0.41	–0.34	–0.40	–1.45**
Highest V	–0.54*	–0.89	–0.57	0.38	0.97
Education					
Less than primary (omitted)					
Primary	–0.12	–0.33	1.49	–1.53**	–1.45**
Secondary	0.09	1.10*	1.96**	0.77	0.47
More than secondary	–0.05	0.97	0.93	0.30	0.00
Self-assessed health					
Good or very good (omitted)					
Moderate	0.79***	1.26**	0.45	0.80*	3.88***
Bad or very bad	1.50***	2.90***	1.91**	0.93	5.11***
People will tell us they are sad	0.27*	–0.72*	0.18	–0.08	0.05
Constant	–4.39***	–11.62***	–11.88**	–6.31***	–11.15***
N	10,635	2,566	3,111	4,917	13,736
Pseudo R^{2a}	.09***	.37***	.50***	.10***	.21***

*p<.05; **p<.01; ***p<.001

[a]p value reflects the significance of Chi squared for the associated Wald statistic

respondent is depressed: in all five countries, people who reported moderate, bad, or very bad health are significantly more likely to be depressed than those in good or very good health.

Discussion

Our analyses show substantial variability across the five countries in the prevalence of a depressive episode in the past year. This variability is well within the range of prior results. As part of the World Health Organization's World Mental Health (WMH) Survey Initiative, 28 countries are participating in an effort to conduct methodologically consistent surveys of adult mental health status using the WHO's Composite International Diagnostic Interview (WHO-CIDI), which uses DSM-IV diagnostic criteria (Demyttenaere et al. 2004). In a summary of the findings from 14 participating countries, the 12-month prevalence for mood disorders varied from the lowest rate observed in Nigeria at 0.8% and the highest rate observed in the United States at 9.6% (Demyttenaere et al. 2004). Reasons for the variation are unclear and could include lack of services and knowledge, lack of prior exposure to this kind of survey, and biological factors. Social desirability of response may also be a contributing factor in differences among countries.

In this study, China shows a remarkably low percentage – about 1% overall – even in high-risk categories: older people (1.3%); divorced, separated, or widowed (2.8%); and those with poor or very poor self-assessed health (3.0%). Is this a function of the assessment using DSM criteria? Cultural norms? Our simple question about whether a sad person would tell us s/he was sad was more widely endorsed in China – nearly three-quarters of the respondents said "yes" – than in any other country. We cannot tell at this point of our analyses whether the results are attributable to the instrument, cultural factors that shape the expression of sadness, or biological resilience in the population. Our work in Taiwan suggests that the last explanation may not be completely out of the question as a contributing – albeit small – factor. The prevalence of protective long (L) and extra long (XL) variants of the 5HTTLPR gene appears to be much higher in that population than elsewhere (Goldman et al. 2010), although identification of the XL variants is only recent and its estimation in populations may be understated.

Parker and colleagues (2001) found that depression was less prevalent among the Chinese and more likely to be expressed somatically, probably a result of a variety of interconnected historical and cultural phenomena. They hypothesized that low levels of reported depression are linked to stigmatization of the disease, cultural factors that protect individuals from depression, an historical political context in which mental distress was viewed as an expression of wrong political thinking, a preference in traditional Chinese epistemology of disease causation for diagnoses of neurasthenia, and an explicit lack, until 1979, of a psychiatric classificatory scheme more consistent with Western diagnostic decision rules (Parker et al. 2001). Other data – two surveys were conducted through the WMH Survey – show an estimate of the 12-month prevalence of major depressive disorder of 2.0%. Such a low prevalence rate in China seems inconsistent with findings that suicide rates in China are quite high: 23 per 100,000 (Phillips et al. 2009).

Some results – most notably the merry widows in Mexico – are likely to be a statistical artifact, a result of using the traditional cut-off of a .05 level of significance (Taubes 1995; Ioannidis 2005). Ionnanidis goes as far as saying that "Most claimed research findings are false" (Ioannidis 2005). In this regard, the importance of the comparative space that the SAGE studies afford us cannot be overstated. The surveys allow us to replicate analyses, if not across time, at least across geography. It is also encouraging that SAGE is planned as a longitudinal survey. Biannual follow-ups are planned with the next waves proposed for 2012 and 2014. These follow-up data, along with measures of well-being that are included in SAGE, will allow analysis of some of these questions and the examination of the relationship among depressive disorders, poor subjective well-being, and health outcomes.

The interpretation of Table 4.2 – our effort to get at unmet need – is complex for a number of reasons. First, we should acknowledge the limitations of our measures. Although the realization of the DSM criteria in the SAGE instruments is quite good, it cannot replace the face-to-face interaction that a trained clinician would have with a patient. We are not assessing demeanor, grooming, interpersonal cues, or other aspects of the subject's mental status exam. And, of course, we are dependent upon the respondent's interpretation of the questions and the willingness and ability of respondent to provide truthful answers. These last constraints affect all survey research: we can never be sure that the thought experiment that a participant responds to is the same thought experiment we had in mind when we asked a question; and we cannot adjust for self-awareness or truthful answers. Future work using other questions that elicit information about depression may help us establish consistency, but even that effort will have its limitations. Second, the comparison between the DSM diagnosis and our estimate of treatment also has its limitations. In some instances, the estimates of the percentages being treated exceed the estimates of persons who had a depressive episode in the past year. This result could well be correct: a person who has been using medications or other therapy might not have had a depressive episode in the past year. With these limitations in mind, however, the results of Table 4.2 still pose a "half-full or half-empty" kind of question. On the one hand, we see that large proportions of people that we identify as depressed are not being treated. The smallest percentage is in South Africa – 25% are untreated – but even that percentage is high in terms of suffering; elsewhere, the percentages are even higher, ranging from about 75 in Mexico to 92 (Ghana) or 93 (India) percent. On the other hand, as a percentage of the overall study populations, the percentages of untreated persons are low – ranging from under 1% in China to just over 7% in India – and the percentages of respondents who were neither depressed according to DSM criteria nor taking medications are high: above 91% in all five countries.

We recognize the difficulties inherent in examining self-assessed health, or indeed any measure of health, in our analyses: the causal direction is uncertain. As noted by Miller and his colleagues, depressive symptoms are associated with morbidity and mortality from heart disease and depression implicated in the occurrence and disease progression of cardiovascular disease (Miller et al. 2009). We cannot sort out the causal direction using an observational study, with one round of data collection; we cannot even identify which came first, however it is a large and significant effect, one that we cannot ignore from a clinical perspective. People who are physically ill are also at risk of depression (or vice versa); it is an important finding that we should consider in treating both. In reporting self-assessed health, respondents may be integrating multiple dimensions: physical, psychological, and cognitive. A fruitful area for additional research may be to explicate the relationship between depression and these various dimensions.

Galen, Aristotle, and the Bible all describe instances of depression, but the definitive work, originally published in 1621, is by Robert Burton – *The Anatomy of*

Melancholy (Burton et al. 1621). Replete with footnotes itself, we might reasonably borrow Alfred North Whitehead's observation about Plato, and say that all work on depression consists of a series of footnotes to Burton – at least with regard to the Western tradition. Here we have confined our inquiry to just a few of the correlates identified by Burton – e.g., poverty, education, age – but we recognize that much remains to be explored.

There is a broad path laid out for future work. We have already mentioned the need to explicate the link between the multiple dimensions of health and depression, other areas that we propose to explore include the characteristics that determine treatment. For example, are there groups that are at particularly high risk of undertreatment? Our work suggests that persons above age 70, continue to be undertreated, additional analyses may suggest other groups that require attention. The sex differential in depression appears to be a fairly robust finding, possibly excepting China and Ghana. Can we dissect the underlying causes? Is there a biological basis or are there cultural and socioeconomic factors that make women more vulnerable – or more likely to report and be treated for depression? Finally, we have not as yet exploited the vignettes that are available as part of the SAGE data. This rich source of information may be an important tool in helping us identify differences across the countries.

Acknowledgments WHO's Study on Global Ageing and Adult Health is supported by the US National Institute on Aging through an Interagency Agreement with WHO and through the NIH grant 1 R01 AG034479-01A1.

References

American Psychiatric Association. (2000). *Diagnostic and statistical manual of mental disorders: DSM-IV-TR*. Washington, DC: American Psychiatric Association.

Andrade, L., Caraveo-Anduaga, J., Berglund, P., Bijl, R., Kessler, R., Demler, O., & Walters, E. (2000). Cross-national comparisons of the prevalences and correlates of mental disorders. WHO International Consortium in Psychiatric Epidemiology. *Bull World Health Organ, 78*(4), 413–426.

Aneshensel, C. S., Frerichs, R. R., & Huba, G. J. (1984). Depression and physical illness: A multiwave, nonrecursive causal model. *J Health Soc Behav, 25*(4), 350–371.

Araya, R., Lewis, G., Rojas, G., & Fritsch, R. (2003). Education and income: Which is more important for mental health? *J Epidemiol Community Health, 57*(7), 501–505.

Burton, R., Lichfield, J., Short, J., & Cripps, H. (1621). *The anatomy of melancholy*. Oxford: Oxford University Press.

Cole, M. G., & Dendukuri, N. (2003). Risk factors for depression among elderly community subjects: A systematic review and meta-analysis. *Am J Psychiatry, 160*(6), 1147–1156.

Demyttenaere, K., Bruffaerts, R., Posada-Villa, J., Gasquet, I., Kovess, V., Lepine, J. P., Angermeyer, M. C., Bernert, S., De Girolamo, G., Morosini, P., Polidori, G., Kikkawa, T., Kawakami, N., Ono, Y., Takeshima, T., Uda, H., Karam, E. G., Fayyad, J. A., Karam, A. N., Mneimneh, Z. N., Medina-Mora, M. E., Borges, G., Lara, C., De Graaf, R., Ormel, J., Gureje, O., Shen, Y., Huang, Y., Zhang, M., Alonso, J., Haro, J. M., Vilagut, G., Bromet, E. J., Gluzman, S., Webb, C., Kessler, R. C., Merikangas, K. R., Anthony, J. C., Von Korff, M. R., Wang, P. S., Brugha, T. S., Aguilar-Gaxiola, S., Lee, S., Heeringa, S., Pennell, B. E., Zaslavsky, A. M.,

Ustun, T. B., & Chatterji, S. (2004). Prevalence, severity, and unmet need for treatment of mental disorders in the World Health Organization World Mental Health Surveys. *JAMA, 291*(21), 2581–2590.

Eshun, S. (2000). Role of gender and rumination in suicide ideation: A comparison of college samples from Ghana and the United States. *Cross-cultural research, 34*(3), 250.

Ferguson, B., Murray, C., Tandon, A., & Gakidou, E. (2003). Estimating permanent income using asset and indicator variables. In C. Murray & D. Evans (Eds.), *Health systems performance assessment debates, methods and empiricism*. Geneva: World Health Organization.

Goldberg, D. P., & Huxley, P. (1992). *Common mental disorders: A bio-social model*. London/New York: Tavistock/Routledge.

Goldman, N., Glei, D. A., Lin, Y. H., & Weinstein, M. (2010). The serotonin transporter polymorphism (5-HTTLPR): Allelic variation and links with depressive symptoms. *Depress Anxiety, 27*(3), 260–269.

Guerra, M., Ferri, C. P., Sosa, A. L., Salas, A., Gaona, C., Gonzales, V., De La Torre, G. R., & Prince, M. (2009). Late-life depression in Peru, Mexico and Venezuela: The 10/66 population-based study. *Br J Psychiatry, 195*(6), 510–515.

Gureje, O., Uwakwe, R., Oladeji, B., Makanjuola, V. O., & Esan, O. (2010). Depression in adult Nigerians: Results from the Nigerian Survey of Mental Health and Well-being. *J Affect Disord, 120*(1–3), 158–164.

Gureje, O., Oladeji, B., & Abiona, T. (2011). Incidence and risk factors for late-life depression in the Ibadan Study of Ageing. *Psychol Med, 41*(9), 1897–1906. doi: 10.1017/S0033291710002643. Accessed Sep 2011.

Hamad, R., Fernald, L. C., Karlan, D. S., & Zinman, J. (2008). Social and economic correlates of depressive symptoms and perceived stress in South African adults. *J Epidemiol Community Health, 62*(6), 538–544.

Ioannidis, J. P. (2005). Why most published research findings are false. *PLoS Med, 2*(8), e124.

Joe, S., Stein, D. J., Seedat, S., Herman, A., & Williams, D. R. (2008). Prevalence and correlates of non-fatal suicidal behaviour among South Africans. *Br J Psychiatry, 192*(4), 310–311.

Kessler, R. C., & Ustun, T. B. (2004). The World Mental Health (WMH) Survey Initiative Version of the World Health Organization (WHO) Composite International Diagnostic Interview (CIDI). *Int J Methods Psychiatr Res, 13*(2), 93–121.

Kessler, R. C., Berglund, P., Demler, O., Jin, R., Koretz, D., Merikangas, K. R., Rush, A. J., Walters, E. E., & Wang, P. S. (2003). The epidemiology of major depressive disorder: Results from the National Comorbidity Survey Replication (NCS-R). *JAMA, 289*(23), 3095–3105.

Kosloski, K., Stull, D. E., Kercher, K., & Van Dussen, D. J. (2005). Longitudinal analysis of the reciprocal effects of self-assessed global health and depressive symptoms. *The Journals of Gerontology. Series B, Psychological Sciences and Social Sciences, 60*(6), P296–P303.

Lorant, V., Deliege, D., Eaton, W., Robert, A., Philippot, P., & Ansseau, M. (2003). Socioeconomic inequalities in depression: A meta-analysis. *Am J Epidemiol, 157*(2), 98–112.

Majodina, M. Z., & Johnson, F. Y. (1983). Standardized assessment of depressive disorders (SADD) in Ghana. *Br J Psychiatry, 143*, 442–446.

Mathers, C., Fat, D. M., & Boerma, J. (2008). *The global burden of disease: 2004 update*. Geneva: World Health Organization.

Medina-Mora, M. E., Borges, G., Lara, C., Benjet, C., Blanco, J., Fleiz, C., Villatoro, J., Rojas, E., & Zambrano, J. (2005). Prevalence, service use, and demographic correlates of 12-month DSM-IV psychiatric disorders in Mexico: Results from the Mexican National Comorbidity Survey. *Psychol Med, 35*(12), 1773–1783.

Medina-Mora, M. E., Borges, G., Benjet, C., Lara, C., & Berglund, P. (2007). Psychiatric disorders in Mexico: Lifetime prevalence in a nationally representative sample. *Br J Psychiatry, 190*, 521–528.

Miller, G., Chen, E., & Cole, S. W. (2009). Health psychology: Developing biologically plausible models linking the social world and physical health. *Annu Rev Psychol, 60*, 501–524.

Mirowsky, J., & Ross, C. E. (1990). Control or defense? Depression and the sense of control over good and bad outcomes. *J Health Soc Behav, 31*(1), 71–86.

Moussavi, S., Chatterji, S., Verdes, E., Tandon, A., Patel, V., & Ustun, B. (2007). Depression, chronic diseases, and decrements in health: Results from the World Health Surveys. *Lancet, 370*(9590), 851–858.
Nolen-Hoeksema, S. (1987). Sex differences in unipolar depression: Evidence and theory. *Psychol Bull, 101*(2), 259–282.
Parker, G., Gladstone, G., & Chee, K. T. (2001). Depression in the planet's largest ethnic group: The Chinese. *Am J Psychiatry, 158*(6), 857–864.
Patel, V., & Kleinman, A. (2003). Poverty and common mental disorders in developing countries. *Bull World Health Organ, 81*(8), 609–615.
Phillips, M. R., Zhang, J., Shi, Q., Song, Z., Ding, Z., Pang, S., Li, X., Zhang, Y., & Wang, Z. (2009). Prevalence, treatment, and associated disability of mental disorders in four provinces in China during 2001–05: An epidemiological survey. *Lancet, 373*(9680), 2041–2053.
Ross, C. E., & Mirowsky, J. (2006). Sex differences in the effect of education on depression: Resource multiplication or resource substitution? *Soc Sci Med, 63*(5), 1400–1413.
Rumble, S., Swartz, L., Parry, C., & Zwarenstein, M. (1996). Prevalence of psychiatric morbidity in the adult population of a rural South African village. *Psychol Med, 26*(5), 997–1007.
Shidhaye, R., & Patel, V. (2010). Association of socio-economic, gender and health factors with common mental disorders in women: A population-based study of 5703 married rural women in India. *Int J Epidemiol, 39*(6), 1510–1521.
Statacorp. (2007). *Stata statistical software: Release 10*. College Station: StataCorp LP.
Stein, D. J., Seedat, S., Herman, A., Moomal, H., Heeringa, S. G., Kessler, R. C., & Williams, D. R. (2008). Lifetime prevalence of psychiatric disorders in South Africa. *Br J Psychiatry, 192*(2), 112–117.
Suliman, S., Stein, D. J., Myer, L., Williams, D. R., & Seedat, S. (2010). Disability and treatment of psychiatric and physical disorders in South Africa. *J Nerv Ment Dis, 198*(1), 8–15.
Sundar, M. (1999). Suicide in farmers in India. *Br J Psychiatry, 175*, 585–586.
Taubes, G. (1995). Epidemiology faces its limits. *Science, 269*(5221), 164–169.
Tomlinson, M., Grimsrud, A. T., Stein, D. J., Williams, D. R., & Myer, L. (2009). The epidemiology of major depression in South Africa: Results from the South African stress and health study. *South African Medical Journal, 99*(5 Pt 2), 367–373.
Vega, W. A., Kolody, B., Hough, R. L., & Figueroa, G. (1987). Depressive symptomatology in northern Mexico adults. *Am J Public Health, 77*(9), 1215–1218.
Weissman, M. M., Bland, R. C., Canino, G. J., Faravelli, C., Greenwald, S., Hwu, H. G., Joyce, P. R., Karam, E. G., Lee, C. K., Lellouch, J., Lepine, J. P., Newman, S. C., Rubio-Stipec, M., Wells, J. E., Wickramaratne, P. J., Wittchen, H., & Yeh, E. K. (1996). Cross-national epidemiology of major depression and bipolar disorder. *JAMA, 276*(4), 293–299.
World Health Organization. (2011). *WHO study on global AGEing and adult health (SAGE)*. Retrieved February 26, 2011, from http://www.who.int/healthinfo/systems/sage/en/

Chapter 5
Population Aging and Health Expenditure in Kerala: An Empirical Analysis

Yadawendra Singh

Introduction

Population aging is a global phenomenon, which has already been experienced in the developed countries and is now being felt in the developing countries too. India is one among such countries which accommodates a large number of elderly. Given the projected duration of life in old age, the emerging concern relates to well-being in terms of freedom from disease and disability, which has implication not only for the individual but also for the household and society at large. The state of Kerala, which achieved below replacement level fertility much ahead of other Indian states, has the highest proportion of elderly. This proportion is going to increase from 10.6% in 2001 to 18.3% in 2026 (India, Registrar General 2006). This evident shift in the population structure indicates intense aging of the Kerala population, which, in turn, has considerable socio-economic implication, viz., meeting health needs and proper nutrition for the elderly, providing pensions and social security, etc. Different aspects of aging have been looked upon in case the of India, but the implication of aging on health expenditure has not been given due attention yet, in the case of either Kerala or India. On this account, this research proposes to attempt an exploration of the issue of population aging and its implications for health expenditure.

There are ample evidences to suggest that the elderly are more likely to have health problems as compared to general population (Omran 1971; Young 1997; Wensing 2001; Prakash et al. 2004; Bhatia et al. 2007). Regardless of physical illness, the aged are more likely to have mental health problems, which arise from senility, neurosis and extent of life satisfaction (WHO 1989). Mental disorders are due not just to brain aging, but also to the losses associated with the quality of life, and socio-economic problems are also responsible for advanced mental problems among the elderly (Prakash et al. 2004).

Y. Singh (✉)
Centre for the Study of Regional Development, Jawaharlal Nehru University, New Delhi, India
e-mail: yadawendra@gmail.com

N. Hoque et al. (eds.), *Applied Demography and Public Health*, Applied Demography Series 3, DOI 10.1007/978-94-007-6140-7_5,
© Springer Science+Business Media Dordrecht 2013

The high prevalence of health problems among the elderly has direct implication on health expenditure. As physical and mental health tends to deteriorate with age, the elderly need much more health care. In addition, the elderly often need medical care, which involves relatively expensive treatment and frequent hospitalisation. As a result, per capita health spending among the elderly is three to five times more than among the young population (Reinhardt 2003). Further, higher incidence of death due to the prevalence of more severe diseases increases health-related costs among the elderly. Seshamani and Gray (2003) show that approaching death affects costs up to 15 years prior to death, and the health care cost increases ten times from 5 years prior to death. The concentration of medical care expenditure in the last years of life is also evident in particular disease categories such as heart disease and cancer (Riley et al. 1987). Studies also find rise in health expenditure in old age, primarily because mortality rates increase with age and health care expenditure increases with proximity to death (Yang et al. 2003; Seshamani and Gray 2004).

Growth in the elderly population in Kerala and prevalence of chronic diseases among the elderly raise concerns regarding the overall burden of care for those with physical and cognitive limitations and regarding the related health care costs. In the Indian context, sufficient evidence exists pertaining to the kind of deterioration in physical and mental health in old age (Gupta et al. 2001; Irudaya Rajan 2004, 2008; Alam 2008), but, there is no systematic exploration regarding the burden of health expenditure that could arise due to the longer life span of the elderly with multiple chronic ailments. Kerala is selected for the analysis because it will be the first state to face the problem of aging[1] and hence it can be a wake-up call for the other Indian states. Another reason for selecting Kerala is the availability of state specific data from Migration Monitoring Study[2] (2007) apart from NSSO, which gives more insight into the situation of the elderly in the state.

Given this background, the study seeks to examine how population aging affects health expenditure at the individual level and to estimate the cost of managing the diseases in future.

This paper is divided into six sections. After the introduction in the first section, section "Data Source and Methodology" discusses the data source and methodology adopted in the study. Morbidity prevalence and cost of diseases are examined in section "Description of Variables" and "Demographic Variables", respectively. Section "Socio-Economic Variables" discusses the regression result, and section "Morbidity Prevalence and Health-Seeking Behaviour Among the Elderly" concludes with some policy implications.

[1]As per projection by census of India, the proportion of elderly in Kerala will rise from 10.6% in 2001 to 18.3% in 2026, which is more than all India and other Indian states' corresponding figure (India, Registrar General 2006).

[2]Migration Monitoring Study (2007) is the third round of the Migration Monitoring Studies conducted by the Research Unit on International Migration of the Centre for Development Studies. Households were randomly selected from all the 14 districts and all the 63 taluks of the state. The thrust areas covered in the survey are migration, remittances and employment. This round of the survey is different from the previous rounds as it also covers topics like education and health, amenities in the households, possession of consumer durables, and household indebtedness.

Data Source and Methodology

Data sources used for the present study are National Sample Survey (NSS)[3] 60th Round (Schedule No. 25, Jan-June, 2004) and NSS 52nd Round (Schedule 25, July–June 1995–1996),[4] population projections provided by India, Registrar General (2006) and Migration Monitoring Study (2007)[5] conducted in Kerala. Life expectancy data has been taken from Sample Registration System (SRS) based abridged life table of 1992–1996 and 2002–2006. NSS 60th Round and 52nd Round provides micro data on morbidity and health care of the whole population, including those aged 60 and above. The surveys of morbidity do not follow any uniform pattern, although objectives are the same, with slight differences in reference period, grouping of diseases, and source and type of treatment. Furthermore, these surveys covered various curative aspects such as utilization of health care services and the expenditure incurred by the households for availing these services. All information is collected for in-patients only, with a 365-day reference period for information for every event of hospitalization of each household member, whether living or deceased at the time of survey. Information on the condition of the elderly and the prevalence of ailments among them was also collected in the survey. Two-stage stratified sampling[6] was followed with census village and urban blocks as the first-stage unit (FSU) for the rural and urban area, respectively, and household as the second-stage unit (SSUs).

Proportion of elderly reporting poor health and prevalence of ailment among them is directly calculated from the NSS data. Prevalence of diseases, utilization of health care, and per capita cost of disease for in-patients in Kerala is also directly calculated from Migration Monitoring Study data.

To estimate the expected economic burden of aging, the future cost of certain diseases for the elderly and the nonelderly is estimated using the following formula:

$$C_d = ASHR * OOP_i^n * P_i^t$$

Where,

Cd = Estimated cost of disease[7]
ASHR = Age specific hospitalisation rate in 2004 = nH_x / nP_x
nH_x = Hospitalised population in the age group x to (x + n);

[3]NSS data is collected by National Sample Survey Organization, which is the Government of India body for collecting information on various aspects of Indian economy through nationwide surveys.

[4]In the schedule data related to the "Morbidity, Health Care and the Condition of the Aged" has been collected on both 52nd and 60th rounds.

[5]Migration Monitoring Study (2007) is the third round of the Migration Monitoring Studies conducted by the Research Unit on International Migration of the Centre for Development Studies, Thiruvananthapuram, India. The survey randomly collected 10,000 sample households from all the 14 districts and all the 63 taluks of Kerala.

[6]For details of sampling strategy and context, see NSS Report No. 441 (52/25.0/1) and 507 (60/25.0/1).

[7]Diseases are grouped into two categories – chronic and non-chronic – according to NSSO classification available in report number 441 of NSSO.

nP_x = Population in the age group x to (x + n);
OOP_i^n = Per capita out of pocket (OOP) expenditure for a given disease for i^{th} age group for year n;
P_i^t = Projected population for i^{th} age group at time period t
OOP_i^n is estimated using the following compound growth rate formula

$$OOP_i^n = OOP_i^0 \left(1 + r / 100\right)^n$$

Where OOP_i^n = cost of disease in period n and OOP_i^0 = cost of disease in the beginning period, r is the compound rate of growth observed between 1995 and 1996 and 2004 and n is the time period.[8] OOP expenditure is adjusted for inflation using GDP deflator for the given years.

Correlates of health expenditure are estimated using dummy variable regression model. Per capita health expenditure is taken as the dependent variable and the independent variables are consumption quintile,[9] literacy, sex, age, type of hospital, type of disease, place of residence, and social group.[10] Dummy variable regression model is used because the explanatory variables are qualitative in nature. Health expenditure is estimated using the following model:

$$PCHE = \beta_0 + \beta_1 d\_hsp + \beta_2 d\_illit + \beta_3 d\_r + \beta 4 d\_chr + \beta 5 d\_sex + \beta 6 d\_sc + \beta 7 d\_st + \beta 8 d\_age + \beta 9 d\_q1 + \beta 10 d\_q2 + \beta 11 d\_q3 + \beta 12 d\_q4 + \mu$$

Where, β_0 is the intercept and β_is (i = 1, 2, 3, …, 12) are constant coefficients and μ is the error term.

Dummies are created on the basis of standard rule for creating dummy variable (i.e. if there are 'm' categories of a variable, then 'm-1' dummy variables are introduced).
d_hsp is dummy for hospital type; 1 if the hospital is private, 0 if it is public
d_illt is dummy for education; 1 if the person is illiterate, 0 otherwise
d_r is dummy for type of residence; 1 if rural, 0 otherwise
d_chr is dummy for type of disease; 1 if disease is chronic, 0 otherwise
d_sex is dummy for sex; 1 if female, 0 for male,
d_sc is dummy for social group; 1 if scheduled caste, 0 otherwise
d_st is dummy for social group; 1 if scheduled tribe, 0 otherwise
d_age is dummy for age; 1 if the person is aged 60 and above, 0 otherwise
d_q1 is dummy for consumption quintile; 1 if the person belongs to quintile 1, 0 otherwise
d_q2 is dummy for consumption quintile; 1 if the person belongs to quintile 2, 0 otherwise

[8] NSS data on morbidity and health care is available for these points of time only in the 52nd and 60th round respectively; therefore growth rate is calculated using the data available in these two time frames.

[9] Consumption quintile is constructed using household consumption expenditure with quintile 1 referring to the lowest income quintile and quintile 5 referring to the highest quintile.

[10] Social group is categorized into three categories – Scheduled tribe (ST), Scheduled Caste (SC), and others.

d_q3 is dummy for consumption quintile; 1 if the person belongs to quintile 3, 0 otherwise

d_q4 is dummy for consumption quintile; 1 if the person belongs to quintile 4, 0 otherwise

Description of Variables

Variables are categorised into two groups (socio-economic variables and demographic variables), which are described below:

Demographic Variables

Children and elderly are more vulnerable to health risk and therefore there is higher chance of high health expenditure among these two groups. Apart from the household composition, household size is also expected to affect the health expenditure (O'Donnell et al. 2005).

Socio-Economic Variables

Household income is expected to affect the OOP expenditure on health care as it determines the household's capacity to pay for health care without affecting the consumption of other necessities. Since NSSO does not provide data on income, consumption expenditure is taken as proxy of income. Based the consumption expenditure, consumption quintile is constructed. Health expenditure of the household in rural India is sensitive to changes in the household income levels (Mathiyazhagan 2003). The other variable that might affect health expenditure is education, which makes the individual more aware about health care and hence leads to reduction in OOP health expenditure (also termed as efficiency mechanism[11]). Education also increases the opportunity cost of ill health, and educated people experience better health than those who are poorly educated (Ross and Wu 1995). Health expenditure is also expected to differ between rural and urban areas.

Type of disease has an influence on health expenditure: the more severe the disease is, the higher will be the health expenditure. Diseases are categorised into two categories – chronic and non-chronic. Chronic diseases are diseases that last for the longer duration. In the Indian context, social group is also an important variable that is likely to affect health expenditure. Social group is divided into three categories – scheduled caste, scheduled tribe, and others.

---

[11] Grossman (1999) and Cowell (2006).

Morbidity Prevalence and Health-Seeking Behaviour Among the Elderly

Before we examine the OOP health expenditure for the elderly, it is relevant to inspect morbidity prevalence among, as it has a direct implication for OOP health expenditure. Inter-state comparison has been done to show the relative health status of the elderly in Kerala. Figure 5.1 shows the perceived health status of the elderly and life expectancy at 60 for 1995–1996 and 2004.[12] The figure reveals that life expectancy at 60 has increased for all India and all Indian states from 1995 to 1996 to 2004. It is interesting to note that the proportion of elderly reporting their health as poor is as high as 37% for Kerala, which is the highest among all Indian states (Fig. 5.1) in 2004. Kerala is followed by West Bengal and Orissa. It can also be noticed from the figure that the proportion of the elderly reporting their health as poor has increased for all India as well as for all Indian states except Himachal, Karnataka, Orissa, and Punjab from 1995 to 96 to 2004. This finding indicates that although life expectancy has improved, it has not been accompanied by good quality of life. Further disaggregation among the elderly suggests that the proportion of the elderly reporting their health as poor increases with the advancement of age (Table A.1).

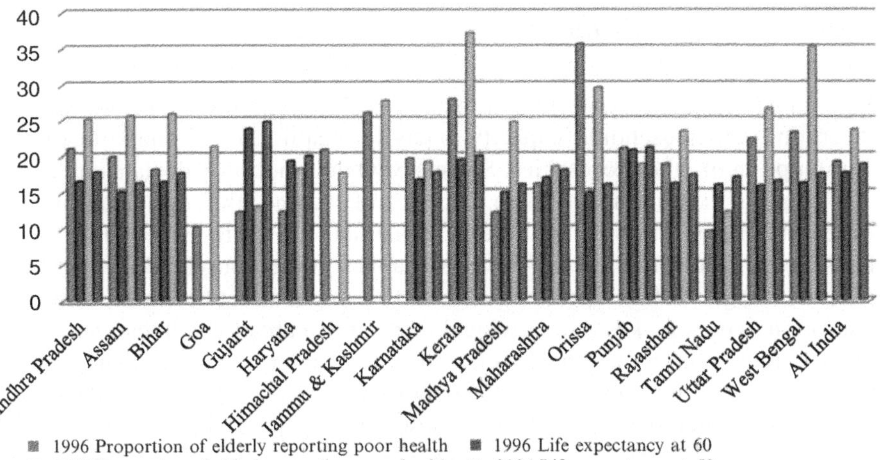

Fig. 5.1 Proportion of the elderly reporting poor health and life expectancy across major Indian states, 1995–1996 and 2004 (Source: Computed by the author using unit level records of National Sample Survey 60th round, 'Morbidity, health care and condition of the aged' (2004) and 52nd round, 'Morbidity and health care'. Life expectancy is taken from SRS based Abridged life table, 2002–2006 and 1992–1996)

[12] Same exercise could not be replicated for morbidity prevalence due to the data inconsistency between NSS 52 round and NSS 60 round for this variable.

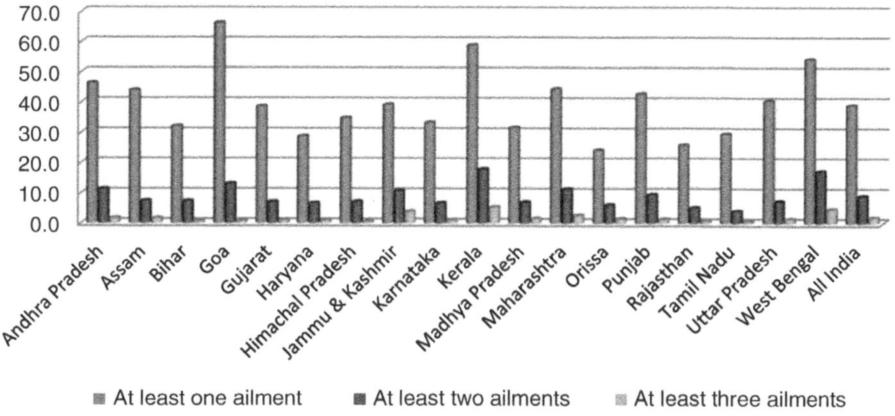

Fig. 5.2 Prevalence of ailments among the elderly, 2004 (Source: Computed by the author using unit level records of National Sample Survey 60th round, 'Morbidity, health care and condition of the aged' (2004))

To further the discussion regarding the impact of aging on deterioration of physical health status, disease prevalence among the elderly is shown in Fig. 5.2. This may provide a clue as to whether the perceived health status reflects the observed ill health as indicated by the prevalence of various ailments among the elderly. Interestingly, the proportion of the elderly having at least one ailment is 59%, which is much higher than in the other Indian states and than the all India average. This result is quite interesting keeping in view the fact that Kerala has the highest life expectancy at birth and the third highest life expectancy at 60 in India (India, Registrar General 2007b). Like prevalence of at least one ailment, prevalence of at least two ailments and at least three ailments among the elderly is found to be highest in Kerala. Further, the results indicated that the prevalence of morbidity increases with the advancement of age.

Apart from the pattern of morbidity among the elderly and the non-elderly population in the state, morbidity from specific diseases is of greater interest in so far as the implications are concerned. Prevalence of disease pattern according to broad age groups in Kerala is shown in Table 5.1. It is evident that the prevalence of selected diseases does increase with advancing age and does intensify beyond the age of 60. Among the selected set of diseases, blood pressure and diabetes are the two diseases which commence early in life (about 30 years of age). Diseases listed in Table 5.1 exhibit the systematic magnitude of intensification with age. Onset prior to the age of 60, coupled with long life expectancy in Kerala suggests rising cost of care relating to aging of the population in Kerala. The high prevalence of these diseases in persons aged 75 and above indicates a need for institutional care, which may add to the financial burden of such care in the state.

To formulate an idea regarding the approximate cost of care in accordance with the prevailing scenario of age and stage of diseases, there is a need to approximate an average age of persons with such diseases. For this purpose, mean age of onset

Table 5.1 Prevalence of diseases (per 1,000) in Kerala, 2007

Age group	0–14	15–29	30–44	45–59	60–74	75 and above
Diabetes	1.0	1.4	19.9	86.9	141.5	139.6
Heart problem	2.5	2.2	6.4	25.5	41.4	44.9
Arthritis	0.6	1.0	6.7	15.2	23.3	30.5
Cholesterol	0.3	0.6	6.5	20.7	19.0	17.4
Blood pressure	0.3	3.9	20.2	71.8	125.6	145.8
Asthma	6.7	3.1	9.9	24.2	42.1	61.1
Cancer	0.2	0.5	1.1	3.5	6.5	3.7
Kidney problem	0.7	0.4	2.2	3.0	3.6	6.2

Source: Computed by the author using Kerala Migration Monitoring Study, 2007

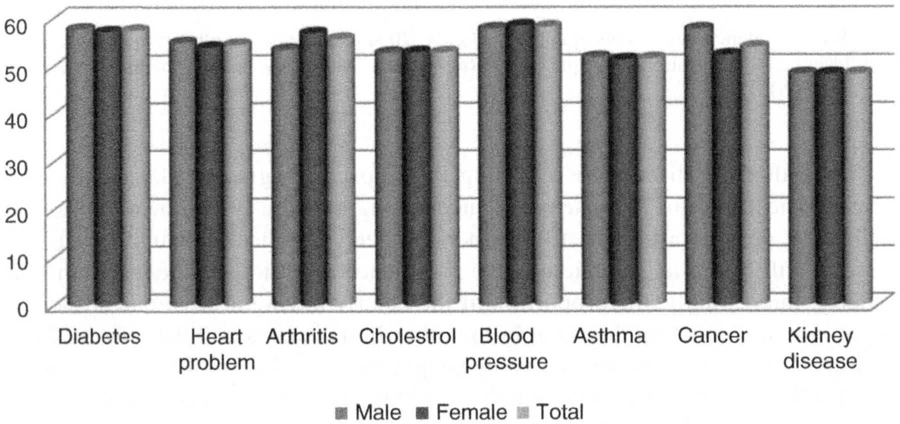

Fig. 5.3 Mean age of onset of chronic diseases in Kerala, 2007 (Source: Computed by the author using Kerala Migration Monitoring Study, 2007)

of diseases has been calculated, which is shown in the Fig. 5.3. It is clear that mean age of onset of most of the diseases is beyond 50, which indicates that people at higher age are more vulnerable to disease. Mean age of onset of diabetes and blood pressure is 59, which is higher than that of any other disease. It can also be noticed from the figure that there is not much difference in the mean age of onset of chronic diseases for males and females in the case of most of the diseases.

Following an understanding of the age pattern of disease prevalence in the state, it becomes pertinent to analyse the kind of care that individuals with different ailments seek. From Fig. 5.4, it becomes very clear that most of the sick people in Kerala seek treatment; only 5% of the sick do not seek treatment. This observation suggests the existence of a well-developed medical system and the positive health-conscious behaviour of people in the state. From the figure, it can also be noted that around 95% of people go to the doctor or health specialist for treatment. Not much gender difference is found in this treatment-seeking behavior.

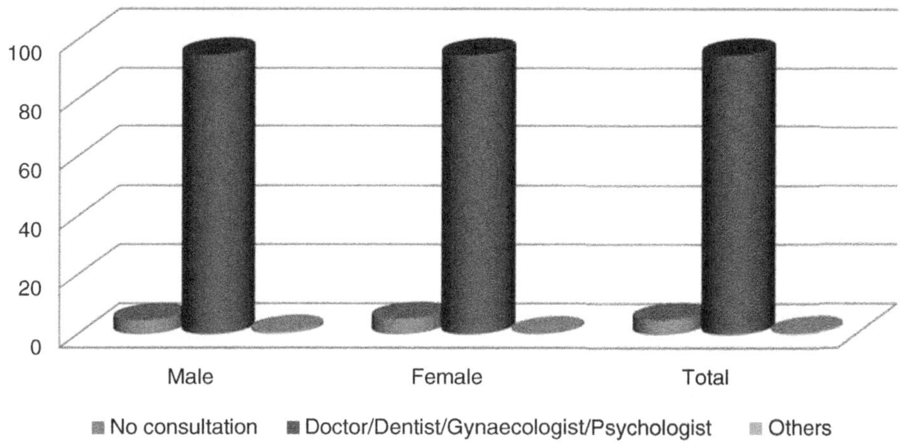

Fig. 5.4 Person contacted for treatment by the elderly in Kerala, 2007 (Source: Computed by the author using Kerala Migration Monitoring Study, 2007)

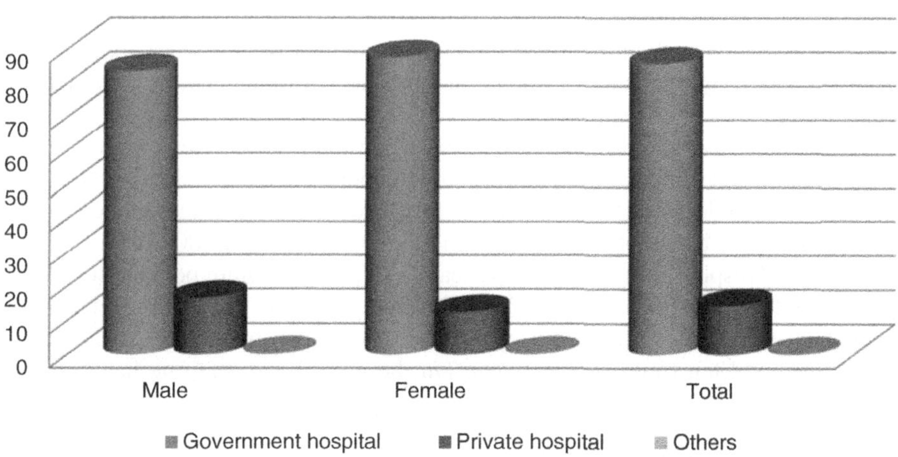

Fig. 5.5 Place of consultation for the medical treatment for the elderly in Kerala, 2007 (Source: Computed by the author using Kerala Migration Monitoring Study, 2007)

Beyond the positive treatment-seeking behaviour, the study also examined the kind of medical institution preferred by the people. If more people are going to public hospitals, they are likely have relatively less income as compared to those who are going to private hospitals for treatment because private hospitals are mostly profit-motivated and hence, expensive. The type of hospital utilisation is shown in Fig. 5.5. The figure reveals that a majority of the elderly are going to government hospitals for treatment, which is in contrast with our previous findings from NSSO.

The reason is likely that when the survey was conducted chickenguniya was widespread all over Kerala and the government hospitals played a major role in eradicating the menace, while private hospitals could not participate in an effective manner.

The figure also demonstrates that the proportion of female elderly going to public hospitals is relatively higher, that is, it is 87.4% for female elderly, whereas it is 83.3% for male elderly.

Cost of Disease

Following an understanding of morbidity prevalence and treatment-seeking behavior, it is also relevant to examine the cost of disease, as it has to be financed mostly by OOP expenditure in India, and this expenditure has a direct implication on household wellbeing. The table reveals that cancer is the most expensive disease (Rs. 764 per capita per month), which is followed by 'kidney problem' and 'heart problem'. It was expected that the diseases would cost more at higher ages, but no definite pattern is found (Table 5.2). Nevertheless, it can be observed that the per capita cost of most of the diseases is higher for the 60–74 age group than the average cost for all ages for all ailments except cholesterol and asthma. These findings are well supported by the study of Zachariah and Irudaya Rajan (2007), in which the results were found to be similar.

To estimate the cost of managing diseases, hospitalisation rate is multiplied by the per capita out of pocket expenditure for in patient and the population in the contemporary period. Per capita out of pocket expenditure is estimated on the basis of compound growth rate observed between 1995 and 1996 and 2004 for estimating future cost. Hospitalisation rate and per capita OOP expenditure per year for 1995–1996 and 2004 are shown in Table 5.3. It is interesting to notice that hospitalisation rate of the elderly for chronic and non-chronic diseases has increased approximately four times and ten times, respectively. On the other hand, the rate has declined

Table 5.2 Per capita cost of diseases per month for those who have paid in Kerala, 2007

Age group	0–14	15–29	30–44	45–59	60–74	75 and above	Total
Diabetes	308	256	214	215	242	336	239
Heart problem	542	303	512	501	579	431	510
Arthritis	194	434	279	243	269	204	258
Cholesterol	216	433	182	237	195	433	234
Blood pressure	90	188	196	191	208	215	201
Asthma	295	233	258	275	239	273	262
Cancer	675	767	407	693	1,048	330	764
Kidney problem	1,105	538	519	425	550	413	540
Others	246	297	304	293	288	264	287

Source: Computed by the Author using Kerala Migration Monitoring Study, 2007

Table 5.3 Hospitalisation rate and OOP expenditure for chronic and non-chronic diseases for 1995–1996 and 2004

	1995–96		2004	
	Chronic	Non chronic	Chronic	Non chronic
Elderly				
Hospitalisation per 10,000	276	176	1,315	1,909
PC exp for in-patient	4,425	2,660	5,236	3,349
Non-elderly				
Hospitalisation per 10,000	51	82	39	18
PC exp for in-patient	4,791	2,565	5,569	4,547

Source: Computed by the author using unit level records of National Sample Survey 60th round and 52nd round, 'Morbidity and health care'

considerably for the non-elderly over a period of time, with an especially steep decline in the hospitalisation rate for non-chronic diseases. Per capita OOP expenditure per year has increased for both elderly and non-elderly in-patient treatment; it has increased from Rs. 4,425 in 1995–1996 to Rs. 5,236 for in-patient treatment of elderly persons for chronic diseases, while the same has increased from Rs. 2,660 to Rs. 3,349 in the respective year for non-chronic diseases. The per capita OOP expenditure for the non-elderly has increased from Rs. 4,791 and Rs. 2,565 in 1995–1996 to Rs. 5,569 and Rs. 4,547 for chronic and non-chronic diseases respectively. As revealed from the table, the elderly have a dual burden; (i) a higher rate of hospitalisation due to high morbidity prevalence, and (ii) an increased cost of hospitalisation. Because the cost of hospitalisation is much more for the elderly, the health of the elderly calls for more care and attention.

Based on the compound growth rate observed between the two NSS rounds of morbidity and health care (1995–1996 and 2004), the future cost of hospitalisation is estimated.[13] Nonetheless, it should be noticed that the growth rate of hospitalisation for elderly is high; therefore if we project the hospitalisation at the same pace, it goes beyond the actual number of elderly. It should, however, be borne in mind that the rate of hospitalisation cannot go beyond a certain limit, and hence current hospitalisation rate (i.e. for 2004) has been taken for the projection of future cost. Table 5.4 clearly reveals that the cost of managing the diseases will increase significantly from Rs. 4,662 million in 2004 to Rs. 11,948 million in 2026, out of which most of the increase will come from the increase in the cost of hospitalisation of the elderly. The OOP expenditure for elderly in-patient will constitute around 80% of the total OOP expenditure for all in-patients. These findings suggest that the high prevalence of morbidity among elderly is reflected in high health expenditure. It indicates that the elderly will face a dual burden of higher morbidity prevalence

[13] It should be kept in mind that the same growth rate, which has been observed during 1995–1996 and 2004, is applied to estimate the cost of hospitalisation. Since the data on such costs is available for these two periods only, it is not possible to include more periods to make the estimation more robust. This is one of the major drawbacks of the study.

Table 5.4 Estimated cost of hospitalisation according to type of diseases per year (in Rs. million) in Kerala

	1996	2004	2011	2016	2021	2026
Elderly						
Chronic	359	2,484	3,394	3,771	4,189	4,654
Non-chronic	138	1,315	3,329	3,844	4,440	5,128
Total	497	3,799	6,723	7,615	8,629	9,782
Non-elderly						
Chronic	673	631	752	826	907	997
Non-chronic	575	232	400	572	818	1,169
Total	1,249	863	1,152	1,398	1,725	2,166
Total	1,745	4,662	7,875	9,013	10,354	11,948

Source: Computed by the author

and high OOP health care expenditure. This result has significant bearing on public policy to finance such health expenditures in order to alleviate the economic burden of the elderly. It should also be observed that OOP expenditure for chronic diseases as well as non-chronic diseases will increase for both elderly and non-elderly persons, and the cost of non-chronic diseases is higher than the cost of chronic diseases.

Results of Regression Analysis

The regression results (Table 5.5) show that all independent variables are significant at the 1% level of significance. As expected, per capita health expenditure (PCHE) of hospital in-patients is less for the individuals who chose public hospitals compared to those who chose private hospitals. Furthermore, health expenditure is less for illiterate persons, who are less likely to be conscious about their health and less likely to seek treatment. Types of disease also have significant effects on per capita health expenditures. The regression result clearly indicates that persons having chronic diseases are more likely to spend on health care as in-patients. The regression analysis further shows that sex is also an important determinant of health expenditure. Per capita health expenditure is likely to be less for males compared to females. Social group also has a substantial effect on PCHE. People categorized as SC and ST are likely to spend less compared to 'others',[14] who tend to be more well off compared to people in the ST and SC categories, and hence are likely to spend more on health care. Age is also an important factor affecting PCHE, as expected PCHE is found to be more for the elderly who are more prone to disease than people in the younger age groups. The regression results also indicate that consumption quintile, which has been taken as a proxy for income, is one of the major determinants of PCHE. People with the lowest income spend the least on health care, and

[14] Social group is categorized into three categories, ST, SC and others.

Table 5.5 Regression results

Independent variables	Beta	t
(Constant)	(2.84)	914.04
d_hsp	−0.11 (2.15)***	−527.94
d_illit	−0.06 (2.19)***	−309.83
d_r	−0.05 (2.35)***	−251.33
d_chr	0.05 (2.11)***	268.13
d_sex	−0.01 (2.08)***	−44.67
d_sc	−0.01 (4.83)***	−49.04
d_st	−0.01 (2.74)***	−64.28
d_age	0.04 (2.73)***	212.53
d_q1	−0.01 (3.45)***	−49.50
d_q2	−0.03 (3.48)***	−113.75
d_q3	−0.03 (3.17)***	−123.22
d_q4	−0.04 (2.99)***	−153.08

Note: Robust standard errors in parentheses
*Indicates significance at 10% level, **indicates significance at 5% level, ***indicates significance at 1% level

people in quintile 2, quintile 3, and quintile 4 are also less likely to spend on health care compared to people in quintile 5.

Conclusion

The paper examined the effect of population aging on health expenditure in India, with specific reference to Kerala. An attempt was made to estimate the future cost of managing diseases. The proportion of the elderly reporting their health as poor is found to be highest in Kerala followed by West Bengal. Prevalence of at least one ailment is second highest in Kerala after Goa. These results are quite surprising as it is well known that Kerala is the most advanced state in India in terms of human development indicators.

To devise an idea regarding the approximate cost of care in accordance with the prevailing scenario of age and stage of diseases, mean age of onset of diseases was calculated and the findings revealed the higher vulnerability of the elderly as the mean age of most of the diseases were found to be more than 50. OOP expenditure according to type of diseases (chronic and non-chronic diseases) was estimated in order to understand the burden according to the type of diseases, and the findings revealed that OOP expenditure was significantly higher for chronic diseases than for non-chronic diseases. Higher morbidity prevalence coupled with higher OOP expenditure among the elderly indicated that the elderly are the most vulnerable sections of the society and hence there is an urgent need for the insurance policies to be especially targeted towards the elderly. The comparative analysis of two rounds of NSSO revealed significant increase in hospitalisation rates as well as OOP expenditures for elderly in-patients. On the other hand, hospitalisation rates declined and OOP expenditure for non-elderly in-patients increased. OOP expenditures for in-patients are estimated to increase significantly from Rs. 1,745 million in 1996 to Rs. 11,948 million in 2026 (OOP expenditures for elderly in-patients are around 80% of the total OOP expenditure). This result has significant bearing on policy formulation, especially in terms of public finance, as the government devises health insurance plans to alleviate the burden of OOP expenditures on health care.

Acknowledgements The author would like to thank Dr. S. Irudaya Rajan, Dr. Lekha Chakraborty, Jatinder Singh, Indervir Singh, Shashi Ranjan Jha and Kaushalendra Kumar for their useful comments.

Appendix

Table A.1 Proportion of elderly reporting their health as poor for 1995–1996 and 2004

	1995–1996	2004
60–64	15.0	23.5
65–69	20.8	31.7
70–74	29.9	39.5
75–79	36.1	52.4
80 and above	45.8	57.3
60 and above	23.6	37.2

Source: Computed by the author using unit level records of National Sample Survey 60th round, 'Morbidity, health care and condition of the aged' (2004) and 52nd round, 'Morbidity and health care'

References

Alam, M. (2008). Ageing, socio-economic disparities and health outcomes: Some evidence from rural India (Working Paper Series no. E/290/2008). Institute of Economic Growth, University Enclave, New Delhi.

Bhatia, S. P. S., Swami, H. M., Thakur, J. S., & Bhatia, V. (2007). A study of health problems and loneliness among the elderly in Chandigarh. *Indian Journal of Community Medicine, 32*(4), 255–258.

Cowell, A. (2006). The relationship between education and health behavior: Some empirical evidence. *Health Economics, 15*, 125–146.

Grossman, M. (1999). The human capital model of the demand for health. National Bureau of Economic Research Working Paper Series no. 7078.

Gupta, I., Dasgupta, P., & Sawhney, M. (2001). 'Health of the elderly in India: Some aspects of vulnerability' (Discussion Paper Series No. 26). Institute of Economic Growth, University Enclave, New Delhi.

India, Registrar General. (2006). *Population projection for India and states 2021–2026*. Report of the Technical Group on Population Projections Constituted by the National Commission on Population, Census of India 2001, New Delhi.

India, Registrar General. (2007b). *Sample registration system abridged life table 2007, analytical studies*. Report No. 3, Office of the Registrar General, Government of India, New Delhi.

Irudaya Rajan, S. (2004). *Population ageing and health in India.* The Centre for Enquiry into Health and Allied Themes, Mumbai. http://www.cehat.org/humanrights/rajan.pdf. Cited 20 July 2010.

Irudaya Rajan, S. (2008). *Social security for the elderly: Experiences from South East Asia.* New Delhi: Routledge.

Mathiyazhagan, M. K. (2003). Rural household characteristics and health expenditure in India; an analysis. *Journal of Social and Economic Development, 5*(1), 86.

Migration Monitoring Study. (2007). Kerala Migration Monitoring Study. Research Unit on International Migration of the Centre for Development Studies.

National Sample Survey Organisation. (1996). Survey on Health Care: NSS 52nd round (July 1995–1996). Department of Statistics, Government of India.

National Sample Survey Organisation. (2004). Morbidity, health care and the conditions of the aged: NSS 60th round (January – June 2004)'. Ministry of Statistics and Programme Implementation, Government of India.

O'Donnell, O., Doorslaer, E., Rannan-Eliya, R., Somanathan, A., Garg, C., Hanvoravongchai, P., Huq, M. N., Karan, A., Leung, G. M., Tin, K., Vasavid, C. (2005). Explaining the incidence of catastrophic expenditures on health care: Comparative evidence from Asia (EQUITAP Project Working Paper No. 5).

Omran, A. R. (1971). The epidemiological transition. *Milbank Memorial Fund*, 49, Part 1, 509–538. Paper 7078, NBER.

Prakash, R., Choudhary, S. K., & Singh, U. S. (2004). A study of morbidity pattern among geriatric population in an urban area of Udaipur Rajasthan. *Indian Journal of Community Medicine, 29*(1), 35–40.

Registrar General of India. (1992–1996). Sample registration system based abridged life table, Office of the Registrar General, Government of India, New Delhi.

Registrar General of India. (2002–2006). Sample registration system based abridged life table, Office of the Registrar General, Government of India, New Delhi.

Reinhardt, U. E. (2003). Does the aging of the population really drive the demand for health care? *Health Affairs, 22*(6), 27–39.

Riley, G. F., Lubitz, J., Prihoda, R., & Rabey, E. (1987). The use and costs of medicare services by cause of death. *Inquiry, 24*, 233–244.

Ross Catherine, E., & Chia-Ling, W. (1995). The links between education and health. *American Sociological Review, 60*, 719–745.

Seshamani, M., & Gray, A. (2003). Health care expenditures and ageing: An international comparison. *Applied Health Economic Health Policy, 2*(1), 9–16.

Seshamani, M., & Gray, A. (2004). The longitudinal study of the effects of age and time to death on hospital costs. *Journal of Health Economics, 23*, 217–235.

Wensing, M. (2001). Functional status, health problems, age and comorbidity in primary care patients. *Quality of Life Research, 10*(2), 141–148.

World Health Organization. (1989). Health of the elderly. Technical support series 779, Report of a WHO Expert Committee. Geneva: WHO.

Yang, Z., Norton, E. C., & Stearns, S. C. (2003). Longevity and health care expenditures: The real reasons for older people spend more. *The Journals of Gerontology, Series B: Psychological Sciences and Social Sciences, 58*(1), S2–S10.

Young, A. (1997). Ageing and physiological functions. *Philosophical Transactions: Biological Sciences, 352*(1363), 1837–1843.

Zachariah, K. C., & Irudaya Rajan, S. (2007). Costs of basic services in Kerala, 2007 education, health, childbirth and finance (loans) (Working Paper No. 406). Thiruvananthapuram: Centre for Development Studies

Part II
Cause-Specific Mortality

Chapter 6
State Estimates of Cause and Condition-Specific Mortality Rates for Diabetes Mellitus

David W. Smith, Stephanie L. McFall, and Benjamin S. Bradshaw

Introduction

Official vital statistics report the death rates due to diabetes in the general population. These are only an indirect indicator of mortality among diabetics since these rates measure deaths due to diabetes in the whole population. A higher rate can mean greater prevalence of diabetes or greater mortality among diabetics or a combination of both. Condition and cause specific death rates directly identify deaths caused by diabetes with the diabetic sub-population in which they occur, giving more specific, focused information since persons diagnosed with diabetes are those most at risk of dying from the disease.

Diabetes is frequently a cause of death. Diabetes was listed as a cause in 8.9% of all deaths in the U.S. in 1999–2001 and was the underlying cause in 2.9% of deaths (obtained from Centers for Disease Control using CDC WONDER, http://wonder.cdc.gov/mcd-v2004.html, April 2, 2010). In 2000 prevalence of diagnosed diabetes among adults 18 years and over varied from 3.8% in Alaska to 7.6% in Mississippi and West Virginia (Centers for Disease Control and Prevention 2000). The national adult prevalence rate was 3.1% (se: 0.08%) in 1995, rose to 4.4% (se: 0.07%) in 2000 and to 5.6% (se: 0.08%) in 2005 (Centers for Disease Control and Prevention 2009). Among adults 20 years of age or older in 1999–2000, the prevalence was 5.9% (95% CI: 4.9–6.9%) and undiagnosed diabetes was at a prevalence of 2.4%

D.W. Smith, Ph.D., M.P.H. (✉)
Consultant, Colchester, UK
e-mail: davidwsmithphd@gmail.com

S.L. McFall, Ph.D.
Institute for Social and Economic Research, University of Essex,
Wivenhoe Park, Colchester, UK

B.S. Bradshaw, Ph.D.
Division of Management, Policy, and Community Health, The University of Texas
School of Public Health, San Antonio, TX, USA

N. Hoque et al. (eds.), *Applied Demography and Public Health*,
Applied Demography Series 3, DOI 10.1007/978-94-007-6140-7_6,
© Springer Science+Business Media Dordrecht 2013

(95% CI: 1.5–3.4%) for a total prevalence rate of 8.3% (95% CI: 6.9–9.8%) (Centers for Disease Control and Prevention 2003).

There is little published information about death rates in diabetic populations. The estimated rate (per 10,000) due to diabetes among diabetics aged 25 and over in the U.S. in 1999–2001 was 162.7 (95% CI: 159.6–165.8), and for diabetes as the underlying cause it was 52.9 (95% CI: 51.9–54.0) (Smith and Bradshaw 2008). Tierney et al. (2001) estimated total and cause specific death rates among diabetics aged 18 and over in North Dakota during 1992–1996 using specially modified death certificates to count deaths and the Behavioral Risk Factor Surveillance System (BRFSS) to estimate the numbers of diabetics.

Estimation of prevalence rates and subpopulation sizes of 5–10% of the total population presents a significant challenge to sample surveys. A typical survey sample size of about 1,000 would yield a subsample of about 50–100 respondents. Even with a larger sample size of 2,000, the total sample of a subpopulation at such prevalence would only be about 100–200. Prevalence rates by sex and age can be more problematic than these small samples would suggest. For estimates for diabetes, for example, the subgroup sample sizes at young ages are unusually small because diabetes occurs disproportionately at older ages. Some age groups could have few or even no diabetic respondents in a randomly sampled survey of typical size. Estimates for wider age intervals can be used and might be thought to ameliorate the problem of estimation. However, the prevalence rates can vary substantially within wide age intervals and such estimates might be difficult to interpret for public health policy. Pooling several years of data to increase sample sizes makes estimates more feasible but annual surveys are not usually designed for this purpose. Sampling weights are usually computed annually, for example, which incorporate the observed mix of respondents by age, sex, and often race and ethnicity, standardized to their estimated population totals. On the other hand, sample sizes of health surveys have increased over the last 20 years, partly to obtain better estimates of low rates and characteristics of small subpopulations.

Estimation of death rates for an estimated subpopulation with a disease or condition is more of a challenge than estimation of prevalence rates because the estimated subpopulation size is used as the denominator of a death rate instead of the numerator of a prevalence rate. Ratios of random variables are statistically difficult to estimate, more so as their denominators become smaller and more variable. These estimates are highly variable when the proportions and numbers are small, as described above. Estimated ratios of random variables are often strongly asymmetric, a consequence of the amount of random variation in the denominator. The usual confidence intervals, using a rate plus and minus a constant times the standard error, may be misleading for such ratios (Hansen et al. 1953, vol. II, pp. 109–111).

We use surveys to estimate the denominators of mortality rates, the population sizes for states, using methods which have been applied successfully to estimates of mortality rates for diabetics in the United States (Smith and Bradshaw 2008). We use information from the survey estimates, the coefficients of variation of the of the population sizes, to assess the reliability of the rates. The estimates provide information about such death rates. They also permit us to evaluate the utility of this method for relatively small populations.

Ratio Estimation Methods and Materials

We estimated death rates among persons diagnosed with diabetes during the period 1999–2001. We included only persons aged 35 and over since diabetes deaths under that age are rare – 1.0% of deaths in 1999–2001 with any mention of diabetes were to persons under 35 – and the diabetic population was small – 5.7% of the total estimated population in 1999–2001. We used age intervals of 10 years from 35 to 74 and pooled those over 74 in order to include older diabetics who, though smaller in number, have high mortality.

Counts of deaths by age group and sex for each state were obtained from the Centers for Disease Control (CDC) using the data tabulation software, CDC WONDER. We obtained the total number of deaths with any mention of diabetes as an underlying or contributing cause of death. We computed death rates for both underlying and total mentions of diabetes. A few deaths are not included in our analyses because age, sex, or race was not available. We estimated the standard deviation (SD) of each total count as the square root of the count, assuming a Poisson distribution for the number of deaths (Alho and Spencer 2005, p. 107).

We used the public use data file of the Behavioral Risk Factor Surveillance System (BRFSS), a large telephone survey sponsored by the Centers for Disease Control and Prevention (CDC) (Centers for Disease Control and Prevention 2005; Holtzman 2003). The BRFSS is a system of random digit dialed telephone interviews conducted by states (as well as territories and the District of Columbia). Each state manages the conduct of its own survey following mutually agreed standards. These standards specify such characteristics as the sample design and sample selection, dates of data collection each month, the number of call-backs to contact a household, making appointments for interviews, and the questionnaire structure and wording. The questionnaire content varies somewhat from year to year with few changes in the core content. Sample sizes vary by year and state but are designed to be large enough in each year to reliably estimate most rates.

The BRFSS core questionnaire for many years has included the question "Have you ever been told by a doctor that you have diabetes?" The coded response categories are: yes, no, only while pregnant, don't know or not sure, and refused. We recoded each response as yes or other to estimate the diabetic population size.

We pooled BRFSS data for 1999–2001 to estimate population sizes. The total number of interviews in 1999 was 159,989, in 2000 it was 184,450, and in 2001 it was 212,510. We computed new sampling weights for the pooled data. Reweighting is especially important for small sub-populations whose relative sample size can vary much more from year to year. For each state we used the original weights and the state sample sizes in each of the 3 years to compute new weights. A respondent's new weight was computed as the original weight times the number of interviews done by the state in the year of the interview divided by the total number of interviews done by the state in all 3 years. In order to collect detailed information in some states, the BRFSS sample size may increase substantially in some states for 1 year and decrease the following year. Our reweighting method allows more even

Table 6.1 Estimated diabetic population aged 35 and over by sex and age, standardized to 1,000,000 – United States: 1999–2001

Age group	Male	Female	Total
35–44	53,322	52,959	106,281
45–54	109,594	101,912	211,506
55–64	129,885	126,742	256,626
65–74	121,126	142,459	263,585
75+	67,925	94,076	162,001
Total	481,852	518,148	1,000,000

weights of respondents in different years, compared with the simplest method of reweighting each year equally, but stops short of complete reweighting by all post-stratification categories, which vary somewhat among states. Estimates of population sizes and variances for the pooled samples were made for males, females, and the total using the survey estimation procedures of StataCorp (Survey Data, 2007).

Each death rate was estimated as the ratio, X/Y, of the total number of deaths, X, during 1999–2001 to the sum of the estimated populations, Y, for 1999–2001. The estimated variance and standard error of the ratio used a formula based on the Taylor series expansion of the ratio (Cochran 1977, p. 319; Hansen et al. 1953, vol. I, pp. 162–167). For two independent random variables, X and Y, both positive, the estimated standard error of the estimated ratio, X/Y, is $se(X/Y) = (X/Y)\ [var(X)/X^2 + var(Y)/Y^2]^{1/2}$. This is somewhat simplified from the usual formula, which has a covariance term for X and Y since our estimates of X and Y are from distinct sources and so uncorrelated. We used Microsoft Excel to calculate the ratios and their standard errors from the counts of deaths and population estimates and their associated variances.

We computed standardized death rates as well as crude or unstandardized rates. For standardized rates we used the estimated diabetic population for the United States by sex and age intervals of 35–44, 45–54, 55–64, 65–74, and 75 or older to directly standardize the rate for each state. The U.S. population sizes, totaling to one million for diabetics aged 35 or over in 1999–2001, are shown in Table 6.1. We report the estimates of death rates per 10,000 and standard errors separately for men and for women for each state. The standardized rate is the linear combination of the age-specific or age-sex specific rates using the proportion of the diabetic population in each age group or age-sex group as the coefficient. The variance is the sum of the weighted variances of the rates for the age groups or age-sex groups and the standard error is the square root of the variance.

We evaluated the resulting estimates partly through the coefficient of variation (CV) of the denominators and of the rate estimates themselves. The CV is the ratio of a standard error to the corresponding estimate. Where these ratios are small, the resulting confidence intervals can be used more reliably. Where the ratios are larger, the confidence intervals are wider but the intervals themselves might be poor estimates, namely, failing to include the underlying true parameter with the degree of confidence specified. For denominators of ratio estimates from surveys, Hansen et al. (1953, vol. I, pp. 162–167) recommended CVs 0.05 or less and Kish (1965, p. 218) recommended 0.10 or less. Their recommendations do not readily apply to the standardized rates, however, since they are weighted averages of ratio estimates. A high value of a CV may be more useful as a cautionary warning when using a particular estimate and less useful as a method to decide whether an estimate or its confidence interval is usable.

Estimates of Death Rates

The total BRFSS sample sizes for 1999–2001 by state ranged from 4,871 to 21,801, with an average of 10,634. The number of diabetics ranged from 248 to 1,611 and averaged 632.

The diabetic population aged 35 or over is shown in Table 6.1, standardized to a total of one million. There were slightly more females, at 52% of the total, though there were more males in each age interval from 35 to 64. The death rates for the whole United States by age group and sex are shown in Table 6.2. Those rates increased with age, sharply after age 75. The rates for diabetes as an underlying cause were higher for men up to age 74 and for women above age 74. The rates for all mentions of diabetes were higher for men at every age.

The death rates and standardized death rates for diabetes as an underlying cause for men, women, and all diabetics are shown for each state in Table 6.3. Figure 6.1 shows the rates and confidence intervals for each state. There was substantial variation in rates among states for males, females, and both. The crude rates ranged from about 37 to almost 100 per 10,000, and were slightly higher among men than women. The standardized rates had a similar range with a slightly lower maximum at about 92 per 10,000. The standard errors were all low relative to the estimates, which indicates that the estimates and confidence intervals using them are reasonably reliable. The standard errors of the standardized rates were generally larger than those of the crude rates.

Comparisons among states are better made with standardized death rates. The four states with the lowest standardized death rates per 10,000 were Nevada at 38.6

Table 6.2 Age specific death rates (per 10,000) due to diabetes among diabetics, any mention and underlying cause, by sex-United States: 1999–2001

	Any mention			Underlying cause		
Age group	Male	Female	Both sexes	Male	Female	Both sexes
18–24	10.9	10.6	10.7	7.0	6.2	6.6
25–34	21.9	16.4	19.1	12.7	8.8	10.7
35–44	37.6	25.6	31.6	17.5	12.0	14.8
45–54	55.4	41.4	48.7	21.5	16.6	19.1
55–64	92.7	75.3	84.1	31.2	27.2	29.2
65–74	182.1	141.3	160.0	55.4	47.9	51.4
75+	400.7	333.3	361.5	166.5	187.8	178.9
Total	136.7	122.1	129.1	50.2	55.6	53.0

Table 6.3 Crude and age standardized death rates for diabetes as an underlying cause of death in the diabetic population, by sex-U.S. states: 1999–2001

		Male				Female				Both sexes			
		Crude		Standardized		Crude		Standardized		Crude		Standardized	
State	Number of sampled diabetics	Rate	SE	Rate	SE	Rate	SE	Rate	SE	Rate	SE	Rate	SE
Alabama	600	45.2	3.7	43.9	3.8	59.9	4.4	62.9	7.1	52.7	3.1	53.7	4.1
Alaska	248	44.3	6.1	68.2	17.6	68.4	9.7	92.7	18.0	54.5	5.4	80.9	12.6
Arizona	440	51.5	4.7	61.3	7.5	54.8	4.6	59.3	6.0	53.0	3.5	60.3	4.8
Arkansas	586	55.0	4.6	60.6	7.5	62.2	4.3	56.9	4.4	58.7	3.2	58.7	4.3
California	671	42.9	3.0	43.9	3.6	43.7	2.9	46.2	3.9	43.3	2.1	45.1	2.7
Colorado	338	41.2	3.7	37.1	3.6	59.6	5.5	54.3	5.9	49.3	3.2	46.0	3.5
Connecticut	830	46.7	3.1	41.9	3.1	56.5	3.4	56.0	4.9	51.5	2.3	49.2	2.9
Delaware	607	47.2	4.4	48.9	5.2	57.9	4.8	58.2	6.1	52.4	3.3	53.8	4.0
District of Columbia	342	57.7	7.0	52.0	6.9	81.3	7.7	77.4	9.0	70.6	5.5	65.2	5.7
Florida	1,037	52.6	3.1	49.2	3.3	51.2	2.5	46.9	2.6	51.9	2.0	48.0	2.1
Georgia	747	36.9	2.6	48.8	5.8	37.6	2.2	43.7	4.1	37.3	1.8	46.1	3.5
Hawaii	671	40.0	3.4	37.5	3.8	43.6	3.8	46.8	5.0	41.6	2.6	42.3	3.2
Idaho	721	59.6	4.9	55.8	5.1	76.3	5.4	68.2	6.1	68.4	3.8	62.2	4.0
Illinois	618	50.6	3.9	50.4	4.9	57.2	3.5	51.8	3.7	54.1	2.7	51.1	3.0
Indiana	569	61.5	5.0	70.7	9.0	62.8	4.2	59.0	4.6	62.2	3.4	64.7	4.9
Iowa	662	48.1	3.6	40.0	3.3	65.0	4.2	51.9	3.6	56.6	2.8	46.2	2.5
Kansas	731	59.5	4.4	54.6	4.8	67.4	4.1	61.5	4.5	63.6	3.1	58.2	3.3
Kentucky	1,611	50.6	2.7	53.2	3.6	60.8	2.7	62.3	3.4	55.9	2.0	57.9	2.5
Louisiana	793	78.3	5.7	93.4	11.5	86.2	4.8	91.7	7.0	82.8	3.9	92.5	6.6
Maine	530	67.0	5.9	61.8	6.1	72.2	5.4	68.0	6.3	69.8	4.1	65.0	4.4
Maryland	788	54.2	3.7	60.1	5.4	62.4	3.8	66.7	6.2	58.4	2.8	63.5	4.1
Massachusetts	1,135	47.9	2.7	44.2	3.0	55.7	2.9	52.1	3.6	51.7	2.0	48.3	2.3
Michigan	599	51.1	3.6	51.6	4.8	59.2	3.9	60.4	5.5	55.4	2.8	56.2	3.7
Minnesota	548	74.8	5.5	69.2	6.5	81.4	5.6	69.4	6.3	78.1	4.0	69.3	4.5
Mississippi	594	40.7	3.4	41.1	4.3	44.5	3.2	45.7	4.0	42.8	2.5	43.5	2.9
Missouri	851	58.5	3.8	55.0	4.0	63.1	3.5	64.3	4.6	60.9	2.7	59.8	3.1

Montana	511	57.2	5.5	60.4	8.2	65.5	5.4	58.8	5.8	61.4	4.0	59.6	5.0
Nebraska	487	61.8	5.8	56.0	5.5	74.9	6.1	64.9	5.5	68.5	4.3	60.6	3.9
Nevada	378	37.2	3.4	36.6	3.6	36.4	3.8	40.5	5.3	36.8	2.6	38.6	3.3
New Hampshire	367	64.7	6.6	60.4	6.7	72.9	6.9	78.2	12.3	68.7	5.0	69.7	7.2
New Jersey	746	63.6	4.1	72.0	7.3	65.1	3.8	65.9	5.4	64.4	2.8	68.8	4.5
New Mexico	630	78.7	5.8	91.4	10.0	64.5	4.5	72.2	6.8	71.0	3.7	81.5	6.0
New York	543	44.3	3.5	43.8	4.0	46.5	3.1	45.0	4.2	45.5	2.4	44.4	2.9
North Carolina	800	52.4	3.4	54.2	4.3	60.1	3.1	56.9	3.6	56.4	2.3	55.6	2.8
North Dakota	332	98.7	11.5	87.1	12.2	82.9	8.2	63.2	7.0	89.8	6.8	74.8	6.9
Ohio	556	65.6	5.1	66.0	6.6	73.7	4.7	81.6	8.1	69.9	3.7	74.1	5.3
Oklahoma	741	53.9	3.6	53.1	4.2	75.9	4.5	78.0	5.8	64.9	2.9	66.0	3.6
Oregon	416	67.8	5.9	65.4	7.4	69.7	5.5	72.8	8.6	68.8	4.2	69.2	5.7
Pennsylvania	668	60.4	4.2	54.7	4.3	67.4	4.1	62.8	5.2	64.2	3.1	58.9	3.4
Rhode Island	616	53.7	4.5	48.6	4.7	71.1	5.8	68.5	7.1	61.9	3.7	58.9	4.3
South Carolina	658	50.6	3.6	60.0	6.3	63.2	4.1	73.9	7.2	57.0	2.9	67.2	4.8
South Dakota	804	64.3	5.6	56.8	5.4	74.8	5.9	60.8	5.1	69.6	4.1	58.9	3.7
Tennessee	576	55.7	4.9	64.8	8.2	58.9	4.0	65.8	6.4	57.5	3.3	65.3	5.1
Texas	968	52.6	3.0	55.6	3.8	61.7	3.1	73.1	5.8	57.3	2.3	64.7	3.5
Utah	439	77.4	7.0	80.0	9.8	88.2	7.5	88.7	8.8	82.8	5.3	84.5	6.6
Vermont	531	78.8	7.9	77.2	9.0	85.8	7.7	73.2	7.1	82.4	5.6	75.1	5.7
Virginia	535	44.5	3.5	50.0	5.7	56.5	4.1	70.8	7.7	50.4	2.9	60.8	4.9
Washington	591	57.5	4.2	56.0	5.1	61.8	4.1	60.2	5.1	59.6	3.0	58.2	3.6
West Virginia	680	64.2	5.3	67.4	6.3	75.8	5.3	76.5	6.4	70.3	4.2	72.1	4.5
Wisconsin	465	56.4	5.0	53.2	6.1	60.0	4.8	51.0	4.9	58.3	3.8	52.1	3.9
Wyoming	341	78.5	9.5	80.1	12.5	82.9	9.0	80.7	10.1	80.8	6.7	80.4	8.0
United States	32,246	52.6	0.8			58.4	0.8			55.6	0.6		
Minimum	248	36.9		36.6		36.4		40.5		36.8		38.6	
Mean	633	57.1		58.0		64.4		63.9		60.8		61.1	
Maximum	1,611	98.7		93.4		88.2		92.7		89.8		92.5	

Rates are standardized to the estimated diabetic population of the United States, 1999–2001

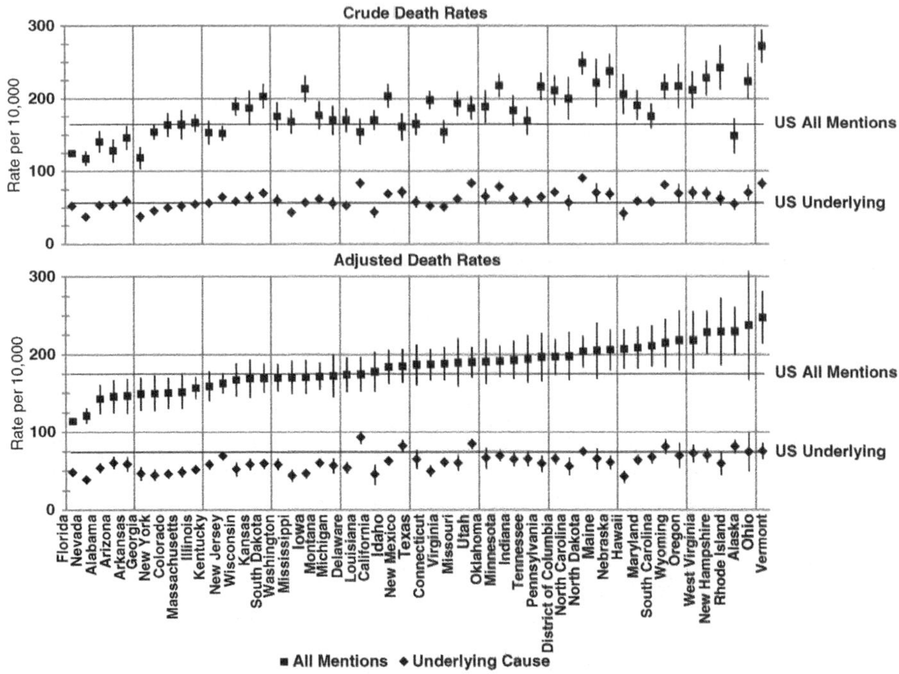

Fig. 6.1 Crude and standardized death rates (per 10,000) due to diabetes among diabetics for each state. Rates are for both any mention of diabetes as a cause and for diabetes as the underlying cause. Standardized rates are standardized to the estimated population of diabetics in the U.S. The rates for the U.S. are shown for reference. States are sorted by the adjusted death rates for any mention of diabetes as a cause

(se: 3.3), Hawaii at 42.3 (se: 3.2), Mississippi at 43.5 (se: 2.9) and New York at 44.4 (se: 2.9). The unstandardized death rates were similar in all four states. The four states with the highest standardized rates were Louisiana at 92.5 (se: 6.6), Utah at 84.5 (se: 6.6), New Mexico at 81.5 (se: 6.0) and Alaska at 80.9 (se: 12.6). The standardized rate for Alaska was observably higher than its unstandardized rate. Three other states had standardized rates that were noticeably higher than their crude rates: New Mexico, Virginia, and South Carolina. Three had noticeably lower standardized rates than crude rates: North Dakota, South Dakota, and Iowa, all with higher proportions of older residents. Alaska was the most unusual state in having the largest difference between its crude rate and standardized rate. Two states might be described as the most typical, Michigan and North Carolina, since both their crude rates and standardized rates are quite close to the national rate.

The death rates and standardized death rates for diabetes as any mention as a cause of death in the diabetic population are shown in Table 6.4 and Fig. 6.1 for men, women, and all diabetics. There was also substantial variation among states for males, females, and both. The crude rates ranged from about 110 to almost 280 per 10,000. The standardized rates had a similar range. The standard errors were all

Table 6.4 Crude and age standardized death rates for any mention of diabetes as a cause of death in the diabetic population, by sex-U.S. states: 1999–2001

State	Number of sampled diabetics	Male				Female				Both sexes			
		Crude		Standardized		Crude		Standardized		Crude		Standardized	
		Rate	SE	Rate	SE	Rate	SE	Rate	SE	Rate	SE	Rate	SE
Alabama	600	125.3	10.0	119.9	10.7	154.8	11.1	162.8	18.8	140.3	8.1	142.1	11.0
Alaska	248	123.5	14.2	205.1	53.5	182.4	22.2	252.6	47.2	148.3	12.5	229.7	35.5
Arizona	440	130.0	11.7	155.6	18.9	126.1	10.3	136.8	13.9	128.1	8.4	145.9	11.6
Arkansas	586	138.8	11.0	154.4	19.4	152.1	9.9	138.7	10.4	145.7	7.7	146.3	10.8
California	671	177.3	12.4	181.9	15.3	163.3	10.6	173.4	15.5	170.0	8.3	177.5	10.9
Colorado	338	143.8	12.3	127.9	12.1	188.4	16.6	170.5	18.3	163.4	10.2	150.0	11.2
Connecticut	830	187.1	11.1	164.9	11.6	209.4	11.4	207.3	17.8	198.1	8.2	186.9	10.8
Delaware	607	155.5	12.1	160.8	15.2	184.5	12.7	185.6	16.7	169.6	9.1	173.6	11.3
District of Columbia	342	192.2	20.7	175.7	20.5	226.8	19.5	216.3	23.6	211.1	15.0	196.8	15.7
Florida	1,037	129.4	7.5	119.8	8.1	119.0	5.6	108.2	6.2	124.2	4.8	113.8	5.1
Georgia	747	117.4	8.0	160.2	19.9	119.0	6.6	138.3	12.8	118.3	5.4	148.9	11.7
Hawaii	671	204.2	14.0	189.9	16.9	208.1	14.3	222.9	21.5	206.0	10.4	207.0	13.8
Idaho	721	202.4	14.1	184.5	16.5	204.8	12.5	182.9	15.1	203.7	9.8	183.7	11.2
Illinois	618	162.8	12.3	161.5	16.3	169.8	10.3	152.6	11.1	166.4	8.3	156.9	9.7
Indiana	569	186.2	14.8	217.8	28.7	181.1	11.7	169.7	13.2	183.5	9.8	192.9	15.4
Iowa	662	200.7	13.6	164.0	13.2	225.8	13.3	176.7	11.9	213.3	9.7	170.5	8.9
Kansas	731	187.9	12.9	168.8	15.0	186.5	10.5	168.6	12.2	187.2	8.5	168.7	9.6
Kentucky	1,611	141.9	6.9	149.7	10.0	163.1	6.5	167.7	8.9	152.8	5.1	159.0	6.7
Louisiana	793	150.5	10.7	182.3	23.3	156.3	8.5	166.6	12.7	153.8	7.0	174.2	13.0
Maine	530	221.1	17.5	202.0	19.1	222.3	15.0	206.8	18.6	221.8	11.8	204.5	13.3
Maryland	788	179.5	11.8	201.0	18.4	201.3	11.8	215.4	19.8	190.6	8.7	208.4	13.5
Massachusetts	1,135	156.2	8.2	142.3	9.6	172.0	8.3	159.9	10.9	163.9	6.0	151.4	7.3
Michigan	599	168.3	11.6	169.9	16.1	171.3	11.1	174.7	15.9	169.9	8.5	172.4	11.3

(continued)

Table 6.4 (continued)

State	Number of sampled diabetics	Male				Female				Both sexes			
		Crude		Standardized		Crude		Standardized		Crude		Standardized	
		Rate	SE	Rate	SE	Rate	SE	Rate	SE	Rate	SE	Rate	SE
Minnesota	548	214.2	15.2	195.7	19.0	220.7	14.7	186.7	16.8	217.4	10.8	191.1	12.6
Mississippi	594	164.4	12.8	164.7	17.3	170.1	11.3	174.9	14.7	167.7	9.1	170.0	11.3
Missouri	851	191.3	11.9	179.0	13.2	194.9	10.3	199.1	14.5	193.2	8.2	189.4	9.8
Montana	511	173.7	14.6	184.1	24.8	180.2	13.0	160.2	14.5	177.0	10.3	171.7	14.1
Nebraska	487	223.4	19.1	196.3	19.3	251.7	18.6	214.3	17.6	237.8	13.9	205.6	13.0
Nevada	378	123.8	10.2	120.1	11.1	109.8	10.5	122.0	15.6	117.5	7.6	121.1	9.7
New Hampshire	367	223.2	20.8	205.4	21.9	233.5	20.1	249.5	37.3	228.2	15.2	228.3	22.0
New Jersey	746	151.8	9.7	172.9	18.3	151.4	8.6	153.4	12.7	151.6	6.5	162.8	11.0
New Mexico	630	175.7	12.2	205.0	22.2	148.1	9.6	166.6	15.0	160.7	7.7	185.1	13.2
New York	543	152.3	11.8	149.8	14.2	155.4	10.2	149.7	14.7	153.9	8.2	149.8	10.2
North Carolina	800	195.7	12.1	203.6	16.7	203.8	10.2	192.1	12.1	200.0	8.0	197.6	10.2
NorthDakota	332	279.7	29.9	242.4	33.1	224.3	19.8	167.4	17.4	248.6	17.0	203.6	18.3
Ohio	556	218.1	16.8	219.3	23.0	228.4	14.3	253.5	25.5	223.6	11.6	237.0	17.2
Oklahoma	741	174.7	11.0	170.7	13.4	202.5	11.5	209.2	15.2	188.6	7.9	190.6	10.2
Oregon	416	222.3	18.6	213.2	25.0	212.2	16.0	222.2	27.6	217.0	12.8	217.8	18.7
Pennsylvania	668	214.8	14.8	191.5	15.8	218.1	13.1	201.1	17.1	216.6	10.2	196.5	11.7
Rhode Island	616	214.8	15.2	193.5	16.9	273.2	19.3	262.3	26.2	242.4	12.6	229.1	15.8
South Carolina	658	163.1	11.2	198.7	22.0	187.3	11.7	221.8	22.5	175.4	8.5	210.7	15.8
South Dakota	804	193.4	13.7	168.8	13.6	212.7	13.6	169.9	12.1	203.1	10.0	169.3	9.1
Tennessee	576	168.9	14.6	198.8	25.9	169.1	11.2	190.2	18.8	169.0	9.6	194.4	15.9
Texas	968	157.2	8.9	166.8	11.9	171.6	8.5	204.6	16.5	164.6	6.4	186.4	10.3

Utah	439	179.7	15.5	184.3	22.4	194.3	15.7	195.0	19.2	187.0	11.5	189.8	14.7
Vermont	531	266.3	22.2	264.4	29.4	277.0	20.6	231.1	19.8	271.9	15.4	247.1	17.5
Virginia	535	137.6	10.6	157.9	19.7	170.2	12.1	216.0	24.0	153.6	8.6	188.0	15.6
Washington	591	175.5	12.3	170.5	16.5	174.8	11.3	169.2	14.7	175.1	8.5	169.8	11.0
West Virginia	680	196.4	15.3	208.1	20.4	226.0	14.9	227.5	18.9	211.8	12.0	218.1	13.9
Wisconsin	465	186.2	16.1	174.0	20.7	191.9	14.8	160.5	15.8	189.1	12.1	167.0	12.9
Wyoming	341	221.5	22.9	225.1	31.9	212.2	19.6	205.2	23.3	216.7	15.4	214.8	19.5
United States	32,246	168.5	2.4			174.1	2.2			171.4	1.7		
Minimum	248	117.4		119.8		109.8		108.2		117.5		113.8	
Mean	633	180.1		181.3		189.7		187.3		184.7		184.4	
Maximum	1,611	279.7		264.4		277.0		262.3		271.9		247.1	

Rates are standardized to the estimated diabetic population of the United States, 1999–2001 low relative to the estimates, which indicates that the estimates and confidence intervals using them are reasonably reliable. The standard errors of the standardized rates were generally larger than those of the crude rates.

The three states with the lowest standardized death rates per 10,000 were Florida, Nevada, and Alabama. The two states with the highest standardized rates were Ohio and Vermont. Four states had standardized rates that were noticeably higher than their crude rates: Alaska, South Carolina, Virginia, and Georgia. Again, Alaska was the most unusual state with this pattern. Four states had noticeably lower standardized rates than crude rates: Nebraska, South Dakota, Iowa, and North Dakota, all with higher proportions of older residents.

The crude and standardized rates for each state are not strictly comparable because the state age specific rates are weighted by different age compositions – i.e., the crude rates result from the implicit weighting of the state age specific rates by the age distribution of diabetics in each state, while the standardized rates result from the explicit weighting of the state age specific rates by the U.S. age distribution of diabetics. Nevertheless, comparing the crude and standardized rates for each state is of interest because it suggests the differences in state and U.S. age composition of diabetics.

The CVs for the estimated diabetic population sizes, the denominators of the crude death rates, ranged from 0.05 to 0.10 for men, from 0.04 to 0.11 for women, and from 0.03 to 0.07 for the totals. These rates almost always meet the standard of 0.10 or less recommended by Kish (1965), but a number of them fail to meet the standard of 0.05 or less recommended in Hansen et al. (1953). While the variation in the rates is adequately low, some confidence intervals may have the nominal 95% coverage usually specified and might require specialized methods of estimation to obtain good intervals.

The CVs for crude death rates using any mention of diabetes were similar for males and females, varying from 0.040 to 0.121 and smaller for all diabetics, varying from 0.033 to 0.085. The CVs for standardized rates were higher, being similar for males and females, between 0.057 and 0.261, and between 0.042 and 0.187. The largest values were for Alaska, which had the largest difference between its crude and standardized rates.

The CVs for crude death rates using the underlying cause were similar for males and females, varying from 0.044 to 0.141 and smaller for all diabetics, varying from 0.036 to 0.100. The CVs for standardized rates were higher, being similar for males and females, between 0.055 and 0.258, and for all diabetics between 0.043 and 0.194. Again, the largest values were for Alaska, which had the largest difference between its crude and standardized rates. The CVs were similar for both kinds of rates, underlying cause and all mentions of diabetes.

While many of these CVs show that the corresponding rates are satisfactory, they also suggest that some rates are more variable than is desirable and indicate that, at least in some states, larger sample sizes might be needed.

Discussion

State death rates due to diabetes among the population of diabetics yield valuable information by restricting the population to the people at risk from the specific cause. These results show it is feasible to estimate cause and condition-specific diabetes death rates for relatively small areas, *i.e.* states, at least when pooled data for 3 years is used. The CVs here were generally acceptable, though some indicated that the sampling variation in some rates might be large enough to warrant caution in their use. These estimates are ratios with sampling variation in the denominator as well as the numerator, which must be accounted for in estimating their standard errors and in assessing their reliability.

If the diabetic population size estimates for age-sex groups in each area are adequately reliable, then indirect standardization could be used. The national rates can be taken from Table 6.2 or computed contemporaneously for the nation using the methods described here. Thus, it is possible to estimate reliable death rates that can be compared across smaller areas or shorter periods.

This information should be interpreted in conjunction with the prevalence rates of diabetes in individual states. States might differ from typical in prevalence rates, in death rates, or in both. Consideration of these differences in mortality and prevalence could suggest different strategies to reduce diabetes in different states.

Using the estimated diabetic population as the standard appears to be a better choice than using the U.S. Standard Million Population (Anderson and Rosenberg 1998). Use of the U.S. Standard Million would have resulted in much lower rates since that standard population has larger numbers at the younger age groups compared with diabetics; the U.S. Standard Million is nearly the inverse of the diabetic population. The standardized rates based on the U.S. Standard Million are not realistic for state diabetic populations, and that is one reason we chose to use the estimated national diabetic population for standardization.

Mortality is a primary indicator of health status, both overall and for sub-populations defined by age, sex, and other characteristics such as race and ethnicity. It could also be useful for sub-populations with a chronic disease or long-term condition such as diabetes mellitus, asthma, physical impairment, smoking, or substance abuse. We focus here on state estimates of diabetes death rates among persons diagnosed with diabetes, that is, deaths due to diabetes among diabetics. Such rates, which are both cause and condition-specific, were reported earlier for the United States (Smith and Bradshaw 2008).

References

Alho, J. M., & Spencer, B. D. (2005). *Statistical demography and forecasting*. New York: Springer.

Anderson, R.N., & Rosenberg H.M. (1998). *Age standardization of death rates: Implementation of the year 2000 standard* (National vital statistics reports Vol. 47, no. 3). Hyattsville: National Center for Health Statistics.

Centers for Disease Control and Prevention. (2000). *Behavioral risk factor surveillance system survey data*. Atlanta: U.S. Department of Health and Human Services, Centers for Disease Control and Prevention. Retrieved April 2, 2010, from http://apps.nccd.cdc.gov/brfss/

Centers for Disease Control and Prevention. (2003, September 5). Prevalence of diabetes and impaired fasting glucose in adults – United States, 1999–2000. *MMWR, 52*(35), 833–837.

Centers for Disease Control and Prevention. (2005). *Behavioral risk factor surveillance system operational and user's guide*, Version 3.0, March 4, 2005. Downloaded Jan 25, 2013 from http://www.cdc.gov/brfss/pdf/userguide.pdf.

Centers for Disease Control and Prevention. (2009). 2001 *Crude and age-adjusted percentage of civilian, noninstitutionalized population with diagnosed diabetes, United States, 1980–2007*. Retrieved April 2, 2010, from http://www.cdc.gov/diabetes/statistics/prev/national/figage.htm. Page last modified July 24, 2009.

Cochran, W. G. (1977). *Sampling techniques*. New York: Wiley.

Hansen, M.H., Hurwitz, W.N., & Madow, W.G. (1953) *Sample survey methods and theory* (Vols. 1 and 2). New York: Wiley.

Holtzman, D. (2003). Analysis and interpretation of data from the U.S. behavioral risk factor surveillance system (BRFSS), chapter 5. In M. Q. David & P. Pekka (Eds.), *Global behavioral risk factor surveillance* (pp. 35–46). New York: Kluwer Academic/Plenum.

Kish, L. (1965). *Survey sampling*. New York: Wiley.

Smith, D. W., & Bradshaw, B. S. (2008). Cause-specific mortality rates in chronic disease populations. *The Open Demography Journal, 1*, 11–14.

StataCorp. (2007). *Stata Statistical Software: Release 10*. College Station, TX: StataCorp LP.

Tierney, E. F., Geiss, L. S., Engelgau, M. M., et al. (2001). Population-based estimates of mortality associated with diabetes: Use of a death certificate check box in North Dakota. *American Journal of Public Health, 91*(1), 84–92. Jan 2001.

Chapter 7
Individual- and County-Level Factors Associated with Racial Disparities in Cause-Specific Infant Mortality: Florida 1980–2000

Jessica C. Bishop-Royse and Isaac W. Eberstein

Introduction

The period 1980–2000 was important for infant health in the United States. During this time, dramatic social change and substantial improvements in medical perinatal care produced striking improvements in infant health and survival. Despite overall declines in infant mortality from all causes some evidence has suggested that relative racial disparities have persisted and even widened during this period. While the maternal socio-demographic factors associated with these racial disparities are well-established, several points remain unclear. First, there is some uncertainty regarding which causes have contributed to the widening racial disparities in infant mortality. Second, it is uncertain how the changing social context may have affected these patterns. Finally, it is unknown which has been more influential, changes in the social context or changes in maternal socio-demographic characteristics.

This study addresses these questions, using linked birth and infant death files on the 1980 and 2000 Florida birth cohorts. There are three main findings. First, the relative racial disparity in infant mortality in Florida increased during the period 1980–2000. Black infants born 1980 had about 60% greater odds of infant death than whites. Even though absolute rates of infant death declined for both groups between 1980 and 2000, the relative racial disparity increased over this period such that in the year 2000 black infants had 80% higher mortality risk than whites. Second, maternal and socio-demographic variables explain less of the black-white mortality differences in 2000 than in 1980. Third, changes in cause specific infant mortality have contributed to the increased disparity.

Changes in deaths due to prematurity and maternal/obstetric conditions contributed the most to the racial disparity in infant mortality, while changes in SIDS and

J.C. Bishop-Royse (✉) • I.W. Eberstein
Department of Sociology, Center for Demography and Population Health, Florida State University, Tallahassee, FL 32306-2240, USA
e-mail: jessibishoproyse@gmail.com; eberstein@fsu.edu

N. Hoque et al. (eds.), *Applied Demography and Public Health*, Applied Demography Series 3, DOI 10.1007/978-94-007-6140-7_7,

© Springer Science+Business Media Dordrecht 2013

congenital anomalies were the least. Findings highlight the need to consider specific causes of death for understanding the racial disparity in infant mortality. We demonstrate that changes in causes of death due to advancing therapeutic technologies and improved distributions of maternal risk factors can influence the overall distribution of infant deaths by race. Additionally, social context should continue to be included in future studies, although new measures may need to be considered.

Background

Infant mortality declined dramatically during the twentieth century (Mathews and MacDorman 2007). At the same time, research has documented widened disparities between blacks and whites (Frisbie et al. 2010, 2004; Reichman et al. 2008; Singh and Yu 1995; Singh and Kogan 2007; Williams and Collins 2001, 1995). Research has moved in two important directions. One is towards incorporating community- and contextual-level influences into analyses on individual infant outcomes. This step has been made possible by the increasing availability of geographic data, which allow for multi-level analyses. Investigations using multi-level data allow researchers to begin separating the effects of place from other social and demographic characteristics.

The second direction of inquiry is based on the increasing ability of investigators to examine birth outcomes beyond all-cause infant mortality, to include cause-specific infant death, prematurity and low birth weight. This development has allowed researchers to examine infant mortality by grouping causes of death together based on similar etiologies and to juxtapose infant health outcomes against technological improvements. For example, researchers were able to examine the dramatic declines in infant death following 1992 recommendations that infants be placed to sleep on their backs (Frisbie et al. 2010; Pollack and Frohna 2002).

Separately, these directions for research are incomplete. One approach provides information on the causes of death associated with racial differences in infant mortality, but virtually none on the community-level factors that may be associated with one cause of death over another. The other approach provides conclusions about the influence of contextual- and community-level variables that affect infant health but little information as to whether all birth outcomes are affected equally by these influences.

We examine the period 1980–2000 because the regionalization of Neonatal Intensive Care Units (NICUs) was most pronounced during this time. The 1976 publication of "Toward Improving the Outcome of Pregnancy" (The Committee on Perinatal Health with The National Foundation of the March of Dimes) offered an organizational structure for providing perinatal and neonatal care through a regionalized model that could dramatically improve health outcomes while lowering costs (National Foundation of the March of Dimes Committee on Perinatal Health 1976). This publication advocated a regionally organized system of delivery of health services utilizing three levels of care based on anticipated risk: level I (basic or routine), level II (moderate risk), and level III (high risk). Included in this system of care was a broad collection of services including maternal risk evaluation, neonatal transports, outreach education, telephone hotlines, and long-term follow-up.

This paper examines racial differentials in cause-specific infant mortality during 1980–2000 in Florida. Using two cohorts of Florida birth certificates linked to infant death records we investigate the influence of both maternal socio-demographic variables and county-level characteristics on racial disparities specific to cause of death. We investigate three main questions:

1. How did racial differences in cause-specific infant mortality change between 1980 and 2000?
2. What is the contribution of county-level variables to racial differences in cause-specific infant mortality during 1980–2000?
3. What is the relative importance of these causes of death to the increasing racial disparity in infant mortality during the period 1980–2000?

The main goal of this research is to determine which individual- and county-level factors are associated with cause-specific infant mortality. Additionally, we are interested in to what degree these factors explain the persistent black-white racial disparity in infant mortality in Florida. We review the relevant literature, discuss methods, and turn to the analyses. We conclude with a brief discussion of our findings.

We focus on the literature on the maternal factors associated with cause-specific infant mortality in the United States, as well as the influence of county level factors on infant health and survival. There have been several comprehensive literature reviews on the factors associated with all-cause infant mortality, such as Frisbie's chapter "Infant Mortality" in Poston and Micklin's *Handbook of Population* (2005). Frisbie also discusses the theoretical and methodological issues associated with demographic research on infant death.

The racial disparity in infant mortality persisted throughout the twentieth century, despite overall improvements in infant mortality rates. This persistence suggests the presence of underlying processes that influence health and survival of African American infants differently than white infants and justifies examining racial disparities across difference causes of death (Binkin et al. 1988; Dollfus et al. 1990; Frisbie et al. 2004, 2010; Powers and Song 2009; Sowards 1997). We begin by reviewing the literature on the regionalization of hospitals and contextual level variables associated with infant health outcomes. Then, we turn to a discussion of cause-specific infant mortality, focusing first on patterns before turning to the ways in which the racial disparity in infant mortality is due to differences in cause-specific infant death.

Hospital/Context/Time Comparison

Changes in health care, public health policy, and medical treatment of infants during the twentieth century have altered the distribution of infant deaths by cause. Regionalization of neonatal intensive care units (NICUs) in the United States has meant that care for the most fragile infants takes place in regional centers with specialized facilities and staff (as opposed to local hospitals and birthing centers). McCormick et al. (1985) conclude that the regionalization of perinatal services actually improved pregnancy outcomes while decreasing costs. This finding led to a stronger push in healthcare during the late 1980s and 1990s to move towards a regionalized model based on formal agreements among providers. This move resulted in an increased supply of specialized physicians or neonatologists, which facilitated regionalization by providing hospitals with a supply of specialized service providers (McCormick and Richardson 1995).

Hospitals designated as Level I centers in the regionalized three-tiered system provide care for healthy newborns without pregnancy complications or concerns for frailty. Facilities designated as Level II provide a full range of health services for certain neonatal conditions, but also uncomplicated deliveries and obstetric conditions. Level III centers are regional hospitals that offer a full range of obstetric and neonatal services and are prepared (with staff and technology) to provide care for the most frail infants and highest risk mothers. Level III centers are considered to be the most appropriate for women whose pregnancies are deemed high risk either because of maternal complications or infant health problems.

While regionalization of NICUs in the form of these Level III centers has increased in Florida, rural facilities providing obstetric services have declined because of rising insurance costs associated with malpractice litigation (Nesbit et al. 1990). This decline can leave rural areas without facilities in which women can give birth (Mayfield et al. 1990) and result in the necessity for pregnant women to travel greater distances to reach hospitals for delivery, which can lead to poor outcomes (Martin and Linda 1990). This relationship is independent of birth weight, suggesting that the risk of poor outcomes for women giving birth outside their county of residence operates through pathways other than preterm birth.

Causes of improvements in rates of infant death that occurred with the regionalization of NICUs are those with medical and physiological origins, such as prematurity-related conditions or maternal/ obstetric conditions. It is highly unlikely that regionalization of care influenced other causes of death, such as homicide and accidents, as these are largely outside the influence of the physiology surrounding prenatal care and pregnancy. It is possible that changes in the structure of hospital care over time contributed to persistent and increasing racial disparities. Frisbie et al. (2004) suggest that these changes in the structure of care might explain continued racial differences in infant death: "the potential for a widening of the relative racial gap in infant mortality is high when innovations in health care occur in a continued context of social inequality." While infant health may have improved absolutely for black and white infants, it may be the case that the widening racial disparity is actually the result of slower improvements for black infants compared to whites.

Cause-Specific Infant Mortality

Changes in health care organization and public health services and medical advances in the treatment of mothers and infants influence infant health and survival two significant ways. The first is by influencing specific cause of death. The second is by altering the distribution of the socio-demographic characteristics associated with cause-specific infant death. One example that illustrates both is necrotizing enterocolitis (NEC), an infection that occurs in infants who cannot digest food. NEC originates in the under-development of digestive organs, which often occurs in premature infants. The etiology of NEC complicates the discussion of cause of infant deaths, because the conditions of the fatal infection originate in the premature birth of the infant. Consequently, the socio-demographic characteristics associated with mortality that is due to NEC are more similar to those related to prematurity-related deaths than infection (Sowards 1997).

One example of the influence of the distribution of the socio-demographic characteristics associated with specific causes of death is deaths due to external/unknown causes. Infants who die of external causes (homicide, drowning, vehicle accidents, etc.) tend to have younger mothers than infants who die from other causes. All other things being equal, the population with the greater proportion of births to young mothers will have a higher infant death rate than a population with fewer births to young women (Eberstein et al. 1990). Conversely, infants with mothers over 35 face greater risks of death because of congenital anomalies and preterm birth. Populations with more infants born to older mothers should have more deaths that are due to these causes.

That all causes of death have not declined at the same pace provides support for employing a cause-specific framework in the investigation of the racial disparity in infant mortality. Eberstein and Parker (1984) suggest that cause-specific analyses are "potentially a fundamental extension of demographic analyses of racial differences in infant mortality." Further, they argue that cause-specific investigations may be more indicative than traditional analytical approaches, allowing for conceptual advancements in the understanding of racially disparate infant mortality experiences. At the very least, a cause-specific framework helps contribute "to a systematic explanation for observed racial inequalities which is unencumbered by the conceptual/methodological imprecision of much research in this area" (Eberstein and Parker 1984).

Moreover, employing a cause-specific framework allows for multiple levels of influence beyond what is known regarding the influence of individual-level factors. In doing so, it becomes possible to examine the differential roles that some factors have on the health and survival of infants born in the U.S.[1] Eberstein (1989) suggests that since demographic research is interested in the diverse linkages between social inequality and mortality, a multi-level perspective is useful, as it allows for

[1] Without knowing specific cause of death, it is difficult to theorize about the individual contribution of factors associated with infant mortality. For example, area-level poverty isn't likely to have a strong influence on deaths due to congenital anomalies. Since infants with congenital anomalies tend to die within minutes of birth, factors that influence the home environment of infants don't usually have much effect on the infant when the infant doesn't even come home from the hospital. Conversely, community-level variables that measure "rurality" or distance to medical facilities are likely to have a strong impact on deaths due to birth asphyxia (which occur when a woman experiences problems during delivery that delay the birth of the infant). If it takes a pregnant woman a significant amount of time from when her water breaks to when she gets care at a hospital, she faces increased risk of losing her infant due to birth asphyxia. Distance to a hospital is not likely to affect the health of an infant born with a congenital anomaly.

the combination of background and proximate factors in infant health. Additionally, a cause-specific framework acknowledges some causes are more susceptible to prevention than others.

Individual-Level Characteristics Related to Racial Differences in Cause-Specific Infant Death

Given that declines in infant mortality have not been observed equally for all causes of death, it is possible that the continued racial disparity in infant survival is the product of differential improvements in cause-specific infant mortality. The distributions of some causes of death seem to be shifting differently for whites than for blacks during the twentieth century. This shift is evident in the distribution of infant death by birth weight,[2] where in pre-surfactant eras black infants actually had a survival advantage at the lowest birth weights compared to their white peers. Frisbie et al. (2004) find that in post-surfactant eras, this advantage was lost, such that African American infants had a greater risk of death at the lowest birth weights.

Additionally, the "Back-to-Sleep" initiative, which started in 1994 helped dramatically reduce the proportion of infant deaths due to SIDS and asphyxia, since a great majority of SIDS deaths are avoidable with proper placement of infants on their backs to sleep (Gershan et al. 2002; Gibson et al. 2000). It is possible that differentials in access to information about the "Back-to-Sleep" initiative might explain differences in SIDS-related infant mortality. Depending on how much of all mortality to a birth cohort is accounted for by SIDS-related mortality, racial differences in infant mortality may be driven in part by the diminished access to information on the "Back to Sleep" initiative by some groups.

Both young and advanced maternal age are hypothesized to influence the odds of preterm birth, in different ways. Some authors have suggested that young maternal age (17 years old or younger) is a risk factor for preterm birth because young maternal age is an indicator for physiological underdevelopment, low social class, poor nutrition, and lack of access to resources such as health care (Abrams et al. 1989; Shiono et al. 1986). Advanced maternal age (greater than 35 years old) is considered a risk factor because older age is often associated with a greater likelihood of having experienced preterm birth/low birth weight birth, stillbirth, and abortion (Cnattingius et al. 1992; Meyer et al. 1976; Seidman et al. 1990; Wen et al. 1990), all of which are associated with preterm birth.

[2]Birth weight is often considered a proxy for prematurity, where the lightest infants are gestationally the most immature. While some (Frisbie et al. 1997) have made the distinction between the etiologies leading to low birthweight as a result of prematurity versus low birthweight as the result of intrauterine growth restriction (IUGR), the majority of research on infant health and survival equates low birthweight with prematurity.

African-American women are more likely to experience preterm labor and delivery than all other racial groups (Kleinman and Kessel 1987; Shiono et al. 1986). Some researchers have suggested that the difference between African-Americans and whites is partially explained by intrinsic differences in gestational age-specific distributions between the two groups (Papiernik et al. 1990), because blacks on average are born a week earlier than whites.

Unmarried women experience higher rates of preterm birth than their married counterparts (Golding et al. 1987; Wen et al. 1990). This relationship doesn't seem to be confined to the financial and socioeconomic resources associated with living with a spouse/partner, as others have demonstrated that cohabiting women are more likely to experience preterm labor and birth than their married peers (Blondel and Zuber 1988).

Women of lower socioeconomic status are more likely to experience preterm birth than women with higher socioeconomic status (Berkowitz and Papiernik 1993; Fedrick and Anderson 1976; Kaminski et al. 1973). It seems likely that the effect of lower socioeconomic status flows through not only access to resources such as prenatal care, but also through its effect on psychosocial influences such as depressive symptomology, stress exposure, and "nerves" (Misra et al. 2001; Peacock et al. 1995).

County-Level Characteristics Related to Racial Differences in Cause-Specific Infant Death

Wilson (1987) and Collins and Williams (1995) attribute the poverty often associated with urban areas to the out-migration of middle class blacks. Massey et al. (1994) go further, adding two additional complementary influences of the selective migration of poor people into black neighborhoods and the net downward mobility into poverty of blacks living in segregated areas. This concentration of poverty in specific regions has been noted in other populations (such as the rural Mississippi delta) by Cossman et al. (2007), who find that areas with lower mortality rates tend to experience less population outmigration by the young and less economic decline than noted in other areas.

The high levels of poverty and deprivation documented in some places are associated with poor health outcomes for inhabitants (Eibner and Sturm 2006), and increased infant mortality (Hummer 2005; Stockwell et al. 2005; Subramanian et al. 2005). Messer et al. (2006) find deprivation related to the unadjusted prevalence of preterm birth and low birth weight for both non-Hispanic whites and non-Hispanic blacks. Others have found that concentrated poverty is an important factor in the association between maternal age and birth weight, accounting for 44% of the variation in that relationship (Cerda et al. 2008). Cossman et al. (2007) note that the risk of intrauterine growth restriction was higher among women with no medical insurance and health care (compared to women with health insurance and health care) and that adverse birth outcomes were lower for women who participated in a supplemental food/nutrition program (compared to women who did not participate). This finding is supported in research on trends in maternal and infant health in urban areas, where the areas that had the most comprehensive health programs to improve infant and maternal health saw the most improvement across all indicators of infant health (Howell et al. 2005).

Data and Method

Data

The data for these analyses are from the Florida Department of Health's Bureau of Vital Registration. These data represent all the births that occurred in Florida in 1980 and 2000. Births that occurred in 1980 were manually matched to subsequent infant deaths in 1980–1981 on the basis of child's name, mother's name, date of birth, county of birth, and race of child. The 2000 birth cohort was available as a linked data set. The link rate on these datasets is nearly complete: 97% of the deaths to the 1980 birth cohort were successfully matched to infant birth records and 99% of the infant deaths in the 2000 birth cohort were successfully matched to birth records.

Since this research is primarily concerned with the racial disparity in infant health, only black and white infants are included in these analyses and ethnicity is considered an independent variable. It is for this reason that only infants whose mother's race was recorded on the birth certificate as "African-American" or "White" were included in these analyses; "Asian", "Native American," "Other," or "Unknown" races were excluded. Additionally, Florida residents giving birth in other states were excluded, as were women who resided in other states but gave birth in Florida. Largely, these exclusions were made because of practical concerns regarding combining county-level data. Also excluded in these analyses are multiple gestation births because of their inherent increased risk of poorer pregnancy outcomes, such as low birth weight (Martin and Park 1999). Additionally, the increased use of IVF therapy for conception raises questions about the differences in the incidence and characteristics surrounding multiple gestation pregnancies in 1980 compared to 2000 that are outside the scope of this investigation (Schieve et al. 2002). The final dataset includes 119,432 births and 1,525 deaths to the 1980 birth cohort and 196,361 births and 1,251 deaths to the 2000 birth cohort.

Individual-level data from mothers were combined with census data on their counties of residence to approximate the conditions in which women lived and worked in Florida. The individual-level factors of interest are those mentioned often in demographic research on infant mortality: maternal age (in years), maternal education (in years), maternal marital status (married or not married), maternal nativity (foreign born or native born), maternal ethnicity (Hispanic or Non-Hispanic), maternal race (white or black), parity (number of pregnancies), and prenatal care utilization. Regarding prenatal care utilization, we used the categorization suggested by Kotelchuck (1994) of adequate plus, adequate, intermediate and inadequate.

Additionally, we constructed a measure of "crisis births," which are births that occur outside maternal county of residence, as a way to approximate the increased risk that comes with traveling outside county of residence to access health care for labor and delivery. We also included four census items based on maternal county of residence in an effort to capture some of the unique characteristics of Florida counties in 1980 and 2000. Specifically, we investigate outcomes associated with certain types of counties in Florida, including counties with proportionally "large" black, Hispanic, and poor populations. We were interested in studying whether there are effects associated with living in rural versus urban counties. To simplify the interpretations of results with county-level variables included, we dichotomized these four items such that 1's indicated that mothers lived in counties where more than 15% of the population was black, where more than 5% of the population was Hispanic, where more than 15% of the population lived below the federal poverty line, and where more than 50% of the population lived in rural areas.

For example, deaths due to Respiratory Distress Syndrome (RDS) and Necrotizing Enterocolitis (NEC) are quite different etiologically. RDS is the result of fetal underdevelopment of the respiratory system and is largely due to premature birth. NEC is an infection that results from an infant's digestive system being unable to digest nutrition because of underdevelopment. While the actual pathways to death are quite dissimilar, the underlying cause of each is premature/preterm birth. Rather than consider these causes separately, we group them together under the broader category of "prematurity related conditions." For the purposes of this research, causes were categorized as: prematurity related conditions, congenital anomalies, sudden infant death syndrome, maternal and obstetric conditions, and external and unknown deaths. The categorizations were based on previous research articles employing similar categorization schemes (Sowards 1997; Dollfus et al. 1990).

Finally, given the relatively small size of the Florida data for the specific causes of death, we collapsed the eight and nine cause categorizations offered by Dollfus et al. (1990) and modified by Sowards (1997) to five causes, including a survival category. Deaths were categorized in five groups of causes: prematurity-related conditions, congenital anomalies, SIDS, maternal and obstetric conditions, and external and unknown causes. Births that did not result in death were categorized as having survived.

Method

We use a series of logistic regression models to assess not only the individual risk of infant death by cause in 1980 and 2000. This series of logistic regressions models racial differences in the odds of death due to one cause versus survival and dying of another cause of death. A series of logistic regressions will allow tests of whether each independent variable has a different relationship with each cause of death. Multi-level models are used to specify risk estimates that include the potential mediating effects of maternal county of residence. Analyses were completed with the 11th edition of Stata software (StataCorp. 2009. Stata Statistical Software: Release 11. College Station, TX: StataCorp LP).

Descriptive Results

There were 1,520 deaths among the 119,432 infants born in Florida in 1980 (IMR = 12.7 deaths per 1,000 births). This is substantially more than in 2000, when there were 1,249 deaths among the 196,361 births (IMR = 6.37 deaths per 1,000 births). In 1980 and 2000, the majority of deaths were due to conditions related to prematurity (39.3% in 1980, 34.7% in 2000). Other noteworthy changes include a 40% decline in SIDS infant mortality and a 33% increase in deaths from maternal/obstetric conditions (Table 7.1).

Table 7.2 presents estimates of racial differences in infant death, which increased over the period for some causes, but not others. Black infants' excess risk of mortality due to prematurity-related conditions, congenital anomalies and maternal/obstetric conditions increased over the period. Racial differences in SIDS mortality and external conditions were reduced dramatically to the point of insignificance.

The association of increased odds of death to maternal age remained relatively stable over time and across cause of death. Maternal age was significant in both cohorts for deaths due to prematurity related conditions and SIDS. It was negatively associated with deaths due to maternal and obstetric conditions in 1980, but this relationship disappeared in 2000. The influence of ethnicity was most pronounced for deaths due to prematurity related conditions, and maternal obstetric conditions, where Hispanic mothers experienced fewer deaths due to these causes. In both cases, the relationship of ethnicity on the odds of death fell over the period. Maternal nativity was marginally related to the odds of infant mortality over the period 1980–2000. Specifically, in 2000, it was associated with deaths due to prematurity related conditions, maternal/obstetric conditions and SIDS, but not for deaths due to external and unknown causes. Maternal education remained important for racial differences in cause-specific infant mortality across the period, where it had ameliorative effects for prematurity related conditions, SIDS, and maternal/obstetric conditions in 1980. While its influence on these causes of death decreased in 2000, strong negative associations remain.

Less than adequate prenatal care is associated with death from prematurity related conditions and external/unknown causes in 1980, but this relationship disappears in 2000. In 1980, marital status is strongly associated with deaths due to prematurity and maternal/obstetric conditions. This relationship continued in 2000. Parity was positively associated with congenital anomalies and maternal obstetric conditions in 2000, but not 1980. The positive relationship between parity and SIDS maintains over the period 1980–2000. Crisis births were related to deaths from prematurity related conditions, congenital anomalies, and maternal/obstetric conditions in 2000.

Each of the county/contextual-level variables included in these analyses was associated with death due to prematurity related conditions in 2000, however; only

Table 7.1 Percent distributions and cause-specific infant death rates by race and year, 1980–2000

	Florida		1980		2000	
	1980	2000	White	Black	White	Black
Prematurity related conditions						
(n)	598	433	348	250	223	210
IMR (n per 1,000 births)	5.01	2.21	3.87	8.44	1.49	4.49
% of column total	39.3%	34.7%	35.2%	44.1%	30.8%	39.8%
Congenital anomalies						
(n)	306	272	232	74	178	94
IMR (n per 1,000 births)	2.56	1.39	2.58	2.50	1.19	2.01
% of column total	20.1%	21.7%	23.5%	13.1%	24.6%	17.8%
SIDS						
(n)	179	87	107	72	65	22
IMR (n per 1,000 births)	1.50	0.44	1.19	2.43	0.43	0.47
% of column total	11.7%	7.0%	10.8%	12.7%	9.0%	4.2%
Maternal and obstetric conditions						
(n)	260	284	163	97	150	134
IMR (n per 1,000 births)	2.18	1.45	1.81	3.28	1.00	2.87
% of column total	17.0%	22.7%	16.5%	17.1%	20.7%	25.4%
External and unknown causes						
(n)	177	173	103	74	107	66
IMR (n per 1,000 births)	1.48	0.88	1.15	2.50	0.72	1.41
% of column total	11.6%	13.8%	10.4%	13.1%	14.8%	12.5%
Births (n)	119,432	196,361	89,845	29,607	149,596	46,765
Deaths (n)	1520	1249	953	567	723	526
IMR (per 1,000 births)	12.7	6.37	11.01	19.15	4.83	11.29

"Black population over 15%" and "Rural population over 50%" were associated in 1980. Except for lower SIDS deaths in high Hispanic counties in 2000, there were no other significant relationships of county-level variables with infant mortality. This is a surprising finding that suggests that county-level characteristics are less salient for infant mortality than was anticipated.

Multivariate Analyses

We discuss the results from the multivariate analyses by cause of death and by model. We begin by describing the results of the base model (Model 1) of racial differences in prematurity-related conditions, then the ways in which those differences are influenced by individual-level maternal characteristics including age, education, marital status, and ethnicity (Model 2). Next we show the racial differences in risk of infant death due to prematurity related conditions while controlling for maternal

Table 7.2 Coefficients of bi-variate associations between maternal factors and cause-specific infant mortality

	Prematurity related conditions		Congenital anomalies		SIDS		Maternal and obstetric conditions		External conditions	
	1980	2000	1980	2000	1980	2000	1980	2000	1980	2000
Black	0.77***	1.10***	–0.03	0.52***	0.71***	0.08	0.58***	1.05***	0.72***	0.68***
Maternal age	–0.03***	–0.03***	0.01	–0.002	–0.03*	–0.04**	–0.05***	–0.00006	–0.01	–0.03*
Hispanic	–0.39***	–0.35**	–0.27*	0.02	–0.21	0.59*	–0.54***	–0.32*	–0.25	–0.39
Foreign born	–0.07	–0.25*	–0.08	0.06	0.30	–1.83***	0.14	–0.42**	–1.46**	–0.30
Maternal education	–0.10***	–0.07***	–0.02	–0.07***	–0.07*	–0.11**	–0.10***	–0.06***	–0.06	–0.10***
Poor prenatal care	0.23**	0.12	–0.07	–0.12	0.05	0.23	0.21	–0.04	0.38*	0.16
Not married	0.73***	0.73***	0.04	0.35**	0.47*	0.32	0.90***	0.52***	0.27	0.69***
Parity	0.05	–0.05	0.00	0.16***	0.10*	0.28***	0.07	0.12**	0.11	0.23***
Crisis birth	0.11	0.46***	0.17	0.35**	–0.09	0.36	–0.11	0.40**	–0.10	0.11
Black population over 15%	0.18*	0.29**	–0.28**	0.11	–0.12	–0.26	–0.05	–0.12	0.07	0.01
Hispanic population over 5%	–0.08	–0.23*	0.03	0.11	0.23	–0.44*	0.04	–0.13	–0.32	0.04
Poor population over 15%	–0.02	0.64**	–0.76	–0.29	0.20	0.87	–0.17	–0.70	–0.51	0.51
Rural population over 50%	0.18*	0.62***	0.10	–0.04	–0.20	0.43	0.02	–0.27	0.24	0.48

* p=.05; ** p=.01; *** p=.001

county-level factors such as "proportion of the population living in rural areas" (Model 3). Finally, we present the full model of racial differences in deaths due to prematurity related conditions with controls for both individual- and county-level maternal characteristics (Model 4). After estimates for prematurity related conditions are discussed, we turn to deaths due to congenital anomalies, SIDS, maternal/obstetric conditions, and external/unknown causes.

Prematurity-Related Conditions

One striking finding in the cause-specific regression analyses is the persistence of the racial disparity in prematurity-related mortality. Without considering controls for individual- or county-level socio-demographic variables, racial differences in deaths due to prematurity-related conditions increase from 1980 to 2000 (Table 7.3, Model 1). Black infants born in the earlier cohort had more than twice the odds[3] (coefficient=0.77) of death as their white peers. This increased in 2000 such that they have over triple the risk odds of death due to this cause compared to white infants (coefficient=1.10).

The inclusion of individual-level variables in multivariate models affects racial disparities in prematurity-related deaths differently in 1980 than in 2000 (Table 7.3, Model 2). In 1980, individual-level controls for maternal age, ethnicity, nativity, prenatal care, education, marital status, parity, and crisis birth reduced the excess risk for black infants but did not eliminate it completely (coefficient=0.54). In 2000, the same model actually increases the racial difference in prematurity related mortality (coefficient=1.12), such that black infants had over three times the odds of death compared to whites. This change may suggest diverging pathways of influence of maternal socio-demographic characteristics on odds of premature infant death. Including contextual/county-level variables does little to explain racial differences in deaths due to prematurity related conditions in 1980 and 2000, although the effect is at least similar for both years (Table 7.3, Model 3). The racial disparity in this cause is reduced somewhat in 1980 and 2000 by including dichotomous indicators of county level variables.

The full model (Table 7.3, Model 4) reduces racial disparities in deaths due to prematurity related conditions in 1980 and 2000. The effect is much stronger in 1980, where the full model indicates that black infants had 68% greater odds of death due to prematurity than whites (coefficient=0.52). Black infants born in 2000 had almost three fold higher risk of death due to these conditions compared to white infants (coefficient=1.09). Model 4 accounted for about 27% of the racial differences in deaths due to prematurity related conditions in 1980, but only about 1% in 2000.

---

[3]While we present regression coefficients in Table 7.3, we discuss them in terms of odds ratios in the narrative. We calculated odds ratios by hand, by exponentiating them, using the formula e^x.

Table 7.3 Coefficients of racial differences by year

	Model 1		Model 2		Model 3		Model 4	
Prematurity related conditions	1980	2000	1980	2000	1980	2000	1980	2000
Coefficient	0.77***	1.10***	0.54***	1.12***	0.75***	1.08***	0.52***	1.09***
Standard error	0.08	0.09	0.10	0.12	0.08	1.08	0.113	0.125
Log likelihood	−3724.2	−3018.4	−3573.3	−2807.0	−3501.8	−3009.6	−3349.5	−2802.2
BIC	7471.9	6061.2	7263.5	5732.9	7085.3	6104.5	6873.7	5787.1
Congenital anomalies								
Coefficient	−0.03	0.52***	−0.08	0.44***	0.03	0.52***	0.01	0.41**
Standard error	0.13	0.12	0.16	0.15	0.13	0.13	0.16	0.16
Log likelihood	−2131.3	−2053.5	−2072.1	−1951.1	−2031.1	−2052.9	−1973.8	−1948.6
BIC	4286.1	4131.3	4260.9	4023.9	4143.7	4191.1	4122.1	4079.9
Sudden infant death syndrome								
Coefficient	0.71***	0.08	0.54**	−0.23	0.71***	0.175	0.54**	−0.16
Standard error	0.15	0.24	0.19	0.28	0.15	.025	0.20	−0.16
Log likelihood	−1332.4	−758.43	−1311.2	−728.2	−1278.3	−744.8	−1258.2	−722.1
BIC	2688.3	1541.2	2739.1	1578.3	2637.9	1574.9	2690.9	1626.7
Maternal/obstetric conditions								
Coefficient	0.58***	1.05***	−0.03	1.21***	0.58***	1.12***	−0.12	1.31***
Standard error	0.12	0.11	0.16	0.14	0.13	0.12	0.17	0.15
Log likelihood	−1843.3	−2103.4	−1784.8	−1974.2	−1759.9	−2097.5	−1698.2	−1969.5
BIC	3710.1	4231.2	3686.3	4070.2	3601.4	4280.4	3571.0	4121.7

External and unknown causes								
Coefficient	0.72***	0.68***	0.75***	0.29	0.76***	0.70***	0.87***	0.28
Standard error	0.18	0.18	0.23	0.22	0.19	0.18	0.24	0.23
Log likelihood	−1319.9	−1382.3	−1290.6	−1327.9	−1228.1	−1380.1	−1199.6	−1326.9
BIC	2663.3	2788.9	2698.2	2777.8	2537.8	2845.5	2573.9	2836.7

Model 1: Race only

Model 2: Race with controls for maternal age, ethnicity, nativity, education, prenatal care, marital status, parity, and crisis birth status

Model 3: Race with controls for residence in counties with over 15% of population black, with over 5% of population Hispanic, over 15% of population poor and with over 50% of population living in rural areas

Model 4: Race with controls for maternal age, ethnicity, nativity, education, prenatal care, marital status, parity, crisis birth status, for residence in counties with over 15% of population black, over 5% of population Hispanic, with 15% of population poor and over 50% of population living in rural areas

$^{*}p$=.05; $^{**}p$=.01; $^{***}p$=.001

Congenital Anomalies

Black infants born in 1980 were no more likely to experience a congenital anomaly related death than were whites (Table 7.3, Model 1). Black infants born in 2000, however, have 68% greater odds of death due to congenital anomalies than white infants (coefficient=0.52). Individual socio-demographic controls reduced this difference to 55% (Table 7.3, Model 2). County-level factors had little effect on the odds of infant death due to congenital anomalies in 1980 and 2000, producing no changes in coefficients for either year. Including both individual- and county-level factors did not produce race-specific differences in deaths due to congenital anomalies in 1980 and did little to reduce disparities present in 2000. Black infants born in 1980 had no discernable excess risk for death due to congenital anomalies in 1980, even when individual- and county-level variables are controlled (coefficient=0.01). However, in 2000, blacks had excess risk of death due to congenital anomalies, which was not attenuated by controls for individual- and county-level variables (coefficient=0.41) as shown in Model 4 of Table 7.3.

Sudden Infant Death Syndrome

Black infants were twice as likely as whites to die of SIDS during the first year of life (Table 7.3, Model 1) in 1980 (coefficient=0.71). This disparity disappeared 2000, such that there were no significant differences between black and white infants (coefficient=0.08). For infants born in 1980, individual-level maternal factors reduced the racial difference in the odds ratio between black and white infants to 1.72 (coefficient=0.54), as indicated in Model 2 of Table 7.3. This suggests that even after controlling for maternal individual-level characteristics, black infants were about 72% more likely to die of SIDS than whites.

Including controls for contextual/county-level variables does little to explain black-white differences in SIDS mortality (Table 7.3, Model 3). Black infants born in 1980 had twice the odds of SIDS death than whites, after accounting for differences in contextual/county-level variables. There appear to be no benefits to controlling for contextual level variables in the full model, as it produces no reduction in the race coefficient in Model 4 (Table 7.3).

Maternal and Obstetric Conditions

Black infants had 79% greater odds (coefficient=0.58) of death due to maternal/obstetric conditions in 1980 than whites (Table 7.3, Model 1). This disparity increased over the period, such that black infants had almost three times the odds of death due to these causes than white infants in 2000 (coefficient=1.05). This change may suggest that the physiological process of pregnancy became more important for survival between 1980 and 2000.

Controls for maternal individual-level characteristics explain virtually all of the racial differences in odds of death due to maternal/obstetric conditions in 1980 (Table 7.3, Model 2). These controls have an opposite effect in 2000, exacerbating the racial differences in deaths due to maternal/obstetric conditions as indicated by increased regression coefficients in Model 2 (coefficient = 1.21) from Model 1 (coefficient = 1.05).

County-level factors fail to explain any of the racial differences in deaths due to maternal and obstetric conditions (Table 7.3, Model 3) in 1980 and actually exaggerate them in 2000. The suppressing effect of county-level variables on the racial disparity in 2000 suggests that if black mothers were equal to white mothers in terms of the counties they live in, the racial disparity in deaths due to maternal/obstetric conditions would be higher. Including individual- and county-level maternal factors in Model 4 virtually eliminates racial differences in 1980 (coefficient = –0.12). The full model illustrates opposite effect for infants born in 2000, exacerbating racial differences in death due to maternal/obstetric conditions (coefficient 1.31). The combination of individual- and county-level variables produces greater racial differences in this cause of death in 2000 than the base model of racial differences for 1980, which may suggest a suppressing influence of these variables on racial differences in deaths due to maternal and obstetric conditions.

External Causes and Unknown Conditions

Black infants had over twice the odds (coefficient = 0.72) of infant death due to external and unknown causes in 1980 than whites (Model 1). This excess risk remains virtually unchanged over the period and is still significant in 2000 (coefficient = 0.68). Individual maternal factors did not explain any of the increased risk for blacks in 1980; in fact including them in Model 2 increases racial differences in deaths due to external causes and unknown conditions. In 2000, however, these factors explained much of the initial racial disparity in external/unknown causes of death where the odds ratio was reduced from 1.97 to 1.33 (the coefficient was reduced from 0.75 to 0.29).

County-level variables did not explain any of the racial differences in external and unknown causes of death in 1980 or 2000 (Model 3). In both years, including these variables increased racial differences between black and white infants. Including these indicators with the full model produces exaggerated racial differences for the 1980 cohort. This suggests that black infants would have 14% higher odds of death due to these conditions, if they had similar distributions of individual- and county-level maternal factors as white infants (coefficient = 0.87). There is no corresponding effect for the 2000 birth cohort, which indicates a complicated relationship between individual- and county-level maternal characteristics and their influence on the risk of this cause of death.

To summarize, there are three main findings from the cause-specific analyses that deserve further consideration:

1. The substantial declines in SIDS-related mortality and racial differences in SIDS-related mortality characterized a substantial portion of the decline in absolute levels of mortality from all causes over the period.
2. The increasing racial disparity in deaths due to maternal and obstetric conditions combined with the inability of maternal characteristics to account for the increased odds of death for black infants suggests that the pathways that result in deaths due to maternal and obstetric conditions are not well understood.
3. Finally, the continue substantial racial disparity in deaths due to prematurity likely signals the growing influence of maternal physical health as well as gestational age and birth weight for infant survival, which may present a future avenue for demographic research on infant health.

Racial differences in SIDS mortality virtually disappeared during the 1980–2000 period, while disparities in deaths due to prematurity-related conditions, congenital anomalies, and maternal/obstetric conditions increased. Individual- and county-level maternal socio-demographic characteristics account for some racial differences in deaths due to prematurity related and maternal/obstetric conditions in 1980 but do not in 2000. Overall, county-level factors were not helpful in explaining racial differences in cause-specific infant death, which was unexpected.

Conclusions

Understanding the persistent excess risk of total infant mortality for black infants requires understanding that the racial disparity is made up of differential risks of specific causes of death and that each of those causes of death is influenced to some degree by individual maternal and county-level characteristics. In 1980, black infants were 2.03 times more likely to die of SIDS than whites. This disparity virtually disappears over the period, such that black infants born in 2000 faced no excess risk of this cause of death than whites. This change was likely a response to the "Back to Sleep" campaign, which educated women on the importance of placing infants in the supine sleep position (which was associated with lower odds of mortality). The virtual amelioration of racial disparities in SIDS mortality is particularly salient because one of the main justifications of the "Back to Sleep" campaign was that it addressed the social and environmental conditions associated with SIDS, which disproportionately affected black infants more than white infants (crowded and unsafe sleeping conditions associated with higher parity, low income housing, maternal romantic relationships, etc.). The campaign was viewed as a way of removing the influence of social and environmental conditions on the racial disparity in infant mortality.

Conversely, the racial disparity deaths that are due to maternal and obstetric conditions increased over the 1980–2000 period. What is remarkable is that these racial differences increased as the ability to explain them with individual- and county-level maternal characteristics decreased. Individual maternal characteristics ameliorated the racial disparity in infant death due to maternal and obstetric conditions in 1980, but actually exacerbated these differences in 2000. The full model, which controls for individual- and county-level characteristics of the mother, produces larger odds ratios than including individual- and county-level characteristics separately. This suggests that there is complex interaction between individual maternal variables and county-level indicators of social context.

It is possible that these factors have direct influences on maternal and obstetric conditions such as utero-placental bleeding disorders and placenta previa and on deaths due to these conditions (Ananth et al. 1996), which include birth asphyxia and maternal infections. Another consideration may be the indirect effects of these maternal characteristics on overall physical health prior to and during pregnancy, which some research has shown to influence infant outcomes (Breton et al. 2009; Gibbs 2001). These analyses are based on data from birth certificates, which are admittedly somewhat inadequate sources of information on maternal physical health. It has been suggested elsewhere that trends in maternal health, such as increasing maternal pre-pregnancy obesity, may result in increased poor infant health outcomes (Cedergren 2004; Sebire et al. 2001), such that persistent racial differences in some causes of death are actually due to differences in the physical health of mothers that are not accounted for by controlling for individual- and county-level factors.

Additionally, the increased racial disparity in maternal and obstetric conditions may be the result of compromised physical health due to cumulative stress exposure (Geronimus 1996), which some research suggests is closely related to maternal infections and other pregnancy conditions (Collins et al. 2004; Stoll et al. 1998). It is possible that mothers' "return on investment" of education and other maternal characteristics (such as marital status and prenatal care) was higher in 1980 than it was in 2000, such that the effect of being poorly educated was stronger in 2000 than it was in 1980.

Given the absolute declines in causes of death such as SIDS, the findings regarding maternal and obstetric conditions may point to a new direction in infant mortality research where the physical health of the mother and her pregnancy is becoming more important for understanding infant health and survival. In fact, such a shift has already been indicated by Atrash et al. (2006) who suggested that the route to improving pregnancy outcomes is in improving the health of mothers before they conceive. The findings presented here regarding maternal and obstetric conditions may provide some evidence for the growing influence of maternal health prior to and during pregnancy on infant health outcomes. This influence may also be evident in the increased racial disparity in mortality due to prematurity related conditions.

Black infants were over twice as likely as whites to die of conditions related to prematurity in 1980. This difference increased over the period, such that by 2000, black infants were over three times as likely to die of these causes as white infants. Individual- and county-level maternal variables explained a much more substantial portion of racial differences in this cause of death in 1980 than they did in 2000. Given a similar effect of these characteristics on deaths due to maternal and obstetric conditions, there may be evidence of the increased importance of the physiological process of pregnancy. The corollary to this is that these effects may also signal the decreasing importance of social/environmental factors on pregnancy outcomes. Future research should explore these relationships more fully to determine what influence gestational age and birth weight have on relationships between race and maternal socio-demographic and county-level characteristics and the risk of infant death.

Regarding the use of multi-level models for determining the factors associated with disparities in cause-specific infant death, the county-level variables that we incorporated into analyses were of limited use in helping to explain racial disparities. In fact, aside from a few somewhat significant associations in terms of deaths due to prematurity-related conditions, the county-level variables we utilized didn't add much to our understanding. There are two possible explanations for this: (1) the indicators that we chose were not accurate measures of our constructs; or (2) there is no relationship between these county-level variables and odds of cause-specific infant mortality. What this may mean is that individual-level socio-demographic factors such as maternal education and marital status exert a much stronger influence on odds of infant death than whether or not a mother lives in a county with a large poor population, and/or that county-level poverty works through or jointly with individual- level characteristics, such that when individual characteristics are controlled, no aggregate effect is apparent.

The main limitations to demographic research utilizing vital records are well known. One of these limitations is the lack of information available on the birth certificate regarding key dimensions of interest, such as socioeconomic status. Additionally, other dimensions that might be helpful for explaining the racial disparity in infant death, such as maternal pregnancy indicators are either not present (i.e. c-reactive protein) or not universally collected (pregnancy weight gain).

Another concern about using vital records for cause-specific infant mortality research is a concern over the numerically rare causes of infant death. These low numbers were a problem in the present study, so we grouped causes of death together in larger categories than we had originally desired. Concern over the small number of cases led us to combine maternal infections, birth asphyxia, and other obstetric conditions into the same category. While there may be questions over the etiological similarities of these conditions, our grouping was done in order to achieve statistical power and to add to interpretation of the results.

The extremely sensitive and precarious nature of the relationship between maternal health and infant survival has been established in previous research (Moos and Cefalo 1987; Institute of Medicine 1985). For many, the circumstances of infant death include poor maternal health, leading to preterm labor and delivery, resulting in death due to prematurity related conditions. We contend that increased racial disparities in deaths due to prematurity and maternal/obstetric conditions signals a growing importance of maternal physical health prior to and during pregnancy. Declining racial disparities in SIDS and unknown/external causes suggests that the importance of social/environmental conditions may have declined.

References

Abrams, B., Newman, V., Key, T., & Parker, J. (1989). Maternal weight gain and preterm delivery. *Obstetrics and Gynecology, 74*(4), 577–583.

Ananth, C. V., Wilcox, A. J., Savitz, D. A., Bowes, W. A., & Luther, E. R. (1996). Effect of maternal age and parity on the risk of uteroplacental bleeding disorders in pregnancy. *Obstetrics and Gynecology, 88*(4 Pt 1), 511–516.

Atrash, H. K., Johnson, K., Adams, M., Cordero, J. F., & Howse, J. (2006). Preconception care for improving perinatal outcomes: The time to act. *Maternal and Child Health Journal, 10*(5 Suppl), S3–S11.

Berkowitz, G. S., & Papiernik, E. (1993). Epidemiology of preterm birth. *Epidemiologic Reviews, 15*(2), 414–443.

Binkin, N. J., Rust, K. R., & Williams, R. L. (1988). Racial differences in neonatal mortality. What causes of death explain the gap? *American Journal of Diseases in Children, 142*(4), 434–440.

Blondel, B., & Zuber, M. C. (1988). Marital status and cohabitation during pregnancy: relationship with social conditions, antenatal care, and pregnancy outcome in France, 2(2), 125–137. http://onlinelibrary.wiley.com/doi/10.1111/j.1365-3016.1988.tb00192.x/abstract

Breton, M. C., Beauchesne, M. F., Lemiere, C., Rey, E., Forget, A., & Blais, L. (2009). Risk of perinatal mortality associated with asthma during pregnancy. *Thorax, 64*, 101–106.

Cedergren, M. I. (2004). Maternal morbid obesity and the risk of adverse pregnancy outcome. *Obstetrics and Gynecology, 103*(2), 219–224.

Cerda, M., Buka, S., & Rich-Edwards, J. (2008). Neighborhood influences on the association between maternal age and birth weight: A multilevel investigation of age-related disparities in health. *Social Science & Medicine, 66*(9), 2048–2060.

Cnattingius, S., Forman, M. R., Berendes, H. W., & Isotalo, L. (1992). Delayed childbearing and risk adverse perinatal outcome. *Journal of the American Medical Association, 268*(7), 886–890.

Collins, D. R., & Williams, C. (1995). U.S. socioeconomic and racial differences in health: Patterns and explanations. *Annual Review of Sociology, 21*, 349–386.

Collins, J. W., David, R. J., Handler, A., Wall, S., & Andes, S. (2004). Very low birth weight in African American infants: The role of maternal exposure to interpersonal racial discrimination. *American Journal of Public Health, 94*(12), 2132–2138.

Cossman, J. S., Cossman, R. E., James, W. L., Campbell, C. R., Blanchard, T. C., & Cosby, A. G. (2007). Persistent clusters of mortality in the United States. *American Journal of Public Health, 97*(12), 2148–2150.

Dollfus, C., Patetta, M., Siegel, E., & Cross, A. W. (1990). Infant mortality: A practical approach to the analysis of the leading causes of death and risk factors. *Pediatrics, 86*(2), 176–183.

Eberstein, I. W. (1989). Demographic research on infant mortality. *Sociological Forum, 4*(3), 409–422.

Eberstein, I. W., & Parker, J. R. (1984). Racial differences in infant mortality by cause of death: The impact of birth weight and maternal age. *Demography, 21*(3), 409–422.

Eberstein, I. W., Nam, C. B., & Hummer, R. A. (1990). Infant mortality by cause of death: Main and interaction effects. *Demography, 27*(3), 413–430.

Eibner, C., & Sturm, R. (2006). US-based indices of area-level deprivation: Results from healthcare for communities. *Social Science & Medicine, 62*(2), 348–359.

Fedrick, J., & Anderson, A. B. (1976). Factors associated with spontaneous pre-term birth. *British Journal of Obstetrics and Gynaecology, 83*(5), 342–350.

Frisbie, W. P. (2005). Infant mortality. In D. Poston & M. Micklin (Eds.), *Handbook of population* (pp. 251–282). New York: Springer.

Frisbie, W. P., Biegler, M., de Turk, P., Forbes, D., & Pullum, S. G. (1997). Racial and ethnic differences in determinants of intrauterine growth retardation and other compromised birth outcomes. *American Journal of Public Health 87*(12), 1977–1983. http://ajph.aphapublications.org/doi/abs/10.2105/AJPH.87.12.1977

Frisbie, W. P., Song, S. E., Powers, D. A., & Street, J. A. (2004). The increasing racial disparity in infant mortality: Respiratory distress syndrome and other causes. *Demography, 41*(4), 773–800.

Frisbie, W. P., Hummer, R. A., Powers, D. A., Song, S. E., & Pullum, S. G. (2010). Race/ethnicity/nativity differentials and changes in cause-specific-infant deaths in the context of declining infant mortality in the U.S.: 1979–2001. *Population Research and Policy Review, 29*, 395–422.

Geronimus, A. T. (1996). Black/white differences in the relationship of maternal age to birthweight: A population based test of the weathering hypothesis. *Social Science & Medicine, 42*(4), 589–597.

Gershan, W. M., Besch, N. S., & Franciosi, R. A. (2002). A comparison of apparent life-threatening events before and after the back to sleep campaign. *Wisconsin Medical Journal, 101*, 39–45.

Gibbs, R. S. (2001). The relationship between infections and adverse pregnancy outcomes: An overview. *Annals of Periodontology/The American Academy of Periodontology, 6*(1), 153–163.

Gibson, E., Dembofsky, C. A., Rubin, S., & Greenspan, J. S. (2000). Infant sleep position practices 2 years into the "back to sleep" campaign. *Clinical Pediatrics, 39*(5), 285–289.

Golding, J., Robinson, J., Henriques, J., & Thomas, P. (1987). Does conception before marriage matter? *British Journal of Obstetrics and Gynaecology, 94*(1), 38–43.

Howell, E. M., Pettit, K. L. S., & Kingsley, G. T. (2005). Trends in maternal and infant health in poor urban neighborhoods: Good news from the 1990s, but challenges remain. *Public Health Reports, 120*(4), 409–417.

Hummer, R. (2005). Income, race, and infant mortality: Comment on Stockwell et al. *Population Research and Policy Review, 24*(4), 405–409.

Institute of Medicine. (1985). *Preventing low birth weight*. Washington, D.C.: National Academy Press.

Kaminski, M., Goujard, J., & Rumeau-Rouquette, C. (1973). Prediction of low birthweight and prematurity by a multiple regression analysis with maternal characteristics known since the beginning of the pregnancy. *International Journal of Epidemiology, 2*(2), 195–204.

Kleinman, J., & Kessel, S. (1987). Racial differences in low birth weight: Trends and risk factors. *The New England Journal of Medicine, 317*(12), 749–753.

Kotelchuck, M. (1994). An evaluation of the Kessner adequacy of prenatal care index and a proposed adequacy of prenatal care index. *American Journal of Public Health, 84*(9), 1414–1420.

Martin, L. M. (1990). *Geographic proximity of maternal and perinatal medical services: Socio-demographic determinants and infant mortality consequences*. Master's thesis, Department of Sociology, Florida State University, Tallahassee.

Martin, J. A., & Park, M. M. (1999). Trends in twin and triplet births: 1980–97. *National Vital Statistics Reports, 47*(24), 1–16.

Massey, D. S., Gross, A. B., & Shibuya, K. (1994). Migration, segregation, and the geographic concentration of poverty. *American Sociological Review, 59*(3), 425–445.

Mathews, T. J., & MacDorman, M. F. (2007). Infant mortality statistics from the 2004 period linked birth/infant death dataset. *National Vital Statistics Reports, 55*(14), 1–32, National Center for Health Statistics.

Mayfield, J. A., Rosenblatt, R. A., Baldwin, L. M., Chu, J., & Logerfo, J. P. (1990). The relation of obstetrical volume and nursery level to perinatal mortality. *American Journal of Public Health, 80*(7), 819–823.

McCormick, M. C., & Richardson, D. K. (1995). Access to neonatal intensive care. *The Future of Children, 5*, 162–175.

McCormick, M. C., Shapiro, S., & Starfield, B. H. (1985). The regionalization of perinatal services summary of the evaluation of a national demonstration program. *Journal of the American Medical Association, 253*(6), 799–804.

Messer, L., Laraia, B., Kaufman, J., Eyster, J., Holzman, C., Culhane, J., Elo, I., Burke, J., & O'Campo, P. (2006). The development of a standardized neighborhood deprivation index. *Journal of Urban Health, 83*(6), 1041–1062.

Meyer, M. B., Jonas, B. S., & Tonascia, J. A. (1976). Perinatal events associated with maternal smoking during pregnancy. *Journal of the American Medical Association, 103*(5), 464–476.

Misra, D. P., O'Campo, P., & Strobino, D. (2001). Testing a sociomedical model for preterm delivery. *Paediatric and Perinatal Epidemiology, 15*(2), 110–122.

Moos, M. K., & Cefalo, R. C. (1987). Pre-conceptional health promotion: A focus for obstetric care. *American Journal of Perinatology, 4*(1), 63–67.

National Foundation of the March of Dimes Committee on Perinatal Health. (1976). *Toward improving the outcome of pregnancy: Recommendations for the regional development of maternal and perinatal health services*. White Plains: National Foundation-March of Dimes.
Nesbit, T., Connell, F., Hart, L., & Rosenblatt, R. (1990). Access to obstetric care in rural areas: Effect on birth outcomes. *American Journal of Public Health, 80*, 814–818.
Papiernik, E., Alexander, G. R., & Paneth, N. (1990). Racial differences in pregnancy duration and its implications for perinatal care. *Medical Hypotheses, 33*(3), 181–186.
Peacock, J., Bland, J. M., & Anderson, H. R. (1995). Preterm delivery: Effects of socioeconomic factors, psychological stress, smoking, alcohol, and caffeine. *British Medical Journal, 311*(7004), 531–535.
Pollack, H. A., & Frohna, J. G. (2002). Infant sleep placement after the back to sleep campaign. *Pediatrics, 109*(4), 608–614.
Powers, D. A., & Song, S. E. (2009). Absolute change in cause-specific infant mortality for blacks and whites in the U.S.: 1983–2002. *Population Research and Policy Review, 28*, 817–851.
Reichman, N. E., Hamilton, E. R., Hummer, R. A., & Padilla, Y. C. (2008). Racial and ethnic disparities in low birthweight among urban unmarried mothers. *Maternal and Child Health Journal, 12*, 204–215.
Schieve, L. A., Meikle, S. F., Ferre, C., Peterson, H. B., Jeng, G., & Wilcox, L. S. (2002). Low and very low birth weight in infants conceived with use of assisted reproductive technology. *The New England Journal of Medicine, 346*(10), 731–737.
Sebire, N. J., Jolly, M., Harris, J. P., Wadsworth, J., Joffe, M., Beard, E. W., Regan, L., & Robinson, S. (2001). Maternal obesity and pregnancy outcome: A study of 287213 pregnancies in London. *International Journal of Obesity, 25*(8), 1175–1182.
Seidman, D. S., Samueloff, A., Mor-Yosef, S., & Schenker, J. G. (1990). The effect of maternal age and socioeconomical background on neonatal outcome. *International Journal of Gynaecology and Obstetrics, 33*(1), 7–12.
Shiono, P. H., Klebanoff, M. A., Graubard, B. I., Berendes, H. W., & Rhoads, G. G. (1986). Birth weight among women of different ethnic groups. *Journal of the American Medical Association, 255*(1), 48–52.
Singh, G. K., & Kogan, M. D. (2007). Persistent socioeconomic disparities in infant, neonatal, and post-neonatal mortality rates in the United States, 1969–2001. *Pediatrics, 119*(4), E928–E939.
Singh, G. K., & Yu, S. M. (1995). Infant mortality in the United States: Trends, differentials, and projections, 1950–2010. *American Journal of Public Health, 85*(7), 957–964.
Sowards, K. A. (1997). Premature birth and the changing composition of newborn infectious disease mortality: Reconsidering "exogenous" mortality. *Demography, 34*(3), 399–409.
Stockwell, E. G., Goza, F. W., & Balistreri, K. S. (2005). Infant mortality and socioeconomic status: New bottle, same old wine. *Population Research and Policy Review, 24*, 387–399.
Stoll, B. J., Holmann, R. C., & Schuchat, A. (1998). Decline in sepsis-associated neonatal and infant deaths in the United States, 1979 through 1994. *Pediatrics, 102*(2), e18.
Subramanian, S., Chen, J., Rehkopf, D., Waterman, P., & Krieger, N. (2005). Racial disparities in context: A multilevel analysis of neighborhood variations in poverty and excess mortality among black populations in Massachusetts. *American Journal of Public Health, 95*(2), 260–265.
Wen, S. W., Goldenberg, R. L., Cutter, G. R., Hoffman, H. J., & Cliver, S. P. (1990). Intrauterine growth retardation and preterm delivery: Prenatal risk factors in an indigent population. *American Journal of Obstetrics and Gynecology, 162*(1), 213–218.
Williams, D. R., & Collins, C. (1995). U.S. socioeconomic and racial differences in health: Patterns and explanations. *Annual Review of Sociology, 21*, 349–386.
Williams, D. R., & Collins, C. (2001). Racial residential segregation: A fundamental cause of racial disparities in health. *Public Health Reports, 116*, 404–416.
Wilson, W. (1987). *The truly disadvantaged: The inner city, the underclass and public policy*. Chicago: University of Chicago Press.

Chapter 8
Estimates of Survival and Mortality from Successive Cross-Sectional Surveys

David W. Smith, Stephanie L. McFall, and Benjamin S. Bradshaw

Introduction

Mortality rates, primary indicators of health status, are usually reported by age and sex and sometimes other characteristics such as race and ethnicity. These rates are constrained by the items on the records used to compute them: vital records and a census. Mortality rates could also be useful measures of the burden of disease for subpopulations of people who have a chronic disease such as diabetes or a long-term condition such as physical impairment. Such potentially useful categories are rarely recorded on death certificates or obtained in a census. This information is often available from surveys that are used to estimate prevalence rates of diseases or conditions. We describe a method to estimate death rates from successive, independent surveys. This is an adaptation of a method that was developed for survival ratios and death rates calculated from successive national censuses (United Nations 1967).

To estimate death rates of subpopulations based on health conditions or chronic diseases obtained in surveys, two successive surveys must ascertain whether a condition or disease is present at the time of interview. The second survey must also ascertain age at onset or year of onset of the condition to determine if the condition was present when the first survey was done. When this information is available, survival from the time of the first survey to the time of the second can be estimated.

D.W. Smith (✉)
London School of Hygiene and Tropical Medicine, London, UK
e-mail: davidwsmithphd@gmail.com

S.L. McFall
Institute for Social and Economic Research, University of Essex,
Wivenhoe Park, Colchester, UK

B.S. Bradshaw
Department of Management, Policy and Community Health, The University of Texas School of Public Health, San Antonio, TX, USA

N. Hoque et al. (eds.), *Applied Demography and Public Health*,
Applied Demography Series 3, DOI 10.1007/978-94-007-6140-7_8,
© Springer Science+Business Media Dordrecht 2013

The information about age of onset is sometimes available in health surveys since it is used to estimate incidence rates of diseases or conditions (Kirtland et al. 2008).

We estimate survival ratios and their variances from two successive, independent surveys and use the survival ratios to estimate death rates and their variances. We illustrate this method by estimating death rates for diabetics in the United States. Diabetes was selected as the case example because of substantive interest in its impact on population health. Diabetes was a cause of 8% of all deaths in the US in 1999–2001 (Smith and Bradshaw 2008). The prevalence of diabetes, 5–10% in recent years, is sufficiently low to challenge the method we use here.

Methods and Findings

Survey Estimates of Population Sizes

Estimates of the initial size of the subpopulation and its variance can be made using standard survey estimation methods which account for sampling weights and the survey design (Hansen et al. 1953). Estimates of the survivors in the second period require special treatment to account for age at interview and age of onset.

The survivors are the respondents in the subpopulation who would have had their chronic condition status identified by the first survey, that is, who were already diagnosed by that time. Onset of a chronic disease is usually obtained by asking how old a respondent was when they were first diagnosed with the disease or condition, though year of diagnosis or time since diagnosis could be asked instead. The difference between the respondent's reported age at the time of interview and age at diagnosis can be compared with the time since the first survey to determine which respondents had already been diagnosed at that time.

If the two surveys are k years apart, respondents in the second survey whose onset was more than k years before or less than k years before can be easily classified as having had the condition or not at the time of the initial survey. Respondents whose onset is equal to k years before cannot be classified, but their estimated total population size can be divided between the two groups. Since the time of the interview is random throughout the year, onset can occur equally before or after a respondent's birthday during the year, on average. Those who were diagnosed k years since onset could equally have had their onset before or after k years before the second survey, so we divide them equally between the two groups.

From the second survey we first estimate the subpopulation sizes of three groups with the given condition by onset time: those with onset before the time of the first survey (Tb), those with onset after the time of the first survey (Ta), and those with onset at the same time as the first survey (Ts). The estimated total of those with onset before the first survey plus one-half the estimated total of those with the condition diagnosed at the same year as the first survey, $X = Tb + Ts/2$, is the subpopulation surviving from the time of the first survey to the second. (The remainder, the total of one-half of those diagnosed at the same age year of age as the first survey plus the total of those diagnosed more recently, $X = Ta + Ts/2$, estimates the incident subpopulation after adjustment for deaths occurring after diagnosis.) The variance of the estimated total is $V(x) = V(Tb) + V(Ts)/4 + Cov(Tb, Ts)$. All the components can be estimated with standard survey software that incorporates weights and sample design. These estimates can also be made by categories of age and sex for sex-specific or age-sex specific rates where the sample sizes are sufficiently large.

Survival Ratios and Annual Probabilities of Death

The survival ratio, $S = X/Y$ is the ratio of the number of those with a previously diagnosed condition who are surviving in the second period (X) divided by the number with the condition during the first period (Y). The variance of the ratio estimate can be estimated, treating the numerator and denominator as random variables (Hansen et al. 1953, vol. I, pp. 162–167). They are independent in this ratio since the two surveys are independent. This simplifies the variance of the estimate somewhat, which is approximately $V(X/Y) = (X/Y)^2\ (V(X)/X^2 + V(Y)/Y^2)$, since the numerator and denominator are uncorrelated. The standard error is the square root of the estimated variance.

The probability of death during the period between the two surveys is $1 - S$. It is useful to estimate annual probabilities since 1 year is the usual reporting period for probabilities of death while the number of years between surveys, k, can vary. If the annual probabilities of death are constant for the whole period, then the annual probability of mortality is $M = 1 - S^{1/k}$ where k is the number of years between surveys. The variance of the estimate of M is approximately $V(M) = (S^{1/k-1}/k)^2\ V(S)$ using the Taylor series method and taking the square root to obtain the standard error. Again, useful estimates can also be made by sex or for age and sex subpopulations where the survey sample sizes are large enough.

Hansen et al. (1953, vol. II, pp. 109–111) recommended that the coefficient of variation of the estimated denominator of a ratio statistic be less than 0.05 in order for the usual, approximate, confidence intervals (the estimate plus or minus its standard error times a critical value) to be good approximations to exact, asymmetric intervals derived by Fieller (1940, 1954), which are more accurate for any value of the coefficient of variation.

Estimates for Diabetics in the United States

We estimated survival ratios and annual probabilities of death for a 5 year period using 3 years of pooled survey data. The initial period was 1996–1998 and the final period was 2001–2003. Effectively, we treated each pooled estimate as an estimate for the middle year, giving a time interval of 5 years for deaths to occur, on average.

We used the public use data files of the Behavioral Risk Factor Surveillance System (BRFSS), a large telephone survey sponsored by the Centers for Disease Control and Prevention (CDC) (Centers for Disease Control and Prevention 2005; Holtzman 2003). The target population is the noninstitutionalized adult population of the United States. Each jurisdiction conducts an independent sample. For 2001–2003, the sample designs were list-assisted with disproportionate stratified sampling (DSS) of telephone numbers, with strata defined by the density of households in the list of numbers. Many states also used geographic strata, primarily to control the sample sizes. For 1996–1998, sample designs were more varied: Mitofsky-Waksberg, DSS, and others.

The response rate routinely reported for the BRFSS is labeled the CASRO (Council of American Survey Research Organizations) response rate. It is the number of respondents divided by the number of in scope units, known units and an estimate of the number in-scope for those of unknown eligibility (Biemer and Larsberg 2003). For the period 1996–1998 the state median response rates ranged from 59.2 to 63.1%. The minimum state response rate was 32.5% and the maximum was 88.9% (CDC, no date). For 2001–2003, the median response rate for states ranged from 57.1 to 58.3%. The minimum response rate for a state in this period was 33.3% and the maximum was 82.6% (CDC 2002, 2003, 2004).

The core of the BRFSS questionnaire for many years has included the question "Have you ever been told by a doctor that you have diabetes?" The response categories are: yes, no, only while pregnant, don't know or not sure, and refused. We recoded each response as yes or other to compute rates of diagnosed diabetes among all respondents. The BRFSS has an optional module of questions for diabetics which includes "How old were you when you were told you have diabetes?" During 2001–2003 every state but Illinois and Oregon used the optional diabetes module in at least 1 year. Our estimates for both periods excluded those two states.

Since age at the time of interview is recorded in years as 18–98 with 99 indicating anyone older than 98, we used an initial age range of 18–94 and a final age range of 23–99, so our estimates apply to diabetics aged 18–94. Diabetics who are initially over age 94 and survive at least 5 years are counted as survivors in our final estimate and slightly increased our estimated survival ratio.

For each period we computed new weights for the pooled samples. For each state we used the original weights and the sample sizes in each of the 3 years. A respondent's new weight was computed as the original weight times the number of interviews done by the state in the year of the interview divided by the total number of interviews done by the state in all 3 years. Our reweighting method allows more even weights of respondents in different years, compared with the simplest method of reweighting each year equally, but stops short of complete reweighting by age, sex, region, and other post-stratification categories. For the second period we used only the 1, 2, or 3 years of data for each state that included the optional diabetes module. For both estimates, we treated states as strata but did not use strata within states.

We also report indirectly standardized mortality ratios for diabetics using the U.S. death rates for 2000 to compute expected deaths by age and sex for 5 years. The age intervals were 15–94 years by 10 years with the first interval providing the

Table 8.1 Estimated diabetic population in 1996–1998 and estimated survivors in 2001–2003 in the U.S. with survival ratios and annual probabilities of mortality (per 1,000)

Sex	Initial pop'n estimate	SE	CV	Final survivor estimate	SE	Survival ratio	SE	Annual prob'y (per 1,000)	SE
Male	4,457,101	77,356	0.017	3,773,302	68,761	0.847	0.021	32.8	4.9
Female	5,104,130	73,976	0.014	4,006,599	63,866	0.785	0.017	47.3	4.1
All	9,561,231	106,305	0.011	7,779,901	94,936	0.814	0.013	40.4	3.2

Standard errors (SE) are shown for all estimates and the coefficients of variation (CV) are shown for the initial population estimate

estimate for survey respondents aged 18–24 years. The death rates for these intervals were weighted by the estimated diabetic population sizes in 1996–1998 to obtain the expected deaths, which were added to get the total expected deaths. The ratio of the survey estimate of the total deaths to the expected number based on US rates is the indirectly standardized ratio for the diabetic population in 1996–1998. The estimated variance and standard error of this ratio used the denominator as a fixed value, though this is subject to sampling variation of the initial sample.

Estimates and derived statistics are shown in Table 8.1. Of diabetics age 18–94 in the U.S. during 1996–8, 81.4% survived 5 years, with a standard error (SE) of 1.3%. The corresponding annual death rate was 41.1 per thousand (SE=3.2%). This was 2.06 (SE=0.16%) times the rate expected for U.S. adults with a similar age-sex composition of the initial sample. Among men the survival ratio was 84.7% (SE=2.1%) and the annual death rate was 32.8 per thousand (SE=4.9%), or 1.50 (SE=0.22%) times the expected rate. Among women the survival ratio was 78.5% (SE=1.7%) and the annual death rate was 47.3 per thousand (SE=4.1%), or 2.7 (SE=0.23%) times the expected rate. All the coefficients of variation of the denominators of the survival ratios are below 0.05.

Discussion

It is feasible to estimate death rates for modest sized subpopulations from large surveys conducted several years apart. Estimates of death rates based on surveys appear to be acceptable for planning, as census-based estimates of population mortality have proven their utility (United Nations 1967). Estimates can be made for characteristics that can be obtained in a survey but are not obtained in a census or from death certificates, such as self-reported chronic diseases or conditions. Systematic collection of the age of onset in surveys would allow estimates of death rates as well as of incidence rates for chronic conditions or diseases.

These estimates are subject to the kinds of errors that occur in surveys, including sampling and nonsampling errors. Since the BRFSS does not obtain the information about age of onset each year in every state, the final sample sizes in our example were quite variable. This increased the variance of the estimates we made and would also increase the variability of estimates for individual states. Systematic collection of the age of onset would reduce this variability and allow publication of regular rates by states.

The usual estimates of death rates are based on two data sources: death certificates and population estimates from a recent census, each with characteristic sources of error. Estimates of death rates for diabetics that link survey responses with death certificates of respondents have also been used (Gu et al. 1998; Saydah et al. 2002), as have estimates that include both surveys and death certificates but without linkage of specific records (Tierney et al. 2001). These estimates are subject to both sampling and nonsampling errors that differ from not only the method we have proposed here but also the standard methods for death rates. The choice of method should be influenced by a better understanding of the errors in the estimates as well as the costs and feasibility of alternative methods.

A next step will be to apply this approach to smaller geographic units, such as states, to examine the impact of smaller sample sizes on the plausibility and precision of estimated mortality as well as provide useful local area estimates. Another step is to apply this method to other chronic conditions where both status and age of onset are obtained in a survey. One example is the Canadian Community Health Survey, which has asked the age of onset of every major chronic condition included in the survey.

References

Biemer, P. P., & Lyberg, L. E. (2003). *Introduction to survey quality*. New York: Wiley.

Centers for Disease Control and Prevention. (2002). *2001 behavioral risk factor surveillance system summary data quality report*. Retrieved March 29, 2010, from ftp://ftp.cdc.gov/pub/Data/Brfss/2001SummaryDataQualityReport.pdf

Centers for Disease Control and Prevention. (2003). *2002 behavioral risk factor surveillance system summary data quality report*. Retrieved March 29, 2010, from ftp://ftp.cdc.gov/pub/Data/Brfss/2002SummaryDataQualityReport.pdf

Centers for Disease Control and Prevention. (2004). *2003 behavioral risk factor surveillance system summary data quality report*. Retrieved March 29, 2010, from ftp://ftp.cdc.gov/pub/Data/Brfss/2003SummaryDataQualityReport.pdf

Centers for Disease Control and Prevention. (2005). Behavioral risk factor surveillance system operational and user's guide, Version 3.0, March 4, 2005.

Centers for Disease Control and Prevention. (no date). *1998 BRFSS summary quality control report*. Retrieved March 29, 2010, from ftp://ftp.cdc.gov/pub/Data/Brfss/98quality.pdf

Fieller, E. C. (1940). The biological standardisation of insulin. *Journal of the Royal Statistical Society (Supplement), 1*, 1–54.

Fieller, E. C. (1954). Some problems in interval estimation. *Journal of the Royal Statistical Society B, 16*, 175–185.

Gu, K., Cowie, C. C., & Harris, M. I. (1998). Mortality in adults with and without diabetes in a national cohort of the U.S. population, 1971–1993. *Diabetes Care, 21*(7), 1138–1145.

Hansen, M. H., Hurwitz, W. N., & Madow, W. G. (1953). *Sample survey methods and theory* (Vols. I and II). New York: Wiley.

Holtzman, D. (2003). Analysis and interpretations of data from the U.S. behavioral risk factor surveillance system. In D. V. McQueen & P. Puska (Eds.), *Global behavioral risk factor surveillance* (pp. 35–46). New York: Kluwer Academic/Plenum Publishers.

Kirtland, K. A., Li, Y. F., Geiss, L. S., & Thompson, T. J. (2008). State-specific incidence of diabetes among adults – participating states, 1995–1997 and 2005–2007. *Morbidity and Mortality Weekly Report, 57*(43), 1169–1173.

Saydah, S. H., Eberhardt, M. S., Loria, C. M., & Brancati, F. L. (2002). Age and the burden of death attributable to diabetes in the United States. *American Journal of Epidemiology, 156*(8), 714–719.

Smith, D. W., & Bradshaw, B. S. (2008). Cause-specific mortality rates in chronic disease subpopulations. *The Open Demography Journal, 1*, 11–14.

Tierney, E. F., Geiss, L. S., Engelgau, M. M., et al. (2001). Population-based estimates of mortality associated with diabetes: Use of a death certificate check box in North Dakota. *American Journal of Public Health, 91*(1), 84–92.

United Nations. (1967). *Methods of estimating basic demographic measures from incomplete data*. New York: United Nations.

Chapter 9
Cancer Screening in the U.S. and Europe: Policies, Practices, and Trends in Cancer Incidence and Mortality

Krista Garcia and Eileen M. Crimmins

Introduction

Population-based data are increasingly used to elucidate the burden of cancer worldwide. Incidence and mortality data from regional and national cancer registries should allow researchers to monitor trends and disparities in cancer occurrence, survival, and mortality in populations and subgroups of the population and to evaluate the effectiveness of screening for cancers amenable to early detection and treatment. Given that the primary purpose of screening is to reduce the number of deaths attributable to cancer, cancer mortality is assumed to be the most important indicator of the effectiveness of screening and the most basic measure of progress against cancer (Hakama et al. 2008; Jatoi and Miller 2003). In setting screening policy, the deaths saved by screening, however, must be weighed against any adverse effects of screening resulting from over identifying or over treating cases, as well as monetary costs.

Recent studies on cancer in the United States (U.S.) and Europe show an overall decline in cancer mortality in recent years; however the magnitude of the decline and current mortality rates are variable across Europe and between the U.S. and other high-income European countries (Jemal et al. 2010; La Vecchia et al. 2010; Crimmins et al. 2010). Declines in screened cancers including breast, prostate, and colorectal cancers have played important roles in the reduction in overall cancer mortality (Jemal et al. 2010; Karim-Kos et al. 2008; Boyle and Ferlay 2005b; Baade et al. 2004; Botha et al. 2003; Quinn et al. 2003). Screening, along with improved diagnostic methods, and therapeutic advances are thought to be responsible for site-specific cancer declines, however the extent to which each of these factors is responsible for the declines remains largely unknown and controversial.

K. Garcia (✉) • E.M. Crimmins
Davis School of Gerontology, Andrus Gerontology Center,
University of Southern California, Los Angeles, CA, USA
e-mail: kegarcia@usc.edu

N. Hoque et al. (eds.), *Applied Demography and Public Health*,
Applied Demography Series 3, DOI 10.1007/978-94-007-6140-7_9,

© Springer Science+Business Media Dordrecht 2013

This paper compares screening policy, screening uptake, and recent trends in cancer incidence and mortality rates in the U.S. and high-income European countries for cancers of the breast, prostate, colon, rectum, and anus among persons aged 50 years and older. As the approaches to screening in the U.S. and Europe have been similar in some, but different in many respects, the comparison allows the outcomes of key differences to be evaluated. We examine mortality trends in two time periods, 1980–1989 and 1990–2005, before and after screening became more widespread, to identify differences in the rate of decline in site-specific cancer deaths across countries with different uptakes of cancer screening. We find that in general, greater declines in mortality coincide with higher uptake of screening, however our results should be interpreted with caution. To conclude, we highlight the challenges and critical issues in this field of research.

Cancer Screening

The aim of cancer screening is to reduce cancer mortality through regular and systematic examinations of asymptomatic persons, so that cancers are detected at earlier stages when they are more responsive to appropriate treatments, thus minimizing the loss of life as well as the social and financial burden of cancer (von Karsa et al. 2008). While many of the technologies used for screening are also used for the diagnosis of cancer among those with symptoms, screening refers to the use of tests and exams among those who are not symptomatic as part of preventative health care. There are risks, as well as benefits, associated with screening and early detection. While screening can identify cancers that will become symptomatic and can cause death, screening also identifies slow-growing and indolent tumors that may result in the diagnosis and treatment of a "cancer" that would otherwise not go on to cause symptoms or death if undetected or untreated (Welch and Black 2010). It is important to note that the term "cancer" represents a continuum of disease, ranging from noninvasive to invasive carcinoma, and screening techniques may detect both of these disease entities as well as noncancerous benign tumors and lesions (Nelson et al. 2009).

Public health policies related to cancer screening have been integrated into preventive health care in many countries; however screening guidelines for particular cancers vary considerably across countries. Screening policies and methods, while generally based on scientific analysis and evidence-based recommendations, can also reflect economic considerations. In Europe, screening guidelines and programs are strictly based on findings from randomized controlled trials (RCT) that have demonstrated a significant reduction in cancer mortality as a result of screening (Hakama et al. 2008). In the U.S., screening guidelines have also been based on observational and diagnostic accuracy studies, rather than relying only on experimental evidence from RCTs. For instance, the recommendation for widespread use of the prostate specific antigen (PSA) test in the U.S. as a screening tool for prostate cancer prior to supporting results from randomized trials serves as an example of intuitive screening practices.

Despite widespread use of screening, optimal screening policy remains controversial. For example, in the U.S., revised recommendations by the U.S. Preventive Services Task Force in 2009, to increase the age at which routine screening should begin from 40 to 50 and reduce the frequency of routine mammograms, conflicted with long-standing recommendations by other medical groups and sparked a great deal of controversy. While RCTs are generally considered the gold standard for determining a screening modality's effectiveness in reducing mortality from a particular cancer, conflicting and inconclusive results among RCTs have generated much debate among the medical community and have created a great deal of confusion among both medical practitioners and the public as to when the benefits of screening outweigh the risk of adverse effects as a result of screening. Another source of confusion is that the mortality benefit of screening not only depends on the type of cancer, but also on age, adding to the difficulty in setting universal sets of screening recommendations.

In the following section we discuss the screening modalities generally used to detect breast, prostate, and colorectal cancer and their effectiveness in reducing cancer-specific mortality. These are major cancers, with breast cancer responsible for 16.5% of all cancer deaths among women, prostate cancer responsible for 9.2% of all cancer deaths among men, and colorectal cancer responsible for 11.2% of all cancer deaths among men and women in the U.S. and Europe in 2008 (Ferlay et al. 2010). Each of these cancers is amenable to screening but each has different issues related to screening effectiveness in reducing cancer-specific mortality and appropriate screening policy.

Breast Cancer

Breast cancer has an asymptomatic phase that can be identified with various screening techniques including screen film and digital mammography, magnetic resonance imaging (MRI), and ultrasound. Our discussion will focus on mammography. For women at high-risk for breast cancer, MRI may be used as a screening modality (Nelson et al. 2009; Warner et al. 2011), however there are currently no studies investigating its effectiveness in reducing breast cancer mortality. Numerous organizations continue to recommend clinical breast exams as a complementary examination to mammography screening, however self examination is no longer recommended by most organizations (Anees et al. 2007). In two RCTs, no mortality benefit to breast self-examination was found (Semiglazov et al. 2003; Thomas et al. 1997).

Screen-film mammography gained widespread use after its introduction in the late 1980s and is the most extensively studied screening modality. When an abnormal mammographic finding is identified, additional imaging and biopsy for tissue sampling may be recommended to further discriminate cancerous and noncancerous conditions and to classify the lesion in more detail.

Mammography screening guidelines are generally based on the findings from eight randomized trials conducted in the U.S., Sweden, United Kingdom, and Canada.

Findings from these trials show mammography to be effective in reducing mortality from breast cancer by 20 to 35% among average-risk women ages 50–69 (Nystrom et al. 2002; Shapiro 1994). It is estimated that 465 women need to be screened (every 24–33 months), for 7 years in order to save one life over 20 years (Tabar et al. 2004). This estimate translates to 1,499 mammographic examinations needed to prevent one death among average-risk women in the 50–69 age range. Recent research on the effectiveness of mammograms among younger women, those between age 40 and 50, indicates that mammography is much less efficient in this age range (Quanstrum and Hayward 2010). It is estimated that more than 1,900 women between the ages of 40 and 49 years need to be screened in order to save one life from breast cancer during 11 years of follow-up (Nelson et al. 2009). If women in this age range are receiving annual mammograms, this estimate translates to 20,944 mammographic examinations needed to prevent one death, indicating that each mammogram has less than a 1 in 20,000 chance of preventing a death from breast cancer among average-risk women in the 40–49 age range (Quanstrum and Hayward 2010; Goldberg 2010). It is this difference in effectiveness that has resulted in the changing of recommendations for mammography screening among women younger than 50.

There are critical evidence gaps on the effectiveness of mammography in decreasing breast cancer mortality among average-risk women aged 75 years and older (Galit et al. 2007). A randomized controlled trial on the efficacy of mammographic screening in women over age 74 has not been conducted. However, data from two cohort studies (McCarthy et al. 2000; McPherson et al. 2002) and one nested case-control study (van Dijck et al. 1994) suggest that mammography screening among women aged 75 years and older with a reasonable estimated life expectancy may be associated with identification of earlier-stage disease and lower breast cancer mortality (Galit et al. 2007).

The potential harms associated with mammography screening include pain during the procedure, along with anxiety and distress, although these effects are usually transient (Lerman et al. 1991; Ekeberg et al. 2001; Lampic et al. 2001). More serious harms include false-positive results that lead to further diagnostic evaluation and unnecessary treatment. The specificity of a single mammographic examination is 94–97%, indicating that 3–6% of women who do not have cancer undergo further diagnostic procedures (Humphrey et al. 2002). The percentage of women experiencing one false-positive result over time, however, is much higher due to the cumulative risk of multiple examinations from routine screenings (Elmore et al. 1998; Croswell et al. 2009). It is estimated that for every one life saved from breast cancer, approximately 2,000 false-positive mammograms will occur among screened women between the ages of 40 and 49 years (Nelson et al. 2009). Approximately 400 false-positive mammograms will occur among screened women between the ages of 60–69 years. Furthermore, there is a 1–3% increase in the relative risk of developing breast cancer due to the small dose of ionizing radiation received during mammography (Nelson et al. 2009).

Prostate Cancer

Digital rectal examination and the PSA test are the two methods used to screen for prostate cancer. PSA testing was developed in the mid 1980s primarily for physicians to monitor the progression of confirmed prostate cancers before and after cancer treatment. However, by the early 1990s, the PSA test, performed in conjunction with a digital rectal examination, had become the primary method for prostate cancer screening in the U.S. (Cookson 2001).

The test measures the amount of prostate-specific antigen, a protein produced by cells in the prostate gland, in the bloodstream. Elevated levels are associated with tumors in the gland, as well as common non-cancerous conditions such as prostatitis (inflammation of the prostate) and benign prostatic hyperplasia (enlargement of the prostate). PSA levels also tend to increase with age. Test results do not distinguish between cancerous tumors and benign prostate conditions; a biopsy is needed for distinction and classification. The common threshold for biopsy is 4 ng/ml, however varying cut-off values have been adopted to increase the test's sensitivity and specificity (Bangma et al. 2007; Holmström et al. 2009).

PSA testing combined with digital rectal examination is simple, minimally invasive, and readily available. Screening for prostate cancer can result in the detection of small volume, low grade, and organ confined prostate tumors diagnosed at an early stage (Catalona et al. 1991; Postma et al. 2006; Draisma et al. 2006). Diagnosis of early stage virulent tumors is important and can save lives. However, most tumors in the prostate grow slowly, are unlikely to spread, and do not become symptomatic or clinically significant for many years or even decades. For this reason, most men with prostate cancer are more likely to die with prostate cancer than from it (Sakr et al. 1994; Brawley et al. 1998). Based on postmortem studies, over 30% of men who died in their seventh decade with no known history of prostate cancer had detectable malignant cancer in the prostate at autopsy (Sanchez-Chapado et al. 2003; Soos et al. 2005; Hass et al. 2007). Because of the test's high rate of identifying tumors that would not cause mortality, there is concern over the adverse effects associated with additional diagnostic and treatment procedures. Biopsy and treatment following a positive diagnosis can result in morbidity and significant declines in quality of life due to the risks of erectile dysfunction and incontinence (Raaijmakers et al. 2002; Potosky et al. 2000; Wilt et al. 2008).

Scientific evidence of a mortality benefit from prostate screening was sought in two landmark randomized controlled trials: the U.S.-based Prostate, Lung, Colorectal, and Ovarian (PLCO) Cancer Screening Trial and the European Randomized Study of Screening for Prostate Cancer (ERSPC). Despite the assumption that the two trials would clarify the effects of prostate cancer screening, findings of the studies led to different conclusions. The American randomized trial reported no evidence of a mortality benefit to screening with up to 10 years of follow-up (Andriole et al. 2009), while the European trial reported a 20% decline in mortality after 9 years of follow-up (Schroder et al. 2009). The European trial indicated that 1,410 men would need to be screened and 48 additional cases would need to be treated to prevent one death from prostate cancer (Schroder et al. 2009).

The disparity in results is attributed to differences in the protocol, execution, and contamination levels between the two trials (Pinsky et al. 2010; La Rochelle and Amling 2010). Because screening for prostate cancer has become a regular part of American health care, PSA tests were being received by approximately 50% of the men in the control group of the American trial. In Europe, the PSA test is less commonly used as a screening tool for prostate cancer. Contamination was projected to be 20% in the design stage of the trial, thus the European trial was less affected in its control arm by screening behavior outside of the study. Nonetheless, high usage of the intervention in the control group reduces the effective sample size and statistical power of each study (Pinsky et al. 2010; Boyle and Brawley 2009), weakening ability to reach a valid conclusion about the mortality benefit from screening. Preston (2009) interprets the results from these two trials to indicate that the United States would gain no mortality benefit by expanding PSA testing beyond its already high screening levels, whereas European countries would benefit from an expansion. The debate over prostate cancer screening continues in light of these findings.

Colorectal Cancer

Several screening test modalities are available for colorectal cancer, including fecal occult blood test (FOBt), sigmoidoscopy, and colonoscopy (Atkin 2003). Studies suggest that colorectal cancer has an asymptomatic phase when benign adenomatous polyps develop into early, localized cancers, before further progressing into advanced and potentially fatal cancers. The average time for an adenoma (pre-cancerous polyp) to progress to carcinoma is approximately 10 years, and tests that detect adenomas, such as endoscopy, can be offered less frequently. It is important to note that 90% of adenomas remain benign, and screening for them can result in overtreatment. For the 10% of adenomas that do develop into carcinoma, it takes approximately 2–3 years for an asymptomatic cancer to become symptomatic, thus screen-detected colorectal cancers are typically diagnosed 2–3 years earlier than clinically detected cancers (Atkin 2003).

The FOBt is the most extensively studied screening modality and has been shown in three randomized trials to reduce colorectal cancer mortality by 20–33% (Mandel et al. 1999; Kronborg et al. 1996; Jørgensen et al. 2002; Hardcastle et al. 1996). The FOBt (home-test kit commonly used) is a noninvasive, inexpensive test that involves placing consecutive stool samples onto cards and mailing them to a lab for processing. Investigation of the colon by endoscopy is generally recommended for positive results. Proponents of the FOBt argue that the test is a cost-effective screening modality by reducing the number of endoscopies administered, although endoscopic examinations have greater sensitivity in detecting adenomatous polyps and early cancers compared to stool tests when considered as a single test (Whitlock et al. 2008).

Colonoscopic screening methods are considered to be the gold-standard due to greater sensitivity for detecting adenomas and carcinomas in both the distal and proximal colon, and the ability to remove pathological lesions within a single examination (Zavoral et al. 2009). Despite these advantages, there is currently no published data from multicenter RCTs on the efficacy of colonoscopy screening in reducing colorectal cancer incidence and mortality. However, findings from a controlled, multicenter randomized study on the efficacy of a once-only flexible sigmoidoscopy screen, which can also remove pathological lesions and detect adenomas and carcinomas of the rectum and sigmoid colon where approximately two-thirds of adenomas and cancers are located, suggest that this examination can reduce colorectal cancer incidence by 23% and reduce mortality by 31%, when offered only once between ages 55 and 64 years (Atkin et al. 2010). Based on the data from this trial, 489 people need to be screened by sigmoidoscopy to prevent one death from colorectal cancer after a median of 11 years of follow-up. These findings suggest that sigmoidoscopy may be a more cost-effective population-based screening modality than colonoscopy, because it is a relatively safe procedure that does not require anesthetics and necessitates less time and preparation for patients (Loeve et al. 2000). Although evidence suggests that population-based screening for colorectal cancer is effective, there is still debate over which screening modality is appropriate (Hawkes and Cunningham 2010).

Comparison of Cancer Screening in the U.S. and Europe

The establishment of organized population-based cancer screening programs in the European Union has distinguished European screening practices from that of the U.S., where cancer screening is predominantly opportunistic. In the U.S., screening behaviors and practices generally depend on individual level circumstances such as one's awareness of, decision to seek, and/or access to care and health insurance. Organized screening programs in Europe, however, operate under a standardized system of care in which nationally implemented guidelines chosen by government or health departments define the target population to be invited, the screening method to be used, and the screening interval followed for particular types of cancers (Miles et al. 2004). With over 50 nationwide screening programs for breast, cervical, and colorectal cancer, the Europe Union leads the way in population-based screening; however in the first implementation report in 2003, less than half of the minimum recommended numbers of screenings took place in the EU each year and more than half of the annual volume of screening examinations (59%) were administered outside of population-based programs (von Karsa et al. 2008).

Significant variation in screening test utilization between the United States and Europe and across European countries is observed (Howard et al. 2009; Stock and Brenner 2010; Preston and Ho 2010). Cancer screening in the U.S. is among the highest compared to other countries, with a generally higher prevalence of screening at both younger and older ages (Preston and Ho 2010; Howard et al. 2009; Cutler 2008).

Recent analyses of the risks and benefits of screening have questioned the health and mortality benefits accruing to the aggressive screening practices at older ages in the U.S., resulting in the recommendations against routine screening for breast cancer in women older than 70 years (USPSTF 2009), for colorectal cancer in adults older than 75 years (USPSTF 2008a), and for prostate cancer in men older than 75 years (USPSTF 2008b). Although age-based limits for routine screenings are relatively new in the U.S., many European countries have targeted persons within a specified age range and have used age-based limits since the implementation of population-based screening programs in the late 1980s and early 1990s (Shapiro et al. 1998; Miles et al. 2004). It is important to note that age-based limits for both breast and colorectal cancer screening vary considerably across Europe, and persons outside the age range can request to continue screening in a number of countries (von Karsa et al. 2008; NHSSP 2006).

Screening Policies and Prevalence

Guidelines for cancer screening in the U.S. and Europe generally differ in the methods used for screening and the populations targeted for screening. In this section, we highlight screening policies and guidelines for individual cancers of the breast, prostate, and colorectal in the U.S. and Europe. We discuss how variations in screening policies and guidelines in the U.S. and Europe have translated to differences in screening practices and patterns. Screening prevalence estimates based on data from nationally represented surveys are presented.

Breast Cancer

Screening mammography guidelines in the United States differ from those in Europe. The Council of the European Union recommends biannual mammography screening for women between the ages 50–69 years of age. Conversely, most major U.S. medical organizations and government agencies such as the American Cancer Society, American College of Radiology, and the American Medical Association, have recommend annual mammography screening for women aged 40 years and older; however, the US Preventative Services Task Force and the American College of Preventative Medicine recently updated their guidelines to include annual or biannual screening for women between the ages of 50–69, resembling European guidelines.

Comparing data from the United States and nine European countries, in 2004, the U.S. had the highest percentage (77.7%) of women between the ages 50–64 reporting that they received a mammogram in the past two years (Howard et al. 2009). Although mammography use declines with age, there is greater variation in the percentage of women screened at older ages and the U.S. has by far the highest screening percentage with almost two-thirds of American women aged 75 and over

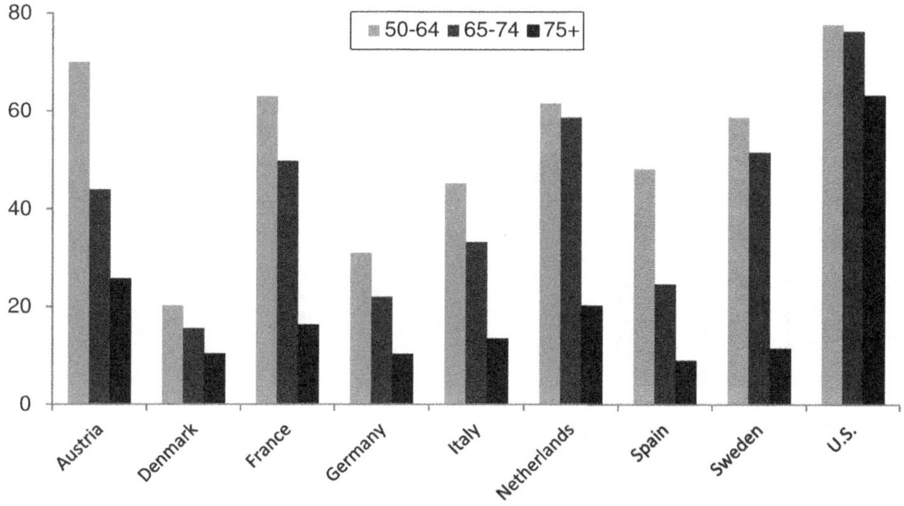

Fig. 9.1 Percentage of women who received a mammogram in previous 2 years, 2004 (Source: Howard et al. 2009; U.S. – 2004 Health and Retirement Study (HRS); Europe – 2004 Survey of Health, Ageing and Retirement in Europe (SHARE))

receiving a mammogram (63.1%), as shown in Fig. 9.1. Screening prevalence among European women aged 75 years and older ranged from 9.0% for Spain, to 25.7% for Austria. The severe drop in mammography use from ages 50–64 to 75 years and older among European women reflects age-based limits in mammography test use in many European countries.

Prostate Cancer

The serum prostate-specific antigen (PSA) test was introduced in the U.S. in the late 1980s and is the most commonly used tool for detecting prostate cancer in the U.S. Although utilization of the PSA test is widespread in the U.S., the Council of the European Union has concluded that there is insufficient evidence to recommend routine screening in Europe.

The U.S. has one of the highest percentages of men receiving a PSA test in the past year across all age groups, as shown in Fig. 9.2. Austria was the only country to have a higher prevalence of PSA test use than the U.S. among men ages 50–64 and 75 years and older, whereas the majority of European countries have a much lower screening prevalence. Austria's higher screening prevalence is likely to be attributed to prostate screening trials, such as in Tyrol, where intensive PSA screening began in 1992 (Micheli et al. 2003). Lower cancer screening prevalence in the rest of the European countries analyzed can be attributed to the European Union's strong sentiment against prostate cancer screening. Higher prevalence of test use amongst older respondents probably reflects the use of PSA as a diagnostic test as well as a screening test.

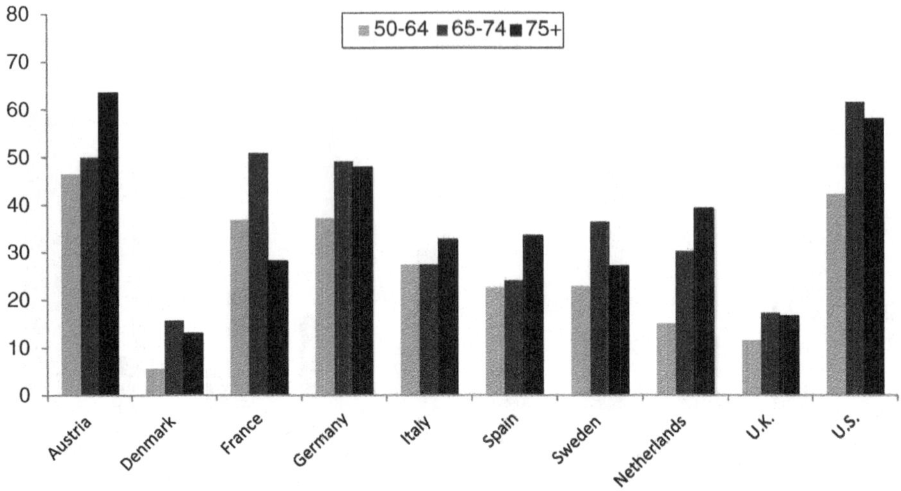

Fig. 9.2 Percentage of men who received a PSA test in previous year, 2006 (Notes: U.S. – ages 65–85, data collection year 2004; Source: Howard et al. 2009; U.S. – 2004 Medical Expenditure Panel Survey (MEPS); Europe – 2006 Eurobarometer)

Colorectal Cancer

There are marked differences in the testing modalities recommended in the U.S. and Europe. Since the mid 1990s, U.S. guidelines have recommended the use of fecal occult blood tests annually in addition to endoscopic examinations (sigmoidoscopy every 5 years or colonoscopy every 10 years) for average-risk adults aged 50 years and older. Over the last decade, colonoscopy has become the most common screening modality in the U.S. (Chen et al. 2008). Substantial increases in its use were noted after Medicare coverage was expanded in 2001 to include colonoscopy for screening purposes for average-risk individuals (Harewood and Lieberman 2004). The fecal occult blood test is the only test recommended by the Council of the European Union and is the most frequently applied method in Europe, whereas colonoscopy is seldom used as a primary screening test (Zavoral et al. 2009; Benson et al. 2007). Many European countries have been reluctant to promote endoscopic screening due to the lack of evidence from randomized trials on their efficacy in reducing colorectal cancer incidence and mortality (Atkin 2003; Pox et al. 2007).

The prevalence of colorectal cancer test use among European countries has only been reported recently (Stock et al. 2010; Stock and Brenner 2010; Howard et al. 2009). Howard and colleagues (2009) report colorectal cancer screening rates based on receipt of the FOBt or endoscopy combined for the U.S. and Europe, in which European rates, with the exception of Austria, were lower than U.S. rates across younger and older age groups. In this section, we highlight the findings by Stock and Brenner (2010), who report prevalence estimates by screening modality among adults aged 50 years and over in Europe based on the 2004 SHARE data. Prevalence

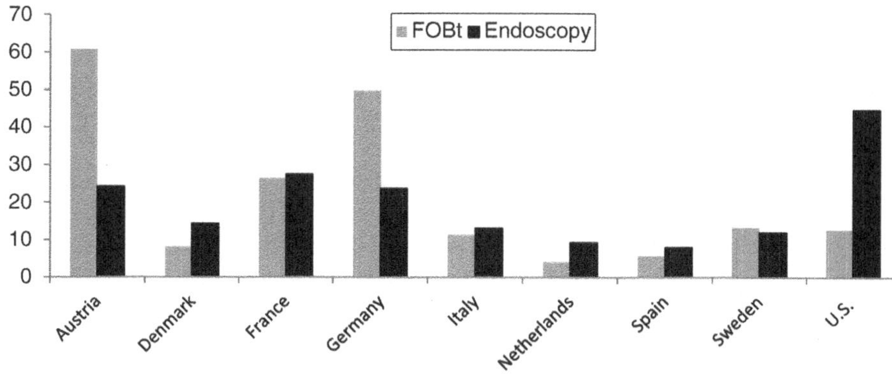

Fig. 9.3 Percentage of men aged 50+ who received a colorectal screening test in last 10 years (Notes: U.S. – FOBt within the last year; Endoscopy, sigmoidoscopy within past 5 years or colonoscopy within past 10 years; Europe – FOBt within the last 10 years; Endoscopy, sigmoidoscopy or colonoscopy within the past 10 years; Source: Stock and Brenner 2010; American Cancer Society 2009; U.S. – 2005 National Health Interview Survey (NHIS); Europe – 2004 Survey of Health, Ageing and Retirement in Europe (SHARE))

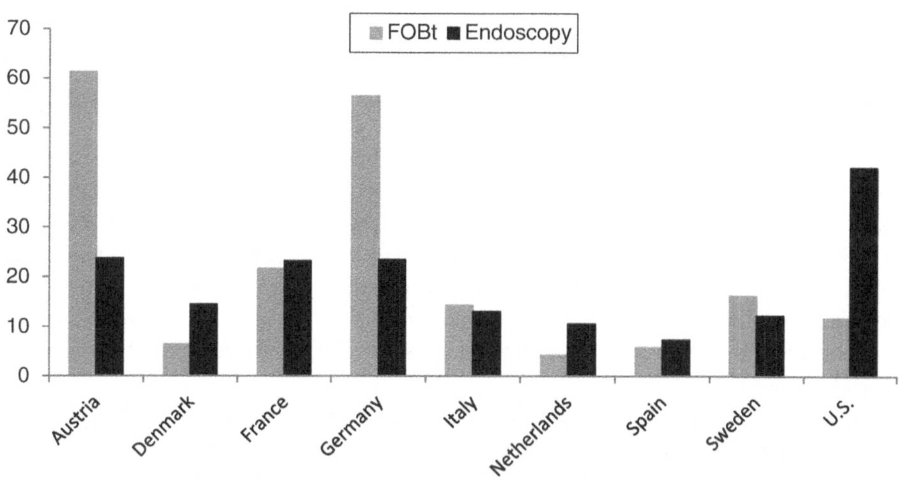

Fig. 9.4 Percentage of women aged 50+ who received a colorectal screening test in last 10 Years (Notes: U.S. – FOBt within the last year; Endoscopy, sigmoidoscopy within past 5 years or colonoscopy within past 10 years; Europe – FOBt within the last 10 years; Endoscopy, sigmoidoscopy or colonoscopy within the past 10 years; Source: Stock and Brenner 2010; American Cancer Society 2009; U.S. – 2005 National Health Interview Survey (NHIS); Europe – 2004 Survey of Health, Ageing and Retirement in Europe (SHARE))

estimates for the United States are based on 2005 NHIS data (American Cancer Society 2009).

Prevalence estimates of FOBt and endoscopy utilization among Europeans aged 50 years and older in the last 10 years were generally less than 20%, as shown in Figs. 9.3 and 9.4. Austria, France and Germany reported prevalence rates above

20% for both men and women across screening modalities. Although the Council of the European Union only recommends the FOBt for colorectal cancer screening, prevalence estimates were higher for endoscopy than for the FOBt in approximately half of the European countries analyzed. There were few significant gender differences in screening prevalence (Stock and Brenner 2010).

In the United States, endoscopy rates are higher than FOBt rates among both men and women aged 50 years and over (Meissner et al. 2006). Although recent endoscopy often includes receipt of a sigmoidoscopy in the past 5 years or colonoscopy in the last 10 years, both men and women report substantially higher prevalence of colonoscopy within the last 10 years (32.2 and 29.8%, respectively) than sigmoidoscopy within the last 5 years (7.6 and 5.9%, respectively) (Meissner et al. 2006). FOBt use in the United States is comparable to that in most European countries, however reported endoscopy use is much higher in the U.S. (Figs. 9.3 and 9.4). We assume this reflects the marked differences in the screening modalities recommended in the U.S. and Europe.

Screening and Cancer Trends

Incidence and mortality data from regional and national cancer registries allow researchers to monitor the disease among various populations and examine differences in cancer occurrence, survival, and mortality by demographic factors. Population-based cancer data have increasingly been used to evaluate the effectiveness of screening for cancers amenable to early detection and treatment on a national-level. Trends in age-standardized incidence and mortality rates from 1980 to 2005 for breast, prostate, and colorectal cancer among persons aged 50 years and older in the U.S. and several countries in Europe are provided. We examine mortality trends in two time periods, 1980–1989 and 1990–2005, to identify differences in the rate of decline in site-specific cancer deaths in relation to the use of population screening across countries.

Cancer disparities and the burden of cancer worldwide have been highlighted due to the availability of comparable regional and national-level data from Cancer Incidence in Five Continents (CI5) and the World Health Organization (WHO) Mortality Database (La Vecchia et al. 2010; Ferlay et al. 2004; Quinn and Babb 2002; Parkin et al. 2001). Cancer Incidence in Five Continents Annual Dataset (CI5*plus*) provides crude and age-standardized annual incidence based on data from national and regional cancer registries (Ferlay et al. 2010).

Incidence and mortality rates are based on the number of new or primary cancer cases and deaths occurring in a given time period in a specified population and expressed per 100,000 persons per year. To increase comparability, incidence and mortality rates are adjusted to the World standard population (Segi 1960). Anatomical sites examined include malignant neoplasms of the breast (ICD code C50), prostate (ICD code C61), and colon, rectosigmoid junction, rectum, anus, and anal canal (ICD code C18–21).

Cancer Incidence

Screening practices have had large influences on cancer diagnosis. As indicated above, screening will increase the diagnosis of more localized, curable cancers, as well as identify clinically insignificant tumors that would never be identified without screening (Bangma et al. 2007; Thompson et al. 2004). Numerous studies have shown changes in cancer incidence that parallel major changes in screening test utilization (Mettlin 2000; Glass et al. 2007; Jørgensen and Gøtzsche 2009). Marked increases in incidence are observed for particular cancers after the introduction of screening. The estimation of overdiagnosis in relation to initiation of screening is complex (Paci and Duffy 2005; Duffy et al. 2008) and varies by cancer site (Welch and Black 2010). In the U.S., overdiagnosis of prostate cancer due to PSA screening is estimated to be 15–37%, depending on race (Etzioni et al. 2002). Estimates of overdiagnosis of breast cancer based on the analysis of incidence rates before and after the implementation of breast screening programs or trials range from less than 1–33% (Paci et al. 2004, 2006; Duffy et al. 2005; Olsen et al. 2006; Zackrisson et al. 2006; Jørgensen et al. 2009), and differ by age and outcome (in situ breast vs. invasive breast cancer). We examine time trends in breast, prostate, and colorectal cancer incidence based on data from regional and national cancer registries across a number of countries. Both levels and trends in cancer incidence vary widely between the U.S. and Europe, and across Europe as well.

Breast Cancer Incidence

From 1980, there was a gradual increase in the reported incidence of breast cancer among women aged 50 years and older in the U.S. and Europe, as shown in Fig. 9.5. From 1980 to 2002, breast cancer incidence rates are higher in the U.S. compared to most European countries analyzed. Higher prevalence of mammography screening in the U.S. relative to other countries may have resulted in the higher rates of diagnosed breast cancer. The increase in incidence rates over time may reflect the progressive adoption of mammography beginning in the 1980s (Glass et al. 2007). It is also possible that some of the increase in breast cancer incidence in the United Sates up through about 2002 may have resulted from widespread use of hormone replacement therapy for potential chronic disease prevention among menopausal women beginning in the 1980s (Glass et al. 2007). The difference in oral hormone therapy use may also contribute to some of the disparities in breast cancer incidence between American and European women (Stefanick 2005).

Prostate Cancer Incidence

Since the 1990s, many European countries have experienced a gradual increase in the reported incidence of prostate cancer among men aged 50 years and older, as

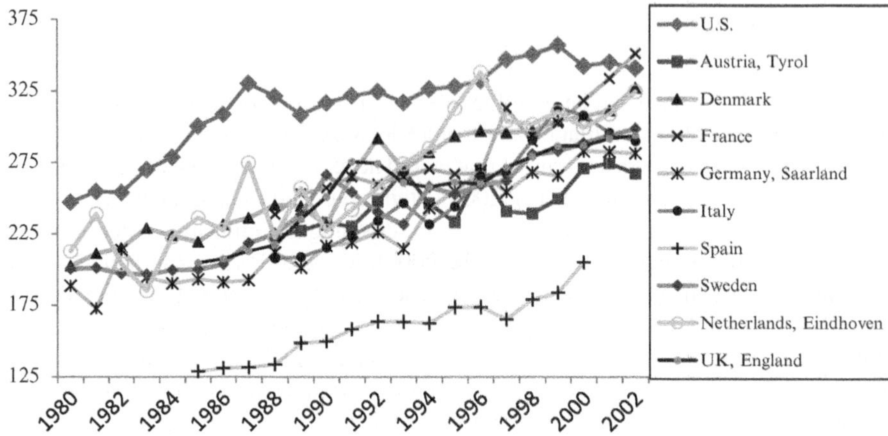

Fig. 9.5 Age-standardized breast cancer incidence among women 50+, 1980–2002 (Source: Ferlay et al. 2010)

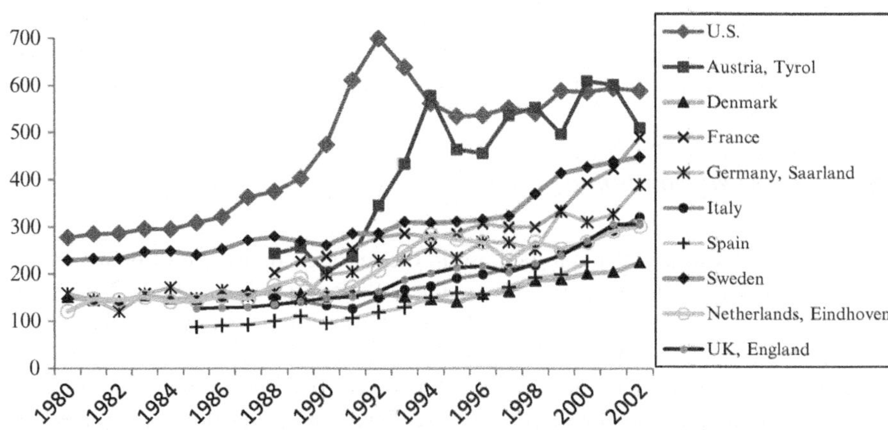

Fig. 9.6 Age-standardized prostate cancer incidence among men 50+, 1980–2002 (Source: Ferlay et al. 2010)

shown in Fig. 9.6. However, in the U.S. and Austria (Tyrol), prostate cancer incidence rates rose rapidly in the early 1990s and then declined in the late 1990s. Despite these declines, recorded prostate cancer incidence rates remained substantially higher in the U.S. and Austria compared to other European countries. This pattern parallels the introduction and widespread use of the PSA test as a screening tool in the U.S. (Quinn and Babb 2002), and the implementation of a mass prostate screening program in Tyrol, Austria (Horninger et al. 1999). The widespread implementation of prostate cancer screening has not only affected trends in prostate cancer incidence, but has also affected the features of the identified cases, such as tumor stage and grade (Rietbergen et al. 1999; Stephenson 1998).

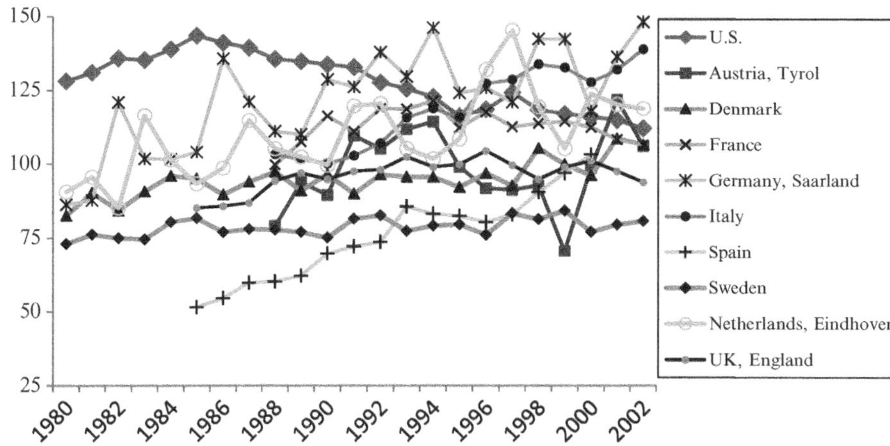

Fig. 9.7 Age-standardized colon cancer incidence among men 50+, 1980–2002 (Source: Ferlay et al. 2010)

Colon Cancer Incidence

From 1980 to 2002, reported colon cancer incidence among men and women aged 50 years and older remained stable or gradually increased in the European countries examined, whereas reported colon cancer incidence decreased among both men and women in the U.S. over this period (Fig. 9.7). It is interesting that in spite of increased screening for colorectal cancer in the U.S. (Chen et al. 2008; CDC 2011), the incidence decreased. It is possible that there have been real declines in incidence as screening prevalence has increased. One difference between screening for colorectal cancers and other cancers is that the removal of polyps that occurs with colorectal screening may reduce the incidence of cancer as well as mortality from diagnosed cancers (Rabeneck et al. 2010). Progressive adoption of colonoscopy in the U.S. is consistent with declining colon cancer incidence trends.

Cancer Survival Rates

Improved cancer survival in the U.S. and Europe is attributed to the advent of earlier diagnosis and advances in effective treatment (Wingo et al. 1998; Sant 2001; Gatta et al. 2002; Mariotto et al. 2002). Over the last 30 years, the 5-year relative survival rate for all cancers diagnosed in the U.S. has significantly increased from 50% between the years 1975 and 1977 to 68% between the years 1999 and 2005 (Horner et al. 2009). In an international comparison, the U.S. had the highest 5-year relative survival for breast, colorectal, and prostate cancer compared to the European countries included in this analysis, as shown in Table 9.1 (Coleman et al. 2008).

Table 9.1 5-year relative survival for select cancers

	Breast	Prostate	Colorectum	
	RS (%) (95% CI)	RS(%) (95% CI)	Males	Females
Austria	74.9 (71.9–78.1)	86.1 (82.9–89.4)	52.7 (48.2–57.6)	55.1 (50.8–59.7)
Denmark	73.6 (72.5–74.7)	38.4 (36.3–40.6)	44.2 (42.7–45.7)	47.7 (46.3–49.2)
France	79.8 (78.2–81.4)	73.7 (70.5–77.1)	55.6 (53.3–58.1)	61.5 (59.2–64.0)
Germany	75.5 (73.3–77.8)	76.4 (72.7–80.4)	50.1 (47.2–53.2)	55.0 (52.3–57.9)
Italy	79.5 (78.8–80.3)	65.4 (63.7–67.2)	50.7 (49.7–51.8)	52.7 (51.7–53.8)
Spain	77.7 (76.4–79.0)	60.5 (57.6–63.6)	52.5 (51.0–54.1)	54.7 (53.1–56.4)
Sweden	82.0 (81.2–82.7)	66.0 (64.7–67.3)	52.8 (51.6–54.1)	56.2 (55.0–57.4)
Netherlands	77.6 (76.6–78.6)	69.5 (67.2–71.9)	53.6 (51.5–55.7)	55.1 (53.3–57.0)
U.K.	69.7 (69.4–70.1)	51.1 (50.4–51.8)	42.3 (41.8–42.8)	44.7 (44.3–45.2)
U.S.	83.9 (83.7–84.1)	91.9 (91.7–92.1)	59.1 (58.8–59.5)	60.2 (59.8–60.5)

Source: Coleman et al. (2008), data for selected countries taken from Table 9.2
Notes: Age-standardized to ICSS weights; Survival estimates based on adults (aged 15–99 years) diagnosed with cancer during 1990–1994 and followed up to 1999

The links between differences in survival rates and changes is survival rates over time, however, must be interpreted with caution due to the effects of screening activities (Farrow et al. 1996). By detecting tumors and precancerous lesions before symptoms are present, the disease may be more treatable and have a better prognosis. However, screening may also lead to the detection of both benign and pre-malignant tumors that will never become symptomatic or progress further. Second, there may also be cases where earlier detection of the disease through screening has no effect on disease outcome, but leads to an artificial increase in individual survival time from diagnosis to death simply as a result of an earlier diagnosis. Slower-growing tumors have a greater likelihood of being detected at preclinical stages by periodic screening, leading to a length bias in survival rates (Walter and Stitt 1987; Prorok et al. 1990). It is probable that higher or improved survival rates result from greater detection of latent, slow-growing tumors that are already associated with a greater likelihood of survival rather than reductions in mortality from tumors of the same size and lethality as those identified before screening. In many respects, trends in cancer mortality may provide a better indication of the effectiveness of cancer control measures than trends in cancer incidence or cancer survival rates.

Cancer Mortality

The examination of population-based cancer mortality trends and retrospective analyses of screening prevalence have been used to infer the extent of the possible public health benefit of population-based screening. In the past two decades, declines in breast, prostate and colorectal cancer mortality have been observed in the U.S. and Europe (Preston and Ho 2010; Rohde et al. 2009; Karim-Kos et al. 2008; Collin et al. 2008; Coleman et al. 2008; Bouchardy et al. 2008; Verdecchia

Table 9.2 Change in breast cancer incidence and mortality, and screening among women ages 50+

	Incidence change (%)		Mortality change (%)			Mammography in past 2 years (%)
	Annual		Annual		Overall	Ages 50–64
	1980–1989	1990–2002	1980–1989	1990–2005	1980–2005	2004
Austria		1.0*	1.6*	−1.4*	−8.6	70.0
Denmark	2.1*	2.1*	0.7*	−1.0*	−12.5	20.2
France		2.5*	0.5*	−0.7*	−2.5	63.0
Germany	2.2*	2.2*	0.8*	−1.0*	−3.2	30.9
Italy		2.6*	1.1*	−1.4*	−5.5	45.2
Spain		2.3*	2.9*	−1.4*	3.9	48.1
Sweden	2.3*	1.3*	−0.8*	−0.8*	−17.2	58.7
Netherlands	2.2*	2.2*	0.3	−1.7*	−20.1	61.6
U.K.		1.0*	0.6*	−2.5*	−26.8	NA
U.S.	3.2*	0.5	0.4*	−2.2*	−26.1	77.7

Source: Ferlay et al. (2010); WHO Mortality Database [http://www.encr.com.fr]; Screening data: Howard et al. (2009); U.S. – 2004 Health and Retirement Study (HRS); Europe – 2004 Survey of Health, Ageing and Retirement in Europe (SHARE)

Notes: Incidence estimates based on regional data for the following countries: Austria (Tyrol), Germany (Saarland), The Netherlands (Eindhoven), United Kingdom (England)

*AAPC is statistically significant (two-sided $p<0.05$)

NA: Not Available

et al. 2007; Ward et al. 2006; Boyle and Ferlay 2005a; Levi et al. 2005; Baade et al. 2004; Tyczynski et al. 2004; Hsing et al. 2000; Pito et al. 2000). Recent declines in cancer-specific mortality in countries with high uptakes of screening tests may be interpreted as some evidence of the effectiveness of screening, however ecological analyses should be interpreted with caution. There are numerous other factors that can affect mortality, including treatment. There is also a lag time between when a cancer is identified and when a death is prevented, making it difficult to relate screening to cancer mortality trends.

The rate of decline in age-standardized breast, prostate, and colorectal cancer mortality rates among persons aged 50 years and older in the U.S. and several countries in Europe are examined below. Joinpoint regression (Joinpoint Version 3.3; National Cancer Institute, Bethesda, MD 2008) is used to estimate average annual percent change (AAPC) to summarize the mortality trend over the intervals 1980–1989 and 1990–2005.

Breast Cancer

From 1980 to 1989, significant increases in breast cancer mortality rates are observed in most countries except for Sweden, where a significant decrease in mortality is observed (Table 9.2). After rising mortality rates throughout the 1980s, significant declines in breast cancer mortality rates are observed in all countries from 1990 to 2005 (Fig. 9.8). In this time period, breast cancer mortality rates

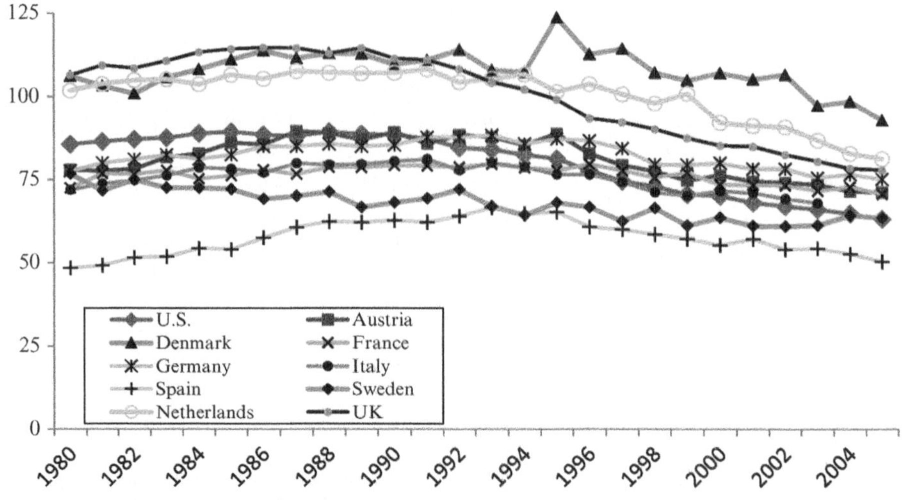

Fig. 9.8 Breast cancer mortality among women 50+, 1980–2005 (Source: WHO Mortality Database [http://www.encr.com.fr])

decreased by an average annual percentage of −0.7 to −2.5% per year, as shown in Table 9.2. The U.S. and U.K. experienced the fastest rates of decline from 1990 to 2005, −2.2 and −2.5% per year, respectively, and experienced the highest overall decline in age-standardized breast cancer deaths of approximately 26% from 1980 to 2005.

The United States and U.K., which experienced the fastest rates of decline and the highest overall decline in breast cancer mortality, have the highest screening prevalence among the group of countries analyzed here. Although self-reported data on current mammography use were not available for the U.K., screening prevalence for mammography among women aged 50–70 years old in 2006/2007 is estimated to be approximately 74% (Patnick 2009). However, from 1990 to 2005, countries with low screening prevalence, such as Denmark and Germany, experienced rates of decline in breast cancer mortality similar to rates experienced by countries with a much higher screening prevalence, such as France. This finding would seem to indicate that screening has played some role in the declines in breast cancer but that other factors, such as improved treatment using adjuvant multiagent chemotherapy and tamoxifen, may have also been important (Mariotto et al. 2002; Harlan et al. 2002).

Prostate Cancer

Between 1980 and 1989, significant increases in prostate cancer mortality rates are observed for all countries except Sweden (Table 9.3). After rising mortality rates from prostate cancer occur throughout the 1980s, significant declines in mortality rates are observed in most countries from 1990 to 2005, as shown in Fig. 9.9. In this period, mortality rates decreased by an average annual change of −0.9 to −3.2% per

Table 9.3 Change in prostate cancer incidence and mortality, and screening among men ages 50+

	Incidence change (%)		Mortality change (%)			PSA test in past year (%)
	Annual		Annual		Overall	Ages 50–64
	1980–1989	1990–2002	1980–1989	1990–2005	1980–2005	2006
Austria		8.8*	1.6*	−1.7*	−14.6	46.5
Denmark	1.0*	2.9*	1.5*	0.3	14.5	33.8
France		6.1*	1.2*	−1.9*	−17.4	36.8
Germany	4.6*	4.6*	1.4*	−1.5*	−7.4	37.2
Italy		8.4*	0.5*	−1.0*	−3.6	27.3
Spain		8.3*	0.6*	−1.1*	−13.2	22.6
Sweden	2.2*	4.4*	0.2	0.1	1.4	22.8
Netherlands	2.5*	4.9	1.4*	−1.2*	−4.5	15.0
U.K.		6.1*	3.2*	−0.9*	17.0	11.5[a]
U.S.	5.0*	1.6	1.0*	−3.2*	−30.4	42.2[b]

Source: Ferlay et al. (2010); WHO Mortality Database [http://www.encr.com.fr]; Screening data: Howard et al. (2009); U.S. – 2004 Medical Expenditure Panel Survey (MEPS); Europe – 2006 Eurobarometer

Notes: Incidence estimates based on regional data for the following countries: Austria (Tyrol), Germany (Saarland), The Netherlands (Eindhoven), United Kingdom (England)

*AAPC is statistically significant (two-sided $p < 0.05$)

[a]Data for Great Britain

[b]2004 data

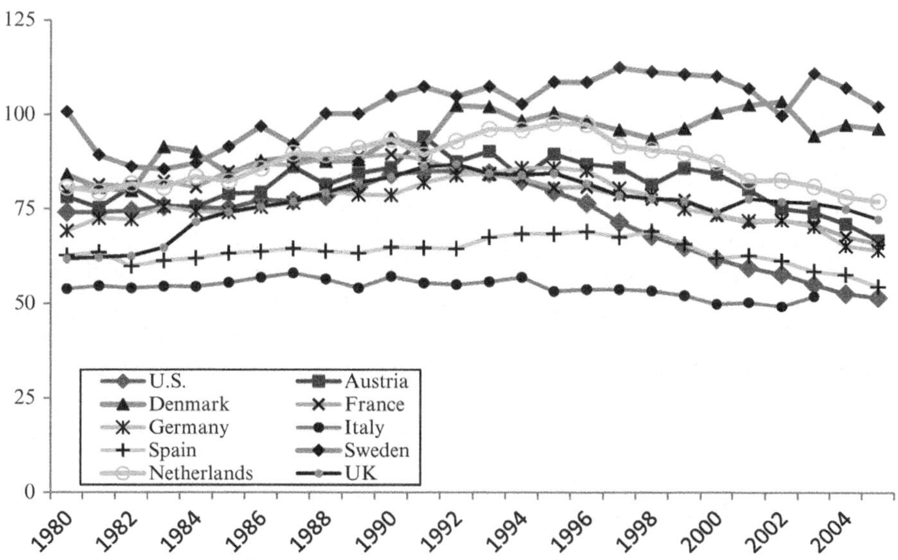

Fig. 9.9 Prostate cancer mortality among men 50+, 1980–2005 (Source: WHO Mortality Database [http://www.encr.com.fr])

year among men aged 50 years and older (Table 9.3). The U.S. experienced the fastest rate of decline of –3.2% per year from 1990 to 2005 and the highest mortality reduction in age-standardized prostate cancer rates from 1980 to 2005, 30.4%.

Countries with the highest screening prevalence, such as the U.S., Austria, France, and Germany, experienced the fastest rates of decline in prostate cancer mortality among men aged 50 years and older from 1990 to 2005 and the greatest overall mortality change from 1980 to 2005. In contrast, countries with the lowest screening prevalence, such as Denmark and the U.K., have experienced little or no decline in prostate cancer mortality from 1990 to 2005 and have actually experienced an increase in overall prostate cancer mortality from 1980 to 2005. Thus, these data suggest that national trends in prostate cancer mortality have been significantly affected by the use of screening.

Colorectal Cancer

From 1980 to 1989, some countries experienced significant increases in colorectal cancer mortality, while other countries experienced stable or small declines in mortality among men (Table 9.4). In this time period, most countries, however, experienced significant declines in colorectal cancer among women. American men and women experienced the fastest decline in mortality from 1980 to 1989, –1.0 and –1.3% per year, respectively. From 1990 to 2005, most countries experienced declines in colorectal cancer mortality among both men and women (Figs. 9.10 and 9.11). American men and women continued to experience one of the fastest mortality declines, of –2.4 and –2.5% per year, throughout this period, and experienced the highest overall decline in age-standardized colorectal cancer deaths between 1980 and 2005, 37.6% and 41.0%, respectively (Table 9.4). The U.K. and Austria experienced the fastest decline in colorectal cancer mortality –2.7% per year among women. Spain and Italy were the only countries to experience a rise in colorectal cancer mortality rates from 1980 to 2005, especially among men. From 1980 to 2005, mortality rates among Spanish women increased by 33%, while rates increased by an alarming 95% among Spanish men.

Similar to patterns seen for breast and prostate cancer, countries with higher colorectal cancer screening prevalence, such as the U.S., Austria, and Germany, experienced faster rates of decline in colorectal cancer mortality, while countries with extremely low screening prevalence, such as Italy and Spain, experienced little or no decline in colorectal cancer mortality.

Issues and Challenges

The reduction in cancer death rates over the past two decades in the U.S. and other high-income European countries appears to be a persuasive argument in support of screening and early detection. Issues surrounding over diagnosis and over treatment

Table 9.4 Change in colorectal cancer incidence and mortality, and screening among 50+, by sex

	Colon cancer incidence change (%)		Rectum and anus cancer incidence change (%)		Colorectal cancer mortality change (%)			Colorectal cancer tests in past 10 years (%); Ages 50+	
	Annual		Annual		Annual		Overall	Endoscopy	FOBT
	1980–1989	1990–2002	1980–1989	1990–2002	1980–1989	1990–2005	1980–2005	2004	2004
Males									
Austria		−0.3		1.5	0.5*	−1.9*	−26.6	24.1	60.7
Denmark	0.7*	0.7*	−0.1	−0.1	−0.1	−1.2*	−13.3	14.3	8.1
France		−0.8*		−0.9*	−0.4*	−1.3*	−22.1	27.4	26.3
Germany	1.7*	1.7*	−2.7	1.6*	0.4*	−1.4*	−19.2	23.6	49.7
Italy		3.0*		0.6	0.8*	−0.1	6.7	13.1	11.3
Spain		3.5*		1.9*	4.2*	1.9*	94.8	7.9	5.6
Sweden	0.3*	0.3*	0.3*	0.3*	−0.6*	−0.6*	−18.2	12.0	13.3
Netherlands	1.3*	1.3*	1.0*	1.0*	−0.4*	−0.4*	−11.7	9.3	4.0
U.K.		−0.1		0.2	0.3	−2.2*	−25.6		
U.S.	0.5	−1.4*	−0.4	−1.4	−1.0*	−2.4*	−37.6	[a]44.6	[a]12.7
Females									
Austria		−1.3		1.1	−1.0*	−2.7*	−39.3	23.7	61.3
Denmark	−0.3	−0.3	0	0	−0.9*	−0.9*	−25.0	14.4	6.4
France		−0.7*		−0.6	−1.2*	−1.2*	−24.6	23.1	21.6
Germany	4.2*	0.2	−2.7	1.2*	−0.5*	−2.5*	−36.2	23.4	56.4
Italy		1.5*		−0.4	0.9	−0.6*	−0.2	13.0	14.3
Spain		2.4*		0.2	3.5*	0.2	33.2	7.3	5.7
Sweden	0	0	0	0	−1*	−1*	−24.2	12.2	16.2
Netherlands	0.8*	0.8*	0.5	0.5	−1.1*	−1.1*	−20.1	10.5	4.2
U.K.		−1.2*		0.3	−1.1	−2.7*	−41.1		
U.S.	−1.0*	−1.0*	−1.2*	−1.2*	−1.3*	−2.5*	−41.0	[a]42.0	[a]11.7

Source: Ferlay et al. (2010); WHO Mortality Database [http://www.encr.com.fr]; Screening data: Europe – 2004 Survey of Health, Ageing and Retirement in Europe (SHARE); Stock and Brenner (2010); U.S. – 2005 National Health Interview Survey (NHIS); American Cancer Society (2009)
Notes: Incidence estimates based on regional data for the following countries: Austria (Tyrol), Germany (Saarland), The Netherlands (Eindhoven), United Kingdom (England)
*AAPC is statistically significant (two-sided $p<0.05$)
[a]2005 data for colorectal cancer tests

remain at the forefront of developing policies for population screening (Elmore et al. 2005; Welch 2009; Jørgensen and Gøtzsche 2009; Esserman et al 2009). Greater emphasis is now placed on quantifying the overall risk-benefit profile of a screening modality in order to determine its value for population screening.

In addition, it is hard to separate the effect of screening from other factors including improved diagnosis through technological advances and development and implementation of more effective therapy (Etzioni et al. 1999; Mariotto et al. 2002; Meng et al. 2002). The recent declines in site-specific cancer mortality can only be attributed to screening if screening is followed by appropriate diagnoses, effective

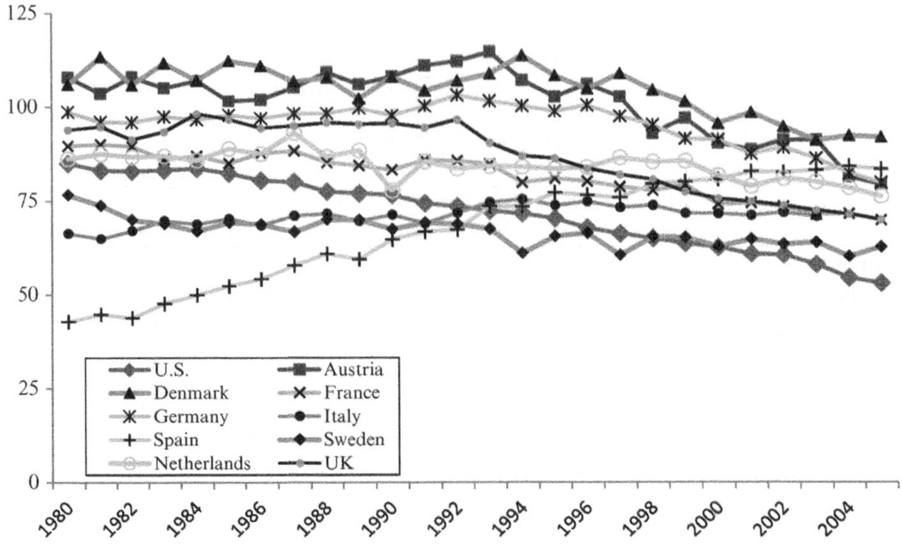

Fig. 9.10 Colorectal cancer mortality among men 50+, 1980–2005 (Source: WHO Mortality Database [http://www.encr.com.fr])

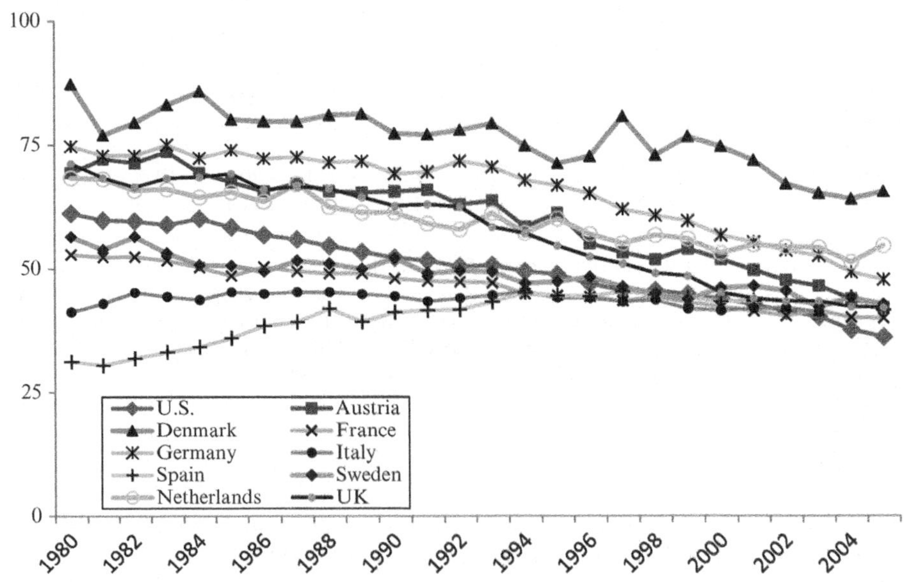

Fig. 9.11 Colorectal cancer mortality among women 50+, 1980–2005 (Source: WHO Mortality Database [http://www.encr.com.fr])

treatment, and follow-up care. The unique impact of screening on cancer mortality is difficult to establish because advances in treatment known to alter disease prognosis occurred concurrently with the widespread use of screening modalities. For example, the advent of nerve-sparing surgical techniques in the early 1980s, followed by innovations in radiotherapy and hormonal treatment, led to curative treatment options, often multimodal, for patients diagnosed with varying stages of cancers in the prostate and breast (Etzioni and Feuer 2008; Nelson et al. 2009).

Treatment patterns and access to cancer care also differ markedly across countries. Vast inequalities in resources for cancer care are reported in Europe including the number of medical oncology facilities and specialists in each country (ESMO 2006). For example, higher numbers of medical oncology facilities per million of the population are reported in Northern Europe than in the Mediterranean countries (ESMO 2006). National and regional variations in the provision of radiotherapy have also been documented (Bentzen et al. 2005). The consequence of inadequate access to radiotherapy is increased waiting times for treatment, which is likely to have detrimental effects on treatment outcomes (Rutqvist 2006).

The quality and availability of cancer prevention and treatment modalities and resulting cancer survival have been linked to macro-economic determinants, such as gross domestic product (GDP), the total public expenditure on health (TPEH), and total national expenditure on health (TNEH) (Micheli et al. 2003). European countries with high TNEH tended to have high cancer survival rates compared to countries with low TNEH. Based on this analysis, it is not surprising that cancer survival rates are among the highest in the U.S., which has the highest total health expenditure among all high-income countries (OECD 2006).

Conclusion

Countries with the highest screening prevalence have generally experienced faster declines in mortality from 1990 to 2005, while countries with lower screening prevalence have experienced increases or little change in cancer mortality in this period. The results in this study reveal that despite higher reported incidence rates for most cancers analyzed, Americans currently have among the lowest breast, prostate, and colorectal cancer mortality rates and experienced some of the fastest declines in breast, prostate, and colorectal cancer mortality rates from 1990 to 2005, compared to their European counterparts. However, this was not the case in the 1980s.

The reduction of cancer death rates over the past two decades in the U.S. and other high-income European countries among persons aged 50 years and older appears to be a persuasive argument in support of screening and early detection. The complexity of the relationship between mortality trends and screening prevalence lies within the countries in the middle. Some countries with moderate prevalence of screening have experienced significant declines in cancer-specific mortality rates comparable to those with the highest prevalence of screening.

The comparison of cancer incidence and mortality rates between regions or countries with different screening uptakes plays an important role in the current debate on the value of population screening (Etzioni and Feuer 2008; Mettlin 2000). Despite their limitations, ecological or geographical studies are useful for monitoring the effectiveness of population interventions, such as screening initiatives and programs. In the absence of conclusive findings from randomized trials, these studies help generate hypotheses about the public health benefit of cancer screening and highlight disparities in the burden of cancer across populations. Continued monitoring of incidence and mortality trends, along with prevention and treatment practices, may increase our understanding of the relationship between screening and mortality reduction.

Acknowledgments This work was supported by grant T32AG0037 from the National Institute on Aging to the University of Southern California.

References

American Cancer Society. (2009). *Cancer prevention & early detection facts & figures 2009*. Atlanta: American Cancer Society.

Andriole, G., Crawford, E., Grubb, R., Buys, S., Chia, D., Church, T., et al. (2009). Mortality results from a randomized prostate-cancer screening trial. *The New England Journal of Medicine, 360*, 1310–1319.

Anees, B., Chagpar, M. D., & McMasters, K. M. (2007). Trends in mammography and clinical breast examination: A population-based study. *Journal of Surgical Research, 140*, 214–219.

Atkin, W. (2003). Options for screening for colorectal cancer. *Scandinavian Journal of Gastroenterology, 38*(Suppl 237), 13–16.

Atkin, W. S., Edwards, R., Kralj-Hans, I., Wooldrage, K., et al. (2010). Once-only flexible sigmoidoscopy screening in prevention of colorectal cancer: A multicenter randomized controlled trial. *Lancet, 375*, 1624–1633.

Baade, P. D., Coory, M. D., & Aitken, J. F. (2004). International trends in prostate-cancer mortality: The decrease is continuing and spreading. *Cancer Causes & Control, 15*, 237–241.

Bangma, C. H., Roemeling, S., & Schroder, F. H. (2007). Overdiagnosis and overtreatment of early detected prostate cancer. *World Journal of Urology, 25*(1), 3–9.

Benson, V. S., Patnick, J., Davies, A. K., Nadel, M. R., Smith, R. A., & Atkin, W. S. (2007). Colorectal cancer screening: A comparison of 35 initiatives in 17 countries. *International Journal of Cancer, 122*, 1357–1367.

Bentzen, S. M., Heeren, G., Cottier, B., Slotman, B., Glimelius, B., Lievens, Y., & van den Bogaert, W. (2005). Towards evidence-based guidelines for radiotherapy infrastructure and staffing needs in Europe: The ESTRO QUARTS project. *Radiotherapy and Oncology, 75*(3), 355–365.

Botha, J. L., Bray, F., Sankila, R., & Parkin, D. M. (2003). Breast cancer incidence and mortality trends in 16 European countries. *European Journal of Cancer, 39*(12), 1718–1729.

Bouchardy, C., Fioretta, G., Rapiti, E., Verkooijen, H. M., Rapin, C. H., Schmidlin, F., et al. (2008). Recent trends in prostate cancer mortality show a continuous decrease in several countries. *International Journal of Cancer, 123*(2), 421–429.

Boyle, P., & Brawley, O. W. (2009). Prostate cancer: Current evidence weighs against population screening. *CA: A Cancer Journal for Clinicians, 59*(4), 220–224.

Boyle, P., & Ferlay, J. (2005a). Mortality and survival in breast and colorectal cancer. *Nature Clinical Practice Oncology, 2*, 424–425.

Boyle, P., & Ferlay, J. (2005b). Cancer incidence and mortality in Europe, 2004. *Annals of Oncology, 16*(3), 481–488.

Brawley, O. W., Knopf, K., & Merrill, R. (1998). The epidemiology of prostate cancer part I: Descriptive epidemiology. *Seminars in Urologic Oncology, 16*, 187–192.

Catalona, W. J., Smith, D. S., Ratliff, T. L., Dodds, K. M., Coplen, D. E., Yuan, J. J., et al. (1991). Measurement of prostate-specific antigen in serum as a screening test for prostate cancer. *The New England Journal of Medicine, 324*(17), 1156–1161.

Centers for Disease Control and Prevention (CDC). (2011). Colorectal cancer screening – United States, 2002, 2004, 2006, and 2008. *Morbidity and Mortality Weekly Report, 60*(Suppl), 42–46.

Chen, X., White, M. C., Peipens, L. A., & Seeff, L. C. (2008). Increase in screening for colorectal cancer in older Americans: Results from a National Survey. *Journal of American Geriatrics Society, 56*(8), 1511–1516.

Coleman, M. P., Quaresma, M., Berrino, F., Lutz, J. M., De Angelis, R., Capocaccia, R., et al. (2008). Cancer survival in five continents: A worldwide population-based study (CONCORD). *The Lancet Oncology, 9*(8), 730–756.

Collin, S. M., Martin, R. M., Metcalfe, C., Gunnell, D., Albertsen, P. C., Neal, D., et al. (2008). Prostate-cancer mortality in the USA and UK in 1975–2004: An ecological study. *The Lancet Oncology, 9*(5), 445–452.

Cookson, M. S. (2001). Prostate cancer: Screening and early detection. *Cancer Control, 8*(2), 133–140.

Crimmins, E. M., Garcia, K., & Kim, J. K. (2010). Are international differences in health similar to international differences in life expectancy? In E. Crimmins, S. Preston, & B. Cohen (Eds.), *International differences in mortality at older ages: Dimensions and sources*. Washington, D.C.: The National Academies Press.

Croswell, J. M., Kramer, B. S., Kreimer, A. R., Prorok, P. C., Xu, J. L., Baker, S. G., et al. (2009). Cumulative incidence of false-positive results in repeated, multimodal cancer screening. *Annals of Family Medicine, 7*(3), 212–222.

Cutler, D. M. (2008). Are we finally winning the war on cancer? *Journal of Economic Perspectives, 22*(4), 3–26.

Draisma, G., Postma, R., Schröder, F. H., van der Kwast, T. H., & de Koning, H. J. (2006). Gleason score, age and screening: Modeling dedifferentiation in prostate cancer. *International Journal of Cancer, 119*(10), 2366–2371.

Duffy, S. W., Agbaje, O., Tabar, L., Vitak, B., Bjurstam, N., Björneld, L., et al. (2005). Overdiagnosis and overtreatment of breast cancer: Estimates of overdiagnosis from two trials of mammographic screening for breast cancer. *Breast Cancer Research, 7*, 258–265.

Duffy, S. W., Lynge, E., Jonsson, H., Ayyaz, S., & Olsen, A. H. (2008). Complexities in the estimation of overdiagnosis in breast cancer screening. *British Journal of Cancer, 99*(7), 1176–1178.

Ekeberg, Ø., Skjauff, H., & Kåresen, R. (2001). Screening for breast cancer is associated with a low degree of psychological distress. *Breast, 10*(1), 20–24.

Elmore, J. G., Barton, M. B., Moceri, V. M., Polk, S., Arena, P. J., & Fletcher, S. W. (1998). Ten-year risk of false positive screening mammograms and clinical breast examinations. *The New England Journal of Medicine, 338*(16), 1089–1096.

Elmore, J. G., Armstrong, K., Lehman, C. D., & Fletcher, S. W. (2005). Screening for breast cancer. *Journal of the American Medical Association, 293*(10), 1245–1256.

Esserman, L., Shieh, Y., & Thompson, I. (2009). Rethinking screening for breast cancer and prostate cancer. *Journal of the American Medical Association, 302*(15), 1685–1692.

Etzioni, R., & Feuer, E. (2008). Studies of prostate-cancer mortality: Caution advised. *The Lancet Oncology, 9*(5), 407–409.

Etzioni, R., Legler, J. M., Feuer, E. J., et al. (1999). Cancer surveillance series; interpreting trends in prostate cancer – Part III: Quantifying the link between population prostate-specific antigen testing and recent declines in prostate cancer mortality. *Journal of the National Cancer Institute, 91*, 1033–1039.

Etzioni, R., Penson, D. F., Legler, J. M., di Tommaso, D., Boer, R., Gann, P. H., & Feuer, E. J. (2002). Overdiagnosis due to prostate-specific antigen screening: Lessons from U.S. prostate cancer incidence trends. *Journal of the National Cancer Institute, 94*(13), 981–990.

European Society of Medical Oncology (ESMO). (2006). *Medical Oncology Status in Europe Survey (MOSES): Phase II*. In R. Labianca (Ed.). Available online: http://www.esmo.org/fileadmin/media/pdf/surveys/MOSES.pdf

Farrow, D. C., Samet, J. M., & Hunt, W. C. (1996). Regional variation in survival following the diagnosis of cancer. *Journal of Clinical Epidemiology, 49*(8), 843–847.

Ferlay, J., Bray, F., Pisani, P., & Parkin, D. M. (2004). *GLOBOCAN 2002: Cancer incidence, mortality and prevalence worldwide* (IARC Cancer Base No. 5 Version 2.0). Lyon: IARC Press. Available from: http://www-dep.iarc.fr

Ferlay, J., Parkin, D. M., Curado, M. P., Bray, F., Edwards, B., Shin, H.R., & Forman, D. (2010). *Cancer incidence in five continents* (Vols. I–IX: IARC CancerBase No. 9 [Internet]). Lyon: International Agency for Research on Cancer. Available from: http://ci5.iarc.fr

Galit, W., Green, M. S., & Lital, K. B. (2007). Routine screening mammography in women older than 74 years: A review of the available data. *Maturitas, 57*(2), 109–119.

Gatta, G., Capocaccia, R., Sant, M., et al. (2002). Understanding variations in colorectal cancer survival in Europe: A EUROCARE high-resolution study. *Gut, 47*, 533–538.

Glass, A. G., Lacey, J. V., Carreon, D., & Hoover, R. N. (2007). Breast cancer incidence, 1980–2006: Combined roles of menopausal hormone therapy, screening mammography, and estrogen receptor status. *Journal of the National Cancer Institute, 99*, 1152–1161.

Goldberg, C. (2010, September 10). DIY mammogram math: 1 in 20,000 odds. *CommonHealth*. Available online: http://commonhealth.wbur.org/2010/09/diy-mammogram-math-1-in-20000-odds/

Hakama, M., Coleman, M., Alexe, D. M., & Auvinen, A. (2008). Cancer screening. In M. O. Coleman, D. M. Alexe, T. Albreht, & M. McKee (Eds.), *Responding to the challenge of cancer in Europe*. Slovenia: Institute of Public Health of the Republic of Slovenia.

Hardcastle, J. D., Chamberlain, J. O., Robinson, M. H., Moss, S. M., Amar, S. S., Balfour, T. W., et al. (1996). Randomized controlled trial of faecal-occult-blood screening for colorectal cancer. *Lancet, 348*(9040), 1472–1477.

Harewood, G. C., & Lieberman, D. A. (2004). Colonoscopy practice patterns since introduction of Medicare coverage for average-risk screening. *Clinical Gastroenterology and Hepatology, 2*, 72–77.

Harlan, L. C., Abrams, J., Warren, J. L., et al. (2002). Adjuvant therapy for breast cancer: Practice patterns of community physicians. *Journal of Clinical Oncology, 20*, 1809–1817.

Hass, G. P., Delongchamps, N. B., Jones, R. F., Chandan, V., Serio, A. M., Vickers, A. J., et al. (2007). Needle biopsies on autopsy prostates: Sensitivities of cancer detection based on true prevalence. *Journal of the National Cancer Institute, 99*, 1484–1489.

Hawkes, E. A., & Cunningham, D. (2010). Flexible sigmoidoscopy-valuable in colorectal cancer. *Nature Reviews Clinical Oncology, 7*(9), 488–490.

Holmström, B., Johansson, M., Bergh, A., Stenman, U. H., Hallmans, G., & Stattin, P. (2009). Prostate specific antigen for early detection of prostate cancer: Longitudinal study. *British Medical Journal, 339*, b3537.

Horner, M. J., Ries, L. A., Krapcho, M., et al. (Eds.). (2009). *SEER cancer statistics review, 1975–2006*. Bethesda: National Cancer Institute. Available online at: seer.cancer.gov/csr/1975_2006/

Horninger, W., Reissigl, A., Rogatsch, H., Volgger, H., Studen, M., Klocker, H., & Bartsch, G. (1999). Prostate cancer screening in Tyrol, Austria: Experience and results. *European Urology, 35*(5–6), 523–538.

Howard, D. H., Richardson, L. C., & Thorpe, K. E. (2009). Cancer screening and age in the United States and Europe. *Health Affairs, 28*(6), 1838–1847.

Hsing, A. W., Tsao, L., & Deves, S. S. (2000). International trends and patterns of prostate cancer incidence and mortality. *International Journal of Cancer (Pred. Oncol.), 85*, 60–67.

Humphrey, L. L., Helfand, M., Chan, B. K., & Woolf, S. H. (2002). Breast cancer screening: A summary of the evidence for the U.S. Preventive Services Task Force. *Annals of Internal Medicine, 137*(5(1)), 347–360.

Jatoi, I., & Miller, A. B. (2003). Why is breast-cancer mortality declining? *The Lancet Oncology, 4*(4), 251–254.

Jemal, A., Ward, E., & Thun, M. (2010). Declining death rates reflect progress against cancer. *PLoS One, 5*(3), e9584.

Joinpoint Regression Program, Version 3.3. (2008, April). *Statistical methodology and applications branch*, Surveillance Research Program. Bethesda: National Cancer Institute.

Jørgensen, K. J., & Gøtzsche, P. C. (2009). Overdiagnosis in publicly organized mammography screening programmes: Systematic review of incidence trends. *British Medical Journal, 339*, b2587.

Jørgensen, O. D., Kronborg, O., & Fenger, C. (2002). A randomized study of screening for colorectal cancer using faecal occult blood testing: Results after 13 years and seven biennial screening rounds. *Gut, 50*, 29–32.

Jørgensen, K. J., Zahl, P. H., & Gøtzsche, P. C. (2009). Overdiagnosis in organized mammography screening in Denmark. A comparative study. *BMC Women's Health, 9*, 36.

Karim-Kos, H. E., de Vries, E., Soerjomataram, I., Lemmens, V., Siesling, S., & Coebergh, J. W. (2008). Recent trends of cancer in Europe: A combined approach of incidence, survival and mortality of 17 cancer sites since the 1990s. *European Journal of Cancer, 44*, 1345–1389.

Kronborg, O., Fenger, C., Olsen, J., Jørgensen, O. D., & Søndergaard, O. (1996). Randomised study of screening for colorectal cancer with faecal-occult-blood test. *Lancet, 348*(9040), 1467–1471.

La Rochelle, J., & Amling, C. L. (2010). Prostate cancer screening: What we have learned from the PLCO and ERSPC trials. *Current Urology Reports, 11*(3), 198–201.

La Vecchia, C., Bosetti, C., Lucchini, F., Bertuccio, E., Negri, E., Boyle, P., & Levi, F. (2010). Cancer mortality in Europe, 2000–2004, and an overview of trends since 1975. *Annals of Oncology, 21*, 1323–1360.

Lampic, C., Thurfjell, E., Bergh, J., & Sjödén, P. O. (2001). Short- and long-term anxiety and depression in women recalled after breast cancer screening. *European Journal of Cancer, 37*(4), 463–469.

Lerman, C., Trock, B., Rimer, B. K., Boyce, A., Jepson, C., & Engstrom, P. F. (1991). Psychological and behavioral implications of abnormal mammograms. *Annals of Internal Medicine, 114*(8), 657–661.

Levi, F., Bosetti, C., Lucchini, F., Negri, E., & La Vecchia, C. (2005). Monitoring the decrease in breast cancer mortality in Europe. *European Journal of Cancer Prevention, 14*(6), 497–502.

Loeve, F., Brown, M. L., Boer, R., van Ballegooijen, M., van Oortmarssen, G. J., & Habbema, J. D. (2000). Endoscopic colorectal cancer screening: A cost-saving analysis. *Journal of the National Cancer Institute, 92*(7), 557–563.

Mandel, J. S., Church, T. R., Ederer, F., & Bond, J. H. (1999). Colorectal cancer mortality: Effectiveness of biennial screening for fecal occult blood. *Journal of the National Cancer Institute, 91*(5), 434–437.

Mariotto, A., Feuer, E., Harlan, L., et al. (2002). Trends in use of adjuvant multi-agent chemotherapy and tamoxifen for breast cancer in the United States: 1975–1999. *Journal of the National Cancer Institute, 94*, 1626–1634.

McCarthy, E. P., Burns, R. B., Freund, K. M., et al. (2000). Mammography use, breast cancer stage at diagnosis, and survival among older women. *Journal of American Geriatrics Society, 48*, 1226–1233.

McPherson, C. P., Swenson, K. K., & Lee, M. W. (2002). The effects of mammographic detection and comorbidity on the survival of older women with breast cancer. *Journal of American Geriatrics Society, 50*, 1061–1068.

Meissner, H. I., Breen, N., Klabunde, C. N., & Vernon, S. W. (2006). Patterns of colorectal cancer screening uptake among men and women in the United States. *Cancer Epidemiology, Biomarkers & Prevention, 15*(2), 389–394.

Meng, M. V., Grossfeld, G. D., Sadetsky, N., et al. (2002). Contemporary patterns of androgen deprivation therapy use for newly diagnosed prostate cancer. *Urology, 60*(3 Supp 1), 7–11.

Mettlin, C. (2000). Impact of screening on prostate cancer rates and trends. *Microscopy Research and Technique, 51*, 415–418.

Micheli, A., Coebergh, J. W., Mugno, E., et al. (2003). European health systems and cancer care. *Annals of Oncology, 14*(5), 41–60.

Miles, A., Cockburn, J., Smith, R. A., & Wardle, J. (2004). A perspective from countries using organized screening programs. *Cancer, 101*(5 Suppl), 1201–1213.

Nelson, H. D., Tyne, K., Bougatsos, C., Chan, B. K., & Humphrey, L. (2009). Screening for breast cancer: An update for the U.S. Preventative Services Task Force. *Annals of Internal Medicine, 151*(10), 727–737.

NHS Screening Programmes. (2006). *Breast screening: Over 70? You are still entitled to breast screening*. London: Department of Health.

Nystrom, L., Andersson, I., Bjurstam, N., Frisell, J., Nordenskjold, B., & Rutqvist, L. E. (2002). Long-term effects of mammography screening: Updated overview of the Swedish randomized trials. *Lancet, 359*, 909–919.

Olsen, A. H., Agbaje, O. F., Myles, J. P., Lynge, E., & Duffy, S. W. (2006). Overdiagnosis, sojourn time, and sensitivity in the Copenhagen mammography screening program. *The Breast Journal, 12*, 338–342.

Organization for Economic Co-operation and Development. (2006). *OECD health data 2006*, from the OECD Internet subscription database. OECD 2006. Available from: http://www.oecd.org/health/healthdata

Paci, E., & Duffy, S. (2005). Overdiagnosis and overtreatment of breast cancer: Overdiagnosis and overtreatment in service screening. *Breast Cancer Research, 7*(6), 266–270.

Paci, E., Warwick, J., Falini, P., & Duffy, S. W. (2004). Overdiagnosis in screening: Is the increase in breast cancer incidence rates a cause for concern? *Journal of Medical Screening, 11*(1), 23–27.

Paci, E., Miccinesi, G., Puliti, D., Baldazzi, P., De Lisi, V., Falcini, F., et al. (2006). Estimate of overdiagnosis of breast cancer due to mammography after adjustment for lead time. A service screening study in Italy. *Breast Cancer Research, 8*, R68.

Parkin, D. M., Bray, F. I., & Devesa, S. S. (2001). Cancer burden in the year 2000: The global picture. *European Journal of Cancer, 37*(suppl 8), S4–S66.

Patnick, J. (Ed.). (2009). *NHS breast screening programme annual review 2009*. NHS Cancer Screening Programs, 2009. Available from: http://www.camcerscreening.nhs.uk

Pinsky, P. F., Blacka, A., Kramer, B. S., Miller, A., Prorok, P. C., & Berg, C. (2010). Assessing contamination and compliance in the prostate component of the Prostate, Lung, Colorectal, and Ovarian (PLCO) cancer screening trial. *Clinical Trials, 7*(4), 303–311.

Pito, R., Boreham, J., Clarke, M., Davies, C., & Beral, V. (2000). UK and USA breast cancer Deaths down 25% in year 2000 at ages 20–69 years. *Lancet, 355*, 1822.

Postma, R., van Leenders, A. G., Roobol, M. J., Schröder, F. H., & van der Kwast, T. H. (2006). Tumour features in the control and screening arm of a randomized trial of prostate cancer. *European Urology, 50*(1), 70–75.

Potosky, A. L., Legler, J., Albertsen, P. C., et al. (2000). Health outcomes after prostatectomy or radiotherapy for prostate cancer: Results from the Prostate Cancer Outcomes Study. *Journal of the National Cancer Institute, 92*(19), 1582–1592.

Pox, C., Schmiegel, W., & Classen, M. (2007). Current status of screening colonoscopy in Europe and in the United States. *Endoscopy, 39*, 168–173.

Preston, S. H. (2009). Prostate-cancer screening. *The New England Journal of Medicine, 361*(2), 202–203.

Preston, S. H., & Ho, J. (2010). Low life expectancy in the United States: Is the health care system at fault? In E. Crimmins, S. Preston, & B. Cohen (Eds.), *International differences in mortality at older ages: Dimensions and sources* (p. 2010). Washington, D.C.: The National Academies Press.

Prorok, P. C., Connor, R. J., & Baker, S. G. (1990). Statistical considerations in cancer screening programs. *The Urologic Clinics of North America, 17*(4), 699–708.

Quanstrum, K. H., & Hayward, R. A. (2010). Lessons from mammography wars. *The New England Journal of Medicine, 363*(11), 1076–1079.

Quinn, M., & Babb, P. (2002). Patterns and trends in prostate cancer incidence, survival, prevalence and mortality. Part I: International comparisons. *BJU International, 90*(2), 162–173.

Quinn, M. J., d'Onofrio, A., Møller, B., Black, R., Martinez-Garcia, C., Møller, H., et al. (2003). Cancer mortality trends in the EU and acceding countries up to 2015. *Annals of Oncology, 14*, 1148–1152.

Raaijmakers, R., Kirkels, W. J., Roobol, M. J., Wildhagen, M. F., & Schrder, F. H. (2002). Complication rates and risk factors of 5802 transrectal ultrasound-guided sextant biopsies of the prostate within a population-based screening program. *Urology, 60*(5), 826–830.

Rabeneck, L., Paszat, L. F., Saskin, R., & Stukel, T. A. (2010). Association between colonoscopy rates and colorectal cancer mortality. *The American Journal of Gastroenterology, 105*(7), 1627–1632.

Rietbergen, J. B., Hoedemaeker, R. H., Kruger, A. E., Kirkels, W. J., & Schroeder, F. H. (1999). The changing pattern of prostate cancer at the time of diagnosis: Characteristics of screen detected prostate cancer in a population based screening study. *The Journal of Urology, 161*, 1192–1198.

Rohde, V., Weidner, W., & Katalinic, A. (2009). Decrease in prostate cancer incidence and mortality in Germany – Effects of opportunistic PSA screening or more? *Urologia Internationalis, 83*, 134–140.

Rutqvist, L. E. (2006). Waiting times for cancer patients-a "slippery slope" in oncology. *Acta Oncologica, 45*, 121–123.

Sakr, W. A., Grignon, D. J., Crissman, J. D., Heilbrun, L. K., Cassin, B. J., Pontes, J. J., & Haas, G. P. (1994). High grade prostatic intraepithelial neoplasia (HGPIN) and prostatic Adenocarcinoma between the ages of 20–69: An autopsy study of 249 cases. *In Vivo, 8*(3), 439–443.

Sanchez-Chapado, M., Olmedilla, G., Cabeza, M., Donat, E., & Ruiz, A. (2003). Prevalence of prostate cancer and prostatic intraepithelial neoplasia in Caucasian Mediterranean males: An autopsy study. *The Prostate, 54*, 238–247.

Sant, M. (2001). Differences in stage and therapy for breast cancer across Europe. *International Journal of Cancer, 93*, 894–901.

Schroder, F., Hugosson, J., Roobol, M., Tammela, T., Ciatto, S., Nelen, V., et al. (2009). Screening and prostate-cancer mortality in a randomized European study. *The New England Journal of Medicine, 360*, 1320–1328.

Segi, M. (1960). *Cancer mortality for selected sites in 24 countries (1950–57)*. Sendai: University School of Public Health.

Semiglazov, V. F., Manikhas, A. G., Moiseenko, V. M., Protsenko, S. A., Kharikova, R. S., Seleznev, I. K., et al. (2003). Results of a prospective randomized investigation [Russia (St.Petersburg)/WHO] to evaluate the significance of self-examination for the early detection of breast cancer. *Voprosy Onkologii, 49*(4), 434–441.

Shapiro, S. (1994). Screening: Assessment of current studies. *Cancer, 74*(1Suppl), 231–238.

Shapiro, S., Coleman, E. A., Broeders, M., Codd, M., de Koning, H., Fracheboud, J., et al. (1998). Breast cancer screening programmes in 22 countries: Current policies, administration and guidelines. *International Journal of Epidemiology, 27*, 735–742.

Soos, G., Tsakiris, I., Szanto, J., Turzo, C., Hass, P. G., & Dezso, B. (2005). The prevalence of prostate carcinoma and its precursor in Hungary: An autopsy study. *European Journal of Urology, 48*, 739–744.

Stefanick, M. L. (2005). Estrogens and progestins: Background and history, trends in use, and guidelines and regines approved by the US food and drug administration. *American Journal of Medicine, 118*(12B), 64–73.

Stephenson, R. A. (1998). Population-based prostate cancer trends in the PSA era: Data from the Surveillance, Epidemiology, and the End Results (SEER) program. *Monographs in Urology, 19*, 3–19.

Stock, C., & Brenner, H. (2010). Utilization of lower gastrointestinal endoscopy and fecal occult blood test in 11 European countries: Evidence from the Survey of Health, Aging and Retirement in Europe (SHARE). *Endoscopy, 42*(7), 546–556.

Stock, C., Haug, U., & Brenner, H. (2010). Population-based prevalence estimates of history of colonoscopy or sigmoidoscopy: Review and analysis of recent trends. *Gastrointestinal Endoscopy, 71*(2), 366–381.

Tabar, L., Vitak, B., Yen, M. F., Chen, H. H., Smith, R. A., & Duffy, S. W. (2004). Number needed to screen: Lives saved over 20 years of follow-up in mammographic screening. *Journal of Medical Screening, 11*(3), 126–129.

Thomas, D. B., Gao, D. L., Self, S. G., Allison, C. J., Tao, Y., Mahloch, J., et al. (1997). Randomized trial of breast self-examination in Shanghai: Methodology and preliminary results. *Journal of the National Cancer Institute, 89*, 355–365.

Thompson, I. M., Pauler, D. K., Goodman, P. J., Tangen, C. M., Lucia, M. S., Parnes, H. L., et al. (2004). Prevalence of prostate cancer among men with a prostate-specific antigen level< or = 4.0 ng per milliliter. *The New England Journal of Medicine, 350*(22), 2239–2246.

Tyczynski, J. E., Plesko, I., Aareleid, T., Primic-Zakelj, M., Dalmas, M., Kurtinaitis, J., et al. (2004). Breast cancer mortality patterns and time trends in 10 new EU member states: Mortality declining in young women, but still increasing in the elderly. *International Journal of Cancer, 112*(6), 1056–1064.

U.S. Preventative Services Task Force. (2008a). Screening for colorectal cancer: U.S. Preventative Services Task Force recommendation statement. *Annals of Internal Medicine, 149*(9), 627–637.

U.S. Preventative Services Task Force. (2008b). Screening for prostate cancer: U.S. Preventative Services Task Force recommendation statement. *Annals of Internal Medicine, 149*(3), 185–191.

U.S. Preventative Services Task Force. (2009). Screening for breast cancer: U.S. Preventative Services Task Force recommendation statement. *Annals of Internal Medicine, 151*(10), 716–726.

van Dijck, J. A., Holland, R., Verbeek, A. L., Hendriks, J. H., & Mravunac, M. (1994). Efficacy of mammographic screening of the elderly: A case referent study in the Nijmegen program in The Netherlands. *Journal of the National Cancer Institute, 86*, 934–938.

Verdecchia, A., Francisci, S., Brenner, H., Gatta, G., Micheli, A., Mangone, L., & Kunkler, I. (2007). Recent cancer survival in Europe: A 2000–02 period analysis of EUROCARE-4 data. *The Lancet Oncology, 8*, 784–796.

von Karsa, L., Anttila, A., Ronco, G., Ponti, A., Malila, N., Arbyn, M., et al. (2008). *Cancer Screening in the European Union: Report on the implementation of the Council Recommendation on cancer screening*. Luxembourg: European Commission.

Walter, S. D., & Stitt, L. W. (1987). Evaluating the survival of cancer cases detected by screening. *Statistics in Medicine, 6*, 885–900.

Ward, E. M., Thun, M. J., Hannan, L. M., & Jemal, A. (2006). Interpreting cancer trends. *Annals of the New York Academy of Sciences, 1076*, 29–53.

Warner, E., Hill, K., Causer, P., Plewes, D., Jong, R., Yaffe, M., et al. (2011). Prospective study of breast cancer incidence in women with a BRCA1 or BRCA2 mutation under surveillance with and without magnetic resonance imaging. *Journal of Clinical Oncology, 29*(13), 1664–1669.

Welch, G. H. (2009). Overdiagnosis and mammography screening. *British Medical Journal, 339*, b1425.

Welch, H. G., & Black, W. C. (2010). Overdiagnosis in cancer. *Journal of the National Cancer Institute, 102*(9), 605–613.

Whitlock, E. P., Lin, J. S., Liles, E., Beil, T. L., & Fu, R. (2008). Screening for colorectal cancer: A targeted, updated systematic review for the U.S. Preventative Services Task Force. *Annals of Internal Medicine, 149*, 638–658.

Wilt, T. J., MacDonald, R., Rutks, I., Shamliyan, T. A., Taylor, B. C., & Kane, R. L. (2008). Systematic review: Comparative effectiveness and harms of treatments for clinically localized prostate cancer. *Annals of Internal Medicine, 148*(6), 435–448.

Wingo, P. A., Ries, L. A., Rosenberg, H. M., et al. (1998). Cancer incidence and mortality, 1973–1995: A report card for the U.S. *Cancer, 82*, 1197–1207.

World Health Organization, mortality database. http://www.who.int/whosis/whosis/

Zackrisson, S., Andersson, I., Janzon, L., Manjer, J., & Garne, J. P. (2006). Rate of overdiagnosis of breast cancer 15 years after end of Malmö mammographic screening trial: Follow-up study. *British Medical Journal, 332*, 689–692.

Zavoral, M., Suchanek, S., Zavada, Z., Dusek, L., Muzik, J., Seifert, B., & Fric, P. (2009). Colorectal cancer screening in Europe. *World Journal of Gastroenterology, 15*(47), 5907–5915.

Part III
Maternal Health and Morbidity

Chapter 10
Prevalence and Correlates of Obstetric Morbidity in India

Pandurang Sontakke and R.S. Reshmi

Introduction

Women's health, particularly reproductive health and maternal health, is a major issue and it has direct implication to maternal morbidity and mortality. Maternal and child health care is one of the eight basic components of primary health care in the declaration of Alma Ata. The *International Conference on Population and Development* (1994) also reiterated the importance of women's health and reproductive health for overall development. Women's health is not only linked to biological factors, but more linked to socio-economic and cultural factors which exist in the society. In many of the societies women are disadvantaged by discrimination rooted in socio-cultural factors and which affect their health (WHO 2011). The issues related to reproductive and sexual health is not much spoken and speaking about is considered as taboo. Consequently women are reluctant to seek treatment for their health problems. Women's lack of information and knowledge of health issues and the inability to recognize symptoms of disease also exacerbate the health problem (WHO 2007).

Pregnancy is one of the important events in woman's life, but in many times it can become dangerous for her life. Pregnancy is a risky event in India and other developing countries because of the lack of medical care and ignorance concerning women's health. Pregnant women experience severe maternal morbidity from direct obstetric causes. Reproductive morbidity refers to the morbidity or dysfunction of the reproductive tract, or any morbidity, which is a consequence of reproductive behaviour including pregnancy, abortion, childbirth, or sexual behavior. Reproductive

P. Sontakke, Ph.D. Scholar (✉)
Department of Research and Development, Tata Institute of Social Sciences
(Deemed University), Mumbai 400088, India
e-mail: pandurang.sontakke@gmail.com

R.S. Reshmi, Ph.D.
Assistant Professor, Institute of Health Management Research, Bangalore 560105, India
e-mail: srreshmi@gmail.com

N. Hoque et al. (eds.), *Applied Demography and Public Health*,
Applied Demography Series 3, DOI 10.1007/978-94-007-6140-7_10,
© Springer Science+Business Media Dordrecht 2013

morbidity includes obstetric morbidity and it refers to ill health in relation to pregnancy and child birth. Obstetric morbidity is one of the major causes for maternal death. Obstetric morbidity is defined as "morbidity in a woman who has been pregnant (regardless of site or duration of the pregnancy) resulting from any cause related to or aggravate by the pregnancy or its management but not from accidental or incidental causes" (WHO 1989).

Women suffer from reproductive morbidity like menstrual disorders, lower abdominal pain, burning sensation during urination, genital itching, vaginal discharge and even painful sex. There are social and medical causes associated with pregnancy complications, such as delay in decisions to seek care and delay in accessing and receiving care. The major reasons for lack of health care seeking behaviour among women are lack of knowledge, economic hardship, shyness to expose to doctor, moreover inadequate service facilities such as 'no female doctor available in the hospital' (Rahman and Shahidullah 2005). Other social causes are inequality in providing proper nutrition, education, and medical treatment. Malnutrition, infection, early and repeated child bearing, and high fertility also play an important role in poor maternal health condition in India. Lack of access to health care along with the poor quality of health care services and its responsiveness to women's need make Indian women more vulnerable to maternal morbidity. Thus, maternal morbidity and reproductive morbidity in general, is an outcome not just of biological factors but of women's poverty, powerlessness, and lack of control over the resources as well (Ramasubban and Jejeebhoy 2000).

The lifetime risk of maternal death is commonly used to measure the obstetric risk in women (Chaurasia 2006). Among the biomedical causes of maternal deaths, more than 70% of the deaths are from direct obstetric complications. In 2005, almost 536,000 women worldwide died from pregnancy complications, and the majority of them were from the developing countries. More than half of the maternal deaths (270,000) occurred in the sub-Saharan Africa region alone, followed by South Asia (188,000). Thus, sub-Saharan Africa and South Asia accounted for 86% of global maternal deaths (World Health Organization 2005). Around one-fifth of the births worldwide and one-fourth of maternal deaths are occurring in India (Ramasubban and Jejeebhoy 2000). Maternal mortality as well as risk of maternal death in central India is well above the national average. The risk of death associated with the complications of pregnancy and delivery is relatively high in central India, indicating that this part of the country has the maximum burden of reproduction-related morbidity and mortality of women. This problem strongly arises not only from economic but also from social and cultural factors, as well as inadequate and under-utilization of health services (Chaurasia 2006). Thus, there is a relation between maternal mortality and obstetric morbidity.

Obstetric morbidity has a negative effect on women's lives; for example women may feel discomfort because of physical symptoms; they may experience social isolation and negative psychological effects; and they may be unable to support themselves economically, be compelled to live separately from family members because of the smell, or be abandoned or divorced by their husbands (Turan et al. 2007). Thus, there is a need for community mobilization, education on safe motherhood, counseling follow up, proper health intervention, increasing access to emergency obstetric care, effective health management and social services for reduction of obstetric morbidity (Cham et al. 2007).

Literature Review

Many studies have been done on reproductive morbidity, including obstetric, gynaecological, and contraceptive morbidity among women in India.

Based on the available literature on maternal morbidity, Narayan (2000) finds that women in rural areas, less educated women, and women from a lower economic status might experience more problems than others. The study further indicates that the perception of women and their relatives regarding obstetric morbidity, low self-esteem, and embarrassment or feelings of guilt are some social barriers to utilization of services for obstetric morbidity.

Jain and Parsuraman (2002) indicate that Madhya Pradesh and Bihar are the states with the highest percentage of obstetric morbidity in the country. A large proportion of women in these states experience almost of all types of complications in these states. The extent of obstetric complications increases with women's age and birth order and decreases with increase in standard of living and education.

Another study by Bansod (2002) examines the association between socioeconomic and demographic variables and the prevalence of contraceptive morbidity in Maharashtra. According to this study, contraceptive morbidity is high among the women belong to scheduled castes (SC), women having low standards of living, non-literate women, and rural women.

In Jharkhand four out of every five scheduled tribes (ST) women suffer from at least one type of obstetric morbidity (Kumar 2004). Among those who suffer from all types of reproductive morbidity, the percentage of obstetric morbidity is found to be high

Sahu (2004) reveals that women in the younger age group, better-educated women, urban women, and women with a higher standard of living have more obstetric morbidity in Orissa. This study also shows significant association between child bearing and obstetric morbidity.

A study based on currently married women in south India (Reshmi and Unisa 2006) reveals that the prevalence of obstetric morbidity is high in Kerala and Andhra Pradesh. The study further shows that treatment-seeking behaviour is low in Andhra Pradesh.

One-third of the women in Karnatka reported symptoms of reproductive morbidity (Bhatia and Cleland 1995). Lack of education and economic status were significant factors affecting the women's health. In another study conducted in Karnataka based on 3,600 mothers with at least one pre-school age child, Bhatia and Cleland (1997) find that approximately two-fifths of the respondents reported at least one morbid condition associated with their last pregnancy. About one-fifth reported at least one problem during the antenatal period, like swelling of hands and face, fits and convulsions, hypertension, etc. Nearly, 8% experienced a problem during delivery, and a little more than one-fourth of them indicated problems during the post-partum period. There is a high percentage of perceived obstetric morbidity in rural Karnataka (Ramakrishna et al. 2000). The factors such as lack of information, time, family support, and resources, poor quality and inadequate services, access to care, transportation issues, and traditional beliefs and practices result in delays in seeking care and in inappropriate use of services. High education, urban residence, high age, and parity have a positive effect on utilization of services. Low household income and women's attitude about services are barriers to use of local health services.

Garg et al. (2001) show that the lack of personal hygiene and abortions are major causes for reproductive health problems. The proportion of women who sought treatment for reproductive health problems was quite low in the study area. The study suggests the need for implementation of more strategic interventions.

Another study (Bang et al. 1989) finds that there is high prevalence of gynaecological diseases as well as high prevalence of anaemia and vitamin 'A' deficiency associated with poor economic status. Also, there are very low levels of treatment due lack of care, but a high percentage of women are aware of their problems.

In Tamil Nadu, the gynaecological morbidity is high among rural women, and the majority of women suffer from one or more gynaecological morbidity. The study highlights an urgent need for suitable health education and awareness about reproductive diseases in both genders (Santhya and Dasvarma 1996).

A study among women in a Mumbai slum (Parikh et al. 1980) finds that women having high income are more likely to report their problems as compared to their counterparts. Similarly, workingwomen are more likely to report their problems than non-working women. The results from this study indicate that neither women's education levels nor their sanitary conditions are related to gynaecological morbidity.

Need for the Study

In India every year, large numbers of women suffer obstetric problems. However, the severity of the problem is still unknown. According to NFHS-3, a considerable proportion of women were suffering from pregnancy and post delivery complications (International Institute for Population Sciences 2007). Although a number of studies have been conducted in India on reproductive morbidity, studies focused on obstetric morbidity and its associated factors are meagre. In addition, most of the studies are based on clinical settings and provide information only on biomedical causes. In India, a large proportion of women do not go to health facilities for their problems. Thus, in most of the cases, the true magnitude of the problem may not be reflected. In this context, the present paper tries to examine and compare the factors associated with obstetric morbidity in India and its states.

Objectives

The objectives of the present study are:

1. To study the levels of obstetric morbidity in the India and its states.
2. To examine the relationship of socioeconomic and demographic factors with obstetric morbidity.

Data and Methodology

The present paper is based on data from the National Family Health Survey – 3 (NFHS-3) conducted in 2005–2006. The study covers 124,385 women in India in the age group of 15–49 years. The present study focuses on currently married women having at least one birth during the 5 years preceding the survey in the four selected states.

NFHS-3 collected information from women on specific problems they had during their pregnancies. For the most recent birth in the 5 year preceding the survey, the mothers were asked whether at any time during the pregnancy they experienced any of the following problems: difficulty with vision during the day light, night blindness, convulsion (not from fever), swelling of legs, body, or face, excessive fatigue, or vaginal bleeding. Every woman who had a birth in the 5 years preceding the survey was asked if she had massive vaginal bleeding or a very high fever – both symptoms of possible post partum complications – at any time during the 2 months after birth of her most recent child. The variables such as 'complications during the pregnancy' and 'post partum complications' were computed separately using the above-mentioned variables. Another variable, 'any obstetric morbidity,' was computed by clubbing the variables 'complications during the pregnancy' and 'post partum complications'.

Mean number of obstetric morbidity was calculated for all women who experienced pregnancy and delivery. The mean value was classified according to states and socioeconomic and demographic characteristics. In order to understand the effect of socioeconomic and demographic characteristics on obstetric morbidity, a logistic regression analysis was carried out. The dependent variable was categorical and dichotomous in nature with two categories: no obstetric morbidity = 0 and any obstetric morbidity = 1.

Results

Type of Obstetric Morbidity

Women reported different types of pregnancy related problems such as excessive fatigue (48%), swelling of leg, body or face (25%), convulsions not from fever (10%), night blindness (9%), difficulty with daylight vision (6%), and vaginal bleeding (4%). More than one tenth of the women reported very high fever and massive vaginal bleeding as post delivery problems. About 62% of the currently married women reported any of the obstetric complication during their pregnancy and childbirth. While more than half of the women reported any of the pregnancy related problems, only one fifth of the women reported any post delivery complications (Table 10.1).

Table 10.1 Distribution of obstetric complication among currently married women in India

Obstetric complications	Percentage	Number*
Pregnancy related problems		
Difficulty with daylight vision	6.3	2,450
Night blindness	8.8	3,449
Convulsions not from fever	10.3	4,009
Leg, body or face swelling	25.1	9,772
Excessive fatigue	47.8	18,643
Vaginal bleeding	4.4	1,714
Any pregnancy complication	**57.4**	**22,317**
Post delivery problems		
Massive vaginal bleeding	12.4	4,825
Very high fever	13.5	5,267
Any post delivery complication	**21.0**	**8,147**
Any obstetric complications	**62.0**	**24,033**

Note: (1) *Number indicates the total number of women who reported a particular obstetric complication
(2) Any obstetric complication was calculated out of 38,745 women who were exposed to any of the obstetric problems

State Variation in Obstetric Morbidity

India is a country comprising 29 states and six union territories and the states vary significantly in terms of geographical area, culture, population size, population health, demographic, and socio-economic characteristics. Therefore, it is important to understand the variation in the level of obstetric morbidity among women in various states of India.

Table 10.2 gives information about the percent distribution of obstetric morbidity among currently married women by states of India. It is evident from the table that there was significant state wise variation in the proportion of women suffering from any pregnancy complications, any post delivery complications and any obstetric complications. For instance, any pregnancy related complications were highest among women in Tripura (89%) and lowest in Haryana (35%). The highest proportion of women who reported any post delivery complications was in Jharkhand (40%) and lowest in Delhi (10%). One of the developed states in western India like Maharashtra shows lower level of obstetric morbidity. In general, the proportion of women with any obstetric problems was relatively lower in southern states except in Kerala.

Mean Number of Obstetric Morbidity

Mean number of pregnancy complications, post delivery complications and any obstetric complications among women was calculated separately for each state. Table 10.3 shows the mean number of obstetric complications among currently married women in India and its states.

Table 10.2 Percent distribution of obstetric morbidity among currently married women by states

States	Any pregnancy complications (%)	Any post delivery complications (%)	Any obstetric complications (%)	Total*
Delhi	51.6	10.3	54.0	375
Haryana	35.4	15.4	40.6	709
Himachal Pradesh	51.4	21.5	57.7	174
Jammu Kashmir	59.1	21.9	64.0	322
Punjab	61.1	31.1	67.2	780
Rajasthan	51.2	16.7	54.3	2,347
Uttaranchal	71.0	22.7	73.3	288
Chhattisgarh	54.8	15.7	59.2	849
Madhya Pradesh	61.9	24.6	65.6	2,501
Uttar Pradesh	54.9	23.5	60.7	7,577
Bihar	78.7	30.5	83.0	4,066
Jharkhand	76.3	40.3	81.2	1,251
Orissa	59.5	18.5	64.0	1,391
West Bengal	64.9	22.6	70.8	3,069
Arunachal Pradesh	69.8	25.0	72.7	43
Assam	60.1	23.1	65.0	1,058
Manipur	43.0	14.0	47.7	85
Meghalaya	61.4	13.2	61.9	113
Mizoram	68.8	12.5	68.8	32
Nagaland	52.6	12.3	55.4	57
Sikkim	68.4	15.8	70.0	19
Tripura	88.8	29.0	90.3	124
Goa	61.4	26.2	67.4	43
Gujarat	66.0	15.7	68.9	1,771
Maharashtra	41.3	11.0	44.7	3,200
Andhra Pradesh	38.5	17.9	45.9	2,276
Karnataka	40.4	14.5	45.9	1,869
Kerala	78.5	12.1	79.5	797
Tamil Nadu	49.0	12.7	51.5	1,559
Total	**57.4**	**21.0**	**62.0**	**38,745**

Note: (1) *Indicates the total number of women who are exposed to any of the obstetric complications

(2) The variation of any pregnancy complications, any post delivery complications and any obstetric complication among women by states was significant at 1% level

It is evident from the table that the average number of obstetric complications reported by women was 1.3. The mean number of pregnancy problems reported was 1.0 while the mean value of post delivery complications was 0.3. The average number of problems varied significantly by states. The mean value of any obstetric complications was highest in Jharkhand (2.2) and lowest in Haryana (0.8). Moreover, Jharkhand show the highest mean value in any pregnancy and any post delivery complications. The average number of obstetric problems was comparatively lower in south Indian states except in Kerala. Although mean value of any post

Table 10.3 Mean number of obstetric complications among currently married women in states of India

	Any pregnancy complications*		Any post delivery complications*		Any obstetric complications*	
States	Mean	Number	Mean	Number	Mean	Number
Delhi	0.8	377	0.1	378	1.0	375
Haryana	0.6	709	0.2	709	0.8	709
Himachal Pradesh	1.0	177	0.3	177	1.2	174
Jammu Kashmir	1.1	323	0.3	324	1.4	322
Punjab	1.1	781	0.4	782	1.5	780
Rajasthan	0.9	2,347	0.2	2,347	1.1	2,347
Uttaranchal	1.5	290	0.3	290	1.7	288
Chhattisgarh	1.0	849	0.2	849	1.1	849
Madhya Pradesh	1.3	2,501	0.3	2,503	1.6	2,501
Uttar Pradesh	1.0	7,597	0.3	7,601	1.3	7,577
Bihar	1.5	4,085	0.4	4,074	1.9	4,066
Jharkhand	1.7	1,260	0.6	1,258	2.2	1,251
Orissa	1.1	1,404	0.2	1,396	1.3	1,391
West Bengal	1.0	3,069	0.3	3,078	1.3	3,069
Arunachal Pradesh	1.4	43	0.3	44	1.7	43
Assam	1.1	1,069	0.3	1,074	1.4	1,058
Manipur	0.7	86	0.2	86	0.9	85
Meghalaya	1.2	114	0.2	114	1.3	113
Mizoram	1.3	32	0.1	32	1.4	32
Nagaland	0.9	57	0.2	57	1.1	57
Sikkim	1.4	19	0.2	19	1.6	19
Tripura	1.7	125	0.3	124	2.0	124
Goa	1.1	43	0.3	43	1.4	43
Gujarat	1.2	1,780	0.2	1,775	1.3	1,771
Maharashtra	0.6	3,212	0.1	3,209	0.8	3,200
Andhra Pradesh	0.6	2,282	0.2	2,277	0.8	2,276
Karnataka	0.7	1,874	0.2	1,895	0.8	1,869
Kerala	1.3	814	0.1	803	1.4	797
Tamil Nadu	0.7	1,559	0.2	1,562	0.9	1,559
Total	**1.0**	**38,875**	**0.3**	**38,879**	**1.3**	**38,745**

*Indicates the variation in mean is significant at 1% level

delivery complications was lowest (0.1) in Kerala, the mean number of pregnancy related problems were much higher (1.3) compared to other south Indian states.

The mean number of obstetric complications by socio-economic characteristics among currently married women in India is given in Table 10.4. The mean number of obstetric complications varied significantly according to socio-economic characteristics. The average number of obstetric complications was highest among women who were in the age group 40–49 years and women who have more than three children. The mean value was highest among women who were Muslims and who belong to scheduled caste, scheduled tribe, and other backward castes. Women who have no education and primary education have highest level of mean number of problems. Rural women have significantly higher (1.3) mean value as compared to urban

Table 10.4 Mean number of obstetric complications by socio-economic characteristics among currently married women in India

Characteristics	Mean	Number
Age**		
15–29	1.3	28,550
30–39	1.3	9,185
40–49	1.4	1,010
Children ever born***		
1	1.3	10,189
2	1.2	11,130
3	1.3	6,666
More than 3	1.4	10,759
Religion***		
Hindu	1.3	30,611
Muslim	1.4	6,324
Others	1.3	1,810
Caste***		
Scheduled caste	1.3	7,777
Scheduled tribe	1.3	3,568
Other backward class	1.3	15,725
Others	1.2	11,675
Education***		
No Education	1.4	18,306
Primary	1.4	5,431
Secondary and above	1.2	15,008
Place of residence***		
Urban	1.1	10,415
Rural	1.3	28,330
Standard of living***		
Low	1.5	10,981
Medium	1.3	11,890
High	1.1	11,797
Work status***		
Not working	1.3	24,328
Working in Primary sector	1.4	12,552
Professional & Service sector	1.2	1,856
Toilet facility***		
No facility at home	1.3	21,755
Facility at home	1.2	13,513
Total	**1.28**	**38,745**

***Significant at 1% level; **significant at 5% level;*significant at 10% level of significance

women (1.1). The average value decreased significantly with an increase in the standard of living. The mean number of problems was significantly higher (1.3) for women who do not have any toilet facility at home. The average number of obstetric complications was lowest (1.2) among women who were working in professional and service sector. Thus, it is clear that the mean number of obstetric complications was relatively higher among women with low socio-economic background.

Results from Logistic Regression

A multiple logistic regression analysis was performed in order to examine the effect of socioeconomic and demographic factors on obstetric morbidity. The dependent variable is dichotomous, that is 'no obstetric morbidity' =0, 'any obstetric morbidity' =1. The independent variables selected are age of the women, children ever born, religion, caste, education of women, work status, place of residence, standard of living, and sanitation facilities.

The odds ratios of the likelihood of obstetric morbidity among currently married women in India are given in Table 10.5. The factors such as children ever born, religion, caste, education of women, work status, place of residence, standard of living, and sanitation facilities show a significant effect on obstetric morbidity. Compared to women with no education, primary educated women are significantly less likely to have any obstetric complications. Rural women have significantly less likely to have any of the obstetric morbidity. The likelihood of having obstetric complications was significantly less among women who have toilet facility at home.

Conclusions

The objective of this paper was to study the levels of obstetric morbidity in the India and its states. The relationship of socio-economic and demographic factors on obstetric morbidity was also analyzed in this paper. The analysis revealed that more than 60% of the currently married women reported any of the obstetric complications during their pregnancy and childbirth. Pregnancy related problems were relatively more as compared to post delivery complications. Obstetric complications among currently married women varied significantly according to states. Further analysis revealed that on an average a currently married woman in India suffers from 1.3 obstetric complications. The mean number of obstetric complications varied significantly according to states and socio-economic characteristics. The mean number of any obstetric complications was highest in Jharkhand. In general, the situation was better among women in southern states of India except in Kerala. The average number of obstetric complications was also relatively higher in Kerala.

Logistic regression results also revealed that the factors such as children ever born, religion, caste, education of women, work status, place of residence, standard of living, and sanitation facilities show a significant effect on obstetric morbidity. Thus, it is clear that obstetric morbidity is a serious reproductive health concern in India. The proportion of women who reported any obstetric morbidity is relatively higher even in the developed states like Kerala. In addition, women in the lower socio-economic strata are still facing reproductive health problems. Therefore, policies should focus on improving the reproductive health status of women especially those who are in the weaker sections of the society.

Table 10.5 Odds ratios of the likelihood of obstetric morbidity among currently married women in India

Variables	Exp (B)
Age of women	
15–29[a]	
30–39	1.0
40–49	0.9
Children ever born	
1–3[a]	
4 & above	0.9***
Religion	
Hindu[a]	
Muslim	0.9*
Others	1.2***
Caste	
SC/ST[a]	
OBC	1.0
Others	1.03
Education of women	
No education[a]	
Primary	0.9***
Secondary & Higher	1.0
Work status	
Not working[a]	
Working	1.0
Residence	
Urban[a]	
Rural	0.8***
Standard of living	
Low[a]	
Medium	1.2***
High	1.1**
Sanitation	
No Facility at home[a]	
Facility at home	0.9***
Constant	**2.2*****

Note: Dependent variable: Obstetric Morbidity (0=No morbidity//1=Any morbidity)
***Significant at 1% level; **significant at 5% level; *significant at 10% level
[a]Reference category

References

Bang, R., Bang, A., Baitule, M., Choudhary, Y., Sarmukaddan, S., & Tale, O. (1989). Community health: High prevalence of gynecological disease in rural India women. *The Lancet, 1*(8629), 85–88.

Bansod, D. (2002). *Contraceptive morbidity and quality care in Maharashtra*. Unpublished M. Phil. Seminar Paper, IIPS, Mumbai.

Bhatia, J. C., & Cleland, J. (1995). Self reported symptoms of gynecological morbidity and their treatment in South India. *Studies in Family Planning, 26*(4), 203–216.
Bhatia, J. C., & Cleland, J. (1997). Obstetric morbidity in South India: Result from community survey. *Studies in Family Planning, 28*(3), 1507–1516.
Cham, M., Vangen, S., & Sundby, J. (2007). Maternal death in rural Gambia. *Global Public Health, 2*(4), 359–372.
Chaurasia, A. (2006). Obstetric risk and obstetric care in Central India. *Social Change, 36*(4), 48–66.
Garg, S., Meenakshi, M., Singh, M. C., & Mehara, M. (2001). Perceived reproductive morbidity and health care behavior among women in urban slum. *Health and Population; Perspectives and Issues, 24*(4), 178–188.
International Institute for Population Sciences. (2007). *National Family Health Survey – 3. (NFHS-3)*, 2005–2006. Mumbai.
Jain, R., & Parsuraman, S. (2002). Maternal morbidity and utilization of antenatal care services: A study of Madhya Pradesh and Bihar population. In T. K. Roy, M. Guruswami, & P. Arokiasamy (Eds.), *Health and development in India*. Mumbai/Jaipur: IIPS/Rawat Publication.
Kumar, B. (2004). *Reproductive morbidity among scheduled tribe women in selected districts of Jharkhand*. Unpublished M.P.S. Seminar Paper, IIPS, Mumbai.
Narayan, K. (2000). *Issues on obstetric morbidity: Finding from community based research*. Paper presented at Workshop on Reproductive Health in India: New Evidences and Issues, Pune.
Parikh, I., Taskar, V., Dharap, N., & Mulgaokar, V. (1980). *Gynecological morbidity among women in bombay slum*. Mumbai: Streehitakarni.
Rahman, M. Mizanur; and Shahidullah M. (2005). *Adolescent self reported reproductive morbidity and health care seeking behaviour in Bangladesh*. Paper prepared for 25th IUSSP International Population Conference, Tours, 18–23 July 2005. http://iussp2005.princeton.edu/download.aspx?submissionId=50506. Accessed May 25, 2011.
Ramakrishna, J., Ganpathy, S., Mathews, Z., Mahendra, S. and Kailaru, A. (2000). *Health, illness and care in the obstetric period: A perspective of women in rural Karnataka*. Paper Presented at the Workshop on Reproductive Health in India, Pune
Ramasubban, R., & Jejeebhoy, S. (2000). *Women's reproductive health in India*. New Delhi: Rawat Publications.
Reshmi, R. S., & Unisa, S. (2006). Reproductive morbidity among currently married women in South India: Evidence from NFHS II. *Journal of Family Welfare, 52*(2), 40–58.
Sahu, H. (2004). *Safe delivery and reproductive (obstetric) morbidity in Orissa: Exploring their possible relationship based on DLHS-RCH*. Unpublished M.P.S. Seminar Paper, IIPS, Mumbai.
Santhya, K. and Dasvarma, G. (1996). *Cultural and behavior factor affecting reproductive morbidity in Southern India*. Paper contributed to Informal Session 1.41: Measuring Adult (Reproductive) Morbidity in Developing Country, Tamil Nadu.
Turan, J., Jonson, K., & Polan, M. (2007). Experiences of women seeking medical care for obstetric fistula in eritrea: Implications for prevention, treatment, and social reintegration. *Global Public Health, 2*(1), 64–77.
World Health Organization (WHO). (1989). *Measuring reproductive morbidity*. Report of a Technical Working Group. Geneva 2: WHO.
World Health Organization (WHO). (2005). Maternal mortality, estimates developed by WHO, UNICEF, UNFPA and World Bank. www.who.int/reproductive-health
World Health Organization (WHO). (2007). Cross-cutting gender issues in women's health in the Eastern Mediterranean Region. http://www.emro.who.int/ghd/PDF/gender_crosscutting_issues.pdf. Accessed May 24, 2011.
World Health Organization (WHO). (2011). Health topic: Women's health. http://www.who.int/topics/womens_health/en/. Accessed May 24, 2011.

Chapter 11
Maternal Health Status and Early Childbearing: A Test of the Weathering Hypothesis

Sarah O. Meadows, Megan K. Beckett, Marc N. Elliott, and Christine Petersen

Introduction

Early childbearing, especially as an adolescent, has been labeled by one former president as the country's "most important social problem" (Clinton 1995). Conventional wisdom suggests that having a child as a teenager is detrimental for maternal well-being, especially educational attainment and labor market outcomes, but also for interpersonal outcomes, such as relationship quality with partners and exposure to intimate violence. Many studies confirm such expectations (see Hayes 1987). Empirically, teenage childbearing has been linked to lower levels of completed education (Hotz et al. 1997; Fletcher and Wolfe 2009), lower wages and earnings and generally worse labor market outcomes (Chevalier and Viitanen 2003; Klepinger et al. 1999), and lower rates of marriage and higher overall fertility (Bennett et al. 1995; Hoffman et al. 1993), although some studies have suggested the negative economic and social consequences of teen pregnancy and childbearing are not as large as once thought (Furstenberg 1991; Lawlor and Shaw 2002; Scally 2002; Rich-Edwards 2002).

Even more noteworthy than these negative consequences, however, are the race/ethnic disparities that surround teenage births. In 2007, the live birth rate per 1,000 teens aged 15–19 was 27.2 among white youths but 64.2 among African American youths and 81.7 among Hispanic youths (Hamilton et al. 2009).[1] These race/ethnic differences are also apparent among even younger teens between the ages of 10 and 14. Thus, while it is important to study early childbearing because of its potential

[1]Throughout the paper we use the terms African American and black and Latino and Hispanic interchangeably.

S.O. Meadows (✉) • M.K. Beckett • M.N. Elliott • C. Petersen
RAND Corporation, 1776 Main Street, Santa Monica, CA 90401, USA
e-mail: smeadows@rand.org

N. Hoque et al. (eds.), *Applied Demography and Public Health*,
Applied Demography Series 3, DOI 10.1007/978-94-007-6140-7_11,
© Springer Science+Business Media Dordrecht 2013

life-long negative consequences for women, it is also important to study because of its implications for the intergenerational reproduction of race/ethnic inequality and disparities in health and well-being.

Much of the research seeking to account for race/ethnic differences in teenage childbearing focuses on family-related factors, such as socioeconomic status. One explanation that has captured the attention of social scientists is the weathering hypothesis (Geronimus 1991). Weathering refers to the physical consequences of social inequality. Specifically, it states that minority women (as well as men) who live in poverty experience early physical deterioration, relative to more advantaged women, because of the biological and social processes associated with poverty and racism. The weathering hypothesis, as it pertains to teenage childbearing (Burton 1990; Geronimus 1991, 1992b, 1996, 2001), suggests that early teen pregnancy and childbearing is rational for many socioeconomically disadvantaged American women if they believe that they will likely age more quickly than other women and have shortened life spans. Early childbearing thus may represent a more normative act among certain segments of the population based on the poor health status of surrounding adults. The young women in these communities may believe that peak reproductive years should shift to earlier stages in the life course given the rapid aging they perceive.

We propose a simple yet, to date, unexplored test of the basic assumption of the weathering hypothesis at a basic ecological level: does an adolescent's mother's health status predict her odds of experiencing pregnancy and childbirth at a young age? If the weathering hypothesis is correct, we would expect that poor maternal health, as a proxy for an adolescent girl's expected health status in adulthood, and teen childbearing are positively correlated among African American and Hispanic youths, but not among white teens. Using a subsample of young women from the Panel Survey of Income Dynamics (PSID) we explore how maternal self-rated health when a young woman is age 14 is associated with her odds of experiencing a pregnancy before age 19, controlling for other individual, maternal, and family level characteristics.

Background

Race/Ethnic Differences in Health

Race/ethnic differences in health are well-documented (Dressler et al. 2005; Geronimus et al. 2001; Wong et al. 2002). For example, Geronimus and Thompson (2004) estimate that in central Harlem and the south side of Chicago, black adults are as or more likely to suffer health-induced functional limitations at age 34 as are 55-year-old whites nationwide; they also find that disability rates among 55-year-old blacks approximate those of 75-year-old whites and that only 30% of teenage African American girls and 20% of African American boys can expect to be alive and able-bodied at age 65. The corresponding figures for whites nationwide are 70 and 60%, respectively.

The weathering hypothesis has been invoked to explain such race/ethnic differences in health status. In particular, the thesis is that African Americans have higher allostatic load, or physiological responses to chronic stress (McEwen 2000) due to characteristics such as poverty, economic hardships, and racism (Geronimus et al. 2006, 2007; Williams 1999). Allostatic load is linked to a "wearing down" (or weathering) of the body's cardiovascular system and ability to fight off disease and illness (McEwen 1998). Evidence links increased stress with chronic diseases, such as hypertension, one of the major contributors to excess mortality among urban blacks (relative to whites) (Geronimus et al. 1996; Geronimus and Thompson 2004; Williams 1999; Williams and Jackson 2005).

With increasing age, the minority gap in health widens as the deleterious effect of cumulative stress exposure takes it toll (Clark and Maddox 1992; Shuey and Willson 2008). Among many minorities, disease, illness, functional limitations, and disabilities are already present by the mid 1920s and early 1930s and rates rise through the 1940s and 1950s (Geronimus et al. 2006). The weathering hypothesis suggests that it is this pervasive health uncertainty that women of childbearing and working age face that is responsible for higher birth rates at younger ages among African Americans. Or as Lancaster et al. (2008) suggest, "weathering is a formidable threat to family economies and caretaking systems" (p. xx). Chronic diseases also complicate pregnancy (e.g., hypertension and diabetes) resulting in an increased number of babies born prematurely, with low birth weight, or who will die before they reach the first year of life (Gilbert et al. 2007; Rosenberg et al. 2005). Thus, having a child early, while still healthy and physically robust, is seen as a positive life event. In the same Harlem sample mentioned above, infant mortality rates among teen mothers were roughly half of what they were for older mothers, who were still in their 1920s (Geronimus 2003).

Weathering and Early Childbearing

Geronimus (1992b, 1996) first reported the paradoxical finding that birth outcomes, such as birth weight, among teen black mothers were better than among older black mothers. For white women, the reverse was true: white women in their 1920s always had better infant health outcomes than white women in their teens. She went on to argue that health deterioration among race/ethnic minorities occurred more rapidly than among whites, given greater cumulative exposure to socioeconomic disadvantage, discrimination, and other structural constraints that result in harsh environments. Her weathering hypothesis postulates that age patterns at birth are an adaptive response to the life conditions that each group experiences and represent women's efforts to take advantage of an optimal age at birth, with black births occurring, on average, earlier than white births.

Wildsmith (2002) suggests that there are two ways to test the weathering hypothesis: (1) by comparing age-specific patterns of health outcomes between socioeconomically advantaged and disadvantaged groups, and (2) by examining within-group variations of these outcomes across age. Using the first strategy,

Geronimus (1992b) examined black-white differences in infant survival and found that black infants had the greatest survival advantage at younger maternal ages whereas white infants have the greatest survival advantage at older ages (see also Ananth et al. 2001; Rich-Edwards et al. 2003). More generally, Geronimus' work has sought to test the weathering hypothesis by seeing whether black women, relative to white women, have worse health during the child bearing years (see Geronimus and Bound 1990; Geronimus et al. 1991b, a; Geronimus and Hillemeier 1992; Geronimus et al. 2007). Using the second strategy, Wildsmith (2002) examined Mexican-origin women, both native and U.S. born, and found some support for the weathering hypothesis. Among U.S. born women, rates of neonatal mortality and hypertension showed a curvilinear relationship with age, reaching the lowest levels between 17 and 18.

As noted above, existing empirical tests of the weathering hypothesis have focused on race/ethnic differences in maternal and infant health outcomes. When more positive health outcomes (e.g., neonatal mortality, birth weight, etc.) are observed among younger disadvantaged sample members, authors typically conclude that they have found support for the weathering hypothesis. We argue, however, that this is not a complete test of the weathering hypothesis. With respect to teenage childbearing, the weathering hypothesis has two components, one explicit and one more implicit. First, the theory explicitly states that blacks and other race/ethnic minorities have worse and more rapidly deteriorating health status compared to whites given differential cumulative exposure to all sorts of structural factors (e.g., poverty, discrimination, violence). Second, and more implicit in the theory, minority teens use the world around them to make assessments about own future health and mortality (see Geronimus 1992a; Geronimus et al. 1999). Such social construction is likely to be based on the physical health of the adults closest to them (i.e., family and community members). In a qualitative study of a black community in the northeast, Burton (1990) finds evidence of what she calls an accelerated family time table. She notes that, "…the community is so homogenous and close-knit that individuals often interpreted their life-course possibilities in light of what happened to individuals around them" (p. 132). She goes on to report that many women, including teenagers, were extremely cognizant of community mortality patterns suggesting the very real possibility of an early death. Many of these women aspired to have children early not only to maximize their own reproductive success but also to allow their own mother, or even grandmother, to take part in the child's life.

Despite the implied importance of intergenerational health for the weathering hypothesis this piece of the theory has never been empirically tested. Geronimus and colleagues (1999) examined the probability that a child's parents or grandparents would live to see the child's 20th birthday across a number of urban U.S. areas and found that blacks were less likely than whites to have family members who survived to the end of the interval and the discrepancy grew as age at birth increased. Although the findings support the first component of the theory, the analysis falls short of explicitly testing whether adult health has a direct impact on teen childbearing decisions and thus does not test the second component of the theory outlined above. We argue that the most theoretically grounded test of the weathering hypothesis with respect to teenage childbearing should focus on the association between adult health and teen pregnancy/childbirth, specifically focusing on the lineage of maternal health status. According to the theory, teens with parents, especially mothers, who are in poor health should have higher odds of teen pregnancy and childbirth. Because health status is likely to vary by race/ethnicity and class, it will be important to test the association between maternal health and teenage childbearing across these dimensions.

Learning Theories and Early Childbearing

Two social psychological theories, derived from learning theory, further suggest that minority adolescents and young adults may use parental health status as a basis for their own fertility intentions: social cognitive theory and the theory of planned action. Both posit that individuals construct new knowledge from their experiences in the social world (Bandura 1977). Social cognitive theory (SCT) explains how people acquire and maintain certain behaviors, while also providing a rationale for intervention strategies (Bandura 1989, 1997). It describes learning in terms of the relationships between behavior, environmental factors, and personal factors (e.g., cognitions, affect, or biological events). Knowledge is gained through experiencing the interplay of these elements of life, and new experiences are evaluated with respect to past experiences such that they help individuals to determine what their own actions will be across a range of situations. In other words, SCT is a learning theory based on the idea that people base their own behavior on the behavior and experiences of others around them (Miller and Dollard 1941). Ultimately the individual comes to believe that certain things will happen because he or she observes them happening to others around him or her, and this element of the theory relies heavily on outcome expectancies. These expectancies are greatly influenced by the individual's environment and for teenagers the family serves as one of the primary environments from which these expectancies are formed.

As previously mentioned, there are large health discrepancies among African American and white adults and these differences are not restricted to objective measures of health status like chronic disease (National Center for Health Statistics 2009), disability (Kelley-Moore and Ferraro 2004), life expectancy (Harper et al. 2007), and mortality (Satcher et al. 2005). Age- and sex-adjusted estimates from the 2008 National Health Interview Survey show that 69.7% of white adults reported very good or excellent health compared to 58.1% of African American adults (Heyman et al. 2009). The percentage for Latino adults reporting very good or excellent health is even lower at 56.8%. Adjusted regression models suggest that African American adults are roughly twice as likely as whites to report fair or poor SRH (Boardman 2004; Borrell and Crawford 2006; Ferraro 1993). Spencer and colleagues (2009) find that, controlling for physical functioning, older white adults were almost four times as likely as older African American adults to report favorable self-rated health. The authors suggest that health pessimism is stronger among the African American elderly population than whites. These studies suggest that African American youths have a higher rate of exposure to adults in poor physical health. Thus, based on social learning theory, one could argue that this difference in the prevalence of morbidity, mortality, and poor subjective health ratings among adult minorities might also lead to lower expectations about future health status among African American youths compared to white youths.

Building on the concept of expectancies, the theory of planned behavior predicts that beliefs and attitudes (i.e., expectations), shared norms, and perceived behavior indirectly determine actual behavior via behavioral intention (Azjen 1991). Beliefs and values about a certain behavior, and more importantly, its consequences, are evaluated with respect to norms surrounding both behavior and outcome. Individuals also assess how much self-efficacy they have with respect to the behavior. That is, for a behavior to occur individuals must believe they are capable of successfully executing that behavior in order to produce the desired result (Bandura 1977). When self-efficacy is high, the behavior is thought to be normative, and both the behavior and especially the outcome are positively valued, the odds of that behavior actually occurring are increased via heightened behavioral intention (Azjen and Fishbein 1980).

Many of the elements of the theory of planned behavior have been applied to early childbearing, including beliefs about age at first pregnancy, norms about early childbearing, and contraceptive use (see Buhi and Goodson 2007; Myklestad and Rise 2007). For some young women, early age at first pregnancy is not viewed in a negative light, but rather is seen as a way to connect with the child's father or grow closer to her family, to force adulthood at a time when most teens struggle with forming an identity, or as motivation to work harder in order to support the child (Rosengard et al. 2006). Some scholars, like Geronimus (1991, 2003) and Burton (1990) have argued that early childbearing can be a normative life course event among certain race/ethnic cultures, especially African Americans. A lack of stigma surrounding teenage childbearing (Mollborn 2009; Olson 1980), and the view that having a child early in life offers more benefits than negative consequences, may lead some adolescents and young adults to view childbearing as a positive event. When these conditions co-exist, some teens and young women may participate in behaviors that facilitate their desired outcome. And indeed, some research on early childbearing suggests that inconsistent and infrequent use of contraception is a planned behavior (Brückner et al. 2004; Davies et al. 2006; Jaccard et al. 2003; Rosengard et al. 2004).

Hypotheses

Lancaster and colleagues (2008) note that how ecologies come to influence fertility timing is an understudied question. They suggest that teens and their elders may make conscious fertility decisions without having explicit knowledge of the statistical odds of death, disability, and disease among the African American community.

Instead, because these events are pervasive in the culture, poor physical health is assumed to be a biological imperative. Qualitative studies of African Americans suggest that fertility-timing decisions in specific high poverty areas do involve socially derived knowledge of the benefits of early childbearing and multi-generational childrearing (Stack and Burton 1993; Geronimus 1996), but similar empirical evidence is lacking.

Based on social cognitive theory, as well as the theory of planned behavior, we expect that teens and young adults will use the health status of their parents as guides for their own fertility behavior. These theories lead us to the following hypothesis:

Hypothesis 1: Young women will use their mother's health status (i.e., maternal self-rated health) to inform pregnancy decisions at early ages.

Along with Geronimus' weathering hypothesis, the theories reviewed above also make powerful predictions about how race and ethnicity interact with environmental cues. In particular, African American teens may be more likely to witness adults with low levels of physical health, given the combined deleterious effects of socioeconomic disadvantage and racism. If, as suggested by social cognitive theory, these young women derive expectations about their own future health status from the observed health of those around them, especially their mothers, they may come to believe that good health occurs only during a brief period, early in the life course. If they then use those beliefs to make decisions about the sexual behavior and timing of pregnancies, as suggested by the theory of planned behavior, we might expect African American teens to enter into motherhood at an earlier age than teens of other race/ethnic groups.

Our second hypothesis is:

Hypothesis 2: The association between maternal self-rated health and fertility behavior (i.e., pregnancy and birth) will be stronger among African-American and Hispanic young women than white young women.

Thus, we propose a direct test of the weathering hypothesis that examines whether a teen's mother's self-rated health status is associated with increased odds of the teen having a child before the age of 20 and if it is, whether this association is stronger among African American versus Hispanic or white young women.

Method

Data

The dataset used to perform the analyses comes from the Panel Study of Income Dynamics (PSID), a national survey of 5,000 American families first interviewed in 1968. The PSID sample was interviewed every year for the first 20 years and every other year since then. The PSID is an excellent data source for examining the effects of parents' health status on adolescent children's fertility because it follows children from the original sample as they have grown into adulthood and formed their own households. Our primary maternal health measure is self-rated health (asked each year since 1984). Although PSID has contained other health items in each wave, health content was not expanded and consistent until the 1990s.

We restrict our analysis to daughters born between 1970 and 1991 who had valid data when they had reached age 14. This resulted in a sample of 3,588 young women. We dropped four cases where the data indicated that a birth occurred before age 19 but age at first birth information was missing. We dropped an additional case where age at first birth was listed as age six. Finally, we dropped 209 cases where no data were available on maternal characteristics. We did not drop, but excluded, cases where a birth occurred before age 14 (n=15 cases where a first birth occurred at ages 12 or 13) because we rely on maternal characteristics when the daughter was age 14. Thus we are left with 3,359 young women in our analytic sample.

The first year in which we observe a daughter's pregnancy or birth outcome is 1984 and the last year in which we observe pregnancy and birth outcomes is 2005, the most recent year for which public use data was available for the analysis. Consequently, the births we observe occur to daughters who were between the ages of 14 and 19 by 1984 and daughters who had reached at least age 14 by 2005. Those who had not yet reached age 14 in 2005 are right-censored.

Measures

Dependent Variable. In the analytic sample, 10.1% had a non-marital birth before age 19 (n=340, see Table 11.1).[2] Compared to previous studies using the PSID, this sample includes teens from cohorts in the 1990s, a period in which birth rates fell (Klein and the Committee on Adolescence 2005). The dependent variable in our analysis is time to event, which in this case is age at first non-marital birth through age 19. Young women who had not had a non-marital birth by age 19 were right censored at age 19 and young women who experienced a marital birth prior to age 19 were censored at the age of first marriage (see footnote 1).

Daughter Characteristics. A number of covariates are included in the model based on the fact that existing literature has shown them to be associated with teen-age childbearing. *Daughter's race/ethnicity* is defined by a series of dichotomous variables for white Non-Hispanic (37.6%), black non-Hispanic (46.4%), Hispanic (13.0%), and other (2.2%), with white as the reference group.

[2]Of the 380 births we observe in the analytic sample only 16 occurred after the daughter was married. In 14 of those 16 cases the birth occurred by the daughter's next birthday which suggests that the young woman may have known of her pregnancy at the time she married (i.e., these may have been "shotgun" weddings). The remaining two cases involved a birth two years after the year of the wedding. Because we only have the year of birth and the year of the marriage we cannot definitively identify whether the young woman would have been aware of her pregnancy at the time of the wedding. An additional 24 cases experience birth and marriage in the same year. All 40 of these cases were considered censored at the time of first marriage.

Table 11.1 Descriptive statistics (analytic sample before imputation)

	Total sample	Black	White	Hispanic	Other
Individual characteristics					
Percent experiencing non-marital birth before age 19	10.1	18.1	5.2	5.3	5.5
Race/ethnicity					
Black, non-Hispanic	37.6	–	–	–	–
White, non-Hispanic	46.4	–	–	–	–
Hispanic	13.0	–	–	–	–
Other	2.2	–	–	–	–
Missing	0.8				
Maternal characteristics					
Health status[a]					
Self-rated health (1–5)[b]	2.5 (1.0)	2.7 (1.0)	2.2 (.9)	2.9 (1.1)	2.8 (1.0)
Percent in fair/poor health	14.6	18.7	7.4	27.5	17.6
Marital status[a]					
Married	65.0	44.0	81.0	68.8	70.3
Divorced/separated	19.6	26.7	15.1	14.5	16.2
Widowed	2.0	2.9	1.0	3.0	4.0
Single	11.4	23.5	1.0	11.2	9.5
Education in years (1–17)	12.2 (2.7)	12.1 (1.9)	13.1 (2.1)	9.1 (4.0)	12.2 (2.9)
Currently employed[a]	85.9	78.0	91.4	88.5	89.2
Percent experiencing birth before age 19	30.2	44.2	18.0	33.5	25.7
Family characteristicsa					
Family income[c]	33.7 (38.2)	21.7 (20.9)	44.7 (47.5)	29.0 (23.5)	32.7 (40.2)
Percent missing family income	28.0	27.5	26.3	34.4	31.1
N	3,359	1,264	1,559	436	74

Notes: Unweighted means or percentages are presented in the table, with ranges and standard deviations in parentheses if applicable. Missing data are included in all tabulations

[a]When teen is age 14

[b]Excellent (1) to poor (5)

[c]In $1,000s

Maternal Characteristics. All maternal characteristics are collected when her daughter was age 14. *Maternal self-rated health* is a continuous variable ranging from 1 (excellent) to 5 (poor) (mean = 2.5, SD = 1.0). Approximately 15% of mothers in the sample were in fair or poor health. *Marital status* is a series of dichotomous variables indicating that the mother was married (65.0%), divorced/separated (19.6%), widowed (2.0%), or single (11.4%), with married as the reference group. *Maternal education* is measured in single years of completed schooling (mean = 12.2, SD = 2.7). *Maternal employment status* is a dichotomous variable indicating that the mother was employed (85.9% were employed). A final dichotomous variable indicates whether the mother herself experienced a *teenage birth* (30.2%).

Family Characteristics. *Family income* (in thousands of dollars) in 1984 is included as a measure of overall family socioeconomic status (mean = $33,700,

SD = \$38,200). We also include (but do not show in the results tables) a flag for missing family income.

Key Independent Variable. An interaction term between maternal self-rated health and daughter's race/ethnicity is used to assess the predicted race/ethnic difference in the association between maternal health status on daughter's fertility decisions.

Analysis

Data estimating age at first teen birth are analyzed using a standard Cox proportional hazard model for adolescents of all race and ethnic groups combined. As shown in Eq. 11.1, the hazard at time *t*, h(*t*), is defined as the likelihood of giving birth in year *t*, given that a young woman did not give birth prior to time *t* or reached age 19 by time *t*:

$$h_i(t) = h_0(t)\exp(\beta_1 x_{i1} + \cdots \beta_k x_{ik}) \quad (11.1)$$

The $h_0(t)$ term represents the baseline hazard at time *t* for an individual *i* who has a 0 on all of the predictor variables in the model. The $\beta_k x_{ik}$ term includes the covariates, or predictor variables, included in the model. Positive coefficient estimates for the predictor variables indicate that higher levels of the variable increase the hazard of an early birth. Negative coefficients have the opposite interpretation. The inverse logarithm of the estimated coefficients is interpreted as the risk ratio. A risk ratio greater than one indicates a higher risk of early childbearing for women with higher levels of the variable compared to women with lower levels.

To test Hypothesis 1 we investigate whether there is a significant first-order, bivariate association between maternal self-rated health and fertility outcomes among young women without including any of the covariates. Stage two of this model includes the covariates described above, including the daughter's race/ethnicity. Stage three of this model includes interaction terms between race/ethnicity and maternal self-rated health to investigate Hypothesis 2. Based on the joint significance of these interaction terms with all predictors in the model ($p < 0.0001$), we present separate models for non-Hispanic white, non-Hispanic black, and Hispanic groups to compare the effects of the covariates on early childbirth across the three groups.

We use multiple imputation to replace missing values in five simulated versions (Rubin 1987). The simulated complete dataset is analyzed by standard methods and the results are combined using the "micombine" command in STATA 10.1 (see Royston 2005). (Descriptive statistics for the imputed sample can be found in Table A.1.) Observations for daughters within the same family are not independent. Therefore, we correct all standard errors and p-values for the complex (clustered) data structure that would be miscalculated in a standard survival time analysis.

Results

Table 11.1 presents descriptive statistics for the non-imputed analytic sample. Not surprisingly, rates of early childbearing are higher among non-Hispanic blacks than non-Hispanic white, Hispanic, or other race/ethnicities ($p < .0001$ level, significance not shown in the table). Mothers of white young women rate themselves as healthier than other mothers ($p < .0001$). In general, white young women are more advantaged than their minority peers in terms of maternal characteristics, including marital status, education, and employment status, as well as family income. Finally, significantly fewer white young women have a mother who herself experienced first birth before the age of 19 than young black, Hispanic, or other race/ethnic women ($p < .0001$ for black and Hispanic; $p < 05$ for other).

Recall that our first hypothesis predicted that young women would use their mother's health status, defined as self-rated health, to inform pregnancy decisions at early ages.

To test this hypothesis we estimate the association between the characteristics of daughters and mothers when daughters are age 14 and time until first teen non-marital birth (see Table 11.2). Model 1 in Table 11.2 shows that each unit increase in mother's self-rated health (representing a decrease in health) is significantly associated with younger age at first birth for daughter in the sample overall (hazard ratio = 1.29, $t = 5.28$). Thus, we do find support for our first hypothesis.

Model 2 adds three controls for daughter's race/ethnicity, comparing each group to white young women. As seen in Table 11.2, black adolescents have the highest risk of early first non-marital birth (hazard ratio = 3.45, $t = 8.82$). Coefficients for Hispanic and other race/ethnicity do not reach statistical significance. The coefficient associated with mother's self-rated health remains largely unchanged when adjusting for race/ethnicity in Model 2 (hazard ratio = 1.19, $t = 3.12$) or other maternal characteristics, including whether the mother herself experienced a birth before age 19, in Model 3 (hazard ratio = 1.62, $t = 4.40$).

To test whether maternal self-rated health status matters similarly in the timing of first non-marital birth across race and ethnic groups, we include the interaction of maternal self-rated health and race/ethnic group. Hypothesis 2 predicted that the association between maternal self-rated health and age at age at first birth would be stronger for black and Hispanic versus white young women, with minority women having a younger average age at first birth what whites. A joint test of significance for all the race/ethnic interactions was significant (chi-square test of joint significance is $p < 0.001$), indicating that the effects of maternal self-rated health when the adolescent is 14 years old on subsequent early childbearing varies across race and ethnic groups.

Before disaggregating our results by race and ethnic group, we also estimated a model that fully interacted race/ethnicity with all other maternal and adolescent characteristics used in Model 3 (see Table 11.2). The chi-square test of joint significance was $p < 0.0001$ again suggesting that disaggregation of Model 3 is appropriate. Thus, we estimated parallel hazard models for each of the three largest race and

Table 11.2 Hazard model of age of early childbearing and mother's self-rated health

	Model 1		Model 2		Model 3	
	Hazard ratio (t)	CI	Hazard ratio (t)	CI	Hazard ratio (t)	CI
Mother's self-rated health (1 = Excellent, 5 = Poor)	1.29 (5.28)	(1.18, 1.43)	1.19 (3.12)	(1.07, 1.33)	1.62 (4.40)	(1.31, 2.00)
Individual characteristics						
Race/ethnicity[a]						
Black, non-Hispanic			3.45 (8.82)	(2.62, 4.54)	8.24 (5.41)	(3.83, 17.7)
Hispanic			1.00 (0.02)	(0.63, 1.61)	6.44 (3.24)	(2.09, 19.9)
Other			1.01 (0.02)	(0.37, 2.76)	0.08 (−1.35)	(0.49, 0.81)
Maternal characteristics[b]						
Race/ethnic interactions						
F/P Health*Black					0.63 (−3.64)	(0.49, 0.81)
F/P Health*Hispanic					0.42 (−4.41)	(0.28, 0.62)
F/P Health*Other					1.82 (0.83)	(0.73, 4.53)
Marital status[c]						
Divorced/separated					1.89 (4.94)	(1.47, 2.43)
Widowed					1.37 (0.94)	(0.71, 2.66)
Single					1.37 (0.94)	(0.71, 2.66)
Education in years (1–17)					0.89 (−3.96)	(0.85, 0.95)
Employed					1.16 (0.88)	(0.84, 1.60)
Mother birth before age 19					1.55 (3.73)	(1.23, 1.95)
Family characteristics[b]						
Family income[d]					1.00 (−1.15)	(0.99, 1.00)
N	3,359		3,359		3,359	

Notes:
[a]White, non-Hispanic is the reference category
[b]When teen is age 14
[c]Married is the reference category
[d]In $1,000s

Table 11.3 Hazard model of age of early childbearing and mother's self-rated health by daughter's race/ethnicity

	White, non-Hispanic		Black, non-Hispanic		Hispanic	
	Hazard ratio (t)	CI	Hazard ratio (t)	CI	Hazard ratio (t)	CI
Mother's self-rated health (1=Excellent, 5=Poor)	1.50 (3.36)	(1.18, 1.90)	1.01 (0.16)	(0.89, 1.15)	0.78 (−1.20)	(0.52, 1.17)
Maternal characteristics[a]						
Marital status[b]						
Divorced/ separated	1.59 (1.74)	(.94, 2.67)	2.10 (4.45)	(1.51, 2.91)	0.98 (−0.04)	(0.33, 2.89)
Widowed	3.03 (1.83)	(.92, 10.0)	1.24 (0.53)	(0.56, 2.75)	–	–
Single	0.73 (–.40)	(.16, 3.39)	1.51 (2.19)	(1.04, 2.19)	1.40 (0.61)	(0.48, 4.12)
Education in years (1–17)	0.78 (−4.29)	(.72, .88)	0.86 (−3.91)	(0.80, 0.93)	1.11 (1.71)	(0.99, 1.24)
Employed	1.83 (1.20)	(.68, 4.93)	1.08 (0.38)	(0.74, 1.56)	1.82 (0.55)	(0.21, 15.50)
Mother birth before age 19	1.67 (1.94)	(1.00, 2.79)	1.40 (2.36)	(1.06, 1.86)	1.35 (0.74)	(0.61, 2.95)
Family characteristics[a]						
Family income[c]	0.99 (−1.25)	(.99, 1.00)	1.00 (0.65)	(1.00, 1.01)	0.98 (−1.55)	(0.95, 1.01)
N	1,559		1,269		451	

Notes:
[a]When teen is age 14
[b]Married is the reference category
[c]In $1,000s

ethnic groups (black non-Hispanic, white non-Hispanic, and Hispanic) to allow for the comparison of the effects of different variables on early childbearing between race and ethnic groups. We drop the other/race ethnic group for this analysis because of the small sample size.

Table 11.3 represents Model 3 stratified by race and ethnicity. Worse maternal self-rated health when adolescent was 14 years old increases the risk of early childbearing for non-Hispanic whites (risk ratio = 1.50, t = 3.36), but not for blacks or Hispanics, controlling for other maternal and household characteristics. Thus, we do not find support for our second hypothesis. Despite earlier evidence that the association between maternal self-rated health status and early fertility behavior among non-Hispanic black young women was stronger than the association among non-Hispanic white and Hispanic young women, once we estimated a fully interactive model the results changed.

Among black young women, having a currently divorced or separated (and not remarried) or single mother when the daughter was age 14, and having a mother who had given birth as a teenager, both increased the likelihood of early childbearing. For all young women, maternal years of education was protective against an early childbearing, although the association did not reach statistical significance at the $p = .05$ level for Hispanic young women. Among Hispanic adolescents, no other variables in the model reached statistical significance, which may reflect the small sample size.

Robustness Check. Although we do find a significant association between maternal self-rated health and early childbearing among the young women in our sample, especially non-Hispanic whites, it is also possible that these young women are actually using *community* rather than maternal information as the basis for fertility behavior. We assess how much adolescents consider conditions in their local community relative to the health status of their mothers to determine the likelihood that they will experience poor health as they reach adulthood. To test the community reference hypothesis, we obtain the residuals from a model that predicts mother's self-rated health using other maternal characteristics. These residuals are a measure of mother's predicted health status relative to women with similar race/ethnicity, education, income, employment, marital status, and early childbearing status (i.e., birth prior to age 19). We then compare the coefficient belonging to the standardized residual to the coefficients belonging to a standardized version of maternal self-rated health from a bivariate model predicting early childbearing. This comparison provides a test of whether adolescents attend more to their mothers' health status in an absolute sense (i.e., excellent versus poor) or relative to what is typical for their mothers' peers. This approach does not provide a direct measure of the health of the neighborhood, but it provides an approximation of what adolescents are seeing in their community.

Results from this analysis showed that the hazard ratio associated with the standardized residuals did not differ significantly from 1.0 (hazard ratio = 0.908, $p = 0.089$), whereas the hazard ratio associated with observed maternal health status was significantly different from 1.0 (hazard ratio = 0.76, $p < 0.0001$). Therefore, we conclude that adolescents' early childbearing is more strongly associated with absolute maternal health status than with maternal health status relative to her mothers' peers (i.e., the community).

Discussion

Existing research finds that early, non-marital childbearing is more common among race/ethnic minorities, especially African Americans and Hispanics, that whites (Hamilton et al. 2009; Santelli et al. 2009). The weathering hypothesis has been used to explain this difference (Geronimus 1992b, 1996). The thesis states that early pregnancy and childbearing is a rational fertility decision for socioeconomically disadvantaged women especially if they believe they will age rapidly and have a shortened life span. Thus, early child bearing may be a more normative behavior among young women who are surrounded by adults in poor health. In particular, young women may use the health of their own mother as a proxy for rapid aging and shift peak reproductive years to an earlier stage in the life course.

Our results present the first direct test of the weathering hypothesis' assumption that young women's fertility decisions incorporate information about the health status of individuals around them. We find evidence that adolescent girls with mothers who have worse self-rated health are more likely to have an early non-marital birth, consistent with the weathering hypothesis as originally proposed. That is, young women consider expectancies about their own health status when making fertility decisions before the age of 19. Contrary to the original thesis, however, we fail to find evidence that these expectancies, as proxied by maternal self-rated health, can account for the race and ethnic differences in the timing of early childbearing. Our results show that a relationship between maternal self-rated health and early childbearing is only evident among non-Hispanic white young women in our study but not among non-Hispanic black or Hispanic young women. In other words, we find support for the weathering hypothesis among non-Hispanic whites, but not among traditionally disadvantaged adolescents.

We can only speculate as to why the weathering hypothesis did not hold for the more disadvantaged young women in our sample. Certainly, black and Hispanic young women had higher rates of non-marital childbearing prior to age 19 than whites in our sample. And when we controlled for race/ethnicity, rather than conditioned on race/ethnicity (i.e., ran separate models for each group), poor maternal self-rated health was associated with significantly higher odds of early childbearing. It may be that other factors, such as family socioeconomic status or the young woman's academic abilities, may mask the association between maternal health and fertility decisions. That is, minority young women may be more aware of their own economic opportunities (or lack thereof), rather than their future health expectancies. If they believe that their life circumstances are unlikely to improve, there is no reason to delay childbearing. In their qualitative work in disadvantaged communities, Edin and Kefalas (2005) found that early childbearing, typically outside of marriage, provided women with a sense of purpose and gave their lives meaning when faced with limited economic prospects. Further, some combination of economic and health expectancies may doubly-disadvantage some groups relative to others. So although this analysis did not find support for the weathering hypothesis among non-Hispanic black and Hispanic young women, it should not be taken as evidence *against* the weathering hypothesis. Instead, the results presented here suggest that the weathering hypothesis may need to be more nuanced, especially in terms of exactly what information young women use to make early fertility decisions.

Limitations

The analysis is not without limitations. First, the PSID is an older dataset and in as much as period effects may be at work the applicability of our findings to current rates of, trends in, and reasons for early childbearing may be in question. Second, the data contain a small number of Hispanic young women and an even smaller number of young women of other race/ethnicities. Because rates of teenage pregnancy and early childbearing vary across this dimension, it would be useful to have information from other race/ethnic groups, especially Asian and Pacific Islanders and Native Americans and American Indians. Third, our analysis uses maternal self-rated health as a proxy for future health because other measures of health, like obesity or specific disease outcomes, are not available in the PSID until much later. Despite the fact that self-rated health is strongly correlated with actual physical health, if we had operationalized health in a different way, our results may have shown more variation across race/ethnicity. Similarly, we have no way of knowing whether a young woman consciously used observed maternal health status as a factor in fertility decision making. Few data sets could allow for such an analysis, which suggests that future studies should consider including queries about reasons that young women give for early pregnancy and childbirth and what their own health expectancies are.

Future research may want to explore why expectancies, as measured by maternal health status, appear to matter for non-Hispanic white, but not other minority young women. It is possible that maternal self-rated health does matter for black and Hispanic women but once other maternal and family characteristics are accounted for the association does not reach statistical significance. It could be that maternal health status is associated with daughters' early fertility decisions but that maternal health status is itself a proxy for socioeconomic status. Our results seem to support this hypothesis. In the race/ethnic specific models, maternal education was a significant protective factor among all groups. Existing research also shows a clear association between educational attainment and health, such that individuals with more education are also healthier (Elo 2009). Although beyond the scope of this paper, the interrelationships between early childbearing, maternal health, and family socioeconomic status should be the focus of future work.

Conclusion

This analysis represents the first attempt to empirically test one of the implicit assumptions of the weathering hypothesis, namely that young women base their own fertility decisions on the health of adults around them. Although the results do suggest that poor maternal self-rated health is associated with early childbearing among young women in the sample, once other maternal and family characteristics are accounted for, this association is only significant for non-Hispanic whites. These findings should not be used to discredit the weathering hypothesis. Rather, they highlight how complicated the causes of early childbearing are.

Acknowledgments This work was funded by a seed grant from the RAND Population Research Center (Meadows and Beckett, PIs). Support was also provided by Panel Study of Income Dynamics (Beckett, and Meadows, PIs).

Appendix A: Descriptive Statistics for the Imputed Sample

Table A.1 Descriptive statistics (imputed sample)

	Total sample	Black	White	Hispanic	Other
Individual characteristics					
Percent experiencing non-marital birth before age 19	11.3	18.7	7.0	6.2	7.0
Race/ethnicity					
Black, non-Hispanic	37.9	–	–	–	–
White, non-Hispanic	46.5	–	–	–	–
Hispanic	13.4	–	–	–	–
Other	2.2	–	–	–	–
Maternal characteristics					
Health status[a]					
Self-rated health (1–5)[b]	2.5 (1.0)	2.7 (1.0)	2.2 (.9)	2.9 (1.1)	2.8 (1.0)
Percent in fair/poor health	16.0	20.8	10.1	29.0	19.5
Marital status[a]					
Married	66.2	45.4	81.9	69.8	72.7
Divorced/separated	20.2	27.6	15.7	15.2	17.4
Widowed	11.5	24.0	1.2	12.2	9.9
Single	2.1	3.0	1.2	2.9	0.0
Education in years (1–17)	12.1 (2.7)	12.1 (1.9)	13.0 (2.1)	9.1 (3.8)	12.1 (2.9)
Currently employed[a]	90.3	84.4	94.5	91.3	96.5
Percent experiencing birth before age 19	32.4	47.2	19.5	35.8	31.6
Family characteristics[a]					
Family income[c]	33.6 (38.0)	22.8 (23.2)	43.7 (46.5)	29.9 (28.8)	29.9 (36.9)
N					

Notes: Unweighted means or percentages are presented in the table, with ranges and standard deviations in parentheses if applicable

[a]When teen is age 14

[b]Excellent (1) to poor (5)

[c]In $1,000s

References

Ananth, C. V., Misra, D. P., Demissie, K., & Smulian, J. C. (2001). Rates of preterm delivery among black women and white women in the United States over two decades: An age-period-cohort analysis. *American Journal of Epidemiology, 154*(7), 657–665.

Azjen, I. (1991). The theory of planned behavior. *Organizational Behavior and Human Decision Processes, 50*, 179–211.

Azjen, I., & Fishbein, M. (1980). *Understanding attitudes and predicting social behavior.* Englewood Cliffs: Prentice-Hall.

Bandura, A. (1977). *Social learning theory*. New York: General Learning Press.

Bandura, A. (1989). Human agency in social cognitive theory. *American Psychologist, 44*, 1175–1184.

Bandura, A. (1997). *Self-efficacy: The exercise of control*. New York: Freeman.

Bennett, N. G., Bloom, D. E., & Miller, C. K. (1995). The influence of nonmarital childbearing on the formation of first marriages. *Demography, 32*(1), 47–62.
Boardman, J. D. (2004). Health pessimism among black and white adults: The role of interpersonal and institutional maltreatment. *Social Science & Medicine, 59*, 2523–2533.
Borrell, L. N., & Crawford, N. D. (2006). Race, ethnicity, and self-rated health status in the behavioral risk factor surveillance system survey. *Hispanic Journal of Behavioral Sciences, 28*, 387–403.
Brückner, H., Martin, A., & Bearman, P. (2004). Ambivalence and pregnancy: Adolescents' attitudes, contraceptive use and pregnancy. *Perspectives on Sexual and Reproductive Health, 36*(6), 248–257.
Buhi, E. R., & Goodson, P. (2007). Predictors of adolescent sexual behavior and intention: A theory-guided systematic review. *Journal of Adolescent Health, 40*, 4–21.
Burton, L. M. (1990). Teenage childbearing as an alternative life-course strategy in multigenerational black families. *Human Nature, 1*(2), 123–143.
Chevalier, A., & Viitanen, T. K. (2003). The long-run labour market consequences of teenage motherhood in Britain. *Journal of Population Economics, 16*(2), 1431–1475.
Clark, D. O., & Maddox, G. L. (1992). Racial and social correlates of age-related changes in functioning. *Journal of Gerontology, 47*, S222–S232.
Clinton, W. J. (1995, January 24). *State of the union address*. Washington, DC: Joint Session of Congress.
Davies, S. L., DiClemente, R. J., Wingwood, G. M., Person, S. D., Dix, E. S., Harrington, K., Crosby, R. A., & Oh, K. (2006). Predictors of inconsistent contraceptive use among adolescent girls: Findings from a prospective study. *Journal of Adolescent Health, 39*(1), 43–49.
Dressler, W. W., Osths, K. S., & Gravlee, C. C. (2005). Race and ethnicity in public health research: Models to explain health disparities. *Annual Review of Anthropology, 24*, 231–252.
Edin, K., & Kefalas, M. (2005). *Promises I can keep: Why poor women put motherhood before marriage*. Berkeley: University of California Press.
Elo, I. T. (2009). Social class differentials in health and mortality: Patterns and explanations in a comparative perspective. *Annual Review of Sociology, 35*, 553–572.
Ferraro, K. F. (1993). Are black older adults health-pessimistic? *Journal of Health and Social Behavior, 34*, 201–214.
Fletcher, J. M., & Wolfe, B. L. (2009). Education and labor market consequences of teenage childbearing: Evidence using the timing of pregnancy: Outcomes and community fixed effects. *Journal of Human Resources, 44*(2), 303–325.
Furstenberg, F. F., Jr. (1991). As the pendulum swings: Teenage childbearing and social concern. *Family Relations, 40*(2), 127–138.
Geronimus, A. T. (1991). Teenage childbearing and social reproductive disadvantage: The evolution of complex questions and the demise of simple answers. *Family Relations, 40*, 463–471.
Geronimus, A. T. (1992a). Teenage childbearing and social disadvantage: Unprotected discourse. *Family Relations, 41*, 244–248.
Geronimus, A. T. (1992b). The weathering hypothesis and the health of African-American women and infants: Evidence and speculations. *Ethnicity & Disease, 2*, 207–221.
Geronimus, A. T. (1996). Black/white differences in the relationship of maternal age to birth weight: A population-based test of the weathering hypothesis. *Social Science & Medicine, 42*, 589–597.
Geronimus, A. T. (2001). Understanding and eliminating racial inequalities in women's health in the United States: The role of the weathering conceptual framework. *Journal of the American Medical Women's Association, 56*(4), 133–136, 149–150.
Geronimus, A. T. (2003). Damned if you do: Culture, identity, privilege, and teenage childbearing in the United States. *Social Science & Medicine, 57*(5), 881–893.
Geronimus, A. T., & Bound, J. (1990). Black/white differences in women's reproductive-related health status: Evidence from vital statistics. *Demography, 27*, 457–466.
Geronimus, A. T., & Hillemeier, M. M. (1992). Patterns of blood lead levels in US black and white women. *Ethnicity & Disease, 2*(3), 222–231.

Geronimus, A. T., & Thompson, J. P. (2004). To denigrate, ignore, or disrupt: The health impact of policy-induced breakdown of urban African American communities of support. *Du Bois Review, 1*(2), 247–279.

Geronimus, A. T., Andersen, H. F., & Bound, J. (1991a). Differences in hypertension prevalence among U.S. black and white women of childbearing age. *Public Health Reports, 106*, 393–399.

Geronimus, A. T., Neidert, L. J., & Bound, J. (1991b). *Age patterns of smoking among U.S. black and white women* (Research Report 91-232). Ann Arbor: University of Michigan Population Studies Center.

Geronimus, A. T., Bound, J., Waidmann, T. A., Hillemeier, M. M., & Burns, P. B. (1996). Excess mortality among blacks and whites in the United States. *The New England Journal of Medicine, 335*(21), 1552–1558.

Geronimus, A. T., Bound, J., & Waidmann, T. A. (1999). Health inequality and population variation in fertility-timing. *Social Science & Medicine, 49*, 1623–1636.

Geronimus, A. T., Bound, J., Waidmann, T. A., Colen, C. G., & Steffick, D. (2001). Inequality in life expectancy, functional status, and active life expectancy across selected black and white populations in the United States. *Demography, 38*, 227–251.

Geronimus, A. T., Hicken, M., Keene, D., & Bound, J. (2006). "Weathering" and age-patterns of allostatic load scores among blacks and whites in the United States. *American Journal of Public Health, 96*, 826–833.

Geronimus, A. T., Keene, D., Hicken, M., & Bound, J. (2007). Black-white differences in age trajectories of hypertension prevalence among adult women and men, 1999–2002. *Ethnicity & Disease, 17*(1), 40–48.

Gilbert, W. M., Young, A. L., & Danielsen, B. (2007). Pregnancy outcomes in women with chronic hypertension. *The Journal of Reproductive Medicine, 52*(11), 1046–1051.

Hamilton, B. E., Martin, J. A., & Ventura, S. J. (2009). *Births: Preliminary data for 2007*. National Center for Health Statistics. Available via http://www.cdc.gov/nchs/data/nvsr/nvsr57/nvsr57_12.pdf. Cited 28 July 2009.

Harper, S., Lynch, J., Burris, S., & Smith, G. D. (2007). Trends in black-white life expectancy gap in the United States, 1983–2003. *Journal of the American Medical Association, 297*(11), 1224–1232.

Hayes, C. (Ed.). (1987). *Risking the future* (Vol. 1). Washington, DC: National Academy Press.

Heyman, K. M., Barnes, P. M., & Schiller, J. S. (2009). *Early release of selected estimates based on data from the 2008 National Health Interview Survey*. National Center for Health Statistics. Available via http://www.cdc.gov/nchs/nhis/released200906.htm#11. Cited 27 July 2009.

Hoffman, S. D., Foster, E. M., & Furstenberg, F. F., Jr. (1993). Reevaluating the costs of teenage childbearing. *Demography, 30*(1), 1–13.

Hotz, V. J., McElroy, S. W., & Sanders, S. G. (1997). The impacts of teenage childbearing on the mothers and the consequences of those impacts for government. In R. A. Maynard (Ed.), *Kids having kids: Economic and social consequences of teen pregnancy* (pp. 55–94). Washington, DC: The Urban Institute Press.

Jaccard, J., Dodge, T., & Dittus, P. (2003). Do adolescents want to avoid pregnancy? Attitudes towards pregnancy as predictors of pregnancy. *Journal of Adolescent Health, 33*(2), 79–83.

Kelley-Moore, J. A., & Ferraro, K. F. (2004). The black/white disability gap: Persistent inequality in later life? *Journal of Gerontology: Social Sciences, 59B*(1), S34–S43.

Klein, J. D., & the Committee on Adolescence. (2005). Current trends and issues. *Pediatrics, 116*(1), 281–286.

Klepinger, D., Lundberg, S., & Plotnick, R. (1999). How does adolescent fertility affect the human capital and wages of young women. *Journal of Human Resources, 34*(3), 421–448.

Lancaster, J. B., Geronimus, A. T., Hamburg, B. A., & Kramer, K. (2008). Introduction to the transaction edition. In J. B. Lancaster & B. A. Hamburg (Eds.), *School-age pregnancy and parenthood* (pp. ix–xxx). Edison: AldineTransaction.

Lawlor, D. A., & Shaw, M. (2002). Too much too young? Teenage pregnancy is not a public health problem. *International Journal of Epidemiology, 31*(3), 552–553.

McEwen, B. S. (1998). Protective and damaging effects of stress mediators. *The New England Journal of Medicine, 338*, 171–179.

McEwen, B. S. (2000). Allostasis and allostatic load: Implications for neuropsychopharmacology. *Neuropsychopharmacology, 22*(2), 108–124.
Miller, N. E., & Dollard, J. (1941). *Social learning and imitation*. New Haven: Yale University Press.
Mollborn, S. (2009). Norms about nonmarital pregnancy and willingness to provide resources to unwed parents. *Journal of Marriage and Family, 71*(1), 122–134.
Myklestad, I., & Rise, J. (2007). Predicting willingness to engage in unsafe sex and intention to perform sexual protective behaviors among adolescents. *Journal of Health Education and Behavior, 34*, 686–699.
National Center for Health Statistics. (2009). *Health, United States, 2008*. Hyattsville: National Center for Health Statistics.
Olson, L. (1980). Social and psychological correlates of pregnancy resolution among adolescent women: A review. *The American Journal of Orthopsychiatry, 50*, 432–445.
Rich-Edwards, J. W. (2002). Teen pregnancy is not a public health crisis in the United States. It is time we made it one. *International Journal of Epidemiology, 31*(3), 555–556.
Rich-Edwards, J. W., Buka, S. L., Brennan, R. T., & Earls, F. (2003). Diverging associations of maternal age with low birthweight for black and white mothers. *International Journal of Epidemiology, 3*, 83–90.
Rosenberg, T. J., Garbers, S., Lipkind, H., & Chiasson, M. A. (2005). Maternal obesity and diabetes as risk factors for adverse pregnancy outcomes: Differences among 4 racial/ethnic groups. *American Journal of Public Health, 95*(9), 1545–1551.
Rosengard, C., Phipps, M. G., Adler, N. E., & Ellen, J. M. (2004). Adolescent pregnancy intentions and pregnancy outcomes: A longitudinal examination. *Journal of Adolescent Health, 35*, 453–461.
Rosengard, C., Pollock, L., Weitzen, S., Meers, A., & Phipps, M. G. (2006). Concepts of the advantages and disadvantages of teenage childbearing among pregnant adolescents: A qualitative analysis. *Pediatrics, 118*, 503–510.
Royston, P. (2005). Multiple imputation of missing values: Update of ice. *The Stata Journal, 5*, 527–536.
Rubin, D. B. (1987). *Multiple imputation for nonresponse in surveys*. New York: Wiley.
Santelli, J. S., Orr, M., Lindberg, L. D., & Diaz, D. C. (2009). Changing behavioral risk for pregnancy among high school students in the United States, 1991–2007. *Journal of Adolescent Health, 45*, 25–32.
Satcher, D., Fryer, G. E., Jr., McCann, J., Troutman, A., Woolf, S. H., & Rust, G. (2005). What if we were equal? A comparison of the black-white mortality gap in 1960 and 2000. *Health Affairs, 24*(2), 459–464.
Scally, G. (2002). Too much too young? Teenage pregnancy is a public health, not a clinical, problem. *International Journal of Epidemiology, 31*(3), 554–555.
Shuey, K. M., & Willson, A. E. (2008). Cumulative disadvantage and black-white disparities in life-course health trajectories. *Research on Aging, 30*, 200–225.
Spencer, S. M., Schulz, R., Rooks, R. N., Albert, S. M., Thorpe, R. J., Jr., Brenes, G. A., Harris, T. B., Koster, A., Satterfield, S., Ayonayon, H. N., & Newman, A. B. (2009). Racial differences in self-rated health at similar levels of physical functioning: An examination of health pessimism in the health, aging, and body composition study. *The Journals of Gerontology: Series B, 64B*(1), 87–94.
Stack, C., & Burton, L. M. (1993). Kinscripts. *Journal of Comparative Family Studies, 24*, 157–170.
Wildsmith, E. M. (2002). Testing the weathering hypothesis among Mexican-origin women. *Ethnicity & Disease, 12*, 470–479.
Williams, D. R. (1999). Race, socioeconomic status, and health. The added effects of racism and discrimination. *Annals of the New York Academy of Sciences, 896*, 173–188.
Williams, D. R., & Jackson, P. B. (2005). Social sources of racial disparities in health. *Health Affairs, 24*(2), 325–334.
Wong, M. D., Shapiro, M. F., Boscardin, W. J., & Ettner, S. L. (2002). Contribution of major diseases to disparities in mortality. *The New England Journal of Medicine, 347*, 1585–1592.

Chapter 12
Maternal Health and Maternal Mortality in Post War Liberia: A Survey Analysis

Komanduri S. Murty and Jimmy D. McCamey Jr.

Introduction

The United Negro College Fund Special Programs (UNCFSP) funded the partnership between Rust College of Holly Springs, Mississippi, and Cuttington University College, Suakoko, Liberia, to implement an intervention project based on three interconnected strategies: training, management and extension, and community engagement. The overall goal of this project is to develop capacity of health practitioners assigned to rural clinics and health centers to deliver better services to the most marginalized communities of women and children in an agrarian society recovering from two decades of war. The first of the five phases, that were proposed to implement this project, was to *conduct needs assessment* to identify and determine the magnitude of priorities of unmet needs.[1] In an attempt to fulfill this objective, three independent surveys were conducted. The first survey focused on knowledge, attitudes, and behaviors relating to HIV/AIDS, and 170 Liberians participated in that survey (Murty 2006). This study reports the findings of the other two surveys that are directly related to maternal health and maternal mortality—that is as perceived by the women in reproductive ages and by health care professionals/providers. Both surveys were conducted in the months of June and July of 2006.

---

[1]The remaining four phases include: curriculum development process to produce 12 in-service training modules; piloting and revisions of the 12 modules; use of the modules to train two target groups—midwives and public health workers; and evaluation and module reproduction and distribution across the country.

K.S. Murty (✉)
Department of Behavioral Sciences and Population Studies Center,
Fort Valley State University, Fort Valley, GA, USA
e-mail: murtyk@FVSU.EDU

J.D. McCamey Jr.
Department of Behavioral Sciences, Fort Valley State University,
Fort Valley, GA, USA

N. Hoque et al. (eds.), *Applied Demography and Public Health*,
Applied Demography Series 3, DOI 10.1007/978-94-007-6140-7_12,
© Springer Science+Business Media Dordrecht 2013

Survey of Women in Reproductive Ages

This survey instrument consisted of a total of 16 questions—name, age, current marital status, number of pregnancies, number of live births, number of children living at present, persons seeking assistance from health workers/professionals for delivering babies (information collected by children's birth order), reasons for not seeking such assistance, status of receiving prenatal care for pregnancies, and from whom, reasons for not seeking such assistance, number of sisters ever had and those surviving, details of deceased sisters, number of sisters dying for maternal causes, perceptions of seriousness of problems of maternal health, and opinions related to common threats of maternal health during and after pregnancy in their region. The questionnaire maintained a balance between open-ended and close-ended questions to optimize the level of difficulty and time required on the respondents' part in providing the information solicited. Only one woman per household participated in the survey.

Data Analysis

A total of 277 women in reproductive ages (13–49) participated in the survey (Table 12.1). One interview in which the woman was reportedly 55 years old was eliminated from the analysis. While 269 women reported an average age of 27.4 ± 0.54 years, the remaining eight respondents said *adult age* without specifying their exact age. While this response made them eligible to participate in the survey, it prevented them to be included in any particular age group. Secondly, only 4 women were 13 or 14 years old and the remaining 265 were in the age group of 15–49 years. Ninety percent of women split equally between *never married* and *currently married* categories and the remaining 10% were *widowed, divorced, or separated*. However, 75% of never married women reported one or more (up to 8) live births (the corresponding percentages were 95 for married women and 96% for widowed, divorced, or separated women). Thus, it can be surmised that it is common for Liberian women to have children without getting married.

Additionally, these women have high fertility patterns with an average number of pregnancies of 3.4 ± 0.16 (range 0–13) and average number of live births of 2.7 ± 0.14 (range 0–10). The average number of live births (or "children ever born") by age of the mother can be seen in Fig. 12.1.[2]

[2]This average number of children ever born per woman up to a certain age, or by the end of reproductive period, is a cohort measure of fertility. For the women of 45 years and above, this mean was 5.5, which reflects on *completed family size* and approximates the total fertility rate for Liberia (6.02) in 2006 (CIA-The World Fact Book). Thus the reproductive behavior of this sample is very close to national average.

Table 12.1 Demographic and reproductive health characteristics among respondents

Variable	Respondents
Age (years) n = 269, mean ± SE (range)	27.4 ± 0.54 (13–49)
Marital status, n = 271	
Never married	121 (44.6)
Currently married	123 (45.4)
Widowed, divorced, separated	27 (10.0)
Number of pregnancies, n = 276, mean ± SE (range)	3.4 ± 0.16 (0–13)
Number of live births, n = 276, mean ± SE (range)	2.7 ± 0.14 (0–10)
Number of children living at present, n = 276, mean ± SE (range)	2.2 ± 0.12 (0–10)
Received assistance for delivering babies, n = 244	188 (77.0)
Births attended by, n = 244	
Trained health professionals (doctors, nurses, midwifes, TTM)	166 (68.0)
Untrained persons (traditional doctors, zoes, TBA)	22 (9.0)
Unattended, delivered alone	56 (23.0)
Reasons for not seeking assistance in delivering babies, n = 56	
Lack of transportation	6 (10.7)
No clinic in the area	15 (26.8)
Distance to clinic is too far	12 (21.4)
Financial difficulties/could not afford	17 (30.4)
Afraid	5 (8.9)
Uncomfortable/Do not think nurses will understand	1 (1.8)
Received prenatal care, n = 239	184 (77.0)
From same person who delivered baby	159(86.4)
From a different person	25 (13.6)
Reasons for not receiving prenatal care, n = 51	
Distance from health clinic/providers	49 (96.1)
Cost (fees, transportation, drugs, supplies, etc.)	49 (96.1)
Multiple demands on my time	12 (23.5)
I cannot decide, even if I want to go	17 (33.3)
I prefer not going	7 (13.7)
I never had any problems, so I didn't see a reason to go	9 (17.6)
I do not trust those people in health clinic	7 (13.7)
Other	1 (2.0)
Perceived seriousness of the problem of maternal health in the region, n = 272	
Very serious	127 (46.7)
Somewhat serious	114 (41.9)
Not serious	31 (11.4)

Unfortunately, this combination of pregnancies and live births also indicates a high level of *fetus risk* or *pregnancy wastage*, with an average number of unsuccessful pregnancies of 0.6764 ± 0.06 (range 0–6).[3] Although the survey did not collect information on age at death of each child, a high rate of child mortality is indicated

[3]Computed by simply subtracting the number of live births from number of pregnancies.

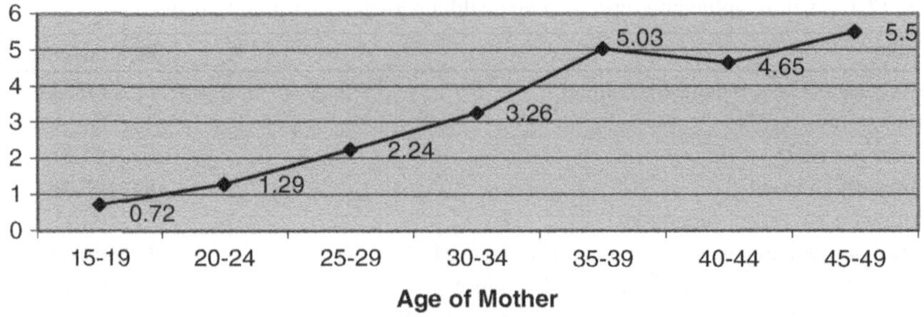

Fig. 12.1 Average number of children ever born

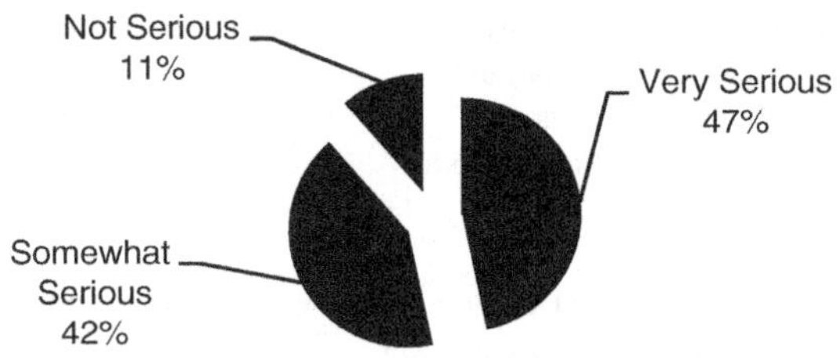

Fig. 12.2 In general, how serious is the problem of maternal health in this region?

when the number of children living at present is compared with the number of live births—there is an average loss of 0.4932±0.056 (range 0–6) children. Looking differently, 276 women reported a total of 936 pregnancies, 751 live births, and 615 children living at present—resulting in the finding of a loss of 185 pregnancies before they turn into live births and a loss of 136 children after they were born. This is an indication of serious risk to child health as well as maternal health among this population. In fact, 47% of the respondents perceived that maternal health is a *very serious* problem and another 42% perceived it as *somewhat serious* problem. Only 11% said it was not a serious problem (Fig. 12.2).

The risks of child health and maternal health may further be substantiated from what the respondents had to say about their dead sisters. The average age of dead sisters, as recalled by 67 respondents, was 26.5±1.9 (range 17–42) years; the average duration of marriage (n=40) was 5.7±0.8 (range 1–9) years; the average number of children ever born (n=64) was 3.5±0.43 (range 1–7); and the average number of children currently living (n=62) was 2.3±0.34 (range 0–5). A total of 132 sisters were reported to be dead; 29 (22%) of them had died for maternal causes (abortion, labor, and postpartum infection) and 54 (42%) for non-maternal causes (malaria, heart failure, typhoid, cholera, and anemia). The cause of death was unknown for the remaining 49 (36%) (Fig. 12.3). Labor among maternal causes (19/29 or 66%) and malaria among non-maternal causes (24/54 or 44%) were leading causes of death. Heart failure was the second most leading non-maternal cause of death, contributing for 14 out of 54 deaths (26%).

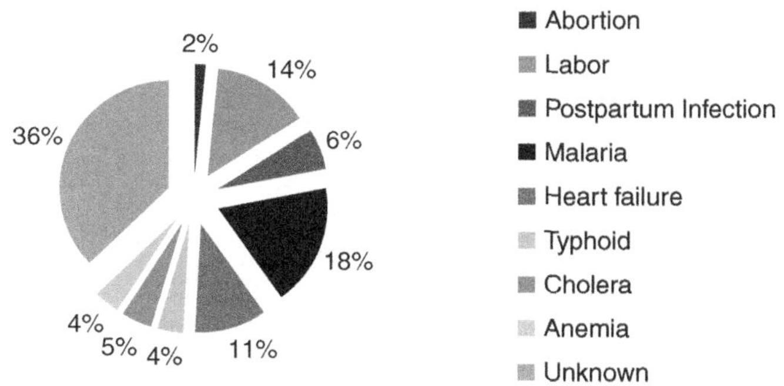

Fig. 12.3 Sister deaths by cause

These respondents described circumstances that lead to their sisters' death in varying degree—some being very specific and others being more general. Following are representative illustrations:

1. Explanations for maternal causes of death:

She died because of a delivery complication during childbirth.

She stayed in pain and both baby and mother died in childbirth.

My sister died while giving birth at home by a TBA (trained birth assistant); because of fear she decided not to go to the clinic. The causes of the death of mother are infection and early child bearing.

Because of age and fear during her delivery, she and her child passed away (died).

My sister, while giving birth to her child that did not live too. The death was as the result of the untrained midwife that was carrying on the delivery process. She bled too much until she was short of blood that we did not know until we rush her to the hospital but it was too late for her.

Because of the war, we were dwelling in the bushes without proper medication or medical care. She went to give birth to her second child under the watchful eyes of an untrained midwife. After which she bled for several days and later passed out (away).

She had cephalopelvic disproportion and died during delivery.

They (referring two sisters) died, as the result of untrained midwife attaining to them during the time delivery, therefore they and the babies did not make it.

Mary had a septic abortion; alone by an untrained health worker who perforated her uterus; when rushed to the hospital the doctors told the relatives that her uterus was perforated, during the surgery when Mary died.

She died because of bleeding heavily during labor.

2. Explanations for non-maternal causes of death:

She died because of snake bite.

My sisters (3) suffered from typhoid, cholera and yellow fever and there was no health service that could help us. They needed money and we never had any money.

My sister suffered from malaria and died while convulsing.

They (2 sisters) suffered from stomach pain and seizures and died.

She suffered from high malaria and high blood pressure; because of the war and the distance from the health center, she was taking herbs but they didn't help her and she passed out (away).

She was crippled and a sickle cell patient.

My sister died when I was eleven (11) years old. But my mother told me that my sister died when she was pregnant and she died from constant headache and convulsion.

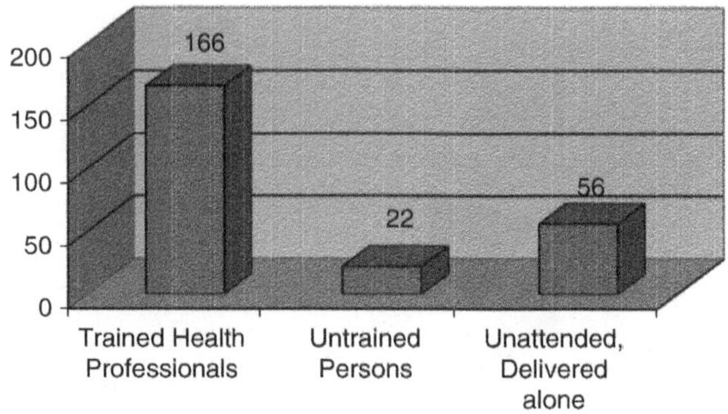

Fig. 12.4 Births attended by:

Anemia; she had malaria and treated herself at home with herbs after two weeks she was then taken to hospital and the doctors said she had low blood.

Both breasts had abscess that burst and made sore.

She had asthma and was told to be treated with herbs by our parents.

She had sickle cell anemia.

3. Explanations for maternal and non-maternal causes of death:

One sister died because of postpartum infection after delivery; and the other sister died of malaria and convulsion while she was pregnant.

One had edema before pregnancy and died of hypertension during labor; one had infection before labor and died; one had prolonged labor and gave birth to a dead child and died.

Even in such alarming conditions of maternal health and maternal mortality, only 77% of the respondents reported to have received prenatal care (184/239) and/or assistance at the time of delivering their babies (188/244) (Fig. 12.4). Of those who received prenatal care (n = 184), 86% received it from the same person who assisted them with delivering their baby and the remaining 14% from a different person. Of the 244 mothers who answered the question of who attended their child's birth, only 68% affirmed their delivery was attended by trained health professionals (doctors-12%, nurses-18%, midwifes-36%, and trained traditional midwifes, TTM-2%) and 9% by untrained persons (traditional/untrained doctor-1%, zoes-2%, and traditional birth attendant, TBA-6%).

The remaining 23% of the births (n = 56) were unattended; women delivered alone because they did not have transportation (11%), no healthcare facility was available in the area (27%), distance to nearest clinic was too far (21%), financial reasons (30%), fear (9%), or they were uncomfortable and did not think that nurses would understand their personal situation (2%) (Fig. 12.5).

Distance to health clinic and cost of healthcare seem to be the major barriers even for receiving prenatal care, as reported by 96% of those who failed to receive such care when they were pregnant. Other barriers included: multiple demands on time (33%), preferred not going to clinic because no one would talk to them until they paid the fees and they had no money to pay (14%), did not feel the need (18%), lack of trust in health professionals (14%), and other (2%).

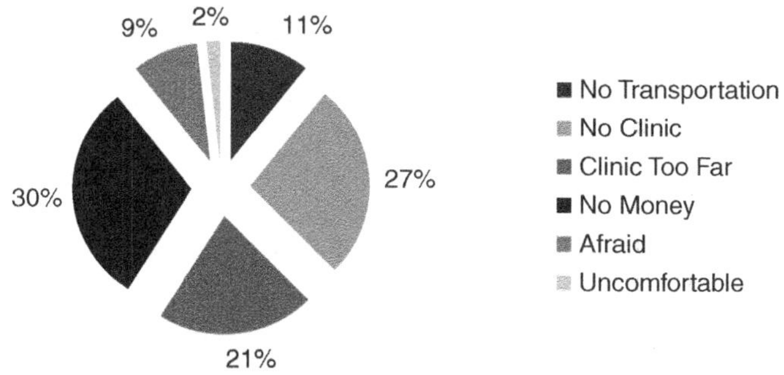

Fig. 12.5 Reasons for unattended births

Estimating Maternal Mortality by Sisterhood Method

The sisterhood method is an indirect technique for deriving survey-based estimates of maternal mortality in high-fertility populations. It substantially reduces sample size requirements because it obtains information by interviewing respondents about the survival of all their adult sisters (see for example, World Health Organization 2005). Graham et al. (1989) developed the sisterhood method from the key simplification of the basic sibling survivorship technique of Hill and Trussell (1977) and published their first field trial results from the Gambia data in 1989. The rationale for this method is based on several principles: first, it assumes that a relationship exists between the number of siblings and their survival probabilities, especially when the questions were restricted to siblings who have survived at least to the point of entry to the adult age groups; second, the number of households that need to be visited in order to obtain information on large numbers of women who reached reproductive age is relatively small, given the average family sizes in high-fertility societies of the developing countries; third, in many of these populations, siblings remain in close contact long after they have left their natal home; fourth, the circumstances of a death of an adult sister would be highly memorable, even when the date and age of death may be forgotten; and finally, sisters may assist each other in the later stages of pregnancy, at the time of childbirth, or during the period immediately following delivery. This rationale convinced us to interview only the women in reproductive ages rather than both genders.

This method uses the proportions of adult sisters dying during pregnancy, childbirth, or the puerperium reported by adults during the survey to derive maternal mortality ratio. Over the last 18 years (i.e. since the method was developed), this technique was applied in many studies and several evaluations of its reliability were undertaken (Rutenberg and Sullivan 1991; Walraven et al. 1994; Wirawan and Linnan 1994; Amowitz 2002). The major advantages of this method include its minimal data requirements, analytical simplicity, and lower sample size requirements (Graham 1994; Daniel et al. 1996).

The method provides a framework for both data collection and data analysis. Four simple questions are asked: (1) How many sisters (born to the same mother) have you ever had who were ever-married (including those who are now dead)? (2) How many of these ever-married sisters are alive now? (3) How many of these ever-married sisters are dead? (4) How many of these dead sisters died while they were pregnant, or during childbirth, or during 6 weeks after the end of pregnancy? While these questions provide guidance as to what information needs to be solicited in order to estimate maternal mortality in a given region by using the *Sisterhood Method*, it raises concerns, at least in our case, in terms of the accuracy of the information that respondents could provide for such broad questions (especially the first three), and most importantly, in terms of sensitivity for a lost family member (which may result in frequent refusals or underreporting). Therefore, we have modified these questions in the following manner:

1. *How many sisters have you ever had?* ______________
2. *Of them, how many are older than you?* ______________
3. *Of them, how many are currently living?* ______________
   (If responses for 2 and 3 are NOT same ask question 4. If they ARE same go to question 5)
4. *For each older sister who died answer the following.*

Name	*Age at death*	*Marital Status*	*Duration of Marriage if married*	*No. of children ever born*	*No. of children currently living*	*Cause of death*

5. *How many younger sisters do you have?* ______________
6. *Of them, how many are currently living?* ______________
   (If responses for 5 and 6 are NOT same ask the following question)
7. *For each younger sister who died answer the following.*

Name	*Age at death*	*Marital Status*	*Duration of Marriage if married*	*No. of children ever born*	*No. of children currently living*	*Cause of death*

8. *How many of these deceased sisters died while they were pregnant, during childbirth, or during the 6 weeks after the end of the pregnancy?* ______________

The required aggregate data were compiled from the above information and used to calculate the proportion of sisters dying during pregnancy, childbirth, or up to 6 weeks after the end of pregnancy (puerperium), and standard adjustment factors[4] are used to convert these proportions into estimates of maternal mortality. The principal indicator obtained is the lifetime risk of maternal death (LTR), which is converted to an estimate of the maternal mortality ratio (MMR) by using appropriate total fertility rate (TFR).[5] As shown in Table 12.2, the LTR for women in the survey

[4]For an explanation of how these adjustment factors are developed, see the Methodological Note of Graham et al. 1989.

[5]The sisterhood method typically recommends to consider the total fertility rate of 10–12 years before data collection. In this case, we have taken the total fertility rate of 1996 for Liberia (6.29), as found in the *CIA's World Fact Book*.

Table 12.2 Maternal mortality estimates using the sisterhood method

Age group of respondent	Number of respondents	Eligible sisters	Maternal deaths	Adjustment factor	Sister units of risk exposure	Lifetime risk of maternal death	Proportion of dead sisters dying of maternal causes
15–19	39	131[a]	3	0.107	14	0.215	0.375
20–24	69	231[a]	4	0.206	48	0.084	0.182
25–29	49	175	6	0.343	60	0.100	0.222
30–34	43	123	3	0.503	62	0.048	0.150
35–39	34	152	9	0.664	101	0.089	0.250
40–44	23	40	3	0.802	32	0.093	0.200
45–49	8	37	1	0.900	33	0.030	0.250
Total	265	889	29	–	350	0.083[b]	0.220

[a]Derived by multiplying the number of respondents by the average number of ever-married sisters per respondent reported for the age groups of 25+, that is, 3.35 (Reported numbers: 15–19=87; 20–24=183)

[b]Lifetime risk of maternal deaths from respondents under age 50=29/350=.0829 or about 1 in 12

[c]Maternal Mortality Ratio (MMR)=$[1-(1-\text{Lifetime risk})^{1/\text{TFR}}]\times[100{,}000]=[1-(1-0.0829050)^{1/6.29}]\times[100{,}000]$=1,366 deaths/100,000 live births (95% confidence interval, 1,199–1.534)

region in Liberia was 0.082905, i.e., 1 in every 12 women who reached reproductive age (defined as 15 years) died during pregnancy, childbirth or the puerperium. A total of 132 participants' sister deaths were reported, and 29 of them (22%) were attributed to maternal causes. The estimated MMR was 1,366/100,000 live-births. These estimates are comparable to the national level for Liberia.[6]

Interestingly, these risk estimates fall in between the health professionals' crude success rate of 81 per 100 pregnant women and their perceived probability of maternal mortality of 6%±0.43 (reported in the next section on the Survey of Health Care Professionals/Providers). Considering that health professionals' perceptions of probability of maternal death are confined to those who are attended by them, one can expect a higher probability when mothers who are unattended or who are attended by untrained persons (e.g. zoe, TBA) are included in the sample. Thus, the LTR of 8% seems to be an accurate estimate.

Self-Vulnerability, Causes and Solutions

In response to the question, *In general, what is the most common cause(s) of mothers in this region to suffer during or after pregnancy and what do you suggest to improve the health of these mothers*, women indicated a high level of self-vulnera-

[6]The WHO estimates in 2000 for Liberia were: LTR=1 in 16; MMR=760 with an uncertainty range from 190 to 1,400 (see *World Health Organization* 2005). It is likely that the survey region has a higher MMR than the national average, and the national MMR itself may have been higher about 10–12 years ago.

bility due to lack of money; lack of a healthcare facility in their vicinity; ignorance of their conditions of health; spread of common diseases like cholera, malaria, typhoid; and frequently, unskilled/untrained health workers experimenting on them. They all requested affordable (if not totally free) health care services, establishment of local/community health clinics, and training for the unskilled health workers like zoes, untrained midwifes, and traditional birth attendants with education for women about their health risks, nutritional facts, and the importance of regular visits to clinics and following health professionals' advice including taking medication as recommended. Here is a representation of statements the respondents made:

> I am a typical example of mothers or women suffering after pregnancy because I drink herbs and rubbed chalk throughout my pregnancy until I gave birth. This practice does not mean well for us because I am presently experiencing the negative of these herbs and chalk that I was taking. So I will like to advice that enough awareness be done in our area so as to enable us use the clinic or nearby health center, although it is a distance. I am also urging the national government through the health ministry to see reason to build for us a health center in our community.
>
> Most common cause of mothers' suffering during or after pregnancy is severe stomach pain, which come as the result of untrained midwife attending to mothers. Malaria and body pain are also some common causes encountered by mothers. I request that trained medical doctors should be sent in our areas.
>
> From where I come from we don't know about medical care. All we do is to seek our native doctors and pray to God for good health until the child is born. I suggest that trained doctors/nurses go into these regions and educate our people about prenatal care/medical care. This will stop the complications, which most women are faced with during pregnancy.
>
> Many young girls get pregnant and abort because of no support. After aborting plenty, it can stop you from bearing sometimes. One common problem is swollen feet. Malaria can cause serious problems. It can even destroy pregnancy. I suggest that contraceptives, pills be free like condoms too. Secondly, young girls should be given businesses and scholarships to help them start supporting themselves.
>
> No clinic here. Don't know what to do if we get sick while pregnant. We only see country doctor who will sometimes tell us to go to the hospital, and the distance is so far and no money. Therefore we sometimes have serious problems that pregnant women even die.
>
> Common causes are urinary tract infection, sexually transmitted infections, malaria, anemia, and postpartum hemorrhage. Suggestions: trained health workers be sent to the rural communities and they should be encouraged to spend longer times with these communities.
>
> These mothers should go to trained doctors, nurses, and good midwife. Seeking good medical care at hospital. You have to train the mothers and educate them well.
>
> Most common cause is due to nurses poorly trained, they don't know how to take care of people because only small schools they can attend. I suggest that students should go to college and good schools to learn more before doing work in hospital, clinic or home.
>
> When pregnant, giving birth outside of the hospital is a problem, not taking vaccines. Women should be taught to visit hospital through radio programs, workshops and field work. Reduce the fees.
>
> Weak back, low blood and lack of transportation. I suggest that the hospital fees should be reduced and the women be educated about their health.
>
> Lack of nutritional status, lack of medical attention are common in this region. In order to improve the health of these mothers training should be provided and teach women on what kinds of food to eat during pregnancy. More health centers should be provided so that women can be assessed and know some of the risk factors during and after pregnancy.

Survey of Health Care Professionals/Providers

The health care professionals/providers survey instrument consisted of 14 questions—name, highest educational qualification, position and rank, age, gender, experience, self involvement in providing prenatal services to pregnant women and/or delivering babies, whether or not trained to deliver babies, record keeping, volume of services rendered to pregnant women and rate of success during the past year, perceived maternal mortality rate and associated causes, organizational description and capacity, perceived roles of health professionals and of adult women in reproductive ages to improve the conditions of maternal health and mortality in their region. The questionnaire maintained a balance between open-ended and close-ended questions to optimize the level of difficulty and time required on the respondents' part in providing the information solicited.

Data Analysis

A total of 203 health professionals/providers participated in the survey—68 (33.5%) males and 130 (64%) females. They were between 20 and 65 years old, with a mean age of 35.8 years. They represented various organizational sizes and types as shown in Table 12.3.[7] About 23% of professionals serving in small agencies specified that their agencies serve rural populations. Nearly 19% of medium agencies said that their agencies were suffering from understaffing and lack of funds/budget cuts.

To what extent the above descriptions represent the respondents' explications may be examined from the following quotes:

1. Responses from large organizations:

> At the hospital I work we do minor and major surgeries, we do prenatal and post natal clinics, well baby clinic. We provide healthcare delivery to the people of county and even people from all other counties...We have over 75 staff and receive about 90–100 patients a day.
>
> This hospital functions as a Pediatric hospital, has a staff of approximately 200 and caters to approximately 200 patients a day.
>
> The hospital that I am working at is government hospital and is by "NGO" (non-governmental organization). It has prenatal, well baby and surgical facilities. It receives about 200 patients daily on a 24 hr. basis. It has over 800 staff. We do 100 deliveries weekly with live babies.
>
> The hospital is a major referral hospital for the southeastern counties of Liberia. It has over 100 workers with many divisions—OB, pediatrics, surgical orthopedic, dentistry, etc. It deliveries over 300 babies annually.
>
> I served at Phebe Hospital. Phebe provides preventive and curative serves for all ages, sex or religion.

[7]These descriptions are compiled from respondents' accounts in response to the question: *Tell me about the hospital/clinic where you serve—in terms of its functions, staff size, number of patients it serves, number of babies delivered,* etc.

Table 12.3 Distribution of respondents by organizational size and type

Organizational size/type	Number of respondents	Percent of respondents	Organizational description
I (Large)	31	15.2	Mostly government owned and often run by NGOs. Serve patients of both genders and of all ages (unless a specialized facility for children) with multiple needs—OB/GYN, pediatrics, orthopedics, vision, etc. Serve population covering wide areas and take referrals from other hospitals/clinics. Capable of handling long-term care inpatients as well a outpatients. Can conduct both major and minor surgeries. Equipped with testing laboratories, X-ray laboratories, ICUs, and other facilities. Staff size ranges from 30 to 500; number of patients served per day ranges from 90 to 1,000. Open 24 h a day and 7 days a week and handle emergencies.
II (Medium)	57	27.9	Owned by private individuals/organizations or government. Serve neighboring communities/ counties. Capable of handling minor surgeries and provide limited emergency care. Provide care for patients without many complications. Limited bed capacity for short-term inpatients. Operate 24 h a day and 7 days a week. Refer complicated cases and major surgeries to large hospitals. Staff size varies from 11 to 25 and number of patients served per day varies from 50 to 300.
III (Small)	98	48.0	Local clinics. Owned by private individuals/ organizations or government Provide outpatient services only. Open only 8 h a day and closed on weekends. Treat symptoms, give vaccines, provide well baby checkups and routine checkups, and perform normal deliveries. Refer all other cases to medium and large hospitals based on level of complication. Staff size varies from 3 to 15 and number of patients served per day from 10 to 100.
Unknown	17	8.8	Descriptions are either not provided or vague.

The Phebe Hospital located in Suacoco, Bang County—is to provide health services to people in all around Liberia, the staff size 680, and number of patients it serves per day is 500–1,000. Number of babies delivered 20 a day.

Has OPD, OBG, Eye Clinic (or HIV/AIDS). Has large number of staff (about 500). Very large number of patient—about a thousand including admission and OPC. Abouts—10 babies deliver every day.

2. Responses from medium organizations:

I am working in a government hospital where we have limited staff. We provide prenatal clinic ... we do minor surgeries and c/section. We serve about 40–50 patients a day and we do about 6 normal deliveries a day. ...live babies.

We offer services such as treating malaria, diarrhea, infections, minor surgeries, etc. We only have limited bed space for short stay. The staff includes 2 Pas, 2 nurse, 2 nurse aids, 1 dispenser, 2 midwives, security, and 4 cleaners. Three doctors because one is on call, if needed.

A government clinic sponsored by MDM providing OPD services and short stay 8 bed-room services. Vaccines are served here. All complications are transferred. 4 midwifes, 3 TTMs, 2 Pas, 2 vaccinators, 2 record keepers, 3 pharmacists, 1 growth monitor, 2 injection room nurse aides and 2 janitors. It serves about 100 patients a day and delivers like 2–5 babies a day.

3. Responses from small organizations:

Within my clinic I have 7 staff and within a day we do about 2–3 normal deliveries. We also serve about 20 patients a day and provide prenatal clinic.

I'm working at a local clinic, which comprises 8 staff and runs from 8 am to 5 pm Monday–Friday. We deal strictly with medical cases excluding deliveries. We only give advice to pregnant women to go to bigger health facilities.

The clinic is far from the main road. We provide immunization, treat symptoms, uncomplicated problems. This clinic has 10 staff and renders services to about 50 patients. Normal deliveries are about 2 babies a day.

This is a 5-room private clinic that gives only outpatient services, with 6 staff: 1LPN, 1PA, 1TBA, 1 Student nurse aide, 1 pharmacist, 1 registrar. We do 1–2 deliveries a day or about 5–10 a week. We don't work on weekends. We see about 25–40 persons a day. We don't deliver people with complications at all. We refer them.

Professional Involvement

A total of 30 positions and ranks were reported by 201 respondents. Only two respondents did not specify their position. Most of the respondents were Midwives (38) or Registered Nurses/Head Nurses (33), followed by Screeners (13), Physician Assistants (12), Bedside Nurses (10), Nurse Aides (10), OICs (8) and Student Nurses (14). Six were college seniors. Registered Nurses and Physician Assistants also frequently had second function as Screeners (13 and 12, respectively). Other positions/ranks involved RNs and Midwives (2), Supervisors (6), Registrar (5), Traditional Birth Attendants (3), Clinic Pharmacist (1), OIC/Screener (1), Ward Nurse (1), Assistant Midwife (1), Registrar and Sanitation Officer (1), Coordinator (1), Dispenser (1), Vaccinator (1), Student Midwife (1), Anesthetist (1), and Shift Supervisor/OB Ward (1).

Most of the respondents appear to have had appropriate academic qualification to the positions/ranks they hold. Thirty percent (n=61) had a diploma in nursing or RN training, 24% (n=48) had certified midwife training, and 17% (n=34) had Physician Assistant (PA) training. Among others, 20% (n=41) were high school graduates and

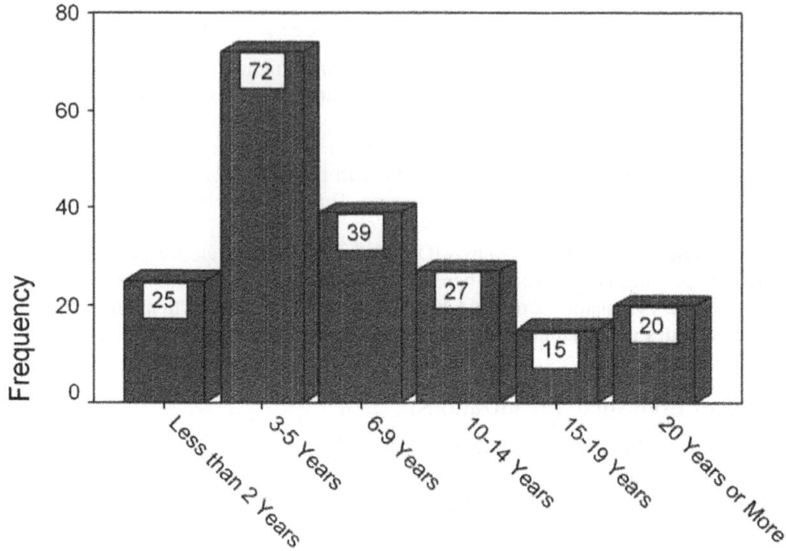

Fig. 12.6 Professional experience

3.4% (n=7) had college education. A comparison of education with position/rank shows an agreement ratio of 82%, indicating that at least 82% of the staff had an academic background that translated into their occupational rank/position.

Most (88%) had at least 3 years of professional experience and only 12% had reportedly been working for 2 years or less (Fig. 12.6). Thirty-six percent had 3–5 years experience; 19% 6–9 years; 13% 10–14 years; 7% 15–19 years; and, 10% had experience of 20 years or more. Eight out every 10 health professionals (n=166) indicated that they provide services to pregnant women and/or deliver babies. A few RNs (16%), RN and Head Nurses, one-half of bedside nurses, registrars, clinic pharmacists, and some student nurses were among those who did not provide these services (Table 12.4).

Apparently everyone who was involved in delivering babies had undergone some formal training. However, some of them had this training long ago and might be in need of some continuing education in lieu of new developments in the medical field and in technology (Table 12.5).

Maternal Health Services and Success Rate

Three questions were posed to respondents: *Do you regularly keep the records of the pregnant women to whom you provide services? If yes, how many pregnant women did you serve in the last 1-year? Of all the pregnant women you served, how many were successful deliveries? (That is, both mother and child surviving after delivery).*

Table 12.4 Professional rank/title by status of providing prenatal services

	Provide prenatal services				Provide prenatal services		
Rank/Title	No	Yes	Total	Rank/title	No	Yes	Total
Registered Nurse (RN)	5	25	30	Bedside nursing	5	5	10
Midwife		38	38	Nurse aide	3	7	10
RN-cum-Midwife		2	2	Registrar	5		5
RN & Head nurse	2	1	3	Clinic pharmacist	1		1
Head nurse		2	2	Ward nurse		1	1
Physician Assistant (PA)		12	12	Assistant midwife		1	1
Screener	1	12	13	OIC/Screener	1		1
PA-cum-Screener	2	10	12	Coordinator		1	1
RN & Screener		13	13	Dispenser	1		1
Student nurse	3	11	14	Vaccinator		1	1
Traditional birth attendant	1	2	3	Supervisor	2	2	4
Office-in-charge (OIC)		8	8	Student midwife		1	1
Supervisor/OPD	1	1	2	Anesthetist		1	1
Registrar & Sanitation officer	1		1	Nursing director		1	1
Shift supervisor/ OB ward		1	1	Senior in college		6	6
				TOTAL	**34 (17.1%)**	**165 (82.9%)**	**199 (100.0%)**

Table 12.5 When trained to deliver babies?

		Frequency	Percent	Valid percent	Cumulative percent
Valid	1960s	2	1.0	1.4	1.4
	1970s	2	1.0	1.4	2.8
	1980s	24	11.8	16.6	19.3
	1990s	41	20.2	28.3	47.6
	2000s	76	37.4	52.4	100.0
	Total	145	71.4	100.0	
Missing	System	58	28.6		
Total		203	100.0		

In response to these questions, 28 (of the 170 providers of maternal health services) said they would not keep records of pregnant women they serve, and the remaining 142 replied that they keep such records. The number of pregnant women they served varied from as low as two women to as many as 4,480 with an average of 228 women in the last year. The number of successful cases in which both mother and

Table 12.6 Number of pregnant women served, number of successful cases, and success rates by the size of organization

Organization type	Number of respondents	Total served (T) vs. success (s)	Number of pregnant women served: Minimum	Maximum	Mean number of cases	Average success rate
I Large	19	T	7	4,480	672	88.9
		S	7	4,240	598	
II Medium	44	T	2	750	128	87.5
		S	2	450	112	
III Small	68	T	6	1,750	177	72.9
		S	5	1,250	129	
All types combined (Pooled sample)	131	T	2	4,480	228	81.1
		S	1	4,240	185	

child survived after delivery varied from 1 to 4,240 with an average of 185 cases. Thus, the crude success rate is 81 per 100 pregnant women. It is important to see how this risk is distributed by the size of the organization. Table 12.6 shows the number of pregnant women served, number of successful cases, and resulting success rates by the size of the organization.

As the above table shows the success rates vary significantly by the size of organizations—that is, it decreases from large to medium moderately, but decreases drastically from medium to small. This large difference may be because of excessive patient turnover, understaffing, inadequate follow-ups due to the nature of 8 h workdays and closings on weekends, lack of equipment to handle last minute emergencies, and/or lack of medical attention right from the beginning of gestation.

What about the provider's knowledge, experience and skill? Do some professionals ensure better success rate than others? Table 12.7 provides the success rates by providers' position/rank. While screeners reported highest success rates (95.1), 'others' (consisting of Screeners/OICs (Office in-charge), bedside nurses, college seniors, nurse aides, supervisors, traditional birth attendants, assistant midwives, coordinator, student nurses, student midwives, etc.) demonstrated the lowest success rate of 67.8. Screeners may have a better understanding about the conditions of the pregnant women they serve and persons in the latter group may lack such ability because of inadequate experience (especially for students) and other administrative distractions (especially for OICs, supervisors, and nurse directors). Physician Assistants also showed a relatively low success rate of 77.1. The success rates of both midwives and RNs were above the success level of the total sample, although midwives had an edge over RNs (89.8 vs. 84.4).

In order to determine the significance of the observed differences in success rates by organizational size, providers' position/rank, and experience, a three-way analysis of variance was conducted. Table 12.8 indicates that not only do these three variables have a significant effect on success rates independently (main affects),

Table 12.7 Number of pregnant women served, number of successful cases, and success rates by providers' position/rank

Providers' position/rank	Number of respondents	Total served (T) vs. success (s)	Number of pregnant women served		Mean number of cases	Average success rate
			Minim.	Maxim.		
RNs and related	40	T	6	4,480	257	84.4
		S	6	4,240	217	
Midwives	35	T	10	1,320	245	89.8
		S	5	1,317	220	
PAs and related	19	T	27	405	131	77.1
		S	9	198	101	
Screeners	12	T	36	180	122	95.1
		S	36	178	116	
Others	32	T	2	1,758	270	67.8
		S	2	1,748	183	

Table 12.8 ANOVA of success rates by organizational size, providers' position/rank and experience

Source	Type III sum of squares	df	Mean square	F	Sig.
Corrected model	39470.113[a]	50	789.402	11.275	.000
Intercept	349330.117	1	349330.117	4989.389	.000
SIZE	471.428	2	235.714	3.367	.040
POSITION	2923.911	4	730.978	10.440	.000
EXPERIEN	6540.395	5	1308.079	18.683	.000
SIZE * POSITION	6631.027	7	947.290	13.530	.000
SIZE * EXPERIEN	6093.186	9	677.021	9.670	.000
POSITION * EXPERIEN	13380.215	17	787.071	11.242	.000
SIZE * POSITION *EXPERIENT	4200.174	6	700.029	9.998	.000
Error	5461.139	78	70.015		
Total	1078040.053	129			
Corrected total	44931.252	128			

Dependent variable: SUCCESS
[a]R squared = .878 (Adjusted R Squared = .801)

they can also affect the outcome jointly (2-way and 3-way interactions). That means, for example, a student nurse or student midwife working at a small organization can have a lower success rate than he/she would at a medium or large organization. Therefore, it is imperative to have high ranking and highly experience professionals at smaller organizations in order to have higher success rates. Finally, these three variables accounted for an R^2 value of 0.878—which means, 87.8% of variance in success rates can be explained by these three variables alone.

Table 12.9 Health professionals' perceived maternal mortality

		Frequency	Percent	Valid percent	Cumulative percent
Valid	None	46	22.7	31.1	31.1
	Less than 3%	21	10.3	14.2	45.3
	3–5%	54	26.6	36.5	81.8
	5–10%	21	10.3	14.2	95.9
	10–20%	6	3.0	4.1	100.0
	Total	148	72.9	100.0	
Missing	System	55	27.1		
Total		203	100.0		

Perceptions of Maternal Mortality

In response to the question, *In your best judgment, keeping [in mind] all the pregnant women you have served over last year, how often have you seen the death of a woman during or within 6 weeks after delivering a baby? (e.g., 1 in 5, 1 in 10, 1 in 20, etc.)*, respondents provided their estimated probabilities. Perceived maternal mortalities based on these probabilities are shown in Table 12.9: 23% responded that no one had died,10% said less than 3% of women they had served had died, nearly 27% felt 3–5% had died, 10% said that 5–10% had died, and yet 3% believed as many as 10–20% had died.

In order to determine what these perceptions might have been based upon, a correlation analysis was conducted between each respondent's perceived maternal mortality (pmmr) and four possible correlates: his/her reported success rate (success), organizational size (size), professional experience (experience), and position/rank (Table 12.10). Interestingly, neither zero-order nor partial correlations showed significant association between perceived maternal mortality and success rate. However, perceived maternal mortality is significantly associated with organizational size, professional experience, and position/rank. In other words, lower maternal mortality rates are likely to be perceived by those affiliated with large organizations, those with longer experience, and those employed as RNs and Midwives. Since these same three factors were found to be significantly associated with success rate earlier, it is possible that success rate may not be directly associated with an individual's perceptions but is predicated through its determinants.

Perceptions of Maternal Health Risk Factors

The questionnaire called for health professionals' ranking of the six most common risk factors,[8] and the results are shown in Fig. 12.7: 36.9% rated severe bleeding during and/or after delivery as the most common cause of maternal death; 29.5%

[8]These risk factors are commonly found in many developing countries. See for example, Strong 1992; United Nations Children's Fund 1996; World Health Organization 1996, 1997; Graham 1997; Tsui et al. 1997; Abouzahr and Warlaw 2001; Reproductive Health Response in Conflict Consortium 2004.

Table 12.10 Zero-order and partial correlation coefficients of perceived maternal mortality (pmmr) with success rate (success), organizational size (size), professional experience (experience) and position/rank

Correlates	Zero-order correlation coefficients/ number of cases/significance level	Third order partial correlation coefficients[a]/number of cases/significance level
Success	.0680	.0856
	(129)	(126)
	p=.440	p=.337
Size	−.2324**	−.2315**
	(137)	(126)
	p=.006	p–.009
Experience	−.1645*	−.1164
	(144)	(126)
	p=.047	p=.191
Position (q3)	.2388**	.2147**
	(145)	(126)
	p=.004	p–.015

Note: [a]Third order partials indicate controlling for all other three variables in the table
* = .05
** = .01 or less

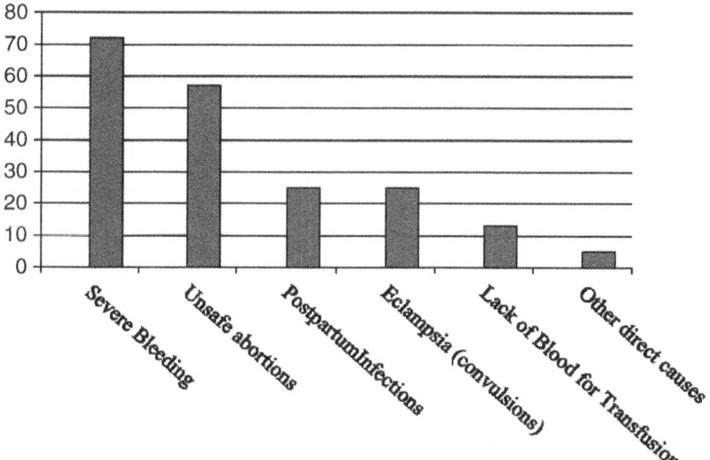

Fig. 12.7 Leading causes of maternal mortality

selected unsafe abortion/septic induced abortion; 13% indicated postpartum infections; another 13% chose eclampsia or convulsions, 6.7% chose lack of blood for transfusions; and, only 3% weighed other direct causes over all the above.

The response patterns for each of these six leading causes of maternal mortality along with corresponding mean values and standard deviations further evidence that severe bleeding and unsafe abortions are the leading two causes of maternal mortality (Table 12.11). The larger mean values are associated with lower ratings, implying that health professionals observed them among fewer cases and vice versa. In addition to these direct causes, *harmful traditional practices during delivery, such as putting a cook-spoon in the mouth of the pregnant woman in labor and setting of*

Table 12.11 Health professionals' rating patterns of leading causes of maternal morality

Cause of maternal mortality	Ratings from *most common (1)* to *least common (6)*						Mean (Std. Dev.)
	1	2	3	4	5	6	
1. Severe bleeding during and/or after delivery (n = 195)	72 (36.9)	51 (26.2)	39 (20.0)	24 (12.3)	7 (3.6)	2 (1.0)	2.23 (1.23)
2. Unsafe abortion/septic induced abortion (n = 193)	57 (29.5)	42 (21.8)	35 (18.1)	31 (16.1)	28 (14.5)	–	2.64 (1.42)
3. Postpartum infections (n = 193)	25 (13.0)	52 (26.9)	58 (30.1)	39 (20.2)	16 (8.3)	3 (1.6)	2.89 (1.21)
4. Eclampsia/convulsions (n = 92)	25 (13.0)	33 (17.2)	42 (21.9)	63 (32.8)	25 (13.0)	4 (2.1)	3.22 (1.30)
5. Lack of blood for transfusions (n = 193)	13 (6.7)	17 (8.8)	19 (9.8)	30 (15.5)	93 (48.2)	21 (10.9)	4.22 (1.39)
6. Other direct causes (n = 168)	5 (3.0)	1 (0.6)	3 (1.8)	6 (3.6)	20 (11.9)	133 (79.2)	5.58 (1.05)

Note: Values in parentheses are row percentages

mortar on the lady's stomach to push the baby out, distance from healthcare center, lack of vehicle to transport pregnant woman to a major hospital in case of emergency, poor nutrition, and preexisting health conditions are specified as indirect causes of maternal mortality.

According to respondents, the morbidity conditions that pregnant women suffer from are malaria, anemia, urinary tract infection, malnutrition, communication inadequacy, backache, etc. during pregnancy and postpartum hemorrhage, postpartum infection, malnutrition, hypertension, and postpartum psychosis after pregnancy.

What Should Health Professionals Dealing with Pregnant Women Know?

Many respondents advocated the need for health professionals to establish an ongoing relationship with their patients (along with their spouses, if possible) and to gain knowledge of their health conditions and history. Respondents also stressed the importance of treating each patient on a case-by-case basis instead of handling them as a routine procedure. For example a Registered Nurse Midwife-OB Supervisor at a large organization stated:

> All health workers should be able to know about their clients as well as their husbands. They should be able to establish nurse-patient relationship between them and their clients. They should be able to make their clients to build confidence and trust in them in order for them (clients) to be able to explain their problems to them. The health worker should teach their clients about the importance of visiting the prenatal clinic regularly and on taking the medication given them while attending the prenatal clinic. All health workers dealing with pregnant women should know which drugs to give their clients per trimester. They should

not conceal any problem pertaining to the pregnancy from the clients and her husband. They should learn to visit their clients as well. They should teach them how to care for themselves and their babies. The best way to make them understand these things is to health educate them and conduct workshop for them as well.

Another Registered Nurse from a large organization emphasized:

All health professionals who deal with pregnant women should know that all women are different and respond to pregnancy changes differently. Also, they should know that the cultural beliefs of pregnant women are very important to them although they may not be true. They are deeply rooted into the lifestyle of these women. They should therefore handle such beliefs with caution if they want these women to open up and be responsive to them.

Some focused on the job knowledge and skill levels on the part of health professionals themselves. The following statement by a Midwife from the medium organization illustrates this angle:

They should know all about OB and GYN from start to end. They should be well educated because nursing is not guessing. They should know how to measure FHT, Fundal height, fetus lie, presenting part, detect weak back, etc. They should know how to prescribe drugs. They should know how to do deliveries and how to handle complications. They should know teamwork and how to transfer complications very early. To help them understand, schools need to really teach them. Also small size workshops for health workers will help those who ar3e working to understand too.

A Traditional Birth Attendant from a small organization echoed along the same lines:

They should know how to keep some money for assisting pregnant women, who can't afford; how to do correct prenatal assessment; know the kinds of exercise pregnant women should take, especially those whose babies are not lying down good; know how to measure pregnancy and how to listen to the baby heart sound; know how to deliver babies good; how to cut and tie the cord, how to check the placenta, how to suction the baby; how to check women well; they should know that their materials should always be kept clean; and they should know how to record the birth records on the health cards.

What Do Health Professionals Think Women in Reproductive Ages Should Know?

Health professionals opined that pregnant women, in general, should learn the importance of regular health clinic visits and checkups, following medical advice, taking preventive care and medication, avoiding risky methods of delivery, practicing safe-sex methods, and maintaining close and honest communication with the health professionals. The following quotations are from health professionals' responses that illustrate these views.

Adult women should know that regular hospital or clinic visitation is essential, this will help in early detection/diagnosis of future problem and can be properly managed. Example, spontaneous abortion, post-partum hemorrhage, pre-eclempsia vaccination and proper prenatal routine drugs absence, which may sometimes lead to irreversible conditions. Adult women should be made to know that during pregnancy certain foods are essential for a healthy mother and baby or drugs for some infections that occur in pregnancy that may progress in to other problems if not treated properly. It is a risk for a previous C-section to attempt to do a home delivery. A healthy mother and child after delivery fully depend on full cooperation of the women listening to professional advice.

They should know about malnutrition, sexually transmitted infection, risks involved delivering the child vaginally in abnormal cases and ways to avoid, nutritional education, and following health professionals' advice.

Women of reproductive age need to know about the deadly disease, HIV/AIDS and how to protect themselves from contracting it. They should know about abstinence, being faithful to a single sex partner, and about the use of condoms.

They should learn the importance of vaccination to avoid polio babies and tetanus. They should always go to a hospital or clinic and stop buying medicines from the street.

All adult women in this region should know the risk of not taking family planning, and refusing to take vaccines during pregnancy.

…risk of not attending pre-natal clinic, poor hygiene, and the intake of harmful drugs.

…risks of teenage pregnancy, malnutrition, and anemia.

…risks of bleeding during pregnancy and after delivery.

They should know that sickle cell patients are not to get pregnant and that alcohol abuse is a risk factor for pregnant women.

…metabolic disorders such as diabetes mellitus are risk factors for women already diagnosed and endeavoring to get pregnant.

Conclusion

The findings of this study are consistent with other national studies. For example, we estimated the maternal mortality at the national level to be at 1,366 per 100,000 live-births and crude success rate (i.e., the survival rate of both mother and child after delivery) at 81 per 100 pregnant women. These estimates are in the acceptable range of the 2005 statistics reported by the World Health Organization: 1,200 maternal deaths per 100,000 live births and 66 neonatal deaths per 1,000 live births (World Health Organization 2008). The 2006–2007 Liberia Demographic and Health Survey showed a 71% increase in maternal mortality compared to its earlier survey in 1999–2000 (Liberia Institute for Statistics and Geo-information Services 2007). The Integrated Regional Information Networks (2008), a website maintained by the humanitarian news and analysis service of the United Nations Office for the Coordination of Humanitarian Affairs, reported that the increase in maternal mortality since the end of Liberia's civil war in 2003 was due to the near "non-existent" healthcare system. Along the lines of our survey findings, the Integrated Regional Information Networks also reported that: (1) doctors say the most common cause of death is vaginal hemorrhaging following childbirth, and (2) fewer births are being attended by trained medical professionals, the number of which declined through the end of the 1990–2003 war. Moreover, a wealth of the first-hand anecdotal information included herein from the reproductive mothers as well as from health professionals pertaining to risks and challenges they routinely encounter underscores the importance of maternal health. Maternal mortality in post-war Liberia is at an all time high, and it is imperative that efforts are made to develop the capacity of health practitioners assigned to rural clinics and health centers in order to deliver better services to these most marginalized communities as they struggle to recover from two decades of war.

References

Abouzahr, C., & Warlaw, T. (2001). Maternal mortality at the end of a decade: Signs of progress? *Bulletin of the World Health Organization, 79*(6), 561–568. Geneva: World Health Organization.

Amowitz, L. L, Reis, C., Iacopino V., & Physicians for Human Rights. (2002). Maternal mortality in herat province, Afghanistan: The need to protect women's rights (pp. 21–22). Boston: Physicians for Human Rights.

Central Intelligence Agency. (2006). *The world fact book*. Washington, DC: Central Intelligence Agency. Available online at https://www.cia.gov/library/publications/the-world-factbook/geos/li.html. Last accessed 2006.

Daniel, I., Graham, W., Stupp, P., & Castillo, P. (1996). Applying sisterhood method for estimating maternal mortality to a health facility-based sample: A comparison with results from a household-based sample. *International Journal of Epidemiology, 25*(5), 1017–1022.

Graham, W. (1994). The sisterhood method for estimating maternal mortality: Seven years' experience. *Kangaroo, 3*(2), 184–189.

Graham, W. (1997). *A question of survival? a review of the safe motherhood*. Kenya: Ministry of Health.

Graham, W., Brass, W., & Snow, R. W. (1989). Estimating maternal mortality: The sisterhood method. *Studies in Family Planning, 20*(3), 125–135.

Hill, K., & Trussell, J. (1977). Further developments in indirect mortality estimation. *Population Studies, 31*(2), 313–334.

Liberia Institute for Statistics and Geo-information Services (LISGIS), & Macro International, Inc. (2007). *Liberia demographic and health survey 2006–2007*. Calverton: Macro International, Inc.

Murty, K. S. (2006). *Maternal mortality and HIV/AIDS: Priorities and strategies to build intervention capacity of rural health services in post war Liberia—analysis of survey data on HIV/AIDS*. Washington, DC: United Negro College Fund Special Programs, Inc.

Reproductive Health Response in Conflict Consortium. (2004). *Emergency obstetric care: critical need among populations affected by conflict*. New York: Women's Commission for Refugee Women and Children. Available online at womensrefugeecommission.org/docs/emoc.pdf. Last accessed 2011.

Rutenberg, N., & Sullivan, J. (1991, August 5–7). *Direct and indirect estimates of maternal mortality from the sisterhood method*. Proceedings of the Demographic and Health Surveys World Conference, Washington, DC, (Vol. 3, pp. 1969–1996). Columbia: Institute for Resource Development/Macro International.

Strong, M. A. (1992). The health of adults in the developing world: The view from Bangladesh. *Health Transition Review, 2*(2), 215–224.

The Integrated Regional Information Networks. (2008). *LIBERIA: Maternal health worsened since war ended*. Available online at http://www.irinnews.org/report.aspx?ReportId=77196. Last accessed 2012.

Tsui, A. O., Wasserheit, J. N., & Haaga, J. G. (1997). *Healthy pregnancy and child bearing. Reproductive health in developing countries: Expanding dimensions, building solutions*. Washington, DC: National Academy Press.

United Nations Children's Fund. (1996). *The progress of nations*. New York: UNCEF.

Walraven, G. E., Mkanje, R. J., van Roosmalen, J., van Dongen, P. W., & Dolmans, W. M. (1994). Assessment of maternal mortality in Tanzania. *British Journal of Obstetrics and Gynaecology, 101*(5), 414–417.

Wirawan, D., & Linnan, M. (1994). The Bali indirect maternal mortality study. *Studies in Family Planning, 25*, 304–309.

World Health Organization. (1996). *Revised 1990 estimates of maternal mortality: A New approach by WHO and UNICEF*. Geneva: World Health Organization.

World Health Organization. (1997). *Coverage of maternal care: A listing of available information*. Geneva: World Health Organization. Available online at www.who.int/healthinfo/statistics/indantenatal/en/index.html. Last accessed 2011.

World Health Organization. (2005). *Maternal mortality in 2000: Estimates developed by WHO, UNICEF, UNFPA* (pp. 6–7). Geneva: Department of Reproductive Health and Research, World Health Organization. Available online at http://www.who.int/whosis/mme_2005.pdf. Last accessed 2012.

World Health Organization. (2008). World Health Statistics 2008. Available online at www.who.int/whosis/whostat/EN_WHS08_Full.pdf. Last accessed 2011.

Part IV
Special Analysis

Chapter 13
Neighborhood Resources and Adolescent Health and Risk Behaviors

Karen A. Snedker, Jerald R. Herting, and Emily Walton

Introduction

Neighborhood conditions – risks and resources – influence a range of individual behaviors for both adults and adolescents. While a growing literature explores the effects of neighborhood resources on individual behaviors, few studies focus on adolescents. Moreover, limited research explores both neighborhood risks and neighborhood resources. Data for this paper are from adolescents (aged 13–18) in the Seattle metropolitan area surveyed from 1998 to 2003. We explore the impact of neighborhood resources on three behavioral and health outcomes (alcohol use, depressed affect, and risky conduct behavior), while controlling for neighborhood disadvantage. By exploring multiple outcomes among adolescents and different features of the neighborhood environment, this paper provides insight into the ways in which positive aspects of neighborhood context matter for youth.

This research is couched at the intersection of demography and public health. The health behaviors – alcohol use, depression affect, and risky conduct behavior – addressed in this paper are precursors to more serious outcomes of substance abuse, depression,

K.A. Snedker (✉)
Department of Sociology, Seattle Pacific University, Seattle, WA, USA

Department of Psychosocial and Community Health, School of Nursing,
University of Washington, Seattle, WA, USA
e-mail: snedker@spu.edu

J.R. Herting
Department of Sociology, Department of Psychosocial and Community Health,
School of Nursing, University of Washington, Seattle, WA, USA
e-mail: herting@u.washington.edu

E. Walton
Department of Sociology Dartmouth College, University of Wisconsin – Madison,
Madison, WI, USA
e-mail: emily.c.walton@dartmouth.edu

N. Hoque et al. (eds.), *Applied Demography and Public Health*,
Applied Demography Series 3, DOI 10.1007/978-94-007-6140-7_13,

© Springer Science+Business Media Dordrecht 2013

juvenile delinquency and crime, all of which are serious public health concerns. Taking a demographic perspective, this paper explores behavioral patterns during a major developmental period of the life course. Adolescence is a key transitional stage that is important for demographic research. Moreover, quantitative approaches to tease apart different types of neighborhood effects from each other and from individual correlates is consistent with demographic methods and conceptual frameworks. This type of demographic health research has implications for public policy and health promotion programming – in terms of creating positive neighborhood spaces and resources – which is a central feature of public health research.

Background

Multiple aspects about neighborhoods have been linked to individual health and behavioral and outcomes. Most neighborhood research focuses on the effects of risk factors, namely economic or social disadvantage, relying on a social disorganization or stress perspective (Jencks and Mayer 1990; Massey 1996; Shaw and McKay 1942; Wilson 1996). Drawing from theories of social capital, an alternative approach explores the ways in which neighborhood resources benefit health. Disadvantage and resource frameworks are not necessarily incompatible. Indeed, researchers assert that economically disadvantaged neighborhoods often contain important neighborhood organizational resources and are sources of positive social support (Sampson et al. 1997; Wilson 1987). In this perspective, resources are not simply the opposite end of the disadvantage continuum, but can co-exist alongside disadvantage in neighborhoods. This paper explores positive dimensions of neighborhood conditions from the perspective that the presence of positive public spaces and service amenities in the environment impact adolescent well-being by providing opportunities for socialization and resource utilization.

Neighborhood Resources

Neighborhoods have resources that may protect individuals against negative health outcomes or risk behaviors associated with negative health outcomes. Services and public places, such as community centers or youth focused services (e.g., Boys and Girls clubs), may decrease unhealthy or problematic behaviors through involvement, socialization, and modeling. Such neighborhood resources provide opportunities for interaction, support and activity. In general, neighborhood resources have implications for social trust (Curley 2010), neighborhood attachment (Greif 2009), employment (Mendenhall et al. 2006), and crime (Peterson et al. 2000). Neighborhood resources are important for social capital in that they enhance or impede social connections and networks. In this area of research, key aspects of social capital include social support, social leverage, informal social control, and neighborhood organization participation (Carpiano 2008). For example, in a study exploring relocation of HOPE VI residents, authors find that neighborhood resources are strong predictors of social capital, which had implications for social trust (Curley 2010).

Several studies explore the influence of neighborhood resources for adults and find support for a protective effect, especially for health outcomes. In a study of female caregivers, Carpiano (2008) reports that three forms of neighborhood social capital have positive implications for health. Moreover, neighborhood resources, support among friends, and community organizations were associated with adherence to self-care behaviors among adult diabetics (Shaw et al. 2006). In addition, supportive neighborhood environments (street connectivity, amenities, lack of incivilities) were associated with lower rates of obesity among public housing residents (Heinrich et al. 2008).

Studies also link neighborhood resources and services to a range of behaviors in childhood and adolescence. Neighborhood resources, including resident support services (e.g., social service agency, parks) were associated with fewer daily hassles (family, peer, school, and neighborhood) reported by youth (Anthony and Nicotera 2008). Youth perceptions of high quality local facilities (e.g., equipment is good and available, facilities are open when needed, and facilities are fun), rather than the total number of facilities, are associated with more physical activity (Romero 2005). A study of middle childhood highlights the importance of family and neighborhood resources for social-emotional functioning (Bryant 1985). Neighborhood organizations or services were associated with lower levels of aggression among urban youth (Molnar et al. 2008). Moreover, Molnar and collaborators conclude that family, peer, and mentoring resources may only be beneficial when found in high concentrations.

In addition to direct neighborhood effects, researchers are increasingly examining the moderating role of neighborhoods in adolescent development and behavior. Moderating effects have been found for multiple adolescent outcomes including drug use (Fuller et al. 2005), internalizing and externalizing behavior (Spencer et al. 1997), and social and behavioral adjustment (Kupersmidt et al. 1995). Neighborhood moderating effects have been reported between neighborhood resources and family factors (Kupersmidt et al. 1995; Klebanov et al. 1994) and neighborhood education, neighborhood minority composition and individual race (Fuller et al. 2005), and neighborhood risk and coping behaviors (Spencer et al. 1997).

This study is innovative in its assessment of multiple health and risk outcomes among adolescents, focusing on alcohol use, depressed affect, and risky conduct behavior. A unique contribution is that we explore the direct and moderating effects of neighborhood resources alongside neighborhood disadvantage, bringing both positive and negative aspects of context together in one study.

Sample and Measures

Data for this paper are from adolescents (aged 13–18) in the Seattle metropolitan area surveyed from 1998 to 2003 as part of the Reconnecting Youth (RY) prevention research project. The sample represents a cross-sectional, random sample of high school youth (aged 14–19). It is stratified by high risk of school dropout; over the period three contiguous school districts (17 high schools) are represented in the survey, with only one high school declining to participate. Students with low school performance (low GPA, high absenteeism, and/or prior dropout/suspension were part of the criteria assessed from school records) were over sampled resulting in the construction and use of sampling weights in analyses. The over sampling of high-risk youth should produce variation in the behavioral and health outcomes, as the selection criteria are related to a variety of problematic outcomes.

Sixteen high schools in the Seattle and surrounding school districts participated in health/drug use interventions and/or surveys over the period. The analyses use data from three separate RY study sources conducted between 1998 and 2003: "Preventing Drug Abuse: Parents and Youths with Schools." (National Institute on Drug Abuse – NIDA), "Reconnecting Youth: Replication of an Indicated Prevention Program in Multicultural Settings" (Department of Education – DoE) and "Assessing Suicide Risk among Adolescents" (Centers for Disease Control – CDC). Merging the datasets increases our sample size and subsequent power and is appropriate given that the data sets are compatible in terms of: (1) the sampling frame and definition of high risk; (2) the content of the survey and format of survey administration; and (3) the region/schools and time period. All study youth agreed to participate, and parents provided consent in accordance with approved University of Washington IRB protocols. The analysis in this paper is based on data obtained prior to participants knowing to which condition within the randomized controlled trial they had been assigned.

For this analysis, we use part of the sample in which detailed resources and service data were available by census tract. This limited the sample to the city of Seattle, including students from nine Seattle high schools. Student home addresses from the individual-level dataset are geocoded and spatially linked to the appropriate census tract. In total, 1,661 individual respondents are included in the combined dataset, and more than 97 census tracts are represented in the data.

Following the research on neighborhood analysis, the neighborhood data in this project are operationalized at the census tract level (Billy and Moore 1992; Crane 1991; Ku et al. 1993). Data are compiled from the 2000 U.S. Census (e.g., population density and economic indicators) and City of Seattle (neighborhood services and public places) from 2000. Measures of neighborhood resources are captured by enumerating the resources in each census tract for three variables: boys and girls clubs, community centers, and public health clinics. The intent is to measure resources expected to provide positive service programs for adolescents and reflect some level of community involvement through local participation (e.g., volunteers). Other possible resources, such as parks or hospitals, were not always clear in their positive valence as a resource. For example, some parks may offer opportunity for negative behaviors rather than necessarily act as a positive resource. Other studies using a similar set of resource measures (Curley 2010) report that these measures capture people's perceptions of key resources (Yen et al. 2007).

A composite measure to represent economic *Neighborhood Disadvantage* is based on a scale constructed by Sampson and collaborators (1997). This index is composed of a mean of four indicators of economic disadvantage at the census tract level: percentages of residents below the federal poverty level, households headed by a female, residents receiving public assistance, and residents aged 16 years or older that are unemployed (reliability = 0.82). *Population density* of the census tract is measured per 1,000 people and is used to control for census tract size.

All outcomes and individual level independent variables come from the Reconnecting Youth High School Questionnaire (HSQ), a detailed self-report questionnaire capturing a range of youth behaviors including substance use, peer and family relations, and school behaviors. We focus on three categories of behavior for adolescents: substance use, mental health, and risky conduct behavior (reflecting early deviance or delinquency). We assess the frequency of alcohol use[1] during the past month (beer, wine, and hard liquor) based on questions derived from Monitoring the Future; frequency was gauged on a 7 point scale from 0 (no use) to 6 (daily use). For mental health we assess a scale of *depressed affect* (reliability between .80 and .89 across different surveys). The scale is a modified 6 item version of the CES-D depression index using a 0–6 Likert scale of frequency; prior work shows this smaller scale to have high reliability and correlates well with the larger scale (Eggert et al. 1994). A composite measure of *risky conduct behavior* includes the frequency of assault, theft, police contact, and disciplined at school for fighting over the past year (based on a 0–6 Likert scale).

We include measures designed to capture psychosocial risk and protective factors: *personal control, family support,* and *peer high risk behavior. Personal control* reflects a mean score based on five items tapping into personal agency and coping abilities (Cronbach's alpha=.82). Representative items include, "I feel confident that I can handle my personal problems," and "When I try, I can make good things happen for me." *Family support* is based on the extent of and satisfaction with help provided by immediate family members comprised of five items (Cronbach's alpha=.89). Representative items include, "My parent(s) support my activities," and "I feel satisfied with the way my family and I share time together." *Peer high risk behavior* captures the amount of close friends involved in five different delinquent behaviors (Cronbach's alpha=.85). Items include responses to the question "How many of your close friends…" for example, "skip school?" and "Have gotten into physical fights with other kids?" Specific details about all of the questions that comprise each construct are available upon request. All scales are adapted from known scales and based on 0–6 Likert items (Thompson et al. 2005). We include controls for age, sex, race and ethnicity, high risk for school dropout, time spent on activities (clubs, volunteering, and attending religious services), family structure and parent's educational attainment.

Statistical Approach

Multilevel techniques (hierarchical linear models-HLM) are used to assess the impact of resource and risk context on adolescent well-being. A hierarchical model explicitly incorporates variables at the individual level and at the contextual level and accounts for the clustering of individuals in the aggregate unit. HLM allows key

[1] We also explored *illicit drugs* (cocaine, opiates, depressants, tranquilizers, inhaled substances, stimulants, and over the counter drugs) but the HLM logit models failed to converge probably due to the limited frequency of affirmative responses for these items.

parameters of interest at the individual level to vary across local contexts, and our interest is to see if this variation is systematically associated with neighborhood factors (Raudenbush and Bryk 2002; Snijders and Bosker 1999). We assess direct influences of neighborhood context on three categories of adolescent behaviors. Specifically, we examine if neighborhood resources have a significant direct effect on predicting adolescent behavioral and health outcomes – substance use, mental health, and risky conduct behavior – while controlling for key individual- and neighborhood-level variables known to be associated with health and risk behaviors among youth. We explore cross-sectional associations among neighborhood characteristics and health and risk behaviors.

In the first model, the three behavior outcomes types (alcohol use, depressed affect, and risky conduct behavior) are regressed separately on the three neighborhood variables (resources, disadvantage, and population density). These models test for any effects of neighborhood dimensions on substance use, depressed affect, or risky conduct behavior without specific individual controls. Second, an individual-level model is added, including personal control, family support/structure, high risk peer behaviors, and basic control variables. This second model tests for any neighborhood effects after controlling for key individual-level factors. All continuous variables (age, parent education, personal control, family support, and high risk peers) are centered on their respective grand means. The individual (level 1) and neighborhood (level 2) can be seen in two equations below where the subscript i represents individuals and j represents neighborhood:

Level 1 – Individual Model

$Yij = \beta_{0j} + \beta_1$ (Hispanic) $+ \beta_2$ (Black) $+ \beta_3$ (Asian) $+ \beta_4$ (Other race) $+ \beta_5$ (Age) $+ \beta_6$ (Sex) $+ \beta_7$ (High risk for dropout) $+ \beta_8$ (Natural family structure) $+ \beta_9$ (Parent education) $+ \beta_{10}$ (Time spent in activities) $+ \beta_{11}$ (Personal control) $+ \beta_{12}$ (Family support) $+ \beta_{13}$ (High risk peers) $+ r_{ij}$

Level 2 – Neighborhood Model: Direct Effects

$\beta_{0j} = \gamma_{00} + \gamma_{01}$ (Population density) $+ \gamma_{02}$ (Disadvantage) $+ \gamma_{03}$ (Boys and girls clubs) $+ \gamma_{04}$ (Community centers) $+ \gamma_{05}$ (Public health clinics) $+ u_{0j}$

We also explore neighborhood moderating effects between the neighborhood resources variables and three psychosocial processes (personal control, family support, and high risk peer behaviors).

Results

Descriptive Statistics

Table 13.1 reports the means, standard deviations and ranges for all variables considered in these analyses. For the 1,661 students in the analysis, the ages ranged from 13 to 18 years, with a mean of 15.70. It is a racially-mixed sample with 38%

Table 13.1 Descriptive statistics (Level-1, N = 1,661; Level-2, N = 97)

Outcomes	Mean	Std. Dev.	Min.	Max.
Alcohol use	0.75	1.10	0.00	6.00
Depressed affect	1.53	1.16	0.00	6.00
Risky behavior (mean of four items)	0.69	1.01	0.00	6.00
Got into a physical fight last year	0.94	1.59	0.00	6.00
Shop-lifted, stolen, damaged property last year	0.98	1.83	0.00	6.00
Got disciplined at school for fighting last year	0.37	1.00	0.00	6.00
Got in trouble with police last year	0.48	1.11	0.00	6.00
Neighborhood explanatory variables				
Population density (in 1,000s)	7.91	3.97	0.71	33.47
Neighborhood disadvantage index (mean of four items)	6.79	3.86	2.57	21.65
Percentage below the poverty level	9.55	4.88	1.10	27.90
Percentage female-headed families	3.35	3.54	0.00	16.60
Percentage receiving public assistance	10.87	8.08	1.80	49.60
Percentage unemployed (over 16 years old)	3.41	1.84	0.50	12.20
Number of resources in tract				
Boys and girls clubs	0.04	0.20	0.00	1.00
Community centers	0.27	0.49	0.00	2.00
Public health clinics	0.03	0.17	0.00	1.00
Individual explanatory variables				
Race/ethnicity				
White	0.38	0.49	0.00	1.00
Hispanic	0.04	0.20	0.00	1.00
Black	0.22	0.42	0.00	1.00
Asian	0.16	0.37	0.00	1.00
Other	0.20	0.40	0.00	1.00
Age	15.70	1.01	13.00	18.00
Female	0.49	0.50	0.00	1.00
High risk for drop out	0.68	0.47	0.00	1.00
Lives with both natural parents	0.45	0.50	0.00	1.00
Parent's highest education	15.23	2.87	9.00	22.50
Time spent in activities	1.72	2.17	0.00	13.33
Personal control	4.28	1.28	1.00	6.00
Family functioning and support	3.44	1.63	0.00	6.00
Peer high-risk behaviors	1.61	1.19	0.00	6.00

white, 22% black, 16% Asian/Pacific Islander, 4% Hispanic, and 20% reporting other race or ethnicity (includes self-reported mixed ethnicity 14%, American Indian/Native Alaskan 3%, other 3%). Sixty-eight percent of the sample were at risk for dropping out of high school based on poor school performance; this reflects the stratified nature of the sample. Just less than half of the students come from homes with a biological mother and father present (45%). Measures of parent educational attainment revealed an average of 15.2 years of schooling. The response options for personal control and family support ranged from 0 to 6, with the averages being 4.28 and 3.44, respectively. Most students reported low levels of peer high risk behavior ($\bar{X} = 1.61$; 0–6 scale). Alcohol use in the past 30 days was generally low, with the average frequency of use falling below once a week. The depressed affect scale had a mean of 1.53 (based on a 0–6 scale) and risky conduct behaviors were low ($\bar{X}$ =0.69 on a 0–6 scale).

There was variability among the 97 census tracts. The mean count of all of the three neighborhood resource variables was less than 1 ranging from 0 to 2. The mean neighborhood disadvantage score for the census tracts in our sample was 6.8, falling within a range of 2.6–21.7. The population density variable reflected a mean of almost 8 ranging from less than 1–33.

Significant variation at the census tract level was found for all outcomes, which justifies incorporating neighborhood level variables into the model. In the first set of models, neighborhood resources, disadvantage, and population density were included in the model to test for effects of neighborhood factors on adolescent alcohol use, depressed affect, and risky conduct behavior without controlling for any individual-level factors. The only significant neighborhood effects were for alcohol and risky conduct behavior. The presence of public health clinics was negatively associated with alcohol use; adolescents living in neighborhoods with more services have lower rates of alcohol use. In addition, neighborhood disadvantage was negatively related to alcohol use; adolescents living in economically disadvantaged neighborhoods had lower rates of alcohol usage. For risky conduct behavior, public health clinics were significantly negatively associated. Surprisingly, no neighborhood constructs achieved significance for the depressed affect scale.

Including the individual-level model did not dramatically alter the influence of the neighborhood variables. For alcohol, both resources and disadvantage and neighborhood services were still significant and in the same directions. For risky conduct behavior, two neighborhood resources – boys and girls clubs and public health clinics – achieved statistical significance. Adolescents living in neighborhoods with more of these resources had lower rates of risky conduct behavior. Similar to the effects found in the first model, there were no neighborhood effects for depressed affect.

In the second set of models individual variables operated in a consistent manner with previous research. Race was important for alcohol but not for depressed affect or risky behavior. For alcohol, white (compared with blacks and Asians) youth reported higher levels of alcohol use (see Table 13.2). Age was only significant for alcohol use where older respondents reported greater use while for risky conduct behavior. There were no significant differences between boys and girls for alcohol use but there were for both depressed affect and risky conduct behaviors, with higher rates for girls and boys, respectively, and consistent with the literature. Being at risk for dropping out of high school was associated with greater alcohol use and risky conduct behaviors but no impact on depressed affect. Spending time in activities had a negative effect for alcohol use but no effect for the other behavioral and health outcomes. Higher parental education, as measured in years, was negative for all three outcomes but never achieved significance. The personal control measure was only significant for depressed affect and was associated with lower reported depressed affect. As expected, higher levels of family support were associated with lower frequency of both depressed affect and risky conduct behavior. Unexpectedly, family support was not related to alcohol use. In line with previous research, having high risk peers was strongly associated with greater alcohol use, depressed affect, and risky conduct behavior.

Table 13.2 HLM of neighborhood resources on various individual outcomes (Level 1, N=1,661; Level 2, N=97)

	Alcohol use		Depressed affect		Risky behavior	
Variable	Model 1	Model 2	Model 1	Model 2	Model 1	Model 2
Intercept	0.647***	0.770***	1.486***	1.499***	0.535***	0.671***
Neighborhood level						
Population density	−0.004	−0.002	0.008	0.010	−0.011	−0.009
Disadvantage index	−0.037***	−0.022**	−0.005	0.004	−0.008	−0.006
Number of resources						
Boys & girls clubs	0.109	0.071	0.046	0.025	−0.092	−0.107**
Community centers	0.055	0.069	0.037	0.073	0.005	0.035
Public health clinics	−0.298**	−0.198**	0.053	0.053	−0.196**	−0.123*
Individual level						
Hispanic		0.009		−0.097		−0.074
Black		−0.390***		−0.130		0.006
Asian		−0.208**		−0.092		−0.079
Other race		−0.116		−0.015		0.089
Age		0.065*		−0.011		−0.047
Female		0.081		0.301***		−0.145**
High risk		0.184**		−0.100		0.163**
Natural family structure		−0.047		−0.022		−0.011
Parent's education		−0.013		−0.010		−0.007
Time spent in activities		−0.026**		−0.011		0.007
Personal control		0.015		−0.401***		−0.021
Family support		−0.018		−0.077**		−0.038*
High risk peers		0.337***		0.124***		0.351***
τ	0.039	0.018	0.065	0.026	0.047	0.022
σ^2	0.925	0.761	1.258	0.906	0.724	0.523
Deviance	4654.47	4370.68	5172.20	4661.05	4266.92	3770.51

***p<.001; **p<.01; *p<.05

Discussion

The results in this paper showed some impact of neighborhood resources – boys and girls clubs and public health clinics – for select adolescent outcomes, specifically alcohol use and risky conduct behaviors. No effect was reported for community centers for any of the three outcome categories (substance use, mental health, or risky conduct behavior). While our measures of neighborhood services are arguably only indirect indicators of social capital, the protective role of these measures are consistent with this perspective and other research for adolescent and adult. The finding that the presence of boys and girls clubs was associated with less risky conduct behavior is also in line with specific research on adolescent behavior. Molnar and colleagues report that neighborhood organizations and services specifically targeting youth were associated with lower levels of aggression among urban youth (Molnar et al. 2008). Specifically, research on Boys and Girls Clubs suggest that they play a significant role in promoting pro-social youth behaviors and that participation in club activities was associated with positive school outcomes and reduced risk and problem behaviors (Anderson-Butcher et al. 2003). Moreover, researchers of adolescent delinquency argue that youth who are socially bonded are less likely to engage in delinquent behavior, such as getting in trouble with the police, and involvement in conventional activities is one of the four key attachments (Hirschi et al. 2002). In addition, one study (Pate et al. 2008) found that vigorous physical activity among 12th graders was positively associated with multipurpose facilities such as recreation centers and youth organizations.

In addition to presence of boys and girls clubs, presence of a public health clinic in the neighborhood was associated with lower levels of both alcohol use and risky conduct behavior among our adolescent sample. In general, the service area for public health clinics is large (e.g., corresponding to multiple census tracts in a region of the city); however, the presence of one of these agencies within the census tract of residence for adolescents corresponds with a lower prevalence of problematic individual behaviors. It could be that public health clinics provide specific information, social support, or awareness of problems or more generally that they are indicative of resources in the local environment. In the case of boys and girls clubs, there are staff, resources, and programming targeting teens and adolescent issues, with a preventative and proactive framework more likely; these types of community services providers might act as protectors against risky behaviors. The same process might also be the case for public health clinics, especially in terms of providing resources for sexual and reproductive health (e.g., sexually transmitted diseases and pregnancy prevention and prevention of drug and alcohol abuse). As part of their mission in King County, public health clinics aim to protect individual health and well-being by providing information and strategic interventions to reduce disparities.

In addition to direct effects of neighborhood resources on adolescent behaviors, neighborhood disadvantage was also significant for one adolescent outcome. In the case of alcohol use, the neighborhood disadvantage effect was in the direction of decreased usage. Adolescents living in neighborhoods with high levels of economic disadvantage have lower rates of alcohol use. Although this is not consistent with social disorganization and stress perspectives, counter results also appear when assessing school-level substance use rates. Based on student, parent, and archival data from a heterogeneous sample of elementary schools in a Midwestern state, lifetime alcohol use was higher for those in schools located in neighborhoods perceived to be more socially advantaged (Ennett et al. 1997). A recent study reports that teens from affluent, suburban families reported higher levels of substance use than their inner-city counterparts (Luthar and D'Avanzo 1999). We argue elsewhere that this is not out of line with the varied results on adolescent alcohol use and might reflect the experimental nature of alcohol use among teenagers (Snedker et al. 2009). Moreover, this relationship holds when controlling for neighborhood alcohol outlet density, but the presence of alcohol outlets in the neighborhood does reduce the protective effect of family resources (Snedker and Herting 2008).

Other spheres that play a pivotal role in adolescent alcohol use, especially the family and peer contexts, might partially explain the direction of these effects. These additional contexts can buffer or exacerbate neighborhood effects. However, we did not find any moderating effects for family support or high risk peers, nor did the inclusion of family or peer variables alter the direction of results. We also speculated that family or parental alcohol/substance use should be controlled at the individual level to insure that the neighborhood effect is accurate. Controlling for the youth's report of family alcohol/substance use in the household did not alter the observed negative effect of neighborhood disadvantage (results available upon request). More research needs to explore how families and parents broker the neighborhood environment and how that impacts adolescent health and risk behaviors.

No neighborhood effects for depressed affect were found in these analyses. This is inconsistent with theory and research in the field for mental health for adults and adolescents (Aneshensel and Sucoff 1996; Mair et al. 2008). It may be that neighborhoods play indirect effects for these outcomes and moderate key individual-level variables. For example, effects of residential poverty, urbanization, and racial/ethnic composition play a role in mental health, but may interact with status characteristics of the individual (McLeod and Edwards 1995). However, several moderating relationships were assessed between the neighborhood resources variables and the three psychosocial processes (personal control, family support, and peer high risk behavior) and no moderating effects were found (results are available upon request). The role of context with respect to mental health and specifically to mental health of adolescents requires continued attention.

The lack of consistent effects across different types of behaviors also raises issues about the uniformity of neighborhood risks or resources on outcomes for adolescence. It may be that neighborhood context has certain effects for some kinds of behavior and different effects for others. Part of the lack of effect or inconsistencies might relate to issues of access and how easily individuals can avail themselves of the services and public places. With this dataset we are unable to assess use of particular neighborhood resources, however we do control for individual club/sports activity, suggesting that the role of these neighborhood resources is in addition to a given youth's own individual activity. We find it especially noteworthy that neighborhood resource effects are still apparent while controlling for neighborhood economic disadvantage and a rich-individual-level model.

It is also worth considering that some resources might actually be risk factors. Yen and colleagues argue that there is some ambiguity between resources and hazards and that distinctions are not always clear (Yen et al. 2007). For example, a local park that is known for gang activity, drug sales, or sexual activity is unlikely to be construed as a positive resource by local residents. Research also suggests that the extent to which the neighborhood resources positively impact behavior might be tied to network integration (Carpiano 2008) and that adolescents who live in neighborhoods with weak social networks report higher levels of hopelessness, even after controlling for SES and depression (Perez-Smith et al. 2002).

The different direction of neighborhood effects, most notably for adolescent alcohol use, reflects that these neighborhood factors are indeed separate constructs and related to different social process, thus having a different impact on behavioral and health outcomes. Notably, research does not always find that these factors are inversely related. Recent analyses unexpectedly find that as poverty rates increase in neighborhoods so do the number of organizational resources, such as childcare centers and grocery stores (Small and McDermott 2006).

Additional conceptual and methodological issues are raised by this analysis. We rely on objective neighborhood indicators of social-structural and physical risks and resources. Research also suggests that perceived conditions might also be important (Anthony and Nicotera 2008). However, research reports that there is a reasonably strong correlation between perceived and actual neighborhood resources (Yen et al. 2007). We note that census tracts are not equivalent of neighborhoods, and the size may be too large to truly capture the impact of local context on behaviors. However, smaller units, such as block-groups, tend to yield few contextual differences with census-tract measures (Diez Roux et al. 2001). In a study of urban women, perceptions of neighborhood boundaries varied by income level, such that women in poorer neighborhoods understood their neighborhoods as smaller (Yen et al. 2007). Different configurations of neighborhood space are needed. In this paper we explore the presence of certain neighborhood resources, but this does not necessarily denote quality presence. Future analyses should tap into individual access to and use of neighborhood resources, which might provide a more complete picture of the impact of neighborhood environments on adolescent behaviors. Finally, there is some concern about the generalizability of the results. While the data set is largely representative of high school age youth in the Seattle metropolitan area, it is unclear how generalizable the results are to all cities; this may especially be true of the larger U.S. cities such as New York where levels of disadvantage may be more pervasive and extreme.

This research has clear implications for those interested in a better understanding of the relationship between neighborhood context and individual-level outcomes. For prevention scientists and practitioners, the linkages between neighborhood conditions and problem behaviors for youth can inform prevention programs and interventions (Kegler et al. 2005). In addition to the neighborhood resources assessed in this paper, other such resources need to be explored. Some neighborhood resources such as churches, schools, and childcare centers are what Small calls "resource brokers" and may be especially important (Small 2006). Further specifying the relationship between neighborhood resources and risky behaviors for youth is an important direction for future research and prevention studies.

Acknowledgements This research was partially funded by CDC (CCR015606), NIDA (DA10317; 5 T32 DAO7257-13; 1 R03 DA019622-01A2) and University of Washington Alcohol and Drug Abuse Institute. The authors would like to thank the University of Washington Reconnecting Youth project team for their comments and assistance with this project.

References

Anderson-Butcher, D., Newsome, W. S., & Ferrar, T. M. (2003). Participation in boys and girls clubs and relationships to youth outcomes. *Journal of Community Psychology, 31*(1), 39–55.

Aneshensel, C. S., & Sucoff, C. A. (1996). The neighborhood context of adolescent mental health. *Journal of Health and Social Behavior, 37*, 293–310.

Anthony, E. K., & Nicotera, N. (2008). Youth perceptions of neighborhood hassles and resources: A mixed method analysis. *Children and Youth Services Review, 30*(11), 1246–1255.

Billy, J. O. G., & Moore, D. E. (1992). A multilevel analysis of marital and nonmarital fertility in the U.S. *Social Forces, 70*(4), 977–1011.

Bryant, B. (1985). The neighborhood walk: Sources of support in middle childhood. *Monographs of the Society for Research in Child Development, 50*, 1–122.

Carpiano, R. M. (2008). Actual or potential neighborhood resources and access to them: Testing hypotheses of social capital for the health of female caregivers. *Social Science & Medicine, 67*(4), 568–582.

Crane, J. (1991). The epidemic theory of ghettos and neighborhood effects on dropping out and teenage childbearing. *The American Journal of Sociology, 96*, 1126–1259.

Curley, A. M. (2010). Relocating the poor: Social capital and neighborhood resources. *Journal of Urban Affairs, 32*(1), 79–103.

Diez Roux, A., Merkin, S., Arnett, D., et al. (2001). Neighborhood of residence and incidence of coronary heart disease. *The New England Journal of Medicine, 345*(2), 99–106.

Eggert, L. L., Thompson, E. A., & Herting, J. R. (1994). A measure of adolescent potential for suicide: Development and preliminary findings. *Suicide & Life-Threatening Behavior, 24*(4), 359–381.

Ennett, S., Flewelling, R., Lindrooth, R., & Norton, E. (1997). School and neighborhood characteristics associated with school rates of alcohol, cigarette, and marijuana use. *Journal of Health and Social Behavior, 38*(1), 55–71.

Fuller, C. M., Borrell, L. N., Latkin, C. A., Galea, S., Ompad, D. C., Strathdee, S. A., & Vlahov, D. (2005). Effects of race, neighborhood, and social network on age at initiation of injection drug use. *American Journal of Public Health, 95*, 689–695.

Greif, M. J. (2009). Neighborhood attachment in the multiethnic metropolis. *City & Community, 8*(1), 27–45.

Heinrich, K. M., Lee, R. E., Regan, G. R., Reese-Smith, J. Y., Howard, H. H., Haddock, C. K., Poston, W. S. C., & Ahluwalia, J. S. (2008). How does the built environment relate to body mass index and obesity prevalence among public housing residents? *American Journal of Health Promotion, 2*(3), 187–194.

Hirschi, T. (2002). *Causes of delinquency*. New Brunswick: Transaction Publishers.

Jencks, C., & Mayer, S. E. (1990). The social consequences of growing up in a poor neighborhood. In L. E. Lynn & M. G. H. McGeary (Eds.), *Inner-city poverty in the United States* (pp. 111–186). Washington, DC: National Academy Press.

Kegler, M. C., Oman, R. F., Vesely, S. K., et al. (2005). Relationships among youth assets and neighborhood and community resources. *Health Education & Behavior, 32*, 380–397.

Klebanov, P. K., Brooks-Gunn, J., & Duncan, G. J. (1994). Does neighborhood and family poverty affect mothers' parenting, mental health, and social support? *Journal of Marriage and the Family, 56*, 441–455.

Ku, L., Sonenstein, F. L., & Pleck, J. H. (1993). Neighborhood, family, and work: Influences on the premarital behaviors of adolescent males. *Social Forces, 72*(2), 479–503.

Kupersmidt, J. B., Griesler, P. C., De Rosier, M. E., Patterson, C. J., & David, P. W. (1995). Childhood aggression and peer relations in the context of family and neighborhood factors. *Child Development, 66*, 360–375.

Luthar, S. S., & D'Avanzo, K. (1999). Contextual factors in substance use: A study of suburban and inner-city adolescents. *Development and Psychopathology, 11*(4), 845–867.

Mair, C., Diez-Roux, A. V., & Galea, S. (2008). Are neighbourhood characteristics associated with depressive symptoms? A review of evidence. *Journal of Epidemiology and Community Health, 62*, 940–946.

Massey, D. S. (1996). The age of extremes: Concentrated affluence and poverty in the twenty-first century. *Demography, 33*(4), 395–412.

McLeod, J. D., & Edwards, K. (1995). Contextual determinants of children's response to poverty. *Social Forces, 73*, 1487–1516.

Mendenhall, R., DeLuca, S., & Duncan, G. (2006). Neighborhood resources, racial segregation, and economic mobility: Results from the Gautreaux program. *Social Science Research, 35*, 892–923.

Molnar, B. E., Cerda, M., Roberts, A. L., & Buka, S. L. (2008). Effects of neighborhood resources on aggressive and delinquent behaviors among urban youths. *American Journal of Public Health, 98*(6), 1086–1093.

Pate, R. R., Colabianchi, N., Porter, D., Almeida, M. J., Lobelo, F., & Dowda, M. (2008). Physical activity and neighborhood resources in high school girls. *American Journal of Preventive Medicine, 34*(5), 413–419.

Perez-Smith, A., Spirito, A., & Boergers, J. (2002). Neighborhood predictors of hopelessness among adolescent suicide attempters: Preliminary investigation. *Suicide & Life-Threatening Behavior, 32*(2), 139.

Peterson, R. D., Krivo, L. J., & Harris, M. A. (2000). Disadvantage and neighborhood violent crime: Do local institutions matter? *Journal of Research in Crime and Delinquency, 37*(1), 31–63.

Raudenbush, S. W., & Bryk, A. S. (2002). *Hierarchical linear models: Applications and data analysis methods*. Thousand Oaks: Sage Publications.

Romero, A. J. (2005). Low-income neighborhood barriers and resources for adolescents' physical activity. *Journal of Adolescent Health, 36*(3), 253–259.

Sampson, R. J., Raudenbush, S. W., & Earls, F. (1997). Neighborhoods and violent crime: A multilevel study of collective efficacy. *Science, 277*(5328), 918–924.

Shaw, C. R., & McKay, H. (1942). *Juvenile delinquency in urban areas*. Chicago: University of Chicago Press.

Shaw, B. A., Gallant, M. P., Riley-Jacome, M., & Spokane, L. S. (2006). Assessing sources of support for diabetes self-care in urban and rural underserved communities. *Journal of Community Health, 31*(5), 393–412.

Small, M. L. (2006). Neighborhood institutions as resource brokers: Childcare centers, interorganizational ties, and resource access among the poor. *Social Problems, 53*(2), 274–292.

Small, M. L., & McDermott, M. (2006). The presence of organizational resources in poor urban neighborhoods: An analysis of average and contextual effects. *Social Forces, 84*(3), 1697–1724.

Snedker, K. A., & Herting, J. R. (2008). The spatial context of adolescent alcohol use: Assessing the role of alcohol availability and neighborhood disadvantage. In Y. F. Thomas, D. Richardson, & I. Cheung (Eds.), *Geography and drug addiction* (pp. 45–65). New York: Springer.

Snedker, K. A., Herting, J. R., & Walton, E. (2009). Neighborhood contextual effects and adolescent substance use: Exploring the moderating role of neighborhoods. *Social Science Quarterly, 90*(5), 1272–1297.

Snijders, T., & Bosker, R. (1999). *Multilevel analysis: An introduction to basic and advanced multilevel modeling*. Thousand Oaks: Sage.

Spencer, M. B., Cole, S. P., Jones, S. M., & Swanson, D. P. (1997). Neighborhood and family influences on young urban adolescents' behavior problems: A multisample, multisite analysis. In J. Brooks-Gunn, G. J. Duncan, & J. L. Aber (Eds.), *Neighborhood poverty: Context and consequences for children* (pp. 200–218). New York: Russell Sage.

Thompson, E. A., Mazza, J. J., Herting, J. R., & Eggert, L. L. (2005). The mediating roles of anxiety, depression, and hopelessness on adolescent suicidal behaviors. *Suicide & Life-Threatening Behavior, 35*(1), 14–34.

Wilson, W. J. (1987). *The truly disadvantaged: The inner city, the underclass, and public policy.* Chicago: University of Chicago Press.

Wilson, W. J. (1996). *When work disappears: The world of the new urban poor*. New York: Vintage Books.

Yen, I. H., Scherzer, T., Cubbin, C., Gonzalez, A., & Winkleby, M. A. (2007). Women's perceptions of neighborhood resources and hazards related to diet, physical activity, and smoking: Focus group results from economically distinct neighborhoods in a mid-sized U.S. city. *American Journal of Health Promotion, 22*(2), 98–106.

Chapter 14
Population Density, Density of Alcohol Retail Outlets, and Point of Consumption's Relation to Violent and Non-violent Crime: A Spatial Analysis

E.B. Mancha and M. Zey

Introduction

This analysis assesses the spatial distribution of 2006 crime within San Antonio, Texas, as a function of alcohol retail outlet density and population density, while controlling for the effects of spatially auto-correlated error. The purpose of this analysis is threefold. First, the nature of association between the variables of interest is significant in its own right, as a way to explore its academic and socio-political implications. Second, the amount of existing research on the subject allows for an invaluable opportunity to substantiate current findings. Ultimately, however, the goal of this analysis is to gauge the benefits of using statistical methods that account for the effects of spatial auto-correlation in the analysis of variables prone to spatial auto-correlation-induced error. The authors purport that this methodological approach to a previously-explored problem represents a unique and significant contribution to the existing research on the association between alcohol retail outlet density and population density.

Specifically, while the existing literature supports a consistent association between the variables of interest, the methodological limitations of existing studies have resulted in contradictory findings when specific questions have been posed. The findings of the present analysis support the conjecture that many of these inconsistencies are the result of the limitations inherent in the measurement of the variables used and the methods employed, which fail to correct for the effects of spatially-autocorrelated induced error.

E.B. Mancha, Ph.D. (✉)
TMF Health Quality Institute, Austin, TX, USA
e-mail: emancha@txqio.sdps.org

M. Zey, Ph.D.
Department of Demography and Organization Studies,
The University of Texas at San Antonio, San Antonio, TX, USA

N. Hoque et al. (eds.), *Applied Demography and Public Health*,
Applied Demography Series 3, DOI 10.1007/978-94-007-6140-7_14,
© Springer Science+Business Media Dordrecht 2013

Background

The ability to gauge the effects of alcohol retail outlet density on crime appears to be dependent on the use of appropriately sized geographic areas of analysis. Specifically, while areas that are too small are difficult to measure and may fail to properly account for variation across an area, the use of very large areas as the geographic unit of analysis allows for little control and assessment of many of the socio-economic variables of interest, also resulting in a failure to detect variation across an area.

There is strong evidence of association between some types of crime and the density of alcohol retail outlets within the extant literature, particularly within small areas of geography (Scribner et al. 1999). Gorman and associates (2001) found an increased incidence of violent crime in census tracts with higher alcohol outlet density. Their report speaks to the need for assessments of small areas of geography, given the limited spatial impact on crime afforded by the density of alcohol retail outlets. More recently Gorman and others (2005) found significant increases in their analytical model attributable to two alcohol outlet density measures and several socio-structural variables, as well as a lack of spatially lagged effects.

Similarly, Gyimah-Brempong (2001) cites the inability of analysts to control for potential environmental variables that can have an unequal impact on crime across a large area. Scribner and associates (2008) cite similar problems as affecting the variance partition across levels of analysis in their multi-level examination of outlet density and college drinking. An earlier study of 223 municipalities in New Jersey found that the density of alcohol outlets was not a significant contributor to the variance in crime rates for those areas (Gorman et al. 1998). However, one longitudinal study of 256 American cities did find a significant relationship between alcohol outlet density and homicide (Gruenewald et al. 1993). The contradictory nature of some of these findings led us to re-examine the relation between alcohol outlet density and crime.

The relationship between alcohol outlet density and crime appears to vary by the manner in which alcohol is distributed to its consumers, specifically, whether outlets sell alcohol for on-site, off-site, or both on- and off-site consumption, and whether the density of total alcohol outlets is taken into consideration. In an analysis of alcohol availability and homicide on college campuses, Scribner and associates (2008) concluded that the relationship holds true even when considering both on and off-site consumption sales. In 2005, Gorman and his colleagues cited the differential impact of alcohol outlet density on crime as a factor of whether outlets that sold alcohol for on-site consumption were included in the model, among other variables (Gorman et al. 2005). A more recent analysis by Gruenewald and others (2006) found assault rates significantly associated with outlets that sold alcohol intended for off-site consumption, however the relationship did not hold for bars. In contrast, a longitudinal analysis conducted in Norway found a significant, positive association between the number of alcohol outlets that provide for on-site consumption of alcohol and violent crime (Norstrom 2000). In an analysis of census tracts within two

Texas cities, total alcohol outlet density significantly affected crime while variables consisting of off-site, on-site and both on-and-off-site consumption did no (Zhu et al. 2004).

The inconsistency of these findings caused us to question if the methods used were responsible for at least some of the differences in findings previously identified in the literature. Specifically, failure to control for the manner in which alcohol is distributed across an area will result in inconsistent findings, to the extent that the nature of alcohol distribution varies across these geographic areas.

The potential associations between population density and crime rates for the purposes of this analysis are twofold. First, areas with denser populations naturally have more potential consumers of alcohol, and subsequently, have an increased likelihood of having higher levels of overall alcoholic consumption. Lipton and Gruenewald (2002) found that the positive association between alcohol outlet density and crime had its greatest effect in densely populated areas. Second, the importance of population density as a significant (and sole) contributor to crime in the analysis of alcohol consumption has been noted in the literature (Gruenewald et al. 2006), particularly because of its strong link to socioeconomic contextual variables such as poverty and education.

Although traditional socio-economic variables, i.e., age, race/ethnicity/income, have been used as predictive factors for the relationship between alcohol availability and crime (Gorman et al. 2001, 2005; Lipton and Gruenewald 2002), precedent mandates this analysis be conducted at a small level of geographic analysis in order to avoid the above-stated limitations surrounding the use of large geographic areas as units of analysis. Given the age of the most recent figures available at the census tract level for the city of San Antonio, namely those from the 2000 U.S. Census, analyses employing demographic variables as independent factors will be limited to the use of population density. Scribner and associates (1999) took a similar approach in ascertaining the strong geographic relationships between homicide rates and two different measures of alcohol outlet density, to the complete exclusion of socio-demographic factors. It is worth noting that this analysis was also conducted at the end of an inter-censual period.

As such, given the potential problems associated with using traditional socio-economic variables in this type of analysis, the established relation between population density and these types of variables, and ultimately, the aim of this analysis to reconcile many of the inconsistencies found in many of the aforementioned studies, the use of population density as the sole predictor variable was deemed preferable as a way to obtain well-grounded and consistent results across our analysis – at the expense of potentially more descriptive findings.

Purpose and Hypotheses

We will first document the extent to which crime rates, alcohol retail outlets, and population density exhibit positive autocorrelation (are clustered) throughout San Antonio. The existence of positive autocorrelation is indicative of the effects that variable values in surrounding areas have on neighboring areas.

Hypothesis 1: Given the relations previously identified in the extant literature, we hypothesize that crime rates, alcohol outlet density, and population density will exhibit significant levels of positive autocorrelation, manifested by clustering within each of the variables.

Hypothesis 2: As further evidence of autocorrelation within variables, variable associations identified through the use of statistical methods that account and correct for autocorrelation-induced error in the analysis of local variance will be greatest when the variables included are highly auto-correlated.

Second, we will determine if correcting for spatially autocorrelated-induced error will result in overall improvement in model fit, when compared to testing the same models using standard Ordinary Least Squares (OLS) regression methods.

Hypothesis 3: A model accounting for spatial autocorrelation will be characterized by an increase in fit when compared with the traditional Ordinary Least Squares (OLS) Model.

Methods

The dependent variable *crime density* is divided into three categories. The first two are exclusive, (1) violent crime density, and (2) non-violent crime density, while the aggregated category of (3) total crime density encompasses both violent and non-violent crime. The need to distinguish between violent and non-violent crimes, in addition to the consideration of total crime is essential because they differ in their nature, i.e., crimes against the individual, as opposed to crimes against property, respectively, and each has been found to have different causes and determents.

We assess the association between alcohol retail outlet density and crime across four types of alcohol retail establishments, based on the point of consumption of their clientele: (1) density of establishments that sell alcohol for on-site consumption only, such as restaurants, bars, and clubs; (2) density of establishments that sell alcohol for off-site consumption only, such as liquor wholesale and retail outlets, drive thru and pick-ups, and carry-outs, (3) density of outlets that sell alcohol for both on-site and off-site consumption, and (4) total outlets, the aggregate sum of on-site, off-site, and outlets that sell alcohol for both on-site and off-site consumption. These gradients are necessary given their relationship to alcohol availability in an area, as well as to build upon previous research.

Population Density Estimates

In order to obtain a valid estimate of population density at the subcounty level for 2006, valid estimates of population size were needed. It was determined that the most appropriate method of estimation was the apportionment method, given its low associated data requirements, and its feasibility. Because the estimation method requires comparable, subcounty population size values across censuses (1990 and 2000), it required the creation of a common set of geographic units from which to ascertain the size and distribution of inter-censual population change.

The 1990 and 2000 Topologically Integrated Geographic Encoding and Referencing (TIGER) System shapefiles containing the outlines of Bexar County, San Antonio, and their associated census tracts were obtained from the U.S. Census Bureau. The U.S. Census Tract Relationship Files were then used to determine areas of change between the two censuses at the census tract level. Regardless of tract union or tract split between 1990 and 2000, tract aggregation was used as the means of reconciling the differences between the shapefiles.

The newly-created, subcounty areas were then assigned unique identifiers that would allow their original composition to be traced if necessary. Values for the population size and area of the original census tracts were then obtained from the Texas State Data Center (2008) and were aggregated in the same manner to produce a modified set of 177 subcounty areas useful for comparative analysis across the 1990 and 2000 U.S. censuses.

Using the apportionment method of small-area estimation outlined in Siegel and Swanson (2004), subcounty area population estimates for 2006 were calculated, with the 2006 population estimate for Bexar County obtained from the Texas State Data Center as the reference population in December 2006. The estimated population size for each subcounty area was then divided by the corresponding subcounty physical area to determine the population density for each of the subcounty areas.

While the crime data used in this analysis provides information for the incidence of crime throughout the City of San Antonio, the Population Density and Alcohol Outlet Density variables were ascertained for the entire county of Bexar. As such, using the rationale proposed in Mitchell (2005) only the subcounty areas whose centroids are located within the San Antonio city limits were selected for final analysis, reducing the number of geographic units available for analysis to 146 subcounty areas. These 146 subcounty areas represent those that fall completely within or mostly within the city limits of San Antonio. Figure 14.1 below shows the relationship between these three areas (county, city, and area of analysis). The subcounty areas in the darker shading represent the 146 selected for analysis.

Alcohol Retail Outlet Density Estimates

An active alcohol retail outlet permit listing from the Texas Alcoholic Beverage Commission (2008) website (www.tabc.state.tx) was obtained for Bexar County, Texas. The listing contained the necessary "permit type" information to classify the information as follows: Those allowing for the consumption of alcohol on-site, off-site,

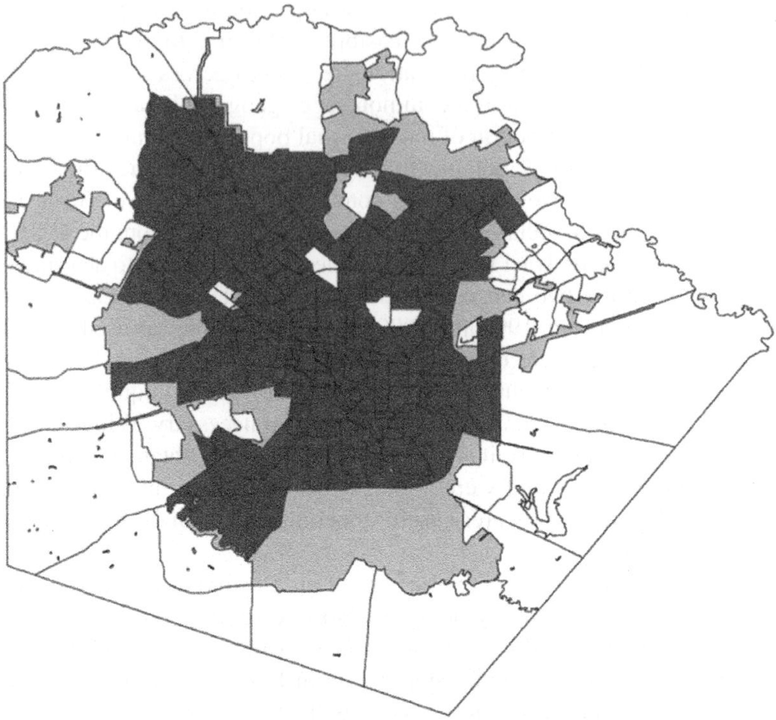

Fig. 14.1 Final 146 subcounty areas super-imposed over images of San Antonio and Bexar county

and both on- and off-site, as well as allowing for their summation as the total number of permits. Since the obtained permit list was for active permits as of April 9, 2008, all permits that had an issue date after December 31, 2006 were excluded (455) from analysis, as were permit types that did not fit into the four consumption categories detailed above (169). Also excluded from analysis were those permits that had been active sometime in 2006, but expired prior to the retrieval of the permit list obtained for this analysis. Other analyses use similar exclusions and data sources (see Gruenewald et al. 2006; Scribner et al. 2008).

The remaining 2,639 permit addresses were geocoded using the ArcView automated geocoding function. The TIGER Texas Roads shapefile for 2000 was used as the reference spatial street database. The process yielded a 100 % match rate and required no manual geocoding for this variable.

Spatial joins using ArcGIS software were then performed to determine the number of alcohol retail outlets within each subcounty area. Densities of alcohol retail outlets (both total and by type) were ascertained by dividing the number of outlets by the total population within each subcounty area. The figure was multiplied by 10,000 to allow for the inclusion of areas with a minimal number of alcohol outlets, and to provide a figure comparable across analyses. All permits outside the boundaries of the 146 subcounty areas deemed useful for analysis were removed from the final sample, yielding frequencies of 1,824 total outlets that sold alcohol within the areas, 781 outlets that sold alcohol for strictly off-site consumption, 473 outlets that sold alcohol for strictly on-site consumption, and 570 outlets that sold alcohol for both on- and off-site consumption.

Crime Density

Data and materials for the dependent variable, crime, were obtained from the San Antonio Police Department website (www.sanantonio.gov/sapd). Obtained were all major crimes that occurred in 2006, consisting of 115,399 individual incidences of crime. Major crimes, as defined by the FBI Crime Index, include all instances of homicide, rape, robbery, assault (aggravated and simple), theft/larceny, burglarized vehicles, vehicle theft, and burglaries. Crimes were then classified and aggregated according to the following dimensions – total crime, violent crimes (homicide, rape, robbery, and assault), and non-violent crimes (theft/larceny, burglarized vehicles, vehicle thefts, and burglaries).

The 115,399 addresses were geocoded using the ArcView automated geocoding function. The TIGER Texas Roads shapefile for 2000 was used as the reference spatial street database. The process yielded a 73 % match rate, through a combination of automated and manual matching. This sample consisted of 84,032 instances of crime throughout San Antonio, Texas.

Spatial joins using ArcGIS software were performed to determine the number of total crimes, violent crimes, and non-violent crimes per subcounty areas. Crime densities (crime rates) were ascertained by dividing the number of crimes (by category) by the total population within each sub county area. The figures were multiplied by 10,000 to allow for the inclusion of subcounty areas with a minimal number of crimes, and to provide figures comparable across analyses. All instances of crime outside the boundaries of the 146 subcounty areas deemed useful for analysis were removed from the final sample, yielding total frequencies of 77,747 total crimes, 24,244 violent crimes, and 53,503 non-violent crimes.

Results

Hypothesis 1: Given the relations previously identified in the extant literature, we hypothesize that crime rates, alcohol outlet density, and population density will exhibit significant levels of positive autocorrelation, manifested by clustering within each of the variables.

Preliminary univariate exploration of the variables to be modeled provides some insight into their individual characteristics, as well as their degree of spatial

Table 14.1 Univariate statistics and raw Moran's I coefficients for all variables

	Mean[a]	SD[a]	Min[a]	Max[a]	Raw Moran's I (p)
Population density (sq. mi.)	4,600.01	2,330.22	22.24	10,430.87	.36 (.01)
Total outlets	31.7	39.78	0	348	.3007 (.01)
On-site outlets	8.42	20.26	0	208	.2808 (.01)
Off-site outlets	12.84	11.08	0	87	.1439 (.01)
On/off site outlets	10.45	15.34	0	123	.3498 (.01)
Total crime	1,120.08	1,156.14	45	9,231	.1626 (.02)
Violent crime	322.49	245.26	8	2,084	.3584 (.01)
Non-violent crime	797.58	972.23	37	8,462	.1212 (.03)

[a]All variables except population density are per 10,000 pop

autocorrelation (clustering). Table 14.1 provides basic univariate statistics and the Raw Moran's I coefficient for each variable in this analysis. The Raw Moran's I coefficient provides a measure of the extent to which the data for one area tend to resemble data from adjacent areas for the same variable. Put simply, it answers the question: "To what extent can similar values of a variable be expected to be found together geographically?"

Given the distinct shape of the final area chosen for analysis, Queen contiguity was used to create the weights matrix used in these calculations. Significance was based on resamplings of 99 permutations. Mean, Standard Deviations, and Range values were calculated using ArcGIS, ArcView software. Moran's I coefficients were calculated using GeoDa.

A cursory analysis of Table 14.1 highlights the wide range of characteristics evident within the subcounty areas. Moreover, all Moran's I coefficients point to the presence of positive autocorrelation within the independent variables ($p=.01$), indicating statistically significant clustering in each case of areas with similar values for each variable. Of interest is the comparatively stronger presence of clustering evident for the total outlet, on-site outlet, and on/off site outlet sites, when compared to outlets that sell alcohol strictly for off-site purposes.

Among the dependent variables, density of violent crime values appear to be the most affected by corresponding neighboring areas with comparable levels of significance, while the impact appears to be comparatively lower and less divergent among the remaining two dependent variables – non-violent crime and total crimes.

Hypothesis 2: As further evidence of autocorrelation within the variables, variable associations identified through the use of statistical methods that account and correct for autocorrelation-induced error in the analysis of local variance will be greatest when the variables included are highly auto-correlated.

The impact of the spatially lagged values (values in neighboring areas) of the independent variables on crime is also important. Table 14.2 shows the Multivariate Moran's I values that are calculated for this analysis, using GeoDa statistical software. Given the distinct shape of the final area chosen for analysis, Queen contiguity was

Table 14.2 Multivariate Moran's I and p values (99 permutations)

	Total crime	Violent crime	Non-violent crime
Population density (p)	.0003	.0577	.0142
	(.99)	(.90)	(.99)
On-site outlet density (p)	.1175	.1909	.0916
	(.12)	(.01)	(.99)
Off-site outlet pop. density (p)	.1618	.2069	.1402
	(.01)	(.01)	(.14)
On and off-site outlet density (p)	.2134	.2876	.1813
	(.01)	(.01)	(.03)
Total alcohol outlet density (p)	.1871	.2657	.1555
	(.01)	(.01)	(.01)

used to create the weights matrix used in these calculations. Significance was based on resamplings of 99 permutations.

While population density appears to have little impact on neighboring crime densities, the density of alcohol retail outlets appears to play a more significant role. Once again, the impact of spatially lagged autocorrelation appears strongest on violent crime, although most of the associations between outlet densities and neighboring crime show some level of statistically significant autocorrelation, as indicated by the corresponding Moran's I and p values. Consideration of total outlet density when assessing the effects of spatially lagged values on crime appears to provide the most consistently significant findings across the types of crime examined.

Hypothesis 3: A model accounting for spatial autocorrelation will be characterized by an increase in fit when compared with the traditional Ordinary Least Squares (OLS) Model.

While the importance of local autocorrelation and local variation is important, the need to model the relationships between the variables on a more global level is critical to gaining an understanding of the interaction between the independent and dependent variables across the geographic area being analyzed.

Ordinary Least Squares (OLS) Regressions were conducted to (1) assess the amount of variance within the different crime variables attributable to the influence of the independent variables, before accounting for spatial autocorrelation, and (2) to provide a platform from which to compare subsequent, spatially adjusted, findings. OLS analyses were conducted using R statistical software. Given the goals of this analysis, the independent variables were regressed against each of the three crime dimensions outlined above. As is evident from Table 14.3 above, the outlet variables alone account for 56 of the variance in the violent crime variable, almost 46 of the variance in the total crime variable, and 37 of the variance in the non-violent variable.

Moreover, while Model 1 appears to contribute a significant amount of variation across the crime variables, relatively little of this contribution is due to the influence of population density on violent crime ($R^2 = .0017$). As such, the global impact of population density appears to be negligible in regards to its impact

Table 14.3 R2, p values, and degrees of freedom of OLS regression models

	Model 1[a]	Model 2[b]	Model 3[c]
	R^2 (p) (dof)	R^2 (p) (dof)	R^2 (p) (dof)
Total crime	.4614 (2.2e–16) (140)	.06086 (.0016) (144)	.4555 (2.2e–16) (141)
Violent crime	.5694 (2.2e–16) (140)	.001684 (.2665) (144)	.5638 (2.2e–16) (141)
Non-violent crime	.3901(9.777e–15) (140)	.07498 (.0005) (144)	.3746 (1.692e–14) (141)

[a]Model 1: Crime = on-site + off-site + on and off-site + total outlet + population density
[b]Model 2: Crime = population density
[c]Model 3: Crime = on-site + off-site + on and off-site + total outlet

Table 14.4 F statistic and p values of F tests for improvement in model fit

	Model 1[a]	Model 1[a]	Model 2[b]	Model 2[b]	Model 3[c]	Model 3[c]
	F1(p)	F2(p)	F1(p)	F2(p)	F1(p)	F2(p)
Total crime	.8908 (.2498)	2.3623 (.001623)	.7935 (.0875)	2.7139 (.0001206)	.9532 (.3918)	1.2606 (.1747)
Total violent crime	.5679 (.001236)	1.7565 (.002533)	.7698 (.06459)	2.2744 (.0004606)	.5727 (.001267)	1.8404 (.001376)
Total non-violent crime	.9173 (.3066)	2.2739 (.003751)	.8115 (.11)	2.6968 (.0001792)	.977 (.4476)	1.1278 (.3061)

[a]Model 1: Crime = on-site + off-site + on and off-site + total outlet + population density
[b]Model 2: Crime = population density
[c]Model 3: Crime = on-site + off-site + on and off-site + total outlet

on violent crime, assessed at the local level when no adjustment for spatial autocorrelation is made – pointing to a non-overlapping relationship between the population density and crime density clusters. This finding is partially consistent with the Multivariate Moran's I analysis in Table 14.2, where the neighboring population density values were found to have the least impact on values for the dependent variables.

In order to compare the effects of adjusting for spatial autocorrelation in regression analyses against the earlier OLS findings, R statistical software was used to conduct a Geographically Weighted Regression (GWR) of the crime variables being analyzed. Determination of improvement to model fit was gauged using two methods proposed by Leung et al. (2000), in which goodness of fit is determined by gauging the significance in the difference for the residual sum of squares and variance, between the OLS (F1 below) and GWR (F2 below) models.

Of all types of crime, violent crime density appears to have most-consistently benefited from GWR analyses, as is evident in the corresponding p values, the large F2 statistics, and the small F1 statistics. This finding supports earlier analyses where the violent crime density variable exhibited relatively high levels of autocorrelation (Table 14.1). Specifically, higher levels of autocorrelation between and among the variables would provide for more significant potential for improvement from the GWR. It is also important to note that total crime density saw improvements in model fit, as gauged by the F2 statistic, in both Models 1 and 2, despite the previous lack of significance associated with population density in the OLS models for violent crime. The phenomenon provides additional support for the spatial nature of the auto-correlation inherent in the population density variable independently, as well as in its relation to other variables of interest, particularly among violent crime.

In contrast, non-violent crime density saw the strongest improvement in Model 2, which included population density as its sole predictor variable, contradictory improvements across the two models that included population density as a predictor, and a consistent lack of improvement in Model 3, which excluded population density as a predictor variable. Such a pattern points to a potentially different relation between population density and different types of crime.

Discussion

First, examination of the Raw Moran's I scores identifies the population density, on-site alcohol outlet density, and violent crime density variables as having the highest level of autocorrelation, while the findings in Table 14.2 point to the spatially lagged effects of neighboring outlet densities on violent crime.

Second, although clusters of areas with similar population densities are evident, they do not appear to be consistently related to clusters of specific outlet types or crime when accounting for spatial autocorrelation. As such, even though the interaction between high population density and easy access to immediate consumption of alcohol does carry with it the potential for an increased density of crime within an area, further analysis is needed to understand the interaction between population density and crime clusters.

Third, as evident in the OLS regression models, population density actually does little to contribute to the variance accounted for within the models predicting violent crime, while the outlet variables alone account for 56 of the variance in the violent crime variable, almost 46 of the variance in the total crime variable, and 37 % of the variance in the non-violent variable. Given the potential contribution of population density to alcohol availability (described above), further exploration of the demographic composition (i.e., age distribution) of these areas would be helpful in ascertaining this apparently contradictory relationship.

Fourth, consistent association between outlet density and total crime is of particular relevance because it emphasizes the need to differentiate across different points of consumption in order to gain a clearer understanding of the underlying mechanisms inherent within this general relationship. For example, violent crime is most strongly associated with the immediate availability of alcohol (reduced time and travel costs). As such, it would also be worth examining whether this relationship holds true among different types of violent crime. The clustering of alcohol outlet types within each of the individual points of consumption also points to the perpetuation of certain types of outlets in certain areas, and provides further support for differentiating across different points of consumption.

Acknowledgements We thank Steve Murdock, Ph.D., and Corey Sparks, Ph.D., for their comments and feedback throughout. All errors and omissions are ultimately the responsibility of the authors.

Selected References

Gorman, D., Speer, P., Labouvie, E., & Subiya, A. (1998). Risk of assaultive violence and alcohol availability. *American Journal of Public Health, 88*, 97–100.

Gorman, D., Speer, P., Gruenewald, P., & Labouvie, E. (2001). Spatial dynamics of alcohol availability, neighborhood structure, and violent crime. *Journal of Studies on Alcohol, 62*, 628–636.

Gorman, D., Zhu, L., & Horel, S. (2005). Drug hot spots, alcohol availability and violence. *Drug and Alcohol Review, 24*, 507–513.

Graham, K. (2006). The relationship between homicide and alcohol, drugs, and psychiatric disorder: Some directions for prevention. *Addiction, 101*, 1071–1072.

Gruenewald, P., Ponicki, W., & Holder, H. (1993). The relationship of outlet densities to alcohol consumption: A time series cross-sectional analysis. *Alcholism: Clinical and Experimental Research, 17*, 38–47.

Gruenewald, P., Freisthler, B., Remer, L., LaScala, E., & Treno, A. (2006). Ecological models of alcohol outlets and violent assaults: Crime potentials and geospatial analysis. *Addiction, 101*, 666–677.

Gyimah-Brempong, K. (2001). Alcohol availability and crime: Evidence from census tract data. *Southern Economic Journal, 68*, 2–21.

Leung, Y., Chang-Lin, M., & Wen_Xiu, Z. (2000). Statistical tests for spatial non-stationarity based on the geographically weighted regression model. *Environment and Planning, 32*, 9–32.

Lipton, R., & Gruenewald, P. (2002). The spatial dynamics of violence and alcohol outlets. *Journal of Studies on Alcohol, 63*, 187–195.

Mitchell, A. (2005). *The ESRI guide to GIS analysis: Vol. 2. Spatial measurements and statistics*. Redlands: ESRI Press.

Norstrom, T. (2000). Outlet density and criminal violence in Norway, 1960–1995. *Journal of Studies on Alcohol, 61*, 907–911.

Scribner, R., Cohen, D., Kaplan, S., & Allen, S. (1999). Alcohol availability and homicide in New Orleans: Conceptual considerations for small area analysis of the effect of alcohol outlet density. *Journal of Studies on Alcohol, 60*, 310–316.

Scribner, R., Mason, K., Theall, K., Simonsen, N., Kessel-Schneider, S., Gomberg-Towvim, L., & DeJong, W. (2008). The contextual role of alcohol outlet density in college drinking. *Journal of Studies on Alcohol and Drugs, 69*, 112–120.

Siegel, J., & Swanson, D. (2004). *The methods and materials of demography* (2nd ed.). San Diego: Elsevier Academic Press.

Texas Alcoholic Beverage Commission. (2008). website. http://www.tabc.state.tx.us/. Accessed 9 Apr 2008.

Texas State Data Center. (2008). Office of the State Demographer. Institute for Demographic and Socioeconomic Research. http://txsdc.utsa.edu/. Accessed 17 Mar 2008.

Zhu, L., Gorman, M., & Horel, S. (2004). Alcohol outlet density and violence: A geospatial analysis. *Alcohol and Alcoholism, 39*, 369–375.

Chapter 15
Determinants of Blood Pressure Control in Hypertensive Diabetic Patients in Rajshahi District of Bangladesh

Md. Nazrul Islam Mondal, Nazrul Hoque, Sabiha Yasmin Moni, and Md. Rocky Khan Chowdhury

Introduction

Hypertension (HTN), also known as high blood pressure (HBP), is one of the most common chronic health conditions prevalent in most of the developed countries. Approximately 1 in 3 or 73 million adults in the United States has HBP. Many people suffer from HTN in the developing countries as well. Blood pressure is essential to move blood from the heart through veins and arteries to all other parts of the body. However, when the pressure is too high, it becomes dangerous, making the heart work harder and increasing the risk for heart problems, such as heart attacks and strokes. Many diabetic patients develop HTN, which increases the potential risk for various problems including kidney disease, diabetes mellitus, renal disease, blindness, and many other deadly diseases. No specific cause for HTN is found in 95% of the cases but it is an extremely common co-morbid condition in diabetes, affecting 20–60% of patients with diabetes, depending on obesity, ethnicity, and age (ADA 2004). Although diabetes mellitus and HTN are not among the top leading causes of deaths, such as cancer and stroke, public attention is increasing as their occurrence increases. Diabetes has been ranked the sixth leading

M.N.I. Mondal, Ph.D. (✉) • M.R.K. Chowdhury
Department of Population Science and Human Resource Development, University of Rajshahi, Rajshahi, Bangladesh
e-mail: nazrul_ru@yahoo.com

N. Hoque, Ph.D.
Department of Demography and Institute for Demographic and Socioeconomic Research, University of Texas at San Antonio, San Antonio, TX, USA

S.Y. Moni, M.Phil.
Department Pharmacology and Therapeutics, Rajshahi Medical College, Rajshahi, Bangladesh

N. Hoque et al. (eds.), *Applied Demography and Public Health*, Applied Demography Series 3, DOI 10.1007/978-94-007-6140-7_15,
© Springer Science+Business Media Dordrecht 2013

cause of death and is also known as costly disease (ADA 2004). Coronary heart disease (CHD) is projected to be the most common cause of death globally by 2020 (Yusuf et al. 2001). HTN is one of the most important modifiable risk factors for CHD in Western and Asian populations (He and Whelton 1999; ESCHDCRG 1998). Studies from India and Bangladesh have shown an increasing trend in the prevalence of HTN (HTN Study Group 2001). The prevalence of diabetes mellitus and HTN increases with age (Moon et al. 2002). It is estimated that more than 220 million people worldwide have diabetes and the number is likely to more than double by 2030 without any intervention, with 80% residing in low and middle income countries. Almost 80% of diabetes deaths occur in low and middle-income countries (Wild et al. 2004). Diabetes increases the risk of coronary events twofold in men and fourfold in women. Hypertensive diabetes patients have approximately twice the risk of cardiovascular disease compared with hypertensive non-diabetic patients. Hypertensive diabetic patients are also at increased risk for diabetes-specific complications including retinopathy and nephropathy along with kidney diseases, diabetic leg ulcers, sexual dysfunction, and sterility.

The prevalence of diabetes is increasing rapidly in the developing countries including Bangladesh. It is a chronic disease that is never cured, but a diabetic patient can lead a normal life by controlling the disease through a planned diet, taking appropriate drugs, and with regular physical exercise. At present, it is estimated that 3.8 million or 4.8% of the people in Bangladesh have diabetes and that number is expected to grow to 7.4 million or 6.1% of the population by 2025 (IDF 2003). This explosion in diabetes prevalence will place Bangladesh among the top ten countries in terms of the number of people living with diabetes by 2025. The increase in diabetes in Bangladesh is expected to follow global gender patterns, whereby more women than men will live with diabetes. The International Diabetes Federation (IDF) and World Health Organization (WHO) predicted that the number of women in the world with diabetes will double in less than 20 years. In Bangladesh, the number of women with diabetes will grow from the current 2 to 4 million by 2025 and during the same period, the number of men with diabetes will rise from 1.8 to 3.4 million (Rahman and Islam 2008). At least 10–15% of Bangladeshis suffer from diabetes and/or HTN, but only the affluent and disciplined can maintain the regimen of diet, regular physical exercise, doctor visits, blood sugar monitoring, and various biochemical laboratory tests needed to prevent disease progression and severe complications. For millions of people in Bangladesh, diabetes is at the root of severe medical complications including eye problems, kidney disease, and foot problems. Importantly, HTN can lead to aneurysms, heart failure, damage to arteries, and other ailments. There is a strong epidemiological connection between HTN in diabetics and adverse outcomes of diabetes. The control of HTN in persons with diabetes has been demonstrated to reduce the rate of progression of diabetic nephropathy and reduce the complications of hypertensive nephropathy, neuropathy, and cardiovascular disease. It is found that in the HTN Optimal Therapy (HOT) study, people with diabetes who kept their DBP (Diastolic Blood Pressure) at 80 (vs 90 mmHg) had 51% lower risk of experiencing a cardiovascular event (Cardiologist 2011).

The United Kingdom Prospective Diabetes Study (UKPDS), a 10-year study of more than 1,000 people who had type-2 diabetes and HTN, clearly demonstrated that BP control is an important issue. Aggressive treatment of even mildly elevated BP was shown to be beneficial. The UKPDS showed that lowering BP to a mean level of 144/82 mmHg significantly reduced vision loss, diabetes related deaths, strokes, heart failure, and various micro vascular complications.

To the best of our knowledge, no recent studies have been conducted on hypertensive diabetic patients in Bangladesh. The goal of this study is to examine the determinants of high blood pressure control among the diabetes patients in Rajshahi district of Bangladesh. At present, Bangladesh, with an estimated 164.4 million people, is the seventh most populous country in the world, and the district of Rajshahi is the third largest city in the country. Given how this condition affects such an enormous population, we believe the findings of this study will contribute to the current body of knowledge by elucidating the socio-demographic status and clinical characteristics associated with diabetes and HTN control and will help policymakers, program planners, and agencies to create more effective public health policy in Bangladesh.

Data and Methods

Data for this study comes from 406 hypertensive diabetic patients (254 male and 152 female) from the Rajshahi Medical College Hospital and Rajshahi Diabetic Centers who are receiving medication for HTN and diabetes. HTN and diabetics were determined by their respective doctors. HTN was determined according to the standard definition of 140 mmHg or more for systolic pressure and 90 mmHg or more for diastolic pressure. HTN controlled was determined by maintaining an average BP of 130/80 mmHg. Three trained research students from the Department of Population Science, University of Rajshahi under the direct supervision of three faculty members collected necessary data. A structured questionnaire was prepared and pretested by a pilot survey (both in English and Bengali). Corrections were made following an evaluation of the pilot survey and a final version of the questionnaire was completed. A Bengali version of the questionnaire was used for more accurate data collection. Responses were then converted to English for data entry and analysis with SPSS (Statistical Package for Social Sciences).

Both bivariate and multivariate analyses were performed for this study. In bivariate analysis, proportions were compared using the chi-square (χ^2) test to analyze the significant association of socio-economic and clinical variables to control HTN. Logistic regression techniques were used to evaluate the effect of a select group of variables on the probability of controlling HTN. When the dependent variable is dichotomous, a logistic regression model is widely used not only to identify the risk factors but also to predict the probability of success. The logistic regression model for the log odds of hypertension control is:

$$\log\left(\frac{p_i}{1-p_i}\right) = \alpha + \beta_i X_{i1} + \beta_2 X_{i2} \ldots + \beta_k X_{ik}$$

where $\log\left(\frac{p_i}{1-p_i}\right)$ is simply the conditional odds of controlling hypertension, given the explanatory variables (X_i), α is the regression intercept, β_i are regression coefficients, and X_i are a set of predictors. P_i can be calculated from the following formula:

$$P_i = \frac{\exp(\alpha + \beta_1 x_{i1} + \beta_2 x_{i2} + \cdots + \beta_k x_{ik}}{1 + \exp(\alpha + \beta_1 x_{i1} + \beta_2 x_{i2} + \cdots + \beta_k x_{ik}}$$

Detailed discussions on logistic regression can be found at Logistic Regression using SAS by Paul D. Allison (1999).

Dependent and Independent Variables

The dependent or response variable in this analyses is HTN control among the diabetes patients, coded 1 for controlled and 0 otherwise. To examine the determinants of HTN control among the diabetes patients, we included several independent variables that have been highly associated with the HTN control. Independent variables are grouped into two categories. These are socio-demographic variables and clinical variables that have been shown in earlier studies to be influential in controlling HTN. The socio-demographic variables are: age, sex, education, occupation, and economic conditions. The clinical variables are: irregularity of taking medicine, side effects of medicine, forgetting to take medicine, kidney diseases, regular physical exercises, occupational stress, mental stress, high levels of salt intake, smoking, and physical activity. Studies have shown that the risk of developing high blood pressure increases with age, weight gain, intake of high sodium foods and with heightened anxiety. Other variables may have significant impact on HTN control, but they have been excluded from the analysis, either because they were not adequately measured or they were not included in the data sets.

Results and Discussion

Distributions of socio-demographic and clinical characteristics of the respondents are given in Table 15.1. A total of 406 patients were recruited for the present study. Out of 406 patients, 254 (or 62.6%) are male and 152 (or 37.4%) are female.

Table 15.1 Distribution of socio-demographic characteristics in controlled and uncontrolled hypertensive diabetic patientsw

Characteristics	Hypertension control Yes	No	Respondents (N)	P values[a]
Demographic and socioeconomic characteristics:				
Sex				
Female	97 (37.5%)	55 (37.4%)	152 (37.4%)	0.994
Male	162 (62.5%)	92 (62.6%)	254 (62.6%)	
Age group				
Adult age (≤40)	25 (9.6%)	7 (4.7%)	32 (7.9%)	0.008
Middle age (41–55)	153 (59.1%)	73 (49.7%)	226 (55.6)	
Old age (≥56)	81 (31.3%)	67 (45.6%)	148 (36.5%)	
Education				
No education	48 (18.5%)	27 (18.4%)	75 (18.4%)	0795
Primary & secondary	151 (58.3%)	90 (61.2%)	241 (59.4%)	
College and above	60 (23.2%)	30 (20.4%)	90 (22.2%)	
Work status/physical activity level				
Extremely inactive	15 (5.8%)	16 (10.9%)	31(7.6%)	0.029
Lightly active	166 (64.1%)	73 (49.7%)	239 (58.9%)	
Moderately active	7 (2.7%)	5 (3.4%)	12 (3.0%)	
Vigorously active	71 (27.4%)	53 (36.0%)	124 (30.5%)	
Economic hardship				
No	67 (25.9%)	34 (23.1%)	101 (24.9%)	0.539
Yes	192 (74.1%)	113 (76.9%)	305 (75.1%)	
Clinical characteristics:				
Physical exercise regularly				
No	28 (10.8%)	29 (19.7%)	57 (14.0%)	0.013
Yes	231 (89.2%)	118 (80.3%)	349 (86.0%)	
Took medicine regularly				
No	176 (67.9%)	104 (70.7%)	280 (69.0%)	0.559
Yes	83 (32.1%)	43 (29.3%)	126 (31.0%)	
Side effect of medicine				
No	251 (96.9%)	129 (87.8%)	380 (93.6%)	0.000
Yes	8 (3.1%)	18 (12.2%)	26 (6.4%)	
Forget to take medicine				
No	198 (76.5%)	99 (67.4%)	297 (73.2%)	0.047
Yes	61 (23.5%)	48 (32.6%)	109 (26.8%)	
Kidney disease				
No	204 (78.8%)	96 (65.3%)	300 (73.9%)	0.003
Yes	55 (21.2%)	51 (34.7%)	106 (26.1%)	
Occupational stress				
No	220 (84.9%)	108 (73.5%)	328 (80.8%)	0.005
Yes	39 (15.1%)	39 (26.5%)	78 (19.2%)	
Mental stress				
No	102 (39.4%)	41 (27.9%)	143 (35.2%)	0.020
Yes	157 (60.6%)	106 (72.1%)	263 (64.8%)	

(continued)

Table 15.1 (continued)

Characteristics	Hypertension control Yes	No	Respondents (N)	P values[a]
Salt intake				
No	173 (66.8%)	103 (70.1%)	276 (68.0%)	0.497
Yes	86 (33.2%)	44 (29.9%)	130 (32.0%)	
Smoking				
In past	40 (15.4%)	22 (15.0%)	62 (15.3%)	0.742
At present	35 (13.5%)	24 (16.3%)	59 (14.5%)	
Never	184 (71.1%)	101 (68.7%)	285 (70.2%)	
Total	259 (100.0%)	147 (100.0%)	406 (100.0%)	

[a]Chi-square test

Among the participants, 259 (or 63.8%) can control HTN while 147 (or 36.2%) cannot control HTN. Age distributions of respondents differ significantly based on whether respondents can control HTN or not. The young (≤40) and the middle age group (41–55 years) can control HTN better than the respondents who are 56 years of age or older. Of respondents who are in the middle age group (i.e., 41–55), 67.7% can control HTN while 32.3% cannot. Only 54.7% of the respondents who are 56 years of age or older can control HTN, while 45.3% cannot. Among the 259 respondents who can control HTN, only 9.65% are from age group 40 or younger, 59.07% are in age group 41–45, and 31.27% are 56 years of age or older. This finding suggests that younger people are not serious about health care and it becomes more difficult to control HTN as people age. In this study, work status variable has been used to measure the physical activity level of the respondents because it has a strong relationship with HTN control. There is no significant difference in HTN control by educational level or economic hardship status. With respect to the clinical variables, we found significant differences for the following variables: regular physical exercise ($p<0.013$), side effects of medicine ($p<0.000$), forgetting to take medicine ($p<0.047$), and kidney disease ($p<0.003$), occupational stress ($p<0.005$), and mental stress ($p<0.020$). Previous studies suggest that regular physical exercise plays a vital role in preventing cardiovascular disease. Moreover regular physical exercise is especially important for a person with diabetes since it helps with blood sugar control, weight loss, and high blood pressure control as well. People with diabetes who exercise regularly are less likely to experience a heart attack or stroke than diabetic patients who do not exercise regularly. Physical exercise generally helps to control blood glucose levels because exercising muscle cells uses more sugar and oxygen. Exercise also helps insulin to work better. Out of 406 respondents, 349 or 85.96% of the respondents exercise on a regular basis, and this exercise showed a significant effect on HTN control ($p<0.013$). For people with diabetes, occupational stress and mental stress can take a greater toll on health. Occupational stress and mental stress increase blood sugar levels, which in turn increases the pressure the blood exerts on the wall of blood vessels. On the other hand, reducing stress can help maintain normal blood pressure. Some mental stress may be a normal part of life, but too much stress can lead to emotional, psychological and even physical problems, including cardiovascular disease, high blood pressure, chest pains or irregular heartbeats. Moreover, mental stress itself is a risk factor for heart disease. Perez and others (2001) found that a high level of psychological stress is strongly associated with HTN. This study found that most of the patients ($n=328$, 80.79%) did not have occupational pressure, but that most of the respondents had mental stress ($n=263$, 64.78%). The χ^2 test showed occupational pressure ($p<0.005$) and mental stress ($p<0.020$) were associated with HTN control. Cigarette smoking and salt intake contribute to cardiovascular disease. As a result, reduced salt intake and smoke cessations are highly recommended as a means to HTN control for the people with diabetes. This study revealed that 276 or 67.98% of the respondents did not take extra salt on their food, and of that number, 173 or 62.70% can control HTN. Two hundred and eighty five (70.20%) patients never smoked, of whom 184 (64.60%) can control HTN (Table 15.1). Cigarette smoking is a risk factor for HTN and smokers have a fivefold increased risk of a hypertensive crisis (Amal et al. 2004). Again, reduction in salt intake and increased physical activity will reduce blood pressure and thus improve in the control of HTN as well (Fagard 1995).

Logistic regression analysis was performed to measure the relative risks of socio-demographic and clinical variables. Results of logistic regressions are presented in Table 15.2. The results show that the variables selected for the analysis are generally important predictors of HTN control among diabetic patients. In Bangladesh, men are more likely to control HTN than are women. The findings show a positive relationship between respondents' age and HTN control. Respondents aged 40 years or younger are 2.6 times more likely to control HTN compared to respondents aged 56 years and above. Similarly, respondents aged 41–55 are 1.66 times more likely to control HTN compared with respondents aged 56 years and above. Respondents with the highest level of education (college/university) are 2.128 times more likely to control HTN than those who had no education. We did not find any significant difference between no education and primary and secondary education. Those who are lightly active in their daily physical activity are two times more likely to control HTN compared with those who are extremely inactive in their daily physical activity. Those who are moderately or vigorously active are almost five times more likely to control HTN than with those who are extremely inactive in their daily physical activity. There is a weak relationship between economic hardship and HTN control.

Among the clinical variables, regular physical exercise, side effects of medication, forgetting to take medicine, kidney disease, occupational stress, and mental stress are significantly associated with HTN control. The respondents who exercised regularly are 1.486 times more likely to control HTN (Odds Ratio [OR] = 1.486, with 95% confidence interval [CI] = 0.783–2.818) compared with those who do not do any physical exercise. The results demonstrated that the patients who took medicine on a regular basis are 1.425 times more likely to control HTN than those who were not taking medicine on a regular basis (OR = 1.425, 95% CI = 0.833–2.438). The patients who experienced side effects of medication are less likely to control

Table 15.2 Logistic regression analysis of socio-demographic and clinical variables of hypertensive diabetic patients

Characteristics	Coefficients (β values)	Standard error (SE)	Odds ratio (OR)	95% Confidence interval (CI)	
				Lower limit	Upper limit
Sex					
Female (RC)					
Male	0.566*	0.336	1.761	0.912	3.400
Age groups					
56+ (RC)					
≤40	0.958*	0.496	2.608	0.987	6.889
1–55	1.501*	0.246	1.663	1.028	2.690
Education					
No education (RC)					
Primary & secondary	−0.092	0.316	0.912	0.491	1.696
College & higher	0.756*	0.422	2.128	0.930	4.869
Work status/physical activity level					
Extremely inactive(RC)					
Lightly active	0.822*	0.446	2.275	0.947	5.462
Moderately active	1.523*	0.469	4.589	1.829	11.518
Vigorously active	1.569*	0.837	4.803	0.931	24.787
Economic hardship					
No (RC)					
Yes	−0.477	0.310	0.621	0.338	1.140
Physical exercise regularly					
No (RC)					
Yes	0.396*	0.327	1.486	0.783	2.818
Took medicine regularly					
No (RC)					
Yes	0.354	0.274	1.425	0.833	2.438
Side effect of medicine					
No (RC)					
Yes	−1.276*	0.493	0.279	0.106	0.733
Forget to take medicine					
No (RC)					
Yes	−0.350*	0.268	0.705	0.417	1.192
Kidney diseases					
No (RC)					
Yes	−0.581*	0.267	0.559	0.332	0.994
Occupational stress					
No (RC)					
Yes	−0.642*	0.307	0.526	0.288	0.961
Mental stress					
No (RC)					
Yes	−0.567*	0.257	0.567	0.343	0.938
Salt intake					
No (RC)					

(continued)

Table 15.2 (continued)

Characteristics	Coefficients (β values)	Standard error (SE)	Odds ratio (OR)	95% Confidence interval (CI) Lower limit	Upper limit
Yes	−0.233	0.253	0.792	0.483	1.300
Smoking					
At present (RC)					
Past	0.394	0.436	1.483	0.631	3.484
Never	0.117	0.371	1.124	0.544	2.324

Note: *OR* odds ratio, *RC* reference category
*p<0.005 or better

HTN compared with the patients who did not experience any side effects of the medication (OR=0.279, 95% CI=0.106–0.733). As expected, the respondents who forgot to take medicine are less likely to control HTN compared with those who did not forget to take medicine (OR=0.705, 95% CI=0.417–1.192). Kidney disease significantly differentiates the control of HTN among diabetic patients; those who suffer from kidney diseases are less likely to control HTN compared with those who do not suffer from kidney diseases (OR=0.559, 95% CI=0.332–0.994). The patients who experience occupational stress are less likely to control HTN than those have not experienced any occupation stress (OR=0.526, 95% CI=0.288–0.961). As expected, the respondents who experience mental stress are also likely to control HTN compared with those who have not experienced any mental stress (OR=0.567, 95% CI=0.343–0.938). The respondents who take extra table salt in their food are less likely to be able to control HTN compared with those do not take extra table salt in their food. In the case of smoking, the respondents are classified into three groups as having never smoked, smoking at present, and smoked in past but not presently. The respondents who smoked in the past but are not smoking at present are 1.483 times more likely to be able to control HTN than those who are smoking at present (OR=1.483, 95% CI=0.631–3.484); and those who have never smoked are 1.124 times more likely to able to control HTN compared with those who are smoking at present (OR=1.124, 95% CI=0.544–2.324).

Conclusion

The main objective of this study was to examine the factors that significantly contribute to the control of high blood pressure among diabetic patients. Diabetes with HTN is currently the fastest growing disease in the world. At least 10–15% of Bangladeshis suffer from diabetes and/or HTN. At present, it is estimated that 3.8 million or 4.8% of the people in Bangladesh have diabetes, and that number is expected to grow to 7.4 million or 6.1% of the population by 2025 (IDF 2003). It is worrying that this explosion in diabetes prevalence will place Bangladesh among the top ten countries in terms of number of people living with diabetes by 2025.

The findings from the bivariate analysis show that statistically significant variations exist across most of the variables selected for the present study. Results of the chi-square and logistics regression analysis suggest it is difficult to control HTN as people age. For the diabetic patients, clinical issues were the significant factors influencing HTN. Occupational pressure, mental stress, and physical exercise had independent effects on HTN. The findings of the study emphasized the importance of maintaining the care and control of HTN among diabetic patients and suggested regular physical exercise, having ongoing medical care, taking medicine on a regular basis, reducing occupational and mental pressure, maintaining a healthy diet, and quitting smoking may help reduce high blood pressure among diabetic patients.

Acknowledgements An earlier version of this paper was published in the *Journal of Biometrics and Biostatistics*. J Biomet Biostat S7:001. Doi: 10.4172/2155-6180.S7-001.

References

Allison, P. D. (1999). *Logistic regression using SAS: Theory and application*. Cary: SAS Institute Inc.

Amal, M. A., Ali, A. A., Majeda, M. A., Huda, S. A., & Bader, N. M. B. A. (2004). Determinants of poor blood pressure control in hypertensive patients – An area-based study. *Kuwait Medical Journal, 36*(4), 270–274.

American Diabetes Association. (2004). Standard of medical care in diabetes. *Diabetes Care, 29*(suppl), S4–S42.

Cardiologist. 2011. *Hypertension in diabetes patients*. Available online at: http://hypertension-highbloodpressure.com/index.php/treatment-of-hypertension/hypertension-in-diabtetes-patients, last accessed July 2011.

ESCHDCRG (Eastern Stroke and Coronary Heart Disease Collaborative Research Group). (1998). Blood pressure, cholesterol, and stroke in eastern Asia. *Lancet, 352*(9143), 1801–1807.

Fagard, R. H. (1995). The role of exercise in blood pressure control: Supportive evidence. *Journal of Hypertension, 13*(11), 1223–1227.

He, J., & Whelton, P. K. (1999). Elevated systolic blood pressure and risk of cardiovascular and renal disease: Overview of evidence from observational epidemiologic studies and randomized controlled trials. *American Heart Journal, 138*, S211–S219.

Hypertension Study Group. (2001). Prevalence, awareness, treatment and control of hypertension among the elderly in Bangladesh and India: A multicentre study. *Bulletin of the World Health Organization, 79*, 490–500.

Moon, R., Kim, N. S., Jang, S. M., Yoon, T. H., & Kim, S. O. (2002). The relationship between body mass index and the prevalence of obesity-related diseases based on the 1995 National Health Interview Survey in Republic of Korea. *Obesity Reviews, 3*(3), 191–196.

Perez, L. H., Gutierres, L. A., Vioque, J., & Torres, Y. (2001). Relation between over weight, diabetes, stress, and hypertension: A case control study in Yarumal – Antioquia, Colombia. *European Journal of Epidemiology, 17*, 275–280.

Rahman, M. M., & Islam, J. M. (2008). Problem with diabetes and awareness to its control: Experience from diabetes patients of Rajshahi City Corporation in Bangladesh. *The Internet Journal of Health, 8*(1), 143–161.

The International Diabetes Federation (IDF). (2003). *Diabetes atlas* (2nd ed.). Brussels: IDF Executive Office.

Wild, S., Sicref, R., Roglic, G., King, H., & Green, A. (2004). Global prevalence of diabetes: Estimates for the year 2000 and projections for 2030. *Diabetes Care, 27*(5), 1047–1053.

Yusuf, S., Reddy, S., & Ounpuu, S. (2001). Global burden of cardiovascular disease. Part II. Variations in cardiovascular disease by specific ethnic groups and geographic regions and prevention strategies. *Circulation, 104*(28), 55–64.

Chapter 16
Active Aging Index and Healthy Life Expectancy in Rajshahi District of Bangladesh

Md. Ismail Tareque, Nazrul Hoque, Towfiqua Mahfuza Islam, Kazuo Kawahara, and Makiko Sugawa

Introduction

The increase in life expectancy in Bangladesh during the twentieth century has been a remarkable achievement. The average life expectancy at birth has increased from about 40 years in 1960 to 66 years in 2010. However, we do not know whether the increase in life expectancy is keeping pace with the healthy life expectancy in Bangladesh. Advancing age may be associated with a higher likelihood of disability, but the processes leading to a decline in health are not irreversible. Studies on health dynamics cite significant evidence of recovery from disability among older people in developed countries, but there is no clear picture of recovery in developing countries. In Japan approximately 30% of older people who were in a state of disability in 1987 regained their functional ability during the following 3 years (Liu et al. 1995). Among older Americans, 20% reported recovery from a disability during a 2 year period (Rogers et al. 1990), although these levels should not be compared given the differences in measures and time frames. A host of socioeconomic and environmental factors were found to explain health recovery including age,

M.I. Tareque, M.Sc. (✉)
Department of Population Science and Human Resource Development, University of Rajshahi, Rajshahi, Bangladesh

Department of Health Care Management and Planning, Graduate School of Medical and Dental Science, Tokyo Medical and Dental University, Tokyo, Japan
e-mail: tareque_pshd@yahoo.com

N. Hoque, Ph.D.
Department of Demography and Institute for Demographic and Socioeconomic Research, University of Texas at San Antonio, San Antonio, TX, USA

T.M. Islam, M.Sc., M.Phil. • K. Kawahara, M.D., Ph.D. • M. Sugawa, M.M.A.
Department of Health Care Management and Planning, Graduate School of Medical and Dental Science, Tokyo Medical and Dental University, Tokyo, Japan

N. Hoque et al. (eds.), *Applied Demography and Public Health*,
Applied Demography Series 3, DOI 10.1007/978-94-007-6140-7_16,
© Springer Science+Business Media Dordrecht 2013

participation in organizational activities, social support, and self-rated health. In particular, younger age and better self-rated health may influence health status by reducing the risk of becoming disabled or dying and by facilitating recovery (Liu et al. 1995). The same study showed that lower education, not being married, and smoking may increase the risk of disability, but they do not have a negative effect on recovery. Health transition analysis (Cruz et al. 2007) indicated a significant proportion of Filipino older people experiencing recovery; while age, sex, place of residence, and health status/behavior indicators (self-assessed health, drinking, and exercise) displayed a significant influence on future health and mortality trajectories, surprisingly, education did not show any significant effect. In some Latin American and Caribbean countries aging is associated with disability or poor quality of health, particularly diabetes and obesity (Palloni and McEniry 2007; Wong and Palloni 2009). Moreover, the cost of medical care for a disabled older person averages three times higher than that of a non-disabled senior (Trupin et al. 1995). According to Ruffing-Rahal (1991), a fundamental goal of health promotion is to facilitate the well-being of older adults on an ongoing basis. Although older adults may suffer from chronic diseases, cognitive impairment, and functional limitations, the choice of a health-promoting lifestyle can minimize health problems and lead to enhanced health outcomes (Ruffing-Rahal 1991). Self-care has been described as a strategy for coping with life events and stressors (McLaughlin and Zeeberg 1993; Chen et al. 2002) and for enhancing quality of life during the aging process (Boyle and Counts 1988), thereby promoting independence and healthy aging. In addition, compared with developed countries, developing countries' pace of aging is much faster, therefore they will have less time to adjust to the consequences of aging, which takes place at much lower socioeconomic levels compared with developed countries. The current and emerging effects of population aging will impact all aspects of life: social, economic, and political (UNPD 2008). Thus, the authors are trying to introduce the concept of active aging in connection with healthy life expectancy (HLE), which is a relatively new concept in Bangladesh. This active aging might be a good step toward suppressing morbidity while allowing individuals to enjoy more disability-free life; efforts will additionally help individuals as well as the nation to reduce medical costs for the elderly. Little is known on the levels of active aging, as its differentials vary across socioeconomic levels, demographic settings, and functional health transition patterns among older people in Bangladesh. Active aging can be applied to both individuals and population groups. It allows people to realize their potential for physical, social, and mental well being throughout their lives and to participate in society according to their needs, desires, and capacities, while providing them with adequate protection, security, and care when they require assistance (WHO 2002). According to WHO (2002), if aging is to be a positive experience, longer life must be accompanied by continuing opportunities for health, participation, and security. Older people who retire from work and those who are ill or live with disabilities can remain active contributors to their families, peers, communities, and nations. Active aging aims to extend healthy life expectancy and quality of life for all people as they age, including those who are frail, disabled, and in need of care (WHO 2002), but there are no statistics about the relationship between active aging and healthy life expectancy, which is a critical enquiry. It is also therefore said that individuals should be aware and should prepare themselves in order to maintain health, independence, and security and produce some benefits for society (WHO 2002; Thanakwang and Soonthorndhada 2006).

Healthy life expectancy that takes into account both mortality and morbidity or disability is increasingly emphasized as an indicator for population health. It can be used to watch the way the health of a population is evolving, to show how it compares with that of other populations, and to suggest, once the trend becomes clear, whether a healthy life expectancy is disability free. The use of healthy expectancy as a measure of a population's health has become an increasingly popular phenomenon and estimates have been published for about 191 countries (Robine and Ritchie 1991; Robine et al. 1993; Mathers et al. 1994, 2001). In addition health policies that focus on health expectancy have increased, particularly in countries characterized by an aging population because a longer life and a healthier life do not necessarily go together (Brønnum-Hansen et al. 2004). Unfortunately, healthy life expectancy cannot be measured for every year in Bangladesh because of the lack of available relevant data.

According to the World Population Prospectus, there were 164.4 million people living in Bangladesh in 2010 (UN 2008), and 6.2% or 10.1 million of them are 60 years of age or older. It is projected that in 2050, 21.2% or 47.2 million will be 60 years of age or older. At present, Bangladesh has not entered into the category of an aging society but it will enter very soon, and it contains the world's third largest number of poor elderly people, preceded only by India and China (HAI 2006). Life expectancy is projected to increase from 66 years in 2010 to 76.2 years in 2050. Very soon Bangladesh is going to face enormous problems associated with aging, particularly for health facilities.

We use a new data set on elderly people from the district of Rajshahi in Bangladesh to measure activeness using the active aging index (AAI) and to compute healthy life expectancy by documenting the health status of elderly people and thus measure the relationship between AAI and HLE. At present, Bangladesh with 164.4 million people is the seventh most populous country in the world and the district of Rajshahi is the third largest city in the country.

To the best of our knowledge, there has not been a similar study examining the relationship between active aging and healthy life expectancy in Bangladesh. This paper is thus unique because it represents the first attempt to examine the relationships between an active aging index and healthy life expectancy in Bangladesh. Although older people are expected to be treated with respect and reverence in Bangladesh, they are facing increased social isolation. The health conditions for older people have not improved, and for older women conditions may have worsened. The infrastructure of Bangladesh is insufficient to help the disabled and older populations. It is, therefore, important to examine the difference between life expectancy and healthy life expectancy, as well as the relationship between active aging and healthy life expectancy, to minimize years of disability in Bangladesh.

Data and Methods

A number of research methods and sources were used to obtain the data necessary for this study. The primary data used for the present study, collected during April 2009, come from a research project entitled "Socio-Demographic Status of the Aged Population and Elderly Abuse: A Study on Rural–urban Differentials in Rajshahi District, Bangladesh." The research project was funded by the Social Science Research Council (SSRC), of the Government of Bangladesh. For the relevance of the project title and because of limited funding, the Rajshahi district had been selected as the study area.

Bangladesh is divided administratively (from large to small) into divisions, districts (zilas), upazilas, and thanas. In rural areas, each thana is divided into several union councils and each union council consists of multiple villages. In metropolitan areas, thanas are divided into several wards and each ward is further divided into multiple mahallas. From the selected district, one Union Council, named Yusufpur Union, has been selected at random. From the selected Union, two villages (smallest administrative unit in rural areas), namely Baduria and Sahapur, have been selected using the probability proportional to size (PPS) technique with random number pairs (01, 0131) and (10, 1003) respectively. All persons 60 years of age and older residing in the households of the two villages have been interviewed.

The urban sample of households and the elderly were selected in a similar way. The Ward number 05, consisting of several Mahallas (smallest administrative unit in urban areas), was selected as the urban sample with random number pairs (05, 0554). All elderly residing in the households of the selected Ward were interviewed. The total number of the selected population sample was 896, with 477 rural and 419 urban residents.

To reach the desired goals of the project, a questionnaire was prepared and pre-tested by a pilot survey. Corrections were made following an evaluation of the pilot survey and a final version of the questionnaire was completed. Finally, field investigators went to the houses of selected areas where they identified eligible persons, asked the questions to the respondents, and recorded answers on questionnaires. To reach the desired response rate, repeated visits were made. The structured survey instrument containing closed questions, with the exception of income information, was designed to collect information on the following: (i) identification of respondents, (ii) details about family members, (iii) health conditions, (iv) daily activities, (v) economic activities, (vi) living conditions, (vii) abuse etc. For more accurate data collection, a Bengali version of the questionnaire was prepared for the interviewees and field investigators. Responses were then converted to English for data entry and analysis with SPSS for Windows, version 15 (SPSS, Inc., Chicago, IL).

Active Aging Index Construction

Active aging depends on a variety of "influences" or "determinants" that surround individuals, families, and nations (WHO 2002). Though WHO tried to accumulate the determinants of active aging under three pillars (see Fig. 16.1), at the same time

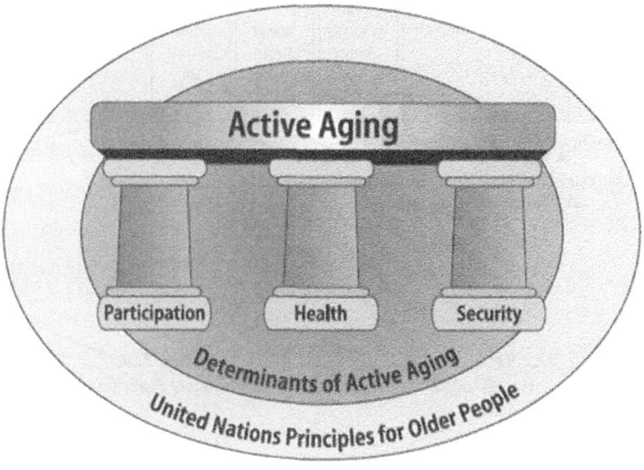

Fig. 16.1 The determinants of active aging according to WHO (2002: 45)

it confirmed that more research is very much needed to clarify and specify the role of each determinant, as well as the interaction between determinants, in the active aging process (WHO 2002).

Thus we tried to include the indicators for constructing an active aging index as recommended by the Active Aging Taskforce of the Western Australian Government (Active Aging Taskforce 2003). We included 15 indicators, used by Thanakwang and Soonthorndhada (2006), which also fall among the determinants of active aging by WHO, under three core or primary dimensions: six indicators for health (three indicators for health and wellness and three indicators for physical activities), three indicators for community participation, and six indicators for security dimension (three indicators for physical security and three indicators for financial security). The composite indices of health, community participation, and security were constructed first. Then the active aging index was constructed by combining these three indices. These indicators are illustrated in the active aging framework in Fig. 16.2.

In this study an attempt has been made to measure active aging in the Rajshahi district of Bangladesh by constructing active aging indices for three major dimensions, namely, (a) health, (b) community participation, and (c) security. The detailed description of these three dimensions with their relevant indicators is given in Table 16.2.

In each dimension, a weighted score for each of the indicators has been calculated. Each composite score is the sum of answers to several indicators within each dimension. However, since there was variability in the range of possible answers to the questions within each composite, a simple summation of answers would not have insured equal contribution of all questions, and there would have been an obvious inequality in the significance of the total variability of the composite score. In order to correct this issue, we applied a method to adjust each composite for the range of answers to each indicator and for the total number of indicators in the composite (McGahan et al. 1986; Thanakwang and Soonthorndhada 2006; Haque et al. 2010). For example, the composite score on the health dimension is composed of six

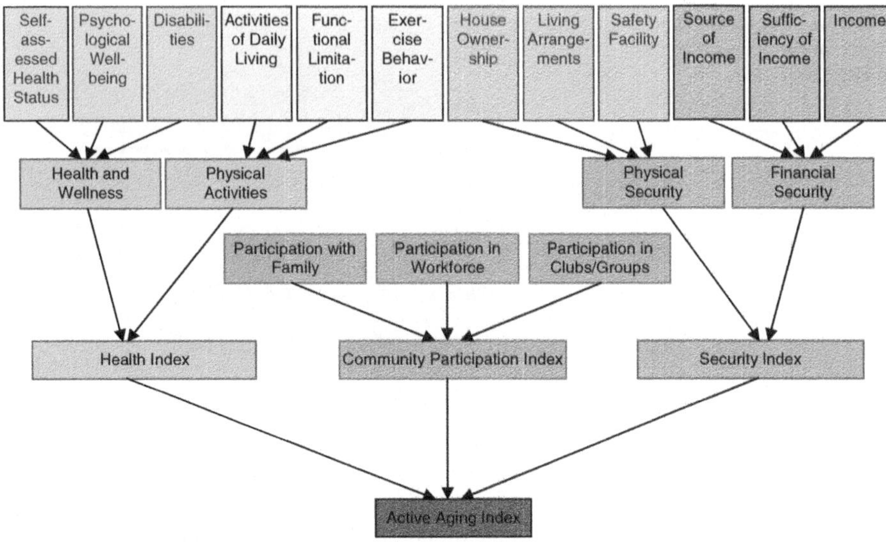

Fig. 16.2 Framework of active aging index

indicators ($H_1 - H_6$). The actual score of each dimension is calculated by summing the positive responses of the respondents in favor of their activeness, as shown in the equation below:

$$\text{Composite score} = H_1 / M_1 \times T + H_2 / M_2 \times T + H_3 / M_3 \times T + H_4 / M_4 \times T + H_5 / M_5 \times T + H_6 / M_6 \times T$$

Where,
H = the score of each indicator
M = the maximum answer value of each indicator
T = the total number of indicators of a dimension

Then an index of each dimension was constructed following the Human Development Index (HDI) constructed by the United Nations Development Programme (UNDP 2006) using the following equation:

$$\textit{Dimension Index} = \frac{\textit{Actual score} - \textit{Minimum score}}{\textit{Maximum score} - \textit{Minimum score}}$$

The maximum and minimum score of each dimension is measured by the performance in each dimension, expressed by 1 or 0 in accordance with the construction method of the HDI, and 1 minus the indices value measures the gap of activeness.

According to the WHO's concept of active aging, health, community participation, and security are inextricably linked. Therefore, the active aging index (AAI) is computed in a straightforward manner as a simple average of these three indices according to the formula below:

$$\text{AAI} = \frac{(\text{health index} + \text{community participation index} + \text{security index})}{3}$$

Each index was classified into three levels based on the UNDP criteria for levels of human development, which constitutes an indicator of the quality of life, as follows:

1. Index value less than 0.5 is low level;
2. Index value between 0.5 and 0.79 is moderate level; and
3. Index value equal or higher than 0.8 is high level.

Computation of Healthy Life Expectancy

To compute healthy life expectancy, we used the method devised by Sullivan (1971). This method partitions total life expectancy into the different health states based on the prevalence of self-rated health within a representative sample at a single point in time. Using the UN (2008) projected population for 2005 and 2010, we first estimated the 2008 and 2009 age- and sex-specific population for Bangladesh based on the exponential growth rate from 2005 to 2010. These estimates for Bangladesh were then proportioned for the Rajshahi district using the 2001 Bangladesh Population Census data to produce 2008 and 2009 population estimates for the district by age and sex for the total as well as for rural–urban areas. Preston and Bennett's (1983) method was then applied to those age distributions to compute five life tables for total and rural–urban areas by sex as well for 2009. By combining the computed life expectancies with age- and sex-specific self-rated disability prevalence rates obtained from the survey, we calculated healthy life expectancy for our study population. Healthy life expectancy values were obtained by dividing total healthy person-years at each age by the survivors at that age from the computed life table, which reflects the current health status of the sample population adjusted for age and mortality levels. For more details on computation of health expectancy using the Sullivan method, see Jagger et al. (2006).

In this study, active aging index (AAI) was constructed using the framework of figure number 2 and HLE using the Sullivan method. Univariate classification analysis has been performed in order to find the percentage of active aging attributes of the elderly population. Mean distribution has been presented to show the differences among study participants for AAI and HLE. Finally, cross-tabulation analyses as well as Pearson's correlation analysis were done to uncover the correlation between AAI and HLE including tests of differences between the correlations.

Results

Table 16.1 provides the distribution of the characteristics of the respondents of the present study. As can be seen from Table 16.1, overall the average age of the respondents is 68.37 years, 57.9% are young-old (i.e., 60–69 years) and 42.0% are old (70 years and above). Overall, 59% of the respondents do not have any education. In rural areas 93.0% women do not have any education compared with 63.6% for men. In urban areas almost 51% of women do not have any education compared with 18.0% for men. In rural areas, only 1.8% of the female respondents have secondary or above education while almost 19% of the male respondents have secondary and above education. In urban areas 17.3% of the female respondents have secondary or above education while 66.3% of the male respondents have secondary and above education. In rural Bangladesh, the female literacy rate is very low, as is a well-known phenomenon (Rahman et al. 2007). About 97% of the respondents are Muslim and about 60% are married. Also of interest, more than 70% of urban elderly live in joint families, while a little over 20% live in nuclear families.

Self-assessments of health are common components of population-based surveys. According to Fillenbaum (1984), self-perceived health status may be a better indicator than actual medical reports. In population studies, self-rated health is probably the most feasible, most inclusive, and most informative measure of human health status as well as a unique and valuable indicator of human health status (Jylhä 2009) and has been used as the first indicator under health dimension for the active aging index. Table 16.2 provides the measurements of indicators and dimensions of constructing active aging index. As can be seen from the Health Index on Table 16.2, almost 96% of elderly respondents reported no disability and about 59% reported either poor or very poor health status. About 85% of elderly indicate psychological well-being. In rural areas 74.3% of males and 62.0% of females have no functional limitations. In urban areas 55.6% of males and 36.9% of females have no functional limitations. Almost all respondents (97.3%) can perform their activities of daily living (ADL) successfully. About 43% of elderly have some functional limitations. The urban females have more limitation than rural females or urban or rural males. About 6 out of 10 elderly participated in some exercise during the last 6 months prior to the survey and male elderly are more active over female elderly in both rural and urban areas.

An overwhelming majority of the elderly supported their family. About 97.8% did not participate in any clubs or any elderly group activities. Particularly in rural areas, no one participated in any groups or clubs; it may be that such facilities are not available in rural areas. About 78% of the rural female and about 61% of the urban female elderly have no income; most strikingly 99% rural elderly were not satisfied with their income. Comparatively, urban elderly have more income than their rural counterparts. About 93% of the elderly live with their spouse, children, or others, while 16.2% of rural female elderly were reported living alone. The most striking finding is that about 35.1% of rural female elderly have no safety facilities and toilet at all.

From the indices, in the health dimension about 40% of elderly are highly active and in good health, with male elderly being more active both in rural and urban

Table 16.1 Elderly characteristics by percent of respondents

	Rural		Urban		
Variables	Male	Female	Male	Female	Overall
Age groups					
60–64	35.0	36.9	36.1	38.3	36.6
65–69	21.4	21.4	21.0	21.5	21.3
70–74	24.8	23.6	19.5	17.8	21.5
75–79	4.9	4.4	8.8	10.3	6.9
80–84	5.3	6.6	4.9	5.6	5.7
85+	8.7	7.0	9.8	6.5	7.9
Average age*	69.02	67.68	68.96	68.07	68.37
Religion					
Islam	97.1	96.7	97.6	96.3	96.9
Hindu	2.9	3.3	0.5	1.9	2.2
Others	–	–	2.0	1.9	0.9
Educational level					
No education	63.6	93.0	18.0	50.9	59.0
Primary	17.5	5.2	15.6	31.8	16.7
Secondary and above	18.9	1.8	66.3	17.3	24.2
Marital status					
Married	89.8	31.4	89.8	37.9	59.7
Others	10.2	68.6	10.2	62.1	40.3
Types of family					
Nuclear	54.4	39.5	26.8	20.1	35.4
Joint	45.6	60.5	73.2	79.9	64.6

Notes: *Indicates average age is calculated for the total population by sex and residence; 45.9 and 54.1% elderly are male and female respectively

areas. In community participation and security dimensions, most of the elderly are moderately active while females are found to be more active in community participation and males are found to be more secured. From the active aging index, we can see that about 79% of elderly are moderately active while male respondents are more active than the female respondents both in rural and urban areas.

Levels of Active Aging Index and Healthy Life Expectancy

Table 16.3 shows the mean values for healthy life expectancy and active aging index, which indicates the level of activeness and disability-free life expected for 60-, 65-, 70-, 80-, and 85-year old individuals by sex with rural–urban differentials. As expected, the results showing mean values of AAI and HLE decrease with the increase of age of the respondents. Comparatively, 60- and 65-year old persons are highly active and have more HLE than the older aged. Male elderly are found to be more active and could expect longer HLE than female elderly in both rural and urban areas. Urban elderly could expect more HLE compared with rural elderly,

Table 16.2 Elderly responses to indicators in the active aging index by dimension types

					Percentage				
					Rural		Urban		
Dimensions	No.	Indicators	Description	Measurements	Male	Female	Male	Female	Overall
Health index	1	Self-assessed health status	Self-assessed health status is an individual's own assessment of his or her health	5 = very good	–	–	1.0	0.5	0.3
				4 = good	8.7	3.7	16.1	5.6	8.1
				3 = Fair	31.6	25.8	41.0	36.0	33.0
				2 = poor	35.0	48.0	30.7	48.1	41.1
				1 = very poor	24.8	22.5	11.2	9.8	17.4
	2	Psychological well-being	The perception of sense of mental wellness in term of self-esteem	3 = high	91.3	80.8	89.3	81.8	85.4
				2 = moderate	6.8	18.5	10.2	16.8	13.5
				1 = low	1.0	0.7	0.5	1.4	0.9
				0 = no	1.0	–	–	–	0.2
	3	Disabilities	The number of handicaps such as paralysis, blindness and deafness	1 = no	95.6	95.2	95.6	95.8	95.5
				0 = 1 or more	4.4	4.8	4.4	4.2	4.5
	4	Activity of daily living (ADL) limitations	ADL limitations consider inability in performing usual daily activities like eating, dressing, bathing etc.	1 = no	97.1	98.5	96.1	97.2	97.3
				0 = 1 or more	2.9	1.5	3.9	2.8	2.7
	5	Functional limitations	Physical limitation, such as squatting, lifting up object weighing 5 kg, walking about 1 km, and climbing stairs (2–3 steps)	1 = no	74.3	62.0	55.6	36.9	57.4
				0 = 1 or more	25.7	38.0	44.4	63.1	42.6
	6	Exercise behavior	Having performed any exercise during last 6 months prior to the interview	1 = yes	63.6	55.0	72.7	43.9	58.4
				0 = no	36.4	45.0	27.3	56.1	41.6

Community participation index	1	Participation in work force	Still participates in paid and unpaid work	1=yes	69.9	77.5	42.0	56.1	62.5
				0=no	30.1	22.5	58.0	43.9	37.5
	2	Interaction with family members	The elderly's support to family members, e.g. food supply, house keeping and child care	1=1 or more	96.6	97.8	95.1	94.9	96.2
				0=no	3.4	2.2	4.9	5.1	3.8
	3	Participation in clubs/groups	The elderly takes part in activity proposed by various groups, i.e. elderly group, funeral group, vocational group, house wife group, cooperatives group, and volunteer scout group	1=1 or more	–	–	9.3	0.5	2.2
				0=no	100	100	90.7	99.5	97.8
Security index	1	Income*	The income is categorized just to show the percentage, not for constructing AAI	4=3001+	13.6	0.7	59.0	15.4	20.5
				3=501 – 3000	61.7	12.5	22.4	22.9	28.6
				2=100 – 500	1.0	8.9	–	0.9	3.9
				1=0	23.8	77.9	18.5	60.7	47.0
	2	Sufficiency of income	The self-assessment by the older persons on whether his/her income is sufficient for a living	2=sufficient	1.0	0.4	23.4	11.4	8.4
				1=not sufficient	75.2	21.7	58.0	27.9	44.6
				0=no income	23.8	77.9	18.5	60.7	47.0
	3	Sources of income	The number of sources of income that the elderly receives, i.e. work, pension, government living allowance, saving/interest, spouse, children, relatives, or others	2=2 or more	16.0	7.7	33.2	18.7	18.1
				1=1 source	83.5	91.9	66.3	81.3	81.6
				0=no	0.5	0.4	0.5	–	0.3
	4	House ownership	The ownership of the dwelling in which older person is living	1=yes	85.4	31.4	77.1	35.0	55.1
				0=no	14.6	68.6	22.9	65.0	44.9

(continued)

Table 16.2 (continued)

					Percentage				
					Rural		Urban		
Dimensions	No.	Indicators	Description	Measurements	Male	Female	Male	Female	Overall
	5	Living arrangement	The co-residence of the elderly with family members or others in their household	1 = with spouse, children or others	97.6	83.8	99.5	93.5	92.9
				0 = living alone	2.4	16.2	0.5	6.5	7.1
	7	Safety facilities	Safety facility denotes to the safe material facilitating in a toilet	1 = yes	73.8	64.9	97.1	96.3	81.8
				0 = no	26.2	35.1	2.9	3.7	18.2
Health index		A composite index constructed from 7 components		3 = high	52.4	35.1	51.7	24.3	40.3
				2 = moderate	42.2	60.9	42.4	70.6	54.7
				1 = low	5.3	4.1	5.9	5.1	5.0
Community participation index		A composite index constructed from 3 components		3 = high	–	–	4.9	0.5	1.2
				2 = moderate	69.4	77.5	41.5	55.6	62.2
				1 = low	30.6	22.5	53.7	43.9	36.6
Security index		A composite index constructed from 5 components		3 = high	0.5	–	16.1	3.7	4.7
				2 = moderate	85.9	25.8	77.6	53.7	58.1
				1 = low	13.6	74.2	6.3	42.5	37.2
Active aging index		A composite index constructed from 3 dimensions	The positive or active living of the elderly based on the WHO concept (a combination of health, community participation and security indices)	3 = high	1.0	–	11.7	1.4	3.2
				2 = moderate	88.3	78.2	76.6	72.0	78.7
				1 = low	10.7	21.8	11.7	26.6	18.1

Note: *Bangladeshi currency – BDT; For indicator number 6 under security index the respondents were asked whether or not they have sanitary toilets and safe materials such as hand rails, no water on the toilet floor, toilet slippers etc. as well?

Table 16.3 Mean values of HLE and AAI by sex and residence

	HLE (AAI)				
	Rural		Urban		
Age	Male	Female	Male	Female	Overall
60	5.88 (0.647)	3.81 (0.580)	8.30 (0.651)	5.58 (0.574)	**5.72 (0.609)**
65	4.63 (0.628)	2.59 (0.561)	5.10 (0.620)	3.50 (0.554)	**3.85 (0.589)**
70	3.26 (0.605)	2.15 (0.540)	3.61 (0.589)	3.41 (0.518)	**2.99 (0.562)**
75	1.29 (0.511)	1.05 (0.496)	1.29 (0.526)	2.22 (0.491)	**1.57 (0.506)**
80	0.93 (0.508)	0.64 (0.487)	0.41 (0.496)	0.98 (0.434)	**0.74 (0.483)**
85	0.00 (0.496)	0.99 (0.487)	0.29 (0.481)	0.45 (0.369)	**0.44 (0.464)**

though some urban age ranges are found to be less active than the respective rural age ranges. In addition if we compare the AAI of urban 60-year old females to rural females of 60 and 65 years of age, it could be easily mentioned that the same level of activeness cannot ensure the same HLE for all. These AAI effects might reflect the effects of morbidity, health declining as age increases, environment, lifestyle, and health facilities.

Differences Between Life Expectancy (LE) and HLE

Life expectancy has frequently been used as an indicator of public health; another indicator, health expectancy, was introduced in the 1970s. Both indicators help us to measure the life expectancy with disability that one would experience in later life. Figure 16.3 shows the LE and HLE by sex and residence.

From Fig. 16.3, it is observed that rural females are expected to live longer than all other elderly, with the little exception found in the 70–74 age group. However, rural female elderly could expect less HLE than all other counterparts except the last age groups. Figure 16.3 also reveals that there is a huge gap between the LE and HLE, i.e. life expectancy with disability that one would experience in later life. For overall areas there is a mean difference of 8.20 years (with 95% confidence interval [CI], 8.06–8.34; $t_{895}=112.08$; $p<0.0001$) between LE and HLE. For rural areas there is a mean difference of 8.40 years (95% CI, 8.13–8.67; $t_{205}=60.99$; $p<0.0001$) for male elderly, and 9.55 years (95% CI, 9.26–9.84; $t_{270}=64.16$; $p<0.0001$) for female elderly. For urban areas there is a mean difference of 6.62 years (95% CI, 6.48–6.76; $t_{204}=93.35$; $p<0.0001$) for male elderly and 7.81 years (95% CI, 7.58–8.04; $t_{213}=67.43$; $p<0.0001$) for female elderly between LE and HLE. So, male elderly could expect less disabled life in comparison with female in both areas. These results might be an indication of the positive effect of active participation in every sector of life for male elderly. This may also indicate lack of comparable facilities for the female elderly both in urban and rural areas.

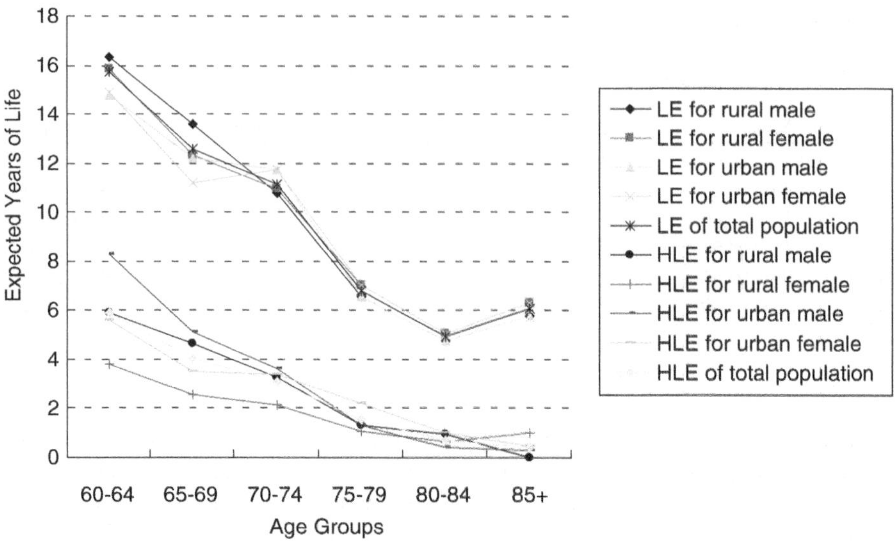

Fig. 16.3 Difference between LE and HLE

Relationship Between HLE and AAI

It is observed from Table 16.3 that the study participants who have more HLE also have high mean values of AAI. The Pearson's correlation coefficient between AAI and HLE has been computed and showed very strong positive significant relationships between the variables in both the rural and urban areas and for both the male and female elderly. The overall correlation between AAI and HLE is 0.979 ($p<0.001$); for rural males the correlation is 0.978 ($p<0.001$), and for rural female it is 0.977 ($p<0.001$). The correlation between AAI and HLE for urban males is 0.969 ($p<0.001$) and for urban females is 0.939 ($p<0.001$). At issue is whether the correlations for males are significantly higher than those for females in both rural and urban areas. Thus tests of differences between correlations were done that revealed Z is 0.25 and 0.43 in rural and urban areas, respectively, and is not significant at the 0.05 level. So, from observing the overall correlation as well as correlation differences, one can conclude that if one wants to lead more disability-free years of life, he/she should be more active in every aspect of life.

Discussion

Traditionally and religiously the elderly people of Bangladesh are very much respected both within their family and in their community. They are considered as the key to family ties and symbols of family identity. They are treated as guardians of ancestral values since time immemorial as well as venerable counselors. For these reasons they are always respected and the younger generations try to take the best care of their elderly relatives in the family. However, due to various socio-economic changes over the years, traditional values and customs are eroding and breaking down traditional joint family living arrangements into nuclear family systems (UNESCO 1992). Increased landlessness and poverty are assumed to weaken the relationship between elder members and other members of the family (Hassan 2007) as well. Because of rural poverty, many adults move in search of employment to urban areas. Women are also joining the urban work force in increasing numbers, and they have less time to take care of elderly family members than they did in the past. It is unclear how long the society will be able to hold the tradition of young family members taking care of the elderly in their family. Thus this paper has tried to introduce self-care (i.e. active aging) by examining the socio-demographic status of the elderly through the dimensions of AAI and the relationship between HLE and AAI as well.

The analysis of 15 indicators of AAI showed that the urban elderly have more income and more education and lead better lives than their rural counterparts. At the same time almost all elderly are dissatisfied with their income, regardless of whether the financial support comes from the family or other sources. About 93% of elderly are found to live with family members, but of the family types observed, 45.9% are nuclear and 54.1% are joint families in rural areas; while 23.4% are nuclear and 76.6% are joint families in urban areas. The financial support from the family might be reduced because of decline in family size. Most of the elderly were not found to be active in any clubs or groups. Therefore, the elderly were asked a multiple choice question, "How do you pass leisure time?" The study found that most of the rural elderly pass leisure time by gossiping, caring for children, and religious work, while urban elderly pass time by gossiping, caring for children, religious work, and reading books or newspapers. In rural areas, almost 99% of the male respondents passed their leisure time by gossiping, 88.3% caring for children, 68.9% with religious work, and 3.9% with reading a newspaper. Almost 99% of the rural female respondents spent their leisure time by gossiping, 87.1% taking care of children, 83% doing religious activities, and 0.4% reading books and or newspapers. In urban areas, 97.6% of the male respondents passed their leisure time by gossiping, 93.2% caring for children, 89.3% with religious work, and 54.6% with reading books and or newspapers. Almost 96% of the urban female respondents spent their leisure time by gossiping, 94.4% taking care of children, 92.5% doing religious activities, and 9.8% reading books and or newspapers. So, most respondents participate in gossiping, whether it is indeed negative or positive, because in Bangladeshi culture the elderly usually have few responsibilities or obligations except taking care of grandchildren. The elderly often hand over their business or properties to their children. This culture should be changed to encourage active aging in every aspect of life. Daily activities can be successfully performed by 97.3% of respondents, and this also could motivate them to remain active in every sector of daily life. Male elderly are also found to be more active than the female elderly. Our study supports studies by Barford et al. (2006) in "Life expectancy: women now on top everywhere," which found that even in the poorest countries, women can expect to outlive men. We found increased levels of disability with advancing age as well as clear gender differences in Bangladesh, which showed that while females outlive males, they are more likely to live a greater part of their remaining life in disability. Still, the very strong positive correlation between AAI and HLE could be a turning point for female elderly as well as for all elderly to be more active for an improved quality of life.

This study is cross-sectional and no direct conclusions can be drawn regarding time trends in healthy life expectancy. The analysis also has a few limitations. First, only the 15 indicators suggested by the Active Aging Taskforce of the Western Australian Government (Active Aging Taskforce 2003) under three pillars have been utilized for constructing the AAI, following the parameters established by Thanakwang and Soonthorndhada (2006). Since the study is based on the WHO concept, more indicators, such as no intoxication habit or coping style, might have been included to construct AAI. Further analysis is also needed to better understand the pathways that explain how these broad aging and lifestyle determinants actually affect health and wellbeing. Second, this study utilized the Preston and Bennett (1983) estimation method for a post-childhood life table where we assumed $l_{85+} = ({}_{5}L_{80} + {}_{15}L_{85})/20$ i.e. the maximum year as 100 years for ${}_{15}L_{85}$ to compute age- and sex-specific life tables since we did not have any persons in 100+ years of age for 2005 and 2010. Usually the Sullivan (1971) method is used with same period mortality, but these data are unavailable for the study area, i.e. for Bangladesh. The Preston and Bennett (1983) method is innovative and yielded estimates that are not as sensitive to certain types of age-misreporting, particularly heaping (UN 1983).

Conclusions

Though Bangladesh will face population aging after 2025, it is much more notable that this elderly population suffers challenges in respect to health and socio-economic issues. The primary objective of this study was to examine the relationships between increased life expectancy and healthy life expectancy in Bangladesh by examining the relationships between AAI and HLE.

People with more education and/or higher incomes live longer and experience fewer adverse health events (Crimmins and Saito 2001). Our study also showed that urban as well as male elderly are more educated, active in all aspects of life, and have longer HLE. These findings indicate that steps should be taken to provide life-long learning as well as pragmatic education with motivation to be active in every aspect of life. The opportunity for positive community participation as well as health and security should also be ensured in later life. Urban amenities such as parks and recreational facilities should be provided in the rural areas. Strengthening family support systems through advocacy and counseling could encourage the responsibility of family members towards elderly members. Many elderly can take care of themselves if physical exercise and income sources are available. These opportunities should be promoted through mass media (i.e. newspapers, television, radio etc.) in a comprehensible manner. Indeed, physical activity plays a central role in the prevention and management of chronic disease (Cyarto et al. 2004), and physical inactivity is identified as a leading cause of disability among older adults (Buchner 1997).

We should bear in mind that the future health of the elderly will be influenced by a range of factors, so it cannot be assumed that healthy life expectancy will remain at current levels. Yong and Saito (2009) conclude that improvements in medical technologies could contribute to longer Japanese healthy life expectancy in the future. Since the Alma Alta Declaration in 1978, Bangladesh has made important gains in providing primary health care. All health indicators show steady gain, and the health status of the population has improved (WHO 2010). As a result, Bangladeshi healthy life expectancy could be increased. At the same time, positive correlations between AAI and HLE suggest that the elderly could enjoy more HLE involving them in all dimensions of AAI. Thus the active aging concept should be properly introduced to the elderly as well as to all people to change their life style so that they may enjoy more disability-free years in later life. Finally, more research on this emerging issue should be done with close monitoring, and this information needs to be scientifically utilized in developing suitable programs to address the needs of poor elderly residents of the Rajshahi district as well as for all the elderly people of Bangladesh and developing countries.

References

Active Aging Taskforce. (2003). *Active aging taskforce: Report and recommendations*. Perth: Government of Western Australia, Minister for Community Development.

Barford, A., Dorling, D., Smith, G. D., & Shaw, M. (2006). Life expectancy: Women now on top everywhere. *British Medical Journal, 332*, 808.

Boyle, J. S., & Counts, M. M. (1988). Toward healthy aging: A theory for community health nursing. *Public Health Nursing, 5*, 45–51.

Brønnum-Hansen, H., Andersen, O., Kjøller, M., & Rasmussen, N. K. (2004). Social gradient in life expectancy and health expectancy in Denmark. *Sozial- und Präventivmedizin, 49*, 36–41.

Buchner, D. M. (1997). Physical activity and quality of life in older adults. *Journal of the American Medical Association, 277*(1), 64–66.

Chen, M. Y., Chang, H. C., & Li, M. Y. (2002). Health promotion behaviors among women with high risk breast cancer: From the self-care perspective. *Journal of Health Science, 4*, 63–74.

Crimmins, E. M., & Saito, Y. (2001). Trends in healthy life expectancy in the United States, 1970–1990: Gender, racial, and educational differences. *Social Science & Medicine, 52*(11), 1629–1641.

Cruz, G. T., Saito, Y., & Natividad, J. N. (2007). Active life expectancy and functional health transition among Filipino older people. *Canadian Studies in Population, 34*(1), 29–47.

Cyarto, E. V., Moorhead, G. E., & Brown, W. J. (2004). Updating the evidence relating to physical activity intervention studies in older people. *Journal of Science and Medicine in Sport, 7*(1 Suppl), 30–38.

Fillenbaum, G. G. (1984). *The wellbeing of the elderly: Approaches to multidimensional assessment* (Publication No. 84). Geneva: World Health Organization.

HAI (Help Age International). (2006). *Social pensions in Bangladesh*. Retrieved November 7, 2009, from http://www.helpage.org/Researchandpolicy/PensionWatch/Bangladesh

Haque, M. M., Tareque, M. I., & Mostofa, M. G. (2010). Women empowerment and its impact on fertility in Bangladesh. *Demography India, 39*(1), 21–34.

Hassan, M. (2007). *Country statement of Bangladesh.* High-level meeting on the regional review of the Madrid International Plan of Action on Aging (MIPAA), Macao, 9–11 October 2007. Retrieved November 3, 2009, from http://www.unescap.org/esid/psis/meetings/AgingMipaa 2007/Bangladesh.pdf

Jagger, C., Cox, B., Le Roy, S., & EHEMU. (2006). *Health expectancy calculation by the Sullivan method* (EHEMU Tech. Rep. 2006-3). Equipe Démographie et Santé, Centre Val d'Aurelle, Parc Euromédecine, 34298 Montpellier cedex 5, France.

Jylhä, M. (2009). What is self-rated health and why does it predict mortality? Towards a unified conceptual model. *Social Science & Medicine, 69*, 307–316.

Liu, X., Liang, J., Muramatsu, N., & Sugisawa, H. (1995). Transitions in functional status and active life expectancy among older people in Japan. *The Journal of Gerontology. Series B, Psychological Sciences and Social Sciences, 50B*(6), S383–S394.

Mathers, C. D., McCallum, J., & Robine, J. M. (Eds.) (1994). Advances in health expectancies. *Proceedings of the 7th meeting of the international network on health expectancy (REVES)*, Canberra.

Mathers, C. D., Murray, C. J. L., Lopez, A. D., Salomon, J. A., Sadana, R., Tandon, A., Ustün, B. L., & Chatterj, S. (2001). *Estimates of healthy life expectancy for 191 countries in the year 2000: Methods and results* (Global Programme on Evidence for Health Policy Discussion Paper No. 38). Geneva: World Health Organization.

McGahan, P. L., Griffith, J. A., Parente, R., & McLellan, A. T. (1986). *Addiction severity index – Composite score manual.* Philadelphia: University of Pennsylvania/Veterans Administration Center for Studies of Addiction.

McLaughlin, J., & Zeeberg, I. (1993). Self-care and multiple sclerosis: A view from two cultures. *Social Science & Medicine, 37*(3), 315–329.

Palloni, A., & McEniry, M. (2007). Aging and health status of elderly in Latin America and the Caribbean: Preliminary findings. *Journal of Cross-Cultural Gerontology, 22*(3), 263–285.

Preston, S. H., & Bennett, N. G. (1983). A census based method for estimating adult mortality. *Population Studies, 37*(1), 91–104.

Rahman, M. M., Tareque, M. I., Rahman, K. M. M., & Islam, T. M. (2007). Dimension of population aging in Bangladesh. *Middle East Journal of Age and Aging, 4*(5), 17–22.

Robine, J. M., & Ritchie, K. (1991). Healthy life expectancy: Evaluation of global indicator of change in population health. *British Medical Journal, 302*, 457–460.

Robine, J. M., Mathers, C. D., Bone, M. R., & Romieu, I. (Eds.). (1993). *Calculation of health expectancies: Harmonization, consensus achieved and future perspectives* (Vol. 226). France: Colloque INSERM/John Libbey Eurotext.

Rogers, A., Rogers, R. G., & Belanger, A. (1990). Longer life but worsening health? Measurement and dynamics. *The Gerontologist, 30*, 640–649.

Ruffing-Rahal, M. A. (1991). Rationale and design for health promotion with older adults. *Public Health Nursing, 8*, 258–263.

Sullivan, D. F. (1971). A single index of mortality and morbidity. *HSMHA Health Reports, 86*, 347–354.

Thanakwang, K., & Soonthorndhada, K. (2006). Attributes of active aging among older persons in Thai land: Evidence from the 2002 survey. *Asia-Pacific Population Journal, 21*(3), 113–135.

Trupin, L., Rice, D. P., & Max, W. (1995). *Medical expenditures for people with disabilities in the United States, 1987.* Washington, DC: US Dept of Education, National Institute on Disability and Rehabilitation Research.

UN (United Nations). (1983). *Mannual X – Indirect techniques for demographic estimation.* New York: United Nations.

UN (United Nations). (2008). *World population prospectus: The 2008 revised population database.* United Nations Population Division. Retrieved September 2010, from http://esa.un.org/unpp/p2k0data.asp

UNDP (United Nations Development Programme). (2006). *Human development report 2006*. New York: United Nations Development Programme.

UNESCO. (1992). *The changing family in ASIA* (RUSHSAP Series on Monographs and Occasional Papers 35). Bangkok: Social and Human Sciences in Asia and the Pacific.

UNPD (United Nations Population Division). (2008). *World population and aging 1950–2050*. New York: Department of Economics and Social Affairs (DESA). Retrieved December 2008, from http://www.un.org/esa/population/publications/worldaging19502050/

WHO. (2010). *Health system in Bangladesh*. Bangladesh: World Health Organization. Retrieved October 29, 2010, from http://www.whoban.org/health_system_bangladesh.html

WHO (World Health Organization). (2002). *Active aging, a policy framework*. Geneva: World Health Organization, Non-communicable Disease Prevention and Health Promotion, Aging and Life Course. A contribution of the World Health Organization to the Second United Nations World Assembly on Aging, Madrid, April 2002.

Wong, R., & Palloni, A. (2009). Aging in Mexico and Latin America. In P. Uhlenberg (Ed.), *International handbook of population aging* (Vol. 1, pp. 231–252). Dordrecht: Springer.

Yong, V., & Saito, Y. (2009). Trends in healthy life expectancy in Japan: 1986–2004. *Demographic Research, 20*, 467–494.

Chapter 17
A Systematic Review of Retirement as a Risk Factor for Mortality

Matthew J. Shim, David Gimeno, Sandi L. Pruitt, Christopher B. McLeod, Margaret J. Foster, and Benjamin C. Amick III

Introduction

Aging, health, and retirement are closely related in modern industrialized societies such as the United States. Starting in the 1800s and continuing through the early 1900s, old age pensions, fixed age retirement, and government sponsored pension plans were introduced by Germany, France and England, which meant that persons no longer had to work until they died or to rely on friends and family for support in their old age (Streib and Schneider 1971). The aging population in the US is dramatically increasing. The U.S. Census Bureau (2006) estimated that 78.2 million people in the baby boomer generation, those born between 1946 and 1964, were alive, a total that represented 30% of the U.S. population. In 2006, the oldest of this

M.J. Shim, Ph.D., M.P.H., M.A. (✉)
15th Aerospace Medicine Squadron, Public Health Flight (15 AMDS/SGPM), Joint Base Pearl Harbor-Hickam, HI, USA
e-mail: matthew.shim@us.af.mil

D. Gimeno, Ph.D.
Division of Epidemiology, Human Genetics & Environmental Sciences, The University of Texas Health Sciences Center at Houston-School of Public Health, San Antonio Regional Campus, San Antonio, TX, USA

Institute for Work & Health, Toronto, ON, Canada
email: david.gimeno@uth.tmc.edu

S.L. Pruitt, Ph.D., M.P.H.
Department of Clinical Sciences, The University of Texas Southwestern Medical Centere, Dallas, TX, USA
email: sandi.pruitt@utsouthwestern.edu

C.B. McLeod, Ph.D.
School of Population and Public Health, The University of British Columbia, Vancouver, BC, Canada
email: chris.mcleod@ubc.ca

N. Hoque et al. (eds.), *Applied Demography and Public Health*, Applied Demography Series 3, DOI 10.1007/978-94-007-6140-7_17,

© Springer Science+Business Media Dordrecht 2013

generation turned 60 years old. The Census also estimates that persons age 65 and older will total about 13% of the U.S. population by 2010, and 19% by 2025 (Campbell 1996). These changes could overwhelm the public and private social security and health care insurance and delivery systems (Gebbie et al. 2005).

Retirement is a change in employment status, from working to non-working, that is usually expected to coincide with a predetermined age (e.g., 65), predetermined length of service (e.g., 20 or 30 years), or health deterioration (e.g., physical disability) (Streib and Schneider 1971). Three basic types of retirement can be defined: (1) on-time retirement, when a worker stops working on or after a predetermined age or length of service; (2) health-related retirement, when a worker stops working either on, after, or prior to a predetermined age or length of service because of ill-health and/or disability; and, (3) early retirement, when a worker stops working prior to a predetermined age or length of service where ill-health and disability are not factors.

The relationship between retirement and health is not well defined (Kasl and Jones 2000). There is no consensus on the definition or measurement of retirement as an exposure or risk factor for mortality. Current social research tends to focus on the association between unemployment, job loss, and/or job transition and health outcomes (Breeze et al. 2001; Gallo et al. 2004; Henriksson et al. 2003; Kasl 1996; vanAmelsvoort et al. 2003) with only a cursory mention of retirement. When retirement is the exposure of interest, the focus has been on the relationship between retirement and mortality without discussing retirement types (Gallo et al. 2004; Marmot and Shipley 1996; Moen 1996).

Two conflicting health beliefs are associated with retirement: (1) retire early and live longer and (2) retire and die sooner (Anderson 1985; Padfield 1996). To date, no research has provided any definitive evidence to support or refute either belief (Anderson 1985; Ekerdt et al. 1983; Haynes et al. 1978; Herzog et al. 1991; Marmot and Shipley 1996; Mein et al. 2003; Ohrui et al. 2004; Quaade et al. 2002; Rosenkoetter and Garris 1998; Ross and Drentea 1998; Schnurr et al. 2005; Sorlie and Rogot 1990).

The role of retirement and its effect on health and mortality is dependent on how retirement is defined and measured. In contrast to the ambiguous results of the relationship between early and on-time retirement as risk factors for illness, both ill-health and disability appear to be strong risk factors for retirement (Krause et al. 1997; Pransky et al. 2005; Siebert et al. 2001). Without considering health-related retirement, it is possible to mistakenly assume that retirement is the risk factor. This systematic review addresses the following research question: "Does the research literature support the view that type of retirement is a risk factor for mortality?"

M.J. Foster, M.S.
Client Services, Texas A&M University Libraries, College Station, TX, USA
email: margaretfoster@library.tamu.edu

B.C. Amick III, Ph.D.
School of Public Health Southwest Center for Occupational and Environmental Health, The University of Texas Health Sciences Center at Houston, Houston, TX, USA

Institute for Work & Health, Toronto, ON, Canada
email: benjamin.c.amick@uth.tmc.edu

Methods

Research related to retirement and mortality was systematically reviewed adapting a Cochrane review protocol (Higgins and Green 2006) and following Slavin's (1995) 'best evidence synthesis' approach and the systematic review protocols of the Institute for Work and Health (IWH) (Brewer et al. 2006). The review team included six researchers from the United States, Canada, and the United Kingdom. Web-based SRS, version 4.0 software (Mobius Analytics 2009) was used for article organization, review, data extraction, and tracking. Team members did not review or extract data from articles they had consulted on, authored, or co-authored.

Eligibility Criteria

Studies were included if they: (1) were written in English; (2) were published or in-press in a peer-reviewed journal; (3) reported data from a longitudinal primary study (i.e., not a review or editorial); (4) measured retirement as an independent variable, main effect, co-variable, or confounder; (5) did not combine retirement with unemployment status or "other" employment categorizations; and (6) measured either all-cause or cause-specific mortality as an outcome.

Literature Search

As of December 2008, no systematic reviews of this literature were identified. A preliminary literature review identified search terms covering three broad areas: (1) retirement, (2) mortality/survival, and (3) epidemiologic study methods. Search and exclusion terms were adapted for six electronic databases that index social, economic, and health related journals published through 2008. The databases, search platforms, and beginning coverage dates included: Academic Search Premier (via EBSCO) 1887, CINAHL (via OVID and EBSCO) 1982, EconLit (via OCLC FirstSearch) 1969, MEDLINE (via OVID) 1950, PsycInfo (via OVID) 1887, and Sociological Abstracts (via CSA) 1967. For all articles eligible for data extraction, we used the Scopus™ web-based database (Elsevier 2007) to identify any additional articles 'cited by' or 'citing' the article that may have been overlooked or missed. Content area experts were also surveyed for potentially eligible articles. The complete search strategy is available from the first author.

Selection for Relevance

First, title and abstract screening (TAS) was conducted to quickly identify and exclude non-relevant studies. Second, full text screening (FTS) was completed for the

Table 17.1 Quality assessment questions, exclusionary response and weights

	Quality assessment question	Weights
1.	Is retirement (or type of retirement) grouped together with non-retirement related categories?	Yes = exclude
2.	The primary research question/objective is clearly stated.	Yes = 1
3.	Is the primary research question/objective related to the systematic review study question that…type of retirement is a risk factor for mortality?	Yes = 2
4.	Were study sample methods (including sample size, inclusion/exclusion criteria and power) adequately described?	Yes = 2
5.	Was non-response to participation in the study addressed and/or adequately described?	Yes = 1
6.	Is retirement the primary exposure or main independent variable in the study?	Yes = 2
7.	Is retirement a main effect, co-variable, confounder or interaction in the study?	Yes = 1
8.	Is mortality a measured outcome in the study? If cause-specific is selected, enter the cause(s) in the text box.	Yes = 1
9.	Did the study measure retirement (exposure) before mortality (outcome)?	Yes = 3
10.	Is the comparison group (or reference group) appropriate? (i.e. does it make sense?)	Yes = 1
11.	Did the study make comparisons between similarly employed/retired populations?	Yes = 1
12.	Were covariates/potential confounders for mortality (e.g. gender, age, pre-existing health conditions) appropriately used to adjust or stratify the analysis and/or adequately described?	Yes = 2
13.	Was loss to follow-up appropriately addressed and/or adequately described in the study?	Yes = 1
14.	Were statistical methods appropriately used and/or adequately described to examine the retirement/mortality relationship?	Yes = 3

remaining studies. One review team member evaluated each article at each step. To reduce agreement bias, reviewers were assigned different articles for TAS and FTS.

To address potential bias due to a single reviewer conducting the TAS, an independent reviewer completed a quality control check by reviewing titles and abstracts of 5% (n = 39) of the 758 excluded articles and 5% (n = 11) of the 210 articles forwarded to FTS. Concordance was high and the team considered the quality of the TAS process acceptable.

Quality Assessment and Ranking

After FTS, articles were forwarded to Quality Assessment (QA) and Ranking (QR) review. Prior to QA, the team developed 14 criteria to assess methodological quality and statistical validity. Following Brewer et al. (2006), the team decided on a three-point weighting scale ranging from "important" (1 point) to "moderately important" (2 points) to "highly important" (3 points) (Table 17.1). A non-weighted exclusionary question (Table 17.1, Item 1) addressed the definition of retirement in each article. Grouping retirement with unemployment status or "other" employment categories was inadequate to assess the study question. Each article was independently reviewed by two team members who were required to reach consensus.

The QR for each article was based on a weighted sum of 13 quality criteria (highest score=21). This QR denominator was reduced by one for each "non applicable" answer. Each article received a QR by dividing the weighted score by the QR denominator and multiplying by 100. Articles were grouped into three categories (Appendix A) determined by consensus following the review methodology literature (Higgins and Green 2006; Slavin 1995): (1) high (90–100%), (2) medium-high (75–89%) and (3) medium-low (£74%).

Data Extraction

To retain only those studies with adequate validity to answer the research question, studies with medium-low quality (MLQ) rankings (£74%) were excluded. Differences between medium-low (MLQ) and medium-high (MHQ) QR studies (Appendix A) varied. The main reasons for lower rankings were: (1) inappropriate use and/or description of statistical methods (MLQ=66%, 19/29 vs. MHQ=0%, 0/9); and (2) lack of statistical adjustment for potential confounders (MLQ=62% 21/29 vs. MHQ=44% 4/9). Also, 44.8% (13/29) of the MLQ studies, but only 22% (2/9) of the MHQ studies, did not compare similarly employed and/or retired populations. Thus, many MLQ studies did not address the healthy worker effect, when lower mortality is observed in employed populations when compared to the general population.

Full data extraction and evidence synthesis was completed on all studies in the "high" (n=4) and "medium-high" (n=9) categories using standardized data extraction questions (Appendix B). Two reviewers performed independent data extraction on each article. The data collected were used to build summary tables and to form the 'best evidence' synthesis basis for the team's conclusions. When studies presented multiple statistical analysis models adjusting for different confounders, data extraction is presented for the fully adjusted models only.

Evidence Synthesis

The studies reviewed were heterogeneous and differed by country, study designs, exposure definitions, mortality outcomes, and statistical methods used. This required a research synthesis approach using Slavin's (1995) 'best evidence synthesis' methodology. Based on quality ranking, quantity of evidence, and consistency among articles, we used the criteria in Table 17.5 to classify evidence as strong, sufficient, mixed, or insufficient (Brewer et al. 2006; Briss et al. 2000; Slavin 1995).

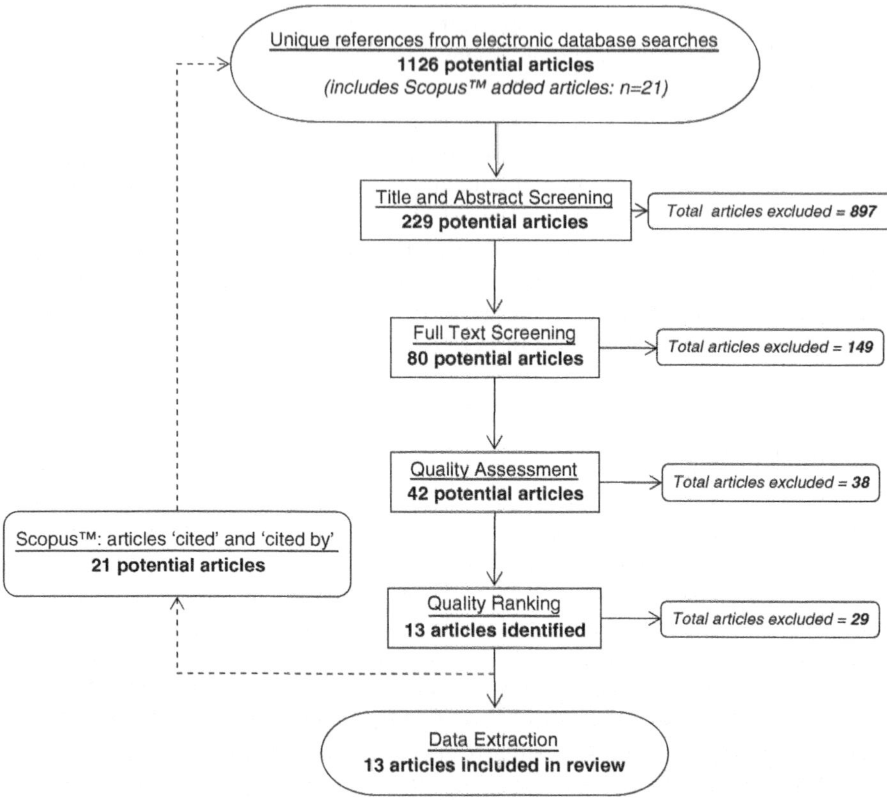

Fig. 17.1 Flowchart of systematic review process

Results

We identified a total of 1,126 articles (Fig. 17.1); 1,084 were excluded during TAS (n=897), FTS (n=149) and QA (n=38). Out of the 42 articles ranked, 29 articles were excluded based on their medium-low quality rankings. Thus, evidence synthesis was conducted on the remaining 13 articles (Table 17.2). These studies were published between 1976 and 2008 and covered the time period of 1953–2006. Cohort sample sizes ranged from 1,235 (Olsen and Jeune 1980) to 170,749 (Munch and Svarer 2005); 54% of the studies had more than 12,000 individuals.

Table 17.3 shows the main study characteristics and illustrates the heterogeneous nature of the studies. The studies included mostly Caucasian men in both white- and blue-collar occupations, and spanned over Asia/Middle-East, Europe, and North America. Study designs were either prospective or retrospective cohort and employed and reported multiple statistical techniques: standardized mortality ratios, survival analysis with hazard ratios (HRs), or logistic regression with relative risks (RRs). All-cause mortality was measured in all studies and six studies provided additional cause-specific mortality. Study results are presented in Table 17.4 and evidence synthesis in Table 17.5.

Table 17.2 Study descriptions

Quality ranking	Author (year)	Primary research question/objective	Time period (years) / Study location / Study design	Sample size (% female)	Employment classifications – definitions (*see notes below*)
High	Jeune (1982)	Estimate the survival prognosis of semi-skilled disability pensioners	1975–1978 Denmark Retrospective cohort	4,439 (0%)	1. **High disability** 2. **Intermediate disability** 3. **Low disability** 4. **Employed**
	Litwin (2007)	Address the association between early retirement and seven-year all-cause mortality in a sample of 2,374 older Jewish Israelis	1997–2004 Israel Prospective cohort	2,374 (39.2%)	1. **Still at work** – not retired 2. **Left work young** – before age 50 3. **Early retirement** – women age 50–59; men age 60–64 4. **On time retirement** – women age 60+; men age 65+ 5. **Missing** – failed to date exit from work
	Olsen (1980)	Compare mortality rates of male pensioners to a matched reference group of employed workers from the same union	1969–1979 Denmark Retrospective cohort	1,235 (0%)	1. **Disability/early old-age pension** – received between 10/1/69 – 9/30/73 2. **Active worker** – present at work 4/1/71 and alive on 9/30/73
	Tsai (2005)	Assess whether there is any survival advantage of early retirement among employees of the petrochemical industry in the United States who retired at 55, 60, and 65	1973–2003 United States Prospective cohort	26,781 (11%)	1. **Retired at 55** 2. **Retired at 60** 3. **Retired at 65** 4. **Working at 55** 5. **Working at 60**

(continued)

Table 17.2 (continued)

Quality Ranking	Author (year)	Primary research question/objective	*Time period (years)* Study location Study design	Sample size (% female)	Employment classifications – definitions (*see notes below*)
Medium-high	Amick (2002)	A person's lifetime exposure to psychosocial work conditions was modeled over the working life course, and its relationship to mortality was assessed in a representative sample of U.S. workers	1968–1992 United States Prospective cohort	25,413 (55.1%)	1. **Retired** – self-report for the year preceding the current interview year 2. **Working** – self-report of working[a] in the past year 3. **Unemployed** – self-reported unemployment status
	Arrich (2005)	Investigate the association between socioeconomic status and mortality of patients with acute ischemic stroke and transient ischemic attack	1998–2002 Austria Prospective cohort	3,607 –47%	1. **Currently unemployed** – at the time of the event 2. **Working in own household** – at the time of the event 3. **Retired early** – before normal retirement age 4. **Retired** – women = age 60; men = age 65
	Bamia (2008)	Determine whether early retirement is a risk factor for all-cause and cause-specific mortality in apparently healthy retirees	1994–2006 Greece Prospective cohort	16,827 (47%)	1. **Employed** – at enrollment in the study 2. **Early retired** – retired at enrollment in the study and before age 65
	Collins (1976)	Describe what would occur in a large scale historical study of steelworkers if retirees only were used for mortality findings instead of all workers in the industry	1953–1966 United States Prospective cohort	58,828 (0%)	1. **Retirees over age 65**[b] 2. **Nonretirees over age 65 who left plant before 65**[c]

Quality ranking					
Medium-high	Morris (1994)	Assess the effect of unemployment and early retirement on mortality in a group of middle aged British men using measures of health and health related behavior made before the loss of employment	1979–1990 United Kingdom Prospective cohort	6,191 (0%)	1. **Employed full time** – continuously employed during follow-up 2. **Retired early for reasons other than illness**
	Munch (2005)	Describe the association between socio-economic status and mortality at the individual level	1992–1997 Denmark Prospective cohort	170,749 (50.5%)	1. **Early retirement** – at age 60 2. **Retired** – through all the years 1988, 1992–1997
	Pensola (2004)	Quantify the contribution of living conditions in the parental home and life-events and trajectories in youth to adult social class differences in mortality from various causes of death	1970–1998 Finland Prospective cohort	186,408 (0%)	1. **Steady employment** – up to end of 1990, with the exception of national service 2. **Short unemployment** – <6 months during 1986–1990 or one spell at the time of the census 3. **Long unemployment** – ≥ 6 months during 1986–1990, or repeated at the time of ≥ 2 censuses 4. **Fragmental employment** - occasional exclusion[d] from labor force
	Wagner (2006)	Establish the life expectancy and standardized mortality ratios of firefighters of the Fire Department of the City of Hamburg, Germany compared to Hamburg and the national reference population with special emphasis on disentangling the suspected strong healthy worker effect in this cohort from the effects of potential chemical exposures and heavy work load	Germany Retrospective cohort	4,557 (0%)	1. Dead 2. **Active firefighter**- full-time professional employees 3. **Left by own request** – left the department for instance to move to a different city 4. **Early retirement** - left for health reasons/disability 5. **Regular retirement**

(continued)

Table 17.2 (continued)

Quality ranking	Author (year)	Primary research question/objective	Time period (years) / Study location / Study design	Sample size (% female)	Employment classifications – definitions (*see notes below*)
Medium-high	Wen (1984)	Present the mortality experience of active, terminated and retired groups from a large refinery cohort	1937–1978 United States Prospective cohort	12,526 (0%)	1. **Active** – employed during the study 2. **Terminated** – left employment with no further financial linkage to the company 3a. **Regular retired** – at or after age 65 3b. **Early retired-regular** – at 55[e]; at 50[f]; before 65[g] with length-of-service criteria 3c. **Early retired-disability** – 15 years of service + medical disability (initiated in 1957)

Notes
[a]Full time, part-time, or temporary; annual working hours >500 h or individual labor income was >$1,000
[b]Management = age ≥65; union = age ≥65 and minimum 15 years at the company
[c]Left plant after usual retirement age, still employed, died while employed
[d]Other than unemployment, retirement, or education
[e]Between 1944–1963
[f]Between 1963–1974
[g]1975-present

Table 17.3 Study characteristics

	Quality ranking												
	High				Medium-high								
Author, year	Jeune (1982)	Litwin (2007)	Olsen (1980)	Tsai (2005)	Amick (2002)	Arrich (2005)	Bamia (2008)	Collins (1976)	Morris (1994)	Munch (2005)	Pensola (2004)	Wagner (2006)	Wen (1984)
Study location													
Europe	X		X			X	X		X	X	X	X	
Middle-East		X											
United States				X	X			X					X
Study design													
Prospective cohort		X		X	X	X	X	X	X	X	X		X
Retrospective cohort	X		X									X	
Study demographics													
Males only	X		X					X	X		X	X	X
Males and females		X		X	X	X	X			X			
Caucasian only	*	X	*	*		*	X		*	*	*	*	X
Multiple ethnicities					X[a]			X[b]					
Retirement data source													
Census data											X		
Employee/retiree records				X				X					X
Municipal records	X		X							X		X	
Self-report		X			X	X	X		X				
Analysis type													
Logistic Regression					X						X		
Standardized Mortality Ratio (SMR)								X			X		X
Survival Analysis	X	X	X	X		X	X		X	X		X	
Mortality outcome(s)													
All-cause mortality	X	X	X	X	X	X	X	X	X	X	X	X	X
Cause-specific mortality							X	X	X	X	X		X
Mortality outcome measure													
Hazard ratio		X		X	X	X	X			X			
Relative Risk	X		X						X		X	X	
Standardized Mortality Ratio (SMR)								X				X	X
Occupational category													
White-collar				X					X		X		
Blue-collar	X			X		X		X	X		X	X	
White/Blue-collar Combined		X	X		X		X			X			X

Note:
*Race/ethnicity of study population not explicitly stated
[a]Ethnicities included white and black
[b]Ethnicities included white and non-white

Table 17.4 Study results and interpretation by quality ranking, author and exposure/referent groups

Quality ranking		Author (Year)	Exposure(E)/Referent(R) groups	Number of events
High		Jeune (1982)	E1. All disability pensioners (n = 1,353) R1. Employed (n = 1,353)	E1. 234 deaths R1. 41 deaths
		Litwin (2007)	E1a. Still at work (n = 486) E1b. Left work young (n = 164) E1c. Early retirement (n = 540) E1d. Missing (n = 219) R1. On time retirement (n = 965)	NP
		Olsen (1980)	E1. Disability pensioners (n = 64) R1. Active workers (n = 121)	E1. 13 deaths R1. 4 deaths
		Tsai (2005)	E1. Retired at 55 (n = 839) E2. Retired at 60 (n = 1,929) R1-2. Retired at 65 (n = 900)	E1. 173 deaths E2. 581 deaths R1. 462 deaths

Measure of association; 95% CI; p value	Statistical Adjustment for Covariables/Confounders	Interpretation
E1. Relative death rate = 1.85; 95% CI NP R1. Relative death rate = 0.28; 95% CI NP **RR (Crowley method) = 6.8; $p < 0.05$**[a,b]	Age	Disability pensioners have 6.8 times the risk of dying than those currently employed. **YES – Health-related retirement is a risk factor for mortality**
E1a. **HR = 0.65; 95% CI 0.48-0.88; $p < 0.01$** E1b. HR = 0.75; 95% CI 0.48-1.19 E1c. **HR = 0.93; 95% CI 0.74-1.16** E1d. HR = 1.17; 95% CI 0.91-1.51	Reason for retirement Gender Age Income Education Diagnosed illness	Those currently employed are 35% less likely to die than those who retire on-time. Although it appears that leaving work while young or retiring early offers some decreased risk of dying, the 95% confidence intervals which include 1.0 do not support the association. **YES – On-time retirement is a risk factor for mortality** **NO – Early retirement is not a risk factor for mortality**
RR = 7.2; $p<0.001$	NP	Disability pensioners have 7.2 times the risk of dying than active workers. **YES–Health-related retirement is a risk factor for mortality**
E1. **HR = 1.37; 95% CI 1.09-1.73** E2. HR = 1.06; 95% CI 0.92-1.22	Gender SES Calendar year of entry to study	Employees that retired at age 55 had a 37% increase in mortality when compared to employees that retired at age 65. **YES – Early retirement is a risk factor for mortality**

(continued)

Table 17.4 (continued)

Quality ranking		Author (Year)	Exposure(E)/Referent(R) groups	Number of events
		Amick (2002)	5-year lag (Karasek job strain) E1a. Retired (n = 7,591) E1b. Age × retired (n = 7,591) 10-year lag (Karasek Job Strain) E2a. Retired (n = 7,746) E2b. Age × retired (n = 7,746) 5-year lag (Job strain quotient) E3a. Retired E3b. Age × retired 10-year lag (Job strain quotient) E4a. retired E4b. Age × retired R1-4. Not retired	5-year lag 10,008 retirements 571 deaths 10-year lag 10,959 retirements 726 deaths
	Medium-high			
		Arrich, (2005)	E1a. Early retired (n = 328) E1b. Retired (n = 1,478) R1. Employed (n = 512)	E1a. 57 deaths E1b. 351 deaths R1. 18 deaths

Measure of association; 95% CI; p value	Statistical Adjustment for Covariables/Confounders	Interpretation
5-year lag (Karasek job strain) E1a. **HR = 5.92; 95% CI 3.40-10.30; p < 0.05**[a,b] E1b. **HR = 0.92; 95% CI 0.90-0.94; p < 0.05** 10-year lag (Karasek job strain) E2a. **HR = 2.85; 95% CI 1.56-5.11; p < 0.05** E2b. **HR = 0.95; 95% CI (0.93-0.97; p < 0.05** 5-year lag (Job strain quotient) E3a. **HR = 5.90; 95% CI 3.39-10.25; p < 0.05** E3b. **HR = 0.92; 95% CI 0.90-0.94; p < 0.05** 10-year lag (Job Strain Quotient) E4a. **HR = 2.83; 95% CI 1.58-5.08; p < 0.05** E4b. **HR = 0.95; 95% CI 0.93-0.97; p < 0.05**	Psychosocial work conditions Age Black race/ethnicity Sex Study year Family income Family size Not working Age × black Age × retired Baseline disability	When compared to those NOT retired, retirees were 5.9 times as likely to die in the 5 year post retirement transition period. When compared to those NOT retired, retirees were 2.8 times as likely to die in the 10 year post retirement transition period. **YES – On-time retirement is a risk factor for mortality**
E1a. **HR = 1.76; 95% CI 0.93-3.36** E1b. **HR = 1.45; 95% CI 0.79-2.67**	SES Age Sex Stroke severity History of stroke Ischemic heart disease Hypertension Elevated plasma lipids Diabetes Peripheral vascular disease Smoking status	When compared to those employed, those that retired and retired early showed an increased risk of dying, however 95% confidence intervals for both measures included 1.0 and offer no conclusive evidence to support the association. **NO – On-time retirement is not a risk factor for mortality** **NO – Early retirement is not a risk factor for mortality**

(continued)

Table 17.4 (continued)

		Author (Year)	Exposure(E)/Referent(R) groups	Number of events
		Bamia (2008)	E1. Early retired *(n = 3,874)* R1. Employed *(n = 12,953)*	E1. 404 deaths R1. 215 deaths
Quality ranking	Medium-high	Collins (1976)	E1. Retirees over 65 (n = 9,688) E2. Nonretirees over age 65 (n = 391) R1. Allegheny county males (n = NP)	E1. 2,637 deaths E2. 97 deaths
		Morris (1994)	E1. Retired early not due to illness (n = 479) R1. Continuously employed (n = 4,112) E2a. Retired early not due to illness – Manual workers E2b. Retired early not due to illness – Non-manual workers R2a. Continuously employed – Manual workers R2b. Continuously employed – Non-manual workers	E1-2. 59 deaths R1-2. 174 deaths
		Munch (2005)	E1a. Early retirement-women (n = NP) E1b. Retired-women (n = NP) R1. Skilled-women (n = NP) E1a. Early retirement-men (n = NP) E1b. Retired-men (n = NP) R1. Skilled-men (n = NP)	NP
Quality Ranking	Medium-High	Pensola (2004)	E1. Retired on disability (n = 4,767) R1. Steady employed (n = 139,716)	E1. 422 deaths R1. 1,493 deaths

Measure of association; 95% CI; p value	Statistical Adjustment for Covariables/Confounders	Interpretation
E1. **HR = 1.51; 95% CI 1.16-1.98; p = 0.002**[a, b]	Age at enrollment Education Smoking status Waist-to-hip ratio Physical activity Body mass index Total energy intake Ethanol intake Stratified by gender	When compared to those still employed at study enrollment, early retirees (persons that were £ age 65 and already retired at study enrollment) in the study had a 51% increase in all-cause mortality. **YES – Early retirement is a risk factor for mortality**
E1. **SMR = 0.851; p < 0.05** E2. **SMR = 1.769 ; p < 0.05**	Age (men > age 65 only)	Retirees over age 65 were 15% less likely to die than their community counterparts. **NO – On-time retirement is not a risk factor for mortality**
E1. **RR =1.86; 95% CI 1.34-2.59** E2a. **RR = 1.57; 95% CI 1.00-2.47** E2b. **RR = 2.51; 95% CI 1.50-4.19**	Age Town Social class Smoking Alcohol intake Pre-existing disease	Those that retire early (not due to illness) are 86% more likely to die than those employed. Those that retire early (not due to illness) are 86% more likely to die than those employed. White collar workers (non-manual) that retire early (not due to illness) are 2.5 times as likely to die as those white collar workers who are employed. **YES – Early retirement is a risk factor for mortality**
E1a. **HR = −0.82**[c]**(−55.96%**[d]**); p = 0.05**[a, b] E1b. HR = −0.01[c] (−0.995%[d]); p > 0.05 E2a. **HR = −0.22**[c]**(−19.75%**[d]**); p = 0.05** E2b. **HR = 0.22**[c]**(24.61%**[d]**); p = 0.05**	City Education Skill level Sector Homeownership	When compared to female skilled workers, women that retire early have a 56% decrease in mortality rate. When compared to male skilled workers, men that retire early have about a 20% decrease in mortality rate. When compared to male skilled workers, men that are retired have about a 25% increase in mortality rate. **YES – On-time retirement is a risk factor for mortality *(men only)*** **NO – Early retirement is not a risk factor for mortality**
RR = 4.72; p < 0.05	Age Social class Parental class Family type Number of siblings Language Region Education Marital path Early parenthood Employment path	Disability retirees have 4.7 times the risk of dying than those steadily employed. **YES – Health-related retirement is a risk factor for mortality**

(continued)

Table 17.4 (continued)

Quality Ranking		Author (Year)	Exposure(E)/Referent(R) groups	Number of events
		Wagner (2006)	E1a. Early retirement-disability (n = 469) E1b. Regular retirement (n = 1,419) R1. German population (n = NP) E2. Early retirees-disabled (n = NP) R2. All other retirees (n = NP)	E1b. 131 deaths E1c. 644 deaths E2. NP R2. NP
	Medium-High	Wen, 1984	E1a. Active (n = 12,526) E1b. Terminated (n = 6,199) E1c. Retired (n = 2,837) E2a. Retired-regular (n = 1,053) E2b. Retired-early (n = 1,784) R1-2. White males in the US by cause of death (n = NP)	E1a. 855 deaths E1b. 1,306 deaths E1c. 1,280 deaths E2a. 246 deaths E2b. 485 deaths

Note:
[a]Meaningful measures of association and interpretations are highlighted in **bold**
[b]statistically significant effects are <u>underlined</u>
[c]Hazard rate coefficient
[d]% change = 100 × (exp(β)-1)
Abbreviations
NP not provided, *HR* hazard ratio, *RR* relative risk, *SMR* standardized mortality ratio

Measure of association; 95% CI; p value	Statistical Adjustment for Covariables/Confounders	Interpretation
E1a. SMR = 1.35; 95% CI 1.13 – 1.60[a, b] E1b. SMR = 0.79; 95% CI 0.73 – 0.85 E2. **RR = 1.71; 95% CI 1.18 – 2.50**	Age-specific SMR Rank group Age at employment Year of employment Duration of employment	Firefighters that retired early on disability were 1.7 times more likely to die than all other firefighter retirees. **YES – Health-related retirement is a risk factor for mortality**
E1a. SMR = 0.68; 95% CI 0.64 – 0.73; p <.01 E1b. SMR = 1.04; 95% CI 0.99 – 1.10 E1c. **SMR = 0.89; 95% CI 0.84 – 0.94; p <.01** E2a. **SMR = 0.87; 95% CI 0.76 – 0.98; p <.05** E2b. **SMR = 0.89; 95% CI 0.82 – 0.98; p <.05**	Cause-specific mortality Age-specific mortality Calendar time-specific mortality	Retirees were 11% less likely to die than the general US white male population Among those that retired, regular retirees were 13% less likely to die than the general US white male population Among those that retired, early retirees were 11% less likely to die than the general US white male population. **NO – On-time retirement is not a risk factor for mortality** **NO – Early retirement is not a risk factor for mortality**

Table 17.5 Evidence synthesis[a]

Quality ranking		Author, year	Is retirement a risk factor for mortality?	Is type of retirement a risk factor for mortality? On-time	Early	Health-related
	High	Jeune (1982)	**Yes**			**Yes**
	High	Litwin (2007)	Mixed	Yes	**No**	
	High	Olsen and Jeune (1980)	**Yes**			**Yes**
	High	Tsai et al. (2005)	**Yes**		Yes	
	Medium-High	Amick et al. (2002)	**Yes**	Yes		
	Medium-High	Arrich et al. (2005)	No	No	**No**	
	Medium-High	Bamia et al. (2008)	**Yes**		Yes	
	Medium-High	Collins and Redmond (1976)	No	No		
	Medium-High	Morris et al. (1994)	**Yes**		Yes	
	Medium-High	Munch and Svarer (2005)	Mixed	Yes	**No**	
	Medium-High	Pensola and Martikainen (2004)	**Yes**			**Yes**
	Medium-High	Wagner et al. (2006)	**Yes**			**Yes**
	Medium-High	Wen et al. (1984)	No	No	**No**	
Evidence synthesis results			Strong and sufficient evidence FOR	Mixed evidence (inconclusive)	Mixed evidence AGAINST	Mixed evidence FOR

[a]Following guidelines set forth by Brewer et al. (2006), **strong** evidence in this review requires a minimum of three high quality studies to converge on the same finding; **sufficient** evidence requires convergence of seven medium-high to high studies; and **mixed** evidence requires a minimum of three medium-high to high studies

Given our primary research question, "Does the research literature support the view that type of retirement is a risk factor for mortality?", we first examined the general question about retirement as a mortality risk factor and then summarized evidence based on three specific types of retirement: (1) on-time (regular) retirement, (2) early retirement (not health-related), and (3) health-related retirement.

Considering *all types of retirement combined*, three high quality studies (Jeune 1982; Olsen and Jeune 1980; Tsai et al. 2005) and five medium-high quality studies (Amick et al. 2002; Bamia et al. 2008; Morris et al. 1994; Pensola and Martikainen 2004; Wagner et al. 2006) found specified categories of retirees with higher risk when compared to either current employees or other retirees. Two studies, one high quality study (Litwin 2007) and one medium-high quality (Munch and Svarer 2005), found mixed evidence. Three medium-quality studies (Arrich et al. 2005; Collins and Redmond 1976; Wen et al. 1984) found no increased risk. *These results suggest both strong and sufficient evidence that retirement (all types combined) is a risk factor for mortality.*

On-Time Retirement

One high quality study (Litwin 2007) found on-time retirement to be associated with an increased risk of dying when compared to current employees. Medium-high quality studies found higher mortality risk among retired men and women, both, when compared to non-retired workers (Amick et al. 2002), higher risk when compared to non-retired workers only among men (Munch and Svarer 2005), lower risk when compared to the general population (Collins and Redmond 1976; Wen et al. 1984), and no evidence of association when compared to those still employed (Arrich et al. 2005). *These results suggest a mixed—and inconclusive—level of evidence neither for nor against on-time retirement as a risk factor for mortality.*

Early Retirement

Two high quality studies showed contradictory results. When compared to on-time retirees, Tsai and colleagues (2005) found an increased mortality risk for early retirees, while Litwin (2007) found no association. The medium-high quality studies results include the following : three studies found no association: Munch and Svarer (2005) and Wen and colleagues (1984) found lower mortality risk when compared to their skilled/employed counterparts in both men and women; Arrich and colleagues (2005) found an inconclusive association; two other studies reported higher mortality risk: Bamia and colleagues (2008) found early retirees (65 years-old and already retired at study enrollment) to have higher all-cause mortality when compared to those still employed at study enrollment and, finally, Morris and colleagues (1994) found higher mortality risk among retired male white-collar workers when compared to actively employed male white-collar workers. *These results suggest a mixed level of evidence against early retirement (not health-related) as a risk factor for mortality.*

Health-Related Retirement

Two of the high quality studies found that disability retirement was shown to increase the risk of dying when compared to current employees (Jeune 1982; Olsen and Jeune 1980). These results were consistent with the medium-high quality studies that showed disability retirees with a higher risk than persons currently employed (Pensola and Martikainen 2004) or than other, non-disability, retirees (Wagner et al. 2006). *These results suggest a mixed level of evidence for health-related retirement as a risk factor for mortality.*

Discussion

Our review suggests that there is strong and sufficient evidence for considering all-type retirement as a risk factor for mortality. However, there is mixed evidence for on-time retirement, early retirement (not health related), and health-related retirement as risk factors for mortality.

These dissimilar findings are not surprising since retirement is commonly used as a general descriptor of employment status—a worker who has permanently stopped working. However, this definition is too broad and includes, at a minimum, three different conceptualizations of retirement. Moreover, there is very little research in this area and the lack of standardized measures of mortality related to retirement makes it difficult to synthesize.

Not only were different outcome measures used, but different exposure groups and numerous operational definitions of retirement make results interpretation more difficult. We identified three main measures used to examine the relationship between retirement and mortality: relative risk, hazard rate, and standardized mortality ratio (SMR). The use of SMR, for instance, may not be the best risk measure since SMRs are usually adjusted for age only and mortality rates of the general population are used as the comparison group. Both Wen and colleagues (1984) and Collins and Redmond (1976) showed the protective effects of retirement on mortality, but using the general population as the comparison group of a work-related population overlooks the healthy worker effect bias.

Because there is a mixed level of evidence for health-related retirement as a risk factor for mortality, special attention is needed to avoid misclassifying health-related retirees as early or on-time retirees. Also if ill-health and disability are strong risk factors for retirement, then it is necessary to differentiate between health and non-health related reasons of early and on-time retirement. This may help clarify the relationship between early/on-time retirement and mortality by controlling for possible confounding of the ill-health and disability risk factors.

Because of the limited number of studies, we were not able to examine in detail the possible roles of gender, race, and/or culture on retirement and mortality. The studies included in the review spanned nine countries over three continents with less than 50% including women and only one study adjusting for ethnicity. Retirement may represent something different for men and women, given different labor market experiences for women compared to men, including lower rates of pay for similar jobs, greater familial obligations outside work, and lower labor force attachment. A focus on how gender affects the relationship between retirement and health should be included in future studies on the relationship between retirement and health.

Retirement is also a life transition that may be influenced by the social and institutional environment. While there were too few studies to examine the relationship between retirement and health by country, welfare state regime, or market economy orientation, these broader based structural factors may play a role in determining who is able to retire and the effect on health. For example the higher rate of health-related retirement in European countries compared to the United States and Canada may mean that the relationship between health-related retirement and health could vary substantially across country clusters. Further, health insurance is tied to employment for most working Americans and creates a selection pressure and pathway though which early retirement could influence health in the U.S. that is not present in other high-income countries that have universal health insurance.

Clearly a gap exists in the current research. If ill health and disability are reasons why people retire, future research will need to identify employee health histories and health status prior to retirement measurements. Health may be a confounder in the relationship between retirement and mortality and retirement may not be a risk factor for mortality when pre-retirement health is considered. More research is needed to determine if health selection into retirement (i.e. people retire based on their health) is the driver of mortality post retirement or if the retirement transition itself is the risk factor.

We consider it important to continue to develop the retirement/mortality literature with an eye toward the complexity—and reality—of the multiple circumstances surrounding the exit of workers from the workforce. Regrettably, the lack of translation resources required the exclusion of 12 non-English language articles that may or may not have been valuable to the evidence synthesis process. There is very little research on retirement as a risk factor for mortality, so development and identification of the grey literature in this area may not be yet possible. Since no comprehensive systematic reviews that addressed the retirement/mortality relationship were identified, the review team decided to focus on the broader research question using the best evidence synthesis versus comparing specific effects using meta-analysis techniques.

The current peer-reviewed literature provides very few high quality studies on the effect of retirement on mortality. Given the large and increasingly growing retired population, there is a critical need for more research in this area.

The views expressed in this paper are those of the authors and do not reflect the official policy or position of the United States Air Force, Department of Defense, or the U.S. Government.

DISTRIBUTION STATEMENT A: Approved for public release; distribution is unlimited. 311 HSW/PA No. 10-294, 30 Jul 2010.

Appendix A: Methodological Quality Assessment Ordered by Quality Ranking and Author

Criteria #	2	3	4	5	6	7	8	9	10	11	12	13	14	Quality
Criteria weight	1	2	2	1	2	1	1	3	1	1	2	1	3	Ranking (%)
High quality ranking														
Jeune (1982)	1	2	2	N/A	2	1	1	3	1	1	2	N/A	3	**100**
Litwin (2007)	1	2	2	N/A	2	1	1	3	1	1	2	N/A	3	**100**
Olsen and Jeune (1980)	1	2	2	N/A	2	1	1	3	1	1	2	N/A	3	**100**
Tsai et al. (2005)	1	2	2	N/A	2	1	1	3	1	1	2	N/A	3	**100**
Criteria Met	4/4	4/4	4/4	N/A	4/4	4/4	4/4	4/4	4/4	4/4	4/4	N/A	5/5	
% Criteria Met	100	100	100	N/A	100	100	100	100	100	100	100	N/A	100	
Medium-high quality ranking														
Bamia et al. 2008	1	2	2	N/A	2	N/A	1	3	1	1	0	1	3	**89**
Collins and Redmond (1976)	1	2	2	N/A	2	N/A	1	3	1	0	0	1	3	**84**
Amick et al. (2002)	1	0	2	1	0	1	1	3	1	1	2	1	3	**81**
Morris et al. (1994)	1	2	2	0	2	N/A	1	3	1	1	0	0	3	**80**
Pensola and Martikainen (2004)	1	0	2	N/A	0	1	1	3	1	1	2	1	3	**80**
Wagner et al. (2006)	1	0	2	N/A	0	1	1	3	1	1	2	1	3	**80**
Arrich et al. (2005)	1	0	2	N/A	0	1	1	3	1	1	2	N/A	3	**79**
Wen et al. (1984)	1	2	2	N/A	2	1	1	3	0	0	0	N/A	3	**79**
Munch and Svarer (2005)	1	0	2	1	0	1	1	3	1	1	2	0	3	**76**
Criteria Met	9/9	4/9	9/9	2/3	4/9	6/6	9/9	9/9	8/9	7/9	5/9	5/7	9/9	
% Criteria Met	100	44	100	67	44	100	100	100	89	78	56	71	100	

(continued)

(continued)

Criteria #	2	3	4	5	6	7	8	9	10	11	12	13	14	Quality
Criteria weight	1	2	2	1	2	1	1	3	1	1	2	1	3	Ranking (%)
Medium-low quality ranking														
Collins and Redmond (1978)	1	0	2	N/A	0	N/A	1	3	1	0	2	1	3	**74**
Haynes et al. (1977)	1	2	2	N/A	2	1	1	3	1	1	0	N/A	0	**74**
Haynes et al. (1978)	1	2	2	N/A	2	1	1	3	1	1	0	N/A	0	**74**
Sweeney et al. (1985)	0	2	2	N/A	0	1	1	3	0	0	2	N/A	3	**74**
Morris et al. (1994)	1	2	2	N/A	2	N/A	1	3	1	1	0	N/A	0	**72**
Boaz (1990)	1	2	0	1	0	1	1	3	1	1	0	1	3	**71**
Ostamo (2001)	1	0	2	1	0	1	1	3	1	1	0	1	3	**71**
Wolfson (1993)	1	0	2	1	0	1	1	3	1	1	0	N/A	3	**70**
Baker (1982)	1	2	2	N/A	2	1	1	3	1	0	0	N/A	0	**68**
McMahan (1955)	1	2	2	N/A	2	1	1	3	0	1	0	N/A	0	**68**
Wong (1985)	0	0	2	N/A	0	1	1	3	1	0	2	N/A	3	**68**
Herttua (2008)	1	0	2	N/A	0	1	1	0	1	1	2	N/A	3	**63**
May (2002)	1	0	2	1	0	0	1	3	1	1	2	1	0	**62**
Quaade et al. (2002)	1	2	2	0	2	N/A	1	0	1	0	0	0	3	**60**
Rushing (1992)	1	0	2	1	0	1	1	3	0	0	2	1	0	**57**
Enterline (1972)	1	0	2	N/A	2	N/A	1	3	0	1	0	N/A	0	**56**
Kingson (1982)	0	2	0	N/A	2	N/A	1	3	1	1	0	N/A	0	**56**
Gamble (2000)	0	2	2	0	2	N/A	1	3	1	0	0	0	0	**55**
Beck (1981)	1	0	2	N/A	2	1	0	3	1	0	0	N/A	0	**53**
Lidgren (2007)	1	0	2	N/A	0	1	1	0	1	1	0	N/A	3	**53**
Studznski (2003)	1	2	2	0	0	0	1	3	1	1	0	0	0	**52**
Weiland (1996)	1	0	2	1	0	1	1	3	1	0	0	1	0	**52**
Saarela (2002)	1	0	2	N/A	0	1	0	0	1	0	2	0	3	**50**
Enterline(1975)	1	0	0	N/A	2	N/A	1	3	1	1	0	0	0	**47**

Pavia (2005)	1	0	2	N/A	0	1	1	0	1	1	2	N/A	0	**47**
Pinto (1977)	1	2	0	N/A	2	N/A	1	3	0	0	0	0	0	**47**
Clarke (1972)	1	0	2	N/A	2	N/A	0	0	1	1	0	N/A	0	**39**
Thomas (1985)	1	0	0	N/A	0	1	1	0	1	0	0	N/A	0	**21**
Heikkinen (1992)	0	0	0	0	0	0	1	0	0	0	0	N/A	0	**5**
Criteria Met	**24/29**	**12/29**	**23/29**	**6/10**	**13/27**	**17/20**	**26/27**	**21/29**	**23/29**	**16/29**	**8/29**	**6/12**	**10/29**	
% criteria Met	**83**	**41**	**79**	**60**	**45**	**85**	**90**	**72**	**79**	**55**	**28**	**50**	**34**	

Appendix B: Data Extraction Questions

1. Write the last name of the first author and the year of publication
2. State the primary research question(s)/objective(s) related to the systematic review study question
3. State the primary hypothesis related to the systematic review study question that
4. State additional hypotheses related to the systematic review study question that are not listed in question #3
5. In what country was the study conducted?
6. In what region/province was the study conducted?
7. In what state was the study conducted?
8. In what city was the study conducted?
9. What is the overall time period covered by the study?
10. What is the study design? (Select only one)
11. What is the main statistical analysis method used? (Select only one)
12. What is the overall study sample size and description?
13. List the detailed characteristics of the study population/study participants/subjects.

13a. Sample size
13b. Follow-up time period
13c. Mean/median age (report stated measure of central tendency and its value to one decimal place)
13d. Standard deviation of age (report to one decimal place)
13e. Age range
13f. Number of males
13g. Number of females
13h. Ethnicities included (separate by comma)
13i. Percent non-white (report as a number to one decimal place)
13j. Occupation
13k. Percent blue-collar workers (manual or technical laborer -report as a number to one decimal place)
13l. Mean/median of employment tenure—years employed at job (report stated measure of central tendency and its value to one decimal place)
13m. Standard deviation of employment tenure (report to one decimal place)
13n. Employment tenure range (include the unit of time – days/months/years)

14. Describe any additional notable/unique characteristics of the study population/study participants/subjects not listed above in Q13
15. For each data type, list the associated data source
16. List the inclusion criteria described in the study
17. List the exclusion criteria described in the study
18. List each employment classification used in the study

19. List associated definition of each employment classification used in the study
20. List the criteria for handling those study participants which are lost to follow-up
21. Select the mortality outcome measured in the study
22. List the location of data in the article
23. List/describe each exposure/referent group related to the systematic review study question
24. List the associated number of people for each exposure/referent group
25. List the mean of age for each exposure/referent group
26. List the SD of age for each exposure/referent group
27. List the age range for each exposure/referent group
28. List the number of females for each exposure/referent group
29. List/describe each exposure/referent group related to the systematic review study question that (from question #23)
30. List the number of events for each exposure/referent group
31. List the outcome measure for each exposure/referent group
32. List the measure of association value for each exposure/referent group
33. List the 95% confidence interval/p-value for each exposure/referent group
34. List the adjustment for each exposure/referent group
35. Describe any additional outcome measures and their associated 95% CIs and p-values not listed in Q29 – Q34 above
36. Describe the significant differences in covariates/confounders between those that participated in the study vs. those that were lost to follow-up
37. State the overall conclusion(s) of the study
38. Please provide YOUR interpretation of the study results plus any noteworthy strengths and limitation of the study. You can also provide any comments, remarks or insights on the study/findings, comparability of the exposure/referent groups or enter other information that is unique about the study that may not be adequately captured elsewhere on the data extraction form
39. Check the names of both data extraction reviewers for this study
40. Is this the consensus–final–version of the data extraction form?

References

Amick, B. C., 3rd, McDonough, P., Chang, H., Rogers, W. H., Pieper, C. F., & Duncan, G. (2002). Relationship between all-cause mortality and cumulative working life course psychosocial and physical exposures in the United States labor market from 1968 to 1992. *Psychosomatic Medicine, 64*(3), 370–381.

Anderson, K. H. (1985). The effect of mandatory retirement on mortality. *Journal of Economics and Business, 37*(1), 81–88.

Arrich, J., Lalouschek, W., & Mullner, M. (2005). Influence of socioeconomic status on mortality after stroke: Retrospective cohort study. *Stroke, 36*(2), 310–314.

Baker, D., Packard, M., Rader, A. D., Reno, V., & Upp, M. (1982, December). Mortality and early retirement. *Social Security Bulletin*, 45(12), 3–10.

Bamia, C., Trichopoulou, A., & Trichopoulos, D. (2008). Age at retirement and mortality in a general population sample: The Greek EPIC study. *American Journal of Epidemiology, 167*(5), 561–569.

Beck, G. J., Schachter, E. N., Maunder, L. R., & Bouhuys, A. (1981, April). The relation of lung function to subsequent employment status and mortality in cotton textile workers. *Chest*, 79(4 Suppl), 26S–30S.

Boaz, R. F., & Muller, C. F. (1990, June). The validity of health limitations as a reason for deciding to retire. *Health Services Research*, 25(2), 361–386.

Breeze, E., Fletcher, A. E., Leon, D. A., Marmot, M. G., Clarke, R. J., & Shipley, M. J. (2001). Do socioeconomic disadvantages persist into old age? Self-reported morbidity in a 29-year follow-up of the Whitehall study. *American Journal of Public Health, 91*(2), 277–283.

Brewer, S., VanEerd, D., Amick, B. C., 3rd, Irvin, E., Daum, K. M., Gerr, F., et al. (2006). Workplace interventions to prevent musculoskeletal and visual symptoms and disorders among computer users: A systematic review. *Journal of Occupational Rehabilitation, 16*(3), 325–358.

Briss, P. A., Zaza, S., Pappaioanou, M., Fielding, J., Wright-De Aguero, L., Truman, B. I., et al. (2000). Developing an evidence-based guide to community preventive services–methods. The task force on community preventive services. *American Journal of Preventive Medicine, 18*(1 Suppl), 35–43.

Campbell, P. R. (1996). *Population projections for states by age, sex, race, and hispanic origin: 1995 to 2025* (No. PPL-47). Washington, DC: U.S. Bureau of the Census, Population Division.

Clarke, N. E., Sr. (1972, June). Silicosis and diseases of retired iron foundry workers. *IMS - Industrial Medicine & Surgery*, 41(6), 22–25.

Collins, J. F., & Redmond, C. K. (1976). The use of retirees to evaluate occupational hazards. *Journal of Occupational Medicine, 18*(9), 595–602.

Collins, J. F., & Redmond, C. K. (1978, April). The use of retirees to evaluate occupational hazards. II. Comparison of cause specific mortality by work area. *Journal of Occupational Medicine*, 20(4), 260–266.

Ekerdt, D. J., Baden, L., Bosse, R., & Dibbs, E. (1983). The effect of retirement on physical health. *American Journal of Public Health, 73*(7), 779–783.

Elsevier, B. V. (2007). *Scopus™*. www.scopus.com

Enterline, P., DeCoufle, P., & Henderson, V. (1972, December). Mortality in relation to occupational exposure in the asbestos industry. *Journal of Occupational Medicine*, 14(12), 897–903.

Enterline, P. E., & Henderson, V. (1975, March). The health of retired fibrous glass workers. *Archives of Environmental Health*, 30(3), 113–116.

Gallo, W. T., Bradley, E. H., Falba, T. A., Dubin, J. A., Cramer, L. D., Bogardus, S. T., Jr., et al. (2004). Involuntary job loss as a risk factor for subsequent myocardial infarction and stroke: Findings from the health and retirement survey. *American Journal of Industrial Medicine, 45*(5), 408–416.

Gamble, J. F., Lewis, R. J., & Jorgensen, G. (2000, July). Mortality among three refinery/petrochemical plant cohorts. II. Retirees. *Journal of Occupational & Environmental Medicine*, 42(7), 730–736.

Gebbie, K. M., Koplan, J. P., Fox, E., & Marks, J. S. (2005). The future of public health: What will it take to keep Americans healthy and safe? *Supplement to Managed Care, 14*(9), 1–23.

Haynes, S. G., McMichael, A. J., & Tyroler, H. A. (1977, January). The relationship of normal, involuntary retirement to early mortality among U.S. rubber workers. *Social Science & Medicine*, 11(2), 05–114.

Haynes, S. G., McMichael, A. J., & Tyroler, H. A. (1978). Survival after early and normal retirement. *Journal of Gerontology, 33*(2), 269–278.

Heikkinen, M., Aro, H., & Lonnqvist, J. (1992, May). The partners' views on precipitant stressors in suicide. *Acta Psychiatrica Scandinavica*, 85(5), 380–384.

Henriksson, K. M., Lindblad, U., Agren, B., Nilsson-Ehle, P., & Rastam, L. (2003). Associations between unemployment and cardiovascular risk factors varies with the unemployment rate: The cardiovascular risk factor study in southern Sweden (CRISS). *Scandinavian Journal of Public Health, 31*(4), 305–311.

Herttua, K., Makela, P., & Martikainen, P. (2008, August). Changes in alcohol-related mortality and its socioeconomic differences after a large reduction in alcohol prices: A natural experiment based on register data. *American Journal of Epidemiology*, 168(10), 1110–1118.

Herzog, A. R., House, J., & Morgan, J. (1991). Relation of work and retirement to health and well-being in older age. *Psychology and Aging, 6*(2), 202–211.

Higgins, J. P. T., & Green, S. (Eds.). (2006). *Cochrane handbook for systematic reviews of interventions 4.2.6 [updated September 2006]*. Chichester: Wiley.

Jeune, B. (1982). Survival experience of semi-skilled disability pensioners in Denmark. *Scandinavian Journal of Social Medicine, 10*(3), 73–76.

Kasl, S. V. (1996). The influence of the work environment on cardiovascular health: A historical, conceptual, and methodological perspective. *Journal of Occupational Health Psychology, 1*(1), 42–56.

Kasl, S. V., & Jones, B. A. (2000). The impact of job loss and retirement on health. In *Social epidemiology* (pp. 118–136). New York: OUP.

Kingson, E. R. (1982, September). The health of very early retirees. *Social Security Bulletin*, 45(9), 3–9.

Krause, N., Lynch, J., Kaplan, G. A., Cohen, R. D., Goldberg, D. E., & Salonen, J. T. (1997). Predictors of disability retirement. *Scandinavian Journal of Work, Environment & Health, 23*(6), 403–413.

Lidgren, M., Wilking, N., & Jonsson, B. (2007). Cost of breast cancer in Sweden in 2002. *European Journal of Health Economics*, 8(1), 5–15.

Litwin, H. (2007). Does early retirement lead to longer life? *Ageing and Society, 27*(5), 739–754.

Marmot, M. G., & Shipley, M. J. (1996). Do socioeconomic differences in mortality persist after retirement? 25 year follow up of civil servants from the first Whitehall study. *BMJ, 313*(7066), 1177–1180.

May, M., McCarron, P., Stansfeld, S., Ben-Shlomo, Y., Gallacher, J., Yarnell, J., Davey Smith, G., Elwood, P., & Ebrahim, S. (2002, January). Does psychological distress predict the risk of ischemic stroke and transient ischemic attack? The Caerphilly Study. *Stroke*, 33(1), 7–12.

McMahan, C. A., Folger, J. K., & Ford, T. R. (1955, May). Longevity of retired army and air force officers. *Human Biology*, 27(2), 125–137.

Mein, G., Martikainen, P., Hemingway, H., Stansfeld, S., & Marmot, M. (2003). Is retirement good or bad for mental and physical health functioning? Whitehall II longitudinal study of civil servants. *Journal of Epidemiology and Community Health, 57*(1), 46–49.

Mobius Analytics. (2009). Systematic Review System (SRS) 4.0 [web-based software]. Ottawa, Ontario, Canada.

Moen, P. (1996). A life course perspective on retirement, gender, and well-being. *Journal of Occupational Health Psychology, 1*(2), 131–144.

Morris, J. K., Cook, D. G., & Shaper, A. G. (1994). Loss of employment and mortality. *BMJ, 308*(6937), 1135–1139.

Munch, J. R., & Svarer, M. (2005). Mortality and socio-economic differences in Denmark: A competing risks proportional hazard model. *Economics and Human Biology, 3*(1), 17–32.

Ohrui, T., Matsui, T., He, M., Ebihara, S., & Sasaki, H. (2004). Relation between retirement and subsequent health status in highly educated older men. *Journal of the American Geriatrics Society, 52*(12), 2145–2147.

Olsen, J., & Jeune, B. (1980). The mortality experience of early old-age and disability pensioners from unskilled- and semiskilled labour groups in Fredericia. *Scandinavian Journal of Social Medicine. Supplementum, 16*, 50–52.

Ostamo, A., & Lonnqvist, J. (2001, January). Excess mortality of suicide attempters. *Social Psychiatry & Psychiatric Epidemiology*, 36(1), 29–35

Padfield, A. (1996). Myths in medicine. Story that early retirement is associated with longevity is often quoted. *BMJ (Clinical Research Ed.), 312*(7046), 1611.

Pavia, M., Nicotera, G., Scaramuzza, G., & Angelillo, I. F. (2005, April). Suicide mortality in Southern Italy: 1998–2002. *Psychiatry Research*, 134(3), 275–279.

Pensola, T., & Martikainen, P. (2004). Life-course experiences and mortality by adult social class among young men. *Social Science & Medicine, 58*(11), 2149–2170.

Pinto, S. S., Enterline, P. E., Henderson, V., & Varner, M. O. (1977, August). Mortality experience in relation to a measured arsenic trioxide exposure. *Environmental Health Perspectives*, 19, 127–130.

Pransky, G. S., Benjamin, K. L., & Savageau, J. A. (2005). Early retirement due to occupational injury: Who is at risk? *American Journal of Industrial Medicine, 47*(4), 285–295.

Quaade, T., Engholm, G., Johansen, A. M., & Moller, H. (2002). Mortality in relation to early retirement in Denmark: A population-based study. *Scandinavian Journal of Public Health, 30*(3), 216–222.

Rosenkoetter, M. M., & Garris, J. M. (1998). Psychosocial changes following retirement. *Journal of Advanced Nursing, 27*(5), 966–976.

Ross, C. E., & Drentea, P. (1998). Consequences of retirement activities for distress and the sense of personal control. *Journal of Health and Social Behavior, 39*(4), 317–334.

Rushing, B., Ritter, C., & Burton, R. P. (1992, June). Race differences in the effects of multiple roles on health: longitudinal evidence from a national sample of older men. *Journal of Health & Social Behavior*, 33(2), 126–139.

Saarela, J., & Finnas, F. (2002). Language-group differences in very early retirement in Finland. *Demographic Research*, 7, 49–66.

Schnurr, P., Lunney, C., Sengupta, A., & Spiro, A. I. I. (2005). A longitudinal study of retirement in older male veterans. *Journal of Consulting and Clinical Psychology, 73*(3), 561–566.

Siebert, U., Rothenbacher, D., Daniel, U., & Brenner, H. (2001). Demonstration of the healthy worker survivor effect in a cohort of workers in the construction industry. *Occupational and Environmental Medicine, 58*(12), 774–779.

Slavin, R. E. (1995). Best evidence synthesis: An intelligent alternative to meta-analysis. *Journal of Clinical Epidemiology, 48*(1), 9–18.

Sorlie, P. D., & Rogot, E. (1990). Mortality by employment status in the national longitudinal mortality study. *American Journal of Epidemiology, 132*(5), 983–992.

Streib, G. F., & Schneider, C. J. (1971). Introduction: Demography and retirement. In *Retirement in American society: Impact and process* (pp. 1–8). Ithaca: Cornell University Press.

Studznski, Z., & Zajewski, W. (2003, January). Factors affecting the survival of 121 patients treated for endometrial carcinoma at a Polish hospital. *Archives of Gynecology & Obstetrics*, 267(3), 145–147.

Sweeney, M. H., Walrath, J., & Waxweiler, R. J. (1985). Mortality among retired fur workers. dyers, dressers (tanners) and service workers. *Scandinavian Journal of Work, Environment & Health, 11*(4), 257–264.

Thomas, T. L., Krekel, S., & Heid, M. (1985, September). Proportionate mortality among male corn wet-milling workers, *International Journal of Epidemiology*, 14(3), 432–437.

Tsai, S. P., Wendt, J. K., Donnelly, R. P., de Jong, G., & Ahmed, F. S. (2005). Age at retirement and long term survival of an industrial population: Prospective cohort study. *BMJ, 331*(7523), 995–998.

U.S. Census Bureau. Facts for features. Special edition: Oldest baby boomers turn 60! January 03, 2006 (Report No.: CB06-FFSE.01-2).

vanAmelsvoort, L. G., Kant, I. J., Bultmann, U., & Swaen, G. M. (2003). Need for recovery after work and the subsequent risk of cardiovascular disease in a working population. *Occupational and Environmental Medicine, 60*(Suppl 1), 83–87.

Wagner, N. L., Berger, J., Flesch-Janys, D., Koch, P., Kochel, A., Peschke, M., et al. (2006). Mortality and life expectancy of professional fire fighters in Hamburg, Germany: A cohort study 1950–2000. *Environmental Health: A Global Access Science Source, 5*, 27.

Weiland, S. K., Mundt, K. A., Keil, U., Kraemer, B., Birk, T., Person, M., Bucher, A. M., Straif, K., Schumann, J., & Chambless, L. (1996, May). Cancer mortality among workers in the German rubber industry: 1981–91. *Occupational & Environmental Medicine*, 53(5), 289–298.

Wen, C. P., Tsai, S. P., Gibson, R. L., McClellan, W., Wen, C. P., Tsai, S. P., Gibson, R. L., & McClellan, W. A. (1984). Long-term mortality of oil refinery workers. II. Comparison of the experience of active, terminated and retired workers. *Journal of Occupational Medicine, 26*(2), 118–127.

Wolfson, M., Rowe, G., Gentleman, J. F., & Tomiak, M. (1993, July). Career earnings and death: A longitudinal analysis of older Canadian men. *Journal of Gerontology*, 48(4), S167–S179.

Wong, O., Morgan, R. W., Kheifets, L., Larson, S. R., & Whorton, M. D. (1985, July). Mortality among members of a heavy construction equipment operators union with potential exposure to diesel exhaust emissions. *British Journal of Industrial Medicine*, 42(7), 435–448.

Part V
Methodological Issues

Chapter 18
Back to Basics or into a Brave New World? The Potential and Pitfalls of Biomarkers in Explaining the Pathways Between Social Engagement and Health

Yumiko Kamiya, Virpi Timonen, Roman Romero-Ortuno, and RoseAnne Kenny

Introduction

The protective influence of social relationships on health is widely recognized in gerontological and social epidemiology research (Berkman and Kawachi 2000; Seeman 1996). Over the last 2 decades, findings from both clinical/experimental studies and population studies (e.g. The Alameda County, Whitehall, Eastern Finland, Pittsburgh Common Cold) studies have been remarkably consistent in demonstrating a beneficial effect of social relations on various health outcomes, including overall mortality (Berkman et al. 1992; Berkman and Syme 1979; House et al. 1982; Kaplan et al. 1988; Orth-Gomer and Johnson 1987; Seeman et al. 1993; Welin et al. 1985) physical and psychiatric morbidity (Berkman 2000; Cohen 1988; House et al. 1988; Seeman 1996; Uchino et al. 2004), activities of daily living (Kondo et al. 2007; Park and Lee 2007) and cognitive decline (Bennett et al. 2006).

Socially integrated persons are less likely to have heart attacks (Kaplan et al. 1988), less likely to develop upper respiratory illness when experimentally exposed to a common cold virus (Cohen et al. 1997), and more likely to survive breast cancer (Funch and Marshall 1983). They are also less likely to suffer from cognitive decline, even in the presence of Alzheimer's disease pathology as seen in post-mortem brain biopsies (Bennett et al. 2006). Conversely, the health risks associated with low levels of social integration are comparable to those linked to smoking, high blood pressure and alcohol excess (House et al. 1988).

Y. Kamiya, Ph.D. (✉) • R. Romero-Ortuno, M.D. • R. Kenny, M.D., Ph.D.
Medical Gerontology, Trinity College Dublin, Dublin, Ireland
e-mail: KAMIYAY@tcd.ie

V. Timonen, D. Phil.
School of Social Work & Social Policy, Trinity College Dublin, Dublin, Ireland

N. Hoque et al. (eds.), *Applied Demography and Public Health*, Applied Demography Series 3, DOI 10.1007/978-94-007-6140-7_18,
© Springer Science+Business Media Dordrecht 2013

Despite the plentiful evidence of an association between social engagement and health, the exact mechanisms or pathways that link social engagement to health are poorly understood. In 1979, Berkman and Syme stated that "adequate tests of the hypothesis that social circumstances alter general susceptibility of disease in humans will not be possible… until data are available on physiologic mechanisms capable of mediating the relationship between social events and disease outcomes" 30 years after Berkman and Syme's seminal study, little is still known about mechanisms by which social engagement influences health outcomes.

Many population surveys in the United States (The Health and Retirement Study (HRS), MacArthur Study of Successful Aging, National Survey of Midlife Development in the United States (MIDUS), National Social Life, Health, and Aging Project (NSHAP), Women's Health and Aging Studies (WHAS)) and in Europe (The English Longitudinal Study on Ageing (ELSA), The Irish Longitudinal Study on Ageing (TILDA), The Italian Longitudinal Study on Ageing (ILSA), The Swedish Adoption/Twin Study of Aging (SATSA), The Rotterdam Study) acquire biomarker information through collection of saliva (for DNA and cortisol), dried blood-spots, or full blood samples (for HbA1c, CRP, IL-6, lipids etc.) (Weinstein et al. 2008). They also collect anthropometric measures of height, weight, hip, and waist, and other biomeasures such as blood pressure, pulse rate, and lung function (Table 18.1). The Chicago Core on Biomarkers in Population–Based Aging research has a list of studies collecting biomarkers (see http://biomarkers.uchicago.edu/studiescollectingbiomarkers.htm). However, as we will argue below, there are some problems associated with measurement and analysis of biomarker data (Table 18.2), which can potentially lead to misconstruing the relationship between these biomarkers, survey respondents' social circumstances, and health outcomes.

The aim of this paper is to provide (1) a concise outline of biological associations linking social engagement to morbidity and mortality; (2) to outline the biomarkers that are currently included in some major longitudinal studies of adult populations, and (3) to discuss the potential for and limitations of some of these biomarkers in throwing light on the relationship between social engagement and health. Addressing these issues, it is hoped, will be helpful to scholars working at the interface of the social and biomedical sciences and seeking to understand the complexity of these interactions.

Pathways Linking Social Engagement to Health Outcomes

Gerontological and social epidemiology research has identified three domains of social engagement associated with health outcomes, namely social networks, social support, and social integration (Cohen et al. 2004; Cohen 1988; House et al. 1988). These domains are not always correlated and each of them may influence health through different, but not necessary independent pathways (Cohen et al. 2004; Uchino 2006). For the purpose of this paper, the term 'social engagement' is an umbrella term referring to a combination of objective measurements of the salient

Table 18.1 Characteristics of longitudinal studies on ageing conducting biomarker collection

Survey name	Sample	Start year	Biomarkers ascertained
Europe			
The English Longitudinal Study of Aging (ELSA)	Nationally representative survey of 12,000 people aged 50 and over	2002	**Fasting Blood Sample**: Total cholesterol, HDL cholesterol, fibrinogen, C-reactive protein, ferritin, glycated haemoglobin and haemoglobin. **Saliva sample**: 24 h salivary cortisol and DNA for a genetic repository **Physical Examination**: 3 readings sitting down blood pressure, waist/hip ratio, weight and height and peak flow rate
The Irish Longitudinal Study on Ageing (TILDA)	Nationally representative survey of 8,500 people aged 50 and over	2010	**Blood Sample**: Total, HDL, LDL cholesterol, and triglycerides **Physical Examination**: Resting and postural blood pressure, pulse wave velocity, heart rate variability, heart rate, height, weight, waist/hip ratio, grip strength, timed up and go, assessment of gait, bone density, visual acuity, contrast sensitivity, retinal photography, macular pigment optical density, visual memory, speed of processing, executive function and global cognition.
The Italian Longitudinal Study on Ageing (ILSA)	Population-based longitudinal study of the health status of 5,493 Italians aged 65–84 years	1992	**Blood Sample**: Total and HDL cholesterol, fibrinogen, Factors VII and VIII, glucose and glucosylated Hb, insulin, sodium potassium, creatinine, uric acid, hemoglobin, hematocrit, RBC, WBC platelet count. T3, T4, FT4, TSH, alanine aminotransferase, aspartate aminotransferase, triglycerides **Physical Examination** Anthropometry: Height, weight, waist and hip circumference Systolic and diastolic blood pressure (3 readings) Examination of heart, lungs, pulses Physical performance tests: Timed chair stand, timed step up, tandem walk, timed one-leg stand, timed 5 m walk, 180° pivot Other exams: Electrocardiogram, spirometry, retinography, hypertension, myocardial infarction, angina pectoris, cardiac arrhythma, congestive heart failure, parkinsonism, Dementia, hypo/hyperthyroidism, intermittent claudication stroke, diabetes, distal symmetric neuropathy of lower limbs, autopsy study of brains from demented Patients, adrenal response to aging, auditory functioning

(continued)

Table 18.1 (continued)

Survey name	Sample	Start year	Biomarkers ascertained
The Rotterdam Study	7,983 persons aged 55 and over	1990	**Blood Sample**: Serum cholesterol, HDL, LDL, triglycerides, glucose and glucose levels **Urine**: Micro albumin and creatinine from intravenous are determined in all participants **Physical Examination**: Dual-Energy X-ray Absorptiometry (bone mineral density), X-rays of hands, thoraco-lumbar spine, hips and knees, an extensive ophthalmologic examination, ultrasound assessment of cardiac dimensions, diameter of the abdominal aorta, carotid arterial wall thickness and plaques thickness, a computerized ECG, blood pressure readings (brachial artery, posterior tibial artery), anthropometry, limited physical examination.
The Survey of Health, Ageing and Retirement in Europe (SHARE)	22,777 individuals aged 50 and over in 11 countries (wave 1)	2004	**Physical Performance**: Grip Strength and walking speed
The Swedish Adoption/Twin Study of Aging (SATSA)	Population-based subset of 958 twin pairs from the Swedish Twin Registry	1984	**Fasting Blood Sample**: Total cholesterol, total triglycerides, HDL cholesterol, LDL cholesterol, apolipoproteins A-1 and B, MaoB H pylori, metals, gamma-glutamyltransferase (gamma-GT), potassium, sodium, telomere length. Whole blood for DNA bank. Plasma at in-person testing occasion 3 for evaluation of a variety of coagulation factors **Urine Sample**: Urea and uric acid, creatinine, electrolytes
North America			
Canadian Study of Health and Aging	Representative sample of 10,263 adults, ages 65+	1991	**Physical Examination**: Cognitive screen 3MS, vital signs, hearing, vision, blood pressure **Biomarkers**: B12, folate, CBC, glucose, VDRL Genetic screen CT scan
Cardiovascular Health Study	Representative sample of 5,000 adults, ages 65+, sampled from Medicare listings for 4 communities (N = 1,250 each; Forsyth County, ND; Sacramento, CA; Washington County, MD; Pittsburgh, PA)	1989	**Blood Sample**: Fasting glucose, insulin, 2-h oral glucose tolerance test, lipid profile (LDL, HDL, triglycerides), albumin, CBC, left ventricular ejection fraction, markers of inflammation and coagulation, ApoE, **Physical Examination**: Resting and postural blood pressure, ankle-arm index, body fat (bioelectric impedance), height, weight, waist/hip ratio, 12-lead ECGs (24-h ambulatory ECGs on subset of 600), forced vital capacity, forced expiratory volume, grip strength, ultrasonography of carotid arteries, m-mode, Doppler echocardiography (for left ventricular mass, ejection fraction, stroke volume and end-systolic stress, regional and segmental wall motion, % fractional shortening)

The Health and Retirement Study	Nationally representative longitudinal survey of ~20,000 people age 51+	1992	**Dried Blood Spots**: CRP, HbA1c, Total Cholesterol, HDL **Saliva** (for which DNA was extracted and stored) **Physical Measures**: Blood pressure, breathing test (peak flow), grip strength, timed walk (8 ft), balance tests (semi-tandem, side-by-side, full tandem), height weight and waist circumference
MacArthur Study of Successful Aging	1,189 men and women, ages 70–79 at baseline	1988	**Blood Sample**: Total/HDL cholesterol, glycosylated hemoglobin, albumin, IL-6, C-reactive protein, fibrinogen, complete blood count (CBC), blood chemistry tests (SMAC-24), DHEAS, antioxidants, homocysteine, vitamin B, folate, ApoE genotyping **Urine**: Norepinephrine, epinephrine, cortisol and dopamine **Physical Examination**: Resting and postural blood pressure, waist/hip ratio, peak flow rate (Mini-Wright meter)
National Survey of Midlife Development in the United States (MIDUS II)	A sub-sample of the MIDUS I population (N = 1350) and on a sub-sample of the Milwaukee African-American sample (N = 200)	2004	**Neuroendocrine**: Salivary cortisol, norepinephrine, epinephrine, DHEAS-S **Cardiovascular**: Blood pressure, cholesterol, fibrinogen, HbA1c, heart-rate variability **Inflammatory**: IL-6, s-IL-6r, CRP, ICAM, E-selection **Physical Examination** Anthropometry: Height, weight, waist and hip circumference Systolic and diastolic blood pressure (3 readings) Functional Assessment: Grip strength, visual acuity, peak flow, chair stands, hearing, teeth condition
National Social Life, Health, and Aging Project (NSHAP)	A nationally representative sample of 3,000 adults aged 57–85	2005	**Dried Blood Spots**: CRP, HbA1c, hemoglobin, EBV antibodies **Saliva**: Oral mucosal transudate (OMT) Vaginal swabs **Physical Examination**: Height, weight, waist circumference, blood pressure, smell, taste, vision, and touch

(continued)

Table 18.1 (continued)

Survey name	Sample	Start year	Biomarkers ascertained
Women's Health and Aging Studies (WHAS)	WHAS I: Cohort of women (n = 1,002) ages 65+ sampled to represent the one-third most disabled Medicare enrollees from the Baltimore, MD, area. WHAS II = cohort of women, age s65+, sampled to represent the remaining two-thirds least disabled women in that age range		**Blood Sample**: Fasted glucose, markers of inflammation, growth factors (IGF-1), genetic information (e.g., IL-6 haplotype), antioxidants, **Physical Examination**: Ambulatory ECG, resting 12-lead ECG, BP (resting, ankle-arm), height, weight, grip strength, spirometry
Australasia			
Social Environment and Biomarkers of Aging Study Taiwan (SEBAS)	4,089 persons aged 60 and older		**Fasting Blood Sample**: Total and HDL cholesterol, Glycosylated hemoglobin, DHEA-S, ApoE genotype Immune function and growth factor: IL-6, IGF-1, Other routine blood tests (e.g., blood cell counts, hemoglobin, glucose, triglycerides) **12-h Urine Sample**: Cortisol, Norepinephrine, Epinephrine, Dopamine and Creatinine **Physical Examination** Anthropometry: Height, weight, waist and hip circumference Systolic and diastolic blood pressure (3 readings) Examination of chest, heart rate, breathing, breasts, abdomen, arms, legs, lymph and thyroid glands for abnormalities (similar to National Health Insurance Exam) Abdominal ultrasound (liver, pancreas, gallbladder, kidneys)

Table 18.2 Limitations of the use of biomarkers

Biological measures	Source	Risk factor[a]	Disease/health outcome	Cautions/confounders
Cardiovascular system				
Systolic blood pressure	Exam	>140/90 mmHg in general population	High blood pressure increases the risk of heart failure, heart attack, stroke, and kidney failure	Blood pressure may be affected by many different conditions, including "White coat hypertension", if the medical visit itself produces extreme anxiety
Dystolic blood pressure	Exam		Low blood pressure may be a sign of a variety of illnesses, including heart failure, infection, gland disorders, and dehydration	
Metabolic system				
BMI	Self-report/ exam	>30 kg/m^2	Being overweight puts strain on heart and can lead to serious health problems such as type 2 diabetes, heart disease, high blood pressure, sleep apnea, varicose veins, and other chronic conditions	Although BMI under 25 is considered healthy, for those older than 65, it is often better to have a BMI between 25 and 27 because a slightly higher BMI may help protect you from osteoporosis
Waist-hip ratio	Self-report/ exam	>0.9 (males), 0.85 (females)	High WHR increases the risk of CHD, hypertension, and diabetes	
HDL	Blood	<0.9(males), <1.0 (females)	The higher HDL, the lower the risk of coronary artery disease	For the most accurate measurements, it needs to be fast for 9–12 h before the blood sample is taken
LDL	Blood	>3.3 mmol/L	The higher LDL, the higher the risk of coronary artery disease	
Homocysteine	Blood	>12 μmol/L is considered high	The higher homocysteine levels in the blood (plasma), the higher the risk of coronary heart disease, stroke and peripheral vascular disease	Homocysteine levels increases by age and are reported to be high in some people with homocystinuria, kidney disease, hypothyroidism, inflammatory bowel disease (IBD), Alzheimer's disease, or certain cancers. Homocysteine levels may also be depleted by a number of drugs. Not getting enough folic acid, vitamin B6, or vitamin B12 also affects homocysteine levels

(continued)

Table 18.2 (continued)

Biological measures	Source	Risk factor[a]	Disease/health outcome	Cautions/confounders
Glycosylated hemoglobin (HbA1c)	Blood	HbA1c is normal if it is 5% or less. Normal ranges may vary slightly depending on the laboratory used	The higher HbA1c, the higher the risk to develop diabetes complications problems such as eye disease, kidney disease, nerve damage, heart disease, and stroke	Undiagnosed diabetes
Triglycerides	Blood	>1.7 mmol/L or >150 mg/dL	High triglycerides may contribute to hardening of the arteries (atherosclerosis) or thickening of the artery walls – which increases the risk of stroke, heart attack and heart disease	High triglycerides are a sign of poorly controlled type 2 diabetes, low levels of thyroid hormones (hypothyroidism), liver or kidney disease, or rare genetic conditions that affect how body converts fat to energy. High triglycerides could also be a side effect of taking medications (tamoxifen, steroids, beta-blockers, diuretics and estrogen)
Inflammation				
IL-6	Blood		It is associated with rheumatoid arthritis, osteoporosis, Alzheimer disease, cardiovascular disease, and type 2 diabetes	High levels of IL-6 are associated with trauma, infection and fever
CRP	Blood	>3.0 mg/L	It is a signal for acute inflammation. A positive test means you have inflammation in the body. This may be due to a variety of different conditions including: cancer, connective tissue disease, heart attack Infection, Inflammatory bowel disease (IBS), lupus, pneumococcal pneumonia, rheumatoid arthritis , rheumatic fever and tuberculosis	High levels of CRP are caused by infections and many long-term diseases. However, a CRP test cannot show where the inflammation is located or what is causing it

Fibrinogen	Blood	The normal range is 200–400 mg per deciliter (mg/dL). (Medline PLUS)	Fibrinogen is involved both in thrombogenesis and in the stimulation of atherogenic cell proliferation, and elevated levels predict the development of coronary heart disease	Fibrinogen is an acute phase reactant, meaning that fibrinogen concentrations may rise sharply in any condition that causes inflammation or tissue damage. Usually elevations in the fibrinogen blood level are temporary, returning to normal after the underlying condition has been resolved. Elevated levels may be seen with: acute infections, cancer, coronary heart disease, myocardial infarction, stroke, Inflammatory disorders (like rheumatoid arthritis and glomerulonephritis)and trauma Certain drugs may cause decreased levels, including anabolic steroids, androgens, Phenobarbital, streptokinase, urokinase, and valproic acid. Moderate elevations in fibrinogen may be seen sometimes with pregnancy, cigarette smoking, and with oral contraceptives or estrogen use
HPA				
Cortisol	Urine blood saliva		Cortisol affects many different body systems and plays a role in increasing glucose metabolism and down regulation of immune function. Persistently elevated levels of cortisol (as in chronic stress) have been found to suppress immune function, facilitate central adiposity (a risk factor for coronary heart disease and diabetes) and to be associated with depression. Nevertheless, cortisol has not been consistently linked to cognitive decline or dementia in prospective epidemiologic studies	Cortisol has a circadian rhythm. To get an accurate picture, it needs to be measured over several days and several times a day. Factors known to influence cortisol: age, gender, smoking, body mass index, emotional stress, hyper or hypothyroidism, obesity, drug (particularly oral contraceptive, hydrocortisone, and spironolactone).

(continued)

Table 18.2 (continued)

Biological measures	Source	Risk factor[a]	Disease/health outcome	Cautions/confounders
DHEAS	Blood		There is a lack of available studies on the long-term effects of DHEA. However, DHEA may cause higher than normal levels of androgens and estrogens in the body, and theoretically may increase the risk of prostate, breast, ovarian, and other hormone-sensitive cancers	Dehydroepiandrosterone (DHEA) and its sulfated metabolite DHEA-S are endogenous hormones secreted by the adrenal cortex in response to adrenocorticotrophin (ACTH). DHEA levels in the body begin to decrease after age 30, and are reported to be low in some people with anorexia, end-stage kidney disease, type 2 diabetes (non-insulin dependent diabetes), AIDS, adrenal insufficiency, and in the critically ill. DHEA levels may also be depleted by a number of drugs, including insulin, corticosteroids, opiates, and danazol
Sympathetic nervous system				
Norepinephrine	Urine plasma	Normal value: 60 ng/100 mL (Medline PLUS)	Cathecolamines increase heart rate, myocardial contractility, blood pressure and bring changes in vascular resistance	Levels of catecholamines are influenced by pain, stress, vigorous exercise, foods and drugs. Foods that can increase catecholamine levels include: coffee, tea, bananas, chocolate, cocoa, citrus, fruits, vanilla. These foods for several days prior to the test, particularly if both blood and urine catecholamines are to be measured. Drugs that can increase catecholamine measurements include: Aminophylline, Caffeine, Chloral hydrate, Clonidine, Disulfiram, Erythromycin, Insulin, Levodopa, Lithium, Methenamine, Methyldopa, Nicotinic acid (large doses), Nitroglycerin, Quinidine, Tetracycline Drugs that can decrease catecholamine measurements include: Clonidine, Disulfiram, Guanethidine, Imipramine, MAO inhibitors, Phenothiazines, Reserpine, Salicylates
Epinephrine	Urine	Normal value: 20 ng/100 mL (ng/mL = nanograms per milliliter) (medline PLUS)		

[a]Values may range from lab to lab

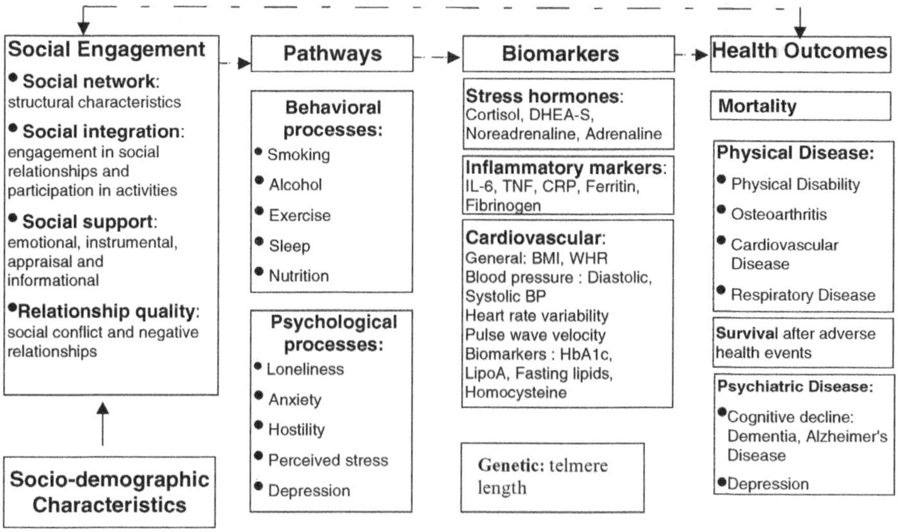

Fig. 18.1 Understanding the pathways: biomarkers, physical assessments

aspects of people's 'social' existence, typically incorporating their social network (the 'structure' within which social interaction takes place), the (different types of) available social support (functional measure), and their level of social integration into the networks that are available to them (the 'content' of the structure).

There are two primary mechanisms that link social engagement to health outcomes, namely *psychological* and *behavioural* processes, which in turn affect physiological pathways (these pathways and mechanisms contained in each pathway are summarised in Fig. 18.1). Of these proposed pathways, the best understood are those that operate via mechanisms that influence health behaviours, lifestyle and access to health and social care. According to the social control hypothesis, 'people obtain normative guidance by comparing their attitudes with those of a reference group of similar others' (Marsden and Friedkin 1994). Normative pressure and example from friends, peers, and family influence the decisions to adopt or maintain (un)healthy behaviours (e.g. a spouse who insists on eating well, drinking less, ceasing smoking and so on or, conversely, peer pressure to start smoking among adolescents). Moreover, fewer social ties provide fewer sources of information and by extension more limited access to appropriate care and less scope to minimize stressful events. Social engagement can attenuate or eliminate stressful experiences by providing a solution to the problem or by giving a new interpretation for adverse events (Cohen 2004), thereby buffering the harmful effects of stress. For example, social engagement can modulate cardiovascular reactivity by reducing sympathetic nervous system activity and/or stress related hormonal activity (via the hypothalamic-pituitary-adrenal cortical axis) (Cohen et al. 2004). Social integration can also influence one's emotional state, giving a sense of purpose, meaning, and belonging and reducing the intensity and duration of negative affective states (Thoits 1982), thus resulting in suppressed neuroendocrine response (Cohen 1988, 2004).

Allostatic load is the composite measure of the body's accommodation to stress from the wear and tear resulting from chronic overactivity or underactivity of physiological systems (McEwen and Stellar 1993; Seeman et al. 2002). In most studies, allostatic load is 'operationalized' as a composite score of the following biomarkers: systolic and diastolic blood pressure, waist/hip ratio, high-density lipoprotein and total cholesterol, glycosylated hemoglobin, cortisol, serum dihydroepiandrosterone sulfate, norepinephrine, and epinephrine (Maselko et al. 2007). Some studies have reported an association between allostatic load and social engagement. Social strain (*negative social relationships and adverse life events/circumstances*) can cause (principally via chronic stress pathways) dysregulation of physiological systems (Glei et al. 2007). In contrast, *positive social relationships* can counteract the effects of chronic stress via the stress-buffering properties of social support (Cohen and Wills 1985; Uchino et al. 2006). More specifically, social support may alter the perception of stressful situations, such that they are no longer perceived as threatening conditions, thus preventing the onset of physiological stress reactivity. Social support may also reduce physiological stress reactivity, helping individuals to cope with negative and stressful experiences (e.g. loss of important social ties for instance following the death of a spouse). Data from two different longitudinal studies, one a cohort of men and women aged 58–59 years (Wisconsin Longitudinal Study) and the other a cohort of men and women aged 70–79 years (MacArthur Study of Successful Aging), found evidence of an association between positive social relationships and lower allostatic load (Seeman and Chen 2002). Furthermore, in the MacArthur Study of Successful Aging, those reported as having greater social integration were significantly less likely to exhibit high allostatic load.

In an example of how non-western societies may differ from the Western ones, data from the Social Environment and Biomarkers of Aging Study (SEBAS) in Taiwan indicates a relationship between social environment characteristics and an index of cumulative biological dysregulation (allostatic load) in persons aged over 54. Linear regression analyses revealed that among those aged 54–70, presence of a spouse was associated with lower allostatic load among men, but not women (Seeman et al. 2004). Among those aged 70 and over, ties with close friends and/or neighbors were found to be significantly related to lower allostatic load for both men and women. Perceived qualities of these social relationships did not show consistent associations with allostatic load. This result contrasts with patterns found in Western societies (MacArthur Study of Successful Aging, Wisconsin data), indicating that cross-cultural differences between Western societies and an East Asian societies may cause differences in the patterns of association between social engagement and physiological substrates of health.

Although the concept of allostatic load has helped to create a framework integrating biological, psychological, and sociodemographic approaches, important questions remain regarding both the concept and measurement of allostatic load. There is no scope for a full exploration of these issues in this article. The Behavioral and Social Research Program at the National Institute on Aging held an exploratory workshop on allostatic load and the documentation of this workshop provides a comprehensive review on these questions (Nielsen et al. 2007).

Biomarkers: How They Shed Light on the Link Between Social Engagement and Health?

Social engagement influences health by affecting behavioral responses (in relation to, for instance, smoking, drinking alcohol, drug use) and psychological processes, as outlined above. However, the precise physiological processes whereby social engagement, through these behavioral and psychological processes, is translated into good or poor health (understood as morbidity and mortality) are not fully understood: 'The research task is to *give an account* of what links social structure to health outcomes – to ask, *what are the intermediary steps*?' (Marmot 2001). The collection of physical measurements and biomarkers is intended to be of assistance in the attempt to unpick these 'intermediary steps'. The third column in Fig. 18.1 lists some of the biomarkers that are believed to play a role in the impact of social engagement on health (Seeman and McEwen 1996; Uchino 2006; Uchino et al. 1996a).

Most of these biomarkers belong to three physiological systems: *inflammatory*, *cardiovascular*, and *neuroendocrine*. The inflammatory system is the body's defense response to infections and other toxic stimuli. The cardiovascular system predominantly reflects the heart, blood vessels and blood pressure. The neuroendocrine system is a network of nerve flares and hormones in the brain and the rest of the body. We will discuss these biomarkers and their proposed relationship to social engagement. The limitations of the use of these biomarkers are also highlighted.

This chapter does not explore the association between the effects of chronic stress (such as caregiving for a very disabled child or caring for a family member with Alzheimer's disease) on telomere length and telomerase activity. Telomere length is largely genetically determined but also affected by age-dependent attrition (Meyer et al. 2008). Therefore, telomere length has been identified as a marker of cellular senescence and is associated with a wide range of age-related disease such as cardiovascular disease. It appears to hold much promise to illuminate the heart of the aging process and for assessing cumulative exposure to stress and/or ability to cope with stress (Damjanovic et al. 2007). However, there are some caveats that pertain to measurement difficulties. Telomere length is highly variable among individuals, including individuals in the same age group. The potential measurement problems are related to high levels of inter-individual variation in telomere length by birth (influenced strongly by genetic polymorphisms), inter-individual variation in telomere attrition after birth, and variation attributed to the techniques used to measure telomere length (Aviv et al. 2006) . Addressing these questions properly would require a separate article devoted to this fascinating new biomarker. It is clear, however, that much work remains to be done on the impact of stress and social engagement on telomere dynamics and that this work has great potential to throw light on the pathways between the social and health aspects of individuals' lives and indeed on the aging process itself.

Inflammatory Biomarkers

The *inflammatory* biomarkers that have been associated with social engagement include pro-inflammatory cytokines (that promote and enhance the inflammation process) such as Interleukin-1 (IL-1), Interleukin-6 (IL-6), Tumor Necrosis Factor (TNF), and acute phase reactants (altered as a result of the inflammatory process) such as C-Reactive Protein (CRP) and Fibrinogen. Higher IL-6 is associated with memory decline (Schram et al. 2007), loss of muscle mass and strength (sarcopenia) (Schaap et al. 2006) and exaggerated arterial thickening (carotid intima media). CRP is a predictor of frailty (Puts et al. 2005), risk factor for the development of cardiovascular conditions such as arterial fibrillation (Aviles et al. 2003), ischemic stroke (Cao et al. 2003), diabetes (Barzilay et al. 2001), and a risk factor for cognition decline (Teunissen et al. 2003). A summary score of CRP, IL-6 albumin and cholesterol is a predictor of mortality and functional decline in high-functioning community-dwelling older persons (Reuben et al. 2002). A combination of high IL-6 and high D-Dimers (a coagulation marker) predicts functional decline and mortality (Cohen et al. 2003). Fibrinogen is associated with coronary disease and stroke and it is one of the markers for the allostatic load (McEwen and Stellar 1993).

The MacArthur Study of Successful Aging reported an inverse association between social integration and CRP in men after adjusting for age, race/ethnicity, smoking, alcohol consumption, physical activity, body mass index, cardiovascular disease, other major or chronic conditions, physical functioning, socioeconomic status, and depression (Loucks et al. 2006a, b). In the same study, social integration was significantly associated with elevated concentrations of fibrinogen (>336 mg/dL) in men after similar adjustments (Loucks et al. 2005). Neither CRP nor fibrinogen is associated with social integration in women.

In the Framingham Heart Study, social engagement (measured by Beckman's Social Network Index) was inversely associated with IL-6 in men ($p=0.03$) after adjusting for potential confounders (Loucks et al. 2006a, b). Friedman et al. (2005) reported that older women with more positive social relations had lower levels of IL-6 and better sleep efficiency. Interestingly, the study also found that social relations and sleep may act to buffer one another; both women with good relationship quality but low sleep efficiency and women with poor social relations but high sleep efficiency had lower levels of IL-6.

However statistically strong, all of these associations should be interpreted with care. Levels of pro-inflammatory cytokines and acute phase reactants alter in response to multiple types of tissue injury, including inflammation, infection, autoimmunity, and malignancy (Provan and Krentz 2002). Inflammatory biomarkers are very *sensitive* (i.e. very likely to be elevated when there is tissue injury in the body) but not very *specific* (i.e. they cannot point towards what *type* of tissue damage is causing their derangement). Pro-inflammatory cytokines and acute phase reactants are a biochemical 'thermometer' of tissue injury in the body: they go up when there's something wrong but don't tell us what the cause is. On the other hand, pro-inflammatory cytokines and acute phase reactants quickly go back to baseline levels once the attack on the body has ceased. For instance, CRP increases within minutes of an inflammatory insult, and falls within 2–3 days of recovery (Longmore et al. 2004). Levels of CRP could therefore be elevated on the day of an assessment if an infection or a recent injury were present, rather than indicative of other age-related processes. Less frequently, tissue damage can occur without an inflammatory response, i.e. without elevation of inflammatory markers. (i.e. false negative) (Pepys and Hirschfield 2003). Conversely, high levels of CRP can be sustained in chronic inflammatory conditions and malignancies. In any case, when inflammatory biomarkers are elevated, some degree of physical damage (reversible or not) is definitely taking place.

In the context of this paper, the key questions are why and how are social relationships linked to morbidity and mortality (Glei et al. 2007). Are social relationships the principal causal factors or are other *unmeasured confounders*, such as underlying infections, systemic inflammations, autoimmune processes or incipient cancers, implicated? Population-based and other research studies control for known variables but are unable to control for *undiagnosed* confounders. Even in longitudinal studies, apparent correlations between social relationships and inflammatory biomarkers do not necessarily indicate the direction of causality. For instance, within the context of population-based studies of social epidemiology, one could imagine a hypothetical case of a person whose longitudinal assessment shows a gradual decline in social relationships coupled with a gradual increase in her/his inflammatory biomarkers, in the absence of past medical history to account for it. Are his/her worsening social relationships causing him/her an inflammatory response? Or is there an undiagnosed medical condition that impairs his/her sociability (i.e. tiredness and fatigue from malignancy)? Thus, the collection of biomarkers in the context of social epidemiology studies can lead to ethical dilemmas in addition to important cost implications, not only arising from the cost of the biomarkers themselves but also from the ethical need to refer participants for a medical opinion. The example highlights the necessity for close collaboration between social scientists and clinicians in socio-epidemiological studies that involve biomarker evaluation.

Cardiovascular Biomarkers

There are ample data supporting an association between the *cardiovascular* system and social factors including the onset of, recovery from, and survival after coronary heart disease (Colantonio et al. 1993; Glass et al. 2000; Orth-Gomer et al. 1993). Social engagement buffers the potentially harmful influences of stress-induced cardiovascular reactivity (usually measured by heart rate, and systolic and diastolic blood pressure) and consequently reduces the incidence of cardiovascular disease (Uchino et al. 2006). However, the studies that have yielded evidence of the impact of social engagement, including functional and structural support, are not based on community samples, but are typically clinical studies (Uchino et al. 1996b).

Laboratory studies show lower cardiovascular reactivity to stressful situations in people accompanied by a supporting other. Several studies used samples of college students performing mental stress tests (arithmetic mental stress task, public speaking, etc.) in the presence/absence of a un/supporting friend, while blood pressure and heart rate were monitored (Chen et al. 2005; Kamarck et al. 1995; Lepore et al. 1993; Phillips et al. 2005).

In the National Heart, Lung, and Blood Institute (NHLBI) Family Heart Study (Knox et al. 2000), women with high risk for the development of coronary heart disease but high social support were found to develop less carotid artery atherosclerosis. Population-based studies have also reported longer survival after CHD in people who are not socially isolated or/and have social support. Negative interaction with social network members has also been associated with biological risk. For instance, poor marital relationships are associated with an increased risk of cardiovascular reactivity (increase in systolic blood pressure, heart rate, and cardiac-output and larger decreases in peripheral vascular resistance and pre-ejection period) (Nealey-Moore et al. 2007) and an increase in Epstein Barr virus antibodies (Kiecolt-Glaser et al. 1988; Kiecolt-Glaser et al. 1987).

Biomarkers of the cardiovascular system and cardiovascular reactivity have important caveats when it comes to measurement validity, reliability, and variability. One example is catecholamines. Catecholamines include epinephrine (adrenaline) and norepinephrine (noradrenaline) and are hormones released by the adrenal medulla upon activation of the sympathetic nervous system. This activation occurs during times of stress such as exercise, heart failure, hemorrhage, emotional stress, excitement or pain.

Catecholamine levels have been collected in population-based surveys and are proposed as an important determinant of allostatic load. However, catecholamine concentrations in serum are subject to tremendous intra and intersubject variability, with changes occurring extremely rapidly according to a variety of external stimuli and every day manouevres such as change in posture from sit to stand (Fitzgerald et al. 2003). This means that even in the calmest of subjects, catecholamine concentrations inevitably go up during the administration of a blood test, to an extent that is individually specific and unpredictable. Therefore, if obtained via a blood test, catecholamine levels are unlikely to represent basal levels for an individual. Twenty-four hour urinary collections may overcome some of these challenges, yet foodstuffs or drinks such as bananas, chocolate, cocoa, citrus fruits, coffee, and tea or vigorous exercise may render interpretation of urinary catecholamine inaccurate. Some surveys collect information on diet and exercise, which enables better control of confounders. Stressful situations and anxiety can also interfere with test results (although this may be valuable to pick up, since stress is a pathway by which social relationships link to health outcomes). Furthermore, extremely high levels of urinary catecholamines should be referred to a physician for consideration of appropriate diagnostic tests for pheochromocytoma, a rare but important tumor that secretes catecholamines.

Another example of a cardiovascular measurement that needs careful evaluation of measurement quality is Heart Rate Variability (HRV). HRV has become a very popular measure in the biomedical sciences, and there is evidence linking decreased HRV with measures of allostatic load , depressive symptoms (Guinjoan et al. 2007; Stein et al. 2008), chronic fatigue (Boneva et al. 2007), chronic stress (Golosarsky 2006), and sleep quality (Sforza et al. 2007). However, the reliability of heart rate variability remains poorly quantified in the light of studies showing large between- and within-subject variation (Sandercock 2007). Reliability coefficients for HRV measures were highly varied, ranging from less than 1% to greater than 100% (Sandercock et al. 2005). In individuals who had two HRV measurements, the second measurement was as high/low as 1.9/0.5 times (best case) and 3.5/0.3 times (worst case) the first measurement, due to random variation alone (Pinna et al. 2007). However, other HRV reliability studies are more optimistic for reliability of HRV measurements (Reland et al. 2005). In any case, social epidemiological studies collecting measurements of HRV should include their own tests of reliability if spurious correlations are to be avoided.

Endocrine Biomarkers

Another biological pathway through which social engagement influences physical health is the *endocrine* system. The endocrine system and the nervous system are so closely associated that they are collectively called the neuroendocrine system. Neural centers in the brain control endocrine glands, and one of the main neural control centers is the hypothalamus. The hypothalamus receives and integrates messages from the central nervous system, which in turn sends messages to the pituitary gland; the pituitary gland, in turn, releases hormones that regulate the body's functions.

One of the most commonly examined endocrine biomarkers is cortisol (Seeman 1996; Uchino 2006). Cortisol is a hormone produced by the adrenal cortex in response to circulating levels of adrenocorticotropic hormone (ACTH), which is produced by the anterior pituitary gland. Normally, cortisol levels rise and fall during the day, following a 24-h cycle (diurnal variation). Cortisol levels are at their highest at about 6–8 a.m. and lowest at about midnight. Physical and emotional stress can increase cortisol levels because during the normal stress response, the pituitary gland increases its release of ACTH. Cortisol affects many different body systems and plays a role in increasing glucose metabolism and down regulation of immune function. Persistently elevated levels of cortisol (as in chronic stress) suppress immune function (Buford and Willoughby 2008), facilitate central adiposity (a risk factor for coronary heart disease and diabetes) (Steptoe et al. 2004), and are associated with depression (Sher 2004). The MacArthur Study of Successful Aging yielded evidence that emotional support is linked to lower levels of urinary cortisol and norepinephrine and epinephrine among older men only. However, there was no significant association between social conflict (high demand and criticism) and endocrine activity (Seeman et al. 2001).

Measurement of cortisol levels in social epidemiological studies is also subject to caveats. Cortisol levels change rapidly in a matter of hours and fluctuate over the 24-h cycle, thus requiring repeated measurements throughout the day and over the course of several days. Studies trying to get a reliable measurement have collected several samples a day over a 3–4 days period, and some researchers recommend ever longer (Stone et al. 2001). Cortisol levels vary with chronic emotional stress lifestyle (e.g. shift work, jet lag), sleep status, alcohol intake, smoking, diet, and exercise. Cortisol may also be increased in Cushing syndrome, hyperthyroidism, acute illness, trauma, sepsis, and chronic renal failure, amongst others. Additionally, a number of drugs can increase cortisol levels, particularly oral contraceptives, hydrocortisone (the synthetic form of cortisol), and spironolactone, and sleep quality and quantity on the previous night affect levels. It is crucial that the first cortisol is taken prior to any physical movement such as getting out of the bed, brushing the teeth, or eating breakfast, since these activities will affect cortisol levels. Obtaining accurate data on cortisol is therefore time-consuming, expensive, and burdensome for the respondents and researchers. Nevertheless, the development of new methods of data collection might reduce respondent burden and help to contain research costs. For example, dried blood spots are a minimally invasive way to collect blood (in comparison with venous blood collection), have been applied in some of large population studies, and can be analyzed for levels of different markers (Lindau and McDade 2008).

Another endocrine biomarker that has been included in studies of allostatic load is glycosylated hemoglobin (HbA1C), which has been classified as a 'secondary mediator of stress response' (Crews 2007). In routine clinical practice, this biomarker is used as a surrogate for blood glucose control in people with diabetes mellitus. One study showed that greater job strain and lower social support at the workplace may be associated with increased concentrations of HbA1c, so increased blood glucose may be a physiological mediator between job strain or social support at the workplace and coronary heart disease (Kawakami et al. 2000). This study appropriately excluded subjects with *known history of diabetes*. However, undiagnosed diabetes is a major public health problem that may pose a source of bias to social epidemiological studies that collect HbA1c. For instance, a recent nationwide study of 35,869 primary care patients in Germany estimated that 0.9% of the population has undiagnosed diabetes, and 2% have impaired fasting glucose (Hauner et al. 2008), both of which increase with advancing years. More than one-fifth of older white British men and women have either undiagnosed diabetes or impaired fasting glucose (Thomas et al. 2005). Surveys based on self-report of medical conditions underestimate true disease prevalence and may falsely relate elevated HbA1c levels *purely* to the effect of negative social relationships. However, the incidence of diabetes is also related to measures of disadvantage, such as education and socioeconomic deprivation, where social relationships do play a role contributing further to the complexity of data interpretation.

Conclusions

The incorporation of biomarkers into multi-disciplinary studies of (ageing) populations is welcome and has potential to shed light on the very poorly understood pathways between 'social engagement' and health. However, it is important to bear a number of precautions in mind. These precautions relate both to measurement issues (e.g. difficulty of collecting reliable biomarker data from large population samples) and to analytical aspects, primarily the difficulty of disentangling the effects and meaning of biomarker data from the effects of possible endogenous (undetected, confounding) factors such as an undiagnosed, underlying pathology. If an insight is to be gained into disease aetiology from the earliest stages of pathology, physiological measurements need to be collected at much more frequent intervals than is in most cases financially and practically feasible in population studies (Mendes de Leon 2005).

At present, we still have a poor understanding of the relative importance of the possible pathways in Fig. 18.1. As has been argued above, the *interpretation* of biomarker data is not as straightforward as is sometimes assumed by researchers interested in understanding the relationship between social factors and health. As such, the efforts to collect biomarkers that relate to the other hypothesized pathways represent a considerable and uncertain investment. It is therefore of great importance to ensure that the biomarkers that are collected are based both on sound hypothesizing about the relative importance of the factors that biomarkers can throw light on, and that the data that are collected are accurate and in fact measure what they purport to measure (and are not interpreted as measuring something that they cannot reliably measure).

Collection of biomarkers has the potential to lead to major advances in our understanding of the causation (and therefore, at least in principle, the prevention and cure) of morbidity; it is very important to ensure that the biomarkers with the greatest potential to yield accurate and useful information are collected. This collection, however, can in some cases have extensive and complex ethical implications and in turn adds considerably to the cost of studies.

Recent growth in the number of studies incorporating biomarkers into larger population-based surveys has yielded a rapidly growing body of evidence linking various aspects of biological functioning not only to major health outcomes, including cognitive and physical functioning and longevity, but also to individual differences in socioeconomic and other social, psychological, and behavioral characteristics. Findings that link aspects of life situations to major biological risk factors provide important evidence on two fronts. First, they provide validation for various bio-psycho-social models of aging and help to elucidate biological pathways through which social, psychological, and behavioral factors affect trajectories of aging and risks for various health outcomes. Second, such evidence provides further support for the potential value of interventions targeting social, psychological, and behavioral factors as a means of altering underlying biological risk profiles. The collection and analysis of biomarker data therefore offers, in principle, the promise of aiding the entry into the 'brave new world' where the pathways between social engagement and health are properly understood (and even positively influenced through various interventions). While the problems associated with both collection and analysis of this data that have been highlighted here do not mean that researchers should go 'back to basics' (i.e. confine themselves to simpler methods of identifying and measuring 'health'), caution in the design of biomarker data collection and use of this data, and further research in biomarker validation, are warranted.

References

Aviles, R. J., Martin, D. O., Apperson-Hansen, C., Houghtaling, P. L., Rautaharju, P., Kronmal, R. A., et al. (2003). Inflammation as a risk factor for atrial fibrillation. *Circulation, 108*(24), 3006–3010. doi:10.1161/01.CIR.0000103131.70301.4F.

Aviv, A., Valdes, A. M., & Spector, T. D. (2006). Human telomere biology: Pitfalls of moving from the laboratory to epidemiology. *International Journal of Epidemiology, 35*(6), 1424–1429.

Barzilay, J. I., Abraham, L., Heckbert, S. R., Cushman, M., Kuller, L. H., Resnick, H. E., et al. (2001). The relation of markers of inflammation to the development of glucose disorders in the elderly: The Cardiovascular Health Study. *Diabetes, 50*(10), 2384–2389.

Bennett, D. A., Schneider, J. A., Tang, Y., Arnold, S. E., & Wilson, R. S. (2006). The effect of social networks on the relation between Alzheimer's disease pathology and level of cognitive function in old people: A longitudinal cohort study. *Lancet Neurology, 5*(5), 406–412. doi:S1474-4422(06)70417-3 [pii].

Berkman, L. F. (2000). Social support, social networks, social cohesion and health. *Social Work in Health Care, 31*(2), 3–14.

Berkman, L. F., & Kawachi, I. (2000). *Social epidemiology*. New York: Oxford University Press.

Berkman, L. F., & Syme, S. L. (1979). Social networks, host resistance, and mortality: A nine-year follow-up study of Alameda County residents. *American Journal of Epidemiology, 109*(2), 186–204.

Berkman, L. F., Leo-Summers, L., & Horwitz, R. I. (1992). Emotional support and survival after myocardial infarction. A prospective, population-based study of the elderly. *Annals of Internal Medicine, 117*(12), 1003–1009.

Boneva, R. S., Decker, M. J., Maloney, E. M., Lin, J. M., Jones, J. F., Helgason, H. G., et al. (2007). Higher heart rate and reduced heart rate variability persist during sleep in chronic fatigue syndrome: A population-based study. *Autonomic Neuroscience, 137*(1–2), 94–101. doi:S1566-0702(07)00446-8 [pii].

Buford, T. W., & Willoughby, D. S. (2008). Impact of DHEA(S) and cortisol on immune function in aging: A brief review. *Applied Physiology, Nutrition and Metabolism, 33*(3), 429–433. doi:h08-013 [pii]10.1139/h08-013.

Cao, J. J., Thach, C., Manolio, T. A., Psaty, B. M., Kuller, L. H., Chaves, P. H., et al. (2003). C-reactive protein, carotid intima-media thickness, and incidence of ischemic stroke in the elderly: The Cardiovascular Health Study. *Circulation, 108*(2), 166–170.

Chen, Y. Y., Gilligan, S., Coups, E. J., & Contrada, R. J. (2005). Hostility and perceived social support: Interactive effects on cardiovascular reactivity to laboratory stressors. *Annals of Behavioral Medicine, 29*(1), 37–43. doi:10.1207/s15324796abm2901_6.

Christakis, N. A., & Fowler, J. H. (2008). The collective dynamics of smoking in a large social network. *The New England Journal of Medicine, 358*(21), 2249–2258. doi:358/21/2249 [pii]10.1056/NEJMsa0706154.

Cohen, S. (1988). Psychosocial models of the role of social support in the etiology of physical disease. *Health Psychology, 7*(3), 269–297.

Cohen, S. (2004). Social relationships and health. *The American Psychologist, 59*(8), 676–684. doi:2004-20395-002 [pii]10.1037/0003-066X.59.8.676.

Cohen, S., & Wills, T. A. (1985). Stress, social support, and the buffering hypothesis. *Psychological Bulletin, 98*, 310–357.
Cohen, S., Doyle, W. J., Skoner, D. P., Rabin, B. S., & Gwaltney, J. M., Jr. (1997). Social ties and susceptibility to the common cold. *JAMA: The Journal of the American Medical Association, 277*(24), 1940–1944.
Cohen, H. J., Harris, T., & Pieper, C. F. (2003). Coagulation and activation of inflammatory pathways in the development of functional decline and mortality in the elderly. *The American Journal of Medicine, 114*(3), 180–187.
Cohen, A. N., Hammen, C., Henry, R. M., & Daley, S. E. (2004). Effects of stress and social support on recurrence in bipolar disorder. *Journal of Affective Disorders, 82*(1), 143–147. doi:S0165032703003173 [pii]10.1016/j.jad.2003.10.008.
Colantonio, A., Kasl, S. V., Ostfeld, A. M., & Berkman, L. F. (1993). Psychosocial predictors of stroke outcomes in an elderly population. *Journal of Gerontology, 48*(5), S261–S268.
Crews, D. E. (2007). Composite estimates of physiological stress, age, and diabetes in American Samoans. *American Journal of Physical Anthropology, 133*(3), 1028–1034. doi:10.1002/ajpa.20612.
Damjanovic, A., Yang, Y., Glaser, R., Kiecolt-Glaser, J., Nguyen, H., Laskowski, B., et al. (2007). Accelerated telomere erosion is associated with a declining immune function of caregivers of Alzheimer's disease patients. *The Journal of Immunology, 179*(6), 4249–4425.
Fitzgerald, R. D., Hieber, C., Schweitzer, E., Luo, A., Oczenski, W., & Lackner, F. X. (2003). Intraoperative catecholamine release in brain-dead organ donors is not suppressed by administration of fentanyl. *European Journal of Anaesthesiology, 20*(12), 952–956.
Friedman, E. M., Hayney, M. S., Love, G. D., Urry, H. L., Rosenkranz, M. A., Davidson, R. J., et al. (2005). Social relationships, sleep quality, and interleukin-6 in aging women. *Proceedings of the National Academy of Sciences of the United States of America, 102*(51), 18757–18762.
Funch, D. P., & Marshall, J. (1983). The role of stress, social support and age in survival from breast cancer. *Journal of Psychosomatic Research, 27*(1), 77–83.
Glass, T. A., Dym, B., Greenberg, S., Rintell, D., Roesch, C., & Berkman, L. F. (2000). Psychosocial intervention in stroke: Families in Recovery from Stroke Trial (FIRST). *The American Journal of Orthopsychiatry, 70*(2), 169–181.
Glei, D. A., Goldman, N., Chuang, Y.-L., & Weinstein, M. (2007). Do chronic stressors lead to physiological dysregulation? Testing the theory of allostatic load. *Psychosomatic Medicine, 69*(8), 769–776. doi:10.1097/PSY.0b013e318157cba6.
Golosarsky, B. (2006). Can heart rate variability timing reflect the body stress? *Medical Hypotheses, 67*(6), 1467–1468. doi:S0306-9877(06)00371-9 [pii]10.1016/j.mehy.2006.05.022.
Guinjoan, S. M., Castro, M. N., Vigo, D. E., Weidema, H., Berbara, C., Fahrer, R. D., et al. (2007). Depressive symptoms are related to decreased low-frequency heart rate variability in older adults with decompensated heart failure. *Neuropsychobiology, 55*(3–4), 219–224. doi:000108381 [pii]10.1159/000108381.
Hauner, H., Hanisch, J., Bramlage, P., Steinhagen-Thiessen, E., Schunkert, H., Jockel, K. H., et al. (2008). Prevalence of undiagnosed Type-2-diabetes mellitus and impaired fasting glucose in German primary care: Data from the German Metabolic and Cardiovascular Risk Project (GEMCAS). *Experimental and Clinical Endocrinology & Diabetes, 116*(1), 18–25. doi:10.1055/s-2007-985359.
House, J. S., Robbins, C., & Metzner, H. L. (1982). The association of social relationships and activities with mortality: Prospective evidence from the Tecumseh Community Health Study. *American Journal of Epidemiology, 116*(1), 123–140.
House, J. S., Landis, K., & Umberson, D. (1988). Social relationships and health. *Science, 241*, 540–545.
Kamarck, T., Annunziato, B., & Amateau, L. (1995). Affiliation moderates the effects of social threat on stress-related cardiovascular responses: Boundary conditions for a laboratory model of social support. *Psychosomatic Medicine, 57*(2), 183–194.
Kaplan, G. A., Cohn, B. A., Cohen, R. D., & Guralnik, J. (1988). The decline in ischemic heart disease mortality: Prospective evidence from the Alameda County Study. *American Journal of Epidemiology, 127*(6), 1131–1142.

Kawakami, N., Akachi, K., Shimizu, H., Haratani, T., Kobayashi, F., Ishizaki, M., et al. (2000). Job strain, social support in the workplace, and haemoglobin A1c in Japanese men. *Occupational and Environmental Medicine, 57*(12), 805–809.
Kiecolt-Glaser, J., Fisher, L. D., Ogrocki, P., Stout, J. C., Speicher, C., & Glaser, R. (1987). Marital quality, marital disruption, and immune function. *Psychosomatic Medicine, 49*(1), 13–34.
Kiecolt-Glaser, J., Kennedy, S., Malkoff, S., Fisher, L., Speicher, C. E., & Glaser, R. (1988). Psychosomatic medicine. *Psychosomatic Medicine, 50*(3), 213–229.
Knox, S. S., Adelman, A., Ellison, R. C., Arnett, D. K., Siegmund, K., Weidner, G., et al. (2000). Hostility, social support, and carotid artery atherosclerosis in the National Heart, Lung, and Blood Institute Family Heart Study. *The American Journal of Cardiology, 86*(10), 1086–1089.
Kondo, N., Minai, J., Imai, H., & Yamagata, Z. (2007). Engagement in a cohesive group and higher-level functional capacity in older adults in Japan: A case of the Mujin. *Social Science & Medicine, 64*(11), 2311–2323. doi:S0277-9536(07)00046-9 [pii] 10.1016/j.socscimed.2007.02.009.
Lepore, S. J., Allen, K. A., & Evans, G. W. (1993). Social support lowers cardiovascular reactivity to an acute stressor. *Psychosomatic Medicine, 55*(6), 518–524.
Lindau, S., & McDade, T. (2008). Minimally-invasive and innovative methods for biomeasure collection in population-based research. In M. Weinstein, J. Vaupel, & K. Wachter (Eds.), *Biosocial surveys, committee on advances in collecting and utilizing biological indicators and genetic information in social science surveys*. Washington, DC: National Academies Press.
Longmore, M., Wilkinson, I. B., & Rajagopalan, S. (Eds.). (2004). *Oxford handbook of clinical medicine* (6th ed.). Oxford: Oxford University Press.
Loucks, E. B., Berkman, L. F., Gruenewald, T. L., & Seeman, T. E. (2005). Social integration is associated with fibrinogen concentration in elderly men. *Psychosomatic Medicine, 67*(3), 353–358.
Loucks, E. B., Berkman, L. F., Gruenewald, T. L., & Seeman, T. E. (2006a). Relation of social integration to inflammatory marker concentrations in men and women 70 to 79 years. *The American Journal of Cardiology, 97*(7), 1010–1016. doi:S0002-9149(05)02221-6 [pii]10.1016/j.amjcard.2005.10.043.
Loucks, E. B., Sullivan, L. M., D'Agostino, R. B., Sr., Larson, M. G., Berkman, L. F., & Benjamin, E. J. (2006b). Social networks and inflammatory markers in the Framingham Heart Study. *Journal of Biosocial Science, 38*(6), 835–842. doi:S0021932005001203 [pii]10.1017/S0021932005001203.
Marmot, M. (2001). Inequalities in health. *The New England Journal of Medicine, 345*(2), 134–136.
Marsden, P. V., & Friedkin, N. E. (1994). Network studies of social influence. In S. Wasserman & J. Galaskiewicz (Eds.), *Advances in social network analysis* (pp. 3–25). Sage: Thousand Oaks.
Maselko, J., Kubzansky, L., Kawachi, I., Seeman, T., & Berkman, L. (2007). Religious service attendance and allostatic load among high-functioning elderly. *Psychosomatic Medicine, 69*(5), 464–472. doi:PSY.0b013e31806c7c57 [pii]10.1097/PSY.0b013e31806c7c57.
McEwen, B. S., & Stellar, E. (1993). Stress and the individual. Mechanisms leading to disease. *Archives of Internal Medicine, 153*(18), 2093–2101.
Mendes de Leon, C. F. (2005). Social engagement and successful aging. *European Journal of Ageing, 2*, 64–66.
Meyer, T. D., Rietzschel, E., Buyzere, M. D., Criekinge, W. V., & Bekaert, S. (2008). Studying telomeres in a longitudinal population based study. *Frontiers in Bioscience, 13*(13), 2960–2970.
Nealey-Moore, J. B., Smith, T. W., Uchino, B. N., Hawkins, M. W., & Olson-Cerny, C. (2007). Cardiovascular reactivity during positive and negative marital interactions. *Journal of Behavioral Medicine, 30*(6), 505–519.
Nielsen, L., Seeman, T., & Hahn, A. (2007). *Background materials and statements from November 2007 workshop participants*. Paper presented at the NIA Exploratory Workshop on Allostatic Load, Washington, DC.
Orth-Gomer, K., & Johnson, J. V. (1987). Social network interaction and mortality. A six year follow-up study of a random sample of the Swedish population. *Journal of Chronic Diseases, 40*(10), 949–957.

Orth-Gomer, K., Rosengren, A., & Wilhelmsen, L. (1993). Lack of social support and incidence of coronary heart disease in middle-aged Swedish men. *Psychosomatic Medicine, 55*(1), 37–43.

Park, K., & Lee, Y. (2007). Association of social support and social activity with physical functioning in older persons. *Journal of Preventive Medicine and Public Health, 40*(2), 137–144.

Pepys, M. B., & Hirschfield, G. M. (2003). C-reactive protein: A critical update. *The Journal of Clinical Investigation, 111*(12), 1805–1812. doi:10.1172/JCI18921.

Phillips, A. C., Carroll, D., Ring, C., Sweeting, H., & West, P. (2005). Life events and acute cardiovascular reactions to mental stress: A cohort study. *Psychosomatic Medicine, 67*(3), 384–392.

Pinna, G. D., Maestri, R., Torunski, A., Danilowicz-Szymanowicz, L., Szwoch, M., La Rovere, M. T., et al. (2007). Heart rate variability measures: A fresh look at reliability. *Clinical Science (London, England), 113*(3), 131–140. doi:CS20070055 [pii]10.1042/CS20070055.

Provan, D., & Krentz, A. (2002). *Oxford handbook of clinical & laboratory investigation*. Oxford: Oxford University Press.

Puts, M. T., Visser, M., Twisk, J. W., Deeg, D. J., & Lips, P. (2005). Endocrine and inflammatory markers as predictors of frailty. *Clinical Endocrinology, 63*(4), 403–411. doi:CEN2355 [pii] 10.1111/j.1365-2265.2005.02355.x.

Reland, S., Ville, N. S., Wong, S., Carrault, G., & Carre, F. (2005). Reliability of heart rate variability in healthy older women at rest and during orthostatic testing. *Aging Clinical and Experimental Research, 17*(4), 316–321. doi:2750 [pii].

Reuben, D. B., Keeler, E., Seeman, T. E., Sewall, A., Hirsch, S. H., & Guralnik, J. M. (2002). Development of a method to identify seniors at high risk for high hospital utilization. *Medical Care, 40*(9), 782–793.

Sandercock, G. (2007). Normative values, reliability and sample size estimates in heart rate variability. *Clinical Science (London, England), 113*(3), 129–130. doi:CS20070137 [pii]10.1042/CS20070137.

Sandercock, G. R., Bromley, P. D., & Brodie, D. A. (2005). The reliability of short-term measurements of heart rate variability. *International Journal of Cardiology, 103*(3), 238–247. doi:S0167-5273(05)00153-1 [pii]10.1016/j.ijcard.2004.09.013.

Schaap, L. A., Pluijm, S. M., Deeg, D. J., & Visser, M. (2006). Inflammatory markers and loss of muscle mass (sarcopenia) and strength. *The American Journal of Medicine, 119*(6), 526.e9–17.

Schram, M. T., Euser, S. M., de Craen, A. J., Witteman, J. C., Frolich, M., Hofman, A., et al. (2007). Systemic markers of inflammation and cognitive decline in old age. *Journal of the American Geriatrics Society, 55*(5), 708–716.

Seeman, T. E. (1996). Social ties and health: The benefits of social integration. *Annals of Epidemiology, 6*(5), 442–451. doi:S1047279796000956 [pii].

Seeman, T. E., & Chen, X. (2002). Risk and protective factors for physical functioning in older adults with and without chronic conditions: MacArthur Studies of Successful Aging. *The Journals of Gerontology. Series B, Psychological Sciences and Social Sciences, 57*(3), S135–S144.

Seeman, T. E., & McEwen, B. S. (1996). Impact of social environment characteristics on neuroendocrine regulation. *Psychosomatic Medicine, 58*(5), 459–471.

Seeman, T. E., Mendes de Leon, C., Berkman, L., & Ostfeld, A. (1993). Risk factors for coronary heart disease among older men and women: A prospective study of community-dwelling elderly. *American Journal of Epidemiology, 138*(12), 1037–1049.

Seeman, T. E., McEwen, B. S., Rowe, J. W., & Singer, B. H. (2001). Allostatic load as a marker of cumulative biological risk: MacArthur studies of successful aging. *Proceedings of the National Academy of Sciences of the United States of America, 98*(8), 4770–4775.

Seeman, T. E., Burton, B. S., Ryff, C., Gayle, L. G. D. L., & Levy-Storms, L. (2002). Social relationships, gender, and allostatic load across two age cohorts. *Psychosomatic Medicine, 64*(3), 395–406.

Seeman, T. E., Glei, D., Goldman, N., Weinstein, M., Singer, B., & Lin, Y. H. (2004). Social relationships and allostatic load in Taiwanese elderly and near elderly. *Social Science & Medicine, 59*(11), 2245–2257. doi:10.1016/j.socscimed.2004.03.027S0277953604001583 [pii].

Sforza, E., Pichot, V., Cervena, K., Barthelemy, J. C., & Roche, F. (2007). Cardiac variability and heart-rate increment as a marker of sleep fragmentation in patients with a sleep disorder: A preliminary study. *Sleep, 30*(1), 43–51.

Sher, L. (2004). Daily hassles, cortisol, and the pathogenesis of depression. *Medical Hypotheses, 62*(2), 198–202. doi:10.1016/S0306-9877(03)00320-7.

Stein, P. K., Barzilay, J. I., Chaves, P. H., Traber, J., Domitrovich, P. P., Heckbert, S. R., et al. (2008). Higher levels of inflammation factors and greater insulin resistance are independently associated with higher heart rate and lower heart rate variability in normoglycemic older individuals: The Cardiovascular Health Study. *Journal of the American Geriatrics Society, 56*(2), 315–321. doi:JGS1564 [pii]10.1111/j.1532-5415.2007.01564.x.

Steptoe, A., Kunz-Ebrecht, S. R., Brydon, L., & Wardle, J. (2004). Central adiposity and cortisol responses to waking in middle-aged men and women. *International Journal of Obesity and Related Metabolic Disorders, 28*(9), 1168–1173. doi:10.1038/sj.ijo.08027150802715 [pii].

Stone, A. A., Schwartza, J. E., Smythb, J., Kirschbaumc, C., Cohend, S., Hellhammerc, D., et al. (2001). Individual differences in the diurnal cycle of salivary free cortisol: A replication of flattened cycles for some individuals. *Psychoneuroendocrinology, 26*(3), 295–306.

Taylor, S. E., Repetti, R. L., & Seeman, T. (1997). Health psychology: What is an unhealthy environment and how does it get under the skin? *Annual Review of Psychology, 48*, 411–447.

Teunissen, C. E., van Boxtel, M. P., Bosma, H., Bosmans, E., Delanghe, J., De Bruijn, C., et al. (2003). Inflammation markers in relation to cognition in a healthy aging population. *Journal of Neuroimmunology, 134*(1–2), 142–150.

Thoits, P. A. (1982). Life stress, social support, and psychological vulnerability: Epidemiological considerations. *Journal of Community Psychology, 10*(4), 341–362.

Thomas, M. C., Walker, M. K., Emberson, J. R., Thomson, A. G., Lawlor, D. A., Ebrahim, S., et al. (2005). Prevalence of undiagnosed Type 2 diabetes and impaired fasting glucose in older British men and women. *Diabetic Medicine, 22*(6), 789–793. doi:DME1516 [pii]10.1111/j.1464-5491.2005.01516.x.

Uchino, B. N. (2006). Social support and health: A review of physiological processes potentially underlying links to disease outcomes. *Journal of Behavioral Medicine, 29*(4), 377–387. doi:10.1007/s10865-006-9056-5.

Uchino, B. N., Cacioppo, J. T., & Kiecolt-Glaser, J. K. (1996a). The relationship between social support and physiological processes: A review with emphasis on underlying mechanisms and implications for health. *Psychological Bulletin, 119*(3), 488–531.

Uchino, B. N., Cacioppo, J. T., Malarkey, W., Glaser, R., & Kiecolt-Glaser, J. K. (1996b). Appraisal support predicts age-related differences in cardiovascular function in women. *Health Psychology, 14*, 556–562.

Uchino, B. N., Holt-Lunstad, J., Smith, T. W., & Bloor, L. (2004). Heterogeneity in social networks: A comparison of different models linking relationships to psychological outcomes. *Journal of Social and Clinical Psychology, 23*, 123–139.

Uchino, B. N., Berg, C. A., Smith, T. W., Pearce, G., & Skinner, M. (2006). Age-related differences in ambulatory blood pressure during daily stress: evidence for greater blood pressure reactivity with age. *Psychology and Aging, 21*(2), 231–239. doi:2006-07381-004 [pii]10.1037/0882-7974.21.2.231.

Weinstein, M., Vaupel, J. W., & Wachter, K. W. (Eds.). (2008). *Biosocial surveys*. Washington, DC: National Academies Press.

Welin, L., Tibblin, G., Svardsudd, K., Tibblin, B., Ander-Peciva, S., Larsson, B., et al. (1985). Prospective study of social influences on mortality. The study of men born in 1913 and 1923. *The Lancet, 1*(8434), 915–918.

Chapter 19
Methodological Aspects of Studying Human Aging, Health, and Mortality

A.I. Yashin, I. Akushevich, K. Arbeev, A. Kulminski, and S. Ukraintseva

Introduction

Age trajectories of mortality rates in human populations characterize individuals' inequality in the duration of life. Various models of mortality rates are used in the analyses of survival data in demographic and epidemiological applications aiming to identify sources of individual differences in life span. Despite existing practice to use estimated model parameters in explanations of differences in mortality rates among different populations, in most cases differences in such estimates are difficult to interpret. The reason for this difficulty is that parameters of many demographic mortality models do not characterize either biological processes developing in aging human organisms or expose to environmental and living conditions. At the same time many processes affecting survival chances are measured in human longitudinal studies of aging, health and longevity, which suggest an opportunity for developing mortality models with parameters that can be interpreted in terms of processes and measured in such studies. The purpose of this paper is to develop an approach to mortality modeling that allows for describing the mortality rate in terms of parameters of physiological processes and declining health status that develops in aging human organisms. In contrast to traditional demographic models, which are difficult to use in the analyses of longitudinal data, our model allows for taking all these data into account. We use diffusion-type continuous time stochastic process for describing evolution of physiological state over the life course and finite-state continuous process for describing changes in health status during this period. We derive equations for respective mortality models, and approximate changes in physiological state by conditional Gaussian process, given health state. We applied this model to the analyses of longitudinal data collected in the Framingham Heart Study. The results of these analyses show that model parameters can be evaluated

A.I. Yashin (✉) • I. Akushevich • K. Arbeev • A. Kulminski • S. Ukraintseva
Center for Population Health and Aging, Duke University, Durham, NC, USA
e-mail: aiy@duke.edu

N. Hoque et al. (eds.), *Applied Demography and Public Health*,
Applied Demography Series 3, DOI 10.1007/978-94-007-6140-7_19,
© Springer Science+Business Media Dordrecht 2013

from longitudinal data and properly interpreted. The analyses indicate important differences in physiological dynamics among healthy and sick individuals.

In demography human aging is represented by the age pattern of mortality rate, which shows how chances of death among survivors to a given age change with this age. Many other dimensions of aging are hidden in the age trajectory of mortality curve. There is growing understanding among demographers about the need to better understand external forces and internal mechanisms forming the age pattern of mortality. Attempts to decipher the information masked in this pattern resulted in different mortality models, which describe certain hypothetical mechanisms affecting mortality rate (see Yashin et al. 2000, and references in it).

An important class of such models deals with hidden heterogeneity or frailty modeling (Vaupel et al. 1979). An advantage of such modeling is that it does not require additional data. All parameters can be estimated from data on life spans for independent individuals. Limitations deal with the assumptions about the proportionality of hazard, parametric structure of baseline mortality rate, and distribution of frailty. All these assumptions are technical and do not have biological justification. However, without such assumptions, the traditional frailty model is not identifiable. It is important to note that the extension of this model to the cases of bivariate or multivariate survival (e.g., survival of twins or other relatives) has better identifiability properties. The baseline hazard in these models should not be parametrically specified. It can be identified semiparametrically from the analyses of bivariate or multivariate survival functions (Yashin et al. 1995). Frailty models play an important educational role. Their use made clear the need of performing a special averaging procedure to proceed from conditional hazard required to describe a frailty model (conditional mortality rate, where the frailty variable is explicitly represented), to unconditional hazard (observed mortality rate), required for the likelihood function of survival data to be used in the parameter estimation procedure. In a more general case, if $\mu(Z,t)$ is conditional hazard rate at age t with unobserved heterogeneity variable Z, and $\bar{\mu}(t)$ is observed mortality rate, then

$$\bar{\mu}(t) = E\left(\mu(Z,t) \middle| T > t\right) \tag{19.1}$$

It is important to note that to get unconditional hazard (observed mortality rate) one has to perform conditional averaging of $\mu(Z,t)$ given $\{T > t\}$. The latter means that averaging has to be performed among those who survived age t. As we will see below, the conditional averaging of hazards describing dependence of mortality from influential variables and processes is required for all types of integrated mortality models that involve unobserved or partly observed influential variables and processes. In case of additional observations on influential processes, additional conditions have to appear in the right hand side of (19.1).

Understanding that some hidden factors affecting mortality risk change with age (e.g., physiological and biological variables) stimulates development of models of changing frailty, describing evolution of aging dependent heterogeneity variables and their effects on mortality risk. Unobserved changes in health and functional status with age can also be considered as cases of hidden heterogeneity, in which changes over age can be described by finite state continuous time stochastic process.

A better understanding of the forces and mechanisms affecting age patterns of the mortality curve requires more details about the processes involved. Data and knowledge from other disciplines have to be involved to better understand demographic phenomena. The need to perform such interdisciplinary studies formed the new discipline called biodemography of aging, health, and longevity.

The involvement of all such variables and processes into description of mortality models results in an increasing number of model parameters that should be evaluated from the data. The use of life span data alone is not enough to identify models' parameters. The data on influential variables and processes affecting mortality could come from different sources, including longitudinal surveys, medical examinations, records of changes in health or disability status, etc. We will refer to differences in additional measurements that are required for identifying parameters of integrated mortality models as to differences in "observational plans". When all influential variables and processes are unobserved, the demographic (unconditional) mortality rate can be obtained by averaging conditional ones with respect to all covariates represented in the conditional mortality rate, taking into account probabilistic properties of respective variables and processes. When some variables and processes are observed or partly observed according to a certain observational plan, such averaging should be conditional to the observations collected in the plan. The conditionally averaged hazard rate is needed to form the likelihood function of the data.

In this paper we will investigate integrated mortality models in which the effects of two different types of processes are taken into account. One deals with changes in an individual's health status, which certainly affects his or her survival chances. Another corresponds to changes in an individual's variables describing physiological state. Traditional (demographic) description of changes in individual health/survival status is performed using continuous-time random Markov process with finite number of states and age-dependent transition intensity functions (transitions rates). Although such a description of the health process plays an important role in describing the connection between health and mortality, it does not allow for studying factors and mechanisms involved in aging-related decline in health/well-being/survival status. Numerous epidemiological studies provide compelling evidence that health transitions rates are influenced by a number of variables. Some of them are fixed at the time of birth (e.g., genetic background). Others experience stochastic changes over the life course. The latter include physiological state, medical costs, behavioral factors, and social-economical factors. Note that these factors also affect mortality risk. It is important to note that the presence of such randomly changing influential factors violates Markov assumption, which makes the description of aging-related changes in health status more complicated.

The dynamics of physiological and other variables in connection with mortality risks has been described using a stochastic process model of human mortality and aging (Woodbury and Manton 1977; Yashin 1985; Yashin and Manton 1997). Recent extensions of this model have been used in the analyses of longitudinal data on aging, health, and longevity collected in the Framingham Heart Study (Akushevich et al. 2005; Yashin et al. 2007, 2008; Arbeev et al. 2009). This model and its extensions are described by stochastic process that has Markov property and satisfies diffusion type stochastic differential equation. The stochastic process is stopped at a random time associated with the individual's death. The quadratic hazard assumption about the form of conditional mortality rate, given covariates values and certain regularity conditions, guarantee Gaussian property of conditional distribution of the covariates values at any given age. This allowed for description of aging-related changes in terms of two first moments of multidimensional Gaussian distribution. When an individual's health status is taken into account, the coefficients of stochastic differential equations become dependent from health states (values of jumping process). Such dependence violates Markov assumption and makes conditional Gaussian property not valid. So the description of this (continuously changing) component of aging-related changes in the body also becomes more complicated. One way to remain within Markov assumption is to increase the dimension of the process by considering the joint evolution of health status and influential variables over the life course and to consider this multidimensional stochastic process as a Markovian. Note that studying age trajectories of physiological state in their mutual connection with changes in health status and mortality risk provides more a realistic scenario for analyzing available longitudinal data. Thus in our model of human aging, health, and mortality, the Markov property takes place for the stochastic process consisting of jumping and continuously changing components. The jumping component is used for description of relatively fast changes in health status. The continuous component describes relatively slow age dynamics of individual physiological state.

Two-Component Markov Process Describing Human Aging, Health, and Mortality

Let $Y_t, t \geq 0$ be K-dimensional stochastic process with continuous components, which satisfies a stochastic differential equation with coefficients depending on the values of stochastic process θ_t:

$$dY_t = A_{\theta_t}(Y_t, t)dt + b_{\theta_t}(t)dW_t, \quad Y_{t_0} \tag{19.2}$$

Here $A_{\theta_t}(Y_t, t)$ is a vector function, $b_{\theta_t}(t)$ is a matrix of respective dimension, Y_{t_0} is a random vector of initial conditions, and W_t is a vector Wiener process with independent components, which is independent from initial value, Y_{t_0}. The process Y_t describes continuous evolution of physiological variables. The process $\theta_t, t \geq 0$ is the finite-state (jumping) continuous time stochastic process (i.e., $\theta_t \in \{1, 2, \ldots, M\}$, where M is the number of states). This process describes jumping changes in individuals' health/well-being status and is completely characterized by conditional transition intensity matrix (from state k to state r)

$$\lambda_{kr}(Y_t, t), \quad k, r = 1, 2, \ldots, M; \quad \text{and} \quad \lambda_{kk}(Y_t, t) = -\sum\nolimits_{r=1, r \neq k}^{M} \lambda_{kr}(Y_t, t) \tag{19.3}$$

and initial probabilities $P(\theta_{t_0} = j), j = 1, 2, \ldots, M$.

Let T be a non-negative random variable describing life span. Its distribution characterizes variability in life span among individuals in human cohorts representing longitudinal data. An individual's death at time T means that the trajectories of θ_t and Y_t are stopped at time T. The conditional distribution of T given trajectories of θ_u, $Y_u, 0 \le u \le t$ is completely characterized by the conditional hazard (mortality) rate $\mu_{\theta_t}(Y_t, t)$. The triple θ_t, Y_t, T describes joint evolution of individual health/well-being/survival status and physiological variables over individuals' age until death at time T.

Likelihood Function of Survival Data

Let $T_1, T_2, \ldots, T_N$ be life span data on N individuals, which health status and physiological state are described by the processes θ_t and Y_t. The likelihood function of these data is:

$$L(T_1, T_2, \ldots, T_N) = \prod_{i=1}^{N} \bar{\bar{\mu}}(T_i)^{\delta_i} \exp\left\{-\int_0^{T_i} \bar{\bar{\mu}}(u)du\right\} \tag{19.4}$$

Here $\bar{\bar{\mu}}(t)$ is total (also called unconditional, observed, or demographic) mortality rate, and δ_i is censoring variable. The ancillary information about connection between θ_t, Y_t and T allows for representation

$$\bar{\bar{\mu}}(t) = E\left(\mu_{\theta_t}(Y_t, t) \middle| T > t\right) \tag{19.5}$$

To estimate parameters of mortality rate, $\bar{\bar{\mu}}(t)$, the likelihood function (19.4) has to be maximized. Note that these parameters describe probability distributions of θ_t, Y_t and T, therefore they have biological interpretation. Since in most interesting cases, hazard (19.5) cannot be represented explicitly as a function of the model's parameters, maximization of the likelihood function (19.4) requires solution of a number of computational problems.

Equations for Conditional P.D.F./Probabilities Needed for Averaging Conditional Hazard

Calculation $\bar{\bar{\mu}}(t)$ in (19.5) requires specifying functional form of the conditional mortality rate and the function $f(y, j|t) = \frac{\partial}{\partial y} P\left(Y_t \le y, \theta_t = j \middle| T > t\right)$, which is the joint conditional probability density function, p.d.f. with respect to Y_t, and the probability with respect to θ_t, given $\{T > t\}$. Using standard Bayesian arguments similar to that used in Yashin et al. (1985, 1995), the following partial differential equation for $f(y, j|t)$ can be derived:

$$\frac{d}{dt} f(y,j|t) = \sum_{i=1}^{M} \lambda_{ij}(y,t) f(y,i|t) - \frac{\partial}{\partial y}\left(A_j(y,t) f(y,j|t)\right) + \frac{1}{2}\frac{\partial^2}{\partial y^2}\left(B_j(t) f(y,j|t)\right) + f(y,j|t)\left(\bar{\bar{\mu}}(t) - \mu_j(y,t)\right),\ f(y,j|t_0) \quad (19.6)$$

Here functions $A_j(y,t)$, are defined in (19.2) and $B_j(t) = b_j(t) b_j(t)^*$. Transition intensities $\lambda_{kr}(y,t)$, $k,r = 1,2,\ldots,M$ are defined by (19.3). Since $f(y,j|t)$ multiplies $\bar{\bar{\mu}}(t)$ in (19.6), this equation is a nonlinear partial differential equation with respect to $f(y,j|t)$. The total mortality rate $\bar{\bar{\mu}}(t)$ can also be represented as follows:

$$\bar{\bar{\mu}}(t) = \sum_{j=1}^{M} \bar{\mu}_j(t) \pi_j(t) \quad (19.7)$$

where $\pi_j(t) = P(\theta_t = j|T > t)$, and

$$\bar{\mu}_j(t) = E\left(\mu_{\theta_t}(Y_t,t)|\theta_t = j, T > t\right) \quad (19.8)$$

To calculate (19.7) and (19.8), one needs $\pi_j(t) = P(\theta_t = j|T > t)$ and conditional p.d.f., $f(y|j,t) = \partial P\left(Y_t \le y|\theta_t = j, T > t\right)/\partial y$ for each $t \ge 0$. Equation for $\pi_j(t)$ can be derived by integrating $f(y,j|t)$ in (19.5) with respect to y:

$$d\pi_j(t)/dt = \sum\nolimits_{k=1}^{M} \bar{\lambda}_{kj}(t)\pi_k(t) + \pi_j(t)\left(\bar{\bar{\mu}}(t) - \bar{\mu}_j(t)\right), \pi_j(t_0) \quad j = 1, 2, \ldots, M \quad (19.9)$$

Here $\bar{\bar{\mu}}(t)$ and $\bar{\mu}_j(t)$ are given by (19.7) and (19.8), and $\bar{\lambda}_{ij}(t)$ is defined as follows:

$$\bar{\lambda}_{ij}(t) = E\left(\lambda_{ij}(Y_t,t)|\theta_t = i, T > t\right) = \int_{R^K} \lambda_{ij}(y,t) f(y|i,t)\,dy. \quad (19.10)$$

Integration in (19.8) and (19.10) requires $f(y|j,t)$, $j = 1,2,\ldots,M$. The equation for this conditional p.d.f. follows from Eqs. (19.6) and (19.9) using Bayes' rule:

$$\frac{\partial}{\partial t} f(y|j,t) = \sum_{i=1}^{N}\left(\lambda_{ij}(y,t) f(y|i,t) - \bar{\lambda}_{ij}(t) f(y|j,t)\right)\frac{\pi_i(t)}{\pi_j(t)} - \frac{\partial}{\partial y}\left(A_j(y,t) f(y|j,t)\right) + \frac{1}{2}\frac{\partial^2}{\partial y^2}\left(B_j(t) f(y|j,t)\right) + f(y|j,t)\left(\bar{\mu}_j(t) - \mu_j(y,t)\right),\quad f(y|j,t_0) \quad (19.11)$$

Note that (19.9) and (19.11) comprise a system of nonlinear (partial and ordinary) differential equations. If these equations could be solved analytically, and integration in (19.8) could be analytically performed one would get parametrically described likelihood function (19.4), and use standard procedures of likelihood maximization to estimate model parameters. In most situations, however, the equations described above admit only numerical solution. This fact makes parameter estimation a computationally extensive procedure because Eqs. (19.9) and (19.11) have to be solved at each step of the numerical likelihood maximization.

Gaussian Approximation

The solutions of Eqs. (19.9) and (19.11) require specification of functional forms for the elements of a conditional-transition-intensities matrix $\lambda_{kr}(Y_t,t)$, a conditional mortality rate $\mu_{\theta_t}(Y_t,t)$ in (19.8) and (19.10), and coefficients, $A_{\theta_t}(Y_t,t)$ and $B_{\theta_t}(t)$ in (19.6) and (19.11). To get $\overline{\overline{\mu}}(t)$, $\overline{\mu}_j(t)$ and $\overline{\lambda}_{ij}(t)$ respective integrations have to be performed. It is convenient and epidemiologically justified to describe these hazard functions as quadratic forms of Y_t:

$$\lambda_{kr}(Y_t,t) = \lambda_{0kr}(t) + \left(Y_t - g_k(t)\right)^* \Lambda_{kr}(t)\left(Y_t - g_k(t)\right) \quad (19.12)$$

$$\mu_{\theta_t}(Y_t,t) = \mu_{0\theta_t}(t) + \left(Y_t - f_{\theta_t}(t)\right)^* Q_{\theta_t}(t)\left(Y_t - f_{\theta_t}(t)\right) \quad (19.13)$$

Here $\Lambda_{kr}(t)$ and $Q_j(t)$ are symmetric non-negative-definite $K \times K$ matrices, $f_{\theta_t}(t)$ is a K-vector function, and $\lambda_{0kr}(t)$ and $\mu_{0r}(t)$ are parametric functions of t for $k, r, j = 1,2,\ldots, M$; $t \geq t_0$. It is convenient to modify Eq. (19.2) to explicitly describe the mechanism of physiological regulation in the presence of external disturbances. This mechanism can be described in terms of linear stochastic differential equation with feedback loops:

$$dY_t = a_{\theta_t}(t)\left(Y_t - f_{1\theta_t}(t)\right)dt + b_{\theta_t}(t)dW_t, \quad Y_{t_0} \quad (19.14)$$

Here $a_{\theta_t}(t)$ is a vector function, $b_{\theta_t}(t)$ is a matrix of respective dimension, Y_{t_0} is a random vector of initial conditions, and W_t is a vector Wiener process with independent components, which is independent from initial value Y_{t_0}. The components of vector function $f_{1\theta_t}(t)$ characterize the effects of allostatic adaptation on physiological state (Yashin et al. 2007, 2008). Equation (19.14) includes negative feedback loops, which reflects basic regularities of organisms' biological functioning.

Conditions (19.12), (19.13), and (19.14), together with the assumptions about normality of the distribution for Y_{t_0} guaranteed Gaussian property of conditional probability distribution of the process Y_t among survivors to age t in the absence of jumping component (Yashin 1985; Yashin and Manton 1997). The presence of jumping process θ_t affecting the structure of the Eq. (19.14) for Y_t, and hence its age dynamics, violates the Gaussian property of this distribution. However, the quadratic forms for conditional transition intensity functions and mortality rates, as well as linear structure of (19.14) allow for using Gaussian approximation of the conditional p.d.f. $f(y|j,t) = \partial P(Y_t \le y|\theta_t = j, T > t) / \partial y$.

The conditional hazard (mortality rate) given health status $\theta_t = j$, and unconditional transition intensity functions can be represented as follows:

$$\bar{\mu}_j(t) = \mu_{0j}(t) + (m_j(t) - f_j(t))^* Q_j(t)(m_j(t) - f_j(t)) + Tr(Q_j(t)\gamma_j(t)) \quad (19.15)$$

$$\bar{\lambda}_{jk}(t) = \lambda_{0jk}(t) + (m_j(t) - g_j(t))^* \Lambda_{jk}(t)(m_j(t) - g_j(t)) + Tr(\Lambda_{jk}(t)\gamma_j(t)) \quad (19.16)$$

where $m_j(t) = E(Y_t|\theta_t = j, T > t)$, and $\gamma_j(t) = E((Y_t - m_j(t))(Y_t - m_j(t))^*|\theta_t = j, T > t)$.

These conditional moments satisfy the following ordinary differential equations:

$$\begin{aligned} \frac{dm_j(t)}{dt} &= \sum_i \frac{\pi_i(t)}{\pi_j(t)}\left[m_{ij}(t)\bar{\lambda}_{ij}(t) - 2\gamma_i(t)\Lambda_{ij}(t)\,\hat{g}_i(t)\right] \\ &\quad - a_j(t)\hat{f}_{1j}(t) + 2\gamma_j(t)Q_j(t)\hat{f}_j(t), \end{aligned} \quad (19.17)$$

$$\begin{aligned} \frac{d\gamma_j(t)}{dt} &= \sum_i \frac{\pi_i(t)}{\pi_j(t)}\Big[\left(\gamma_i(t) - \gamma_j(t) + m_{ij}(t)m_{ij}^*(t)\right)\bar{\lambda}_{ij}(t) \\ &\quad + 2\left(\gamma_i(t)\Lambda_{ij}(t)\gamma_i(t) - \gamma_i(t)\Lambda_{ij}(t)\hat{g}_i(t)m_{ij}^*(t) - m_{ij}(t)\hat{g}_i^*(t)\Lambda_{ij}(t)\gamma_i(t)\right)\Big] \\ &\quad + a_j(t)\gamma_j(t) + \gamma_j(t)a_j^*(t) + B_j(t) - 2\gamma_j(t)Q_j(t)\gamma_j(t). \end{aligned} \quad (19.18)$$

Here $\bar{\lambda}_{ij}(t)$ is given by (19.15), $m_{ij} = m_i - m_j$, "hat" variables are defined as $\hat{f}_j = f_j - m_j$, $\hat{f}_{1j} = f_{1j} - m_j$, $\hat{g}_i = g_i - m_i$.

After these transformations, the likelihood function (19.4) becomes a function of parameters determining dynamic properties of Eqs. (19.9) and (19.15, 19.16, 19.17, and 19.18). The fact that all these parameters have a clear biological interpretation is an important advantage of our model compared to other parametric models of mortality used in demographic applications. There is a price for having proper interpretation, however: the Eqs. (19.9), (19.17), (19.18) do not have an explicit analytical solution. Therefore they have to be solved numerically at each step of the likelihood maximization procedure.

Observational Plans

The parameters describing mortality rate in (19.5) also characterize properties of Eqs. (19.9) and (19.11), or (19.9), (19.17), and (19.18). Since the number of such parameters could be large, the survival data alone may be not sufficient to make the model's parameters identifiable. The use of additional data on the processes affecting life span distribution may improve the situation. Since theoretical results on the effects of additional observations on the accuracy of parameter estimates in this model are not available, we performed simulation study to investigate how the use of different observational plans affects the quality of the estimation procedure. We distinguish among three different observational plans. The plan #1 is characterized by discrete-time observations of continuously changing physiological variables. In this plan the changes in health status are unobserved. In the plan #2 physiological variables are not measured, but health transitions are observed. The plan #3 is characterized by availability of both plan #1 and plan #2 data, i.e., measurements of physiological state and a sequence of health transitions data are available for each individual. The results of our simulation experiments showed that observational plan #3 provides enough information for identifying model parameters. Here we will describe the likelihood function of the data for observational plan #3, outline an approach to parameter estimation, and show the results of analyses of longitudinal data for the original cohort in the Framingham Heart Study.

Discrete Time Observations of Physiological State and Health Transitions

Let us assume that continuously changing variables are measured at ages $t_0, t_1, t_2 \ldots, t_n; t_n \le T$. Denote by $Y_0^t = \{Y_{t_0}, Y_{t_1}, Y_{t_2}, \ldots, Y_{t_n}; t_n \le t < T\}$ the random vector of observations of Y_t at these ages. It follows from these notations that $Y_0^{t_k-} = Y_0^{t_{k-1}}$, and $Y_0^t = Y_0^{t_k}$, if $t_k \le t < t_{k+1}$. Here $t_k - = \lim_{u \uparrow t_k} u$. Let $\tau_1, \tau_2, \ldots, \tau_m$ be ages at which changes in person's health status took place (jump-times of the process θ_t) and $\theta_0^t = \{\theta(t_0), \theta(\tau_1), \theta(\tau_2), \ldots, \theta(\tau_m), t_m \le t < T\}$ be the health history of the process up to time t. Let $\bar{f}(y,t) = \frac{\partial}{\partial y} P\left(Y_t \le y \middle| Y_0^t, \theta_0^t, T > t\right)$ be conditional probability density function of Y_t given observations Y_0^t, θ_0^t, and $\{T > t\}$. Using standard Bayesian arguments one can show that this function satisfies the following equation at the intervals between subsequent observations

$$\begin{aligned}\frac{\partial}{\partial t}\bar{f}(y,t) &= -\frac{\partial}{\partial y}\left(A_{\theta_t}(y,t)\bar{f}(y,t)\right) + \frac{1}{2}\frac{\partial^2}{\partial y^2}\left(B_{\theta_t}(t)\bar{f}(y,t)\right) \\ &+ \bar{f}(y,t)\left(\sum_{k=1,k\ne\theta_{t-}}^{M} \bar{\lambda}_{\theta_{t-},k}(t) - \sum_{k=1,k\ne\theta_{t-}}^{M} \lambda_{\theta_{t-},k}(y,t)\right) \\ &+ \bar{f}(y,t)\left(\bar{\mu}_{\theta_{t-}}(t) - \mu_{\theta_{t-}}(y,t)\right) \qquad (19.19)\end{aligned}$$

The presence of two selection terms on the right side of Eq. (19.19) is easy to understand because at the interval $[t_0, \tau_1)$ $\bar{f}(y,t) = \frac{\partial}{\partial y} P\left(Y_t \le y \middle| \tau_1 > t, T > t\right)$, and similarly at other intervals between jumps of θ_t. To avoid multiple hierarchical indexing we will use notation $\theta_t \equiv \theta(t)$. The initial conditions at the beginning of each interval $[\tau_1,\tau_2),[\tau_2,\tau_3),\ldots,[\tau_m,T)$ are

$$\widehat{f}(y,\tau_p)=\widehat{f}(y,\tau_p-)\frac{\lambda_{\theta(\tau_p-),\theta(\tau_p)}(y,\tau_p-)}{\widehat{\lambda}_{\theta(\tau_p-),\theta(\tau_p)}(\tau_p-)} \tag{19.20}$$

Here $\widehat{f}(y,\tau_p-)=\frac{\partial}{\partial y}P\left(Y_{\tau_p}\le y\middle|Y_0^{\tau_p},\theta_0^{\tau_{p-1}},T>\tau_p\right)$ is the solution of Eq. (19.19) at the interval $[\tau_{p-1},\tau_p)$ at the time just before the *p-th* jump of the process θ_t at time τ_p, $\widehat{\lambda}_{\theta_{t-},k}(t)$ and $\widehat{\mu}_{\theta_{t-}}(t)$ are

$$\widehat{\lambda}_{\theta_{t-},k}(t)=E\left(\lambda_{\theta_{t-},k}(Y_t,t)\middle|Y_0^t,\theta_0^{t-},T>t\right) \tag{19.21}$$

and

$$\widehat{\mu}_{\theta_{t-}}(t)=E\left(\mu_{\theta_{t-}}(Y_t,t)\middle|Y_0^t,\theta_0^{t-},T>t\right) \tag{19.22}$$

at each interval resulted from combining and ordering two sequences $t_1,t_2,\ldots,t_n$ and $\tau_1,\tau_2,\ldots,\tau_m$. If the interval starts with t_k, then Eq. (19.19) for $\widehat{f}(y,t)$ have to be used with initial condition

$$\widehat{f}(y_{t_k},t_k)=\delta(y-y_{t_k}) \tag{19.23}$$

If the interval starts with τ_p then these equations have to be used with initial conditions

$$\widehat{f}(y,\tau_p)=\widehat{f}(y,\tau_p-)\frac{\lambda_{\theta(\tau_p-),\theta(\tau_p)}(y,\tau_p)}{\widehat{\lambda}_{\theta(\tau_p-),\theta(\tau_p)}(\tau_p)} \tag{19.24}$$

where

$$\widehat{\lambda}_{\theta(\tau_p-),\theta(\tau_p)}(\tau_p)=E\left(\lambda_{\theta(\tau_p-),x}(Y_{\tau_p},\tau_p)\middle|Y_0^{\tau_p},\theta_0^{\tau_p-},T>\tau_p\right)\Big|_{x=\theta(\tau_p)} \tag{19.25}$$

For the *i-th* individual the process Y_t is measured at $t_0^i,t_1^i,t_2^i,\ldots,t_{n(i)}^i$, with recorded values: $y_{t_1^i}^i,y_{t_2^i}^i,\ldots,y_{t_{n(i)}^i}^i$. Here $t_{n(i)}^i$ is the last measurement of physiological state for individual *i* before death or censoring. The values of process θ_t are recorded at times $t_0^i,\tau_1^i,\tau_2^i,\ldots,\tau_{m(i)}^i$, with values: $\theta^i(t_0^i),\theta^i(\tau_1^i),\theta^i(\tau_2^i),\ldots,\theta^i(\tau_{m(i)}^i)$, $t_{n(i)}^i<T_i$, and $\tau_{m(i)}^i<T_i$, where $\tau_{m(i)}^i$ is the time of last jump of the health transition process θ_t before death or censoring. Each individual is characterized by the ordered sequence of ages at which different measurements took place. For example, for the *i-th* individual the sequence, $t_0^i,t_1^i,t_2^i,\tau_1^i,t_3^i,\tau_2^i,\tau_3^i,t_4^i,\ldots,\tau_{m(i)}^i$, indicates that the first health transition happened between the second and third measurements of physiological state, the second and third health transitions occurred between the third and forth physiological measurements, etc. It is clear that such sequences could be different for different study participants. Note that in our model $P(\tau_k=t_r)=0$ for any *k* and *r*.

An example of likelihood function for *i-th* individual with observations occurred at a sequence of times $t_1^i, t_2^i, \tau_1^i, t_3^i, \tau_2^i, \tau_3^i, \ldots, \tau_{m(i)}^i, t_{n(i)}^i, T^i$ in case of observational plan #3 is:

$$
\begin{aligned}
&\widehat{L}_i(y_{t_1^i}^i, y_{t_2^i}^i, \ldots, y_{t_{n(i)}^i}^i, \theta^i(\tau_1^i), \theta^i(\tau_2^i), \ldots, \theta^i(\tau_{m(i)}^i), T_i) \\
&= \widehat{f}\left(y_{t_1^i}, t_1^i -\right)\widehat{f}\left(y_{t_2^i}, t_2^i -\right)\widehat{f}\left(y_{\tau_1^i}, \tau_1^i -\right)\widehat{f}\left(y_{t_3^i}, t_3^i -\right)\widehat{f}\left(y_{\tau_2^i}, \tau_2^i -\right) \\
&\widehat{f}\left(y_{\tau_3^i}, \tau_3^i -\right)\ldots\widehat{f}\left(y_{s^i}, s^i -\right) \times p(\theta^i(t_0^i))\prod_{p=1}^{m(i)}\widehat{\lambda}_{\theta^i(\tau_p^i -), \theta^i(\tau_p^i)}(\tau_p^i) \\
&\widehat{\mu}_{\theta^i(T_i)}(T_i)^{\delta_i}\exp\left\{-\int_{t_0^i}^{T_i}\left(\sum_{k=1, k\neq\theta^i(t-)}^{M}\widehat{\lambda}_{\theta^i(t-), k}(t) + \widehat{\mu}_{\theta^i(t-)}(t)\right)dt\right\}
\end{aligned}
\tag{19.26}
$$

Here $s^i = \max\left\{t_{n(i)}^i, \tau_{m(i)}^i\right\}$, and M is the number of states of the process θ_t, $\widehat{f}(y, t_k^i -) = \frac{\partial}{\partial y}P\left(Y_{t_k^i} \leq y \middle| Y_0^{t_k^i -}, \theta_0^{t_k^i -}, T > t_k^i\right)$ is the solution of Eq. (19.19) either at the interval $[\tau_p^i, t_k^i)$, or at the interval $[t_{k-1}^i, t_k^i)$, assuming that these intervals do not contain other observations; $\widehat{f}(y, \tau_k^i -) = \frac{\partial}{\partial y}P\left(Y_{\tau_k^i} \leq y \middle| Y_0^{\tau_k^i -}, \theta_0^{\tau_k^i -}, T > \tau_k^i\right)$ is the solution of Eq. (19.19) either at the interval $[\tau_{k-1}^i, \tau_k^i)$, or at the interval $[t_{k-1}^i, \tau_k^i)$, assuming that these intervals do not contain other observations.

Gaussian Approximation

Let $\widehat{m}(t) = E\left(Y_t \middle| Y_0^t, \theta_0^t, T > t\right)$ and $\widehat{\gamma}(t) = E\left((Y_t - \widehat{m}(t))(Y_t - \widehat{m}(t))^* \middle| Y_0^t, \theta_0^t, T > t\right)$ be the first two moments of the conditional probability density function $\widehat{f}(y, t) = \frac{\partial}{\partial y}P\left(Y_t \leq y \middle| \widetilde{Y}_0^t, \theta_0^t, T > t\right)$. These moments satisfy equations

$$
\frac{d\widehat{m}_j(t)}{dt} = -a_j(t)\widehat{f}_{1j}(t) + \sum_{k\neq j}2\widehat{\gamma}_j(t)\Lambda_{jk}(t)\widehat{g}_j(t) + 2\widehat{\gamma}_j(t)Q_j(t)\widehat{f}_j(t),
\tag{19.27}
$$

$$
\begin{aligned}
\frac{d\widehat{\gamma}_j(t)}{dt} &= a_j(t)\widehat{\gamma}_j(t) + \widehat{\gamma}_j(t)a_j^*(t) + B_j(t) \\
&\quad - \sum_{k\neq j}2\widehat{\gamma}_j(t)\Lambda_{jk}(t)\widehat{\gamma}_j(t) - 2\widehat{\gamma}_j(t)Q_j(t)\widehat{\gamma}_j(t).
\end{aligned}
\tag{19.28}
$$

Here we use index j to indicate dependence of these moments on the value of the process θ_t at time t. Strictly speaking, these moments depend on the entire trajectory of θ_t at the interval $[t_0, t)$. Equations (19.27) and (19.28) have to be solved at the intervals $[\tau_1, \tau_2), [\tau_2, \tau_3), \ldots, [\tau_m, T)$, i.e., between subsequent jumps of the process θ_t. When $\theta(\tau_p-)=k$ and $\theta^i(\tau_p)=j$, and $\lambda_{kj}(Y_t,t)$ is described by (19.11), we have for the initial values $\widehat{m}_j(\tau_p)$ and $\widehat{\gamma}_j(\tau_p)$:

$$\widehat{m}_j(\tau_p)=\widehat{m}_k(\tau_p-)-\frac{2\widehat{\gamma}_k(\tau_p-)\Lambda_{kj}(\tau_p)\widehat{g}_k(\tau_p-)}{\widehat{\lambda}_{kj}(\tau_p-)} \tag{19.29}$$

$$\widehat{\gamma}_j(\tau_p)=\widehat{\gamma}_k(\tau_p-)+\frac{2\widehat{\gamma}_k(\tau_p-)\Lambda_{kj}(\tau_p)\widehat{\gamma}_k(\tau_p-)}{\widehat{\lambda}_{kj}(\tau_p-)} \tag{19.30}$$

with

$$\widehat{g}_k(\tau_p-)=g_k(\tau_p)-\widehat{m}_k(\tau_p-) \tag{19.31}$$

and

$$\widehat{\lambda}_{kj}(t)=\lambda_{0kj}(t)+\left(\widehat{m}_k(t)-g_k(t)\right)^*\Lambda_{kj}(t)\left(\widehat{m}_k(t)-g_k(t)\right)+Tr\left(\Lambda_{kj}(t)\widehat{\gamma}_k(t)\right) \tag{19.32}$$

at each interval resulted from combining and ordering $t_1, t_2, \ldots, t_n$ and $\tau_1, \tau_2, \ldots, \tau_m$.

If the interval starts with t_k, then Eq. (19.27) for $\widehat{m}(t)$ start with initial condition $\widehat{m}(t_k)=y_{t_k}$ and for $\widehat{\gamma}(t)$ with condition $\widehat{\gamma}(t_k)=0$. If the interval starts with τ_p then Eq. (19.27) start with initial condition Eq. (19.29) and Eq. (19.28) with condition (19.30). The likelihood function of the data for the *i-th* individual in case of observational plan #3 is

$$\begin{aligned}
&\widehat{L}_i^G(y^i_{t^i_1}, y^i_{t^i_2}, \ldots, y^i_{t^i_{n(i)}}, \theta^i(\tau^i_1), \theta^i(\tau^i_2), \ldots, \theta^i(\tau^i_{m(i)}), T_i)\\
&=\prod_{j=1}^{n(i)+m(i)}\left(\left(2\pi\left|\widehat{\gamma}^i(u^i_{t^i_j}-1)\right|\right)^{-\frac{K}{2}}\exp\left\{-\frac{1}{2}\left(y^i_{u^i_j}-\widehat{m}^i(u^i_j-)\right)^*\widehat{\gamma}^i_k(u^i_{t^i_j}-)^{-1}\left(y^i_{t^i_j}-\widehat{m}^i(u^i_j-)\right)\right\}\right)\\
&\times p(\theta^i(t^i_0))\prod_{p=1}^{m(i)}\widehat{\lambda}_{\theta^i(\tau^i_p-),\theta^i(\tau^i_p)}(\tau^i_p)\widehat{\mu}_{\theta^i(T_i)}(T_i)^{\delta_i}\\
&\exp\left\{-\int_{t^i_0}^{T_i}\left(\sum_{k=1,k\neq\theta^i(t-)}\widehat{\lambda}_{\theta^i(t-),k}(t)+\widehat{\mu}_{\theta^i(t-)}(t)\right)t\right\}
\end{aligned} \tag{19.33}$$

Here $u^i_k, k=1,2,\ldots,n(i)+m(i)$ is the element of an ordered sequence combined from $t^i_1, t^i_2, \ldots, t^i_{n(i)}$ and $\tau^i_1, \tau^i_2, \ldots, \tau^i_{m(i)}$. If the interval starts with t^i_k then Eqs. (19.27) and (19.28) start with initial conditions $m_{t^i_k}=y_{t^i_k}, \gamma_{t^i_k}=0$. If the interval starts with τ^i_p then Eqs. (19.27) and (19.28) start with initial conditions (19.29), (19.30).

$$\widehat{\mu}(t)=\mu_0(t)+\left(\widehat{m}(t)-f_j(t)\right)^*Q_j(t)\left(\widehat{m}(t)-f_j(t)\right)+Tr\left(Q_j(t)\widehat{\gamma}(t)\right) \tag{19.34}$$

The transition intensities $\widehat{\lambda}_{kj}(t)$ are:

$$\widehat{\lambda}_{kj}(t)=\lambda_{0kj}(t)+\left(\widehat{m}(t)-g_k(t)\right)^*\Lambda_{kj}(t)\left(\widehat{m}(t)-g_k(t)\right)+Tr\left(\Lambda_{kj}(t)\widehat{\gamma}(t)\right) \tag{19.35}$$

Note that the approach described above can be used for joint analyses of data collected using different observational plans (here plans #1 and #2).

Application to Framingham Heart Study Data

The developed model is capable of describing data collected in the original cohort of the Framingham Heart Study (Dawber 1980). Each study participant could be characterized by a continuously changing physiological index Y_t, whose dynamics are described by the stochastic differential equations (19.14), and are in one of two (healthy, or unhealthy) discrete states. Also we assumed that individual mortality rates (state specific) and incidence rate can be described by the quadratic hazard models (19.13) and (19.12), respectively. Thus, we considered process θ_t with two states (healthy [marked by '*H*'] and unhealthy [marked by '*D*' (diseased)]). The following specifications for model parameters in Eq. (19.14) were made: (i) time and age independence of parameters describing the dynamics in both states, i.e., a_H, a_D, b_H, b_D, (ii) quadratic age dependence for f_{1H}, and f_{1D}, e.g., $f_{1H} = f_{1H0} + f_{1H1}(age-50) + f_{1H2}(age-50)^2$, (iii) the Gompertz function for $\mu_{0i}(t) = \mu_{0i}\exp(\alpha_i t)$, $i = H, D$, and for $\lambda_{0HD}(t) = \lambda_{0HD}\exp(\alpha_{HD}t)$, and (iv) time independence of other parameters describing transition probabilities, i.e., Q_H, Q_D, f_H, f_D, Λ_{HD} and g_H. Here f_{1H}, f_{1D}, f_H, f_D, g_H, b_H, and b_D are in the units of the used covariate (e.g., mmHg for blood pressure), a_H, a_D, μ_{0H}, α_H, μ_{0D}, α_D, λ_{0HD}, and α_{HD} are in year^{-1}, and, finally, Q_H, Q_D, and Λ_{HD} are in year^{-1} multiplied by the reciprocal of the covariate unit squared.

Four calculations corresponding to a different choice of a covariate were performed. These include: (i) pulse pressure, (ii) diastolic blood pressure (DBP), (iii) serum cholesterol, and (iv) hematocrit. In all these cases CVD was considered as a disease characterizing unhealthy state. Missing data in covariate trajectories were filled using linear interpolation. The mean time period between evaluated covariates was 1 year.

The estimation scheme based on maximization of the likelihood (19.33) was applied. Some useful specifications of the likelihood to simplify the programming of optimization procedure using SAS Proc NLP are as follows. For the case of two discrete states (healthy and unhealthy) the likelihood function (19.33) can be represented as a product of terms whose functional forms depend on the type of observational events forming respective age intervals. These events are associated with: (i) measurements of physiological state, (ii) changes in health status, and (iii) transitions to death/censoring. There are five types of such interval-specific contributions:

Measurement → Measurement $\quad \bar{\bar{f}}\left(y_{t_k}, t_{k-1}, t_k -\right) S_c(t_{k-1}, t_k)$ for $c = H, D$

Measurement → Jumping (HD) $\quad \bar{\bar{\lambda}}_{HD}(\tau) S_H(t_k, \tau)$

Measurement → Death/censoring $\quad \bar{\bar{\mu}}_c(T)^{\delta_i} S_c(t_k, T)$ for $c = H, D$

Jumping → Measurement $\quad \bar{\bar{f}}\left(y_{t_k},\tau,t_k-\right)S_D(\tau,t_k)$

Jumping → Death/censoring $\quad \bar{\bar{\mu}}_D(T)^{\delta_i}\, S_D(\tau,T)$

Here

$$S_H(t_{k-1},t_k)=\exp\left\{-\int_{t_{k-1}}^{t_k}\left(\bar{\bar{\lambda}}_{HD}(t)+{}_H(t)\right)dt\right\},\ S_D\left(t_{k-1},t_k\right)=\exp\left\{-\int_{t_{k-1}}^{t_k}(\bar{\bar{\mu}}_D(t))dt\right\},$$

$$S_D(\tau,t_k)=\exp\left\{-\int_{\tau}^{t_k}(\bar{\bar{\mu}}_D(t))dt\right\}.\ S_H(t_k,\tau)=\exp\left\{-\int_{t_k}^{\tau}\left(\bar{\bar{\lambda}}_{HD}(t)+\bar{\bar{\mu}}_H(t)\right)dt\right\},$$

and

$$\bar{\bar{f}}\left(y_{t_k},u,t_k-\right)=\left(2\pi\left|\bar{\bar{\gamma}}\,(t_k-)\right|\right)^{-\frac{1}{2}}\exp\left\{-\frac{1}{2}\left(y_{t_k}-\bar{\bar{m}}\,(t_k-)\right)^{*}\bar{\bar{\gamma}}\,(t_k-)^{-1}\left(y_{t_k}-\bar{\bar{m}}\,(t_k-)\right)\right\},$$

$c=H,$ *if* $t_k<\tau;$ and $c=D,$ *if* $t_{k-1}>\tau;$ $\bar{\bar{m}}(t)$ and $\bar{\bar{\gamma}}(t)$, are obtained as solutions of (19.27) and (19.28), with initial conditions $\bar{\bar{m}}(\tau)=\bar{\bar{m}}(\tau-)-\dfrac{2\bar{\bar{\gamma}}(\tau-)\Lambda_{HD}g(\tau-)}{\bar{\bar{\lambda}}_{HD}(\tau-)}$ and $\bar{\bar{\gamma}}(\tau)=\bar{\bar{\gamma}}(\tau-)+\dfrac{2\bar{\bar{\gamma}}^2(\tau-)\Lambda_{HD}(\tau-)}{\bar{\bar{\lambda}}_{HD}(\tau-)}$ if interval starts with τ. When the interval starts with t_k the initial conditions are: $m(t_k)=y_{t_k},\gamma(t_k)=0.$

The results of parameter estimation are presented in Table 19.1.

The empirical estimates of age-specific means of a covariate and three hazard rates were compared with the theoretical two-stage model, which can be specified for these two stages as follows. The conditional hazard (mortality rate) given health status and unconditional transition intensity functions (19.12, 19.13) are specified as:

$$\begin{aligned}\bar{\mu}_H(t)&=\mu_{0H}(t)+\left(m_H(t)-f_H(t)\right)^2Q_H(t)+Q_H(t)\gamma_H(t),\\ \bar{\mu}_D(t)&=\mu_{0D}(t)+\left(m_D(t)-f_D(t)\right)^2Q_D(t)+Q_D(t)\gamma_D(t),\end{aligned}\tag{19.36}$$

$$\bar{\lambda}_{HD}(t)=\lambda_{0HD}(t)+\left(m_H(t)-g_H(t)\right)^2\Lambda_{HD}(t)+\Lambda_{HD}(t)\gamma_H(t)\tag{19.37}$$

The differential equations for the conditional moments become:

$$\frac{dm_H(t)}{dt}=2\gamma_H(t)\Lambda_{HD}(t)\hat{g}_H(t)-a_H(t)\hat{f}_{1H}(t)+2\gamma_H(t)Q_H(t)\hat{f}_H(t),\tag{19.38}$$

$$\begin{aligned}\frac{dm_D(t)}{dt}&=\frac{\pi_H(t)}{\pi_D(t)}\left[m_{HD}(t)\bar{\lambda}_{HD}-2\gamma_H(t)\Lambda_{HD}\hat{g}_H(t)\right]\\ &\quad-a_D(t)\hat{f}_{1D}(t)+2\gamma_D(t)Q_D(t)\hat{f}_D(t),\end{aligned}\tag{19.39}$$

$$\frac{d\gamma_H(t)}{dt}=-2\gamma_H^2(t)\Lambda_{HD}(t)+2a_H(t)\gamma_H(t)+b_H^2(t)-2\gamma_H^2(t)Q_H(t).\tag{19.40}$$

Table 19.1 The results of estimating model parameters for the four covariates

		Pulse pressure	DBP	Serum cholesterol	Hematocrit
a_H	Year^{-1}	−0.053	−0.059	−0.033	−0.050
a_D	Year^{-1}	−0.049	−0.056	−0.017	−0.029
b_H	[C]	23.6	12.9	119.5	1.5
b_D	[C]	35.3	15.5	83.0	1.2
f_{1H0}	[C]	59.2	82.6	270.0	46.8
f_{1H1}	Year^{-1}[C]	1.55	−0.067	−3.65	−0.11
f_{1H2}	Year^{-2}[C]	−0.027	−0.017	0.012	−0.0024
f_{1D0}	[C]	57.6	81.4	248.1	49.2
f_{1D1}	Year^{-1}[C]	2.41	−0.71	−10.1	−0.47
f_{1D2}	Year^{-2}[C]	−0.060	0.00095	0.20	0.0052
$\mu_{0H} \times 10^5$	Year^{-1}	0.59	0.36	0.54	0.33
α_H	Year^{-1}	0.11	0.12	0.11	0.12
$\mu_{0D} \times 10^5$	Year^{-1}	6.99	7.00	13.7	9.63
α_D	Year^{-1}	0.088	0.087	0.080	0.085
$Q_H \times 10^5$	$\text{Year}^{-1}[\text{C}]^{-2}$	0.39	1.25	0.033	10.1
$Q_D \times 10^5$	$\text{Year}^{-1}[\text{C}]^{-2}$	1.28	5.61	0.10	22.9
$\lambda_{0HD} \times 10^5$	Year^{-1}	46.0	35.6	56.2	49.1
α_{HD}	Year^{-1}	0.049	0.057	0.051	0.052
$\Lambda_{HD} \times 10^5$	$\text{Year}^{-1}[\text{C}]^{-2}$	0.68	1.05	0.028	5.07
f_H	[C]	59.8	78.0	281.8	43.6
f_D	[C]	75.8	82.2	222.4	43.7
g_H	[C]	33.3	70.7	185.3	37.7

[C] denotes dimensionality of a covariate: pulse pressure and DBP are measured in millimeters of mercury (mmHg), serum cholesterol is measured in mg/100 ml, and hematocrit is measured in percentages

$$\begin{aligned}\frac{d\gamma_D(t)}{dt} &= \frac{\pi_H(t)}{\pi_D(t)}\Big[\big(\gamma_H(t)-\gamma_D(t)+m_{HD}^2(t)\big)\bar{\lambda}_{HD}(t)\\ &\quad +2\big(\gamma_H^2(t)\Lambda_{HD}(t)-2\gamma_H(t)\Lambda_{HD}(t)\hat{g}_H(t)\cdot m_{HD}(t)\big)\Big]\\ &\quad +2a_D(t)\gamma_D(t)+b_D^2(t)-2\gamma_D^2(t)Q_D(t).\end{aligned} \tag{19.41}$$

and finally, the equations for the conditional probabilities of being in healthy and unhealthy states are:

$$\begin{aligned}\frac{d\pi_H(t)}{dt} &= -\pi_H(t)\bar{\lambda}_{HD}(t)+\pi_H(t)\big(\pi_H(t)\bar{\mu}_H(t)+\pi_D(t)\bar{\mu}_D(t)-\bar{\mu}_H(t)\big),\\ \frac{d\pi_D(t)}{dt} &= \pi_H(t)\bar{\lambda}_{HD}(t)+\pi_D(t)\big(\pi_H(t)\bar{\mu}_H(t)+\pi_D(t)\bar{\mu}_D(t)-\bar{\mu}_D(t)\big).\end{aligned} \tag{19.42}$$

Here $m_{HD}(t)=m_H(t)-m_D(t)$.

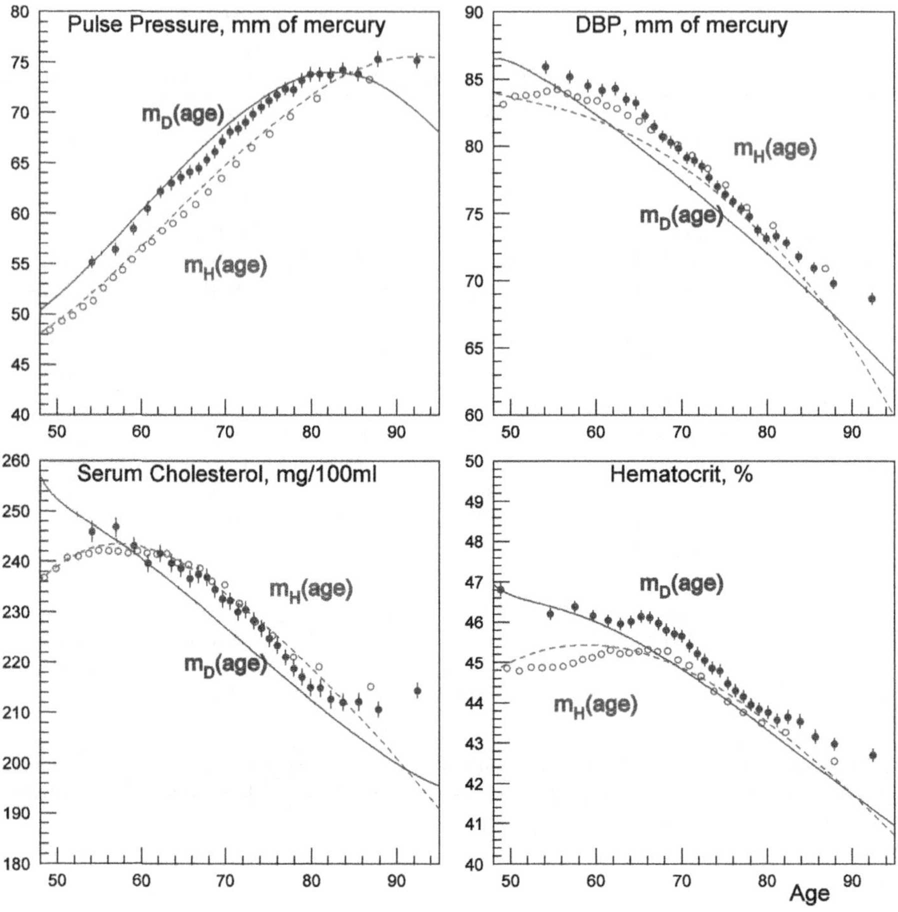

Fig. 19.1 Empirical estimates (*closed dots* for unhealthy state and *open dots* for healthy state with error bars) and theoretical predictions using models with estimated parameters (*solid lines* for unhealthy state and *dashed line* for healthy state) for age patterns of first moments for healthy and disease states, $m_H(t)$, and $m_D(t)$ for four different covariates (DBP, serum cholesterol, hematocrit, and pulse pressure)

Figures 19.1 and 19.2 illustrate the quality of data reproduction for average age patterns of dynamic covariates and the risks of mortality and disease onset specified by the model with estimated parameters. Specifically, they compare theoretical curves, corresponding to equations derived above and calculated with parameters used in data simulation procedure, and the age patterns of respective characteristics in cohorts empirically estimated using FHS data.

One can see from these figures that age patterns of characteristics produced by theoretical model with parameters estimated from the data mainly correspond to empirical estimates of these characteristics.

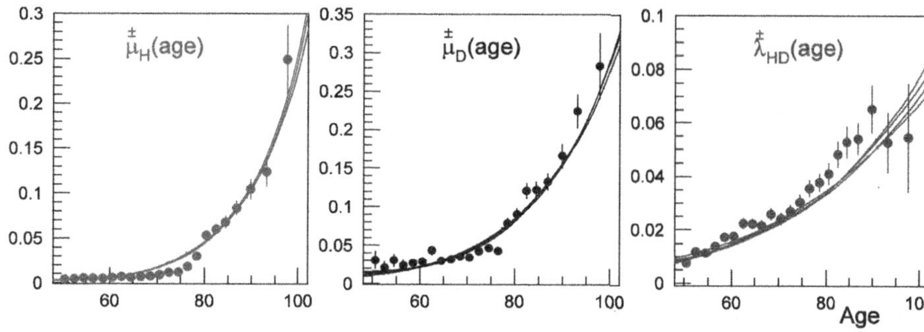

Fig. 19.2 Empirical estimates (*dots* with error bars) and theoretical predictions (*solid lines*) for age patterns of mortality rates from healthy and unhealthy states and transition rate from healthy to unhealthy states. *Different lines* at the same plots correspond to four different dynamic covariates (DBP, serum cholesterol, hematocrit, and pulse pressure). These lines are practically identical for both mortality rates (from healthy and from diseased states). For incidence rate (transition rate from healthy to diseased state) the lines correspond to (from the *top* to *bottom* in the region of advanced ages): DBP, serum cholesterol, hematocrit, and pulse pressure

Discussion

The possibility of postponing or slowing down aging in humans might contribute to the increase in healthy and productive lives, if the individual aging process contributes to development of chronic conditions. That is why the connection between human aging and development of chronic conditions is one of the crucial research questions that gerontologists address today (Le Bourg and Rattan 2010; Yashin 2010). To evaluate this connection, one has to investigate the joint evolution of a system of indices representing aging-related changes in humans and indicators of human health. Such joint evolution is represented in a number of datasets collected in longitudinal studies of aging, health, and longevity. A good example of such a dataset is given by the Framingham Heart Study, in which data on the original cohort contain the results of biannual examinations of physiological state, biological indicators, and ages at onset of a number of chronic conditions, such as cardiovascular disease, cancer, and type 2 Diabetes Mellitus, performed over more than 60 years. The progress in this field depends to a large extent on the possibility of joint analyses of large amounts of data describing the processes of aging-related changes and disease development. Such analyses require appropriate mathematical description of such processes and efficient statistical methods for estimating parameters of respective processes from available longitudinal data. The results of this study indicate that comprehensive analyses of available longitudinal data on human aging, health, and longevity can be successfully performed.

The results of this study open a new avenue in analyzing age patterns of human mortality curves by providing a new parametric description of mortality models.

The parameters of mortality models used in demographic and actuarial applications cannot be properly interpreted to characterize aging-related decline in health status or changes in physiological or other indices affecting chances of death. Despite the existing practice to use mortality rates (survival functions) for comparing effects of different interventions in experimental studies of aging, the results of such comparisons are often controversial and have a limited use for biological applications (Yashin et al. 2002). The use of the approach described in this paper allows for estimating model parameters that characterize both age dynamics of physiological variables and changes in health and survival characteristics. To estimate these parameters, one has to use more sophisticated datasets and use more sophisticated estimation algorithms than currently are used in demography, epidemiology, and biostatistics. In contrast to traditional demographic and actuarial models, our model is appropriate to analyses of a wide spectrum of longitudinal data on aging, health, and longevity with health and survival outcomes.

The use of diffusion type continuous time stochastic process for describing evolution of physiological state over the life course allows us to take recent findings in the area of aging into account and to incorporate them into the model of aging-related changes in physiological state. The use of finite state continuous time stochastic process with transition rates depending on current value of physiological variable for describing changes in health status during this period captures important connections between aging-related changes and morbidity and mortality risks. We derive equations for respective mortality models and approximate changes in physiological state by the conditional Gaussian process, given the health state. The results of statistical analyses of data show that model parameters can be successfully estimated.

Conclusions

In this paper we showed that developing mortality models in which parameters can be interpreted in terms of aging-related decline in physiological functions and deterioration in health/well-being status requires the use additional longitudinal data. The parameter estimation procedures become computationally more extensive compared to those used in traditional analyses of survival data. The analyses, however, can be successfully performed using modern computers. The reward for these efforts is a better understanding of how changes that are developing in aging human organisms affect risks of diseases and survival. The approach, described and tested above, can be extended to evaluate properties of individualized dynamic mechanisms involved in regulation of aging-related changes in each study participant. These types of analyses will contribute to new scientific knowledge promoting development of personalized preventive and treatment strategies.

References

Akushevich, I., Kulminski, A., & Manton, K. (2005). Life tables with covariates: Dynamic model for nonlinear analysis of longitudinal data, *Mathematical Population Studies, 12*, 51–80.

Arbeev, K. G., Akushevich, I., Kulminski, A. M., Arbeeva, L. S., Akushevich, L., Ukraintseva, S. V., Culminskaya, I. V., & Yashin, A. I. (2009). Genetic model for longitudinal studies of aging, health, and longevity and its potential application to incomplete data. *Journal of Theoretical Biology, 258*, 103–111.

Dawber, T. R. (1980). *The framingham study: The epidemiology of atherosclerotic disease*. Cambridge, MA: Harvard University Press.

Le Bourg, E., & Rattan, S. I. (2010). Is hormesis applicable as a pro-healthy aging intervention in mammals and human beings, and how?: Introduction to a special issue of dose–response. *Dose-Response, 8*(1), 1–3.

Vaupel, J. W., Manton, K. G., & Stallard, E. (1979). The impact of heterogeneity in individual frailty on the dynamics of mortality. *Demography, 16*, 439–454.

Woodbury, M. A., & Manton, K. G. (1977). A random walk model of human mortality and aging. *Theoretical Population Biology, 11*, 37–48.

Yashin, A. I. (1985). Dynamics in survival analysis: Conditional Gaussian property vs. Cameron-Martin formula. In N. V. Krylov, R. S. Lipster, & A. A. Novikov (Eds.), *Statistics and control of stochastic processes* (p. 446). New York: Springer.

Yashin, A. I. (2010). Hormesis against aging and diseases: Using properties of biological adaptation for health and survival improvement. *Dose-Response, 8*(1), 41–47.

Yashin, A. I., & Manton, K. G. (1997). Effects of unobserved and partially observed covariate processes on system failure: A review of models and estimation strategies. *Statistical Science, 12*, 20–34.

Yashin, A. I., Manton, K. G., & Vaupel, J. W. (1985). Mortality and aging in a heterogeneous population: A stochastic process model with observed and unobserved variables. *Theoretical Population Biology, 27*, 154–175.

Yashin, A. I., Manton, K. G., Woodbury, M. A., & Stallard, E. (1995). The effects of health histories on stochastic process models of aging and mortality. *Journal of Mathematical Biology, 34*, 1–16.

Yashin, A. I., Iachine, I. A., & Begun, A. S. (2000). Mortality modeling: A review. *Mathematical Population Studies, 8*(4), 305–332.

Yashin, A. I., Ukraintseva, S. V., Boiko, S. I., & Arbeev, K. G. (2002). Individual aging and mortality rate: How are they related? *Social Biology, 49*(3–4), 206–217. Fall-Winter.

Yashin, A. I., Arbeev, K. G., Akushevich, I., Kulminski, A., Akushevich, L., & Ukraintseva, S. V. (2007). Stochastic model for analysis of longitudinal data on aging and mortality. *Mathematical Biosciences, 208*, 538–551.

Yashin, A. I., Arbeev, K. G., Akushevich, I., Kulminski, A., Akushevich, L., & Ukraintseva, S. V. (2008). Model of hidden heterogeneity in longitudinal data. *Theoretical Population Biology, 73*, 1–10.

Chapter 20
Understanding Society – The UK Household Longitudinal Survey: A Resource for Demographers

Stephanie L. McFall and Nick Buck

Introduction

Many demographers are already familiar with the British Household Panel Survey (BHPS), conducted from 1991 forward (Buck et al. 1994). The BHPS has been heavily used by researchers within and outside the United Kingdom (UK) and by government departments, resulting in more than 150 publications per year. The potential for scientific advance has led to the UK Household Longitudinal Survey-(UKHLS). This new survey was modeled on the BHPS and is the largest and most ambitious panel survey in the world. We describe this new social and health survey and some of the opportunities it offers for research in demography and health.

The household panel design has proved extremely powerful in understanding the dynamics of populations and the determinants of behavior and outcomes at household and individual levels. *Understanding Society* is based on developments in this design going back to the Panel Study of Income Dynamics (PSID) established in the USA in the late 1960s. It forms part of an international network of studies with currently active panels in the USA, Germany, Australia, Switzerland, South Africa, Israel, Canada, Korea, and other countries.

The initial support for *Understanding Society* was raised by the Economic and Social Research Council (ESRC) from the Large Facilities Capital Fund. The Large Facilities Capital Fund supports major scientific infrastructure, e.g., big telescopes. Funding of social science research resources is a recent departure. Additional funding was allocated by the ESRC from resources previously earmarked for a longitudinal study of ethnic minorities. Finally, there is support from a consortium of governmental

S.L. McFall, Ph.D. (✉) • N. Buck, Ph.D.
Institute for Social and Economic Research, University of Essex, Colchester, UK
e-mail: smcfall@essex.ac.uk

N. Hoque et al. (eds.), *Applied Demography and Public Health*,
Applied Demography Series 3, DOI 10.1007/978-94-007-6140-7_20,

© Springer Science+Business Media Dordrecht 2013

departments including the Department of Work and Pensions, the Department for Education, the Department for Transport, the Department of Culture, Media and Sport, the Department for Community and Local Government, the Scottish Government, the Welsh Assembly Government, the Department of Environment and Rural Affairs, and the Food Standards Agency.

The scientific leadership of *Understanding Society* is from the Institute for Social and Economic Research (ISER), University of Essex, with colleagues from the University of Warwick and the Institute of Education. The survey research organizations are National Centre for Social Research (NatCen), a large non-profit organization in London, and the Central Survey Unit of the Northern Ireland Statistics and Research Agency of Belfast.

In establishing *Understanding Society:* the UK Household Longitudinal Study, the ESRC set out the following key aims:

> The Study will provide valuable new evidence about the people of the UK, their lives, experiences, behaviours and beliefs, and will enable an unprecedented understanding of diversity within the population. It will inform research on issues of importance to a wide scientific community of interest and will assist with understanding the long term effects of social and economic change, as well as of policy interventions designed to impact upon the general wellbeing of the UK population. (Background and aims of the UK Household Longitudinal Study, paper for the first meeting of the Governing Board)

First, we briefly summarize the research agenda which may be pursued using *Understanding Society,* with an emphasis on its potential contributions to demography and health. This is followed by a description of the study design and data collection processes. We then describe the data from other sources that will augment the basic survey interviews. We conclude by describing how to access the data.

Research Agenda

Seven attributes shape the research agenda that can be pursued using the UKHLS. The first three features relate to the basic design of the sample for the main survey.

Size of the Survey

The survey's large sample size is a key attribute. The target sample size of 40,000 households (approximately 100,000 persons) supports research for which many other surveys, in particular longitudinal surveys, have been too small. Demographers with applied interests may be interested in the ability to conduct detailed analyses at the regional or sub-regional levels. Many relatively rare events or subpopulations can be studied with the survey. As an example, with approximately 1,000 births per year, it will be possible to study births to teenaged mothers.

A Survey of Households

A second feature is the study's household focus. Demographers have long studied population changes in the composition of households. Households make many key decisions related to consumption and life plans of its members. Household members also shape the behaviors of other members. A focus on households or related concepts of family structure provides a good opportunity to examine these mutual influences. For example, household panel surveys have contributed to the study of resident and non-resident parents and their contributions to outcomes of children (Ermisch 2008). They also permit examination of changing patterns in partnerships, such as dissolution and cohabitation, timings of marriages and births, and repartnering in relation to childbearing and employment outcomes.

A Survey of All Ages

A third feature is that the survey collects data on the full age range. Many other longitudinal studies in the UK are limited to a particular age range or cohort. The English Longitudinal Study of Ageing (Marmot et al. 2003), for example, is of persons aged 50 or older. There are several examples of birth cohort studies, defined with birth years of 1946, 1958 and 1970 (Ferri et al. 2003). The newer Millennium Cohort Study has a sample of children born in 2000 (Dex and Joshi 2005). However, having data from household members of all ages will support a wide range of research and complement analyses conducted with age-specific studies such as the birth cohort studies.

An Emphasis on Ethnicity Research

Understanding Society is also noteworthy for its ability to contribute to the understanding of ethnic minorities. The U.S. has a strong emphasis on race and ethnicity in its country's official statistics and research. However, the UK did not collect census information on ethnicity until 1991 (Bradby 2003). The UK population can be characterized as having a relatively large number of minority groups each with small population shares. Study of ethnic variation in general population surveys requires over-representation, on samples, for minorities.

The UKHLS will provide important new information about ethnic minorities through oversampling of ethnic minorities and the collection of additional measurements relevant to their life experiences. These additional measures are asked of members of the boost sample (oversample), of members of ethnic minority groups not sampled as part of the boost sample, and by a comparison group of around 1,000 adults from the general population sample. Examples of the additional ethnicity-relevant measures include ethnic identity, discrimination and harassment, questions about ethnicity and social networks, and questions about remittances. The overall emphasis is on social and health outcomes of minority group members and on ethnic identity.

The questionnaire instruments and survey materials have been translated into nine languages: Bengali, Punjabi in Urdu and Gurmukhi scripts, Welsh, Arabic, Somali, Cantonese, Urdu, and Gujarati. Software development of the Language Management Utility (LMU) (Harkness 2005) supports the work of multiple translators and is important for the CAPI scripting of non-Roman scripts and languages not read left to right. In the translated interviews, interviewers can toggle between English and the alternative questionnaire.

Novel Measures and Methods of Data Collection

The fifth and sixth features relate to the augmentation of conventional interview data with novel data collection methods and measures. The fifth feature is the combination of conventional interviewing with other data collection methods. Applied demographers may be particularly interested in the ability to make use of spatial data and linked administrative data. These data sources will be described in section "Links to Other Types of Data".

An Innovation Panel of approximately 1,500 households is a testbed for research related to longitudinal survey methods. It is intended to guide decisions about the study and contribute to longitudinal survey research methods in a realistic survey context similar to the general *Understanding Society* design. Some of the research conducted with the Innovation Panel has included methodological experiments on incentives, alternative question working, and the use of dependent interviewing on measures of change (Burton et al. 2008).

Collection of Biomeasures

The sixth feature is the collection of a relatively wide range of biomeasures and other health indicators. The study has been designed to support biomedical and social science research. Health scientists will find the study a rich source of information about social and economic factors that may influence health status at a single time point or may influence the trajectory of health outcomes. The particular markers included are relevant to risks of cardiovascular and metabolic conditions including diabetes and obesity, which are health problems of high policy interest as well as leading contributors to mortality and morbidity. Social scientists may wish to evaluate the effects of objective health measures on social resources and attainments. For example, there is utility to having objective health measures not influenced by the individual's life circumstances, in contrast to self-reported health measures. There is also substantial interest in gene-environment linkages as potential explanations of behavior and disease etiology (Moffitt et al. 2006; Hobcraft 2009).

A Multi-topic Survey

The combination of these features and a wide ranging process of consultation has contributed to a survey that will support broad ranging multidisciplinary and interdisciplinary research. The research agenda of household panel studies has in the past focused particularly on issues of family dynamics and household organisation, household income and welfare, and labor market participation. The agenda has become broader, focusing on other issues including health and well-being, social participation, and a range of other behaviours. *Understanding Society* is extending this agenda yet further with for example questions tapping psychological attributes and attitudes related to environmental behaviors. As a multitopic survey aiming to support this broad range of research agendas, there is a clear need to prioritize measures within the questionnaires. Measures were selected to be useful in describing and explaining change at the individual and household levels and to provide breadth and balance of coverage in topic. The long-term content plan has questions that are asked each year, and question modules that rotate on various schedules. Questions are also triggered by events, e.g., moving, or by the respondent's ages.

Study and Sample Design

Understanding Society has four sample components: (a) the general population sample, (b) the ethnic minority boost sample, (c) the innovation panel, and (d) the sample of participants from the BHPS. The sample designs are similar in having multistage sample designs mostly with stratification and clustering. However, each sample component has some unique features in its sample design.

General Population Sample Component

The general population sample is a stratified, clustered, equal probability sample of residential addresses drawn to a uniform design throughout the whole of the UK (including north of the Caledonian Canal), with the exception of Northern Ireland, which is not clustered. The Primary Sampling Units (PSU's) are postal sectors stratified by Government Office Region (GOR), population density, and minority ethnic density. 2,640 postal sectors were selected systematically with probability proportional to size (number of addresses). Within each sampled sector, 18 addresses were selected systematically, resulting in an equal-probability sample of a total of 47,520 addresses in Great Britain. In Northern Ireland, 2,400 addresses were selected systematically from the Land and Property Services Agency list of domestic properties, thus making a total of 49,920 selected addresses in UK. The overall sample was allocated to 24 monthly sub-samples, each independently representative of the UK population.

Ethnic Minority Boost Sample Component

The goal for the ethnic minority boost sample was to provide samples of at least 1,000 adults in each of the five largest ethnic minority groups: Indian, Pakistani, Bangladeshi, Caribbean, and African. Such a sample would support group specific analyses of these ethnic groups (Berthoud et al. 2010). While the sampling targets are defined in terms of numbers of adults, the sample is of households.

The sampling approach first identifies geographic areas with at least 5% density of ethnic minority groups. Because the 2001 Census was becoming outdated, the density estimates were adjusted using more recent survey estimates. The high density sectors (at least 5% of their adult population in minority groups) were 36% of the total sectors and accounted for 85% of all members of minorities. Further subsampling of the high density areas was done to increase the efficiency of the yield. That is, a higher sampling fraction was used for areas anticipated to yield three or more households while successively smaller fractions were used for areas expected to yield two, one or zero households (Berthoud et al. 2010).

At selected addresses, households were screened for the presence of a member of a minority ethnic group. The screening question is, "Do you come from or have parents or grandparents who come from any of the following ethnic groups?" The response categories are Indian, mixed Indian, Pakistan, Bangladeshi, Sri Lankan, Caribbean/West Indian, Mixed Caribbean/West Indian, North African, Black African, African Asian, Chinese, Far Eastern, Turkish, Middle Eastern/Iranian, or other. At the screening stage all households with the smaller ethnic groups are selected and there is some deselection of larger groups, e.g., Indians (Berthoud et al. 2010).

Following the first 6 months of data collection the procedures were reviewed and modified. One change was to increase the number of addresses issued in areas estimated to be high in Bangladeshi. This is the smallest of the five main ethnic groups.

One result of the screening procedure is that people from North Africa and the Middle East, who are sometimes recorded as 'white' will be included with the boost sample, the former within the African category. Thus the proposed screening question identifies persons in the following categories in addition to the five target groups: Chinese, other Far Eastern, Sri Lankan, and Middle Eastern. While it is useful to be able to identify members of these ethnic groups, the number of cases will be well below 1,000. White minorities are not selected in the screening but can be identified by survey questions in the general sample.

BHPS Sample Component

Understanding Society incorporates the BHPS sample members into the overall sample design. The extensive longitudinal data of the BHPS has great scientific value, including the opportunity for early longitudinal analyses of *Understanding Society*. The BHPS was a random sample of Great Britain excluding the Scottish Highlands and Islands. In its first wave in 1991 it achieved a sample of 5,500 households. Boost samples of Scotland and Wales were added in 1999 and of Northern Ireland in 2001. These modifications were motivated by interest in analyses in these countries related to political changes associated with devolution in the UK.

Wave 18, the last wave of the BHPS, was conducted in 2008. As a sample component of *Understanding Society*, the former BHPS participants will be distributed over the 12 months of the first year of data collection, beginning in wave 2 (Laurie 2010).

The Innovation Panel

The final sample component is the Innovation Panel (IP). The purpose of the IP is to test methods of data collection and data collection instruments relevant to the conduct of the main survey. As far as practical it has identical design and procedures as the other samples. Its sample design began with 2,760 households drawn from 120 areas of Britain. Northern Ireland and Scotland north of the Caledonian Canal are not included.

The achieved wave 1 sample was targeted at 40,000 households: approximately 26,000 from the general population sample, 4,000 from the ethnic minority boost, 1,500 from the Innovation Panel, and 8,400 from the BHPS participants. The overall sample design is complex and researchers may wish to use the data in a variety of ways. Consequently, the weighting strategy is also complex to support such uses as cross-sectional analyses, calendar year analyses, and longitudinal analyses involving one or more of the sample components.

Data Collection

This section describes some important features of the study in relation to data collection. It includes the timing of data collection, following rules for the continuity and maintenance of the longitudinal sample, modes of data collection, and description of the survey instruments and topics.

Understanding Society is a household panel survey with annual measurements. A sample of households is selected, data are collected from all adult household members, and sample members are followed in subsequent years. Each wave is collected over 2 years or 24 months, such that the first wave of data was collected between January 2009 and December 2011. The second wave of data collection began in January 2010 with those interviewed in the first month of the first wave and concluded in December 2012 with those interviewed in the last month of the first wave. The IP is collected in the spring of the year before the main survey wave.

Households are the first stage of sampling, and household composition determines the rules for following individual respondents over time. The individuals found at selected households in the first wave were designated as Original Sample Members (OSM). We attempt to maintain OSM respondents as part of the sample as long as they live in the UK. Individuals joining the household of an OSM after the sample selection/first interview are temporary sample members (TSM). However, births to an OSM become an OSM. We attempt to interview TSM participants in successive waves as long as they live in the household of an OSM. TSMs are not followed for interviews when they leave the household, but OSMs are.

The following rules mimic the demographic processes by which population is reproduced, including births and deaths, partnership formations and dissolutions, and emigration. The one exception is that there is no direct way in which the following rules capture immigrants into the UK. With this exception, the sample remains representative of the UK as it changes over time, subject to weighting for attrition. The sampling of new immigrants remains an issue to be decided in the future development of the study.

Most of the data collection uses computer assisted personal interviewing (CAPI). There are several instruments for members in selected households. The structure is similar to the BHPS. The basic structure has a household interview and completion of the household grid conducted with one member of the household. The household questionnaire is about 15 min. Each person aged 16 or older has the individual adult interview and self-completed questionnaire. The individual interview is approximately 30 min. There is also an 8 min self-completion interview for adults. Youth aged 10–15 are asked to respond to a self-completion questionnaire, which is a paper and pencil instrument. Information about younger children is provided by the responsible parent in the household and adult interviews. There is a brief proxy interview about adults unable to be interviewed.

The content plan balances having a broader range of information with reducing the burden of data collection. Content that is asked of all respondents is either annual or rotating. Compared to the BHPS there is a greater use of rotating question modules. Modules can also be done by subsets defined by age or other status characteristics. For example, a module on parenting styles in Wave 3 is asked of parents with children of specific ages. Other content is triggered by events such as birth of a child, marriage, or migration. (The long term content plan can be found at www.understandingsociety.org.uk.)

The initial three waves of data collection are face to face, a mode of administration that is typically more costly but more likely to reduce attrition when we are establishing the study. An experiment in the second wave of the IP compared groups issued to face-to-face interviewing vs. those initially issued to telephone administration with varied procedures for interviewing outstanding household members in face-to-face (Burton et al. 2010). This experiment has provided information about the reduction in response rates and costs of different interviewing options. Implementation of multi-mode data collection will move forward in Waves 4 or 5.

The household level response rate of 59.2% is in line with the target rate of 60%. This rate is typical for surveys of this sort in the UK. The target for household response rate in Wave 2 is greater than 80% and for Wave 3 is greater than 90%.

Ethical review in the UK is frequently conducted by external organizations. For health research, this is done through the National Research Ethics Service (NRES) of the National Health Service. This arrangement is congruent with the NHS's dominance of health care delivery. In addition, research centres and professional societies frequently adopt an ethical framework. ISER has adopted the framework of the Social Research Association (Social Research Association 2003), and the ESRC has published a detailed framework of research ethics (Economic and Social Research Council 2010). In addition, universities organize ethical committees for the research of faculty and staff. *Understanding Society* has received ethical approval for research related to the first three waves of the study from a local research ethics committee of the NRES.

Links to Other Types of Data

The ability to link *Understanding Society* survey data with other data sources is a central goal for the study. The added data will greatly enhance its scientific research capacity.

Administrative Data

Linkages with administrative data can be used to supplement the interview data and reduces respondent burden by adding data that would otherwise be collected in the interview or is a potential source of validation for the survey data (Calderwood and Lessof 2009). Respondents were asked in Wave 1 for consents to link health and educational administrative records for themselves and for their children. The health records are held by the National Health Service (NHS), the NHS Central Registers, the Departments of Health, the General Registration Office, and the Office for National Statistics. Consent to link to education records was requested of parents of children aged 4–15 and by young adults aged 16–24 who were currently attending school or had attended school in the UK in the past.

Because of this volume's emphasis on public health, we will describe the health data linkages. For those who consented, fields from their survey data will be sent to the NHS to establish a flag in the Central Register. The Central Register records the registration of the individual with a general practitioner and is frequently updated following births, moves, name changes, and major events like marriages and deaths. With the flag established, the study will be notified when the Central Register is updated for a study participant. In addition, we will link to medical records like the Hospital Episode Statistics (HES). The type of data in HES includes dates of the episode, information about the facility, procedures and treatments, diagnoses, and waiting times. The data systems in Scotland, Wales, and Northern Ireland vary somewhat but similar procedures will be followed for the linkages.

Spatial Data

While this information is not publicly released, participants' postal codes can be used to identify several geographic variables that are released. Postal codes in each wave can be linked to geographic designations of interest including parliamentary constituencies, local educational authorities, travel to work areas, local authority districts, and primary care trusts. Parliamentary constituencies are geographic areas used to elect members of Parliament. Local authority districts are local governments units which have some social service responsibilities. The education department of a local authority district is frequently referred to as a local educational authority. Primary care trusts are responsible for providing health services to an area and contracting for additional services such as hospitals. The travel to work areas are similar to classifications set up by the U.S. Census for commuting distances. The rural–urban classification categorizes localities by population size and the sparseness of surrounding areas. For a useful description of these geographical classifications see A Beginners' Guide to UK Geographies (Office for National Statistics 2010).

Biomeasures

Biomeasures have been included in several major longitudinal surveys, including the 1946 and 1958 British Cohort studies (Ferri et al. 2003), and the English Longitudinal Study of Ageing (ELSA) (Marmot et al. 2003). The addition of biomeasures to *Understanding Society* permits the examination of objective biological, anthropometric, and functional measures within a large sample that spans many ages and that can be studied within a household context. The measurement of biomarkers in BHPS participants will permit researchers to examine questions that rely on longitudinal psycho-social data immediately.

Collection of the biomeasures began with some components of the Wave 2 general population sample of adults. Data collection was conducted in a separate visit by trained nurses. The measures include anthropometric information (height, weight, waist circumference, and body fat from bioelectrical impedance), blood pressure, lung function (spirometry), grip strength, and the collection of whole blood through venepuncture. The blood analytes are total cholesterol, high density lipids, c-reactive protein, cystatin-c, and glycated haemoglobin (HbA1C). Respondents were asked to provide written consent to store blood for future research and to conduct genetic studies.

Qualitative Studies

In the longer term *Understanding Society* will be significantly enriched by the collection of a wider range of data that will help address research issues that questionnaire data on its own cannot address. Examples include using the survey data as a sampling frame for longitudinal qualitative research, the use of diaries to collect more accurate measurement such as time use information or specific health behaviours, and experiments to test specific hypotheses. An example of a structured experiment is an experiment on trust (Uhrig et al. 2009).

The instructions and terms of agreement for proposing such coordinated studies can be found on the study website: www.understandingsociety.org.uk.

Data Access

The first data release took place in late 2010 and included Wave 1, year 1 data and the first two waves of the Innovation Panel. Subsequently, full waves of data have been released yearly.

The data are released through the UK Data Archive (UKDA). The UKDA is the curator of the largest collection of digital data in the social sciences in the UK. Its staff is experienced in the preservation and dissemination of data resources. In particular, the UKDA collaborates with ISER in the Longitudinal Economic and Social Data Service (ESDS).

The UKDA has different levels of data security. In the usual case, researchers register with the ESDS and agree to the conditions of the regular End User License. The chief conditions are to not use the data to attempt to discover the identity of individuals or households in the data set and to follow the requirements of the Data Protection Act (Information Commissioner 2001). Researchers are also asked to report publications resulting from the data.

Somewhat higher levels of restriction (Conditional Access) are used for data with greater but still small risk of disclosure. These include geocoded data to relatively large geographic units such as Primary Care Trusts. Special Access is required for data with greater risk of personal disclosure, often because the geographic units are smaller. Such units include census wards.

Finally, the UKDA has implemented a Secure Data Service for data with greater sensitivity. Examples of this would be the survey data linked with administrative health or education records.

Entirely new procedures must be established to permit access to biological samples for genetic research by qualified researchers. Not only are these data considered sensitive but the biological samples are a limited resource.

Documentation is maintained both at the UKDA and on the *Understanding Society* webpage. Documentation includes study- and variable-level information, specific guides about major content areas such as the biomeasures or cognitive measures, and guides for issues that are frequently problematic for users such as selection of appropriate weights.

A research conference for the BHPS and *Understanding Society* was held in 2011 and subsequently in odd-numbered years. The conference is an opportunity to present research findings and methodological research to others using the studies' data and to network with the study investigators. User group sessions are scheduled for the conference period. They are an opportunity to gain support in the analysis of the data and to give input into the study.

Conclusion

Understanding Society, the UKHLS, is a new household panel survey funded by the UK ESRC and multiple UK governmental departments. The study is ambitious in scope and coverage and has great potential for interdisciplinary research spanning social and health sciences. The integration of interview data, administrative health record linkages, and the direct assessment of biomeasures will contribute richly to the potential for research in demography and public health. The design of this longitudinal study, similar design to that adopted in a number of other countries, including the PSID in the USA, provides scope for cross-national comparative research on the dynamics of population.

References

Berthoud, R., et al. (2010). *Design of the ethnic minority boost sample for Understanding Society*. Colchester: Institute for Social and Economic Research.

Bradby, H. (2003). Describing ethnicity in health research. *Ethnicity and Health, 8*(1), 5–13.

Buck, N., et al. (Eds.). (1994). *Changing households: The British Household Panel Survey, 1990–1992*. Colchester: ESRC Research Centre on Micro-Social Change.

Burton, J., Laurie, H., & Uhrig, S. C. N. (2008). *Understanding society. Some preliminary research from the wave 1 Innovation Panel* (Understanding Society Working Papers). Colchester: Institute for Social and Economic Research.

Burton, J., Laurie, H., & Uhrig, S. C. N. (Eds.). (2010). *Understanding society innovation panel wave 2: Methodological experiments*. Colchester: Institute for Social and Economic Research.

Calderwood, L., & Lessof, C. (2009). Enhancing longitudinal surveys by linking to administrative data. In P. Lynn (Ed.), *Methodology of longitudinal surveys*. Chichester: Wiley.

Dex, S., & Joshi, H. (Eds.). (2005). *Children of the 21st century; From birth to nine months*. Bristol: Policy Press.

Economic and Social Research Council. (2010). *ESRC research ethics framework (2010)*. Swindon: ESRC.

Ermisch, J. (2008). Child support and non-resident fathers' contact with their children. *Journal of Population Economics, 21*(4), 827–853.

Ferri, E., Bynner, J., & Wadsworth, M. (Eds.). (2003). *Changing Britain, changing lives: Three generations at the turn of the century*. London: Institute of Education.

Harkness, J. (2005). SHARE translation procedures and translation assessment. In A. Borsch-Supan & H. Jurges (Eds.), *The survey of health, aging, and retirement in Europe – Methodology* (pp. 24–29). Mannheim: Mannheim Research Institute for the Economics of Aging (MEA).

Hobcraft, J. (2009). Reflections on the incorporation of biomeasures into prospective surveys: An international perspective. *Biodemography and Social Biology, 55*(2), 252–269.

Information Commissioner. (2001). *Data Protection Act 1998: Legal guidance*. Available from: http://www.dataprotection.gov.uk/dpr/dpdoc.nsf

Laurie, H. (2010). *Continuity and innovation in the design of Understanding Society: The UK Household Longitudinal Study*. Colchester: Institute for Social and Economic Research.

Marmot, M., et al. (Eds.). (2003). *Health, wealth, and lifestyles of the older population in England: The 2002 English Longitudinal Study of Ageing*. London: Institute for Fiscal Studies.

Moffitt, T. E., Caspi, A., & Rutter, M. (2006). Measured gene-environment interactions in psychopathology. *Perspectives on Psychological Science, 181*, 5–27.

Office for National Statistics. (2010). *A beginners' guide to UK geographies*. 26 Apr 2010 [cited 17 June 2010]. Available from: http://www.statistics.gov.uk/geography/beginners_guide.asp

Social Research Association. (2003). *Ethical guidelines*. London: Social Research Association.

Uhrig, S. C. N., et al. (2009). Measuring people's trust. *Journal of the Royal Statistical Society, Series A, 172*, 749–769.

Chapter 21
The Applicability of the Lee-Carter Method to Forecast Health Services Use in Brazil

Cristina Guimarães Rodrigues, Mônica Viegas Andrade, Bernardo Lanza Queiroz, and Carla Jorge Machado

Introduction

The world population age structure has been going through major changes in the past few decades (Bloom 2011; Lee 2011). The average age of the population by 2050 will be 41.9 years old, and the percentage of elderly will rise from 7.6 to 16.2% in the same period (United Nations 2011). Population aging is increasing the concern about the sustainability of health care systems and health care costs around the world.

In addition to these demographic changes in recent years, most of health care systems are going through important reforms (WHO 2008; Docteur and Oxley 2003; Paris et al. 2010), aiming to control the raising of health care costs (Barer et al. 1995; Zweifel et al. 1999, 2004; Hagist and Kotlikoff 2005). In general, these reforms have focused on strengthening primary health care, the promotion of healthy lifestyle and new forms of care – long term care and home care, as well as

C.G. Rodrigues (✉)
Department of Accounting and Actuarial Science,
University of São Paulo (USP), São Paulo, Brazil
e-mail: guimaraes.cristina@gmail.com

M.V. Andrade
Department of Economics, Federal University
of Minas Gerais (UFMG), Belo Horizonte, Brazil

B.L. Queiroz
Department of Demography, Federal University
of Minas Gerais (UFMG), Belo Horizonte, Brazil

C.J. Machado
School of Medicine, Federal University
of Minas Gerais (UFMG), Belo Horizonte, Brazil

N. Hoque et al. (eds.), *Applied Demography and Public Health*,
Applied Demography Series 3, DOI 10.1007/978-94-007-6140-7_21,
© Springer Science+Business Media Dordrecht 2013

the adoption of mechanisms to control supply-induced demand, i.e. managed care (Salkever 2000; WHO 2008; Paris et al. 2010: Menec et al. 2007; Forget et al. 2008; Moineddin et al. 2010). These reforms have also considered the incorporation of new technologies and how it could affect health care expenditures for both private and public sectors (Baker et al. 2003; Mendes 2006).

In order to develop and propose adequate reforms, there are a growing number of studies attempting to forecast health services use and costs overtime (Lee and Miller 2002; Reinhardt 2003; Chan et al. 2004; Brockmann and Gampe 2005; Busse et al. 2007). Usually these papers have considered the impact of demographic changes keeping the level and profile of health care utilization constant (Finlayson et al. 2004; Schulz et al. 2004; Tate et al. 2004; Strunk et al. 2006). Very few studies have incorporated changes in utilization rates based on historical trends (Evans et al. 2001; Finlayson et al. 2004).

This paper contributes to the methodological debate about forecasting in health services research. The aim is to forecast admission rates in the public health care system in Brazil using a probabilistic method. We adapt the Lee-Carter method (Lee and Carter 1992) – originally created to forecast mortality – to forecast public hospital admission rates in Brazil. There are two main innovations in this approach. First we apply the Lee-Carter method for a new variable. The Lee-Carter method was developed to forecast mortality, and it has very few applications with other variables (Frees 2006). Second we use a stochastic approach to forecast health services utilization with probabilistic confidence intervals. This is not a traditional method of forecasting in the field of health services research. The appealing advantage of using the Lee-Carter method is that it provides a simple way to model the age pattern of the demographic variables and to forecast joint probability distributions of age-specific rates (Lee 2004).

We applied this method to the State of Minas Gerais in Brazil. Minas Gerais is in the Southeast region and is one of the most populous states in the country. According to the Brazilian Population Census Bureau (IBGE), in 2010 about 10% of the Brazilian population lived in Minas Gerais. In Brazil, it is more appropriate to forecast health care utilization considering states as units of analysis. State information is more feasible from the standpoint of decision-making, since Brazil is a federation and its states manage health care service delivery autonomously. The 1988 Constitution empowered the states to make decisions regarding the allocation of infrastructure services (Medici 2002; Gerschman and Santos 2006).

Traditional Methods of Forecasting Health Care Use

There are different methods to forecast health care service demand. The traditional method assumes fixed utilization rates by age aiming to estimate the pure demographic effect (Finlayson et al. 2004; Schulz et al. 2004; Tate et al. 2004; Strunk et al. 2006). This procedure takes into account the population size and age composition of health care utilization. The fixed utilization rates are calculated by age and other attributes using the last period of data available. Other attributes could include type of health services, for example inpatient and outpatient care; and individual characteristics, such as sex and health status.

This type of forecasting is of particular interest in short run analyses. It can also be applied in contexts when the population age structure is changing quickly and utilization rates by age are relatively stable over recent years. The main caveat of such method is that it does not incorporate historical trends into health care utilization rates (Evans et al. 2001). The fixed rate assumption can generate bias in the total estimated utilization if the rates are changing over time. Therefore, in order to better organize the supply and delivery of health care services, health policy planning should incorporate historical changes in utilization rates across age groups. Large variation in utilization rates across age groups and over time has also been observed in both developed and developing countries (Tate et al. 2004; Rodrigues 2010).

Currently health care planners and scholars have tried to accurately forecast the use of health care services based on different approaches using time series data (Evans et al. 2001; Finlayson et al. 2004). Some studies stand on simple trend extrapolation, which means that utilization rates fluctuate only deterministically over time. The underlying assumption is that the average growth rates observed over a historical period will be constant over time.

Other studies use regression analysis with panel data including a trend term in order to forecast health care services utilization for a given locality. Usually the dependent variable is the total utilization rate for the locality, regressed on covariates to verify if other factors can influence utilization rates. Some examples of covariates are income per capita, health care services supply, the educational level of the population, and private health insurance coverage (Tate et al. 2004). A counterfactual estimation can also be conducted to simulate policy effects (Hancock et al. 2003). This method allows for controlling factors that affect the use of health care services, while incorporating trends in utilization rates.

Time series approaches may offer plausible estimates of future utilization. Their accuracy depends on the availability of historical time series data and on the assumptions about the behavior of utilization rates. Besides this, different scenarios can be built in order to incorporate uncertainty in forecasts. These scenarios are usually built based on expert opinion and judgments about the future of the rates. Moreover the uncertainty assessed by scenarios lacks probabilistic meaning (Booth 2004; Goldstein 2004). Health service utilization depends on many factors, such as political and economic performance, population health status, age patterns, and so on. Thus, the predictability of these models may not be so reliable over long periods. These scenarios are subjectively chosen and devoid probabilities of occurrence. In order to have more realistic forecasting, health care specialists should indicate how likely the utilization rates are to occur in the future.

Data

In order to calculate admission rates for public health care in Minas Gerais, Brazil, we used data from two sources: Hospital Information System from the Unified Health System (SIH/SUS) and National Sample Household Survey of the Brazilian Institute of Geography and Statistics (PNAD-IBGE), both from 1993 to 2010. The Hospital Information System provides administrative records from the federal government about all public hospitalizations in Brazil. We used the Hospital Information System to obtain the number of admissions in public hospitals by age, and PNAD to obtain population distribution by age. The hospital admission rates were calculated by dividing the number of hospital admissions by the population per 100 inhabitants. We calculated hospital admission rates from 1993 to 2010.[1]

Trends in Admission Rates

In 2010, the admissions in Minas Gerais represented about 10% of all public hospitalizations in the country. Figure 21.1 shows trends of standardized admission rates for 1993–2010 in Minas Gerais and Brazil. The figures are very similar, although the level is a little different in the first years of the series. The pattern of the state of Minas Gerais reproduces the pattern for the whole country, except for the 1993 and 1994 admission rates, for Brazil.

The sharp decline in admission rates in Minas Gerais occurs at an average of about 3.2% a year and is more pronounced from 1993 to 1996. From 1996 to 2010 there is a decrease in number and rate of hospital admissions, 16 and 32%, respectively. The total number of admissions in 2010 was 1,129,845, corresponding to a 5.42 admissions per 100 populations. The variation in the rates over time may reflect both differences in number of people treated or variation in multiple admissions per individual.

There are two main explanations for the decline of admission rates in Brazil. The first is related to institutional changes in the health care system. These changes include the introduction of regulatory mechanisms both in private and public sectors and incentives to primary health care programs (Neto et al. 2008). These institutional changes can reduce the need for inpatient care over time. There is also evidence, for Brazil and other countries, that the government has established financial barriers to avoid the growth of inpatient care, such as budget cuts, and the direct control over the supply of health services, especially hospital beds (Paris et al. 2010).

In Brazil, the government has adopted quotas for admissions for which a limited supply of hospital services is available (Neto et al. 2008). Until 1993 hospital expenses were paid without the establishment of budgetary limits in the number of procedures performed in hospital. From 1994 it was established that the amount of quotas authorized at each location would depend on a fixed proportion according to population size. The quotas were then fixed at 10% of the population in 1994, but they are decreasing over time.

---

[1]The number of admissions by age is available in the database only after 1993.

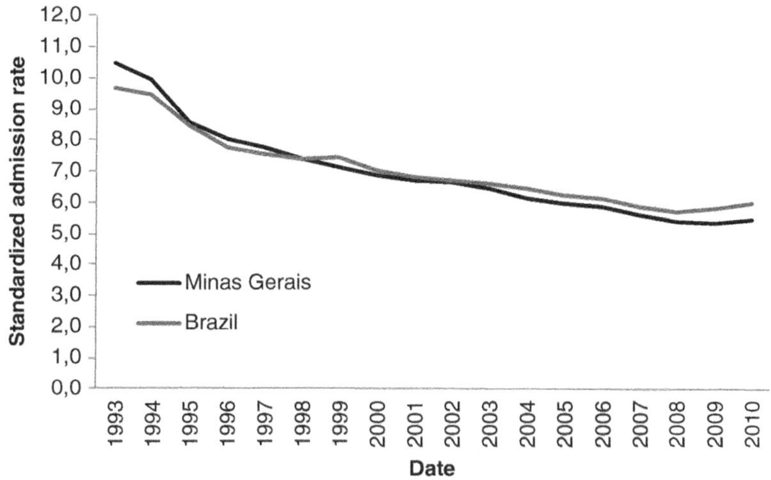

Fig. 21.1 Total admission rates by year (standardized rate) – Minas Gerais and Brazil, 1993–2010 (Source: SIH/SUS and National Household Sample Survey (PNAD) – 1993–2010)

Moreover, priority has been given to primary health care, such as Brazil's Family Health Program, which could help to prevent injuries and promote the health of the population. Some studies discuss the importance of expanding and consolidating the Family Health Program in order to reduce the incidence of hospital admissions, especially for admissions that could be avoided by the provision of quality ambulatory care (Perpétuo and Wong 2006; Oliveira 2007; Alfradique et al. 2009).

The second explanation is the improving health status of the population, resulting in reduced demand for hospital services. The changes in population health and its effects on reducing admission rates may result from several factors. One of them, as addressed earlier, refers to the improvement of primary prevention programs and sanitary conditions that act as inhibiting factors for hospital admissions (Francisco et al. 2004). Evidence for Minas Gerais, and the whole country, suggests that admissions for causes linked to sanitary conditions, like diarrhea, were greatly reduced in recent years (Perpétuo and Wong 2006). Another factor may be the reduction of risk factors in the population observed in the last years, such as alcohol consumption, smoking, and physical inactivity, accompanied by a decreased likelihood of disease (Barata 2008).

Forecasting Methods

We adapted the Lee-Carter method (Lee and Carter 1992) to forecast admission rates in Brazil. It combines a demographic model with a time-series method of forecasting. The method involves a model of two factors, age and time, and uses matrix decomposition to extract a single time-varying index of the level of admissions, which is then forecast using a time-series model. The Lee-Carter method has been considered a powerful method to forecast mortality due to its precision and simple way to model age distribution of mortality rates (Li et al. 2002). The more linear the trends in age-specific rates, the more robust the method (Booth et al. 2006).

We model admission rates similarly to mortality rates, based on a matrix of age-specific log admission rates ${}_nU_x(t)$. The first step of the Lee-Carter method consists of modeling these admission rates as

$$\ln\left({}_nU_{x,t}\right) = {}_n a_x + {}_n b_x \bullet k_t + {}_n \varepsilon_{x,t} \tag{21.1}$$

where ${}_na_x$, ${}_nb_x$ and k_t are parameters to be estimated and ${}_n\mu_{x,t}$ is a set of random disturbances. The solution of this regression is made by applying the Singular Value-Decomposition approach (SVD) on the log of the historical rates matrix ${}_nU_x(t)$. The method imposes two constraints to obtain a unique solution: ${}_na_x$ is calculated as the average of $\ln\left({}_nU_{x,t}\right)$ over time, that is the average pattern of hospital admissions by age over time; ${}_nb_x$ sums up to 1 and is the relative proportional rates of change of hospital admissions by age; k_t sums up to zero and represents an index of the level of admissions at time *t*. Both ${}_na_x$ and ${}_nb_x$ are fixed over time. Once all the parameters are defined, k_t is then forecasted with time-series methods.

As we are modeling the rates to obtain the three parameters with the maximum precision, it is appropriate to minimize the variance in the series, assuming structural similarity of the process (Li et al. 2002). To test for structural changes in the historical data, we applied the Chow Predictive Test (Greene 2000). This test analyzes whether there is a break in the historical stability trend of the series. The main advantage of this test is that it gives a more robust choice of the relevant historical period to use as the time series.

To perform the Chow Predictive Test, we first estimated a regression model for several sub-periods from 1993 to 2010. Then we compared the parameters regarding each sub-period to the ones estimated for the whole period. Test results showed that the statistical stability trend in the time series is estimated to the period from 1996 to 2010. Therefore we use this time frame for the remaining part of the study.

The second step of the method is to extrapolate k_t using ARIMA time-series models. The most appropriate ARIMA model in the context of linear trends in the age-specific rates is the random walk with drift (Li et al. 2002; Booth et al. 2006). The forecasting model is given by $k_t = c + k_{t-1} + u_t$, where *c* is the drift parameter, representing the average annual change in k_t. After forecasting k_t, it is possible to derive all future admission rates by age and their respective probability distributions.

In order to compare the applicability of the Lee-Carter method to our data, we also applied a deterministic model of forecasting. In the deterministic model, the trend in the admission rates is given by a fixed annual variation of the rates, as adapted from Spiegel and Hyman (1998):

$$\frac{1}{2}\ln\left(\frac{1-{}_nU_x^z}{{}_nU_x^z}\right) = \frac{1}{2}\ln\left(\frac{1-{}_nU_x^i}{{}_nU_x^i}\right) * \left[1 + {}_n w_x * \left(t^z - t^i\right)\right] \tag{21.2}$$

where z and i are the superscripts to final and initial year of the forecasting, respectively; ${}_nw_x$ is the average of the annual variation observed in the rates by 5-year age groups between period t and $t+n$, (t) being the initial year and ($t+n$) the final year of the historical data. We also used the Brass logit transformation (Brass et al. 1968) to smooth the admission rates over age and time; otherwise the projected rates could be less than zero. The advantage of this transformation is that as the admission rates can be considered a type of probability that ranges from 0 to 1, the logit of ${}_nU_x$ takes all the values between $-\infty$ and $+\infty$. As the ${}_nw_x$ and the forecasted rates are calculated on this basis, the anti-logit of ${}_nU_x$ by the expression $\frac{\exp(2*{}_nU_x)}{1+\exp(2*{}_nU_x)}$ will map into a value between 0 and 1. Within the respective limits, the projected rate will be zero, but never negative.

The hospital admission rates were then forecasted from 2011 until 2020. In order to evaluate the method, we performed an out-of-sample forecasting from 2006 to 2010 and compared it to the actual admission rates in this period. We used the information from 1996 to 2005 to perform the back cast test to our model.

Results

The Fitted Model

After estimating the parameters ${}_na_x$, ${}_nb_x$ and k_t, we re-estimated the admission rates for the period between 1996 and 2010 to evaluate the adjustment of the method. The results are presented in Fig. 21.2a for age groups until 19 years old and

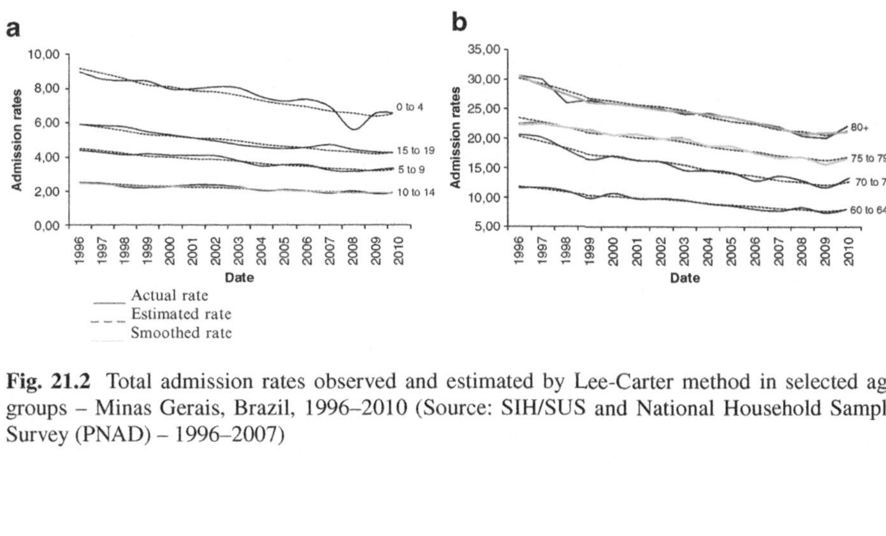

Fig. 21.2 Total admission rates observed and estimated by Lee-Carter method in selected age groups – Minas Gerais, Brazil, 1996–2010 (Source: SIH/SUS and National Household Sample Survey (PNAD) – 1996–2007)

Table 21.1 Proportion of variance accounted by Lee-Carter model, by age groups – Minas Gerais, Brazil, 1996–2010

	Variance[a] (%)	
Age groups	Observed rate	Smoothed rate
0–4	92.0	92.0
5–9	95.4	95.4
10–14	85.6	98.7
15–19	85.7	94.4
20–24	91.0	91.0
25–29	93.5	93.5
30–34	98.1	98.1
35–39	91.3	91.3
40–44	96.5	96.5
45–49	97.9	97.9
50–54	95.4	95.4
55–59	94.5	94.5
60–64	96.4	96.4
65–69	94.9	94.9
70–74	92.7	92.7
75–79	91.8	100
80+	61.9	100
Global variance	**91.5**	**95.5**

Source: SIH/SUS – 1993 to 2010 and IBGE/PNAD – 1993, 1995–1999, 2001–2009 and IBGE/Censo – 2000 and 2010

Note: [a]The proportion of variance is expressed by $\frac{\left({}_{n}s_{x} - {}_{n}\hat{s}_{x}\right)}{{}_{n}s_{x}} - 1$, where s_x is the variance of the rate observed in age group x to x + n at the historical period of available data and ${}_{n}\hat{s}_{x}$ is the variance of estimated rate by the model in the same age group and time t (Lee and Carter 1992)

Fig. 21.2b for 60–64, 70–74, 75–79, and 80 and over. The black line represents the observed rate while the dotted line is the Lee-Carter estimation. As the axis scale is different, we plotted the figures in different graphs.

Results showed that the model has a good fit for all age groups, except for the 0–4 and the elderly. The global variance accounted for the model was 91.5% (Table 21.1) while the lowest variance explained concerned individuals 80+ (61.9%). This result reflects the erratic trend observed for the elderly over the past years. The more erratic the trend, the larger is the error in the forecasting.

In order to smooth trend disturbances, we applied a simple smoothing technique based on centered moving averages over time from three adjacent years. This procedure was applied when the explained percentage of the variance was lower than 90%. It occurred for the following age groups: 10–14, 15–19, and 80 and over. Data smoothing reduces seasonality and noise and makes trends more visible and less disturbing (Shmueli 2011). The smoothing rate is shown by a gray solid line in Fig. 21.2.

After smoothing we estimated the Lee-Carter method again. The smoothing technique increased the variance explained by the model, accounting for nearly 100% for the selected age groups. The smoothing procedure is necessary to improve the quality of forecasting.

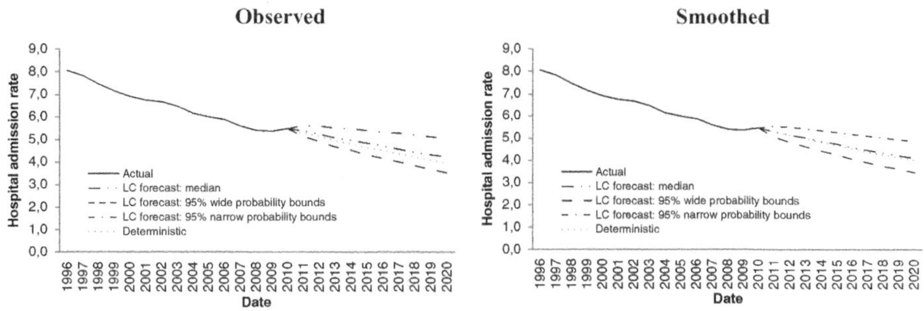

Fig. 21.3 Actual admission rates and forecasts – Minas Gerais, Brazil, 1996–2020 (Source: SIH/SUS and National Household Sample Survey (PNAD) – 1996–2010)

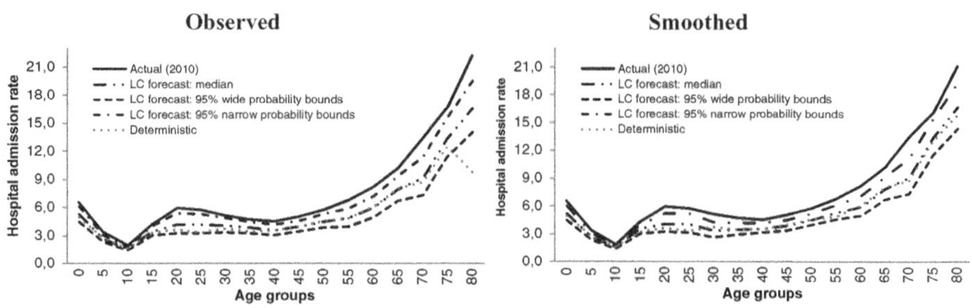

Fig. 21.4 Actual admission rates (2010) and forecasts (2020) by age groups – Minas Gerais, Brazil (Source: SIH/SUS and National Household Sample Survey (PNAD) – 1996–2010)

Forecasting Results

Figure 21.3 plots observed admission rates for the years 1996–2010 and the forecasted values for 2011–2020. The first of two graphs shows results without smoothing. The second one depicts the results regarding the smoothed data. Admission rates forecasting follows the declining historical trends. The wide bound of the 95% probability intervals of Lee-Carter method incorporates a sharp decline in admissions, while the narrow bound considers a more conservative trend of admission rates decline. The comparison of deterministic and probabilistic methods shows very similar results. After data smoothing the deterministic and median Lee-Carter findings are nearly coincident. Admission rates are 25 and 29% lower in 2020, compared to 2010, in Lee-Carter median and deterministic forecasting, respectively. It means an expected reduction of 300,000 admissions in Minas Gerais.

Figure 21.4 shows the actual admission rates in 2010, and forecasts for 2020 by age groups. The decrease in admission rates observed between 1996 and 2010 is followed by a more dramatic decline at some ages than at others. The most striking decline occurs to reproductive and older age groups. Individuals aged 20–24 have a 30% reduction in admission rates while older individuals present a decline of about 32% for the 70–74 age group and 21% for ages 80 and over. For the younger groups we observe small differences between the projected rate for 2020, and the observed

Table 21.2 Actual admission rates and forecasts – Minas Gerais, Brazil, 2006–2010

Ano	Actual admission rate	LC forecast: median		LC forecast: 95% wide probability bounds		LC forecast: 95% narrow probability bounds		Deterministic	
		Rate	Error (%)	Rate	Error (%)	Rate	Error (%)	Rate	Error (%)
Observed rate									
2006	5.86	5.79	−1.11	5.65	−3.57	5.94	1.42	5.77	−1.53
2007	5.60	5.60	0.11	5.40	−3.55	5.82	3.93	5.55	−0.89
2008	5.39	5.42	0.54	5.17	−4.12	5.69	5.45	5.34	−1.03
2009	5.34	5.25	−1.69	4.96	−7.13	5.56	4.09	5.14	−3.78
2010	5.46	5.08	−6.94	4.76	−12.86	5.43	−0.57	4.95	−9.42
Smoothed rate									
2006	5.86	5.83	−0.49	5.67	−3.15	5.99	2.25	5.81	−0.86
2007	5.60	5.65	0.87	5.42	−3.09	5.88	5.01	5.60	0.10
2008	5.39	5.47	1.43	5.20	−3.61	5.76	6.76	5.41	0.25
2009	5.34	5.30	−0.70	4.99	−6.58	5.64	5.60	5.22	−2.26
2010	5.46	5.14	−5.88	4.79	−12.29	5.52	1.06	5.04	−7.75

Source: SIH/SUS and National Household Sample Survey – 2006–2010

one for 2010. This is due to the low level of the admission rate in these age groups and the less erratic trends over years.

The comparison of forecasting with and without data smoothing shows different results for the deterministic method. For individuals aged 80 and over the deterministic method without smoothing shows a trend breakdown that is not forecasted in the Lee-Carter method. A possible explanation for this difference is that the Lee-Carter approach also takes into account joint variation in all age groups to estimate the behavior of each age group (Booth et al. 2006). This dependency across age groups is not present in the deterministic estimation. As a consequence of the independence among age groups in the deterministic method, the erratic trends in the admission rates are reflected at higher extension in the forecasting by this method than by the Lee-Carter. However, after smoothing, results for the deterministic method are very similar to the Lee-Carter forecasting for this age group.

Forecasting Evaluation

In order to evaluate the performance of the methods, admission rates were forecasted for the period between 2006 and 2010 and compared to the observed data in the same period. We used data from 1996 to 2005 as the historic time series. This performance evaluation is only possible for short-term forecasts because of the limited data availability, but still can shed some light on our estimations procedures.

Table 21.2 shows the results for observed rates with and without smoothing data. In both types of data, the Lee-Carter median forecast fit better than the deterministic

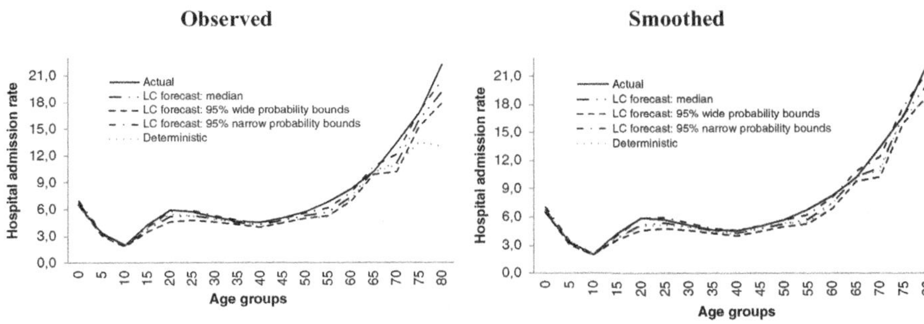

Fig. 21.5 Actual admission rates and forecasts by age groups – Minas Gerais, Brazil, 2010 (Source: SIH/SUS and National Household Sample Survey (PNAD) – 1996–2010)

method, presenting an error lower than 2% for the first 4 years. In 2010, the error was a slightly higher than before, around 7%, probably because of the declining trend reversion in this year, as shown in Fig. 21.1.

Figure 21.5 shows the back cast forecasting by age groups for 2010. The forecasted admissions were very similar to the observed data, especially for the ages below 10. The largest underestimation was verified for the age group 80+. As already mentioned, this age group presents the most irregular trend among all age groups (Fig. 21.2). The use of the smoothing technique reduced the forecasting error by nearly 25%.

Conclusion

In general, methods of forecasting health care services are concerned with utilization levels in the future (Barer et al. 1995; Zweifel et al. 1999, 2004; Finlayson et al. 2004; Schulz et al. 2004; Tate et al. 2004). The level of utilization for each age group is determined by multiplying its utilization rate by the population projections. These methods usually assume a constant utilization rate for all forecasting periods. However, in the context of large variations in health care utilization rates, it is worthwhile to consider time trends in these rates, mainly if these changes are not homogeneous across age groups (Evans et al. 2001).

The main contribution of this paper is to quantify uncertainty in health services utilization through a stochastic approach. Methods of stochastic forecasting in the field of health services research are relatively new and largely unexplored. Partially, these methods are limited by the availability of reliable data and long time series for health care services. We adapt the Lee-Carter method (Lee and Carter 1992) – originally developed to forecast mortality – to forecast public hospital admission rates in Brazil. This method combines a demographic model and a reliable method of time series forecasting.

The specific use of the Lee-Carter method in this field was first made by Lee and Miller (2002) to forecast Medicare expenditures from the year 2020–2075. The authors used 30 years as time series and a fixed age pattern of expenditures. Like in other methods of forecasting health care services, we assume the number of future admissions by multiplying specific age admission rates by population projections by age. However, our model differs from the others as age rates follow a random path being forecasted with confidence probabilistic intervals. Additionally, we compare the Lee-Carter method with deterministic methods of forecasting in health services research.

One caveat of our estimation is the use of short time-series to forecast health care utilization rates. Reliable series of admission rates are only available after 1995. Despite this shortcoming our procedure fit the data well, both for the total admission rates and for the age groups. The global variance explained by the model was, on average, over 90%. Probably the gain in accuracy would be largest if the fitting period was longer or if age-specific admission rates moved slowly over time, which is not the case for people aged 80. Nevertheless, simple smoothing techniques, which do not require complex statistical procedures, also can minimize the variance of the rates and make more reliable estimates. After smoothing data for selected age groups the variance explained reached nearly 100%. Other studies also use data smoothing for the estimation improvement when the Lee-Carter method is used for short time-series (Zhao 2012).

The major advantage of our approach is to produce estimates with confidence intervals. Additionally, uncertainty is incorporated through probabilistic techniques. Therefore this approach is an advance as probabilistic techniques are an objective way to measure uncertainty in opposition to deterministic methods that usually build subjective scenarios to incorporate uncertainty.

The expected admission rate for 2020 is about 4 per 100 population, 23% lower than the one observed in 2010. The Lee-Carter method was evaluated by comparing forecast admission rates with actual admission rates from 2006 to 2010. The results suggest the best fitted model was the Lee-Carter method, which presented a forecasting error lower than 10%. The results for Lee-Carter and deterministic method turned out to be very similar after data smoothing.

Regarding the age groups, we observed a very steep decline in utilization rates in reproductive ages and for elderly people. The decline of admission rates in reproductive ages might be caused by the striking reduction in fertility in Brazil in the last decades. As the most hospitalizations in these age groups are for obstetric causes, this change can explain part of the decrease in admission rates in these groups. For the elderly, some studies explain the health status improvement over the last years due to increased access to primary health care and the increase of vaccine coverage (Francisco et al. 2004).

This study contributes to the literature that investigates forms of forecasting health care use and costs. Although it is a difficult task to forecast the use of health care services, especially in a scenario of rapid change in both population and medical technology, we show that this work is important to generate estimates that can be used to support evidence-based policy.

References

Alfradique, M. E., et al. (2009, June). Internações por condições sensíveis à atenção primária: a construção da lista brasileira como ferramenta para medir o desempenho do sistema de saúde (Projeto ICSAP – Brasil). *Cad. Saúde Pública, Rio de Janeiro, 25*(6), 1337–1349.

Baker, L., et al. (2003). *The relationship between technology availability and health care spending*. Health Affairs – Web exclusive, Millwood. doi:10.1377/hlthaff.W3.537. Disponível em: http://content.healthaffairs.org/cgi/content/full/hlthaff.w3.537v1/DC2. Acesso em 18 fev 2010.

Barata, R. B. (2008). Determinantes e desigualdades sociais no acesso e na utilização de serviços de saúde. In L. Giovanella, et al. (Orgs.), *Políticas e sistema de saúde no Brasil* (pp. 167–214). Rio de Janeiro: FIOCRUZ.

Barer, M. L., Evans, R. G., & Hertzman, C. (1995). Avalanche or glacier: Health care and demographic rhetoric. *Canadian Journal on Aging (Cambridge), 14*, 193–224.

Bloom, D. (2011). 7 billion and counting. *Science, 333*(6042), 562–569.

Booth, H. (2004). On the importance of being uncertain: Forecasting population futures for Australia. *People and Place, 12*(2), 1–12.

Booth, H., et al. (2006, October). Lee-Carter mortality forecasting: A multi-country comparison of variants and extensions. *Demographic Research (Rostock), 15*(9), 289–310.

Brass, W., et al. (1968). *The demography of tropical Africa*. Princeton: Princeton University Press. 539 p.

Brockman, K., & Gampe, J. (2005). *The cost of population aging: Forecasting future hospital expenses in Germany* (Working Paper 2005–2007). Rostock: MPIDR.

Busse, R., Krauth, C., & Schwartz, F. W. (2007, April). Use of acute hospital beds does not increase as the population ages: Results from a seven year cohort study in Germany. *Journal of Epidemiology and Community Health (London), 56*(4), 289–293.

Chan, W. S., Li, S. H., & Fong, P. W. (2004). An actuarial analysis of long-term care demand in Hong Kong. *Geriatrics and Gerontology International, 4*(1), S143–S145.

Docteur, E., & Oxley, H. (2003). *Health care systems: Lessons from the reform experience*. London: OECD.

Evans, R. G., et al. (2001). Apocalypse no: Population aging and the future of health care systems. *Canadian Journal on Aging (Cambridge), 20*(Suppl. 1), 160–191.

Finlayson, G. S., et al. (2004, September). Anticipating change: how many acute care hospital beds will Manitoba regions need in 2020? *Canadian Journal on Aging (Cambridge), 24*(Suppl. 1), 133–140.

Forget, E. L., Roos, L. L., Deber, R. B., & Walld, R. (2008). Variations in lifetime health care costs across population. *Health Care Policy, 4*(1), e148–e167.

Francisco, P. M. S. B., Donalisio, M. R., & Lattorre, M. R. D. O. (2004). Internações por doenças respiratórias em idosos e a intervenção vacinal contra influenza não Estado de São Paulo. *Revista Brasileira de Epidemiologia Sao Paulo, 7*(2), 220–227. dez. 2004.

Frees, E. (2006). Forecasting labor force participation rates. *Journal of Official Statistics, 22*(3), 453–485.

Gerschman, S., & Santos, M. A. B. (2006, June). O Sistema Único de Saúde como desdobramento das políticas de saúde do século XX. *Revista Brasileira de Ciências Sociais, São Paulo, 21*(61), 177–227.

Goldstein, J. R. (2004, April). Simpler probabilistic population forecasts: Making scenarios work. *International Statistical Review (Edinburgh), 72*(1), 93–106.

Greene, W. H. (2000). *Econometric analysis* (4th ed.). Upper Saddle River: Prentice-Hall. 1.004 p.

Hagist, C., & Kotlikoff, L. J. (2005). *Who's going broke? Comparing healthcare costs in ten OECD countries* (NBER Working Paper 11833, 41 pages). National Bureau of Economic Research. Available at http://www.nber.org/papers/w11833.

Hancock, R., Comas-Herrera, A., Wittenberg, R., & Pickard, L. (2003). Who will pay for long-term care in the UK? Projections linking macro-and-micro simulation models. *Fiscal Studies, 24*(4), 387–426.

Lee, R. (2004). *Quantifying our ignorance: Stochastic forecasts of population and public budgets* (CEDA Papers). Berkeley: Institute of Business and Economic Research, University of California at Berkeley.

Lee, R. (2011). The outlook for population growth. *Science, 333*(6042), 569–573.

Lee, R., & Carter, L. R. (1992). Modeling and forecasting U.S. mortality. *Journal of the American Statistical Association, 87*(419), 659–671.

Lee, R., & Miller, T. (2002). An approach to forecasting health expenditures, with application to the U.S. Medicare System. *Health Services Research (Ann Arbor), 37*(5), 1365–1386.

Li, N., Lee, R. D., & Tuljapurkar, S. (2002). Using the Lee-Carter method to forecast mortality for population with limited data. *International Statistical Review (Edinburgh), 72*(1), 19–36.

Medici, A. C. (2002). *Financing health policies in Brazil: Achievements, challenges and proposals. Sustainable development* (Technical Department Papers Series). Washington, DC: Inter-American Development Bank.

Mendes, E. V. (2006). *Uma agenda para a saúde* (2nd ed.). São Paulo: Hucitec. 300 p.

Menec, V. H., Lix, L., Nowick, S., & Ekuma, O. (2007). Health care use at the end of life among older adults: Does it vary by age? *Journal of Gerontology, 62A*(4), 400–407.

Moineddin, R., Nie, J. X., Wang, L., Tracy, C. S., & Upshur, R. E. G. (2010). Measuring change in health status of older adults at the population level: The transition probability model. *BMC Health Services Research, 10*, 306.

Neto, F. C. B., Barbosa, P. R., & Santos, I. S. (2008). Atenção hospitalar: evolução histórica e tendências. In L. Giovanella, et al. (Orgs.), *Políticas e Sistema de Saúde no Brasil* (pp. 665–704). Rio de Janeiro: FIOCRUZ.

Oliveira, A. C. (2007). Ensaios sobre a atenção pública à saúde em Minas Gerais. 2007. 153 f. Dissertação (Mestrado em Economia) – Centro de Desenvolvimento e Planejamento Regional. Belo Horizonte: Universidade Federal de Minas Gerais.

Paris, V., Devaux, M., & Wei, L. (2010). *Health systems institutional characteristics: A survey of 29 OECD countries*. Paris: OECD, 140 p (OECD Working Papers, 50). Disponível em: http://www.olis.oecd.org/olis/2010doc.nsf/LinkTo/NT000029DA/$FILE/JT03282545.PDF. Acesso em: 22 maio 2010.

Perpétuo, I. H. O., & Wong, L. R. (2006). Atenção hospitalar por Condições Sensíveis à Atenção Ambulatorial (CSAA) e as mudanças no seu padrão etário: uma análise exploratória dos dados de Minas Gerais. In: SEMINÁRIO DE ECONOMIA MINEIRA, 12, 2006, Diamantina. Anais... Belo Horizonte: UFMG/CEDEPLAR.

Reinhardt, U. E. (2003, March/April). Does the aging of the population really drives the demand for health care? *Health Affairs (Millwood), 22*(6), 27–39.

Rodrigues, C. G. (2010). Dinâmica demográfica e internações hospitalares: uma visão prospectiva para o Sistema Único de Saúde (SUS) em Minas Gerais, 2007 a 2050. p. 249. Tese (Doutorado em Demografia) – Centro de Desenvolvimento e Planejamento Regional, Universidade Federal de Minas Gerais, Belo Horizonte.

Salkever, D. S. (2000). Regulation of prices and investment in hospitals in the United States. In: A. J. Culyer & J. P. Newhouse (Eds.), *Handbook of health economics* (pp. 1489–1535). Amsterdam: Elsevier, v. 2, cap. 28.

Schulz, E., Leidl, R., & Konig, H. H. (2004, January). The impact of ageing on hospital care and long-term care – The example of Germany. *Health Policy (Amsterdam), 67*(1), 57–74.

Shmueli, G. (2011). *Practical time series forecasting: A hands-on guide*. College Park: University of Maryland. 77 p.

Spiegel, A. D., & Hyman, H. H. (1998). *Strategic Health Planning: Methods and techniques applied to marketing and management*. Norwood: Ablex Publishing Corporation. 440 p.

Strunk, B. C., Ginsburg, P. B., & Banker, M. I. (2006, January/June). The effect of population aging on future hospital demand. *Health Affairs (Millwood), 25*, w141–w149. Web exclusive supplement.

Tate, R. B., MacWilliam, L., & Finlayson, G. S. (2004). A methodology for estimating hospital bed need in Manitoba in 2020. *Canadian Journal on Aging (Cambridge), 24*(Suppl. 1), 141–151.

United Nations. (2011). Population Division of the Department of Economic and Social Affairs of the United Nations Secretariat. World Population Prospects: The 2010 Revision. Available at: about here.

World Health Organization. (2008). *The world health report 2008: Primary health care – Now more than ever*. Geneva: World Health Organization. 128 p.

Zhao, B. B. (2012). A modified Lee-Carter model for analyzing short-based-period data. *Population Studies, 66*(1), 39–52.

Zweifel, P., Felder, S., & Meier, M. (1999, September). Ageing of population and health care expenditure: A red herring? *Health Economics (Chichester), 8*(6), 485–496.

Zweifel, P., Felder, S., & Werblow, A. (2004, October). Population ageing of population and health care expenditure: new evidence on the "Red Herring". *The Geneva Papers on Risk and Insurance, 29*(4), 652–666.

Index

N. Hoque et al. (eds.), *Applied Demography and Public Health*,
Applied Demography Series 3, DOI 10.1007/978-94-007-6140-7,
© Springer Science+Business Media Dordrecht 2013

The manufacturer's authorised representative in the EU is Springer Nature Customer Service Centre GmbH, Europaplatz 3, 69115 Heidelberg, Germany. If you have any concerns regarding our products, please contact ProductSafety@springernature.com

Printed and bound by CPI Group (UK) Ltd, Croydon, CR0 4YY
22/09/2026
02220985-0006